Effective Human Relations

Barry L. Reece | Rhonda Brandt

CENGAGE
Learning™

Australia • Brazil • Japan • Korea • Mexico • Singapore • Spain • United Kingdom • United States

CENGAGE
Learning

Effective Human Relations

Barry L. Reece | Rhonda Brandt

Executive Editor:
Maureen Staudt
Michael Stranz

Senior Project Development Manager:
Linda de Stefano

Marketing Specialist:
Sara Mercurio
Lindsay Shapiro

Production/Manufacturing Manager:
Donna M. Brown

PreMedia Supervisor:
Joel Brennecke

Rights & Permissions Specialist:
Kalina Hintz
Todd Osborne

Cover Image:
Getty Images*

For product information and technology assistance, contact us at
Cengage Learning Customer & Sales Support, 1-800-354-9706

For permission to use material from this text or product, submit all requests online at **cengage.com/permissions**
Further permissions questions can be emailed to
permissionrequest@cengage.com

Source: EFFECTIVE HUMAN RELATIONS 10E, ISBN#061878327X,
Barry L. Reece | Rhonda Brandt, 2008 South Western Cengage Learning

ISBN-13: 978-1-4240-7677-2

ISBN-10: 1-4240-7677-3

Cengage Learning
5191 Natorp Boulevard
Mason, Ohio 45040
USA

Cengage Learning is a leading provider of customized learning solutions with office locations around the globe, including Singapore, the United Kingdom, Australia, Mexico, Brazil, and Japan. Locate your local office at:
international.cengage.com/region

Cengage Learning products are represented in Canada by Nelson Education, Ltd.

For your lifelong learning solutions, visit **www.cengage.com/custom**

Visit our corporate website at **www.cengage.com**

Printed in the United States of America
1 2 3 4 5 6 7 14 13 12 11 10

BRIEF CONTENTS

PART I   HUMAN RELATIONS: THE KEY TO PERSONAL GROWTH AND CAREER SUCCESS   1

1   Introduction to Human Relations   2
2   Improving Personal and Organizational Communications   27

PART II   CAREER SUCCESS BEGINS WITH KNOWING YOURSELF   55

3   Understanding Your Communication Style   56
4   Building High Self-Esteem   84
5   Personal Values Influence Ethical Choices   108
6   Attitudes Can Shape Your Life   132
7   Motivating Yourself and Others   154

PART III   PERSONAL STRATEGIES FOR IMPROVING HUMAN RELATIONS   179

8   Improving Interpersonal Relations with Constructive Self-Disclosure   180
9   Achieving Emotional Balance in a Chaotic World   204
10   Building Stronger Relationships with Positive Energy   229
11   Developing a Professional Presence   252

PART IV   IF WE ALL WORK TOGETHER . . .   275

12   Team Building: A Leadership Strategy   276
13   Resolving Conflict and Dealing with Difficult People   301

PART V   SPECIAL CHALLENGES IN HUMAN RELATIONS   327

14   Responding to Personal and Work-Related Stress   328
15   Valuing Work Force Diversity   354
16   The Changing Roles of Men and Women   381

PART VI   YOU CAN PLAN FOR SUCCESS   407

17   A Life Plan for Effective Human Relations   408

APPENDIX   Human Relations Abilities Assessment Form—Student and Instructor Websites

The NWNL Workplace Stress Test—Student and Instructor Websites

Student and Instructor websites can be accessed at:
college.hmco.com/pic/reece10e.

CONTENTS

ABOUT THE AUTHORS xi

PREFACE xii

PART I HUMAN RELATIONS: THE KEY TO PERSONAL GROWTH AND CAREER SUCCESS 1

1 INTRODUCTION TO HUMAN RELATIONS 2

The Nature, Purpose, and Importance of Human Relations 4
The Forces Influencing Behavior at Work 10
The Development of the Human Relations Movement 14
Major Themes in Human Relations 17
Human Relations: Benefits to You 20

Looking Back ▪ Career Corner ▪ Key Terms ▪ Applying What You
Have Learned ▪ Internet Insights ▪ Role-Play Exercise

Case 1.1 **Challenges in the New Economy** 24
Case 1.2 **In Search of Work/Life Balance** 25

2 IMPROVING PERSONAL AND ORGANIZATIONAL COMMUNICATIONS 27

Communicating Effectively in a High-Tech World 29
The Communication Process 29
Communication Filters 31
How to Improve Personal Communication 38
Communications in Organizations 42
Communicating via Technology 45

Looking Back ▪ Career Corner ▪ Key Terms ▪ Applying What You
Have Learned ▪ Internet Insights ▪ Role-Play Exercise

Case 2.1 **Fluid Communications** 52
Case 2.2 **Reading Nonverbal Cues** 53

PART II CAREER SUCCESS BEGINS WITH KNOWING YOURSELF 55

3 UNDERSTANDING YOUR COMMUNICATION STYLE 56

Communication Styles: An Introduction 57
The Communication Style Model 60
Versatility: The Third Dimension 74
A Final Word of Caution 78

Looking Back ▪ Career Corner ▪ Key Terms ▪ Applying What You
Have Learned ▪ Internet Insights ▪ Role-Play Exercise

Case 3.1 **Steve Ballmer Keeps the Good Times Rolling at Microsoft** 82
Case 3.2 **A Matter of Style** 83

4 BUILDING HIGH SELF-ESTEEM 84

The Power of Self-Esteem 85
Self-Esteem Influences Your Behavior 90
How to Build Self-Esteem 92
Organizations Can Help 100

Looking Back ▥ Career Corner ▥ Key Terms ▥ Applying What You
Have Learned ▥ Internet Insights ▥ Role-Play Exercise

Case 4.1 The Power of Mentoring 105
Case 4.2 "Popeye" Lives On 106

5 PERSONAL VALUES INFLUENCE ETHICAL CHOICES 108

Character, Integrity, and Moral Development 110
How Personal Values Are Formed 110
Values Conflicts 116
Personal Values and Ethical Choices 118
Corporate Values and Ethical Choices 119
Values and Ethics in International Business 125

Looking Back ▥ Career Corner ▥ Key Terms ▥ Applying What You
Have Learned ▥ Internet Insights ▥ Role-Play Exercise

Case 5.1 Employee Theft 129
Case 5.2 Whistleblowers' Rights 130

6 ATTITUDES CAN SHAPE YOUR LIFE 132

Attitudes Are Learned 134
How Attitudes Are Formed 137
Attitudes Valued by Employers 139
How to Change Attitudes 142
Organizations' Efforts Toward Improving Employees' Attitudes 147

Looking Back ▥ Career Corner ▥ Key Terms ▥ Applying What You
Have Learned ▥ Internet Insights ▥ Role-Play Exercise

Case 6.1 Life Is Good at the Pike Place Fish Market 151
Case 6.2 An A-Mazing Way to Deal with Change 152

7 MOTIVATING YOURSELF AND OTHERS 154

The Complex Nature of Motivation 156
Influential Motivational Theories 159
Contemporary Employee Motivation Strategies 164
Motivating the Generations 168
Self-Motivation Strategies 169

Looking Back ▥ Career Corner ▥ Key Terms ▥ Applying What You
Have Learned ▥ Internet Insights ▥ Role-Play Exercise

Case 7.1 Let the People Have the Power 175
Case 7.2 What Drives Them? 176

**PART III PERSONAL STRATEGIES FOR IMPROVING
HUMAN RELATIONS 179**

8 IMPROVING INTERPERSONAL RELATIONS WITH CONSTRUCTIVE
SELF-DISCLOSURE 180

Self-Disclosure: An Introduction 182
The Johari Window: A Model for Self-Understanding 185
Appropriate Self-Disclosure 188
Barriers to Self-Disclosure in an Organizational Setting 193
Practice Self-Disclosure 197

Looking Back ■ Career Corner ■ Key Terms ■ Applying What You
Have Learned ■ Internet Insights ■ Role-Play Exercise

Case 8.1   **The Art of Giving Criticism** 201
Case 8.2   **360-Degree Feedback Uncovers Blind Spots** 202

9 ACHIEVING EMOTIONAL BALANCE IN A CHAOTIC WORLD 204

Emotions—An Introduction 206
Factors That Influence Our Emotions 210
Coping with Your Anger and the Anger of Others 212
Violence in the Workplace 215
Emotional Styles 217
Strategies for Achieving Emotional Control 220

Looking Back ■ Career Corner ■ Key Terms ■ Applying What You
Have Learned ■ Internet Insights ■ Role-Play Exercise

Case 9.1   **Romance at Work** 226
Case 9.2   **Coping with Grief** 227

10 BUILDING STRONGER RELATIONSHIPS WITH POSITIVE ENERGY 229

How Positive Energy Contributes to Improved Interpersonal
Relationships 231
Our Need for Positive Experiences 233
Positive Reinforcement—Creating Positive Energy 235
Barriers to Positive Reinforcement 240
Rewarding Individual and Team Performance 243

Looking Back ■ Career Corner ■ Key Terms ■ Applying What You
Have Learned ■ Internet Insights ■ Role-Play Exercise

Case 10.1   **Incentives: The Good, the Bad, and the Ugly** 249
Case 10.3   **Does Pride Matter More Than Money?** 250

11 DEVELOPING A PROFESSIONAL PRESENCE 252

Professional Presence—An Introduction 253
The Image You Project 257

Looking Back ■ Career Corner ■ Key Terms ■ Applying What You
Have Learned ■ Internet Insights ■ Role-Play Exercise

Case 11.1   **The Importance of Class** 272
Case 11.2   **Do You Want to Be Your Own Brand?** 273

PART IV   IF WE ALL WORK TOGETHER . . .   275

12   TEAM BUILDING: A LEADERSHIP STRATEGY   276

Leadership Challenges in a Changing Workplace   278
Basic Beliefs About Teamwork   282
Team-Building Skills for Leaders   285
Situational Leadership   290
Teamwork: The Employee's Role   292

Looking Back ▪ Career Corner ▪ Key Terms ▪ Applying What You
Have Learned ▪ Internet Insights ▪ Role-Play Exercise

Case 12.1   Coaching to Improve Human Performance   298
Case 12.2   Can You Become a Leader?   299

13   RESOLVING CONFLICT AND DEALING WITH DIFFICULT PEOPLE   301

A New View of Conflict   303
Finding the Root Causes of Conflict   303
Learn to Negotiate Effectively   309
Conflict Resolution Process   314
The Role of Labor Unions in Conflict Resolution   317

Looking Back ▪ Career Corner ▪ Key Terms ▪ Applying What You
Have Learned ▪ Internet Insights ▪ Role-Play Exercise

Case 13.1   The Global Union Movement   323
Case 13.2   Couples Combat   324

PART V   SPECIAL CHALLENGES IN HUMAN RELATIONS   327

14   RESPONDING TO PERSONAL AND WORK-RELATED STRESS   328

The Stress Factor in Your Life   330
Major Causes of Stress   331
Warning Signals of Too Much Stress   337
Stress Management Strategies   337
Coping with Psychological Disorders   344

Looking Back ▪ Career Corner ▪ Key Terms ▪ Applying What You
Have Learned ▪ Internet Insights ▪ Role-Play Exercise

Case 14.1   Vacation Starvation   350
Case 14.2   Drugs on Campus   351

15   VALUING WORK FORCE DIVERSITY   354

Work Force Diversity   355
Prejudiced Attitudes   357
The Many Forms of Discrimination   360
The Economics of Valuing Diversity   368
Managing Diversity   369
Affirmative Action: Yesterday and Today   373

Looking Back ▪ Career Corner ▪ Key Terms ▪ Applying What You
Have Learned ▪ Internet Insights ▪ Role-Play Exercise

Case 15.1   Quality Education Through Enhanced Diversity   378
Case 15.2   The Baggage of Bigotry   379

16 THE CHANGING ROLES OF MEN AND WOMEN 381

Traditional Roles Are Changing 383
Problems Facing Women in Organizations 387
Problems Facing Men in Organizations 391
Challenges and Opportunities for Working Men and Women 392
How to Cope with Gender-Biased Behavior 395
Learn to Understand and Respect Gender Differences 398

Looking Back ■ Career Corner ■ Key Terms ■ Applying What You
Have Learned ■ Internet Insights ■ Role-Play Exercise

Case 16.1   Salomon Smith Barney Learns the Hard Way 404
Case 16.2   Creating a Balance 405

PART VI **YOU CAN PLAN FOR SUCCESS   407**

17 A LIFE PLAN FOR EFFECTIVE HUMAN RELATIONS 408

Achieving Balance in a Chaotic World 409
Toward a New Definition of Success 410
Toward Right Livelihood 414
Developing a Healthy Lifestyle 424
Planning for Changes in Your Life 427
The Choice Is Yours 429

Looking Back ■ Career Corner ■ Key Terms ■ Applying What You
Have Learned ■ Internet Insights ■ Role-Play Exercise

Case 17.1   Toward Right Livelihood 432

APPENDIX Human Relations Abilities Assessment Form—Student and Instructor
Websites

The NWNL Workplace Stress Test—Student and Instructor Websites

*Student and Instructor websites can be accessed at:
college.hmco.com/pic/reece10e.*

NOTES   435

CREDITS   453

NAME INDEX   457

SUBJECT INDEX   467

ABOUT THE AUTHORS

Effective Human Relations: Personal and Organizational Applications, tenth edition, represents a compilation of more than thirty years of research by authors Barry Reece and Rhonda Brandt. Their combined years of post-secondary teaching experience and on-site consulting with business, industry, and educational institutions provide the basis for their real world approach to human relations skill building. With their diverse backgrounds, they work together to consistently offer their readers up-to-date information and advice in this best-selling text.

Barry L. Reece is a professor at Virginia Polytechnic Institute and State University. He received his Ed.D. from the University of Nebraska. Dr. Reece has been actively involved in teaching, research, consulting, and designing training programs throughout his career. He has conducted more than 500 workshops and seminars devoted to leadership, human relations, communications, sales, customer service, and small business operations. He has received the Excellence in Teaching Award for classroom teaching at Virginia Tech and the Trainer of the Year Award presented by the Valleys of Virginia Chapter of the American Society for Training and Development. Dr. Reece has contributed to numerous journals and is author or co-author of thirty-two books. He has served as a consultant to Lowe's Companies, Inc., Wachovia Corporation, WLR Foods, Kinney Shoe Corporation, and numerous other profit and not-for-profit organizations.

Rhonda Brandt teaches interpersonal and business communications, human resources management, and various related courses in the Business and Marketing Division of Ozarks Technical Community College in Springfield, Missouri. She received her bachelor's degree in business education with vocational certification from the University of Northern Iowa and a master's degree in Practical Arts and Vocational/Technical Education from the University of Missouri. She has served as a faculty member at Hawkeye Community College and Administrative Support Department Chair at Springfield College. Ms. Brandt is currently serving as Executive Director of the International Association of Online Teachers (*www.online-teachers.org*), an organization dedicated to providing teachers from all disciplines the opportunity to enhance their professional credentials and online teaching opportunities, while at the same time providing educational institutions access to experienced and credentialed faculty. Rhonda continues to conduct workshops and seminars for teachers, small businesses, and large corporations throughout the nation, just as she has done for more than twenty-five years.

PREFACE

Contrary to popular belief, a lack of technical skills is not the primary reason why new hires fail to meet expectations and experienced workers falter on the road to career success. Interpersonal and communication skills, the ability to work effectively within a team, and personal ethics and integrity are the attributes that are ranked highest by those who make hiring and promotion decisions today. We have seen the evolution of a work environment that is characterized by greater cultural diversity, more work performed by teams, and greater awareness that quality relationships are just as important as quality products in our global economy.

The goal of each revision of *Effective Human Relations: Personal and Organizational Applications* is to develop the most practical and applied text available. The revision process begins with a thorough review of several hundred articles, books, and research reports as well as text and ancillary reviews performed by teachers of the Human Relations course nationwide. One of the major outcomes of the literature review is the discovery of real world examples that help clarify various human relations concepts and develop student interest.

Building on Traditional Strengths

Effective Human Relations: Personal and Organizational Applications is one of the most widely adopted human relations texts available today. This book has been successful because the authors continue to build on strengths that have been enthusiastically praised by instructors and students.

- The **"total person" approach** to human relations has been expanded and enriched in this edition. We continue to believe that human behavior at work and in our private lives is influenced by many interdependent traits such as emotional balance, self-awareness, integrity, self-esteem, physical fitness, and healthy spirituality. This approach focuses on those human relations skills needed to be well-rounded and thoroughly prepared to handle a wide range of human relations problems and issues.

- This edition, like all previous editions, provides the reader with an in-depth presentation of the **seven major themes of effective human relations:** Communication, Self-Awareness, Self-Acceptance, Motivation, Trust, Self-Disclosure, and Conflict Resolution. These broad themes serve as the foundation for contemporary human relations courses and training programs.

- Some of the most important human relations concepts are covered in more than one chapter. The various dimensions of the **communication** theme, for example, are discussed in Chapters 2, 3, and 8. Some of the additional chapters focus on specific communication issues and problems. Ethics is another topic that receives coverage in more than one chapter. Ethical issues and concerns are integrated throughout this edition and featured in Chapter 5, "Personal Values Influence Ethical Choices." Students can also complete the instructional game "Ethical Decision Making."

■ **Self-assessment and self-development opportunities** are strategically placed throughout the entire text. One of the few certainties in today's rapidly changing workplace is the realization that we must assume greater responsibility for developing and upgrading our skills and competencies. In many cases, self-development begins with self-awareness. The text provides multiple opportunities to complete self-assessment activities and then reflect on the results. Employers tell us that they want employees who can apply theory learned in college courses. Consequently, this edition has a very strong skill development orientation.

■ A hallmark of this edition, and all previous editions, is the use of many **real world examples** of human relations issues and practices. These examples build the reader's interest and promote understanding of major topics and concepts. Many of the organizations cited in the tenth edition have been recognized by the authors of *The 100 Best Companies to Work for, The 100 Best Corporate Citizens, 100 Best Companies for Working Mothers,* and *America's 50 Best Companies for Minorities.* The tenth edition also includes many examples from successful smaller companies featured in *Inc.* and *Fast Company* magazines and from America's trading partners within the international community.

■ Each edition is a concise, **tightly focused textbook.** Information not essential to coverage of the topic or concept has been removed. The finished product is very "reader friendly" because the text is focused on important "must know" information. Real world examples that enhance student interest and clarify important concepts are provided in every chapter.

Staying on the Cutting Edge—New to This Edition

The tenth edition of *Effective Human Relations: Personal and Organizational Applications* has been updated to reflect the growing importance of the human element in our service-oriented, information-saturated, global economy. It is a practical text designed to help students achieve insight, knowledge, and relationship skills needed to deal with a wide range of people-related problems. Staying on the cutting edge requires improvements in every edition.

Major Changes and Improvements   These significant changes and improvements can be found in the tenth edition:

■ Fifteen of seventeen chapter opening vignettes are new.

■ Every chapter includes a new Critical Thinking Challenge designed to motivate in-depth thinking about a topic or concept.

■ There are sixteen new Human Relations in Action boxed inserts.

■ There are fifteen new Total Person Insights.

■ There are fourteen new Internet Insight exercises.

- There are sixteen new Skill Development Challenge exercises
- Nine of the Career Corner items have been revised and updated.
- Twelve of the chapter-closing cases are new.
- Nine of the chapter-closing cases have been updated.
- Ten end-of-chapter learning activities are new.
- Every chapter includes a new role-play activity.
- Coverage of diversity themes and issues has been expanded.
- A more compact design has shortened the book.

New Topics

- Changing work patterns that create new opportunities and new challenges (Chapter 1).
- The creation of Web logs (Chapter 2).
- The concept of mirroring (Chapter 3).
- The importance of identifying your dominant talents. Major references come from the book *Now, Discover Your Own Strengths* (Chapter 4).
- The concept of guided imagery (Chapter 4).
- The importance of focusing on your life's purpose (Chapter 5).
- The importance of being an empathizer. Major references come from the book *A Whole New Mind* (Chapter 6).
- The quality of *grit* as a major indicator of success (Chapter 7).
- The Sedona Method program, a process that helps us release unwanted emotions (Chapter 9).
- How positive energy affects our productivity at work (Chapter 10).
- Key concepts from the bestselling book *How Full Is Your Bucket?* (Chapter 10).
- Pride as a source of positive energy (Chapter 10).
- The impact of your emotional focus on making a good first impression (Chapter 11).
- Major determinants of team effectiveness (Chapter 12).
- Four steps in coaching for peak performance (Chapter 12).
- Basic negotiating tips that recur in bestselling books (Chapter 13).
- Major concepts from the authors of *The Stress of Organizational Change* (Chapter 14)
- The importance of resilience as a stress management strategy (Chapter 14).
- The economic benefits of diversity (Chapter 15).
- The current status of women in the work force (Chapter 16).

- Pregnancy discrimination (Chapter 16).

- The new My Pyramid program that provides an individualized approach to improving diet and lifestyle (Chapter 17).

Chapter Organization

This book is divided into six parts. **Part I, "Human Relations: The Key to Personal Growth and Career Success,"** provides a strong rationale for the study of human relations and reviews the historical development of this field. One important highlight of Chapter 1 is a detailed discussion of the major developments influencing behavior at work. This material helps students develop a new appreciation for the complex nature of human behavior in a work setting. The communication process, the basis for effective human relations, is explained from both an individual and organizational level in Chapter 2.

Part II, "Career Success Begins with Knowing Yourself," reflects the basic fact that our effectiveness in dealing with others depends in large measure on our self-awareness and self-acceptance. We believe that by building high self-esteem and by learning to explore inner attitudes, motivations, and values, the reader will learn to be more sensitive to the way others think, feel, and act. Complete chapters are devoted to such topics as communication styles, building high self-esteem, personal values and ethical choices, attitude formation, and motivation.

Part III, "Personal Strategies for Improving Human Relations," comprises four chapters that feature a variety of practical strategies that can be used to develop and maintain good relationships with coworkers, supervisors, and managers. Chapters on constructive self-disclosure, learning to achieve emotional control, positive energy, and developing a professional presence are featured in this part of the text.

In **Part IV, "If We All Work Together . . . ,"** the concepts of team building and conflict resolution are given detailed coverage. Because employers are increasingly organizing employees into teams, the chapter on team-building leadership strategies (Chapter 12) takes on major importance. The chapter on conflict resolution (Chapter 13) describes several basic conflict resolution strategies, discusses ways to deal with difficult people, and provides an introduction to the role of labor unions in today's work force.

Part V, "Special Challenges in Human Relations," is designed to help the reader deal with some unique problem areas—coping with personal and work-related stress, working effectively in a diverse work force, and understanding the changing roles of men and women. The reader is offered many suggestions on ways to deal effectively with these modern-day challenges.

Part VI, "You Can Plan for Success," features the final chapter which serves as a capstone for the entire text. This chapter offers suggestions on how to develop a life plan for effective human relations. Students will be introduced to a new definition of success and learn how to better cope with life's uncertainties and disappointments. This chapter also describes the nonfinancial resources that truly enrich a person's life.

Tools That Enhance the Teaching/Learning Process

The extensive supplements package accompanying the tenth edition of *Effective Human Relations: Personal and Organizational Applications* includes a variety of new and traditional tools that will aid both teaching and learning. The supplements emphasize learning by doing.

Student Support

Online Study Center The Online Study Center is the student-centered, text-specific website that accompanies the tenth edition of *Effective Human Relations: Personal and Organizational Applications.* You can access it at **college.hmco.com/pic/reece10e**. In addition to valuable pass-key protected content, the Online Study Center provides detailed information about every chapter of the text through Chapter at a Glance outlines, Learning Objectives, Looking Back review information, quick ACE self-tests, and a map to the integrated materials within the *Effective Human Relations* program.

Your Guide to an A Passkey The Your Guide to an A passkey is the key to success for *Effective Human Relations*. It protects valuable study content and student support, such as ACE self-tests; MP3 summaries and quizzes to help students learn on the go; and interactive study content originally found in the Classroom Activities Manual. The Your Guide to an A passkey will be automatically shrink-wrapped with all new textbooks and is readily available to purchase through our e-commerce system.

Classroom Activities In order to support classroom interaction and improve communication skills, the authors have enhanced the classroom activities for this edition. The Classroom Activities Manual has been transferred to an online environment. As a Web resource, the activities previously found in the CAM have been more clearly defined to help guide students to the particular resources and support they need. All activities—multiple-choice questions, matching exercises, end-of-chapter review homework, Internet Inquiries, Journal Exercises, Reinforcement Exercises and Assessments—will be protected by the Your Guide to an A passkey, as earlier described. The passkey will be automatically shrink-wrapped with all new textbooks and is readily available to purchase through our e-commerce system.

Instructor Support

Online Teaching Center The Online Teaching Center is the instructor-centered, text-specific website accompanying the tenth edition of *Effective Human Relations: Personal and Organizational Applications*. This website houses all instructor support materials, including the Instructor's Resource Manual, PowerPoint® slides, Class Response System (CRS), Instructional Games, answers to classroom activities and additional exercises, and a guide to integrating program resources throughout the course. You can access the Online Teaching Center at **college.hmco.com/pic/reece10e**.

Instructor's Resource Manual   The Instructor's Resource Manual is a complete teaching guide. The opening material provides a review of the most important **teaching and learning principles** that facilitate human relations training, a review of several **teaching methods,** and a description of suggested **term projects.**

Chapter Teaching Resources provides a chapter preview; chapter purpose and perspective; a presentation outline; and suggested responses to case problem questions for every chapter in the text. Answers, when applicable, are also provided for the text's application exercises.

Additional application exercises are included. Between the material in the textbook and the Instructor's Resource Manual, the instructor can now choose from over 100 application exercises.

The Instructor's Resource Manual also includes two **instructional games** entitled "Ethical Decision Making" and "Coping with Organizational Politics." The ethics game stimulates in-depth thinking about the ethical consequences of certain decisions and actions. Politics surface in every organization and the politics game prepares the student to cope effectively with common political situations. Each game simulates a realistic business environment where employees must make difficult decisions. Students play these games to learn without having to play for keeps. This section of the Instructor's Resource Manual includes complete instructions on how to administer these learning activities in the classroom.

HM Testing   This electronic version of the test items allows instructors to generate and change tests easily. The program includes an online testing feature by which instructors can administer tests via their local area network or over the Web. It also has a gradebook feature that lets users set up classes, record and track grades from tests or assignments, analyze grades, and produce class and individual statistics.

Call-in Test Service   This service lets instructors select items from the Test Bank and call our toll-free faculty services number (800–733–1717) to order printed tests.

Video Program   The video package that accompanies the text includes several segments that illustrate important concepts from the text. The videos focus on topics that include ethics, motivation, diversity, leadership, and organizational culture. These videos provide examples from real world organizations and bring chapter content to life. The accompanying **Video Guide** provides a description of each video, suggested uses, and issues for discussion.

Online/Distance Learning Support   Instructors can create and customize online course materials to use in distance learning, distributed learning, or as a supplement to traditional classes. The **Blackboard Course Cartridge** and **WebCT e-Pack** that accompany the text include a variety of study aids for students, as well as course management tools for instructors.

The Search for Wisdom

The search for what is true, right, or lasting has become more difficult because we live in the midst of an information explosion. The Internet is an excellent source of mass information, but it is seldom the source of wisdom. Television often reduces complicated ideas to a sound bite. Books continue to be one of the best sources of knowledge. Many new books, and several classics, were used as references for the ninth edition of *Effective Human Relations: Personal and Organizational Applications.* A sample of the books we used to prepare this edition follows:

How Full Is Your Bucket? by Tom Rath and Donald O. Clifton
A Whole New Mind by Daniel H. Pink
Now Discover Your Strengths by Marcus Buckingham and Donald O. Clifton
The Success Principles by Jack Canfield
The Leadership Challenge by James M. Kouzes and Barry Z. Posner
The Sedona Method by Hale Dwoskin
The Art of Happiness by the Dalai Lama and Howard C. Culter
Be Your Own Brand by David McNally and Karl D. Speak
Civility—Manners, Morals, and the Etiquette of Democracy by Stephen L. Carter
Complete Business Etiquette Handbook by Barbara Pachter and Majorie Brody
Creative Visualization by Shakti Gawain
Do What You Love . . . The Money Will Follow by Marsha Sinetar
Emotional Intelligence by Daniel Goleman
Empires of the Mind by Denis Waitley
The Four Agreements by Don Miquel Ruiz
Getting to Yes by Roger Fisher and William Ury
How to Control Your Anxiety Before It Controls You by Albert Ellis
How to Win Friends and Influence People by Dale Carnegie
The Human Side of Enterprise by Douglas McGregor
I'm OK—You're OK by Thomas Harris
Minding the Body, Mending the Mind by Joan Borysenko
Multiculture Manners—New Rules of Etiquette For a Changing Society by Norine Dresser
The 100 Absolutely Unbreakable Laws of Business Success by Brian Tracy
1001 Ways to Reward Employees by Bob Nelson
The Power of 5 by Harold H. Bloomfield and Robert K. Cooper
Psycho-Cybernetics by Maxwell Maltz
Self-Matters: Creating Your Life from the Inside Out by Phillip C. McGraw
The 7 Habits of Highly Effective People by Stephen Covey
The 17 Essential Qualities of a Team Player by John C. Maxwell
The Situational Leader by Paul Hersey
The Six Pillars of Self-Esteem by Nathaniel Branden
Spectacular Teamwork by Robert R. Blake, Jane Srygley Mouton, and Robert L. Allen
Working with Emotional Intelligence by Daniel Goleman
You Just Don't Understand: Women and Men in Conversation by Deborah Tannen

Acknowledgments

Many people have made contributions to *Effective Human Relations: Personal and Organizational Applications*. Throughout the years the text has been strengthened as a result of numerous helpful comments and recommendations. We extend special appreciation to the following reviewers and advisors who have provided valuable input for this and prior editions:

James Aldrich, *North Dakota State School of Science*
Thom Amnotte, *Eastern Maine Technical College*
Garland Ashbacker, *Kirkwood Community College*
Sue Avila, *South Hills Business School*
Shirley Banks, *Marshall University*
Rhonda Barry, *American Institute of Commerce*
C. Winston Borgen, *Sacramento Community College*
Jane Bowerman, *University of Oklahoma*
Jayne P. Bowers, *Central Carolina Technical College*
Charles Capps, *Sam Houston State University*
Lawrence Carter, *Jamestown Community College*
Cathy Chew, *Orange County Community College*
John P. Cicero, *Shasta College*
Anne C. Cowden, *California State University Sacramento*
Michael Dzik, *North Dakota State School of Science*
John Elias, *University of Missouri*
Marilee Feldman, *Kirkwood Community College*
Mike Fernsted, *Bryant & Stratton Business Institute*
Dave Fewins, *Neosho County Community College*
Dean Flowers, *Waukesha County Technical College*
Jill P. Gann, *Ann Arundel Community College*
M. Camille Garrett, *Tarrant County Junior College*
Roberta Greene, *Central Piedmont Community College*
Ralph Hall, *Community College of Southern Nevada*
Sally Hanna-Jones, *Hocking Technical College*
Daryl Hansen, *Metropolitan Community College*
Carolyn K. Hayes, *Polk Community College*
John J. Heinsius, *Modesto Junior College*
Stephen Hiatt, *Catawba College*
Jan Hickman, *Westwood College*
Larry Hill, *San Jacinto College—Central*
Bill Hurd, *Lowe's Companies, Inc.*
Dorothy Jeanis, *Fresno City College*
Marlene Katz, *Canada College*
Robert Kegel, Jr., *Cypress College*
Karl N. Kelley, *North Central College*
Vance A. Kennedy, *College of Mateo*
Kristina Leonard, *Westwood College*
Deborah Lineweaver, *New River Community College*
Thomas W. Lloyd, *Westmoreland County Community College*

Jerry Loomis, *Fox Valley Technical College*

Roger Lynch, *Inver Hills Community College*

Edward C. Mann, *The University of Southern Mississippi*

Paul Martin, *Aims Community College*

James K. McReynolds, *South Dakota School of Mines and Technology*

Russ Moorhead, *Des Moines Area Community College*

Marilyn Mueller, *Simpson College*

Erv J. Napier, *Kent State University*

Barbara Ollhoff, *Waukesha County Technical College*

Leonard L. Palumbo, *Northern Virginia Community College*

James Patton, *Mississippi State University*

C. Richard Paulson, *Mankato State University*

Naomi W. Peralta, *The Institute of Financial Education*

William Price, *Virginia Polytechnic Institute and State University*

Shirley Pritchett, *Northeast Texas Community College*

Linda Pulliam, *Pulliam Associates Chapel Hill, N.C.*

Lynne Reece, *Alternative Services*

Jack C. Reed, *University of Northern Iowa*

Lynn Richards, *Johnson County Community College*

Khaled Sartawi, *Fort Valley State University*

Robert Schaden, *Schoolcraft College*

Mary R. Shannon, *Wenatchie Valley College*

J. Douglas Shatto, *Muskingum Area Technical College*

Marilee Smith, *Kirkwood Community College*

Camille Stallings, *Pima Community College*

Lori Stearns, *Minnesota West Community Technical College*

Cindy Stewart, *Des Moines Area Community College*

Rahmat O. Tavallali, *Wooster Business College*

Jane Tavlin, *Delgado Community College*

V. S. Thakur, *Community College of Rhode Island*

Linda Truesdale, *Midlands Technical College*

Wendy Bletz Turner, *New River Community College*

Marc Wayner, *Hocking Technical College*

Tom West, *Des Moines Area Community College*

Steven Whipple, *St. Cloud Technical College*

Burl Worley, *Allan Hancock College*

We would also like to thank Tricia Penno of the University of Dayton for her assistance in revising the test items and MP3 summaries and quizzes for the student website; Jill Whaley for preparing the PowerPoint slides; and Brenny Bachoo of St. John's College for his work in the ACE files.

Over 200 business organizations, government agencies, and nonprofit institutions provided us with the real world examples that appear throughout the text. We are grateful to organizations that allowed us to conduct interviews, observe workplace environments, and use special photographs and materials.

The partnership with Houghton Mifflin, which has spanned nearly three decades, has been very rewarding. Several members of the Houghton Mifflin College Division staff have made important contributions to this project. Sincere appreciation is extended to Suzanna Smith, who has worked conscientiously on the text from the planning stage to completion of the book. We also offer sincere thanks to other key contributors: George Hoffman, Kristen Truncellito, Susan McLaughlin, Mike Schenk, and Erin Lane.

BARRY L. REECE
RHONDA BRANDT

PART I

HUMAN RELATIONS: THE KEY TO PERSONAL GROWTH AND CAREER SUCCESS

1 INTRODUCTION TO HUMAN RELATIONS

2 IMPROVING PERSONAL AND ORGANIZATIONAL COMMUNICATIONS

1

INTRODUCTION TO HUMAN RELATIONS

Chapter Preview

After studying this chapter, you will be able to

- Understand how the study of human relations will help you achieve career success and increased work/life balance.

- Explain the nature, purpose, and importance of human relations in an organizational setting.

- Identify major developments in the workplace that have given new importance to human relations.

- Identify major forces influencing human behavior at work.

- Review the historical development of the human relations movement.

- Identify seven basic themes that serve as the foundation for effective human relations.

Fred Harp has a clear memory of the advice given to him by his uncle. He told Mr. Harp to "get a job and stay with it." Mr. Harp has tried to follow that advice. After graduating from North Bend High School in North Bend, Oregon, he set his sights on a career in the timber industry and started work at a nearby plywood mill. Nine months later the mill closed, and he was out of work. Changing environmental laws, which reduced the amount of timber available for logging, had a major impact on Oregon's timber industry.

Next Mr. Harp found a job in the paper industry, a traditional source of good jobs in Oregon. Four years later the mill closed during a slump created by excess factory capacity and stronger global competition.

Mr. Harp concluded that old-line industries such as timber and paper were a thing of the past. He decided his future lay in electronics. Oregon's economic planners were busy recruiting high-tech manufacturers, and he wanted to work in that growing industry. Soon he began working in a large compact-disc plant opened by Sony Corporation. He enjoyed Sony's team culture and training programs that prepared workers for advancement. As demand for high-tech workers increased, Mr. Harp quit his job at Sony and took a better paying job at a nearby HMT Technology disk-drive plant. A few years later, he and most of his coworkers were given pink slips. The company was bought by Komag Incorporated, and all U.S. production jobs were moved to Malaysia.

After losing yet another job, Mr. Harp decided to return to the classroom. The electric power industry was very healthy in Oregon, so he enrolled in a thirteen-month course in energy management. Unfortunately, by the time

Soon after Oracle completed a $10.3 billion takeover of rival PeopleSoft, 5,000 employee layoff notices were delivered to workers. Most of the affected employees worked for PeopleSoft. These two PeopleSoft employees attempt to console each other.

he graduated the demand for power in Oregon had declined sharply, and he was not able to find work. Today Mr. Harp works for the Lane County facilities-maintenance department. He is hoping this job will not disappear.[1]

The career path followed by Fred Harp reminds us that today's labor market is characterized by a great deal of uncertainty. The old *social contract* between employer and employee was based on the notion of lifetime employment. The new social contract emphasizes personal responsibility for self-development. Today's employers expect employees to assume greater responsibility for increasing their value. Self-development is a major theme of this text.

The Nature, Purpose, and Importance of Human Relations

Each year *Fortune* magazine publishes a list of the 100 best companies to work for in America. The list always includes a variety of small and large companies representing such diverse industries as health care, retailing, finance, manufacturing, and hospitality. Job seekers study the list carefully because these are the companies where morale is high and relationships are characterized by a high level of trust and teamwork. These companies provide a strong foundation for employees to focus on their necessary self-development, therefore enhancing a positive peer-to-peer working environment. America's best companies realize that all work is done through relationships. This chapter focuses on the nature of human relations, its development, and its importance to the achievement of individual and organizational goals.

Human Relations Defined

The term **human relations** in its broadest sense covers all types of interactions among people—their conflicts, cooperative efforts, and group relationships. It is the study of *why* our beliefs, attitudes, and behaviors sometimes cause relationship problems in our personal lives and in work-related situations. The study of human relations emphasizes the analysis of human behavior, prevention strategies, resolution of behavioral problems, and self-development.

Human Relations in the Age of Information

The restructuring of America from an industrial economy to an information economy has had a profound impact on human relationships. Living in an age in which the effective exchange of information is the *foundation* of most economic transactions means making major life adjustments. Many people feel a sense of frustration because they must cope with a glut of information that arrives faster than they can process it. The age of information has spawned the information technology revolution, and many workers experience stress as they try to keep up with ever changing technology.

Increased reliance on information technology often comes at a price—less human contact. Sources of connection away from work are also being trimmed way back. Unfortunately, a human-contact deficiency weakens the spirit, the mind, and the body.[2] To thrive, indeed to just survive, we need warm-hearted contact with other people.

The authors of *The Social Life of Information* describe another price we pay for living in the age of information. A great number of people are focusing on information so intently that they miss the very things that provide valuable balance and perspective. Neglecting the cues and clues that lie outside the tight focus on information can limit our effectiveness. Think about written proposals negotiated on the Internet and signed by electronic signature. Such transactions lack the essence of a face-to-face meeting: a firm handshake and a straight look in the eye. Today's knowledge worker needs to take more account of people and a little less of information.[3]

The Importance of Interpersonal Skills

One of the most significant developments in the age of information has been the increased importance of interpersonal skills in almost every type of work setting. Technical ability is not enough to achieve career success. Studies indicate that communication and interpersonal skills are highly rated by nearly all employers who are hiring new employees. They want to know how new hires will treat coworkers and customers, how they speak and listen at meetings, and how well they extend the minor courtesies that enhance relationships. Your people skills will often make the difference in how high you rise in the organization.[4]

Several important developments in the workplace have given new importance to human relations. Each of the following developments provides support for human relations in the workplace.

- *The labor market has become a place of churning dislocation caused by the heavy volume of mergers, acquisitions, business closings, bankruptcies, downsizings, and outsourcing of jobs to foreign countries.* Layoffs in America, which often exceed 200,000 workers per month, have many negative consequences. Large numbers of companies are attempting to deal with serious problems of low morale and mistrust of management caused by years of upheaval and restructuring. Employees who remain after a company reduces its ranks also suffer; they often feel demoralized, overworked, and fearful that in the next round of cuts they will be targeted.[5]

- *Changing work patterns create new opportunities and new challenges.* The Bureau of Labor Statistics reports that about 30 percent of the U.S. work force is made up of self-employed, temporary, and part-time workers. In recent years we have seen the creation of a phenomenon called *Free Agent Nation*, the growth of self-employed workers who are engaged in consulting and contract work. About 16 million people are now "soloists." Strong demand for temps has surfaced in such diverse fields as medical services, banking, heavy manufacturing, and computers. Many temps land full-time jobs after proving themselves in temporary positions.[6]

- *Organizations are increasingly oriented toward service to clients, patients, and customers.* We live in a service economy where relationships are often more important than products. Restaurants, hospitals, banks, public utilities, colleges, airlines, and retail stores all must now gain and retain the patronage of their clients and customers. In any service-type firm, there are thousands of "moments of truth," those critical incidents in which customers come into contact with the organization and form their impressions of its quality and service.

  In the new economy almost every source of organizational success—technology, financial structure, and competitive strategy—can be copied in an amazingly short period of time.[7] However, making customers the center of the company culture can take years.

> *We live in a service economy where relationships are often more important than products.*

TOTAL	**HARRY E. CHAMBERS**
PERSON	AUTHOR, *THE BAD ATTITUDE SURVIVAL GUIDE*
INSIGHT	"No matter what we do, we do it with people. People create the technology. People implement the technology. People make it all happen. People ultimately use whatever it is we create. No matter how small your organization or how technical its process, it takes people to be successful."

- *Workplace incivility is increasingly a threat to employee relationships.* A popular business magazine featured a cover story entitled "The Death of Civility."[8] The author describes an epidemic of coarse and obnoxious behavior that weakens worker relationships. At a team meeting, a member's cell phone rings several times and is finally answered. As the person talks loudly on the phone, the rest of the team members wait. An employee routinely brushes his teeth at the drinking fountain, and the boss takes three phone calls during an important meeting with an employee. Stephen L. Carter, author of *Civility,* believes that rudeness, insensitivity, and disrespect are the result of people believing in "me" rather than "we." He says civility is the sum of many sacrifices we are called on to make for the sake of living and working together.[9]

■ *Many companies are organizing their workers into teams in which each employee plays a part.* Organizations eager to improve quality, improve job satisfaction, increase worker participation in decision making and problem solving, and improve customer service are turning to teams.

   Although some organizations have successfully harnessed the power of teams, others have encountered problems. One barrier to productivity is the employee who lacks the skills needed to be a team member. In making the transition to a team environment, team members need skills in group decision making, leadership, conflict resolution, and communications.[10]

■ *Diversity has become a prominent characteristic of today's work force.* A number of trends have contributed to greater work force diversity. Throughout the past two decades, participation in the labor force by Asian Americans, African Americans, and Hispanics has increased; labor force participation by adult women has risen to a record 60 percent; the employment door for people with physical or mental impairments has opened wider; and larger numbers of young workers are working with members of the expanding 50-plus age group. Within this heterogeneous work force we will find a multitude of values, expectations, and work habits. There is a need to develop increased tolerance for persons who differ in age, gender, race, physical traits, and sexual orientation. The major aspects of work force diversity are discussed in Chapters 15 and 16.

■ *Growing income inequality has generated a climate of resentment and distrust.* Most measures of income and wage distribution indicate that the wage gap continues to exist. The top 20 percent of American families on average earn about $10 for every dollar earned by the bottom 20 percent. About 37 million people live in poverty, and over 45 million do not have health insurance.[11] Scientists are finding that socioeconomic status—our relative status influenced by income, job, education, and other factors—impacts our physical and mental health. Most agree that psychological factors such as pessimism, stress, and shame are burdens of low social class.[12]

HUMAN RELATIONS IN ACTION

Dartmouth Number One Again

The 2005 Wall Street Journal/Harris Interactive business school poll placed the Dartmouth College MBA program number one. The Hanover, New Hampshire, college has won this award on two previous occasions. MBA recruiters, who are participants in the poll, like students from Dartmouth for their collegiality and teamwork. Dartmouth students are considered impressive because of their humble attitudes, maturity, and strong work ethic. Relationship skills and the ability to work well across an organization are highly valued today.

These developments represent trends that will no doubt continue for many years. Many other developments have also had an unsettling impact on the U.S. work force in recent years. In 2001 the economy was jarred by the collapse of several hundred dot.com companies. The World Trade Center terrorist attack on September 11, 2001, crippled the airline and aerospace industries. In 2002 public trust in the corporate establishment was shaken by a wave of corporate scandals that involved Enron, Tyco, Merrill Lynch, Arthur Anderson, WorldCom, and many other companies.

It is safe to say that no line of work, organization, or industry will enjoy immunity from these developments. Today's employee must be adaptable and flexible to achieve success within a climate of change and uncertainty.

The Challenge of Human Relations

To develop and apply the wide range of human skills needed in today's workplace can be extremely challenging. You will be working with clients, customers, patients, and other workers who vary greatly in age, work background, communications style, values, cultural background, gender, and work ethic.

Human relations is further complicated by the fact that we must manage three types of relationships (see Figure 1.1). The first relationship is the one with ourselves. Many people carry around a set of ideas and feelings about themselves that are quite negative and in most cases quite inaccurate. People who have negative feelings about their abilities and accomplishments and who engage in constant self-criticism must struggle to maintain a good relationship with themselves. The importance of high self-esteem is addressed in Chapter 4.

FIGURE 1.1	Major Relationship Management Challenges

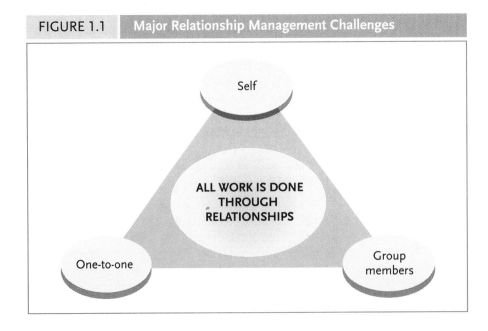

The second type of relationship we must learn to manage is the one-to-one relationships we face in our personal and work lives. People in the health care field, sales, food service, and a host of other occupations face this challenge many times each day. In some cases, racial, age, or gender bias serves as a barrier to good human relations. Communication style bias, a topic that is discussed in Chapter 3, is another common barrier to effective one-to-one relationships.

The third challenge we face is the management of relationships with members of a group. As already noted, many workers are assigned to a team on either a full-time or a part-time basis. Lack of cooperation among team members can result in quality problems or a slowdown in production.

The Influence of the Behavioral Sciences

The field of human relations draws on the behavioral sciences—psychology, sociology, and anthropology. Basically, these sciences focus on the *why* of human behavior. Psychology attempts to find out why *individuals* act as they do, and sociology and anthropology concentrate primarily on *group* dynamics and social interaction. Human relations differs from the behavioral sciences in one important respect. Although also interested in the why of human behavior, human relations goes further and looks at what can be done to anticipate problems, resolve them, or even prevent them from happening. In other words, this field emphasizes knowledge that can be *applied* in practical ways to problems of interpersonal relations at work or in our personal life.

Human Relations and the "Total Person"

The material in this book focuses on human relations as the study of *how people satisfy both personal and work-related needs.* We believe, as do most authors in the field of human relations, that such human traits as physical fitness, emotional control, self-awareness, self-esteem, and values orientation are interdependent. Although some organizations may occasionally wish they could employ only a person's physical strength or creative powers, all that can be employed is the **total person**. A person's separate characteristics are part of a single system making up that whole person. Work life is not totally separate from home life, and emotional conditions are not separate from physical conditions. The quality of one's work, for example, is often related to physical fitness or one's ability to cope with the stress created by family problems.

Many organizations are beginning to recognize that when the whole person is improved, significant benefits accrue to the firm. These organizations are establishing employee development programs that address the total person, not just the employee skills needed to perform the job. At 3M Corporation employees attend lunchtime seminars on financial planning, parenting, and other topics that help them achieve work/life balance. J. Rolfe Davis Insurance Company offers employees an on-site Weight Watchers class and a "Strides for Pride" walking program.[13]

TOTAL	**DANIEL GOLEMAN**
PERSON	AUTHOR, *WORKING WITH EMOTIONAL INTELLIGENCE*
INSIGHT	"The rules for work are changing, and we're all being judged, whether we know it or not, by a new yardstick—not just how smart we are and what technical skills we have, which employers see as givens, but increasingly by how well we handle ourselves and one another."

The Need for a Supportive Environment

Lee Iacocca, the man who was credited with helping Chrysler Corporation avoid bankruptcy, said that all business operations can be reduced to *people*, *product*, and *profit*. He believed that people come first. Iacocca understood that people are at the heart of every form of quality improvement.

Some managers do not believe that total person development, job enrichment, motivation techniques, or career development strategies help increase productivity or strengthen worker commitment to the job. It is true that when such practices are tried without full commitment or without full management support, there is a good chance they will fail. Such failures often have a demoralizing effect on employees and management alike.

A basic assumption of this book is that human relations, when applied in a positive and supportive environment, can help individuals achieve greater personal satisfaction from their careers and help increase an organization's productivity and efficiency.

> **CRITICAL THINKING CHALLENGE**
>
> You are in the process of preparing a résumé that will be used in conjunction with several upcoming job interviews. Assume that you cannot include any past employment experience, training programs, degrees, awards, or community service. The only data you can put on your résumé are the interpersonal skills that you have developed. What would they be?

The Forces Influencing Behavior at Work

A major purpose of this text is to increase your knowledge of factors that influence human behavior in a variety of work settings. An understanding of human behavior at work begins with a review of the six major forces that affect every employee, regardless of the size of the organization. As Figure 1.2 indicates, these are organizational culture, supervisory-management influence, work group influence, job influence, personal characteristics of the worker, and family influence.

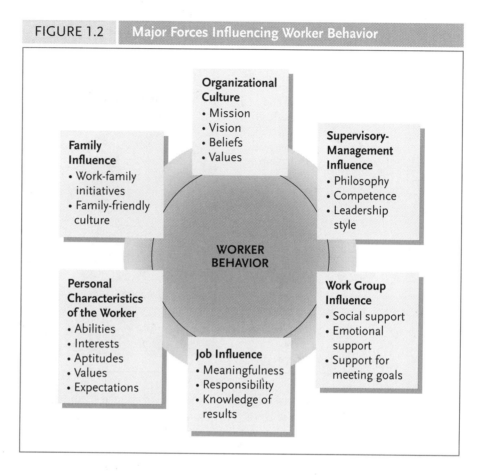

FIGURE 1.2 | Major Forces Influencing Worker Behavior

Organizational Culture

Every organization, whether a manufacturing plant, retail store, hospital, or government agency, has its own unique culture. The **organizational culture** is the collection of shared values, beliefs, rituals, stories, and myths that foster a feeling of community among organizational members.[14] The culture of an organization is, in most cases, the reflection of the deeply held values and behaviors of a small group of individuals. In a large organization, the chief executive officer (CEO) and a handful of senior executives will shape the culture. In a small company, the culture may flow from the values held by the founder.[15]

Enron Corporation, the second-largest company in U.S. history to file for bankruptcy, maintained a corporate culture that pushed everything to the limits: business practices, laws, and personal behavior. This culture drove Enron to dizzying growth, but it eventually collapsed under the weight of greed, deception, and corruption.[16]

By contrast, eBay, the auction website company, has developed a culture that emphasizes customer service and a loyal work force. The culture is based on two principles: "We believe people are basically good" and "We believe everyone has something to contribute."[17]

Maria Benjamin, Wegmans Food Markets employee, offers a cookie to a young customer. Wegmans is usually ranked near the top of Fortune magazine's list of 100 best companies to work for. This Rochester-based chain is beloved by its employees and customers.

Many employees are fired or choose to quit their jobs because they are a poor fit with the corporate culture. It's a good idea to carefully study the organizational culture of a company before accepting employment there.

Supervisory-Management Influence

Supervisory-management personnel are in a key position to influence employee behavior. It is no exaggeration to say that supervisors and managers are the spokespersons for the organization. Their philosophy, competence, and leadership style establish the organization's image in the eyes of employees. Each employee develops certain perceptions about the organization's concern for his or her welfare. These perceptions, in turn, influence such important factors as productivity, customer relations, safety consciousness, and loyalty to the firm.

TOTAL **WILLIAM RASPBERRY**

PERSON SYNDICATED COLUMNIST

INSIGHT "Jobs do a lot more than merely provide income. They provide the opportunity to learn and enhance skills, to have some control over one's fate and, perhaps most important, to gain a sense of self-worth, a sense of carrying one's own weight."

Work Group Influence

In recent years, behavioral scientists have devoted considerable research to determining the influence of group affiliation on the individual worker. This research has identified three functions of group membership. First, it can satisfy *social needs*. When employees feel more connected to their colleagues at work, they are generally more productive.[18] Many people find the hours spent at work enjoyable because coworkers provide needed social support. Second, the work group can provide the *emotional support* needed to deal with pressures and problems on or off the job. Finally, the group provides *assistance in solving problems* and *meeting goals*. A cohesive work group lends support and provides the resources we need to be productive workers.

Job Influence

> *"We spend most of our waking hours doing our jobs, thinking about work, and getting to and from our workplaces."*

Work in modern societies does more than fulfill economic needs. When we find meaning and fulfillment in our jobs, we become more complete as human beings.[19] As one organizational consultant noted, work has taken center stage in the lives of most people: "We spend most of our waking hours doing our jobs, thinking about work, and getting to and from our workplaces. When we feel good about our work, we tend to feel good about our lives. When we find our work unsatisfying and unrewarding, we don't feel good."[20] Unfortunately, many people hold jobs that do not make them feel good. Many workers perceive their jobs to be meaningless and boring. Some workers experience frustration because they are powerless to influence their working conditions.

Personal Characteristics of the Worker

Every worker brings to the job a combination of abilities, interests, aptitudes, values, and expectations. Worker behavior on the job is most frequently a reflection of how well the work environment accommodates the unique characteristics of each worker. For more than half a century, work researchers and theorists have attempted to define the ideal working conditions that would maximize worker productivity. These efforts have met with some success, but unanswered questions remain.

Identifying the ideal work environment for today's work force is difficult. A single parent may greatly value a flexible work schedule and child care. The recipient of a new business degree may seek a position with a new high-tech firm, hoping to make a lot of money in a hurry. Other workers may desire more leisure time.

Coming into the workplace today is a new generation of workers with value systems and expectations about work that often differ from those of the previous generation. Today's better-educated and better-informed workers value identity and achievement. They also have a heightened sense of their rights.

Family Influence

A majority of undergraduates name balancing work and personal life as their top career goal.[21] Most people want time for family, friends, and leisure pursuits.

However, finding employers who truly support work/life balance can be difficult, especially during a slowing economy.

The New Economy is a 24/7 economy. When businesses operate twenty-four hours a day, seven days a week, the result is often a culture of relentless overwork. In many cases workers must live with on-call-all-the-time work schedules.

The number of dual-income families has doubled since 1950. Both parents have jobs in 63 percent of married-couple homes. When both partners are working long hours, it is more difficult to stay committed to a good life together. Marital distress often has a negative impact on organizational productivity.

Many organizations have found that family problems are often linked to employee problems such as tardiness, absenteeism, and turnover. The discovery has led many companies to develop work-family programs and policies that help employees juggle the demands of children, spouses, and elderly parents.[22]

The Development of the Human Relations Movement

The early attempts to improve productivity in manufacturing focused mainly on trying to improve such things as plant layout and mechanical processes. But over time, there was more interest in redefining the nature of work and perceiving workers as complex human beings. This change reflected a shift in values from a concern with *things* to a greater concern for *people*. In this section we briefly examine a few major developments that influenced the human relations movement.

The Impact of the Industrial Revolution

The Industrial Revolution marked a shift from home-based, handcrafted processes to large-scale factory production. Prior to the Industrial Revolution, most work was performed by individual craftworkers or members of craft guilds. Generally, each worker saw a project through from start to finish. Skills such as tailoring, carpentry, and shoemaking took a long time to perfect and were often a source of pride to an individual or a community. Under this system, however, output was limited.

The Industrial Revolution had a profound effect on the nature of work and the role of the worker. Previously, an individual tailor could make only a few items of clothing in a week's time; factories could now make hundreds. However, the early industrial plants were not very efficient because there was very little uniformity in the way tasks were performed. It was this problem that set the stage for research by a man who changed work forever.

Taylor's Scientific Management

In 1874 Frederick W. Taylor obtained a job as an apprentice in a machine shop. He rose to the position of foreman, and in this role he became aware of the inefficiency and waste throughout the plant. In most cases workers were left on their own to determine how to do their jobs. Taylor began to systematically study each job and break it down into its smallest movements. He discovered ways to reduce the number of motions and get rid of time-wasting efforts. Workers willing to follow Taylor's instruction found that their productivity soared.[23]

Frederick W. Taylor started the **scientific management** movement, and his ideas continue to influence the workplace today. Critics of Taylor's approach say that the specialized tasks workers perform often require manual skills but very little or no thinking. It's fair to say that Taylor's ideas gave workers the means to work more efficiently, but they left decisions about how the work should be done to foremen and supervisors.[24]

TOTAL	**JAMES BAUGHMAN**
PERSON	DIRECTOR OF MANAGEMENT DEVELOPMENT, GENERAL ELECTRIC CO.
INSIGHT	"You can only get so much more productivity out of reorganization and automation. Where you really get productivity leaps is in the minds and hearts of people."

Mayo's Hawthorne Studies

Elton Mayo and his colleagues accidentally discovered part of the answer to variations in worker performance while conducting research in the mid-1920s at the Hawthorne Western Electric plant, located near Chicago. Their original goal was to study the effect of illumination, ventilation, and fatigue on production workers in the plant. Their research, known as the **Hawthorne studies**, became a sweeping investigation into the role of human relations in group and individual productivity. These studies also gave rise to the profession of industrial psychology by legitimizing the human factor as an element in business operations.[25]

After three years of experimenting with lighting and other physical aspects of work, Mayo made two important discoveries. First, all the attention focused on workers who participated in the research made them feel more important. For the first time, they were getting feedback on their job performance. In addition, test conditions allowed them greater freedom from supervisory control. Under these circumstances, morale and motivation increased and productivity rose.

Second, Mayo found that the interaction of workers on the job created a network of relationships called an **informal organization**. This organization exerted considerable influence on workers' performance.

Although some observers have criticized the Hawthorne studies for flawed research methodology,[26] this research can be credited with helping change the way management viewed workers.

From the Great Depression to the New Millennium

During the Great Depression, interest in human relations research waned as other ways of humanizing the workplace gained momentum. During that period, unions increased their militant campaigns to organize workers and force employers to pay attention to such issues as working conditions, higher pay, shorter hours, and protection for child laborers.

After World War II and during the years of postwar economic expansion, interest in the human relations field increased. Countless papers and research studies on worker efficiency, group dynamics, organization, and motivational methods were published. Douglas McGregor, in his classic book *The Human Side of Enterprise*, argued that how well an organization performs is directly proportional to its ability to tap human potential.[27] Abraham Maslow, a noted psychologist, devised a "hierarchy of needs," stating that people satisfied their needs in a particular order. Later Frederick Herzberg proposed an important theory of employee motivation based on satisfaction. Each theory had considerable influence on the study of motivation and is explored in detail in Chapter 7.

Since the 1950s, theories and concepts regarding human behavior have focused more and more on an understanding of human interaction. Eric Berne in the 1960s revolutionized the way people think about interpersonal communication when he introduced transactional analysis, with its "Parent-Adult-Child" model. At about the same time, Carl Rogers published his work on personality development, interpersonal communication, and group dynamics. In the early 1980s, William Ouchi introduced the Theory Z style of management, which is based on the belief that worker involvement is the key to increased productivity.

There is no doubt that management consultants Tom Peters and Robert Waterman also influenced management thinking regarding the importance of people in organizations. Their best-selling book *In Search of Excellence*, published in 1982, describes eight attributes of excellence found in America's best-run companies. One of these attributes, "productivity through people," emphasizes that excellent companies treat the worker as the root source of quality and productivity. The editors of *Fast Company* magazine say that *In Search of Excellence* "fired the starting gun in the race to the New Economy."[28]

We have provided you with no more than a brief glimpse of selected developments in the human relations movement. Space does not permit a review of the hundreds of theorists and practitioners who have influenced human relations in the workplace. However, in the remaining chapters, we do introduce the views of other influential thinkers and authors.

HUMAN RELATIONS IN ACTION

Big-Book Blockbusters

Each year between 4,000 and 5,000 new books claiming to be about business are published. Here is a list of four heavyweights:

- ■ *The One Minute Manager* by Kenneth Blanchard and Spencer Johnson. (Published in 1982 and still making best-seller lists.)
- ■ *Reengineering the Corporation* by Michael Hammer and James Champy. (A *Business Week* reviewer said, "May well be the best-written book for the managerial masses since *In Search of Excellence*.)
- ■ *Built to Last* by Jim Collins. (According to *USA Today*, it's "one of the most eye-opening business studies since *In Search of Excellence*.)
- ■ *In Search of Excellence* by Tom Peters and Robert Waterman. (Described by the *Wall Street Journal* as "one of those rare books on management that are both consistently thought provoking and fun to read.")

Major Themes in Human Relations

Seven broad themes emerge from the study of human relations. They are communication, self-awareness, self-acceptance, motivation, trust, self-disclosure, and conflict resolution. These themes reflect the current concern in human relations with the twin goals of (1) personal growth and development and (2) the achievement of organizational objectives. To some degree, these themes are interrelated (see Figure 1.3), and most are discussed in more than one chapter of this book.

Communication

It is not an exaggeration to describe communication as the "heart and soul" of human relations. **Communication** is the means by which we come to an understanding of ourselves and others. To grow and develop as persons, we must develop the awareness and the skills necessary to communicate effectively. Communication is the *human* connection. That is why the subject is covered in more than one section of this book. In Chapter 2 we explore the fundamentals of both personal and organizational communication. It is these fundamentals that provide the foundation for all efforts to improve communication. Chapter 3 provides an introduction to communication styles and outlines several practical tips on how you can cope with communication style bias. Chapter 8 explains how constructive self-disclosure, an important form of personal communication, can be used to improve human relationships.

> *It is not an exaggeration to describe communication as the "heart and soul" of human relations.*

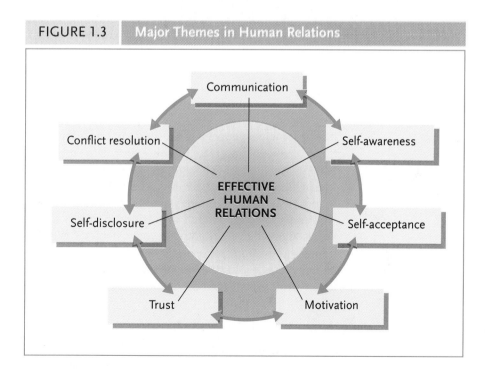

FIGURE 1.3 Major Themes in Human Relations

Self-Awareness

One of the most important ways to develop improved relationships with others is to develop a better understanding of ourselves. With increased **self-awareness** comes a greater understanding of how our behavior influences others. Stephen Covey, author of *The Seven Habits of Highly Effective People*, says that self-awareness enables us to stand apart and examine the way we "see" ourselves, as well as to see other people.[29]

The importance of self-awareness is being recognized by an increasing number of authors, trainers, and educators. Daniel Goleman, author of the best-selling book *Emotional Intelligence*, has given us new insights into the importance of self-awareness. Goleman says IQ accounts for only about 20 percent of a person's success in life. The rest, he says, you can credit to "emotional intelligence." Of all the elements that make up emotional intelligence, Goleman asserts, self-awareness is the most important. He notes that a deficit in self-awareness can be damaging to one's personal relationships and career.[30] Self-awareness is discussed in greater detail in the chapters that are featured in Part II.

Self-Acceptance

The degree to which you like and accept yourself is the degree to which you can genuinely like and accept other people. **Self-acceptance** is the foundation of successful interaction with others. In a work setting, people with positive self-concepts tend to cope better with change, accept responsibility more readily, tolerate differences, and generally work well as team members. A negative self-concept, however, can create barriers to good interpersonal relations. Self-acceptance is crucial not only for building relationships with others but also for setting and achieving goals. The more you believe you can do, the more you are likely to accomplish. Chapter 4 explains why high self-esteem (complete self-acceptance) is essential for effective human relations. That chapter also helps you identify ways to achieve greater self-acceptance.

Motivation

Most people who engage in the study of **motivation** seek answers to two questions: "How do I motivate myself?" and "How do I motivate others?" If you are really committed to achieving peak performance, you must motivate yourself from within.[31] Inner drives for excellence can be very powerful. To motivate others, you need to understand time-proven, well-researched theories and well-established motivation strategies. Chapter 5 will help you identify the priorities and values that motivate you. Chapter 7 explores the complex nature of human motivation, particularly of self and others, and examines various motivation strategies. In Chapter 10 you will learn how incentives and various positive reinforcement methods serve as external motivators.

Trust

Trust is the building block of all successful relationships with coworkers, customers, family members, and friends. There is compelling evidence that low levels of trust in a work force can lead to reduced productivity, stifled innovation, high stress, and slow decision making.[32] When a lack of trust exists in an organization, a decline in the flow of information almost always results. Employees communicate less information to their supervisors, express opinions reluctantly, and avoid discussions. Cooperation, so necessary in a modern work setting, deteriorates. When a climate of trust is present, frank discussion of problems and a free exchange of ideas and information is more likely to take place. The concept of trust is discussed in Chapters 8 and 12.

Self-Disclosure

Self-disclosure and trust are two halves of a whole. The more open you are with people, the more trust you build up. The more trust there is in a relationship, the safer you feel to disclose who you are. Self-disclosure is also part of good communication and helps eliminate unnecessary guessing games. Managers who let their subordinates know what is expected of them help those employees fulfill their responsibilities. Chapter 8 emphasizes the need of individuals to verbalize the thoughts and feelings they carry within them and provides many practical suggestions on how to use constructive self-disclosure.

Conflict Resolution

Conflict in one form or another surfaces almost daily in the lives of many workers. You may experience conflict during a commute to work when a careless driver cuts you off at a freeway exit ramp. If your job includes supervisory-management responsibilities, you will spend a great deal of time in **conflict resolution**, attempting to resolve conflicts among members of your staff. As a team member, you may assume the role of mediator when other team members clash. Conflict also surfaces when working parents attempt to balance the demands of both work and family. Stressful conditions at home often interfere with work performance, and on-the-job pressures create or magnify problems at home.[33] The ability to anticipate or resolve conflict can be an invaluable skill. Although Chapter 13 deals specifically with the topic of conflict resolution, the chapters devoted to communication, achievement of emotional control, and team building provide many valuable suggestions on how conflict can be handled constructively.

SKILL DEVELOPMENT CHALLENGE

To achieve a better understanding of the major themes in human relations, complete the sentences below. Work quickly and don't worry too much about the ending. Sentence completion exercises can be powerful vehicles for self-discovery and personal growth.

To become more self accepting I need to…

To build a more trusting relationship with others, I need to…

My greatest strength in the area of communication is…

To grow in the area of self-awareness I need to…

I am motivated to give my best when…

Conflict at work is quite common, so the ability to anticipate or resolve disagreements can be an invaluable skill. Stressful conditions at work or at home often create or magnify problems.

Human Relations: Benefits to You

As previously noted, the work force is currently characterized by downsizing, mergers, buyouts, business closings, and other disruptive forces. We are seeing more emphasis on quality products and quality services. In addition, diversity has become a more prominent characteristic of today's work force. These conditions will very likely continue in the new millennium. One of the best ways to cope with these changes is to develop and apply the interpersonal skills needed for success in today's working world.

Many leaders feel that courses in human relations are important because very few workers are responsible to themselves alone. These leaders point out that most jobs today are interdependent. If people in these jobs cannot work effectively as a team, the efficiency of the organization will suffer.

LOOKING BACK: Reviewing the Concepts

■ Understand how the study of human relations will help you achieve career success and increased work/life balance.

Human relations covers all types of interactions among people—their conflicts, cooperative efforts, and group relationships. The importance of interpersonal relations can be summarized in one concise law of personal and organizational success: All work is done through relationships. Employees are more productive when they have the ability to develop effective relationships with their supervisor, fellow workers, customers, and clients.

■ Explain the nature, purpose, and importance of human relations in an organizational setting.

The healthy functioning of any organization, large or small, depends on teamwork. Effective human relations is the very foundation of teamwork. Human relations, when applied in a positive and supportive environment, can help increase an organization's productivity and efficiency.

■ Identify major developments in the workplace that have given new importance to human relations.

The restructuring of America from an industrial economy to an information economy has had profound implications for the study of human relations. Several major developments in the workplace have given new importance to this branch of learning. Some of these developments include churning dislocation in the labor market, changing work patterns, the need for higher service standards, increasing workplace incivility, greater reliance on team-based structures, work force diversity, and growing income inequality.

■ Identify major forces influencing human behavior at work.

A major purpose of this text is to increase understanding of major factors that influence human behavior in a variety of work settings. These include organizational culture, supervisory-management influence, work group influence, job influence, personal characteristics of worker, and family influence.

■ Review the historical development of the human relations movement.

Early attempts to improve productivity in manufacturing focused on such things as plant layout and mechanical processes. With the passing of time there was more interest in redefining the nature of work and perceiving workers as complex human beings. Two landmarks in the study of motivation and worker needs are Frederick Taylor's work in scientific management and Elton Mayo's Hawthorne studies. Later research by Douglas McGregor, Frederick Herzberg, Carl Rogers, William Ouchi, and others contributed greatly to our understanding of how to achieve productivity through people.

■ Identify seven basic themes that serve as the foundation for effective human relations.

Seven major themes emerge from a study of human relations: communication, self-awareness, self-acceptance, motivation, trust, self-disclosure, and conflict resolution. These themes reflect the current concern in human relations with personal growth and satisfaction of organization objectives.

● Career Corner

Q: The daily newspapers and television news shows are constantly reporting on mergers, business closings, and downsizing efforts. With so much uncertainty in the job market, how can I best prepare for a career?

A: You are already doing one thing that is very important—keeping an eye on labor market trends. During a period of rapid change and less job security, you must continuously study workplace trends and assess your career preparation. Louis S. Richman, in a *Fortune* magazine article entitled "How to Get Ahead in America," said, "Climbing in your career calls for being clear about your personal goals, learning how to add value, and developing skills you can take anywhere." Richard Bolles, author of the bestselling job-hunting book, *What Color Is Your Parachute?*, says you must do a systematic inventory of the transferable skills that you already possess. Then identify the skills that you still need to develop. Keep in mind that today's employers demand more, so be prepared to add value to the company from day one. Search for your employer's toughest problems and make yourself part of the solutions.

The skills you can take anywhere are those transferable skills required by a wide range of employers. These are important because there are no jobs for life. Be prepared to work for several organizations, and anticipate changing careers.

● Key Terms

human relations	self-awareness
total person	self-acceptance
organizational culture	motivation
scientific management	trust
Hawthorne studies	self-disclosure
informal organization	conflict resolution
communication	

● Applying What You Have Learned

1. Throughout this book you will be given many opportunities to engage in self-assessment activities. Self-assessment involves taking a careful look at the human relations skills you need to be well rounded and thoroughly prepared for success in your work life and fulfillment in your personal life. To assess your human relations skills, complete the Human Relations Abilities Assessment Form found on the website (*college.hmco.com/pic/reece10e*). This assessment form will provide you with increased awareness of your strengths and a better understanding of the abilities you may want to improve. Each item offers an opportunity for goal setting to achieve personal development. Goal setting guidelines are described in Chapter 4.

2. In his book, *The Success Principles*, Jack Canfield describes fifty principles that will increase your confidence, help you tackle daily challenges, and

teach you how to realize your ambitions. Number one on his list is "Take 100% responsibility for your life." This includes the quality of your relationships, your health and fitness, your income, your career success—everything! He says most of us have been conditioned to blame events outside of our life for those parts of our life we dislike. Reflect on your life up to this point and identify situations in which you blamed someone or something else for your failure to achieve a goal or improve in some area. Do you see any situations in which you felt justified in blaming others or refused to take risks?[34]

3. The seven broad themes that emerge from the study of human relations were discussed in this chapter. Although these themes are interrelated, there is value in examining each one separately before reading the rest of the book. Review the description of each theme and then answer these questions:

a. When you take into consideration the human relations problems that you have observed or experienced at work, school, and home, which themes represent the most important areas of study? Explain your answer.

b. In which of these areas do you feel the greatest need for improvement? Why?

Internet Insights

Companies featured in *Fortune's* list of the 100 best companies to work for in America are characterized by openness, fairness, camaraderie among employees, job security, opportunities for advancement, and sensitivity to work/family issues. These companies are concerned about the total person, not just the skills that help the company earn a profit. Here are some of the companies that have made the "best companies" list:

Company	Location	Type of Business
Southwest Airlines	Dallas, TX	Airline
SAS Institute	Carey, NC	Computer software
MBNA	Wilmington, DE	Issuer of credit cards
Harley-Davidson	Milwaukee, WI	Manufacturing
Nordstrom	Seattle, WA	Retailing

Develop a profile of two of these companies by visiting their websites and reviewing the available information. Also, visit Hoover's Online, a resource that provides access to profiles of about 2,800 companies. Additional information on each of these companies may be found in *Business Week, Forbes, Fortune,* and other business publications.

Role-Play Exercise

The college you attend offers career counseling, job placement assistance, and help finding summer internships. You plan to meet with a career counselor and seek help finding a summer internship with a well-established company. You will be meeting with a class member, who will assume the role of career counselor. The purpose of this meeting is to give the counselor some basic information about your career plans and the type of company you would like to work for. Prior to the meeting, prepare a written outline of information you plan to present during the meeting. The outline should focus on answers to the following questions:

- What type of work would be most meaningful?
- What type of organizational culture would be most appealing to you?
- What do you find to be the basic rewards of work?

Case 1.1   Challenges in the New Economy

At the beginning of the new millennium, a growing number of social researchers, economists, and consultants tried to predict what the world of work would be like in the years ahead. We pay close attention to these and to even more recent forecasts because work is a central part of our identities. As one writer has noted, our working life—in a few short decades—adds up to life itself. Work can also be one of the major fulfillments in life. What will the New Economy be like from a worker's viewpoint? Here are three predictions:

- *In the New Economy, everyone is an entrepreneur.* This is the view expressed by Thomas Petzinger, Jr., author and former columnist for the *Wall Street Journal*. He reports on factories where shop floor employees handle customer service calls and create new ways to solve customer problems. At UPS the drivers are the eyes and ears of the sales force. They help identify new customers and help solve customer service problems. Many bank tellers are actively involved in sales and service activities.[35] Today the term *intrapreneur* is used to describe an employee who takes personal "hands-on responsibility" for developing ideas, products, or processes. To become an intrapreneur in a corporate setting often means using your creativity more often, taking some risks, and moving beyond your job description. The new economy will give many workers an opportunity to take more responsibility for their work.

- *The New Economy features the art of the relaunch.* How often will you change jobs during your lifetime? Five times? Ten? Fifteen? The New Economy offers more career options, more challenges, and more uncertainty. Chances are, you will need to relaunch your career several times. Molly Higgins held a career track job in the human resources department of a large company. When she discovered that in the entire department there wasn't a single position she aspired to, it was time to relaunch her career. In recent years, thousands of people joined the ranks of new dot.com companies, only to lose their jobs in a matter of weeks or months. One analyst says that changing jobs will require using your learning skills and applying the skills you have already learned.[36]

■ *In the New Economy, getting a job may be easier than getting a life.* We have, in recent years, seen an increase in the standard of living. The price we pay for a bigger home, a nicer automobile, or a vacation in Italy is often a more demanding work life. Some people choose to work harder in order to acquire more "things." In some cases, corporate downsizing has left fewer people to do the same amount of work. Working more hours and working harder during those hours can result in greater stress, a breakdown in family life, and a decrease in leisure time.[37]

Questions

1. Would you feel comfortable assuming the duties of an entrepreneur within an existing company, or would you rather start your own business?

2. You are likely to relaunch yourself several times during the years ahead. Does the prospect of several relaunches seem frightening to you, or do you look forward to the challenge?

3. What steps would you take to achieve better work/life balance?

Case 1.2   In Search of Work/Life Balance

A growing number of workers do not feel there's a healthy balance between work and personal life. Some are tired of working 10- to 12-hour days and weekends. Many want a better balance between work and family. These employees search for companies that offer family-friendly features such as flexible scheduling, telecommuting, and child care. Each year *Working Mother* magazine publishes a list of the 100 best companies for working mothers. Let's look at two of the companies that made the 2005 list.

■ Arnold & Porter is a large law firm with almost seven hundred lawyers practicing in its U.S. and international operations. New mothers get a combined eight-week maternity and eight-week parental leave at full pay. New fathers get an eight-week parental leave, also at full pay. An on-site children's center is available for parents who want to bring their children to work.

■ DuPont Company is a science company that employs seventy-nine thousand employees. About half work outside of the United States. Employees can use job sharing, part-time scheduling, and telecommuting. About twelve thousand data lines have been installed in employees' homes for telecommuting, and roughly 30 percent of DuPont's work force are telecommuters.

Managers can encourage or discourage the use of family-friendly services by mothers and fathers. At Citigroup Corporation, managers attend seminars on various work/life issues and are encouraged to support programs developed for employees.[38]

Questions

1. A majority of today's workers do not think there is a healthy balance between work and personal life. How do you feel?

2. Some companies develop work/life programs that focus primarily on mothers and fathers who have children. What are the advantages and disadvantages of this approach?

INTEGRATED RESOURCES

VIDEO: "Organizational Structure at Green Mountain Coffee Roasters"

CLASSROOM ACTIVITIES (*college.hmco.com/pic/reece10e*)

Human Relations Abilities Assessment Questionnaire
Discover Classmates' Diversity
Journal Entry: Why Are People Fired?

business.college.hmco.com/students

ACE

Self-tests

2

IMPROVING PERSONAL AND ORGANIZATIONAL COMMUNICATIONS

Chapter Preview

After studying this chapter, you will be able to

■ Understand the communication process and the filters that affect communication.

■ Explain how each filter can distort communication.

■ Identify ways to improve personal communication, including developing listening skills.

■ Understand how communications flow throughout an organization and how to improve the flow when necessary.

■ Learn how to effectively communicate through technology.

Workers employed by Automatic Elevator, a Durham, North Carolina, company, performed routine maintenance on the elevators at two Duke University Health System hospitals. Following the completion of their service, employees of Automatic Elevator emptied used petroleum-based hydraulic fluid into several empty detergent drums. Duke employees discovered the drums, assumed they were surplus stock, and returned them to the original vendor, Cardinal Health, a hospital-supply company. Employees at Cardinal Health failed to detect the contents of the detergent drums and delivered the drums to two Duke hospitals. Later, Duke University Health System administrators found that the used hydraulic fluid was piped into the instrument cleaning systems at both hospitals.

Duke administrators were slow to notify the nearly 3,800 surgical patients who may have had contact with the improperly cleaned surgical instruments. Many of these patients reported suffering infections, poor healing, achy joints, weight loss, and extreme fatigue during the months following their surgery. Some of these patients, feeling that Duke should have made more information available sooner, have hired lawyers.[1]

Ineffective communication can negatively influence the lives of many people. In this case, literally thousands of people were affected because someone "failed to communicate." As you reflect on this situation, think about all the frontline employees who were in a position to prevent this crisis.

Effective communication can play a critical role in every aspect of the modern organization. In one form or another, it is the key to improving customer service, resolving conflict, creating productive work teams, improving employee morale, and achieving many other goals. Communication is also the key to effective personal relationships and career success.

Shelley Bassett, seated, is one of several hundred Duke surgical patients who may have had contact with improperly cleaned surgical instruments. In response to patients' concern, Duke University Health System is providing medical services to any patient who is experiencing unusual symptoms.

Communicating Effectively in a High-Tech World

Not everyone is in the communication business, but everyone is in the business of communicating.

The new millennium has ushered in the age of information, led by rapid advances in technology-based communication. But technology without the involvement of people can create more problems than it solves. Developing new technology to move more information faster is critical to staying competitive in today's global marketplace. But the leaders of successful organizations realize that their primary goal continues to be creating an organizational culture that fosters teamwork, which involves effective communication among its workers so that they are motivated to do their best and thereby improve customer service.

Not everyone is in the communication business, but everyone is in the business of communicating. Workers today are bombarded with information transmitted via technology. Cell phones are now able to search the Internet and serve as personal digital assistants (PDAs). These phones can transmit voice and text messages. Text messages often include photos and complete documents.

Often individuals must wade through useless data to find the information they are seeking—and this data glut has become a serious issue in the workplace. Although the speed and volume of information have increased, the average person cannot process it any faster. A young narrator in a television commercial for Volkswagen expressed the feelings of many people:

> I've got gigabytes, I've got megabytes, I'm voice-mailed. I'm e-mailed. I surf the Net. I'm on the Web. I am Cyber-Man. So how come I feel so out of touch?[2]

As the speed and number of messages increase, workers often find themselves distracted and unable to concentrate. This often leads to a breakdown in communication, which can result in human relations problems that may be hard to fix once the damage is done.

The Communication Process

Most people take communication for granted. When they write, speak, or listen to others, they assume that the message given or received is being understood. In reality, messages are often misunderstood because they are incomplete or because different people interpret messages in different ways. The diversity of today's work force calls for a greater understanding of how to communicate effectively, through technology or face to face, with people from different cultures, countries, and lifestyles. Yet even though people and communication methods may be diverse, the basic communication process remains the same.

Impersonal Versus Interpersonal Communication

In a typical organization the types of communication used to exchange information can be placed on a continuum ranging from "impersonal" on one end to "interpersonal" on the other.[3] **Impersonal communication** is a one-way process that transfers basic information such as instructions, policies, and financial data. Generally, organizations use this information-delivery process when they use electronic bulletin boards or memos as quick, easy ways to "get the word out." Their effectiveness is somewhat limited because there is little, if any, possibility for the person receiving the information to clarify vague or confusing information.

Interpersonal communication is the exchange of information between two or more people. Such words as *share*, *discuss*, *argue*, and *interact* refer to this form of two-way communication. Interpersonal communication can take place in meetings, over the phone, in face-to-face interviews, or even during classroom discussions between instructors and students. If interpersonal communication is to be effective, some type of **feedback**, or response, from the person receiving the information is necessary. When this exchange happens, those involved can determine whether the information has been understood in the way intended. This is one of the reasons that some managers still prefer person-to-person meetings and telephone calls instead of e-mail. The speed of technology can be invaluable when it comes to impersonal information giving, but it cannot replace the two-way, interpersonal communication process when feedback and discussion are necessary.

TOTAL
PERSON
INSIGHT

ERIC MAISEL

AUTHOR, *20 COMMUNICATION TIPS @ WORK*

"Many skills are valuable at work, but one skill is essential: the ability to communicate. Whether you are presenting your ideas at a commitee meeting, dashing off fifteen e-mails in a row, chatting with a coworker at a copy machine, evaluating an employee, or closing a deal over the phone, what you are doing is communicating. These exchanges are the backbone and the life blood of every organization and every relationship."

Sender—Message—Receiver—Feedback

Effective communication is a continuous loop that involves a sender, a receiver, the message, and feedback that clarifies the message.[4] To illustrate, suppose your friend phones from your neighborhood convenience store and asks for directions to your home. You give your friend the appropriate street names, intersections, and compass directions so that he can drive to your door without getting lost. When your friend repeats his understanding of your directions, you clarify any misunderstandings, and he drives directly to your home. A simplified diagram of this communication process would look like Figure 2.1.

Now suppose you are late for an appointment, and the plumber you had requested three days ago calls you from her cell phone and asks directions to your house. She explains that she has gotten lost in this neighborhood before, and it is obvious that English is her second language. The communication process becomes much more complicated, as shown in Figure 2.2. As your message travels from you to your plumber, it must pass through several "filters," each of which can alter the way your message is understood. Most communications flow through this complex process.

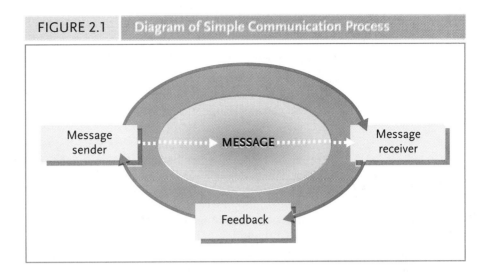

FIGURE 2.1 — Diagram of Simple Communication Process

Communication Filters

Messages are sent—and feedback is received—through a variety of filters that can distort the intended message. (See Figure 2.2.) When people are influenced by one or more of these filters, their perception of the message may be totally different from what the sender was attempting to communicate. Both sender and receiver must be keenly aware of these possible distortions so that they can intercept any miscommunication.

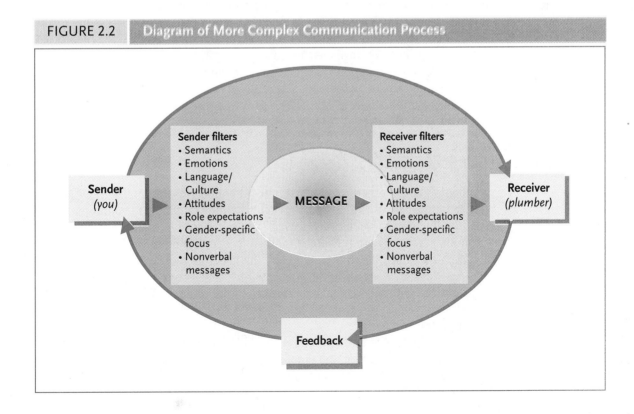

FIGURE 2.2 — Diagram of More Complex Communication Process

Semantics

We often assume that the words we use mean the same things to others, but this assumption can create problems. **Semantics** is the study of the relationship between a word and its meaning(s). Words have associated meanings and usages. We can easily understand what words like *typewriter*, *computer*, or *envelope* mean. But more abstract terms, such as *job satisfaction*, *downsizing*, or *internal customers*, have less precise meanings and will be used and interpreted by different people in different ways. The more abstract the term, the less likely it is that people will agree on its meaning.

■ When Enron wanted to cover up questionable business practices, employees developed some creative accounting jargon. One report included the following sentence: "Enron entered into share settled costless collar arrangements. . . . The transactions resulted in noncash increases to noncurrent assets and equity."[5]

■ Corporate employees often use important-sounding jargon that is almost incomprehensible. Better Communications, a firm that teaches writing skills to employers, clipped this statement from a memo circulated at a *Fortune* 500 company: "Added value is the keystone to exponentially accelerating profit curves."[6]

■ Every industry has its own jargon that can be confusing to those outside that industry. The same is true for young people entering the work force who have communicated extensively via Internet chat rooms. They often assume that their Internet jargon, or cyberlingo, is understood by everyone. Cyberlingo is a feature of the online culture that crosses race, gender, and geography, as this language is accepted and understood by young people all over the world. However, when cyberlingo is used in the mainstream of communication within organizations, it can be confusing to those who are unfamiliar with "words" such as *FAQ* (frequently asked questions), *GMTA* (great minds think alike), *IMHO* (in my humble opinion), and *OTOH* (on the other hand).[7]

Language and Cultural Barriers

When organizations throughout the world connect to the Internet, the people within those organizations must be ready, willing, and able to communicate in a multilingual, multicultural working environment. Although English is the dominant language in the global marketplace, everyone must adjust his or her communication style to accommodate the needs of those whose first language is not English. Keep in mind how muddled a message might get when it is translated from one language to another in the mind of the receiver. To avoid the damage this filter might cause, avoid using industry-specific jargon or culture-specific slang.

The needs of a multicultural work force are getting more attention today because of globalization and employers' growing support for cultural diversity among their workers. The culture in which we are raised strongly influences

HUMAN RELATIONS IN ACTION

Jargon Predates Bubble Burst at WorldCom

Long before massive fraud was uncovered at WorldCom Incorporated, critics said its employees were using strange new words to describe services and to close deals. Some of the jargon used sounded like language from another world. Promotional software was "seedware." WorldCom technologists didn't troubleshoot; they "blamestormed." An embarrassing bug in a sales pitch was a "blevit." Members of the sales force often invented words that were designed to impress the customer. Although some customers were thoroughly perplexed, they were too intimidated to ask questions. Soon after WorldCom filed for bankruptcy, there was a backlash against invented words. In an effort to pacify stockholders, creditors, and other injured parties, a WorldCom spokesperson said, "We're making a really concerted effort to call things what they are."

our values, beliefs, expressions, and behaviors. It also influences the way we interpret the values, beliefs, expressions, and behaviors of others.

When the sender and receiver understand each others' cultural background, each should make the effort to adjust and improve their messages accordingly. For example, people living in the United States, Canada, Europe, Israel, or Australia usually prefer direct-approach communication; they tend to say more or less exactly what they mean. Their cultures value clarity, fluency, and brevity in communication. Many people from Asia, Arab countries, and much of Africa prefer a more indirect style of communication and therefore value harmony, subtlety, sensitivity, and tact more than brevity. They try hard to connect with their listeners.[8]

These Indian employees work at Gecis, an international call center based in Gurgaon. In order to answer calls from outside of India, they must learn foreign accents and be prepared to help customers solve a wide range of technical problems.

Emotions

Strong emotions can either prevent people from hearing what a speaker has to say or make them too susceptible to the speaker's point of view. If they become angry or allow themselves to be carried away by the speaker's eloquence, they may "think" with their emotions and make decisions or take action they regret later. They have shifted their attention from the content of the message to their feelings about it.

You may have had the experience of your spouse or parent angrily demanding to know why you forgot to run an errand. If you allow someone else's anger to trigger your own, the conversation may quickly deteriorate into an argument. The real issue—what happened and what is to be done about it—is lost in the shouting match. Detaching yourself from another's feelings and responding to the content of the message is often difficult. It is hard to realize that another person's emotional response is more likely about fear or frustration than it is about you as an individual. Yet many jobs require that employees remain calm and courteous regardless of a customer's emotional state. Emotional control is discussed in Chapter 9.

Attitudes

Attitudes can be a barrier to communication in much the same way as emotions. The receiver may have a negative attitude toward the sender's voice, accent, gestures, mannerisms, dress, or delivery. These negative attitudes create resistance to the message and can lead to a breakdown in communication. Perhaps the listener has an established attitude about the speaker's topic. For example, a person who is strongly opposed to abortion will most likely find it difficult to listen with objectivity to a pro-choice speaker. Keep in mind, however, that an overly positive attitude can also be a barrier to communication. When biased in favor of the message, the listener may not effectively evaluate the speaker's information. More is said about the power of attitudes in Chapter 6.

Role Expectations

Role expectations influence how people expect themselves, and others, to act on the basis of the roles they play, such as boss, customer, or subordinate. These expectations can distort communication in two ways. First, if people identify others too closely with their roles, they may discount what the other person has to say: "It's just the boss again, saying the same old thing." A variation of this distortion occurs when we do not allow others to change their roles and take on new ones. This often happens to employees who are promoted from within the ranks of an organization to management positions. Others may still see "old Chuck" from accounting rather than the new department head.

Second, role expectations can affect good communication when people use their roles to alter the way they relate to others. This is often referred to as "position power." For example, managers may expect employees to accept what they say simply because of the authority invested in the position. Employees are not allowed to question the manager's decisions or make suggestions of their own, and communication becomes one-way information giving.

Gender-Specific Focus

Gender roles learned throughout childhood can influence the way men and women communicate. After all, boys and girls do grow up in different worlds, and they are conditioned to approach communication in different ways. Girls are socialized as children to believe that talking holds relationships together. As adults, women use conversation to seek and give confirmation and support and to reach a consensus with others. Boys are socialized to maintain their relationships primarily through their activities. As a result, men are more likely to perceive conversation as a form of competition during which they must negotiate to gain the upper hand and protect themselves from being put down.[9] Chapter 16, "The Changing Roles of Men and Women," discusses specific strategies you can use to communicate more effectively with those whose gender differs from your own.

Nonverbal Messages

When we attempt to communicate with another person, we use both verbal and nonverbal communication. **Nonverbal messages** are "messages without words" or "silent messages." These are the messages (other than spoken or written words) we communicate through facial expressions, voice tone, gestures, appearance, posture, and other nonverbal means. Research indicates that our nonverbal messages have much more impact than verbal messages. The late Peter Drucker, author of numerous management books, said, "The important thing in communication is to hear what isn't being said."[10] He recognized that when someone else is speaking, your understanding of what is said depends very heavily on what you see.

> *"The important thing in communication is to hear what isn't being said."*

Some people will walk into a meeting with their shoulders slumped forward and head down. They will slouch in their chair, lean their chin on the palm of their hand, play with a pencil or paperclip on the table, or clutch their arms across their chest. Others will walk into the room with chin held high and shoulders back, sit straight in their chairs, and lean slightly forward with both arms "open" to whomever is speaking during the meetings. Experts agree that the words you say during a meeting, no matter how powerful, are often forgotten or disregarded unless your nonverbal presence commands respect.[11] This chapter limits its discussion to the form of nonverbal communication commonly referred to as "body language." Physical appearance, another powerful form of nonverbal communication, is discussed in Chapter 11.

Many of us could communicate more clearly, more accurately, and more credibly if we became more conscious of our body language. We can learn to strengthen our communications by making sure our words and our body language are consistent. When our verbal and nonverbal messages match, we give the impression that we can be trusted and that what we are saying reflects what we truly believe. But when our body language contradicts our words, we are often unknowingly changing the message we are sending. If a manager says to an employee, "I am very interested in your problem," but then begins to look at her watch and fidget with objects on her desk, the employee will most likely believe the nonverbal rather than the verbal message.

You can improve your communication by monitoring the nonverbal messages you send through your eye contact, facial expressions, gestures, and personal space.

Eye Contact   Eyes transmit more information than any other part of the body. Because eye contact is so revealing, people generally observe some unwritten rules about looking at others. People who hold direct eye contact for only a few seconds, or avoid eye contact altogether, risk communicating indifference. However, a direct, prolonged stare between strangers is usually considered impolite, even potentially aggressive or hostile. Continuous eye contact is especially offensive in Asian and Latin American countries. As a general rule, when you are communicating in a business setting, your eyes should meet the other person's about 60 to 70 percent of the time. This timing is an effective alternative to continuous eye contact.

Facial Expressions   If you want to identify the inner feelings of another person, watch facial expressions closely. A frown or a smile will communicate a great deal. We have all encountered a "look of surprise" or a "look that could kill." Most of our observations are very accurate. However, facial expressions can be intentionally manipulated. When a person is truly happy, the muscles used for smiling are involuntarily controlled by the body's limbic system. When you force a smile, the cerebral cortex (under voluntary control) activates and the person appears to have a "fake" look when he or she smiles. That is why actors often recall a past emotional experience to produce the emotional state they want.[12] If we are able to accurately assess the facial expressions of others and draw conclusions accordingly, we can be sure that others are doing the same to us.

Gestures   Gestures send messages to people about how you are reacting to them and to the situation in which you find yourself. They often add an element that is perceived as a lively speaking style that keeps the attention of others. In some cultures, if you fail to gesture, you may be perceived as boring and stiff.[13] Be aware that some gestures that may be common in one culture may have dramatically different meaning to people from another culture. The examples in Figure 2.3 illustrate how the same gesture can have very different meanings.

Personal Space   Research conducted by Edward Hall provides evidence that people use the space around them to define relationships. It is possible to make others uncomfortable by standing too close to them or too far away from them. A customer may feel uncomfortable if a salesperson stands too close. A job applicant may feel uncomfortable if the interviewer maintains a distance of several feet. Hall identified four "zones" of comfortable distances that help us understand this nonverbal effect on others:[14]

1. *Intimate distance* includes touching to approximately 18 inches from another person. Most people will respond with defensiveness when strangers intrude into this territory.

FIGURE 2.3	Same Sign, Different Meanings

OK SIGN
France: You're a zero;
Japan: Please give me coins;
Brazil: an obscene gesture;
Mediterranean countries: an obscene gesture.

THUMB AND FOREFINGER
Most countries: money;
France: Something is perfect;
Mediterranean: a vulgar gesture.

THUMBS-UP
Australia: Up yours;
Germany: The number one;
Japan: The number five;
Saudi Arabia: I'm winning;
Ghana: An insult;
Malaysia: The thumb is used to point rather than the finger.

Source: Atlanta Committee for Olympic Games, by Sam Ward, *USA Today*. Taken from Ben Brown, "Atlanta Out to Mind Its Manners," *USA Today*, March 14, 1996, p. 7c. Copyright © 1996 *USA Today*. Reprinted with permission.

2. *Personal distance* ranges from 18 inches to 4 feet. This distance is usually reserved for people we feel close to, such as spouses or close friends.

3. *Social distance* is 4 to 12 feet and is used for most business meetings and impersonal social gatherings. Business can be conducted with a minimum of emotional involvement.

4. *Public distance*, which usually involves one-way communication from a speaker to an audience, is 12 to 15 feet.

Hall's research involved the culture of only the United States and should prove helpful to those from other cultures who are attempting to communicate better with Americans. Americans should realize that the distances Hall describes may be different when they are attempting to effectively communicate with those from another culture. For example, Asians are accustomed to close contact. Watch for signals of discomfort, such as leg swinging, foot or finger tapping, and gaze aversion, caused by invading the other person's space.[15]

Who Is Responsible for Effective Communication?

The sender and the receiver share *equal* responsibility for effective communication. The communication loop, as shown in Figure 2.2, is not complete if the message the receiver hears, and acts upon, differs from the one the sender intended. When the sender accepts 100 percent of the responsibility for sending a clear, concise message, the communication process begins. But the receiver must also accept 100 percent of the responsibility for receiving the message as the sender intended. Ideally receivers should provide senders with enough feedback to ensure that an accurate message has passed through all the filters that might alter it.

SKILL DEVELOPMENT CHALLENGE

As you build your human relations skills, it is very important to establish an acute sensitivity to the impact communication filters have on your interpersonal relationships at home and at work. Review Figure 2.2 and identify the communication filters that were in place during a recent face-to-face conversation, argument, or confrontation you had with another person. Did any of these filters interfere with your ability to send or receive the information being transmitted during the exchange? Explain how, if you were to repeat the interaction with this person again, you could reduce the impact of these filters and thereby improve your ability to effectively communicate the messages you were sending and receiving.

How to Improve Personal Communication

Now that you understand the communication process and the various filters messages must pass through, you can begin to take the necessary steps to improve your own personal communication skills.

Send Clear Messages

Send clear, concise messages with as little influence from filters as possible so that you can avoid being misunderstood. A new employee stood before the paper shredder in her new office. An administrative assistant noticed her confused look and asked if she needed some help. "Yes, thank you. How does this thing work?" "It's simple," said the assistant and took the thick report from the new employee and fed it through the shredder. "I see," she said, "but how many copies will it make?" This kind of miscommunication could easily have been avoided if both parties had followed these simple rules:

- *Use clear, concise language.* Avoid slang; jargon; or complex, industry-specific semantics that the receiver might not understand. Tailor your messages to your receivers by using words and concepts they understand.

- *Use repetition.* When possible, use parallel channels of communication. For example, by sending an e-mail and making a phone call, you not only gain the receiver's attention through dialogue but also make sure there is a written record in case specific details need to be recalled.

- *Use appropriate timing.* An important memo or e-mail may get no attention simply because it is competing with more pressing problems facing the receiver. When you need someone's cooperation, be acutely aware of his or her schedule and workload so that you can avoid causing any inconvenience or frustration. Timing the delivery of your message will help ensure that it is accepted and acted on.

■ *Consider the receiver's preferences.* Some people prefer to receive information via e-mail, and others prefer telephone calls or face-to-face contact. Monitor and discover the preferences of those you communicate with on a regular basis, and adjust your communications with them accordingly.

Develop Effective Listening Skills

We may be born with the ability to hear, but we have to learn how to listen. We may think we are good listeners, but the truth is that most people don't listen at all. Too often we simply speak and then think about what we are going to say next, rather than concentrating on what the other person is trying to say.

At Hewlett Packard, employees take listening courses in which they listen, mirror back what they heard, and then elaborate on what it meant. Participants learn that two customers might say similar things, but their messages might have totally different meanings because they have had their own unique experiences that influence their messages. Two employees experiencing a similar frustration at work may take their concerns to management for corrective action. Yet each employee has a unique perspective on the problem, and both need to be heard before management can take effective, appropriate action.

Effective listening can often evoke creative, "out-of-the-box" ideas. An engineer at Hewlett Packard took his listening-skills training seriously and started "coffee talks" in his department every Friday afternoon to improve the listening skills among his coworkers. The resulting lively conversations generated new ideas that stimulated the creation of new products that led to millions of dollars in profits.[16]

A well-known furniture company delivered hundreds of desks to their customers, but many of the desks arrived damaged and unusable because of inadequate packaging. The company's crate builder estimated that one desk model alone was returned twenty times per month. The company lost hundreds of thousands of dollars when they had to replace the damaged desks. Why didn't the company identify this problem earlier? Senior managers simply did not listen to the concerns from the packaging department or from their customers. They took action only after a customer called complaining that the same desk was ruined twice.[17]

TOTAL	**KEN JOHNSON**
PERSON	AUTHOR *(www.listen.org/quotations/quotes_effective.html)*
INSIGHT	"Listening effectively to others can be the most fundamental and powerful communication tool of all. When someone is willing to stop talking or thinking and begin truly listening to others, all of their interactions become easier, and communication problems are all but eliminated."

HUMAN RELATIONS IN ACTION

> ### Career Advice
>
> A recent college graduate wrote to Anne Fisher, career advice columnist for *Fortune* magazine, and asked: "I just graduated from Yale and am about to start my first real job, and I'm curious about something. If you had to pass along just one piece of advice on which to build a career, what would it be?"
>
> Anne answered, "I've always liked Albert Einstein's dictum: 'If A equals success, then the formula is $A = X + Y + Z$. X is work. Y is play. And Z is, Keep your mouth shut.' Or as my dad used to say, 'Nobody ever learns anything while they're talking.' If you make it a habit to listen more than you speak, you can't go too far wrong."

Active Listening **Active listening** is fueled by curiosity and requires your complete concentration on what you are hearing, body language that exhibits your listening attitude, and feedback as to what you think the speaker is trying to tell you. In some cases a simple statement such as "Please tell me more about that" will help you become an active listener. Susan Scott, author of *Fierce Conversations*, offers this advice: "Dig for full understanding. Use paraphrasing and perception checks; don't be satisfied with what's on the surface."[18] When you become an active listener, you will make fewer mistakes, learn new information, and build stronger relationships.

> *Active listening is fueled by curiosity.*

If you would like to pursue additional resources to help you become a better listener, access the information available through the International Listening Association at *www.listen.org*. In addition, carefully examine Table 2.1, Active Listening Skills, and make every effort to implement its recommendations when you are interacting with others. You may be surprised by the impact you can make.

TABLE 2.1	Active Listening Skills

1. *Develop a listening attitude.* Regard the speaker as worthy of your respect and attention. Drop your expectations as to what you are going to hear or would like to hear. Maintain good eye contact and lean slightly forward. Don't rush the speaker. Be patient and refrain from planning what to say in response until the speaker has finished talking.

2. *Give the speaker your full attention.* This is not easy because the messages you hear are often spoken at a much slower rate than you are able to absorb them. This allows your mind to roam. Your senses are constantly receiving extraneous information that may divert your attention. To stay focused, you may want to take notes, if it is appropriate to do so.

3. *Clarify by asking questions.* If something is not clear because the speaker has referred to a person or an event that you are not familiar with, ask him or her to back up and explain. If you want the speaker to expand on a particular point, ask open-ended questions such as "How do you feel about that?" or "Can you tell us some ways to improve?"

4. *Feed back your understanding of the speaker's message.* Paraphrase, in your own words, your understanding of what the speaker has just said: for example, "*Do you mean . . . ?*" "*Am I right in assuming that we should . . . ?*" "*What I hear you saying is . . .*" or "*In other words, we . . . .*"

Critical Listening   To add depth to your active listening skills, consider honing your critical listening skills. **Critical listening** is the attempt to see the topic of discussion from the *speaker's* point of view and to consider how the speaker's perception of the situation may be different from your own. To improve your ability to critically view new information, be sure to listen for evidence that challenges as well as confirms your own point of view. This is especially important when there is no opportunity for feedback, such as when you are viewing "tabloid" television, listening to network TV news "sound bites," or reading Internet blogs. Analyze the source of the information and determine its validity and credibility. Ask yourself, "Why have I been given this information? Is it relevant or am I just being used to advance the agenda of another person or group?" Critical listening skills will help you avoid perpetuating erroneous information simply because you heard it through gossip, saw it on TV, or read it on the Internet.

All of the communications filters identified in Figure 2.2 tend to distort your ability and willingness to listen, so activating your critical listening skills will take some effort. To help you in this skill development process, ask yourself:

- Does the speaker's reasoning make sense?

- What evidence is being offered to support the speaker's views?

- Do I know each point to be valid based on my own experience?

- Is each point based on a source that can be trusted?[19]

This supervisor listens carefully to an employee who needs assistance. He will ask questions and use his active listening skills to acquire the information needed to help the employee with a work-related problem. Active listening is a skill that can be learned.

Empathic Listening Another dimension to becoming a better listener involves empathy, which means understanding another person's feelings. Many workers today face serious personal problems and feel the need to talk about them with someone. They do not expect specific advice or guidance; they just want to spend some time with an empathic listener. Stephen Covey, the noted author and consultant, described **empathic listening** as listening with your ears, your eyes, and your heart.[20] If you want to practice empathic listening, adopt the following practices:

> *Ask yourself, "Why have I been given this information?"*

- *Avoid being judgmental.* Objectivity is the heart and soul of empathic listening. The person is communicating for emotional release and does not seek a specific response.

- *Acknowledge what is said.* You do not have to agree with what is being said, but you should let the person know you are able to understand his or her viewpoint.

- *Be patient.* If you are unable or unwilling to take the time to hear what the person has to say, say so immediately. Signs of impatience send a negative message to the person needing to talk.[21]

We live in a culture where empathic listening is quite rare. Interrupting has become all too common as people rush to fill every gap in the conversation. Nevertheless, empathic listening is greatly valued by those with personal or work-related problems—people want to spend time with a good listener.[22]

CRITICAL THINKING CHALLENGE

Each conversation we have with a coworker, a customer, or a significant other can enhance or weaken the relationship. A conversation that has the power to truly transform a relationship requires some silence. Yet for most Americans, silence in a conversation is almost unendurable. Interrupting the other person or responding too quickly with little or no thought can weaken a relationship. Every important conversation requires moments of silence—time to reflect on what the other person has said and consider our response. During most conversations, do you use silence to improve communication?

Communications in Organizations

Strong teams depend on the effective exchange of information among all the team members so that they can reach their goals. Poor communication can create an atmosphere of mistrust. It is therefore critically important that every team member understands how to get his or her point across by using the appropriate communication channels within the organization's structure. They have a choice of the organization's formal communication channels or its informal "grapevine."

Formal Channels: Horizontal and Vertical

Most organizations establish a formal structure through which official information travels. **Horizontal channels** are used to move information among people on the same level of authority, such as all the store managers of a national retail clothing store chain, all department chairpersons within a college, or all the administrative assistants within an organization. **Vertical channels** move information up and down through all levels of authority within an organization. A message from the president of the organization will move down to the vice president(s), then to the manager(s), and then to the workers. Communicating down vertical channels is fairly routine. Communicating back up can be more difficult because top managers sometimes have the mistaken impression that their subordinates' messages are less important. Often, if a lower-level employee has a message for an upper-level manager, he or she must "go through the channels" before the message gets to the intended person. Note that e-mail has dramatically changed the formal communication structure by allowing employees at all levels to communicate directly with higher level individuals without anyone in between misinterpreting, sabotaging, or blocking the message.

Messages sent through both horizontal and vertical channels can be delivered on the phone, electronically, in writing, or face to face. Many managers find that brief phone calls to their staff members are generally more effective than e-mails or memos because phone calls are quick and allow for immediate feedback. E-mail is quick and efficient and provides a permanent record of the exchange of information. When signatures are necessary before action can be taken on the message, the message should probably be sent as a traditional hard-copy memo or letter. Keep in mind that sensitive matters are best handled face to face. When these formal communication channels are working effectively, everyone authorized to initiate and receive companywide communications will receive the same information in a timely manner. If the level of trust among those sending and receiving the information is fairly high, these messages will usually be understood, believed, accepted, and acted on. If the level of trust is low, however, workers will tend to put more faith in rumors, even if such information conflicts with the formal message.

Informal Channel: The Grapevine

Messages passed through the horizontal and vertical channels can usually be tracked through linear paths, but the pathway of rumors may look more like a cobweb interwoven throughout the organizational chart. The **grapevine**, the informal communication channel, carries unofficial information and exists in every organization. It can have either positive or negative effects. Many times the grapevine will clarify orders sent through the formal channels. At times, however, messages that move through the grapevine may be exaggerated, distorted, or completely inaccurate. These rumors develop quickly when at least two conditions exist in an organization: high degrees of anxiety and a great deal of uncertainty. To quell rumors, top management has to communicate in a timely and honest way.[23]

© King Features Syndicate

Rumors about individuals, or gossip, in the workplace can undermine morale, weaken authority, ruin reputations, and leave even the best teams decimated in its wake. It's no wonder gossip is often referred to as "verbal terrorism."[24] Unless you know for sure that the information is fact, never participate in gossip. Once you are identified as a gossip, others will not trust you again. This can destroy all your efforts to build solid future relationships within that organization. You will discover that others will not share confidential information with you—information that might be important to your career.

> *Once you are identified as a gossip, others will not trust you again.*

How to Improve Organizational Communication

SUPERVISOR: "We've really got to get closer to our employees, communicate with them better."

TRAINER: "Yes, we have a big problem there."

SUPERVISOR: "They don't understand the new changes, even though they have all the details."

TRAINER: "We just need to spend time with them."

SUPERVISOR: "Yes, you're right. We've got to educate them."

In this dialogue, notice the quick deterioration from "get closer" and "communicate" to "they don't understand" and "educate them." Note how quickly the concept of two-way communication was transformed into one-way instruction.

Encourage Upward Communication **Upward communication**, the process of encouraging employees to share their feelings and ideas with their managers, is one of the most effective ways to improve organizational communication and is common among the best companies to work for in America. Employees with limited power are naturally very cautious about discussing mistakes, complaints, and failings with a more powerful person. However, when managers demonstrate the desire to listen to their subordinates, ideas, suggestions, and complaints begin to flow upward. Here are a few examples of leaders who have taken steps to improve upward communication:

- ■ "Ask Al" is an area on the Born Information Services Inc. intranet where employees can anonymously ask president Alan Bauman questions. He willingly posts his responses for everyone to see and encourages debate.[25]

- ■ Winnebago Industries, maker of recreational vehicles, uses a well-established suggestion system to obtain ideas from employees. Over 10,000 suggestions have come from employees since the program began in 1991.[26]

- ■ Peter Brabeck, CEO of Nestlé, meets with twelve to fourteen employees each month over lunch. Their bosses are not in attendance. He encourages the employees to talk frankly about their work and to ask questions.[27]

These organizations actively pursue ways to remove barriers that prevent open communication. They recognize that improving communications will inevitably help build trust among all employees, regardless of their position in the organization.

Communicating via Technology

The traditional memos, letters, phone calls, and face-to-face conversations seem to be the exception rather than the rule in today's high-tech communications environment. Many organizations now maintain **virtual offices**, networks of workers connected by the latest technology. These workers can "set up shop" wherever they are—at home, on an airplane, in a motel room—and communicate with coworkers via e-mail, cell phone, instant messaging, fax, or some other method. **Telecommuting**, an arrangement that allows employees to work from their homes, enables people scattered all over the world to stay connected.

The advantages of using these technology-based communication alternatives are obvious. Time efficiency is unsurpassed because people can transmit simple or detailed information across all time zones, and receivers can retrieve the information at their convenience. Cost effectiveness is unsurpassed because fiber-optic and satellite transmissions cost the consumer virtually pennies compared to traditional transworld phone calls.

In all the frantic speed with which information now flows, many people forget that communication still must be carefully created before it is transmitted. Voice mail can be frustrating and time-consuming if it is not handled properly, and poorly written e-mails can leave the impression that the sender is either poorly educated or careless.

Voice Mail

Now that everyone is adjusting to the opportunities that immediate communication systems offer, nothing is more dismaying than playing phone tag (the exchange of several voice mails without successful transmission of the message). Whether you are on the sending or the receiving end, though, there are ways to avoid this counterproductive exercise in frustration.

When people call you and connect with your voice mail, be sure your recorded message includes your full name and when you will be retrieving your messages. If, for some reason, you will not be returning your calls for an extended time, edit your standard message to reflect this information so that your friends, customers, and colleagues will understand the delay and avoid repeated calls and duplicate messages. Forward your calls to another person's extension, if possible, or explain how the caller can reach a live person if the call is urgent. When you retrieve your messages, write down essential information, prioritize the messages in the order of importance, and return all of the calls as soon as possible.

When you are connected to another person's voice mail, state your full name, *a brief explanation of what information or action you need from that person* (the component most often neglected), your phone number, and the best time to reach you. All four components are necessary in order to avoid phone tag. Then, if the receiver reaches your voice mail when calling back, he or she can simply leave you a voice message with the information you wanted. The communication loop is complete.

E-mail

Technology has accelerated the pace of exchanging information today. People want answers and action now! Therefore, e-mail has become the standard format for most business and personal communication. In some cases, however, e-mail may be slower than a phone call or face-to-face meetings because you may have to wait days for a response to your message; plus, it takes time to compose an effective and accurate message.

HUMAN RELATIONS IN ACTION   **E-mail Tips**

- Do not send e-mail when you are angry or exhausted.
- When a face-to-face meeting is necessary, do not use e-mail as a substitute.
- When receiving large amounts of e-mail, selectively choose which ones you want to read by scanning the subject lines and deleting those that do not need a response.
- Make every attempt to create e-mail messages that are error-free. Messages that contain errors may misrepresent your competence and give the wrong impression.

- Do not use e-mail to share rumors or innuendos or to say anything sensitive or critical that touches on someone's job competence.
- Avoid using unprofessional abbreviations such as BCNU for "Be seeing you," GG for "Got to go," or J/K for "Just kidding."
- Confine junk e-mail or personal e-mail to your friends and home computer and never transmit it through your company's computer system. Junk e-mail often contains attachments with viruses that could potentially shut down your entire organization.

E-mail takes careful planning and new writing skills. Those who read your e-mail will make judgments about your intelligence, competence, and attitude whether you want them to or not. Therefore, you need to carefully monitor not only what you write about but also how you word your messages. Here are some guidelines to follow:

Know Your Company's Policies Most organizations monitor their employees' e-mail carefully. Keep in mind that even deleted messages live on indefinitely in the company's hard drives and may resurface. E-mail that might be sexually offensive could be considered sexual harassment and have serious ramifications.

Keep work-related messages professional and avoid sending personal e-mail messages on company time. A young analyst working in the Carlyle Group's Seoul office sent friends an e-mail in which he described his glamorous life that included a "harem of chickies," bankers catering to his "every whim," and other comments. Several people receiving the e-mail forwarded it to others in the financial community. Excerpts of it even appeared in the *New York Times*. The analyst was promptly fired.[28]

If you plan to join the millions of people who have created their own Web log, or [blog], pay attention to your employer's policy. IBM has developed an eleven-point policy for employees who develop their own blog. Three of the IBM policy points are:

■ Identify yourself and write in the first person. You must make it clear that you are speaking for yourself and not on behalf of IBM.

■ Don't cite or reference clients, partners, or suppliers without their approval.

■ Respect your audience. Don't use ethnic slurs, personal insults, or obscenities.[29]

Keep in mind that the information you include in your blog will be public for a long time.

Create an Appropriate E-mail Address Carefully design your e-mail address to give the impression you want to convey. Addresses such as Crazylady @_____.com or Buddyboy@_____.com may be acceptable for personal e-mail but should never be used in a business setting. Your organization will generally have a specific format for your e-mail address that includes variations of your first and last names.

Although this may seem obvious, *always* make sure you are sending an e-mail to the correct address. This quick double-check will prevent delays and embarrassment for everyone involved if your message contains negative or potentially libelous comments about colleagues, or semiprivate information.

Use the *Subject*: Line One of the best ways to set the stage for effective communications is to learn how to appropriately use the *Subject*: line available on all e-mail messages. It usually appears next to the sender's name on the receiver's screen. This brief introduction to your message will cue the receiver as to the probable content of your message. If your message is time-critical, add *Urgent* to the subject line, but be careful of overuse. When responding to another person's e-mail, be sure to forward the original subject line so that the receiver knows you are responding to his or her original request.

Watch Your Language The biggest clue to your competence will be the words you use. Be sure they are all spelled correctly and that there are no typographical errors. E-mails filled with typing errors convey an attitude of disrespect toward the reader. Be sure that you have selected the appropriate word—when choosing, for example, from *there/their/they're; sight/site/cite; then/than; which/ witch*, and so on. Do your verbs agree with their subjects? If your writing skills are limited, use software that includes grammar- and spelling-checkers.

Keep your messages brief by summarizing your main points, indicate the action or response you are seeking, and be sure you provide all the details the receiver needs. Be very careful about the *tone* of your messages. Remove any potentially offending words and phrasing from your documents. Some people feel that they have to use stronger language to get a message across because the receiver cannot "hear" them. If you use solid capital letters in your e-mail, though, readers may think you are shouting at them.[30]

The missing element in e-mail and other electronic communication is *rapport*, that bonding state that is easier to establish in person or by phone. Facial expressions, tone of voice, gestures—important social cues—are missing in e-mail.[31] Neither the sender nor the receiver can assume anything about the correspondent's frame of mind. Readers will not be able to tell if you are serious or being sarcastic, prying or simply curious, angry or merely frustrated. After creating your message, reread it as a stranger might. If words or phrases might be misconstrued, rewrite it so as to make clear *exactly* what you mean to say.

HUMAN RELATIONS IN ACTION

Freddie Mac Acts Quickly!

As companies merge with others, management sometimes fails to communicate the changes to the lower-level employees. The result is often an active rumor mill that permeates the atmosphere, creating tension and fear among the workers. When officials at the Federal Home Loan Mortgage Corporation (Freddie Mac) implemented a major reorganization, they did not want workers to discover the impending changes in the media. So, on the day the changes took place, workers were greeted with an e-mail posted on the *Home Front*, the company's intranet. It announced that the president/chief operating officer had been fired, the chief executive/chairman had retired, and the chief financial officer had resigned. At the company's headquarters in Herndon, Virginia, interim executives invited managers to attend a 10 a.m. meeting to hear the details and ask questions, and workers were invited to 11 a.m. or noon meetings so that they could ask questions, too. Employees in Dallas, Chicago, New York, Los Angeles, and Atlanta attended via teleconference. By announcing the news quickly and thoroughly to all employees, the company helped them face the changes with enthusiasm about the future instead of fear and distrust. One worker said, "It was actually quite exciting. Everyone was clapping; there was definitely a sense of excitement in the air."

If your organization has been kind enough to provide you with Internet access and e-mail capabilities, respect the gift and use your account properly. In the information age, e-mail etiquette is just as important as other forms of business etiquette.[32]

● LOOKING BACK: Reviewing the Concepts

■ Understand the communication process and the filters that affect communication.

The age of information has given us major advances in technology-based communication. However, successful communication in a work setting requires human involvement. The diversity of today's work force calls for a greater understanding of how to communicate effectively. Impersonal one-way communication methods can be used effectively to share basic facts, policies, and instructions. If feedback is necessary, rely on interpersonal communication that involves a two-way exchange. As noted in this chapter, two-way communication is often a complex process.

■ Explain how each filter can distort communication.

Messages are sent—and feedback is received—through a variety of filters that often distort the messages. Figure 2.2 provides a summary of the most common filters that can challenge both senders and receivers of messages. For example, body language conveys information through eye contact, facial expressions, gestures, and the use of personal space. When you are influenced by one or more of these filters, the message you receive may be totally different from what the sender was attempting to communicate.

■ Identify ways to improve personal communication, including developing listening skills.

The sender and the receiver share equal responsibility for effective communication. Therefore, both sender and receiver should take the necessary steps to improve their personal communication skills. Individuals can make their messages clearer by choosing words carefully, using repetition, timing the message correctly, and considering the receivers' preferences. Personal communication can also be improved by the use of active, critical, and empathic listening skills.

■ Understand how communications flow throughout an organization and how to improve the flow when necessary.

Effective communication in organizations unifies group behavior, builds teamwork, and contributes to improved productivity. Formal communication channels can be vertical or horizontal. The grapevine uses an informal approach to rapidly transmit information, but rumors or gossip may have a negative effect if the information is untrue. Progressive organizations are constantly searching for ways to improve upward communication. They recognize that frontline employees are often in the best position to recommend ways to improve the organization.

■ Learn how to effectively communicate through technology.

Memos, letters, phone calls, and face-to-face conversations have been replaced, in many situations, by technology-based communication alternatives. Virtual offices, networks of workers connected by the latest technology, are now quite common. These communication technologies are time efficient and cost-effective for organizations. However, the increase in the use of e-mail, voice mail, teleconferencing, and other high-tech communication methods often creates human relations problems. Employees often forget that communication must still be carefully created before it is transmitted.

● Career Corner

Q: I have just been "released" from the job I held for twelve years because my company was bought out by our competitor. I am highly skilled, competent, and dependable, but it's been a long time since I went on a job interview, and I'm scared to death. How should I communicate my strengths and commitment to a prospective employer? What happens if I blow it?

A: Fear is your greatest enemy, so be confident that many employers want to know that you are available. Remember that no one wants to hire a "victim," so do not refer to your "release" or your previous employer in a negative way. Memorize a positive statement that explains why you are looking for a new opportunity. It should focus on your strengths rather than on why you were released: for example, "My computer skills far exceeded the needs of my company's new owner." Be aware that your degree, references, wardrobe, and handshake get you in the door, but that interviews today often include probing questions that test your ability to react and respond quickly. Most interviewers expect applicants to ask their own series of questions, such as: How does this position fit into the organizational structure? Why is the position vacant? What are the opportunities for advancement? If you want the job at the conclusion of the interview, ask for it! Be sure to send a follow-up note to the interviewer that reemphasizes your strengths. If you feel you blew it, contact the interviewer by phone or letter to correct misleading or misinterpreted information. This type of persistence will show that you sincerely want the job. If you don't get the job, consider the interview a great practice session and enter the next one with renewed confidence!

● Key Terms

impersonal communication
interpersonal communication
feedback
semantics
nonverbal messages
active listening
critical listening

empathic listening
horizontal channels
vertical channels
grapevine
upward communication
virtual offices
telecommuting

Applying What You Have Learned

1. During the next week, study the listening habits of students in another class in which you are enrolled. Keep a journal of your observations by identifying the nonverbal behaviors you witness. Are they barriers to effective communication between the instructor and the student or do they enhance communication? How do you believe the students' nonverbal behaviors might affect the relationship between the instructor and the students?

2. Print out the most recent e-mails that you have sent or received and bring them to class. Analyze their effectiveness in terms of the e-mail tips in this chapter. Did the messages violate any of the tips? If so, which ones? How could these messages be improved?

3. Many times we take the conversation away from others and make it our own. This practice not only wastes time, but is a major relationship killer. Here is how it works: At the beginning of the conversation, you tell the other person about a problem you are dealing with and, before you finish the story, the other person says, "I know what you mean," and then describes a personal experience that may or may not have anything to do with your problem. Once the other person takes over the conversation, a valuable exchange of ideas is probably lost. During the next week, monitor your conversations with friends, family members, and coworkers. How often did the other person attempt to take the conversation away from you? How often did you attempt to take over the conversation?[33]

Internet Insights

1. Assume that you are currently employed by Avaya, an international communications company with offices in several countries. Next week you will travel to Germany and Italy to check on the installation of new telecommunications equipment. Your manager has told you that *most* of the people you will work with speak English. However, you want to be able to greet people and say "yes," "no," "thank you," and "goodbye" in the languages of the countries you will visit. Go to *www.travlang.com*, scroll down to the bottom, and select "Foreign Languages for Travelers." Then follow the two steps for the language of your choice and click on the option "basic words." Select, record, and practice the appropriate words.

2. Now go to *www.kwintessential.co.uk/resources/country-profiles.html* and click on the country that corresponds with the language you learned in the exercise above. Learn more about the country's social customs, such as rules and taboos of doing business, verbal and nonverbal communication techniques, decision-making techniques, and meeting, gift-giving, and dining etiquette. Discover the country's family values, religion, and expressive communication techniques. Write a brief report on your discoveries.

Role-Play Exercise

This role-play exercise is designed to improve your active listening skills. Carefully study Table 2.1, Active Listening Skills, and prepare to meet with another class member who wants to talk about his or her career plans. As this person talks, make every effort to apply the four active listening skills. Once the other person has finished speaking, discuss your career plans. When both of you have finished talking, discuss whether each felt the partner was really engaged in active listening. Did either of you find that the other person was distracted and not really paying attention? Be prepared to share your insights with your role-play partner, your instructor, and other class members.

Case 2.1　Fluid Communications

At the beginning of this chapter, you were introduced to the problems the administrators at Duke University Health System experienced when they discovered that for two months their surgeons had unknowingly used instruments that had been washed in a mixture of water and used hydraulic fluid instead of detergent and then sterilized with heat. Initially, no one noticed the mistake because the detergent containers had not been relabeled and the detergent normally used and the hydraulic fluid were the same color and were both odorless. Because surgical instruments are routinely treated with lubricants to prevent rusting, hospital administrators did not detect the problem despite complaints from medical staff that the surgical instruments seemed *unusually* slick and oily.

A few hours after the discovery, however, a crisis team had gathered to determine how to handle the potentially devastating situation. Within one week, letters went out to all 3,800 affected patients and their physicians apologizing for the mixup and telling them that it should pose little risk to their health. They were invited to call a hotline to report any changes in their health. A website was created to offer them information about the effects of hydraulic fluid on the body. The goal of the crisis team was to balance the urgency of getting the information out with the need for accuracy, especially in a world of business scandals where corporate attorneys prefer top executives say nothing and public relations advisers want leaders to be frank.

Behind the scenes, Duke's Infection Control physicians began a vigilant surveillance program to monitor any spike in infections among the affected patients. The hotline calls were recorded, monitored, and analyzed. Scientists were brought in to conduct a chemical analysis of the used hydraulic fluid and to determine how it might harm humans. Surgery complications, new illnesses, and unusual complaints were analyzed and compared against normal rates for these problems. Despite these efforts, patients contacted attorneys and formed a support group claiming that Duke officials failed to take their concerns about ongoing health problems seriously.

In hindsight, hospital administrators admit they should have been more responsive to their patients' concerns. They discovered that sharing scientific results was not enough and that they needed to sympathize with their patients by considering not only their medical issues but also their concerns and anxieties. Dr. Michael Cuffe, Duke's vice president for medical affairs and patient-physician liaison, reported that administrators were doing all the right things internally, but they were not telling their patients what steps were being taken and did not provide the appropriate feedback to their concerns. Cuffe believes that patients who wanted to visit in person and talk about their concerns should have had that opportunity.[34]

Questions

1. Dr. Cuffe stated: "I see a heightened need to make sure the administration hears the concerns of patients. Not that they're deaf to it. But that's what needs to improve."[35] What steps could Duke administrators, or managers of any other organization, take to make sure the concerns of customers are heard?

2. How could the original problem have been intercepted before it became a health care crisis?

3. What filters were in place to block effective communication between the hospital administrators, medical staff, and affected patients?

Case 2.2   Reading Nonverbal Cues

Gestures, body movements, tone of voice, and facial expressions are to speech what periods, commas, and exclamation points are to written language. They can make your message meaningful or confusing. They can confirm or contradict what you are trying to say. Without a word, seemingly insignificant changes in your body language can communicate confidence or fear, trust or mistrust, curiosity or boredom.

Because of this powerful, often subconscious communication process, law enforcement officials across the world are being trained to use "behavior profiling" rather than "racial profiling." When they identify suspicious individuals, they ask them pointed questions to increase their stress levels. In addition to listening for inconsistencies in what is said, law enforcement officials then look for minute physical reactions on the faces of people being questioned.

Following the terrorists' attacks on September 11, 2001, the FBI has started teaching nonverbal behavior analysis to all new recruits. Airport personnel and law enforcement officials are being trained to watch for travelers who exhibit nonverbal signals such as darting eyes and hand tremors. Systems are under development to enhance security cameras so that they can monitor certain nonverbal behaviors, and computer software with voice-stress sensors are being installed at various airport checkin desks.

All U.S. customs agents are required to watch videos teaching them techniques for studying body language in order to identify potential terrorists and drug traffickers. One international traveler caught the attention of a customs inspector at John F. Kennedy Airport in New York because his lips were dry and chapped to the point of being almost white. His carotid artery was visibly throbbing. After questioning the man, inspectors discovered he had paid cash for a business-class ticket, even though he was a low-paid service worker from South America. When they x-rayed him, they found he had swallowed several bags of heroin pellets.[36]

Questions

1. Do you believe "behavior profiling" is a viable method of interpreting a person's actions? Why or why not?

2. There is no simple codebook of nonverbal cues that is accepted across all the cultures of the world. How would you enhance the training programs discussed in this case so that they compensate for cultural diversity?

3. How do you feel about hidden security devices that monitor your nonverbal signals yet protect you from those who might cause you harm?

INTEGRATED RESOURCES

VIDEOS: "Communicating Across Cultures at IDG"
"Organizational Structure at Green Mountain Coffee Roasters"
"Interpersonal Communications—Video Cases"

CLASSROOM ACTIVITIES (*college.hmco.com/pic/reece10e*)

Paper Clip Project
English: Official Language? Pro/Con Discussion
Journal Entry: Nonverbal Communication Awareness

business.college.hmco.com/students

ACE

Self-tests

PART II

CAREER SUCCESS BEGINS WITH KNOWING YOURSELF

3 UNDERSTANDING YOUR COMMUNICATION STYLE

4 BUILDING HIGH SELF-ESTEEM

5 PERSONAL VALUES INFLUENCE ETHICAL CHOICES

6 ATTITUDES CAN SHAPE YOUR LIFE

7 MOTIVATING YOURSELF AND OTHERS

3

UNDERSTANDING YOUR COMMUNICATION STYLE

Chapter Preview

After studying this chapter, you will be able to

- Understand the concept of communication style bias and its effect on interpersonal relations.

- Realize the personal benefits that can be derived from an understanding of communication styles.

- Discuss the major elements of the communication style model.

- Identify your preferred communication style.

- Improve communications with others through style flexing.

amille Wright Miller, a talented trainer, consultant, and author, has worked with many effective leaders throughout the years. She has noted that many of these leaders have the ability to "mirror" the behaviors of persons they communicate with. Psychologists and sociologists use the term **mirroring** to describe a situation where one person intentionally matches the body language of the individual they are meeting with.

Mirroring is based on the premise that we are more likely to develop a kinship with those who are like ourselves. In many cases, subtle shifts in how you present yourself can increase the comfort level of the other person. If you participate in a job interview, observe key elements of the person's style. If the person speaks slowly and seems to deliberately select each word, consider slowing your own speech pattern. Your goal is not to manipulate the other person, nor mimic the person, but to avoid a situation where the other individual is distracted by differences.[1]

We form impressions of people by observing their behavior. The thoughts, feelings, and actions that characterize someone are generally viewed as **personality**.[2] Mirroring requires that we pay even closer attention to the speech patterns and gestures of the person we are talking to.

Communication Styles: An Introduction

Have you ever wondered why it seems so difficult to talk with some people and so easy to talk with others? Can you recall a situation where you met someone for the first time and immediately liked that person? Something about the individual made you feel comfortable. You may have had this experience when you started a new job or began classes at a new school. A major goal of this chapter is to help you understand the impact your communication style has on the impression others form of you. This chapter also provides you with the information you will need to cope effectively in today's workplace, which is characterized by greater diversity and more emphasis on teamwork.

Communication Style Defined

The impressions that others form about us are based on what they observe us saying and doing. They have no way of knowing our innermost thoughts and feelings, so they make decisions about us based on what they see and hear.[3] The patterns of behavior that others can observe can be called **communication style**.

Accurate self-knowledge is truly the starting point for effectiveness at work.

Each person has a unique communication style. By getting to know your style, you can achieve greater self-awareness and learn how to develop more effective interpersonal relations with coworkers. Accurate self-knowledge is truly the starting point for effectiveness at work. It is also essential for managing the three key relationships described in Chapter 1: relationships with self, with another person, and with members of a group. If your career objective is to become a supervisor or manager, you will benefit by being more aware of your employees' communication styles. Job satisfaction and productivity increase when employees feel that their leaders understand their personal needs and take these into consideration.

It is sometimes difficult for us to realize that people can differ from us and yet not be inferior. Understanding other people's communication styles improves working relationships by increasing our acceptance of other people and their way of doing things. Knowledge of the various communication styles helps us communicate more effectively with people who differ from us.

In recent years, educational programs that help people understand the fundamental concepts supporting communication styles have been very popular. Wilson Learning Corporation (*wilsonlearning.com*) has developed a self-assessment questionnaire that provides insight into your observable style of communicating with others. Over seven million people worldwide have completed Wilson Learning seminars that help enrollees better understand their communication style.[4]

Fundamental Concepts Supporting Communication Styles

This may be your first introduction to communication styles. Therefore, let's begin by reviewing a few basic concepts that support the study of this dimension of human behavior.

1. *Individual differences exist and are important.* Length of eye contact, use of gestures, speech patterns, facial expressions, and the degree of assertiveness people project to others are some of the characteristics of a personal communication style. We can identify a person's unique communication style by carefully observing these patterns of behavior.[5]

2. *Individual style differences tend to be stable.* The basics of communication style theory were established by Swiss psychiatrist Carl Jung. In his classic book *Psychological Types*, he states that every individual develops a primary communication style that remains quite stable throughout life. Each person has a relatively distinctive way of responding to people and events.[6] Many psychologists now believe that people are born with a predisposition to prefer some behaviors (actions) over others. Because these preferred behaviors are easily and naturally used, they are exercised and developed further over least preferred preferences.

3. *There is a limited number of styles.* Jung observed that people tend to fall into one of several behavior patterns when relating to the world around them. He describes four behavior styles: intuitor, thinker, feeler, and sensor.[7] Those in the same behavior category tend to display similar traits. The thinker, for example, places a high value on facts, figures, and reason.

4. *A communication style is a way of thinking and behaving.* It is not an ability but instead a preferred way of using the abilities one has. This distinction is very important. An *ability* refers to how well someone can do something. A *style* refers to how someone likes to do something.[8]

5. *To create the most productive working relationships, it is necessary to get in sync with the behavior patterns (communication style) of the people you work with.*[9] Differences between people can be a source of friction unless you develop the ability to recognize and respond to the other person's style. The ability to identify another person's communication style, and to know

We form an impression of others by observing their behavior. Bill Gates, Chairman of Microsoft, is described as a quiet, reflective person who often seems preoccupied with other matters. Steve Ballmer, CEO of Microsoft, has been described as frank, demanding, assertive, and determined.

how and when to adapt your own preferred style to it, can give you an important advantage in dealing with people. Learning to adapt your style to fit the needs of another person is called "style flexing," a topic that is discussed later in this chapter.

Learning to Cope with Communication Style Bias

Several forms of bias exist in our society. People over 50 sometimes complain that they are victims of age discrimination. Gender bias problems have made headlines for years. And people of color—blacks, Hispanics, Asians, Native Americans—say that racial and ethnic bias is still a serious problem today. Communication style bias represents another common form of prejudice.

Almost everyone experiences **communication style bias** from time to time. The bias is likely to surface when you meet someone who displays a style distinctly different from your own. For example, a quiet, reflective person may feel uncomfortable in the presence of someone who displays a dynamic, outgoing style. If, however, the person you encounter has the same communication style as yours, communication style bias is less likely to occur. We could say, using the analogy of radio, that you are both on the same wavelength.

TOTAL PERSON INSIGHT	**DAVID W. MERRILL AND ROGER H. REID**
	AUTHORS, *PERSONAL STYLES AND EFFECTIVE PERFORMANCE*
	"Everyone has had the experience of saying or doing something that was perfectly acceptable to a friend or coworker and then being surprised when the same behavior irritated someone else."

At this point, you may be saying to yourself, "But in the world of work, I don't have a choice—I have to get my message across to all kinds of people, no matter what their communication style is." You are right. Office receptionists must deal with a variety of people throughout each day. Bank loan officers cannot predict who will walk into their offices at any given time.

How can you learn to cope with communication style bias? First, you must develop awareness of your own unique style.[10] Recall from Chapter 1 that self-awareness is one of the major themes of this text. Accurate self-knowledge is essential for developing strong interpersonal relationships. Knowledge of your communication style gives you a fresh perspective and sets the stage for improved relations with others. The second step in coping with communication style bias is learning to assess the communication style of those people with whom you have contact. The ability to identify another person's communication style, and to know how and when to adapt your own preferred style to it, can afford you a crucial advantage in dealing with people. The ability to "speak the other person's language" is an important relationship-management skill that can be learned.

The Communication Style Model

This section introduces a model that encompasses four basic communication styles. This simple model is based on research studies conducted over the past seventy years and features two important dimensions of human behavior: dominance and sociability. As you study the communication style model, keep in mind that it describes your *preferences*, not your *skills* or *abilities*.

The Dominance Continuum

In study after study, those "differences that make a difference" in interpersonal relationships point to dominance as an important dimension of style. **Dominance** can be defined as the tendency to display a "take-charge" attitude. Every person falls somewhere on the **dominance continuum**, illustrated in Figure 3.1. David W. Johnson in his book *Reaching Out—Interpersonal Effectiveness and Self-Actualization* states that people tend to fall into two dominance categories: low or high.[11]

1. *Low dominance.* These people are characterized by a tendency to be cooperative and eager to assist others. They tend to be low in assertiveness and are more willing to be controlled by others.

FIGURE 3.1	Dominance Continuum

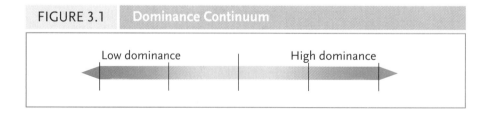

2. *High dominance.* These people give advice freely and frequently initiate demands. They are more assertive and tend to seek control over others.

The first step in determining your most preferred communication style is to identify where you fall on the dominance continuum. Do you tend to be low or high on this scale? To answer this question, complete the dominance indicator form in Figure 3.2. Rate yourself on each scale by placing a checkmark at a point along the continuum that represents how you perceive yourself. If most of your checkmarks fall to the right of center, you rank high in dominance. If most fall to the left of center, you are low in dominance.

Another way to assess the dominance dimension is to ask four or five people who know you well to complete the dominance indicator form for you. Their assessment may provide a more accurate indication of where you fall on the continuum. Self-assessment alone is sometimes inaccurate because we often lack self-insight.[12] Once you have received the forms completed by others, try to determine if a consistent pattern exists. (Note: It is best not to involve parents, spouses, or close relatives. Seek feedback from coworkers or classmates.)

Where Should You Be on the Dominance Continuum?

People who are high in dominance must sometimes curb their desire to express strong opinions and initiate demands.

Is there any best place to be on the dominance continuum? Not really. Successful people can be found at all points along the continuum. Nevertheless, there are times when people need to act decisively to influence the adoption of their ideas and communicate their expectations clearly. This means that someone low in dominance may need to become more assertive temporarily to achieve an objective. New managers who are low in dominance must learn to influence others without being viewed as aggressive or insensitive. The American Management Association offers a course entitled "Assertiveness Training for Managers," which is designed for managers who want to exercise a greater influence on others, get their proposals across more effectively, and resolve conflict situations decisively yet diplomatically.[13]

People who are high in dominance must sometimes curb their desire to express strong opinions and initiate demands. A person who is perceived as being extremely strong-willed and inflexible will have difficulty establishing a cooperative relationship with others.

CRITICAL THINKING CHALLENGE

After you have determined your own place on the dominance scale, think about your closest coworkers and friends. Who is most dominant in your circle? Who is least dominant? Can you recall occasions when either low dominance or high dominance created a barrier to effective interpersonal relations?

| FIGURE 3.2 | Dominance Indicator Form |

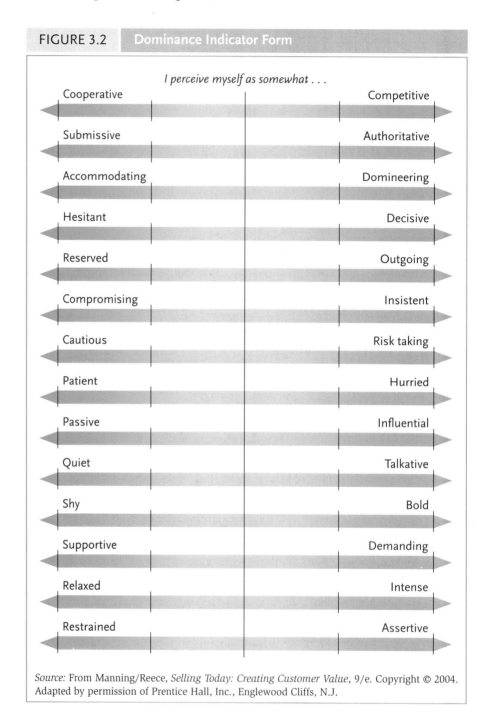

I perceive myself as somewhat . . .

Cooperative	Competitive
Submissive	Authoritative
Accommodating	Domineering
Hesitant	Decisive
Reserved	Outgoing
Compromising	Insistent
Cautious	Risk taking
Patient	Hurried
Passive	Influential
Quiet	Talkative
Shy	Bold
Supportive	Demanding
Relaxed	Intense
Restrained	Assertive

Source: From Manning/Reece, *Selling Today: Creating Customer Value,* 9/e. Copyright © 2004. Adapted by permission of Prentice Hall, Inc., Englewood Cliffs, N.J.

The Sociability Continuum

Have you ever met someone who was open and talkative and who seemed easy to get to know? An individual who is friendly and expresses feelings openly can be placed near the top of the **sociability continuum**.[14] The continuum is illustrated in Figure 3.3. **Sociability** can be defined as the tendency to seek and enjoy social relationships.

Sociability can also be thought of as a measure of whether you tend to control or express your feelings. Those high in sociability usually express their feelings freely, whereas people low on the continuum tend to control their feelings. The person who is classified as being high in sociability is open and talkative and likes personal associations. The person who is low in sociability is more reserved and formal in social relationships.

The second step in determining your most preferred communication style is to identify where you fall on the sociability continuum. To answer this question, complete the sociability indicator form shown in Figure 3.4. Rate yourself on each scale by placing a checkmark at a point along the continuum that represents the degree to which you feel you exhibit each of the characteristics. If most of your checkmarks fall to the right of center, you are high in sociability. If most fall to the left of center, you are low in sociability.

The sociability indicator form is not meant to be a precise instrument, but it will provide you with a general indication of where you fall on each of the scales. You may also want to make copies of the form and distribute them to friends or coworkers for completion. (Remember, it is advisable not to involve parents, spouses, or close relatives in this feedback exercise.)

Where Should You Be on the Sociability Continuum?

Where are successful people on the sociability continuum? Everywhere. There is no best place to be. People at all points along the continuum can achieve success

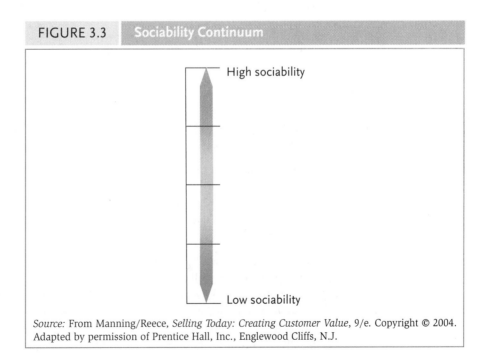

FIGURE 3.3	Sociability Continuum

High sociability

Low sociability

Source: From Manning/Reece, *Selling Today: Creating Customer Value*, 9/e. Copyright © 2004. Adapted by permission of Prentice Hall, Inc., Englewood Cliffs, N.J.

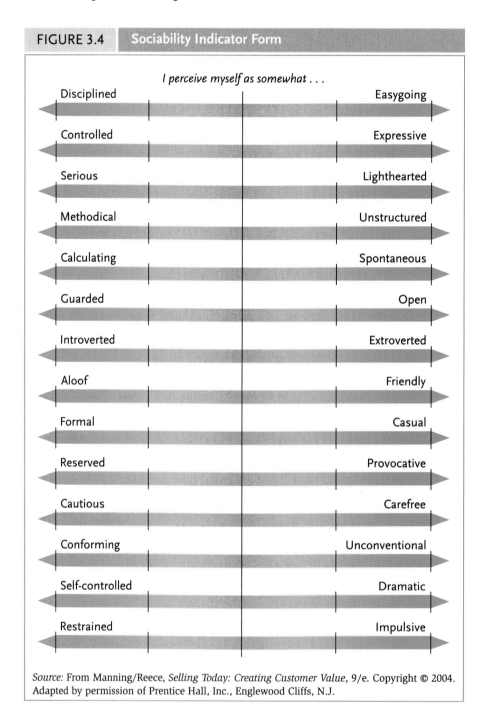

FIGURE 3.4 | Sociability Indicator Form

I perceive myself as somewhat . . .

Disciplined				Easygoing
Controlled				Expressive
Serious				Lighthearted
Methodical				Unstructured
Calculating				Spontaneous
Guarded				Open
Introverted				Extroverted
Aloof				Friendly
Formal				Casual
Reserved				Provocative
Cautious				Carefree
Conforming				Unconventional
Self-controlled				Dramatic
Restrained				Impulsive

Source: From Manning/Reece, *Selling Today: Creating Customer Value*, 9/e. Copyright © 2004. Adapted by permission of Prentice Hall, Inc., Englewood Cliffs, N.J.

in an organizational setting. Nevertheless, there are some commonsense guidelines that persons who fall at either end of the continuum are wise to follow.

A person who is low in sociability is more likely to display a no-nonsense attitude when dealing with other people. This person may be seen as impersonal and businesslike. Behavior that is too guarded and too reserved can be a barrier to effective communication. Such persons may be perceived as unconcerned about the feelings of others and interested only in getting the job done. Perceptions are critical in the business world, especially among customers. Even a hint of indifference can create a customer relations problem.

People who are high in sociability openly express their feelings, emotions, and impressions. They are perceived as being concerned with relationships and therefore are easy to get to know. At times, emotionally expressive people need to curb their natural exuberance. Too much informality can be a problem in some work relationships. The importance of adapting your style to accommodate the needs of others is discussed later in this chapter.

CRITICAL THINKING CHALLENGE

After you have determined your position on the sociability scale, think about your closest coworkers and friends. Who is highest on the sociability indicator? Who is lowest? Can you recall an occasion when high sociability or low sociability created a barrier to effective interpersonal relations?

 Four Basic Communication Styles

The dominance and sociability continua can be combined to form a rather simple model that will tell you more about your communication style (see Figure 3.5). The **communication style model** will help you identify your most

FIGURE 3.5	When the dominance and sociability dimensions are combined, the framework for communication style classification is established.

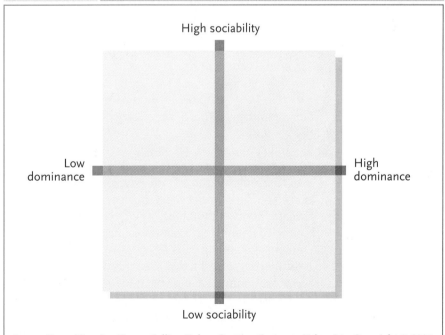

Source: From Manning/Reece, *Selling Today: Creating Customer Value*, 9/e. Copyright © 2004. Adapted by permission of Prentice Hall, Inc., Englewood Cliffs, N.J.

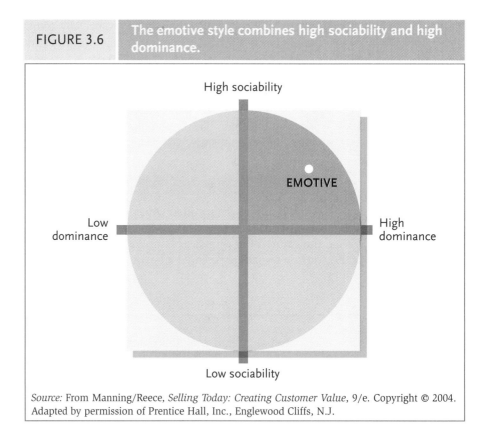

FIGURE 3.6   The emotive style combines high sociability and high dominance.

High sociability

EMOTIVE

Low dominance

High dominance

Low sociability

Source: From Manning/Reece, *Selling Today: Creating Customer Value*, 9/e. Copyright © 2004. Adapted by permission of Prentice Hall, Inc., Englewood Cliffs, N.J.

preferred style. Dominance is represented by the horizontal axis and sociability by the vertical axis. The model is divided into quadrants, each representing one of four communication styles: emotive, director, reflective, or supportive. As you review the descriptions of these styles, you will likely find one that is "most like you" and one or more that are "least like you."

Emotive Style   The upper-right-hand quadrant combines high sociability and high dominance. This is characteristic of the **emotive style** of communication (Figure 3.6).

You can easily form a mental picture of the emotive type by thinking about the phrases used earlier to describe high dominance and high sociability. A good example of the emotive type of person is comedian Jay Leno. Rosie O'Donnell also projects an outspoken, enthusiastic, and stimulating style. Richard Branson, founder of Virgin Atlantic Airways, displays the emotive style. He is animated, frequently laughs at himself, and seems to like an informal atmosphere. Larry King, popular talk-show host, and Jeff Bezos, CEO of *Amazon.com*, also project the emotive communication style. Here is a list of verbal and nonverbal clues that identify the emotive person:

1. *Displays spontaneous, uninhibited behavior.* The emotive person is more apt to talk rapidly, express views with enthusiasm, and use vigorous hand gestures. David Letterman and Jim Carrey fit this description.

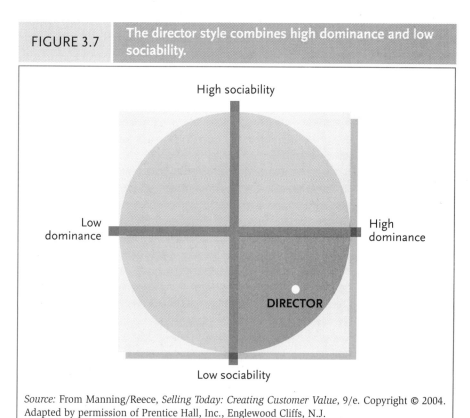

FIGURE 3.7   The director style combines high dominance and low sociability.

High sociability

Low dominance

High dominance

DIRECTOR

Low sociability

Source: From Manning/Reece, *Selling Today: Creating Customer Value*, 9/e. Copyright © 2004. Adapted by permission of Prentice Hall, Inc., Englewood Cliffs, N.J.

2. *Displays the personality dimension described as extroversion.* Extroverts typically enjoy being with other people and tend to be active and upbeat. The emotive person likes informality and usually prefers to operate on a first-name basis.

3. *Possesses a natural persuasiveness.* Combining high dominance and high sociability, this person finds it easy to express his or her point of view dramatically and forcefully.

Director Style   The lower-right-hand quadrant represents a communication style that combines high dominance and low sociability—the **director style** (Figure 3.7). Martha Stewart and Vice President Dick Cheney, project the director style. So does Tom Peters, the hard-driving management consultant. Bob Dole, former presidential candidate, easily fits the description of this communication style. All these people have been described as frank, assertive, and very determined. Some behaviors displayed by directors include the following:

1. *Projects a serious attitude.* Mike Wallace, one of the reporters on the popular television show *60 Minutes*, usually communicates a no-nonsense attitude. Directors often give the impression that they cannot have fun.

2. *Expresses strong opinions.* With firm gestures and a tone of voice that communicates determination, the director projects the image of someone

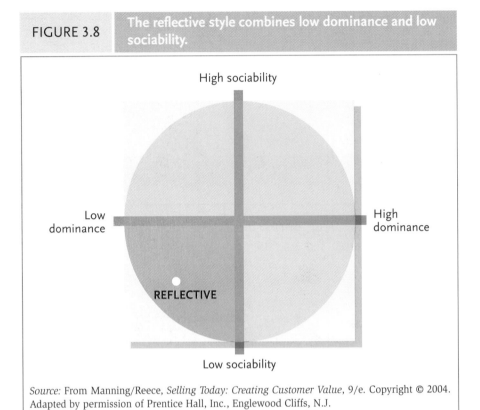

FIGURE 3.8	The reflective style combines low dominance and low sociability.

Source: From Manning/Reece, *Selling Today: Creating Customer Value*, 9/e. Copyright © 2004. Adapted by permission of Prentice Hall, Inc., Englewood Cliffs, N.J.

who wants to take control. Judge Judith Sheindlin of the *Judge Judy* television show displays this behavior.

3. *May project indifference.* It is not easy for the director to communicate a warm, caring attitude. He or she does not find it easy to abandon the formal approach in dealing with people.

Reflective Style The lower-left-hand quadrant of the communication style model features a combination of low dominance and low sociability. This is the **reflective style** of communication (Figure 3.8).

The reflective person is usually quiet, enjoys spending time alone, and does not make decisions quickly. The late physicist Albert Einstein fits this description. He once commented on how he liked to spend idle hours: "When I have no special problem to occupy my mind, I love to reconstruct proofs of mathematical and physical theorems that have long been known to me. There is no goal in this, merely an opportunity to indulge in the pleasant occupation of thinking."[15] Alan Greenspan, former chairman of the Federal Reserve, former president Jimmy Carter, and Dr. Joyce Brothers (psychologist) also display the characteristics of the reflective communication style. Some of the behaviors characteristic of this style are as follows:

| FIGURE 3.9 | The supportive style combines low dominance and high sociability. |

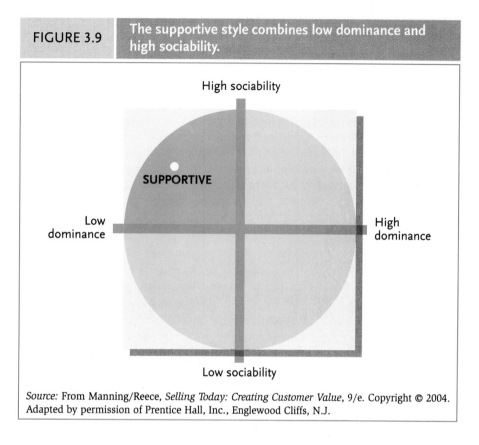

Source: From Manning/Reece, *Selling Today: Creating Customer Value*, 9/e. Copyright © 2004. Adapted by permission of Prentice Hall, Inc., Englewood Cliffs, N.J.

1. *Expresses opinions in a disciplined, deliberate manner.* The reflective person does not seem to be in a hurry. He or she expresses measured opinions. Emotional control is a common trait of this style.

2. *Seems to be preoccupied.* The reflective person is rather quiet and may often appear preoccupied with other matters. As a result, he or she may seem aloof and difficult to get to know. Bill Gates displays this personality trait.

3. *Prefers orderliness.* The reflective person prefers an orderly work environment. At a meeting, this person appreciates an agenda. A reflective person enjoys reviewing details and making decisions slowly.

Supportive Style   The upper-left-hand quadrant combines low dominance and high sociability—the **supportive style** of communication (Figure 3.9). People who possess this style tend to be cooperative, patient, and attentive.

The supportive person is reserved and usually avoids attention-seeking behavior. Additional behaviors that commonly characterize the supportive style include the following:

1. *Listens attentively.* Good listeners have a unique advantage in many occupational settings. This is especially true of loan officers, sales personnel, and supervisors. The talent comes more naturally to the supportive person.

HUMAN RELATIONS IN ACTION	Closing the Sale

Rich Goldberg, CEO of Warm Thoughts Communications, a New Jersey–based marketing communications company, sensed he was about to lose an important client. He met with his staff, and together they created a profile based on their knowledge of the client's communication style. It soon became apparent that there was a mismatch between the client and the salesperson who called on that person. The customer was low in sociability but high in dominance. The customer was also described as someone who needed facts and figures. The salesperson was spending too much time on relationship building, and this approach was agitating the client. Goldberg counseled his staff to keep conversations with this customer brief, use facts and figures frequently, and clearly spell out the company's commitment to the client.

2. *Avoids the use of power.* Supportive persons are more likely to rely on friendly persuasion than power when dealing with people. They like to display warmth in their speech and written correspondence. The late Charles Kuralt, CBS News journalist; Neil Armstrong, Apollo 11 crew member; and actress Julia Roberts fit this description.

3. *Makes and expresses decisions in a thoughtful, deliberate manner.* Supportive persons appear low-key in a decision-making role. Meryl Streep, Paul Simon, Meg Ryan, Kevin Costner, the late Princess Di, and Mary Tyler Moore all display characteristics of this style.

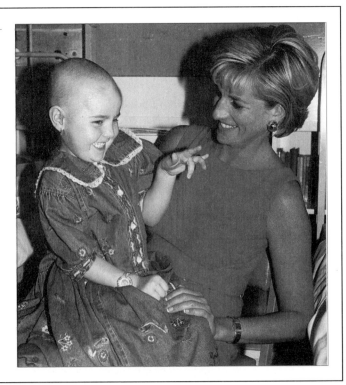

The late Princess Diana displays the characteristics of the supportive style. Persons with this communication style are generally observed as warm, patient, and easygoing; they tend to avoid the use of power.

Did you find one particular communication style that is most like yours? If your first attempt to identify your most preferred style was not successful, do not be discouraged. No one conforms completely to one style. You share some traits with other styles. Also, keep in mind that communication style is just one dimension of personality. As noted previously, your personality is made up of a broad array of psychological and behavioral characteristics. It is this unique pattern of characteristics that makes each person an individual. *Communication style* refers only to those behaviors that others can observe.

Did you discover a communication style that is least like yours? In many cases, we feel a sense of tension or discomfort when we have contact with persons who speak or act in ways that are at odds with our communication style. For example, the person with a need for orderliness and structure in daily work may feel tension when working closely with someone who is more spontaneous and unstructured.

Variation Within Your Communication Style

Communication styles also vary in intensity. For example, a person may be either moderately or strongly dominant. Note that the communication style model features zones that radiate outward from the center, as illustrated in Figure 3.10. These dimensions might be thought of as **intensity zones**.

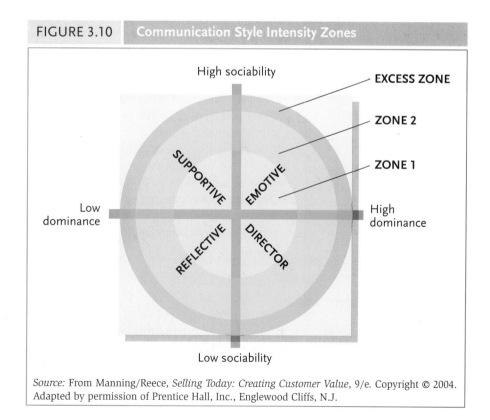

FIGURE 3.10 Communication Style Intensity Zones

High sociability

EXCESS ZONE

ZONE 2

ZONE 1

SUPPORTIVE   EMOTIVE

Low dominance — High dominance

REFLECTIVE   DIRECTOR

Low sociability

Source: From Manning/Reece, *Selling Today: Creating Customer Value*, 9/e. Copyright © 2004. Adapted by permission of Prentice Hall, Inc., Englewood Cliffs, N.J.

Zone 1   People who fall within Zone 1 will display their unique behavioral characteristics with less intensity than people in Zone 2. This means that it may be more difficult to identify the preferred communication style of people in Zone 1. They will not be as obvious in their gestures, tone of voice, speech patterns, or emotional expressions. You may have trouble picking up the right clues to identify their communication style.

Zone 2   People who fall within Zone 2 will display their behavioral characteristics with greater intensity than those in Zone 1. For example, on the following dominance continuum, Sue, Mike, Harold, and Deborah each fall within a different zone.

Low Dominance   High Dominance

    Sue   Mike   Harold   Deborah

In terms of communication style identification, it is probably easier to distinguish between Sue and Deborah (who are in Zone 2) than between Mike and Harold (who are in Zone 1). Of course, the boundary line that separates Zone 1 from Zone 2 should not be viewed as a permanent barrier. Under certain conditions, people will abandon their preferred style temporarily.

You can sometimes observe this behavior change when a person is upset or angry. For example, Sue is a strong supporter of equal rights for women. At school she hears a male student say, "I think a woman's place is in the home." At that point, she may express her own views in the strongest possible terms. This forcefulness will require temporarily abandoning the comfort of her low dominance style to display assertive behavior.

Inflexible and rigid communication styles are likely to lead to a breakdown in human relations.

Excess Zone   The **excess zone** is characterized by a high degree of intensity and rigidity. It can also be labeled the "danger" zone. When people occupy this zone, they become inflexible and display a lack of versatility (see Table 3.1). Extreme intensity in any quadrant is bound to interfere with good human relations.

People often move into the excess zone when they are under stress or not feeling well. A person who feels threatened or insecure may also move into the excess zone. Even a temporary excursion into the excess zone should be avoided if at all possible. Inflexible and rigid communication styles are likely to lead to a breakdown in human relations.

Tips on Style Identification

To identify a person's communication style, focus your full attention on observable behavior. The best clues for identifying styles are nonverbal. Learn to be observant of people's gestures, posture, and facial expressions, and the

TABLE 3.1	Behaviors Displayed in the Excess Zone
Supportive Style	Attempts to win approval by agreeing with everyone Constantly seeks reassurance Refuses to take a strong stand Tends to apologize a great deal
Director Style	Is determined to come out on top Will not admit to being wrong Appears cold and unfeeling when dealing with others Tends to use dogmatic phrases such as "always," "never," or "you can't"
Emotive Style	Tends to express highly emotional opinions Is outspoken to the point of being offensive Seems unwilling to listen to the views of others Uses exaggerated gestures and facial expressions
Reflective Style	Tends to avoid making a decision Seems overly interested in detail Is very stiff and formal when dealing with others Seeks to achieve perfection

rapidity and loudness of their speech.[16] Animated facial expressions and high-volume, rapid speech are characteristic of the emotive communication style. Infrequent use of gestures, speaking in a steady monotone, and few facial expressions are characteristic of the reflective style. Of course verbal messages will also be helpful. If a person tends to be blunt and to the point and makes strong statements, you are likely observing a director.

We have noted that communication style is determined by where a person falls on the sociability continuum and the dominance continuum. Once you have identified as many verbal and nonverbal clues as possible, use this information to place the person on each continuum. Let's assume that the clues indicate that the person is low in dominance. This means you can automatically eliminate the emotive and director styles because both are characterized by high dominance. The next step is to place the person on the sociability continuum. If the clues indicate that the person is low in sociability, you automatically eliminate the supportive style. By the process of elimination, you conclude that this person is probably reflective. The authors of *People Styles at Work*, however, warn that your initial perception of another person's style should not be carved in stone. You should continue to collect new information and reassess your initial observations.[17]

Keep in mind that different situations bring out different behaviors. If you observe someone participating in a classroom discussion, then later observe the same person relaxing with friends at a local restaurant, you may witness two different behavioral patterns. Getting to know someone is hard work, and it's best not to look for shortcuts.[18]

HUMAN RELATIONS
IN ACTION

| Yeeeaaahh!

Many political observers believe that Howard Dean's presidential campaign was undone by one unscripted scream. After losing the Iowa Democratic caucus, he met with his dispirited supporters and promised the campaign would continue. After listing all the states he planned to visit in the weeks ahead, he ended the speech with an emotional promise: "And then we're going to Washington, DC, to take back the White House. Yeeeaaahh!" What followed was a near-saturation replay of that scream on cable, radio, and network television. On that cold night in Iowa, Dean created the impression that his passion had crossed over to anger. A move into the excess zone can have unexpected consequences.

Versatility: The Third Dimension

Earlier in this chapter we described two important dimensions of the communication style model: dominance and sociability. You will recall that these dimensions of human behavior are independent of each other. Now we are ready to discuss versatility, an important third dimension of human behavior.

Persons who can create and maintain interpersonal relations with others, regardless of their communication styles, are displaying versatility. **Versatility** can be defined as acting in ways that earn a social endorsement. Endorsement means simply other people's approval of our behavior. People give us their endorsement when they feel comfortable and nondefensive with us.[19]

The dimension of versatility is independent of style. This means that the emotive style is no more or less likely to be versatile than is the reflective style. Communication style remains relatively stable throughout life, whereas versatility is changeable.

Versatility is a trait we exhibit ourselves rather than elicit from others. Versatile people recognize that they can control their half of relationships and that it is easier to modify themselves than it is to modify others. The versatile person asks, "What can I do to make it easier for the other person to relate to me?"[20]

Research on versatility conducted by Wilson Learning Corporation indicates that the ability to adapt to another person's communication style greatly improves interpersonal relationships. People are divided nearly equally across the four communication styles, so we share our own style with only one out of four persons we have contact with. Once we develop and apply versatility skills, a greater number of people will feel comfortable and nondefensive in our presence.[21]

Achieving Versatility Through Style Flexing

Getting classified according to communication style doesn't mean you are "type-cast" for life. You can always learn to strengthen areas of your most preferred communication style in order to get along better with others.[22] One way to broaden your personality is to engage in **style flexing**, which is the deliberate attempt to change or alter your style to meet the needs of another person. It is a temporary effort to act in harmony with the behavior of another person's communication style. Style flexing is communicating in a way that is more agreeable to persons of other styles. As noted earlier in this chapter, you can learn to adapt your style to accommodate others.

TOTAL   **KIMBERLY ALYN AND BOB PHILLIPS**

PERSON   AUTHORS, *ANNOYING PEOPLE*

INSIGHT   "The best way to break a habit is to establish another habit. For example, if you're a constant talker, stop talking. Work at it."

Style Flexing at Work   To illustrate how style flexing can be used in an organizational setting, let's take a look at a communication problem faced by Jeff Walker, buyer of sporting goods for a small chain of sporting goods stores. Jeff has a strong emotive communication style and usually gets along well with other emotive communicators. His immediate supervisor is Rhonda Greenbaum, a reflective person who tends to approach her work in an orderly, systematic manner. Jeff finds it difficult to curb his stimulating, promotional style and therefore is sometimes viewed as "unstable" by Ms. Greenbaum.

What might Jeff do to improve communication with his supervisor? Jeff is naturally an open, impulsive communicator. During meetings with a reflective person, he should appear less spontaneous, slow his rate of speech, and avoid the use of dramatic gestures. He should try to appear more reserved.

The reflective person admires orderliness, so Jeff should be sure he is well prepared. Prior to each meeting, he should develop a mental agenda of items that he wants to cover. At the beginning of the meeting he might say, "Ms. Greenbaum, there are three things I want to discuss." He would then describe each item concisely and present information slowly and systematically. This disciplined approach will be appreciated by the reflective supervisor.

How could Jeff's boss use style flexing to foster better communication? She could avoid appearing too stiff and formal. During meetings, the reflective person should try to avoid being "all business." (The emotive person does not object to small talk during meetings.) The reflective communicator might also be more informal about starting and ending meetings exactly on time, might allow the emotive person to depart from the agenda now and then, or might bring up an item spontaneously. The reflective person should try to share feelings and concerns more openly in the presence of an emotive person.

Strategies for Adapting Your Style

Once you have identified the dominant style of the other person, begin thinking of ways to flex your style to gain a social endorsement. Remember, you can control your half of the relationship. What can be done to meet the interpersonal needs of the other person? Here are a few general style adaptation strategies:

Flexing to the Emotive Style

- Take time to build a social as well as a business relationship. Leave time for relating and socializing.
- Display interest in the person's ideas, interests, and experiences.
- Do not place too much emphasis on details. Emotive people like fast-moving, inspirational verbal exchanges.
- Maintain a pace that is fast and somewhat spontaneous.

Flexing to the Director Style

- Be specific, brief, and to the point. Use time efficiently.
- Present the facts logically, and be prepared to provide specific answers to questions.
- Maintain a pace that is fast and decisive; project an image of strength and confidence.
- Messages (written or oral) should be short and to the point.

Flexing to the Reflective Style

- Appeal to the person's orderly, systematic approach to life. Be well organized.
- Approach this person in a straightforward, direct manner. Get down to business quickly.

- Be as accurate and realistic as possible when presenting information.

- Messages (written or oral) should be detailed and precise. The pace of verbal messages should be slow and systematic.

Flexing to the Supportive Style

- Show a sincere interest in the person. Take time to identify areas of common interest.

- Patiently draw out personal views and goals. Listen and be responsive to the person's needs.

- Present your views in a quiet, nonthreatening manner. Do not be pushy.

- Put a priority on relationship building and communication.

In those situations where you are attempting to win the support or cooperation of another person, look and listen for clues that identify the individual's preferred communication style. Once you are able to recognize and adjust to communication styles different from your own, gaining a social endorsement will be much easier.

Style Flexing: Pitfalls and Possibilities

Is style flexing just another way to manipulate others? The answer is yes if your approach is insincere and your only objective is to get something for yourself. The choice is yours. If your objective is to build an honest, constructive relationship, then style flexing can be a valuable and productive communication skill.

In an organizational setting, style flexing is especially critical when something important is at stake. Let's assume that you are head of a major department in a large hospital. Tomorrow you will meet with the hospital administrator and propose the purchase of new x-ray equipment that will cost a large amount of money. This is a good time to think about the administrator's communication

---

HUMAN RELATIONS IN ACTION | **Al "Chainsaw" Dunlap Seemed Comfortable in the Excess Zone**

Patricia Sellers, a reporter for *Fortune* magazine, has vivid memories of her last telephone conversation with Al "Chainsaw" Dunlap. The embattled CEO of Sunbeam Corporation was about to be fired by the board of directors. Dunlap, famous for his booming voice, abruptness, and strong opinions, wasn't pleased to learn from Sellers that *Fortune* planned to report that several large Sunbeam investors wanted him out: "Geez, this idea that Dunlap's in jeopardy. That's bull!" he raved. Soon after that conversation Dunlap was tossed out by the board. The man who rose to prominence by taking over large corporations and then firing tens of thousands of people was fired for using unorthodox accounting practices. Sellers says, "My ears are still ringing from the shrill sound of Al Dunlap fighting to hold on to his job." Dunlap always seemed comfortable in the excess zone.

style and consider your style-flexing strategies. Every decision is influenced by both reason and emotion, but the weight given to each of these elements during the decision-making process can vary from one person to another. Often we make the mistake of focusing too much attention on the content of our message and not enough on how to deliver that message.[23]

A Final Word of Caution

It is tempting to put a label on someone and then assume the label tells you everything you need to know about that person.

A discussion of communication styles would not be complete without a few words of caution. It is tempting to put a label on someone and then assume the label tells you everything you need to know about that person. In *The Name of Your Game*, Stuart Atkins says we should be careful not to use labels that make people feel boxed in, typecast, or judged. He says we should not classify *people*; we should classify their *strengths* and *preferences* to act one way or another under certain circumstances.[24] As noted in Chapter 1, the "total person" is made up of such interdependent traits as emotional control, values orientation, self-esteem, and self-awareness. To get acquainted with the whole person takes time and effort. Atkins makes this observation: "It requires much more effort to look beyond the label, to experience the person as a dynamic process, to look at the fine print on the box and carefully study the ingredients inside the package. We have been conditioned to trust the label and look no further."[25]

You must also be careful not to let the label you place on yourself become the justification for your own inflexible behavior. If you discover that your most preferred communication style is reflective and take the position that "others will simply have to get used to my need for careful analysis of data before making a decision," then you are not displaying the characteristics of a versatile person. Try not to let the label justify or reinforce why you are unable to communicate effectively with others.[26]

Strength/Weakness Paradox

As noted previously in this chapter, there is no "best" communication style. Each style has its unique strong points. Supportive people are admired for their easygoing, responsive style. Directors are respected for the thoroughness and determination they display. The stimulating, personable style of emotive persons can be very refreshing. And the emotional control and disciplined nature of reflective persons are almost universally admired.

Problems arise when people overextend or rely too much on the strengths of their style. The director who is too demanding may be viewed by others as "pushy." The supportive person may try too hard to please others and risk being viewed as "wishy-washy." An emotive person may be viewed as too excitable or not serious enough in a business setting. The reflective person who cannot seem to make a decision without mountains of information may be viewed as too cautious and inflexible. Some people rely too heavily on established strengths and fail to develop new skills that will increase their versatility.

To get along with people at all levels of an organization, you must be able to build rapport with those who are different from you. Customizing your communication style often requires learning *how to overcome your strengths*.[27]

LOOKING BACK: Reviewing the Concepts

■ Understand the concept of communication style bias and its effect on interpersonal relations.

Communication styles are our patterns of behaviors that are observable to others. Each of us has a distinctive way of responding to people and events. Communication style bias is likely to surface when you meet someone who displays a style distinctly different from your own.

■ Realize the personal benefits that can be derived from an understanding of communication styles.

By getting to know your communication style, you can achieve greater self-awareness and learn how to develop more effective interpersonal relations with others. Accurate self-knowledge is truly the starting point for effectiveness at work.

■ Discuss the major elements of the communication style model.

The communication style model is formed by combining two important dimensions of human behavior: dominance and sociability. Combinations of these two aspects create four communication styles—emotive, director, reflective, and supportive.

■ Identify your preferred communication style.

With practice you can learn to identify your communication style. The starting point is to rate yourself on each scale (dominance and sociability) by placing a checkmark at a point along the continuum that represents how you perceive yourself. Completion of the dominance and sociability indicator forms will help you achieve greater awareness of your communication style. You may also want to ask others to complete these forms for you.

■ Improve communication with others through style flexing.

A third dimension of human behavior—versatility—is important in dealing with communication styles that are different from your own. You can adjust your own style to meet the needs of others—a process called style flexing.

We must keep an open mind about people and be careful not to use labels that make them feel typecast or judged. Keeping an open mind requires more thought than pigeonholing does.

● Career Corner

Q: The company I work for discourages personal phone calls during working hours. I am a single parent with two young children. How can I convince my supervisor that some personal calls are very important?

A: Placing personal phone calls during working hours is an issue that often divides employers and employees. From the employer's point of view, an employee who spends time on nonwork calls is wasting time, a valuable resource. Also, many organizations want to keep telephone lines clear for business calls. From your point of view, you need to know about changes in child-care arrangements, serious health concerns of family members, and similar problems. In fact, you will probably perform better knowing that family members are safe and secure. Explain to your supervisor that some personal calls will be inevitable. It is very important that you and your supervisor reach an agreement regarding this issue. When possible, make most of your personal calls during your lunch hour or during work breaks. Encourage friends to call you at home.

To improve communications with your supervisor, get acquainted with his or her communication style. Once you have identified this person's dominant style, use appropriate style-flexing strategies to gain a social endorsement.

● Key Terms

mirroring	emotive style
personality	director style
communication style	reflective style
communication style bias	supportive style
dominance	intensity zones
dominance continuum	excess zone
sociability continuum	versatility
sociability	style flexing
communication style model	

● Applying What You Have Learned

1. Oprah Winfrey has become one of America's most popular talk-show hosts. Consider the behaviors she displays on her show, and then complete the following exercises:

   a. On the dominance continuum, place a mark where you feel she belongs.

   b. On the sociability continuum, place a mark where you feel she belongs.

   c. On the basis of these two continua, determine Oprah Winfrey's communication style.

   d. In your opinion, does Oprah Winfrey display style flexibility?

2. To get some practice in identifying communication styles, watch two or three television shows and attempt to identify the style of individuals portrayed on

the screen. To fully develop your skills of listening and observing, try this three-step approach:

a. Cover the screen with a towel or newspaper and try to identify the style of one or two persons, using voice only.

b. Turn down the volume, uncover the screen, and attempt to identify the style of the same persons, using visual messages only.

c. Turn up the volume and make another attempt to identify the communication style of the persons portrayed on the screen. This time the identification process should be easier because you will be using sight and sound.

These practice sessions will help you learn how to interpret the nonverbal messages that are helpful in identifying another person's communication style. When you select TV shows, avoid situation comedies that often feature persons displaying exaggerated styles. You may want to watch a talk show or a news program that features interviews.

3. Self-awareness is very important. As we get to know ourselves, we can identify barriers to acceptance by others. Once you have identified your most preferred communication style, you have taken a big step in the direction of self-awareness. If you have not yet determined your most preferred communication style, take a few minutes to complete the dominance indicator form (Figure 3.2) and the sociability indicator form (Figure 3.4). Follow the instructions provided.

Internet Insights

The primary purpose of this chapter is to provide you with an introduction to communication styles and prepare you to apply at work and in your personal life the concepts presented here. You now have the foundation you need to continue your study. A great deal of information related to communication styles can be found on the Internet. Using your search engine, type in the following keywords, and then review the resources available:

communication styles
personality types
personality profiles
psychological types
Jungian personality types

Examine the resources (such as books, articles, and training programs), and then prepare a brief summary of your findings. Pay special attention to new information that was not covered in your textbook.

 ## Role-Play Exercise

For the purpose of this role play, read Case 3.2 and assume the role of Tyler West, who is described as an outspoken, enthusiastic person who displays the emotive communication style. You will meet with Madison Fitz, who is also described in the case problem. Prior to the role play, study the chapter material on style flexing and on how to communicate effectively with persons who display the reflective communication style. Prepare for the first 5–7 minutes of the meeting. How will you present yourself during the initial contact? What would be the best way to get the meeting off to a good start?

Case 3.1   Steve Ballmer Keeps the Good Times Rolling at Microsoft

Bill Gates, chairman of Microsoft Corporation, and Steve Ballmer, CEO of Microsoft, met as undergraduates at Harvard University. Both were math whizzes. Gates eventually dropped out of Harvard to form Microsoft, and Ballmer ended up teaching at the Stanford Business School. When Gates needed a tough-minded manager at his fledgling company, he gave Ballmer the assignment. Ballmer built a sales organization to compete with IBM in large corporate accounts.

Gates and Ballmer have different communication styles. Gates displays the reflective style; he is impressed by proposals that are supported by data. Ballmer displays the director style; he is a take-charge person who can be quite demanding.

During the early years at Microsoft, Ballmer was known as a very aggressive executive with little patience. His explosive temper was legendary, and he often terrified his staff members. He once needed throat surgery because he yelled so much. He had a domineering management style and was unwilling to delegate decision making; still, he accomplished a great deal. Ballmer was promoted to president in 1998 and then to chief executive officer in January of 2000. As CEO, he has managed to fortify Microsoft's position as an industry leader.

Today Ballmer's leadership style is more diplomatic, and he's more likely to delegate decision-making authority. One of his goals is to do a better job of developing managers and leaders. Many people at Microsoft say Steve Ballmer has mellowed. In 2003 *Business Week* named him one of the nation's best managers.[28]

Questions

1. If Steve Ballmer and Bill Gates met for the first time, would any form of communication style bias surface? Explain.

2. What are Steve Ballmer's primary communication needs?

3. If you made a sales call on Steve Ballmer and you wanted to develop an effective business relationship, how would you speak and act during the meeting?

Case 3.2   A Matter of Style

Tyler West is a sales representative for the World Travel Agency, a firm that specializes in packaged tours to foreign countries. Tyler has spent two months training for this position and is now working with customers. Tyler is an expressive person who is very enthusiastic about travel planning. Tyler possesses all the characteristics of the emotive communication style: outspoken, excitable, and very personable.

Monday morning Tyler has an appointment with Madison Fitz, executive director of an association of bank loan officers. Madison wants to arrange a package tour in England for about fifty persons that will include transportation, hotel accommodations, meals, and tickets to special events. Madison is classified as reflective in terms of communication style and is viewed as industrious, cautious, and well organized. Madison is all business when it comes to representing the bankers' association.

Questions

1. At the initial meeting, do you anticipate that communication style bias will surface? If so, why? If not, why?

2. What will be Madison's primary communication needs?

3. How should Tyler speak and act throughout the meeting to develop an effective business relationship with Madison?

INTEGRATED RESOURCES

CLASSROOM ACTIVITIES (*college.hmco.com/pic/reece10e*)

Communication Style Profile Instrument/Analysis
Improve Your People-Reading Skills Project
Practice Style Flexing?

business.college.hmco.com/students

ACE

Self-tests

4

BUILDING HIGH SELF-ESTEEM

Chapter Preview

After studying this chapter, you will be able to

- Define self-esteem and discuss its impact on your life.

- Discuss how self-esteem is developed.

- Identify the characteristics of people with low and high self-esteem.

- Identify ways to raise your self-esteem.

- Understand the conditions organizations can create that will help workers raise their self-esteem.

Shoshana Zuboff likes to reflect on some of the special students she taught at the Harvard Business School. Some students, she recalls," "threw themselves at learning as if their lives depended on it." One of those students, Edward, had a troubled past. His parents split up when he was a small boy, and he was on his own much of the time as his mother needed to work. Edward and his mother lived in a neighborhood where drugs and gangs were common. By the sixth grade, he was a drug dealer, and later he ended up in a penitentiary. Then he had the good fortune to meet a judge who offered him two years in a drug rehabilitation program in return for good behavior. After rehab, he got a job, enrolled in a community college, and made the dean's list several times. A counselor encouraged Edward to set his sights high, so he applied and was accepted to an Ivy League school, where he studied business and economics. This success led to his acceptance into the Harvard Business School, where he met Professor Zuboff.

Although Edward had accomplished a great deal since leaving the penitentiary, he felt a growing sense of shame over things he did not know. During one lecture, Professor Zuboff briefly mentioned the name of an author who had written about Auschwitz. After class, Edward asked, "What is Auschwitz?" Because of his disadvantaged childhood, he had missed out on many learning experiences that most students take for granted. To avoid giving away his deep-seeded, inner secret, he mastered many defense strategies to protect his image amongst his peers. Professor Zuboff noted, "he was haunted by the sense of not knowing what he didn't know or how to learn it."

With help from this caring professor and her husband, who agreed to serve as his mentor, Edward began a program of study designed to fill in the gaps in his education. His self-esteem improved greatly as his program of self-improvement unfolded. Today Edward runs a successful consulting firm that focuses on leadership and emotional intelligence.[1]

The Power of Self-Esteem

The importance of self-esteem as a guiding force in our lives cannot be overstated. Tschirhart Sanford and Mary Ellen Donovan, the authors of *Women & Self-Esteem*, describe the power of self-esteem as follows:

> *The importance of self-esteem as a guiding force in our lives cannot be overstated.*

> Our level of self-esteem affects virtually everything we think, say, and do. It affects how we see the world and our place in it. It affects how others in the world see and treat us. It affects the choices we make—choices about what we will do with our lives and with whom we will be involved. It affects our ability to both give and receive love. And, it affects our ability to take action to change things that need to be changed.[2]

■ Self-Esteem = Self-Efficacy + Self-Respect

Nathaniel Branden, author of *The Six Pillars of Self-Esteem* and *Self-Esteem at Work*, has spent the past three decades studying the psychology of self-esteem. He states that the ultimate source of **self-esteem** can only be internal: It is the

The Power of Strong Self-Efficacy

Over the years many people we now know to be extremely intelligent and talented have had to develop a strong belief in themselves. If they had relied on others' opinions of their capabilities and potential, who knows where this world would be!

Walt Disney was fired by a newspaper editor for lack of ideas. He went bankrupt several times before he built Disneyland.

Thomas Edison's teacher said he was "too stupid to learn anything."

Fred Astaire recalls the 1933 memo from the MGM casting director that stated, "Can't act. Can't sing. Slightly bald. Can dance a little."

Vince Lombardi, successful football coach and motivational speaker and writer, recalls an expert's description of his talents: "He possesses minimal football knowledge and lacks motivation."

Albert Einstein did not speak until he was 4 years old and did not read until he was 7. His teacher described him as "mentally slow, unsociable, and adrift forever in foolish dreams."

relationship between a person's self-efficacy and self-respect. **Self-efficacy** is the belief that you can achieve what you set out to do.[3] When your self-efficacy is high, you believe you have the ability to act appropriately. When your self-efficacy is low, you worry that you might not be able to do the task, that it is beyond your abilities. Your perception of your self-efficacy can influence which tasks you take on and which ones you avoid. Albert Bandura, a professor at Stanford University and one of the foremost self-efficacy researchers, views this component of self-esteem as a resilient belief in your own abilities. According to Bandura, a major source of self-efficacy is the experience of mastery, in which success in one area builds your confidence to succeed in other areas.[4] For example, an administrative assistant who masters a sophisticated computerized accounting system is more likely to tackle future complicated computer programs than is a person who feels computer illiterate and may not even try to figure out the new program, regardless of how well he or she *could* do it.

Self-respect, the second component of self-esteem, is what you think and feel about yourself. Your judgment of your own value is a primary factor in achieving personal and career success. People who respect themselves tend to act in ways that confirm and reinforce this respect. People who lack self-respect may put up with verbal or physical abuse from others because they feel they are unworthy of praise and deserve the abuse. Nathaniel Branden believes that the healthier our self-esteem, the more inclined we are to treat others with respect, benevolence, goodwill, and fairness since we do not tend to perceive them as a threat, and since self-respect is the foundation of respect for others.[5]

Self-efficacy and self-respect are central themes of the definition of self-esteem adopted by the National Association for Self-Esteem. NASE defines self-esteem as "The experience of being capable of meeting life's challenges and being worthy of happiness."[6] It is having the conviction that you are able to make appropriate choices and decisions, and can be effective in the many roles you play in life, such as that of friend, daughter or son, husband or wife, employee or employer, leader, and so on. Your sense of competence is strengthened through accomplishing meaningful goals, overcoming adversities, and bouncing back from failure.

The NASE definition of self-esteem helps us make the distinction between authentic (healthy) self-esteem and false (unhealthy) self-esteem. Authentic self-esteem is not expressed by self-glorification at the expense of others or by the attempt to diminish others so as to elevate oneself. Arrogance, boastfulness, and overestimation of your abilities are more likely to reflect inadequate self-esteem rather than, as it might appear, too much self-esteem.

How Self-Esteem Develops

To understand the development of self-esteem, it is helpful to examine how you formed your self-concept. Your **self-concept** is the bundle of facts, opinions, beliefs, and perceptions about yourself that are present in your life every moment of every day.[7] The self-concept you have today reflects information you have received from others and life events that occurred throughout childhood, adolescence, and adulthood. You are *consciously* aware of some of the things you have been conditioned to believe about yourself. But many comments and events that have shaped your self-concept are processed at the *unconscious* level and continue to influence your judgments, feelings, and behaviors whether you are aware of them or not.[8]

"Just remember, son, it doesn't matter whether you win or lose—unless you want Daddy's love."

Childhood   Researchers in the field of **developmental psychology** are concerned with the course and causes of developmental changes over a person's lifetime. They pay close attention to genetic and environmental factors (nature versus nurture).[9] Although space does not permit a detailed discussion here of cognitive, social, and emotional development during early childhood, we can state with conviction that developmental experiences during the first few years of life are extremely important. For example, too little attention from nurturing parents and too much television viewing can hinder healthy childhood development.[10]

Because childhood events are retained in your brain, poor performance in school, abusive or uncaring parents, or a serious childhood accident can be defining experiences in your life. Messages from siblings, teachers, and various authority figures can have a lasting impact on your self-concept. Consider the father who repeatedly says, "Real men don't cry," or places undue emphasis on successful performance during contact sports. These childhood experiences can form the foundation for your level of self-esteem that emerges later in life.

Adolescence   The transition from childhood to adulthood can be a long and difficult period. At about age 11, children begin to describe themselves in terms of social relationships and personality traits. By the end of early adolescence, most youth are ready to develop a personal identity as a unique individual. Identity formation, the central task of adolescence, is usually more difficult for youth if their infancy and childhood resulted in feelings of shame, guilt, and inferiority.[11]

Most adolescents are attempting to resolve questions about self-worth, sexuality, and independence. David Rocky Mountain, a 13-year old Lakota Native American surveys a traditional campsite constructed by troubled teens from the Cheyenne River Sioux tribe in South Dakota. This "spiritual boot camp" provides youngsters with the opportunity to bond with their elders who offer many valuable life lessons.

As adolescents attempt to resolve questions about self-worth, sexuality, and independence, they may "try out" alternative identities.[12] Teens often turn to movies, music videos, and magazines for guidance and attempt to emulate the unrealistic body images and fashions that their peers deem worthwhile. Adolescence can last well into the 20s as each person attempts to develop his or her own unique identity.

Parents and teachers can have a powerful effect on their teenagers' self-esteem. When they offer encouragement, support, enthusiasm, and commendation for achievements, they enable teens to learn how to take healthy risks, tolerate frustration, and feel proud of their accomplishments.

Adulthood When you reach adulthood, you are greatly influenced by a time-reinforced self-concept that has been molded by people and events from all your past experiences. You have been bombarded over the years with positive and negative messages from your family, friends, teachers, supervisors, and the media. You may compare yourself to others, as was so common in adolescence, or you may focus on your own inner sense of self-worth. Emmett Miller, a noted authority on self-esteem, says that as adults we tend to define ourselves in terms of:[13]

1. ***The things we possess.*** Miller says this is the most primitive source of self-worth. If we define ourselves in terms of what we have, the result may be an effort to accumulate more and more material things to achieve a greater feeling of self-worth. The idea that we can compensate for self-doubt and insecurity with our checkbook is widely accepted in America.[14] People who define themselves in terms of what they have may have difficulty deciding "what is enough" and may spend their life in search of more material possessions.

2. ***What we do for a living.*** Miller points out that too often our self-worth and identity depend on something as arbitrary as a job title. Amy Saltzman, author of *Downshifting*, a book on ways to reinvent (or redefine) success, says, "We have allowed our professional identities to define us and control us."[15] She points out that we have looked to outside forces such as the corporation, the university, or the media to provide us with a script for leading a satisfying, worthwhile life.

3. ***Our internal value system and emotional makeup.*** Miller says this is the healthiest way for people to identify themselves:

   If you don't give yourself credit for excellence in other areas of life, besides your job and material possessions, you've got nothing to keep your identity afloat in emotionally troubled waters. People who are in touch with their real identity weather the storm better because they have a more varied and richer sense of themselves, owing to the importance they attach to their personal lives and activities.[16]

As an adult, you will be constantly adjusting the level of your self-esteem as you cope with events at work and in your personal life. The loss of a job or being passed over for a promotion may trigger feelings of insecurity or depression.

A messy divorce can leave you with feelings of self-doubt. An unexpected award may raise your spirits and make you feel better about yourself.

The Past Programs the Future Phillip McGraw, better known as "Dr. Phil," has developed a one-sentence guide to understanding the importance of your self-concept: *The past reaches into the present, and programs the future, by your recollections and your internal rhetoric about what you perceived to have happened in your life.*[17] Past experiences and events, which McGraw describes as "defining moments," can influence your thinking for a lifetime and program your future. They get incorporated into your deepest understanding of who you are because they are often the focus of your internal dialogue—a process we call "self-talk." Later in this chapter, we will discuss how to avoid the influence of negative self-talk and build upon positive messages.

TOTAL **DON MIGUEL RUIZ**

PERSON AUTHOR, *THE FOUR AGREEMENTS*

INSIGHT "How many times do we pay for one mistake? The answer is thousands of times. The human is the only animal on earth that pays a thousand times for the same mistake. The rest of the animals pay once for every mistake they make. But not us. We have a powerful memory. We make a mistake, we judge ourselves, we find ourselves guilty, and punish ourselves. . . . Every time we remember, we judge ourselves again, we are guilty again, and we punish ourselves again, and again, and again."

CRITICAL THINKING CHALLENGE

Oprah Winfrey says, "Each of us arrives with all we need to feel valued and unique, but slowly that gets chipped away." She is correct, but some life experiences do cause us to increase the value we place on ourselves. After careful reflection on your childhood and adolescence, identify five events or people who had a significant impact (positive or negative) on your self-esteem. Think of these experiences as "defining moments" in your life.

Self-Esteem Influences Your Behavior

Your level of self-esteem can have a powerful impact on your behavior. Your sense of competence and resulting self-respect, the two components of self-esteem, stem from the belief that you are generally capable of producing the results in life that you want by making appropriate, constructive choices. This confidence makes you less vulnerable to the negative views of others, which then enables you to be more tolerant and respectful of others. People with healthy self-esteem tend to have a sense of personal worth that has been strengthened through various achievements and through accurate self-appraisal.[18]

Characteristics of People with Low Self-Esteem

When we rely too heavily on validation from external sources, we can lose control over our lives.

1. ***They tend to maintain an external locus of control.*** People who maintain an **external locus of control** believe that their life is almost totally controlled by outside forces and that they bear little personal responsibility for what happens to them.[19] When something goes wrong, they have a tendency to blame something or someone other than themselves. Even when they succeed, they tend to attribute their success to luck rather than to their own expertise and hard work. They continually rely on other people to make them feel good about themselves, and therefore need an ever-increasing dose of support from others to keep them going. When we rely too heavily on validation from external sources, we can lose control over our lives.[20]

2. ***They are more likely to participate in self-destructive behaviors.*** If you do not like yourself, there is no apparent reason to take care of yourself. Therefore, people with low self-esteem are more likely to drink too much, smoke too much, and eat too much. Some may develop an eating disorder such as bulimia or anorexia, often with devastating results.

3. ***They tend to exhibit poor human relations skills.*** Individuals with low self-esteem may have difficulty developing effective interpersonal skills. Workers with low self-esteem may reduce the efficiency and productivity of a group: They tend to exercise less initiative and hesitate to accept responsibility or make independent decisions and are less likely to speak up in a group and criticize the group's approach.

Characteristics of People with High Self-Esteem

1. ***They tend to maintain an internal locus of control.*** People who believe they are largely responsible for what happens to them maintain an **internal locus of control**. They make decisions for their own reasons based on their standards of what is right and wrong. They learn from their mistakes, but are not immobilized by them. They realize that problems are challenges not obstacles. In his book *They All Laughed: From Lightbulbs to Lasers*, Ira Flatow examines the lives of successful, innovative people who had to overcome major obstacles to achieve their goals. He discovered that the common thread among these creative people was their ability to overcome disappointing events and press on toward their goals.

2. ***They are able to feel all dimensions of emotion without letting those emotions affect their behavior in a negative way.*** They realize emotions cannot be handled either by repressing them or by giving them free rein. Although you may not be able to stop feeling the emotions of anger, envy, and jealousy, you can control your thoughts and actions when you are under the influence of these strong emotions. Say to yourself, "I may not be able to control the way I feel right now, but I can control the way I behave."

3. ***They are less likely to take things personally.*** Don Miguel Ruiz, author of the best-selling book *The Four Agreements,* cautions us to avoid taking others' comments personally: "When you make it a strong habit not to take anything personally, you avoid many upsets in your life." He says that when you react strongly to gossip or strongly worded criticism ("You're so fat!"), you suffer for nothing. Ruiz notes that many of these messages come from people who are unable to respect you because they do not respect themselves.[21]

4. ***They are able to accept other people as unique, talented individuals.*** They learn to accept others for who they are and what they can do. Our multicultural work force makes this attitude especially important. Individuals who cannot tolerate other people who are "different" may find themselves out of a job. (See Chapter 15, "Valuing Workforce Diversity.") People with high self-esteem build mutual trust based on each individual's uniqueness.

5. ***They have a productive personality.*** They are optimistic in their approach to life and are capable of being creative, imaginative problem solvers. Because of this, they tend to be leaders and to be skillful in dealing with people. They have the ability to evaluate the dynamics of a relationship and adjust to the demands of the interaction. They do not resort to shifting the blame onto others if something goes wrong; instead, they help others accept the responsibility for their own actions. They are able to handle stress in a productive way by putting their problems and concerns into perspective and maintaining a balance of work and fun in their lives.[22]

SKILL DEVELOPMENT CHALLENGE

People with high self-esteem tend to associate with others who exhibit self-confidence and self-respect. Conversely, people with low self-esteem find comfort associating with people who share negative self-images. Can you identify these people in your circle of friends, classmates, and colleagues? Practice your people-reading skills by considering all those people in your life right now, and then mentally decide in which of the two categories they belong: low self-esteem or high self-esteem. What qualities do these people exhibit that helped you make your decisions? In order to build your own self-esteem, which of these people should you associate with more often?

How to Build Self-Esteem

"The level of our self-esteem is not set once and for all in childhood," says Nathaniel Branden. It can grow throughout our lives or it can deteriorate.[23] Healthy self-esteem comes from realizing what qualities and skills you have that you can rely on and then making a plan to build those qualities and skills that you want in the future. The person you will be tomorrow has yet to be created. Your new, higher level of self-esteem will not happen overnight. Such a change is the result of a slow, steady evolution that begins with the desire to overcome low self-esteem.

Search for the Source of Low Self-Esteem

Many people live with deep personal doubts about themselves but have difficulty determining the source of those feelings. They even have difficulty finding the right words to describe those negative feelings. People with low self-esteem are less likely to see themselves with great clarity. The self-image they possess is like a reflection in a warped funhouse mirror; the image magnifies their weaknesses and minimizes their strengths. To raise your self-esteem requires achieving a higher level of self-awareness and learning to accurately perceive your particular balance of strengths and weaknesses.[24]

To start this process, take time to list and carefully examine the defining moments in your life. Pay special attention to those that were decidedly negative, and try to determine how these moments have shaped your current self-concept. Next, make a list of the labels that others have used to describe you. Study the list carefully, and try to determine which ones you have internalized and accepted. Have these labels had a positive or negative influence on your concept of yourself? Phillip McGraw says, "If you are living to a label, you have molded for yourself a fictional self-concept with artificial boundaries."[25]

Identify and Accept Your Limitations

Become realistic about who you are and what you can and cannot do. Demanding perfection of yourself is unrealistic because no one is perfect. The past cannot be changed: Acknowledge your mistakes; learn from them; then move on.

Acting as an observer and detaching yourself from negative thoughts and actions can help you break the habit of rating yourself according to some scale of perfection and can enable you to substitute more positive and helpful thoughts. A good first step is learning to dislike a behavior you may indulge in, rather than condemning yourself. Criticizing yourself may make the behavior worse. If you condemn yourself for being weak, for example, how can you muster the strength to change?

Take Responsibility for Your Decisions

Psychologists have found that children who were encouraged to make their own decisions early in their lives have higher self-esteem than those who were kept dependent on their parents for a longer period of time. Making decisions helps you develop confidence in your own judgment and enables you to explore options. Take every opportunity you can to make decisions both in setting your goals and in devising ways to achieve them.

TOTAL	**FRAN COX AND LOUIS COX**
PERSON	AUTHORS, *A CONSCIOUS LIFE*
INSIGHT	"There is little understanding in our culture that being an adult is an ongoing process of learning and self-correcting: Life is always changing, revealing what was previously unknown and unplanned for."

The attitude that you must be right all the time is a barrier to personal growth. With this attitude you will avoid doing things that might result in mistakes. Much unhappiness comes from the widespread and regrettable belief that it is important to avoid making mistakes at all costs.[26] Taking risks that reach beyond what you already know how to do can often be fun and extremely rewarding.

Engage in Strength Building

Over the past thirty years, the Gallup International Research and Education Center has researched the best way to maximize a person's potential. One of the most important findings can be summarized in a single sentence: Most organizations take their employees' strengths for granted and focus on minimizing their weaknesses. The research findings suggest that the best way to excel in a career is to maximize your strengths.[27]

The Gallup Organization research has been summarized in *Now, Discover Your Strengths* by Marcus Buckingham and Donald Clifton. The first step toward strength building is to discover your greatest talents. A **talent** is any naturally recurring pattern of thought, feeling, or behavior that can be productively applied. It is important to distinguish your natural talents from things you can learn. With practice, of course, we can all get a little better at doing most things. However, to reach consistent, near perfect performances through practice alone is very difficult. Many successful salespeople have a talent for making new acquaintances and derive satisfaction from breaking the ice to make a connection with new people. They are intrigued with the unique qualities of each customer. They have a natural gift, enhanced through practice, for figuring out how to customize their sales presentation so it appeals to the unique needs of each customer. Without these talents, salespeople will struggle to achieve success.[28]

Strength building also requires the acquisition of knowledge and skill. As we prepare for a career, we must acquire certain factual knowledge. An accountant must know how to prepare a statement of cash flow. Nurses must know exactly how much Novocain is needed for a procedure. Skill, the application of knowledge, might be thought of as the "doing" part of strength building.[29]

Identifying Your Dominant Talents   Marcus Buckingham states that when we are not doing what we are truly good at, we are not living up to our greatest performance capabilities. He says that one effective way to identify your dominant talents is to step back and watch yourself as you try out different activities. Pay close attention to how you feel about these experiences. Take an elective course, volunteer to be chair of a committee, complete a summer internship, or accept a part-time job in an area that appeals to you. If you flourish in some activities, but wither in others, analyze why this happened.

Buckingham's research indicates that the best managers spend 80 percent of their time trying to amplify their employees' strengths.[30] Chances are, however, you will not be working for a boss who encourages strength building. So, be prepared to assume responsibility for identifying your natural talents and building your strengths.

The authors of the best-selling book *Now, Discover Your Strengths* encourage us to identify our dominant talents. Get involved in a wide range of activities and then pay close attention to how you feel about these experiences.

FROM THE COAUTHOR OF THE NATIONAL BESTSELLER
FIRST, BREAK ALL THE RULES COMES...

NOW,
DISCOVER
YOUR STRENGTHS

The revolutionary program that shows you how to develop your unique talents and strengths —and those of the people you manage. Based on the Gallup study of over two million people

TAKE GALLUP'S STRENGTHSFINDER.COM PROFILE AND LEARN YOUR TOP 5

MARCUS BUCKINGHAM &
DONALD O. CLIFTON, Ph.D.

Seek the Support and Guidance of Mentors

Chip Bell, author of *Managers as Mentors: Building Partnerships for Learning*, defines a **mentor** as "someone who helps someone else learn something the learner would otherwise have learned less well, more slowly, or not at all."[31] In most organizations mentoring is carried out informally, but formal programs that systematically match mentors and protégés are common.

Most people who have had a mentoring experience say it was an effective development tool. However, many surveys indicate that only a small percentage of employees say they have had a mentor. In today's fast-paced work environment, where most people have a heavy workload, you must be willing to take the initiative and build a mentor relationship. Warren Bennis, founding chairman of the Leadership Institute at the University of Southern California, states, "Being mentored isn't a passive game. It's nothing less than the ability to spot the handful of people who can make all the difference in your life."[32] Here are some tips to keep in mind.

1. ***Search for a mentor who has the qualities of a good coach.*** Mentors need to be accomplished in their own right, but success alone does not make someone a good mentor. Look for someone whom you would like to emulate, both in business savvy and in operating style. Be sure it is someone you trust enough to talk with about touchy issues.[33]

HUMAN RELATIONS IN ACTION

Mentoring Programs at General Mills

The mentoring programs at General Mills are extensive and designed to enculturate new employees, bridge the gaps between genders and cultures, and give established employees experience in facilitated coaching and knowledge transfer.

- The Corporate Mentoring Program matches newly hired employees of color with more senior mentors.
- The Senior Co-Mentoring Program matches corporate officers with high-potential women and people of color at the director level and above.
- The human resource division has a mentoring program that focuses on building relationships, developing competencies, and shaping leadership abilities.
- The Women in Finance/Information Systems Network runs mentoring circles

among seven to nine female employees and a facilitator whose purpose is to encourage networking and skills development through collaboration.

- The sales organization has an informal, self-selected mentoring program for salespeople to learn more about mentoring as well as how to mentor others and is supported by online mentoring resources.
- The Menttium 100, a cross-company mentoring program, matches high-potential women with senior-level mentors from other companies.
- The company also offers a guidebook that provides content and direction for conversations among mentoring pairs, including rules, a working agreement, and a workbook for recording notes on the progress of the relationship.

2. ***Market yourself to a prospective mentor.*** The best mentor for you may be someone who is very busy. Sell the benefits of a mentoring partnership. For example, point out that mentoring can be a mutually rewarding experience. Describe specific steps you will take to avoid wasting the time of a busy person. You might suggest that meetings be held during lunch or agree to online mentoring.[34]

3. ***Use multiple mentors.*** Some people feel the need for both internal and external mentors. An internal mentor, an experienced associate or supervisor, can provide guidance as you navigate the organizational bumps and potholes. An external mentor, someone who does not work for your company, can provide an objective, independent view of your skills and talents.[35] Many people benefit from short-term "learning partners" who will coach them on specific skills.

Although mentors are not mandatory for success, they certainly help. Indeed, there will always be days when you feel nothing you do is right. Your mentor can help repair damaged self-esteem and encourage you to go on. With the power of another person's positive expectations reinforcing your own native abilities, it is hard to fail.

Set Goals

Research points to a direct link between self-esteem and the achievement of personal and professional goals. People who set goals and successfully achieve them are able to maintain high self-esteem. Why? Because setting goals en-

Beth Lay, left, and Christy Woodruff joined a mentoring program at Siemens Westinghouse Power Generation. Both women are veterans at this Orlando, Florida–based firm, but Lay is relatively new to management, while Woodruff is one of the company's highest-ranking women.

ables you to take ownership of the future. Once you realize that just about every behavior is controllable, the possibilities for improving your self-esteem are endless. Self-change may be difficult, but it's not impossible. Some people lack self-esteem because they haven't achieved enough goals and experienced the good feelings that come from success.[36]

The major principles that encompass goal setting are outlined in Table 4.1. Goal setting should be an integral part of your efforts to break old habits or form

TABLE 4.1	Goal-Setting Principles

Goal setting gives you the power to take control of the present and the future. Goals can help you break old habits or form new ones. You will need an assortment of goals that address the different needs of your life. The following goal-setting principles should be helpful.

1. *Spend time reflecting on the things you want to change in your life.* Take time to clarify your motivation and purpose. Set goals that are specific, measurable, and realistic. Unrealistic goals increase fear, and fear increases the probability of failure.

2. *Develop a goal-setting plan that includes the steps necessary to achieve the goal.* Put the goal and the steps in writing. Change requires structure. Identify all activities and materials you will need to achieve your goal. Review your plan daily—repetition increases the probability of success.

3. *Modify your environment by changing the stimuli around you.* If your goal is to lose five pounds during a one-month period, make a weight chart so you can monitor your progress. You may need to give up desserts and avoid restaurants that serve huge portions. Gather new information on effective weight loss techniques, and seek advice from others. This may involve finding a mentor or joining a support group.

4. *Monitor your behavior, and reward your progress.* Focus on small successes, because each little success builds your reservoir of self-esteem. Reinforcement from yourself and/or others is necessary for change. If the passion for change begins to subside, remind yourself why you want to achieve your goal. Be patient—it takes time to change your lifestyle.

new ones. Before you attempt to set goals, engage in serious reflection. Make a list of the things you want to achieve, and then ask yourself this question: What goals are truly important to me? If you set goals that really excite you, desire will fuel your will to achieve them.[37]

Practice Guided Imagery

Guided imagery is one of the most creative and empowering methods for achieving your goals available today. It provides you with a way to harness the power of the mind and imagination to succeed at something. It can be used to help you relax, set goals (like losing weight), or prepare for a challenging opportunity such as interviewing for a new job. Some heart surgeons use guided imagery to calm their patients to help speed recovery. With a Walkman headphone, the patient hears carefully crafted, medically detailed messages that urge the person to relax and imagine themselves in a safe, comfortable place: "Feel the new strength flowing through you, through arteries that are wider and more open, more flexible with smoother surfaces than before."[38]

To **visualize** means to form a mental image of something. It refers to what you see in the mind's eye. Once you have formed a clear mental picture of what you want to accomplish, identify the steps needed to get there and then mentally rehearse them. The visualization process needs to be repeated over and over again.

Many athletes choreograph their performance in their imagination before competitions. Studies by the U.S. Olympic Training Center show that 94 percent of the coaches use mental rehearsal for training and competitions.[39] Artists rarely begin a work of art until they have an image of what it is they are going to create. Dancers physically and mentally rehearse their performances hundreds of times before ever stepping on stage. The same techniques can be used in the workplace.

Let's assume your team members have asked you to present a cost-saving plan to management. The entire team is counting on you. The visualization process should begin with identifying the steps you will take to get approval of the plan. What information will you present? What clothing will you wear? Will you use PowerPoint or some other visual presentation method? Will you use any printed documents? Once you have identified all important contingencies and strategies for success, visualize the actual presentation. See yourself walking into the room with your chin up, your shoulders straight, and your voice strong and confident. Picture yourself making appropriate eye contact with people in the room. The focus of your preparation should be on things within your control.

Use Positive Self-Talk

Throughout most of your waking moments, you talk to yourself. **Self-talk** takes place in the privacy of your mind. It can be rational and productive, or it can be irrational and disruptive. When the focus of this internal conversation is on negative thoughts, you are usually less productive.[40] Some psychologists refer to these negative thoughts as your **inner critic**. The critic keeps a record of your failures but never reminds you of your strengths and accomplishments. A major step toward improving your self-esteem is to understand how to respond to the negative influence of your inner critic.[41]

Self-talk takes place in the privacy of your mind.

FIGURE 4.1	Self-Esteem Cycles

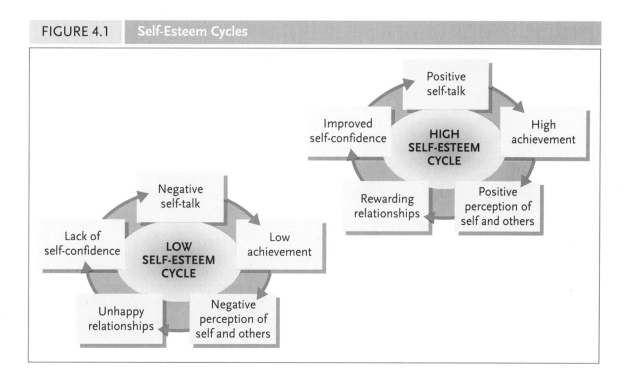

When your inner critic talks to you, ask yourself, "Who is this voice that is reminding me of my past failures?" (see Figure 4.1). The chances are it is not your current boss or spouse, but someone in your past such as a teacher, coach, harsh parent, or sibling. Recognize that this critical voice is probably no longer relevant and take the necessary steps to replace those negative messages with positive ones.[42] You can create effective, positive self-talk statements for each of your goals by using the following guidelines:

1. Be *specific* about the behavior you want to change. What do you want to do to increase your effectiveness? You should firmly believe that what you want is truly possible.

2. Begin each self-talk statement with a first-person pronoun, such as *I or my.* Use a present-tense verb, such as *am, have, feel, create, approve, do,* or *choose.* Don't say "My ability to remember the names of other people *will* improve." Instead, focus on the present: "I *have* an excellent memory for the names of other people."

3. Describe the results you want to achieve. Be sure to phrase the statement as though you have already achieved what you want. Table 4.2 offers several general self-talk statements that might help you improve your self-esteem.[43]

This last step is critical. Because your brain is merely a computer filled with various data from all your past experiences, you need to use, literally, the correct words. When you think of the words *spider, tornado,* or *blue,* your brain develops an automatic understanding of each word and a response or image based on years of conditioning and training. If you are attempting to quit smoking, don't

TABLE 4.2	Creating Semantically Correct Self-Talk	
Wrong	**Right**	
I can quit smoking.	I am in control of my habits.	
I will lose twenty pounds.	I weigh a trim _____ pounds.	
I won't worry anymore.	I am confident and optimistic.	
Next time I won't be late.	I am prompt and efficient.	
I will avoid negative self-talk.	I talk to myself, with all due respect.	
I will not procrastinate.	I do it now.	
I'm not going to let people walk all over me anymore.	I care enough to assert myself when necessary.	

mention the word *smoke* in your self-talk because your brain will react to the word. "I will not smoke after dinner" conjures an image in your subconscious mind, and your behavior follows accordingly. If your self-talk statements use the word *not,* you are probably sending the wrong message to your brain. Say instead, "I am in control of my habits" or "My lungs are clean."

Consider the following statement: "I will not eat chocolate for dessert." Now remove the word *not* from the statement, and the remaining words represent the message being sent to your brain. Does the remaining statement represent your goal? Be careful to semantically design your self-talk statements so that they take you in the direction you want to go; otherwise, they will take you straight toward what you don't want.

Keep in mind that positive self-talk that is truly effective consists of thoughts and messages that are realistic and truthful. It is rationally optimistic self-talk, not unfounded rah-rah hype. Positive internal dialogue should not be a litany of "feel good" mantras; it should be wholly consistent with your authentic self.[44]

Organizations Can Help

Even though each of us ultimately is responsible for raising or lowering our own self-esteem, we can make that task easier or more difficult for others. We can either support or damage the self-efficacy and self-respect of the people we work with, just as they have that option in their interactions with us. Organizations are beginning to include self-esteem modules in their employee- and management-training programs.

When employees do not feel good about themselves, the result will often be poor job performance. This view is shared by many human resource professionals. Many organizations realize that low self-esteem affects their workers' ability to learn new skills, to be effective team members, and to be productive. Research has identified five factors that can enhance the self-esteem of employees in any organization[45] (see Figure 4.2).

- *Workers need to feel valuable.* A major source of worker satisfaction is the feeling that one is valued as a unique person. Self-esteem grows when an

FIGURE 4.2	Factors That Enhance the Self-Esteem of Employees

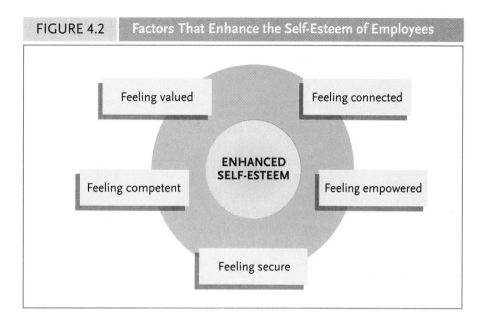

organization makes an effort to accommodate individual differences, to recognize individual accomplishments, and to help employees build their strengths.

■ *Workers need to feel competent.* Earlier in this chapter we noted that self-efficacy grows when people feel confident in their ability to perform job-related tasks. One of the best ways organizations can build employee confidence is to involve employees in well-designed training programs.

■ *Workers need to feel secure.* Employees are more likely to feel secure when they are well informed and know what is expected of them. Managers need to clarify their expectations and provide employees with frequent feedback regarding their performance.

■ *Workers need to feel empowered.* Progressive organizations recognize that every employee has something to contribute to the organization and that limiting employees' contributions limits the organization's progress. When all employees are treated with respect and given the latitude for individual action within the defined limits of the organization, they are free to use their creativity and ingenuity to solve problems and make customers happy. This enables workers to develop a sense of personal responsibility and self-respect. To inhibit this freedom could induce resentful and eventually rebellious attitudes. Restrictions that suppress individuality can make people feel stunted and handicapped in the use of their personal skills, abilities, and resources.[46]

■ *Workers need to feel connected.* People are likely to achieve high self-esteem when they feel their coworkers accept, appreciate, and respect them. Many companies are fostering these feelings by placing greater emphasis on mentoring and teamwork. Team-building efforts help promote acceptance and cooperation.

LOOKING BACK: Reviewing the Concepts

■ Define self-esteem and discuss its impact on your life.

Self-esteem is a combination of self-respect and self-efficacy. If you have high self-esteem, you are more likely to feel competent and worthy. If you have low self-esteem, you are more likely to feel incompetent, unworthy, and insecure. Self-esteem reflects your feelings of adequacy about the roles you play, your personality traits, your physical appearance, your skills, and your abilities. High self-esteem is the powerful foundation for a successful personal and professional life.

■ Discuss how self-esteem is developed.

A person starts acquiring and building self-esteem from birth. Parents, friends, associates, the media, and professional colleagues all influence the development of a person's self-esteem. Adolescents often depend on social relationships to define their value and may compare themselves to media personalities. Adults often define themselves in terms of their possessions, jobs, or internal values.

■ Identify the characteristics of people with low and high self-esteem.

People with high self-esteem tend to maintain an internal locus of control, manage their emotions, rarely take things personally, accept other people as unique and talented, and have productive personalities. People with low self-esteem tend to maintain an external locus of control, are likely to participate in self-destructive behaviors, and exhibit poor human relations skills. They often rely on the opinions of others to establish their inner self-worth.

■ Identify ways to raise your self-esteem.

To build high self-esteem, individuals must accept their limitations, take responsibility for their decisions, engage in strength building, identify their talents, and work with a mentor. Taking responsibility for your decisions and living with the consequences, positive or negative, can also help build self-esteem. Goal setting is an integral part of raising one's self-esteem. Guided imagery and positive self-talk can help overcome the inner critic that often interferes with personal and professional success.

■ Understand the conditions organizations can create that will help workers raise their self-esteem.

Many organizations now realize that they need to help build employees' self-esteem and are doing so by making workers feel valuable, competent, and secure. Employers are empowering their employees to use their creativity and ingenuity to solve problems and make customers happy, which allows workers to develop a sense of personal responsibility.

● Career Corner

Q: The company I worked for recently merged with a giant corporation and I lost my job. Even though my previous employer has guaranteed that they will pay the expense of retraining me for a new career, I just can't seem to get motivated. I signed up for one class, but soon dropped it. I should have known I couldn't handle it. My former colleagues who are in the same situation are all much smarter than I am. I know that I'll never be as good as they are, so why should I even try? I'm not sure what there is in me that makes me avoid going back to school, but it is powerful. What can I do to gain more confidence?

A: It sounds like you are feeling down right now, and that is perfectly normal. Your world, as you knew it, has changed. Many people are going through the same thing in today's ever changing world of mergers, acquisitions, and company closings, so don't feel alone. Nevertheless, your self-esteem has been damaged and you need to take the necessary steps to repair and improve it. You need to stop comparing yourself to others, take a good look at your strengths, and build on them. Determine your skills, your values, and all those facets that make you unique. Though it may not be easy, it is not impossible to feel better about yourself. Trust your thoughts and intuitions. Do what makes you feel happy and fulfilled. Set realistic goals for yourself and take pride in your achievements, big and small. Replace negative self-talk with positive affirmations about your future. Exercise, eat right, and get plenty of sleep. Being exhausted and out of shape can leave you feeling more vulnerable, insecure, and anxious. Don't wait for someone else to take charge of your life and determine how you feel about yourself. Get acquainted with your potential and go for it!

● Key Terms

self-esteem	talent
self-efficacy	mentor
self-respect	guided imagery
self-concept	visualize
developmental psychology	self-talk
external locus of control	inner critic
internal locus of control	

● Applying What You Have Learned

1. Review Table 4.1, Goal-Setting Principles. Work through each of the four principles in light of something you would like to change in your world. It could be a physical characteristic such as weight control or beginning an exercise regimen. It might be a component of your personality such as becoming more confident or assertive. Perhaps you would like to reexamine your career goals. Whatever your choice, write out your plan for change; then follow it through.

2. This chapter identified five characteristics of people with high self-esteem. Read each of the statements below and rate yourself with this scale: U = Usually; S = Sometimes; I = Infrequently.

	U	S	I
I maintain an internal locus of control	☐	☐	☐
I am able to feel all dimensions of emotions without letting these emotions affect my behavior in a negative way.	☐	☐	☐
I do not take things personally.	☐	☐	☐
I am able to accept other people as unique, talented individuals	☐	☐	☐
I feel I have a productive personality.	☐	☐	☐

3. Draw a line down the center of a piece of paper and write HIGH Self-Esteem on top of the left column and LOW Self-Esteem on the top of the right column. In each column, record how your personal and professional interpersonal relationships might change if you maintained that level of self-esteem. Share your insights with your classmates.

 Internet Insights

1. Building your self-esteem is often a do-it-to-yourself project. No one can wrap a package of self-esteem and give it to you for your birthday. If you, or someone you care about, need more support in building this life-skill, visit *www.coping.org/selfesteem* and discover the tools presented by Self-Esteem Seekers Anonymous (SEA).

2. This text attempts to help you understand how the concepts discussed in each chapter influence you as a total person, since it is difficult to separate your personal and professional lives. It may appear that building your self-esteem is a personal issue, but it is important to understand how self-esteem can impact your chosen career. Regardless of your career focus, you will be connected to an organization of some kind. For example, nurses are part of a major organization, car mechanics can be part of a small business or a giant corporation, and even public school teachers work for an organization. To help you understand how your self-esteem can influence your business, visit *http://www.smallbusinessbible.org/developingyourselfesteem.html*. Click on the various topics within the Leadership and Development column at the top left of this site. Discover why organizations should be concerned about the self-esteem of their workers. Review this material not only as a potential employee, but also as a potential employer.

 Role-Play Exercise

Your have accepted a summer job with Bank of America. Throughout the summer you will replace tellers who are on vacation. In addition to earning money to pay next fall's college tuition, you anticipate that this job will help you develop your customer service skills. To maximize the learning opportunities, and explore another area within the bank, you want to develop a mentor relationship with a senior vice president in the loan department. You have an appointment with Erin Brown, an experienced loan officer, tomorrow. In this role-play situation, you will meet with a class member who will assume the role of the loan officer who is very busy and has scheduled the meeting to last no more than 15 minutes. During this short period of time you will need to explain why you need a mentor and market yourself to this prospective mentor. Prior to the role-play activity, review the information on mentoring in this chapter.

Case 4.1   The Power of Mentoring

At the beginning of this chapter, you were introduced to Shoshana Zuboff and her husband, who served as mentors to Edward, the troubled youth who became a successful businessman with their support and guidance. Where would Edward be today if he had not met the Zuboffs? Tim Murphy, head football coach at Harvard University, explains the impact a mentor can have on young people. He sees his mentor role as that of a parent: you are not your mentees' buddy, so don't try to please them. Treat them with respect and expect the same in return. He found that some 18-, 19-, 20-year-olds think they have all the answers, and it is not until they go through the bumps in life that they realize what their mentors told them was good advice after all.[47] Ronna Lichtenberg, author of *It's Not Business, It's Personal*, remembers when her mentor took her aside and said, "No, Ronna, you may not do that. . . . This is how we get things done."[48]

Betsy Bernard, president of AT&T, enjoys her role as a mentor to others within her organization. She listens to her mentees and determines the next opportunity for their development. She describes to them what she is dealing with on a daily basis to give mentees the opportunity to see things in a holistic way. Paul Muldoon, professor of creative writing at Princeton University and Pulitzer Prize winner for poetry, describes the responsibility of a mentor as extraordinary. He believes that mentors have to be enthusiastic and nurturing and states, "I want them to find a place where they can flourish." Dee Hock, founder and CEO emeritus of Visa International, compares the mentor/mentee relationship to "hitching a boat to an elegant cabin cruiser and being towed along in its wake."[49]

Many organizations today realize the value of developing formal and informal mentoring relationships among their employees. They know these relationships are critically important when it is time to pass knowledge along to the next generation of workers. Larry Aloz, author of *Effective Teaching and Mentoring*, declares, "I think what people are finding is that in times of change and turmoil, we reach out for stability and guidance. Mentors give us a sense of continuity. They have been there before. They have advice for us. They have experience to pass on."[50] Mack Tilling, CEO of Instill Corporation, says, "Being able to talk about your work with an experienced executive can help anyone—even a CEO—make better decisions. Mentors help you see things in a way that you might not have thought about."[51]

1. Mentoring programs help bring new employees up to speed with what is going on in the organization and they often help employees advance in the organization. What elements of a mentoring program contribute to building an employee's self-esteem?

2. A well-developed mentoring program can make a major contribution to the success of an organization, yet many companies do not have such programs. What are some reasons why some organizations do not support mentoring programs?

3. Would you prefer the formal approach to mentoring programs within organizations, or would you prefer the informal approach? Explain your reasoning.

Case 4.2   *"Popeye" Lives On*

Dave Longaberger's grandfather and father were master craftsmen and worked in the Dresden Basket Company until it closed during the Depression. Even then, Dave's father hand-made baskets at home after working all day in the paper mill. In his autobiography, completed just before his death, Dave attributed his strong work ethic to his father's powerful influence. "Although I never gave it much thought as a kid, our parents and the environment where we grow up have a strong influence on who we become as adults. We grew up knowing we had to work hard, be honest, and help others."[52] Dave's eleven brothers and sisters provided peer pressure of a different kind from that usually encountered today. Neither he nor his siblings wanted to do anything that might hurt or embarrass their parents because they had so much love and respect for them.

Although his home life was loving and stable, Dave's early years were not easy. His grandfather nicknamed him "Popeye" at birth, he spent two years in first grade and three years in fifth grade because of a learning disorder, and he stuttered so badly that few people could understand anything he said. But his family's strong work ethic gave him the desire to work. Throughout his childhood, he stocked shelves for a local grocer, shoveled snow, delivered papers, mowed grass, and hauled trash. His father gave him a new label: "the 25-cent millionaire." After Dave finally graduated from high school at age 21, he sold Fuller Brushes door to door to improve his speech. Following a stint in the army, he bought a small restaurant and subsequently a grocery store of his own. His lack of a college education never deterred him.

During the 1970s, Dave noticed a growing interest in baskets and asked his father to make a dozen, which sold immediately. In 1973, Dave sold his profitable restaurant and grocery store, hired five weavers, and started The Longaberger Company utilizing independent distributors conducting in-home product shows. He led his employees and distributors with consistent positive attitudes, a constant emphasis on teamwork, an environment that made everyone feel valued, and a strong sense of humor. When he died, Dave Longaberger's company employed more than seven hundred people, supported over fifty thousand independent sales associates, and topped $1 billion in sales. His daughter, Tami, took over the company following Dave's death. When she was asked what she learned from her father, she said: "You can't inherit respect. You have to earn it. . . . If you respect people around you, whether it's employees, customers, sales associates, or vendors, they will respond positively and constructively."[53]

Questions

1. What role did Dave Longaberger's self-esteem play in the success of his businesses?

2. Explain what dynamics were present in Dave Longaberger's life that helped him maintain his self-esteem and motivation, even though he faced seemingly insurmountable obstacles as a child.

3. Another generation has now taken control of this family business. Explain how Dave's obvious self-respect and self-confidence might still be evident in his company, even though he has passed on.

INTEGRATED RESOURCES

VIDEO: "Interpersonal Communications—Video Cases"

CLASSROOM ACTIVITIES (*college.hmco.com/pic/reece10e*)

Self-Efficacy Scale Instrument/Analysis
Self-Esteem Inventory
Guidelines for Designing Positive Self-Talk

business.college.hmco.com/students

ACE
Self-tests

5

PERSONAL VALUES INFLUENCE ETHICAL CHOICES

Chapter Preview

After studying this chapter, you will be able to

- Explain the personal benefits of developing a strong sense of character.

- Understand how personal values are formed.

- Understand values conflicts and how to resolve them.

- Learn how to make the right ethical decisions based on your personal value system.

- Understand the danger of corporate crime and the steps being taken to eliminate it.

Scott Sullivan, former chief financial officer at WorldCom, was looking forward to living in his new 30,000-square-foot estate located in Boca Raton, Florida. The house has ten bedrooms, twelve bathrooms, and seven hand-carved stone fireplaces. It features an eighteen-seat movie theater and a two-bedroom boathouse overlooking a private lake. Instead of moving into this luxury house, Mr. Sullivan will be spending the next five years in a federal prison. He was found guilty of participating in the $11 billion accounting fraud at WorldCom (since renamed MCI). Sullivan and his boss, former CEO Bernie Ebbers, were at the center of the largest accounting fraud in corporate history.[1]

During the past few years we have seen a large number of corporate scandals involving publicly traded companies. Managers employed by Enron, Adelphia Communications, Tyco International, Rite Aid, ImClone, and other well-known companies have been found guilty of various white-collar crimes. Later in this chapter, we will examine some of the factors that motivate corporate leaders to engage in fraud and other crimes.[2]

Of course, it would not be fair to focus our attention on unethical behavior at the top of the organization and ignore the misdeeds of employees in the lower ranks. One third of all employees steal from their employers, and employee theft is the fastest-growing crime in the United States.[3]

The new generation of workers are occupationally and educationally ambitious. They are coming of age at a time when our culture is placing a great deal of emphasis on self-gratification, the crossing of many moral boundaries, and the breaking of many social taboos. This chapter will help you understand how to make the right ethical decisions based on a value system that embraces honor and integrity. It will help you understand how your values are formed, how to clarify which values are important to you, and how to resolve human relations problems that result when your personal values conflict with others' values.

Scott Sullivan, former chief financial officer at WorldCom Incorporated, helped engineer an $11 billion fraud. He was sentenced to five years in prison. Reading from a prepared statement at his sentencing, Sullivan said, "My actions are inexcusable."

Character, Integrity, and Moral Development

If you have character, that's all that matters; and if you don't have character, that's all that matters, too.

Former U.S. senator Al Simpson said, "If you have character, that's all that matters; and if you don't have character, that's all that matters, too."[4] **Character** is composed of personal standards of behavior, including honesty, integrity, and moral strength. It is the main ingredient we seek in our leaders and the quality that earns us respect in the workplace. In *The Corrosion of Character*, author Richard Sennett says that we have seen a decline of character that can be traced to conditions that have grown out of our fast-paced, high-stress, information-driven economy.[5] He notes that many people are no longer connected to their past, to their neighbors, and to themselves.

Integrity is the basic ingredient of character that is exhibited when you achieve congruence between what you know, what you say, and what you do.[6] When your behavior is in tune with your professed standards and values—when you practice what you believe in—you have integrity. When you say one thing but do something else, you *lack* integrity.

How important is it to be viewed as a person with integrity and a strong sense of character in the eyes of your friends, family members, fellow workers, and leaders? When you look closely at the factors that contribute to warm friendships, strong marriages, successful careers, and successful organizations, you quickly come to the conclusion that character and integrity are critical.

You are not born with these qualities, so what can a person do to build his or her character? One approach, recommended by author Stephen Covey, is to keep your commitments. "As we make and keep commitments, even small commitments, we begin to establish an inner integrity that gives us the awareness of self-control and courage and strength to accept more of the responsibility for our own lives."[7] Covey says that when we make and keep promises to ourselves and others, we are developing an important habit. We cannot expect to maintain our integrity if we consistently fail to keep our commitments.

TOTAL	**ROY CHITWOOD**
PERSON	PRESIDENT, MAX SACKS INTERNATIONAL
INSIGHT	"A person's true character can be judged by how he treats those who can do nothing for him."

How Personal Values Are Formed

Hyrum Smith, author of *The 10 Natural Laws of Successful Time and Life Management*, says that certain natural laws govern personal productivity and fulfillment. One of these laws focuses on personal beliefs: Your behavior is a reflection

Once you are aware of your value priorities, you are in a better position to place and initiate life-changing activities.

of what you truly believe.[8] **Values** are the personal beliefs and preferences that influence your behavior. They are deep-seated in your personality. To discover what really motivates you, carefully examine what it is you value.

Table 5.1 details the values clarification process. These five steps can help you determine whether or not you truly value something. Many times you are not consciously aware of what is really driving your behavior because values exist at different levels of awareness.[9] Unless you clarify your values, life events are likely to unfold in a haphazard manner. Once you are aware of your value priorities, you are in a better position to plan and initiate life-changing activities.

Identifying Your Core Values

Hyrum Smith says that everything starts with your **core values**, those values that you consistently rank higher than others. When you are able to identify your core values, you have a definite picture of the kind of person you want to be and the kind of life you want to have. Anne Mulcahy, an executive at Xerox Corporation and a mother of two sons, says she and her husband make decisions at

---

TABLE 5.1	A Five-Part Valuing Process to Clarify and Develop Values

Thinking

We live in a confusing world where making choices about how to live our lives can be difficult. Of major importance is developing critical thinking skills that help distinguish fact from opinion and supported from unsupported arguments. Learn to think for yourself. Question what you are told. Engage in higher-level thinking that involves analysis, synthesis, and evaluation.

Feeling

This dimension of the valuing process involves being open to your "gut level" feelings. If it doesn't "feel right," it probably isn't. Examine your distressful feelings such as anger, fear, or emotional hurt. Discover what you prize and cherish in life.

Communicating

Values are clarified through an ongoing process of interaction with others. Be an active listener and hear what others are really saying. Be constantly alert to communication filters such as emotions, body language, and positive and negative attitudes. Learn to send clear messages regarding your own beliefs.

Choosing

Your values must be freely selected with no outside pressure. In some situations, telling right from wrong is difficult. Therefore, you need to be well informed about alternatives and the consequences of various courses of action. Each choice you make reflects some aspect of your values system.

Acting

Act repeatedly and consistently on your beliefs. One way to test whether something is of value to you is to ask yourself, "Do I find that this value is persistent throughout all aspects of my life?"

Source: Howard Kirschenbaum, *Advanced Values Clarification* (La Jolla, Calif.: University Associates, 1977).

home and work based on their core values: "Our kids are absolutely the center of our lives—and we never mess with that."[10] Maura FitzGerald, CFO of FitzGerald Communications, Inc., a public relations firm, asks all her employees to adhere to the "FitzGerald Family Values" before accepting a job with her company. All her workers carry with them a wallet-size card listing the organization's basic operating principles, one of which is "Never compromise our integrity—this is our hallmark."[11]

We often need to reexamine our core values when searching for a job. Joanne Ciulla, author of *The Working Life,* says taking a job today is a matter of choosing among four core values: high salary, security, meaningful work, and lots of time off.[12] Needless to say, most jobs would require putting at least one of these values on the back burner.

Focus on Your Life's Purpose

Jack Canfield, Brian Tracy, and other authorities on the development of human potential emphasize how important it is to define your purpose in life. Canfield says, "Without purpose as the compass to guide you, your goals and action plans may not ultimately fulfill you." To get from where you are today to where you want to be, you have to know two things: where are you today and where you want to get to.[13] Once you have identified your core values, defining your purpose in life will be much easier.

CRITICAL THINKING CHALLENGE

To create your future, look to the future, not the past. Find a quiet place, close your eyes, and create images of what the ideal life would look like if you could have it exactly the way you want it in each of the following categories:

■ The financial area of your life: Where are you living? In what type of home? How much money do you have in savings and investments? What kind of car are you driving?

■ Your job or career: Where are you working? What are you doing? What is your compensation?

■ Your personal relationships: Are you closely connected to your family? Who are your friends?

Note: This visualization exercise can be expanded to include other important areas of your life such as physical and mental health, spirituality, and leisure time.

Influences That Shape Your Values

As you engage in the values clarification process, it helps to reflect on those things that have influenced your values, such as people and events of your generation, your family, religious groups, your education, the media, and people you admire.

TABLE 5.2	People and events have influenced the formation of values for four groups of Americans: Matures, Baby Boomers, Generation X, and Generation Y (sometimes called Millennials). This means that today's work force represents the broadest range of ages and values in American history.			
	Matures (born 1928–1945)	**Baby Boomers** (born 1946–1964)	**Generation X** (born 1965–1976)	**Generation Y** (born 1977–1994)
	Eisenhower	Television	AIDS	Corporate downsizing
	MacArthur	The Cold War	The Wellness movement	Ethics scandals
	The A-bomb	The space race	Watergate	Digital technology
	Dr. Spock	The Civil Rights Act	Glasnost	24/7 economy
	John Wayne	The pill	The Oklahoma City bombing	Jeff Bezos
	The Great Depression	The drug culture	MTV	9/11 terrorist attacks
	World War II	Gloria Steinem	The World Wide Web	Iraq War
	The New Deal	The Vietnam War	Information economy	Income gap
		JFK and MLK assassinations	Work/Life balance concerns	Globalization

People and Events   Table 5.2 provides a summary of some of the key events and people that have shaped the values of four generations: the Matures, the Baby Boomers, Generation X, and Generation Y, sometimes called Millennials. Although workers of different ages want basically the same things—the opportunity for personal growth, respect, and a fair reward for work done well—they can have very different ideas about what these mean. An older baby boomer might believe that respect is due when someone spends many years on the job. To a Generation Xer, respect is expected when someone displays competence. Someone born during the early years of the baby-boom generation might be satisfied with feedback during annual or semiannual performance reviews. Generation Xers, as a group, have a need to see results almost daily and receive frequent feedback on their performance. Analyzing the traits of any large population can lead to unfair and unrealistic stereotyping. But generational differences shaped by sociological, political, and economic conditions can be traced to differences in values.[14]

Your Family   Katherine Paterson, author of books for children, says being a parent these days is like riding a bicycle on a bumpy road—learning to keep your balance while zooming full speed ahead, veering around as many potholes as possible.[15] Parents must assume many roles, none more important than moral teacher. In many families in contemporary society, one parent must assume full responsibility for shaping children's values. Some single parents—those overwhelmed with responsibility for career, family, and rebuilding their own personal lives—may lack the stability necessary for the formation of the six pillars of character. And in two-parent families, both parents may work outside the home and at the end of the day may lack the time or energy to intentionally direct the development of their children's values. The same may be true for families experiencing financial pressures or the strains associated with caring for elderly parents.

Religious Groups   Many people learn their value priorities through religious training. This may be achieved through the accepted teachings of a church, through religious literature such as the Koran and the Bible, or through individuals in churches or synagogues who are positive role models. Some of the most powerful spiritual leaders do not have formal ties to a particular religion. John Templeton is one example. He is a successful investor and one of the greatest philanthropists of the modern age. Templeton says the only real wealth in our lives is spiritual wealth. Over the years, he has given over $800 million to fund forgiveness, conflict-resolution, and character-building projects.[16]

Religious groups that want to define, instill, and perpetuate values may find an eager audience. Stephen Covey and other social observers say that many people are determinedly seeking spiritual and moral anchors in their lives and in their work. People who live in uncertain times seem to attach more importance to spirituality.[17] Healthy spirituality is discussed in Chapter 17.

Education   Many parents, concerned that their children are not learning enough about moral values and ethical behavior, want character education added to the curriculum. In support of these views, Thomas Lickona, professor of education at the State University of New York, says children have very little sense of right and wrong, so schools must help out. Educators are concerned about the constant barrage of messages children are getting about behavior in corporate America. Twenty grade schools, middle schools, and high schools in New York and Chicago are currently testing an ethics curriculum created by Junior Achievement, whose mission is to teach youngsters about the free-enterprise system.[18]

Several nonprofit organizations have responded to the call for more character education in our public schools, colleges, and universities. The Josephson Institute of Ethics (*www.josephsoninstitute.org*) has formed the Character Counts Coalition, an alliance of organizations that addresses the issue of character development in educational institutions and organizations throughout the country. This coalition has developed a variety of grassroots training activities involving what it refers to as the "six pillars of character": trustworthiness, respect, responsibility, fairness, caring, and citizenship.[19]

The Character Education Partnership (*www.character.org*) is attempting to rally business leaders to champion character education within their companies and encourage character training within the schools located in their communities. The Institute for Global Ethics, or IGE (*www.globalethics.org*), is dedicated to promoting ethical action in a global context. The Center for Corporate Ethics, or CCE (*www.ethics-center.com*), is a division of the IGE. The CCE has developed tools, techniques, and training programs aimed at reducing the likelihood and risks of ethical lapses.

The Media   Some social critics say that if you are searching for signs of civilization gone rotten, you can simply tune into the loud and often amoral voices of mass entertainment on television, radio, and the Internet. They point out that viewers too often see people abusing and degrading other people without any

"I swear I wasn't looking at smut—I was just stealing music."

significant consequences. Mainstream television, seen by a large number of young viewers, continues to feature a great deal of violence and antisocial behavior.

Is there a connection between violence in the media and violence in real life? The American Academy of Pediatrics and the American Psychiatric Association report that repeated exposure to violent imagery desensitizes children and increases the risk of violent behavior.[20] Research has also found a connection between heavy television viewing and depressed children. More research is needed to help us fully understand the extent of the influence of media on our culture's values.

People You Admire In addition to being influenced by the media, you have probably also done some **modeling**—you have shaped your behavior to resemble that of people you admire and embraced the qualities those people demonstrate. The heroes and heroines you discover in childhood and adolescence help you form a "dominant value direction."[21] The influence of modeling is no less important in our adult life. Most employees look to their leaders for moral guidance. Unfortunately, there is a shortage of leaders who have a positive impact on ethical decision making. A recent survey found that less than half of employees in large organizations think their senior leadership is highly ethical.[22] In addition to role models at work, you may be influenced by religious leaders, sports figures, educators, and others whom you admire.

Avoiding Values Drift

Once you have examined the various influences on your values and have clarified what is important to you now that you are an adult (see Table 5.1), you also need to be aware of **values drift**, the slow erosion of your core values over time—those tiny changes that can steer you off course. When you observe lying, abuse, theft, or other forms of misconduct at work or feel pressure to make ethical compromises, carefully and intentionally reflect on the values you hold dear and choose the appropriate ethical behavior that maintains your character and integrity. Monitor your commitment to your values and make adjustments when necessary to get your life back on track. In his book *Conversations with God*, Neal Donald Walsch discusses the process of building a strong foundation for your daily decisions as they lead you toward your life's goals. He suggests: "Do not dismantle the house, but look at each brick, and replace those which appear broken, which no longer support the structure."[23] This careful examination of each of your values in light of each day's decisions will help keep you on track throughout your life.

Values Conflicts

One of the major causes of conflict within an organization is the clash between the personal values of different people. There is no doubt about it; people are different. They have different family backgrounds, religious experiences, educations, role models, and media exposure. These differences can pop out anywhere and anytime people get together. Many observers suggest that organizations look for **values conflicts** when addressing such problems as declining quality, absenteeism, and poor customer service. The trouble may lie not so much in work schedules or production routines as in the mutual distrust and misunderstanding brought about by clashes in workers' and managers' value preferences. The late Peter Drucker, author of *The Practice of Management*, said: "Organizations are no longer built on force but on trust. The existence of trust between people does not mean that they like one another. It means that they understand one another. Taking responsibility for relationships is therefore an absolute necessity. It is a duty."[24]

Internal Values Conflicts

A person who is forced to choose between two or more strongly held values is experiencing an **internal values conflict.** Soon after the World Trade Center was attacked by terrorists, many people began to reexamine their values. Some decided to spend more time with family and friends, thinking that although overtime might be an opportunity to make more income, it was also an obstacle to maintaining a commitment to their family. Some workers also decided that their "work and spend" lifestyle no longer made sense. Before the terrorist attacks, a 28-year-old market research manager described herself as "very driven" and motivated to acquire things. Following September 11 she said, "Maybe I don't need all this stuff."[25]

A recent study of Generation Xers by Catalyst, a group that seeks to advance women in business, found that members of this group are seeking a well-rounded life. They are not frenetic job hoppers as some social commentators maintain, but traditionalists at heart. They value company loyalty and are inclined to stay with their current company. Earning a great deal of money is not nearly as important to these Xers as having the opportunity to share companionship with family and friends. They are able to prioritize their values and make their decisions accordingly.[26]

How you resolve internal values conflicts depends on your willingness to rank your core values in the order of their importance to you. Prioritizing your values will help you make decisions when life gets complicated and you have to make difficult choices. If one of your values is to be an outstanding parent and another is to maintain a healthy body, you should anticipate an internal values conflict when a busy schedule requires a choice between attending your daughter's soccer game and your weekly workout at the fitness center. However, when you rank which value is most important, the decision will be much easier.

■ Values Conflicts with Others

As we have noted, four distinct generations have come together in the workplace. Employees from each generation bring with them different experiences and expectations. Values conflicts are more likely in this environment. These conflicts require effective human relations skills.

How will you handle a tense situation where it is obvious your values conflict with those of a colleague? You may discover your supervisor is a racist and you strongly support the civil rights of all people. One option is to become indignant and take steps to reduce contact with your supervisor. The problem with being indignant is that it burns your bridges with someone who can influence your growth and development within the organization. The opposite extreme would be to do nothing. But when we ignore unethical or immoral behavior, we compromise our integrity, and the problem is likely to continue and grow.[27] With a little reflection, you may be able to find a response somewhere between these two extremes. If your supervisor tells a joke that is demeaning to members of a minority group, consider meeting with her and explaining how uncomfortable these comments make you feel. When we confront others' lapses in character, we are strengthening our own integrity.

HUMAN RELATIONS IN ACTION | **The Fall of Arthur Anderson**

When Barbara Toffler was a consultant for Arthur Anderson, she and some of her colleagues were under considerable pressure to sell their consulting services at inflated prices. Ironically, Toffler was at the time head of the Ethics and Responsible Business Practices Group at Arthur Anderson. In her book *Final Accounting—Ambition, Greed and the Fall of Arthur Anderson*, she recalls a difficult luncheon meeting with a former client. At one point he said, "You were selling us stuff you didn't think we needed." Then he spoke the words that were most painful: "Barbara, this is not the you I used to know." The company that once stood for trust and accountability ended ninety years of service under a cloud of scandal and shame.

Personal Values and Ethical Choices

Ethics refers to principles that define behavior as right, good, and proper. Your ethics, or the code of ethics of your organization, does not always dictate a single moral course of action, but it does provide a means of evaluating and deciding among several options.[28] Ethics determines where you draw the line between right and wrong.

As competition in the global marketplace increases, moral and ethical issues can become cloudy. Although most organizations have adopted the point of view that "good ethics is good business," exceptions do exist. Some organizations encourage, or at least condone, unethical behaviors. Surveys show that many workers feel pressure to violate their ethical standards in order to meet business objectives.[29] Thus, you must develop your own personal code of ethics.

Every job you hold will present you with new ethical and moral dilemmas. And many of the ethical issues you encounter will be very difficult. Instead of selecting from two clear-cut options—one right, one wrong—you often face multiple options.[30]

TOTAL	**WILLIAM J. BENNETT**
PERSON	AUTHOR, *THE BOOK OF VIRTUES*
INSIGHT	"If you want young people to take notions like right and wrong seriously, there is an indispensable condition: they must be in the presence of adults who take right and wrong seriously."

How to Make the Right Ethical Choices

According to the Association of Certified Fraud Examiners, unethical acts by workers cost U.S. businesses more than $600 billion a year.[31] The following guidelines may help you avoid being part of this growing statistic.

Learn to Distinguish Between Right and Wrong.   Although selecting the right path can be difficult, a great deal of help is available through books, magazine articles, and a multitude of online resources. Support may be as close as your employer's code of ethics, guidelines published by your professional organization, or advice provided by an experienced and trusted colleague at work. In some cases, you can determine the right path by *restraining* yourself from choosing the *wrong* path. For example:

- Just because you have the power to do something does not mean it is the proper thing to do.

- Just because you have the right to do something does not mean it is right to do.

- Just because you want to do something does not mean you should do it.

- Choose to do more than the law requires and less than the law allows.[32]

Don't Let Your Life Be Driven by the Desire for Immediate Gratification. Progress and prosperity have almost identical meanings to many people. They equate progress with the acquisition of material things. One explanation is that young business leaders entering the corporate world are under a great deal of pressure to show the trappings of success—a large house or an expensive car, for example.

Some people get trapped in a vicious cycle: They work more so that they can buy more consumer goods; then, as they buy more, they must work more. They fail to realize that the road to happiness is not paved with Rolex watches, Brooks Brothers suits, and a Lexus. Chapter 17 offers support for finding satisfaction through nonfinancial resources that make the biggest contribution to a fulfilling life.

Make Certain Your Values Are in Harmony with Those of Your Employer. You may find it easier to make the right ethical choices if your values are compatible with those of your employer. Many organizations have adopted a set of beliefs, customs, values, and practices that attract a certain type of employee (see Figure 5.1). Harmony between personal and organizational values usually leads to success for the individual as well as the organization. Enlightened companies realize that committed employees give them their competitive edge and are taking values seriously. They realize that reconciling corporate and employee values helps to cement the ethical environment within the organization. Before you select an organization in which to build your career, determine what the organization stands for and then compare those values to your own priorities.[33]

BMS Software in Houston, Texas, provides a work environment where you can find sustenance for the whole self—mind, body, and spirit. Employees can pump iron in the gym, enjoy a gourmet meal, or participate in massage therapy. The self-contained community offers an array of services (banking, dry cleaning, hair salon, etc.), and there is a large kitchen with free fruit, popcorn, soda, and coffee on each floor of the company's two glass towers. You live comfortably at BMS, but you also work long hours. Many employees work 10- to 12-hour days.[34] Some people would feel comfortable working for this company, but others would be unhappy about the long hours.

TOTAL PERSON INSIGHT	**DAN RICE AND CRAIG DREILINGER**
	MANAGEMENT CONSULTANTS; AUTHORS, "RIGHTS AND WRONGS OF ETHICS TRAINING"

"Nothing is more powerful for employees than seeing their managers behave according to their expressed values and standards; nothing is more devastating to the development of an ethical environment than a manager who violates the organization's ethical standards."

Corporate Values and Ethical Choices

When organizations consistently make ethical decisions that are in the best interest of their stakeholders—employees, customers, stockholders, and the community—they are considered good corporate citizens because they are

FIGURE 5.1	Biogen's Values

Biogen's Values

Biogen's success is based on its people. Everyone is considered a leader. The core of leadership is integrity and courage—characteristics they seek in every Biogen employee. The shared values listed below represent how they aspire to lead and work together. Part of the biotech company's performance-appraisal process includes evaluating whether employees lived up to these company values.

- Hire only the highest quality talent.
- Communicate and then obtain alignment to our strategy and goals.
- Tell the truth.
- Face the facts, admit mistakes, accept criticism, learn from it, and improve.
- Build teams.
- Forcefully resist adding layers, procedures, and bureaucracy.
- Assume your position responsibilities are a starting point, not a limitation.
- Weigh the risks carefully but do not hesitate to innovate or to encourage and reward innovation and initiative.
- See change as an opportunity, not a threat.
- Serve and defend with equal energy our customers', our employees', and our shareholders' interests.

Source: Watson Wyatt Data Services, "Watson Wyatt's Human Capital Index," *Workforce,* August 2002 [cited 17 November 2005]. Available from www.workforce.com/archive/article/23/27/06; INTERNET.

socially responsible. The list "The 100 Best Corporate Citizens" published by *Business Ethics* magazine reminds us that a company can be socially responsible and still achieve excellent earnings. In her *Business Week* article "A Conscience Doesn't Have to Make You Poor," Susan Scherreik interviewed stockholders who invest only in companies that are good corporate citizens. One stated, "I see the damage that many companies do to people's health and the environment by polluting or creating dangerous products. Investing in them makes no sense because these companies won't flourish in the long run."[35]

Corporate Crime

Many organizations have gotten into serious trouble by ignoring ethical principles. In recent years, the media have carried headlines concerning organizations involved in corporate crime.

SKILLS DEVELOPMENT CHALLENGE

Practice making ethical choices based on your value priorities in the following scenarios.

■ You are offered a great job, but you have to relocate to a distant city. Your family agrees that the decision is yours to make, but you know they do not want to move. What do you do?

■ You have discovered that your boss lied on her résumé about her academic credentials. She is being considered for a new position in your organization, but you believe you are more qualified than she is. Will you tell the hiring panel about your boss's indiscretion?

■ You are the assistant manager of a retail store. Your manager has asked you out to dinner and a movie. The company rules clearly state that socializing with coworkers is cause for immediate termination. Do you accept the date? Do you notify the appropriate authorities of your manager's actions?

■ You are taking an online college class and have been offered the final exam from a student who printed a copy for you after taking the exam yesterday. The correct answers are not on the test copy. You are in danger of failing the class and losing your financial aid. Do you accept the document and use it to study for your exam?

■ A top Air Force acquisition official admitted that she steered billions of dollars worth of contracts to Boeing Company out of gratitude for Boeing's hiring of her daughter. The procurement scandal cost Boeing billions in lost defense contracts.[36]

■ Bernard Ebbers was found guilty of masterminding a record $11 billion accounting fraud that toppled WorldCom. Investors, former employees, and others experienced large financial losses.[37]

■ A unit of Exide Technologies, the maker of automotive batteries, agreed to plead guilty to fraud and pay criminal fines of $27.5 million. Exide admitted to supplying inferior batteries to Sears, Roebuck & Company, trying to cover up the defects, and spending $80,000 to bribe a Sears battery buyer.[38]

Those items represent only a small fraction of the corporate crime that took place in recent years. Many offenders are not caught or brought to trial. But, on the positive side, recent surveys indicate that a large majority of America's major corporations are actively trying to build ethics into their organizations.

■ At Simmons Bedding Company, the commitment to conducting business with integrity can be traced to 1870, the year the company was founded. Every Simmons employee is guided by a four-part code of ethics: be fair, respect the individual, act from integrity, and foster growth and development.[39]

■ At Harley-Davidson the soul of the "Hog" can be traced to values that emphasize strong working relationships. The company's idea of a healthy working relationship is embedded in five formal values that constitute a code of behavior for everyone:[40] tell the truth; be fair; keep your promises; respect the individual; and encourage intellectual curiosity.

■ Honesty tops the list of employee expectations at Swanson Russell Associates, a marketing communications firm in Lincoln, Nebraska. The mandate is carefully reviewed during new employee orientation and it's posted in every employee's work area.[41]

Many say they have difficulty determining the right course of action in difficult "gray-area" situations. And even when the right ethical course of action is clear, competitive pressures sometimes lead well-intentioned managers astray.[42] Tom Chappell, author of *The Soul of a Business*, explains why organizations often have difficulty doing what is morally right and socially responsible: "It's harder to manage for ethical pursuits than it is to simply manage for profits."[43]

How to Prevent Corporate Crime

Establish and Support a Strong Code of Ethics.   We have recently seen an increase in ethical initiatives that make ethics a part of core organizational values. **Codes of ethics**, written statements of what an organization expects in the way of ethical behavior, can give employees a clear indication of what behaviors are acceptable or improper.[44] An ethics code can be a powerful force in building a culture of honesty, but only if it is enforced without exception. The list of corporate values at Enron Corporation included respect, integrity, communication, and excellence. As events have shown, these values did not prevent unethical conduct at the highest levels of the company. Empty values statements create cynical and dispirited employees and undermine managerial credibility.[45]

Hire with Care.   Thomas Melohn, president of North American Tool & Die, Inc., located in San Leandro, California, says the key to operating a successful company is to first identify a guiding set of values and then "make sure you find people who have those values and can work together."[46] He says the hiring process should be given a very high priority. Melohn never hires any employee without checking references and conducting a lengthy job interview.

Some companies use integrity tests (also called honesty or character tests) to screen out dishonest people. Two standardized tests designed to measure honesty are the Reid Report (*www.reidlondonhouse.com*) and the newer Career Ethic Inventory (*www.careerethic.com*). These tests are helpful, but they are not a substitute for rigorous interviewing and reference checks. Résumés that include exaggerations or outright fabrications tell you a lot about the integrity of the applicants.[47]

Provide Ethics Training.   Many ethical issues are complex and cannot be considered in black-and-white moral terms. It is for this and other reasons that ethics training has become quite common. In some cases, the training involves

Business schools are trying a host of new methods to teach MBAs lasting lessons in ethical behavior. Duke University is encouraging students to think about the importance of ethical decision making by requiring them to sign an ethics pledge.

little more than a careful study of the company ethics code and its implications for day-to-day decision making. In other cases, employees participate in in-depth discussions of ethical decisions.

Can colleges and universities teach ethics? In the wake of numerous corporate scandals, business schools have been criticized for producing graduates who are obsessed with making money regardless of the ethical consequences. In response to this criticism, business schools are trying a host of new methods including required ethics courses and honor codes. At Ohio University, the Fisher College of Business created a new honor code that students are required to sign. The code states: "Honesty and integrity are the foundation from which I will measure my actions."[48]

Develop Support for Whistleblowing. When you discover that your employer or a colleague is behaving illegally or unethically, you have three choices. You can keep quiet and keep working. You can decide you can't be party to the situation and leave. Or you can report the situation in the hope of putting a stop to it. When you reveal wrongdoing within an organization to the public or to those in positions of authority, you are a **whistleblower**.

TOTAL	**EDMUND BURKE**
PERSON	NINETEENTH-CENTURY ENGLISH POLITICAL PHILOSOPHER
INSIGHT	"All that is necessary for evil to triumph is for good men to do nothing."

FBI attorney Coleen Rowley wrote a memo to FBI director Robert Mueller claiming that the department ignored the pleas of the Minneapolis field office to investigate Zacarias Moussaoui, who was subsequently indicted as a September 11 co-conspirator. Cynthia Cooper informed WorldCom's board of directors that illegal accounting procedures covered up $3.8 billion in corporate losses. Enron vice president Sherron Watkins wrote a letter to Enron chairman Kenneth Lay alerting him to the illegal accounting procedures that misled stockholders about Enron's financial picture. All three of these women tried to keep their concerns "in house" by speaking the truth to executives in a position of power, not to the public. As details exploded in the media, these women were plunged into the public eye. *Time* magazine proclaimed them "Persons of the Year for 2002" and made them national celebrities, but their personal and professional lives were permanently altered, as their jobs, their health, and their privacy were threatened.[49]

Because of these women—and a multitude of other whistleblowers—organizations now have a legal responsibility to support whistleblowing. Executives who attempt to retaliate can be held criminally liable. The Occupational Safety and Health Administration (OSHA) fields the complaints of individuals

Cynthia Cooper, Coleen Rowley, and Sherron Watkins, whistleblowers at three prominent organizations, were selected as *Time* magazine's "Persons of the Year." They helped give corporate and government misconduct national attention.

TABLE 5.3	Whistleblower Checklist

Experts say that people who are thinking about blowing the whistle on their company should ask themselves four important questions before doing so.

1. Is this the only way?

Do not blow the whistle unless you have tried to correct the problem by reporting up the normal chain of command and gotten no results. Make sure your allegations are not minor complaints.

2. Do I have the goods?

Gather documentary evidence that proves your case, and keep it in a safe place. Keep good notes, perhaps even a daily diary. Make sure you are seeing fraud, not merely incompetence or sloppiness.

3. Why am I doing this?

Examine your motives. Do not act out of frustration or because you feel underappreciated or mistreated. Do not embellish your case, and do not violate any confidentiality agreements you may have.

4. Am I ready?

Think through the impact on your family. Be prepared for unemployment and the possibility of being blacklisted in your profession. Last but not least, consult a lawyer.

Source: Paula Dwyer and Dan Carney, with Amy Borrus and Lorraine Woellert in Washington and Christopher Palmeri in Los Angeles, "Year of the Whistleblower," *Business Week,* December 16, 2002, pp. 107–108.

who make a disclosure—to a supervisor, law enforcement agency, or congressional investigator—that could have a "material impact" on the value of the company's shares. If the company attempts to retaliate, the whistleblower has ninety days to report the incident to the Department of Labor, which can order the organization to rehire the whistleblower without going to court.[50]

Your fellow colleagues may resent the disruption your revelations cause in their lives. They may be impressed with your integrity, but not everyone will be on your side in your struggle to do what is right and ethical. Your efforts may result in months or even years of emotional and financial turmoil. A survey conducted by the National Whistleblower Center in Washington, D.C., showed that half of the whistleblowers were fired because of their actions. Most reported being unable to acquire new jobs because prospective employers perceived them as troublemakers. Others faced demotions or were placed in jobs with little impact or importance.[51]

Each individual must make his or her own decision as to whether the disturbing unethical offense is worth the personal cost. Table 5.3 lists four questions potential whistleblowers should ask themselves before taking action.

Values and Ethics in International Business

If the situation is complex on the domestic scene, values and ethical issues become even more complicated at the international level. American business firms are under great pressure to avoid doing business with overseas contractors that permit human rights violations such as child labor, low wages, and long hours in their factories. The 1977 Foreign Corrupt Practices Act prohibits U.S. companies from using bribes or kickbacks to influence foreign officials, and many industrial nations have signed a multinational treaty outlawing corporate bribery. But monitoring illegal activities throughout the world is a difficult task. Doing business in the global marketplace continues to be an ethical minefield with illegal demands for bribes, kickbacks, or special fees standing in the way of successful transactions. American businesses acknowledge that it is difficult to compete with organizations from other countries that are not bound by U.S. laws. However, according to the International Business Ethics Institute (*www.business-ethics.org*) there has been significant progress in the last few years, thanks to both national imperatives and polite but firm pressure from the

> *Doing business in the global marketplace continues to be an ethical minefield.*

American business community. Kevin Tan, the Shanghai director of the marketing research firm Frank, Small & Associates, believes U.S. companies have been a very positive role model for the rest of the business world. Even though it is understood by many in the global business community that violations do occur, the question is often one of degree. Paul Jensen, a consultant working for U.S., European, and Japanese interests in China, suggests: "What every internal manager has to do is find what he's personally comfortable with. That's a combination of the company's standards and his personal standards."[52]

LOOKING BACK: Reviewing the Concepts

■ Explain the personal benefits of developing a strong sense of character.

A strong sense of character grows out of your personal standards of behavior. When you consistently behave in accordance with your values, you maintain your integrity.

■ Understand how personal values are formed.

Your values are the personal importance you give to an object or idea. People's values serve as the foundation for their attitudes, preferences, opinions, and behaviors. Your core values are largely formed early in life and are influenced by people and events in your life, your family, religious groups, your education, the media, and people you admire.

■ Understand values conflicts and how to resolve them.

Internal values conflicts arise when you must choose between strongly held personal values. Value conflicts with others, often based on age, racial, religious, gender, or ethnic differences, require skilled intervention before they can be resolved.

■ Learn how to make the right ethical decisions based on your personal value system.

Once you have clarified your personal values, your ethical decisions will be easier. You must learn to distinguish right from wrong, avoid the pursuit of immediate gratification, and choose an employer whose values you share. Shared values unify employees in an organization by providing guidelines for behavior and decisions.

■ Understand the danger of corporate crime and the steps being taken to eliminate it.

Corporate values and ethics on both the domestic and the international levels are receiving increasing attention because of the devastating effect and expense of corporate crime. Many organizations are developing ethics codes to help guide employees' behavior, hiring only those individuals who share their corporate values, offering ethics training opportunities to all employees, and supporting whistle-blowing. As multinational organizations increase in number, the individuals involved will need to consciously examine their values and ethical standards to deal effectively with differing values structures around the world.

Career Corner

Q: I will soon graduate from college and would like to begin my career with an organization that shares my values. I have carefully examined what is most important to me and believe I know the type of organizational culture in which I can thrive. But how do I discover the "real" values of an organization when my interviews are permeated with buzzwords such as *family-friendly* and *teamwork-oriented*? How can I determine whether they truly mean what they seem to say?

A: Getting beyond the standard questions about your hours, pay, and job title is important if you want to build a satisfying and successful career within an organization. But direct questions about an organization's values often result in well-rehearsed answers from the interviewer. Try using *critical incident* questions such as "How did your organization handle the September 11 crisis?" or "Tell me about the heroes in your organization." Ask whether they have a formal code of ethics and how ethical misconduct is disciplined. And don't depend solely on the interviewer's answers. Seek out an honest current or former employee who will tell you the unvarnished truth about the organization. Listen carefully to the language used during your interviews. Do you hear a lot of talk about "love," "caring," and "intuition," or do you hear statements like "We had to send in the SWAT team," "They beat their brains out," and "We really nailed them!" If possible, sit in on a team meeting with your potential coworkers. Be forthright about work/life values, and make them a standard part of your interview process. A perfect match between your values and your potential employers' values is hard to find, so be patient. You may need to compromise.

Key Terms

character	values conflict
integrity	internal values conflict
values	ethics
core values	codes of ethics
modeling	whistleblower
values drift	

Applying What You Have Learned

1. Guilt and loss of self-respect can result when you say or do things that conflict with what you believe. One way to feel better about yourself is to "clean

up" your integrity. Make a list of what you are doing that you think is wrong. Once the list is complete, look it over and determine if you can stop these behaviors. Consider making amends for things you have done in the past that you feel guilty about.[53]

2. In groups of four, discuss how you would react if your manager asked you to participate in some sort of corporate crime. For example, the manager could ask you to help launder money from the company, give a customer misleading information, or cover up a budget inaccuracy and keep this information from reaching upper management. You might want to role-play the situation with your group. Follow up with class discussion.

3. One of the great challenges in life is the clarification of our values. The five-part valuing process described in Table 5.1 can be very helpful as you attempt to identify your core values. Select one personal or professional value from the following list, and clarify this value by applying the five-step process.

   a. Respect the rights and privileges of people who may be in the minority because of race, gender, ethnicity, age, physical or mental abilities, or sexual orientation.

   b. Conserve the assets of my employer.

   c. Utilize leisure time to add balance to my life.

   d. Maintain a healthy lifestyle.

   e. Balance the demands of my work and personal life.

 Internet Insights

1. Visit the website of the Josephson Institute at *www.josephsoninstitute.org*. Navigate through the various icons available. Take notes on those items you consider relevant to your life at work, home, or school. Report your discoveries to your class members.

2. The Center for Public Integrity, *www.publicintegrity.org*, offers investigative journalism on current events that are in the public interest. Visit the site and read about the issues that are detailed. Report to your classmates your reaction to any or all of the stories.

 Role-Play Exercise

You are currently employed by a pharmaceutical wholesaler that sells prescription drugs to hospitals in a three-county area. Each morning you help other employees fill orders that arrive via computer or the telephone. Once the orders are completed and loaded into delivery vans, you spend the rest of the day delivering products to hospitals. Although others help fill the orders, you are responsible for the accuracy of each order and for timely delivery. Corey Houston, a fellow employee, performs the same duties, but delivers items to hospitals in a different territory. Over the past two months you have noticed that Corey sometimes makes poor ethical choices. For example, the company's reimbursement for lunch is a maximum of $8. Corey packs each day's lunch and never eats at a restaurant. At the end of each week, however, Corey's reimbursement form claims the maximum amount for each meal. Once Corey bragged about earning an extra $40 each week for meals that were not purchased. Corey owns a small landscaping business on the side and sometimes uses the company van to transport items to customers. Recently you drove by a Home Depot store and noticed Corey loading bags of mulch into the company van. At one point you thought about talking with the supervisor about these ethical lapses, but decided to talk with Corey first. Another class member will assume the role of Corey Houston. Try to convince Corey that some of these on-the-job activities are unethical.

Case 5.1   Employee Theft

The media often focuses on corporate crime and the executives involved. However, as we mentioned in the opening vignette of this chapter, the fastest growing crime in the United States is employee theft. Recent surveys indicate that companies lose over $50 billion annually as employees steal time, money, and supplies from their employers. Employee theft comes in a variety of forms.

- Employees who pilfer pens, scissors, tape, and other office supplies may begin to refer jokingly to the supply room as the "gift shop."

- Padding an expense account with an extra meal or exaggerated tips to servers and baggage handlers may provide enough extra income to pay for the extended child care necessary while an employee is on a business trip.

- A salesperson who is a single parent may tell the boss that a customer needs additional time so returning to the office will be delayed, when in reality the employee's child has a dental appointment.

- An employee's aging father "dies" each time the employee changes employers, thus gaining the employee the paid time off for bereavement leave.

- The person in charge of arrangements for various luncheons within an organization routinely over orders and takes the "extra" food home.

Theft of this nature is often rationalized as a perk of the job. Some employees may feel that they are underpaid and that they are entitled to these little extras. This larcenous sense of entitlement may come from disgruntled employees who feel they are not appreciated, so they take matters into their own hands. It is true that there are a lot of bad examples at the top of many organizations, and it may be easy to blame top executives for fostering a culture of dishonesty, but does that justify the lack of character and integrity of lower-level employees?[54]

Questions

1. Research indicates that employee misconduct tends to increase in companies where mergers, acquisitions, and restructurings are under way. Why do you think this happens?

2. If your boss is so demanding that you have to lie to protect family time, will you do it? For example, if you have to miss a staff meeting or refuse a business trip to fulfill the needs of your family, will you fabricate work-related or health reasons? Are there any alternatives to lying? Explain.

3. If you were the employer, how would you handle each of the instances above?

Case 5.2 Whistleblowers' Rights

The U.S. Congress passed the Sarbanes-Oxley law in 2002 to protect employees who blow the whistle on their employers' illegal actions. If the charges are confirmed, employers must reinstate employees who were fired for blowing the whistle, plus pay their back wages and their legal fees. However, the employee has the burden of proof, not the employer. The law is enforced by OSHA, a division within the Department of Labor, but OSHA does not have subpoena power and therefore cannot force companies to turn over documents, require witnesses to testify, or place anyone under oath. The majority of these cases have been dismissed or withdrawn by the complainant.[55]

However, the Civil War era False Claims Act, including its qui tam (whistleblower) provisions, remains legally solid. It was initially enacted at the urging of President Lincoln in 1863 in response to reports of widespread fraud by Civil War profiteers. Under this law, citizens with knowledge of fraud against the government were encouraged to come forward by authorizing them to file a civil suit in the name of the government and by rewarding them with a percentage of the recovery. Private citizens who bring suits under the act can receive up to 30 percent of the recovery. Because it takes a great deal of courage for any employee to risk his or her career to serve the public interest, those individuals who step forward with their evidence should be celebrated and rewarded.

■ Three private citizens filed suit on behalf of the U.S. government against Schering-Plough, which offered kickbacks to Cigna, one of the nation's largest health insurers. The kickbacks in effect lowered the price Cigna subscribers paid for Claritin below the price the U.S. government paid for the same drug for its Medicaid patients, a blatant violation of Medicaid rules that require that the government receive the lowest price. Schering-Plough paid $346 million to settle charges, and the three complainants and their attorneys received $31.7 million.

■ Dr. Joseph Gerstein was the medical director of the Tuft's University health plan when he was offered a $40,000 unrestricted grant by TAP Pharmaceuticals if he would keep the company's prostate cancer drug, Lupron, on the HMO's list of preferred drugs. Outraged by TAP's attempts to bribe him, Dr. Gerstein filed suit to try to stop the corruption. In the end, TAP Pharmaceuticals settled his case, and another related whistleblower lawsuit, for a total of $875 million. Dr. Gerstein split his portion of the reward with Tufts and a science-literacy fund in Roxbury, Massachusetts.

■ Brett Roby was a quality-control engineer at Soeca, the contractor that made gears for Boeing's Chinook heavy-lift transport helicopters used by the U.S. Army. Because of defects in the casting of the metal used in the gears, several helicopters crashed, and fifteen soldiers and two Boeing engineers were killed. Although Speco and Boeing were told about the defects, both companies ignored the warnings. Boeing settled the case for $54 million plus attorney fees, and the U.S. Army replaced the defective gears in the helicopters. Mr. Roby said, "My primary goal in this litigation was to ensure the safety of the men and women who fly in these aircraft."[56]

Questions

1. In the bright light of hindsight, most of us would probably say we would blow the whistle on these instances had we been a witness to them, especially since there was so much money involved. But in reality, if you had to keep your job in order to feed your family, would you really step forward with your allegations, knowing that the legal process would take years?

2. What steps do you believe the government should take to reinforce the viability of the Sarbanes-Oxley Law?

3. Most employees do not disclose the fraud and corruption they observe in the workplace, and, therefore, criminal and immoral behaviors continue to flourish. Who or what can intercept this lack of moral fortitude?

4. The moral dilemmas you will face during your career may not be of the magnitude of those presented in this case, but may very well resemble those presented in Case 5.1. If you were to make your ethical decisions based on your value priorities, how would your interpersonal relationships be affected? List the positives and the negatives.

INTEGRATED RESOURCES

VIDEO: "Alex and Melinda: Values Conflict and Ethical Choices"

CLASSROOM ACTIVITIES (*college.hmco.com/pic/reece10e*)

Clarify Your Value Priorities
Ethics Questionnaire
Ethics Games: Vision 2000
Coping with Organizational Politics

business.college.hmco.com/students

6

ATTITUDES CAN SHAPE YOUR LIFE

Chapter Preview

After studying this chapter, you will be able to

- Understand the impact of employee attitudes on the success of individuals as well as organizations.

- List and explain the ways people acquire attitudes.

- Describe attitudes that employers value.

- Learn how to change your attitudes.

- Learn how to help others change their attitudes.

- Understand what adjustments organizations are making to develop positive employee attitudes.

Workers at Seattle's famous Pike Place Fish Market have a cold, wet job. Fish guts, blood, and scales produce a strong stench during their 12-hour shifts. However, when you visit the fish market, you will find that the workers are not downtrodden about their environment.[1] They laugh and joke as they toss fish to each other and over the heads of those who are standing at the counter waiting to pay for their purchases. Some customers even participate in the fish-tossing antics and make spectacular "catches" themselves. Pike Place employees' attitudes, expressed through their energetic clowning, seem contagious.

Not all organizations encourage this type of atmosphere at work. In companies where managers are very controlling, *play* is a four-letter word that means activities that disrupt efforts to be efficient. That's one of the reasons John Christensen, CEO of ChartHouse Learning, coauthored the training books *Fish!*, *Fish! Tales*, and *Fish! Sticks* and created video and management training programs based on the workplace atmosphere at Pike Place. He wanted to provide an opportunity for managers to learn how to instill a positive, productive atmosphere at work. He knew that a playful corporate culture can be created but cannot be mandated. Customers can tell the difference between employees who truly enjoy their jobs and those who are following a company mandate to have a positive attitude. Even Pike Place's owner, John Yokoyama, admits that he was once a grouchy and difficult boss. Then he "got some training" and realized that change was possible.[2] Yokoyama and millions of others have discovered that joyful, lighthearted attitudes occur naturally when people enjoy what they are doing.

Those who embrace what has become known as the "Fish Movement" believe in two basic ideas. First, they believe that a positive attitude is a good

Aly Wagner, U.S. women's soccer team midfielder, holds aloft a salmon she caught during a fish tossing demonstration at Seattle's famous Pike Place Fish Market. This business is known for its playful company culture that creates a high energy, fun atmosphere.

thing. Second, they believe that in most situations one can learn to adapt and accept one's current circumstances even if at first they seem undesirable.[3] It's all a matter of attitude.

Attitudes Are Learned

Attitudes are merely thoughts that you have accepted as true and that lead you to think, feel, or act positively or negatively toward a person, idea, or event. They represent an *emotional readiness* to behave in a particular manner.[4] You are not born with these thoughts; you learn them. Therefore, it is reasonable to conclude that you can learn new attitudes and/or change old ones.

Your values, those beliefs and preferences you feel are important, serve as a foundation for your attitudes. For example, if you believe your religion is important, you may form negative attitudes toward those people and activities that restrict your religious privileges and positive attitudes toward those who support your convictions. Your attitudes, in turn, serve as a motivation for your behavior (see Figure 6.1). So, when someone attempts to interfere with your right to practice your religion, you might become angry and retaliate. But you also have the freedom to choose another response. Perhaps another value comes into play—peace—and it seems more important than "defending" yourself. So, instead of retaliating, you decide to just ignore the interference. The most amazing things can happen once you realize that you can choose which attitude you will act upon.

Root Causes of Negative Attitudes

Some people are positive thinkers and see daily obstacles as opportunities rather than roadblocks. Others tend to dwell on things that can go wrong. Generally speaking, positive attitudes generate positive results and negative attitudes generate negative results. If attitudes are a choice (we can choose our thoughts), why would anyone *choose* to think negatively? There are several factors that exist individually or blend together to produce negative attitudes. We will briefly describe some common root causes of negative attitudes.[5]

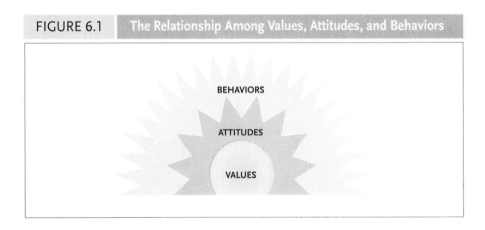

| FIGURE 6.1 | The Relationship Among Values, Attitudes, and Behaviors |

Low Self-Esteem In Chapter 4 we describe people with low self-esteem as those who lack a sense of personal worth and tend to embrace negative thoughts about the future. This negative outlook influences their ability to get along with others.

Unresolved Conflict Unresolved conflict can be very costly in terms of lost productivity at work, broken marriages, and lost friendships. Chapter 13 is devoted to conflict resolution strategies.

Work That Is Not Satisfying Many workers rebel against the monotony of repetitive job functions or working for a boss who fails to recognize work well done. In Chapter 7, "Motivating Yourself and Others," we will discuss job designs that provide a sense of achievement, challenge, variety, and personal growth.

Fear or Uncertainty Negative attitudes can sometimes be traced to feelings of fear or uncertainty. This can happen when someone takes a sliver of fact, rumor, or observation and expands it into something dramatically negative. Fear and other emotions will be discussed in Chapter 9, "Achieving Emotional Balance in a Chaotic World."

TOTAL	**PRICE PRITCHETT**
PERSON	CHAIRMAN, *EPS SOLUTIONS*
INSIGHT	"The biggest career challenges these days are *perceptual . . . psychological.* Not technical. Not even skills-based. The major adjustments we need to make are mental. For example, how we frame things at work. The way we process events in our head. Our attitudes and outlook about how our jobs and organizations now have to operate."

The Powerful Influence of Attitudes

One of the most significant differences between high and low achievers is choice of attitude. People who go through life with a positive attitude are more likely to achieve their personal and professional goals. People who filter their daily experiences through a negative attitude find it difficult to achieve contentment or satisfaction in any aspect of their lives. Jack Welch, the former chairman and CEO of General Electric, believes that an organization needs people with "positive energy" and needs to get rid of those people who inject the workforce with "negative energy"—even if they are high performers.[6]

Attitudes represent a powerful force in any organization. An attitude of trust, for example, can pave the way for improved communication and greater cooperation between an employee and a supervisor. But when trust is absent, a manager's sincere attempts to improve something may be met with resistance. These same actions by management, filtered through attitudes of trust and hope, may result in improved worker morale.

The Age of Information Mandates Attitude Changes

During the early stages of the information age, many of the best jobs were filled by people who were proficient at reasoning, logical thinking, and analysis. But as the information age unfolded and the global economy heated up, organizations discovered that it often takes more than quick and accurate information communicated through advanced technology to retain their clients and customers. In many cases, two competing firms, such as banks, may offer customers the same products at the same prices and use the same information technology. The competitive advantage is achieved through superior customer service provided by well-trained employees with effective interpersonal skills.

Daniel Pink, author of *A Whole New Mind*, says we are moving from the information age to the conceptual age. He predicts that one of the major players in the conceptual age will be the **empathizer**. Empathizers have the ability to imagine themselves in someone else's position and understand what that person is feeling. They are able to understand the subtleties of human interaction.[7] For example, several medical schools have come to the conclusion that empathy is a key element of compassionate medical care. Medical school students at Harvard, Columbia, and Dartmouth are learning that an important part of health care diagnosis is contained in the patient's story. They are trained how to identify the subtle details of a patient's condition through caring, compassionate attitudes.[8]

Technology, in its many forms, will continue to make a major contribution to the workplace. However, we must seek a better balance between "high tech" and "high touch." Leadership, for example, is about empathy. It is about having the ability to relate to and to connect with people. Pink states: "Empathy builds self-awareness, bonds parent to child, allows us to work together, and provides the scaffolding for our morality."[9]

Daniel H. Pink, author of *A Whole New Mind*, predicts that one of the major players in the New Conceptual Age will be the empathizer. These workers have the ability to imagine themselves in someone else's position and understand what that person is feeling.

How Attitudes Are Formed

Throughout life you are constantly making decisions and judgments that help form your attitudes. These attitude-shaping decisions are often based on behaviors your childhood authority figures told you were right or wrong, behaviors for which you were rewarded or punished. The role models you select and the various environmental and organizational cultures you embrace also shape your attitudes.

Socialization

The process through which people are integrated into a society by exposure to the actions and opinions of others is called **socialization**.[10] As a child, you interacted with your parents, family, teachers, and friends. Children often feel that statements made by these authority figures are the "proper" things to believe. For example, if a parent declares, "People who live in big, expensive houses either are born rich or are crooked," the child may hold this attitude for many years. In some cases, the influence is quite subtle. Children who observe their parents recycling, using public transportation instead of a car to get to work, and turning off the lights to save electricity may develop a strong concern for protection of the environment.

Peer and Reference Groups

As children reach adolescence and begin to break away psychologically from their parents, the **peer group** (people their own age) can have a powerful influence on attitude formation. In fact, peer-group influence can sometimes be stronger than the influence of parents, teachers, and other adult figures. With the passing of years, reference groups replace peer groups as sources of attitude formation in young adults. A **reference group** consists of several people who share a common interest and tend to influence one another's attitudes and behaviors. The reference group may act as a point of comparison and a source of information for the individual member. In the business community, a chapter of the American Society for Training and Development or of Sales & Marketing Executives International may provide a reference group for its members.

Rewards and Punishment

Attitude formation is often related to rewards and punishment. People in authority generally encourage certain attitudes and discourage others. Naturally, individuals tend to develop attitudes that minimize punishments and maximize rewards. A child who is praised for sharing toys with playmates is more likely to develop positive attitudes toward caring about other people's needs. Likewise, a child who receives a weekly allowance in exchange for performing basic housekeeping tasks learns an attitude of responsibility.

As an adult, you will discover that your employers will continue to attempt to shape your attitudes through rewards and punishment at work. Many organizations are rewarding employees who take steps to stay healthy, avoid accidents, increase sales, or reduce expenses.

Role Model Identification

Role models can exert considerable influence—for better or for worse—on developing attitudes.

Most young people would like to have more influence, status, and popularity. These goals are often achieved through identification with an authority figure or a role model. A **role model** is that person you most admire or are likely to emulate. As you might expect, role models can exert considerable influence—for better or for worse—on developing attitudes.

In most organizations, supervisory and management personnel have the greatest impact on employee attitudes. The new dental hygienist and the recently hired auto mechanic want help adjusting to their jobs. They watch their supervisors' attitudes toward safety, cost control, accuracy, grooming, and customer relations and tend to emulate the behavior of these role models. Employees pay more attention to what their supervisors *do* than to what they *say*.

Cultural Influences

Our attitudes are influenced by the culture that surrounds us. **Culture** is the sum total of knowledge, beliefs, values, objects, and ethnic customs that we use to adapt to our environment. It includes tangible items, such as foods, clothing, and furniture, as well as intangible concepts, such as education and laws.[11]

Today's organizations are striving to create corporate cultures that attract and keep productive workers in these volatile times. When employees feel comfortable in their work environment, they tend to stay.

■ When it comes to providing a strong, "fun," corporate culture, Icarian Inc., a provider of online software that helps companies hire and manage their work forces, is a prime example of going the extra mile. Balloons and roller-hockey gear are everywhere, and pet dogs frolic in the hallways. Employees work hard, and at break time they play hard with chess, Ping-Pong, and other games in the lunchroom. Employees are encouraged to work at home, and community volunteerism is rewarded with time off to participate. After-hours events include wine tasting and barbecues. Happy workers, CEO Doug Merritt believes, are bound to be productive.[12]

■ Executives at MBNA, the highly successful credit card company, understand that satisfied employees are more likely to provide excellent customer service. Every day the 23,000 MBNA employees are given a gentle reminder that the customer comes first. The words THINK OF YOURSELF AS A CUSTOMER are printed over every doorway of every office. Each year this Delaware-based company makes *Fortune* magazine's list of the 100 best companies to work for.[13]

■ The U.S. Marines have developed an eleven-week basic training program that has a dramatic impact on those who complete it. Recruits emerge as self-disciplined Marines who are physically fit, courteous to their elders, and drug free. Many have had to overcome deep differences of class and race and have learned to live and work as a team. They live in an organizational culture where a hint of racism can end a career and the use of illegal drugs is minimized by a zero tolerance policy.[14]

CRITICAL THINKING CHALLENGE

Identify at least one strong attitude you have for or against an event, a person, or a thing. How did you acquire this attitude? Is it shared by any particular group of people? Do you spend time with these people? Now think of an attitude that a friend or coworker holds but that you strongly disagree with. What factors do you believe contributed to the formation of this person's attitude?

Attitudes Valued by Employers

Many organizations have discovered the link between workers' attitudes and profitability. This discovery has led to major changes in the hiring process. Employers today are less likely to assume that applicants' technical abilities are the best indicators of their future performance. They have discovered that the lack of technical skills is not the primary reason why most new hires fail to meet expectations. It is their lack of interpersonal skills that counts.[15]

Whether you are looking for your first career position, anticipating a career change, or being retrained for new opportunities, you may find the following discussion helpful concerning what attitudes employers want in their employees.

Basic Interpersonal Skills

In this information-based, high-tech, speeded-up economy, we are witnessing an increase in workplace incivility. Rude behavior in the form of high-decibel cell-phone conversations, use of profanity, or failure to display simple courtesies such as saying "thank you" can damage workplace relationships. As we note in Chapter 11, incivility is the ultimate career killer.

Self-Motivation

People who are self-motivated are inclined to set their own goals and monitor their own progress toward those goals.

People who are self-motivated are inclined to set their own goals and monitor their own progress toward those goals. Their attitude is "I am responsible for this job." They do not need a supervisor hovering around them making sure they are on task and accomplishing what they are supposed to be doing. Many find ways to administer their own rewards after they achieve their goals. Employers often retain and promote those employees who take the initiative to make their own decisions, find better ways of doing their jobs, read professional publications to learn new things, and monitor the media for advances in technology.

Dennis the Menace
© NAS. NORTH AMERICA SYNDICATE.

Openness to Change

In the age of information, the biggest challenge for many workers is adjusting to the rapidly accelerating rate of change. Some resistance to change is normal merely because it may alter your daily routine. However, you will get into trouble if you choose the following three attitudes:[16]

1. *Stubbornness* Some workers refuse to be influenced by someone else's point of view. They also find fault with every new change.

2. *Arrogance* Employees who reject advice or who give the impression that they do not want retraining or other forms of assistance send the wrong message to their employer.

3. *Inflexibility* Displaying a closed mind to new ideas and practices can only undermine your career advancement opportunities.

Team Spirit

In sports, the person who is a "team player" receives a great deal of praise and recognition. A team player is someone who is willing to step out of the spotlight, give up a little personal glory, and help the team achieve a victory. Team players are no less important in organizations. Employers are increasingly organizing employees into teams (health teams, sales teams, product development teams) that build products, solve problems, and make decisions. Chapter 12 contains some tips on how to become a respected team member.

Health Consciousness

The ever growing cost of health care is one of the most serious problems facing companies today. Many organizations are promoting wellness programs for all employees as a way to keep costs in line. These programs include tips on healthy eating, physical-fitness exercises, and stress management practices, as well as other forms of assistance that contribute to a healthy lifestyle. Employees who actively participate in these programs frequently take fewer sick days, file fewer medical claims, and bring a higher level of energy to work. Some companies even give cash awards to employees who lose weight, quit smoking, or lower their cholesterol levels. Chapters 14 and 17 discuss health and wellness in greater detail.

Appreciation of Coworker Diversity

To value diversity in the work setting means to make full use of the ideas, talents, experiences, and perspectives of all employees at all levels within the organization. People who differ from each other often add richness to the organization. An old adage states: If we both think alike, one of us is not necessary.

Development and utilization of a talented, diverse work force can be a key to success in a period of fierce global competition. Women and people of color make up a large majority of the new multicultural, global work force. Many people, however, carry prejudiced attitudes against those who differ from them. They tend to "prejudge" others' value based on the color of their skin, gender, age, religious preference, lifestyle, political affiliation, or economic status. Although deeply held prejudices that often result in inappropriate workplace behaviors are difficult to change, employers are demanding these changes. Chapter 15 contains specific guidance on how to develop positive attitudes toward joining a diverse work force.

Honesty

Honesty and truthfulness are qualities all employers are searching for in their employees. This is because relationships depend on trust. An honest employee's attitude is "I owe my coworkers the truth." If you cannot be honest with your employer, customers, fellow workers, and friends, they cannot trust you, and strong relationships will be impossible.

How to Change Attitudes

If you are having difficulty working with other team members, if you feel you were overlooked for a promotion you should have had, or if you go home from work depressed and a little angry at the world, you can almost always be sure you need an attitude adjustment. Unfortunately, people do not easily adopt new attitudes or discard old ones. It is difficult to break the attachment to emotionally laden beliefs. Yet attitudes *can* be changed. There may be times when you absolutely hate a job, but you can still develop a positive attitude toward it as a steppingstone to another job you actually do want. There will be times as well when you will need to help colleagues change their attitudes so that you can work with them more effectively. And, of course, when events, such as a layoff, are beyond your control, you can accept this fact and move on. It is often said that life is 10 percent what happens to you and 90 percent how you react to it. Knowing how to change attitudes in yourself and others can be essential to effective interpersonal relations—and your success—in life.

It is often said that life is 10 percent what happens to you and 90 percent how you react to it.

Changing Your Own Attitude

You are constantly placed in new situations with people from different backgrounds and cultures. Each time you go to a new school, take a new job, get a promotion, or move to a different neighborhood, you may need to alter your attitudes to cope effectively with the change. The following attitudes will help you achieve positive results in today's world.

Choose Happiness   In his best-selling book *The Art of Happiness*, the Dalai Lama presents happiness as the foundation of all other attitudes. He suggests that the pursuit of happiness is the purpose of our existence. Survey after survey has shown that unhappy people tend to be self-focused, socially withdrawn, and even antagonistic. Happy people, in contrast, are generally found to be more sociable, flexible, and creative and are able to tolerate life's daily frustrations more easily than unhappy people.[17]

HUMAN RELATIONS IN ACTION

Who Moved My Cheese?

Several years ago, Spencer Johnson wrote *Who Moved My Cheese?* In this small book, which has been on the bestseller list for more than seven years, Johnson introduces the reader to a fable on how to cope positively with change. He recognizes that change is a basic fact of life, so learning to cope with it is an important life strategy. Johnson's most important message is that instead of seeing change as the end of something, you need to learn to see it as a beginning. Breaking through your fear of change is a very important attitude shift in our fluid, ever changing working world.

Michael Crom, executive vice president of Dale Carnegie Training, believes that happiness is the state of mind that permits us to live life enthusiastically. He views enthusiasm as an energy builder and as the key to overcoming adversity and achieving goals.[18] But how can you become happy and enthusiastic when the world around you is filled with family, career, and financial crises on a daily basis? Most psychologists, in general, agree that happiness or unhappiness at any given moment has very little to do with the conditions around us, but rather with how we perceive our situation, how satisfied we are with what we have.[19] For example, if you are constantly comparing yourself to people who seem smarter, more attractive, or wealthier, you are likely to develop feelings of envy and frustration. By the same token, you can achieve a higher level of happiness by reflecting on the good things you have received in life.[20]

Embrace Optimism   Optimistic thoughts give rise to positive attitudes and effective interpersonal relationships. When you are an optimist, your coworkers, managers, and—perhaps most important—your customers feel your energy and vitality and tend to mirror your behavior.

It does not take long to identify people with an optimistic outlook. Optimists are more likely to bounce back after a demotion, layoff, or some other disappointment. According to Martin Seligman, professor of psychology at the University of Pennsylvania and author of *Learned Optimism*, optimists are more likely to view problems as merely temporary setbacks on their road to achieving their goals. They focus on their potential success rather than on their failures.[21]

TOTAL	**HIS HOLINESS THE DALAI LAMA AND HOWARD C. CUTLER**
PERSON	COAUTHORS, *THE ART OF HAPPINESS*
INSIGHT	"We don't need more money, we don't need greater success or fame, we don't need the perfect body or even the perfect mate—right now, at this very moment, we have a mind, which is all the basic equipment we need to achieve complete happiness."

Pessimists, in contrast, tend to believe bad events will last a long time, will undermine everything they do, and are their own fault. A pessimistic pattern of thinking can have unfortunate consequences. Pessimists give up more easily when faced with a challenge, are less likely to take personal control of their life, and are more likely to take personal blame for their misfortune.[22] Often pessimism leads to **cynicism**, which is a mistrusting attitude regarding the motives of people. When you are cynical, you are constantly on guard against the "misbehavior" of others.[23] If you begin to think that everyone is screwing up, acting inconsiderately, or otherwise behaving inappropriately, cynicism has taken control of your thought process, and it is time to change.

If you feel the need to become a more optimistic person, you can spend more time visualizing yourself succeeding, a process that is discussed in Chapter 4. Monitor your self-talk, and discover whether or not you are focusing on the negative aspects of the problems and disappointments in your life or are looking at them as learning experiences that will eventually lead you toward your personal and professional goals. Try to avoid having too much contact with pessimists, and refuse to be drawn into a group of negative thinkers who see only problems, not solutions. Attitudes can be contagious.

Think for Yourself One of the major deterrents to controlling your own attitude is the power of "group think," which surfaces when everyone shares the same opinion. Individuals can lose their desire and ability to think for themselves as they strive to be accepted by team members, committee members, or coworkers in the same department. You are less likely to be drawn into group think if you understand that there are two overlapping relationships among coworkers. *Personal relationships* develop as you bond with your coworkers. When you share common interests and feel comfortable talking with someone, the bonds of friendship may grow very strong. You form small, intense groups. But there still exists the larger group—the organization. Within this setting, *professional relationships* exist for just one purpose: to get the job done.[24] Having two kinds of relationships with the same people can be confusing.

Let's assume you are a member of a project team working on a software application. The deadline for completion is rapidly approaching, yet the team still needs to conduct one more reliability test. At a team meeting, one person suggests that the final test is not needed because the new product has passed all previous tests, and it's time to turn the product over to marketing. Another member of the team, a close friend of yours, enthusiastically supports this recommendation. You have serious concerns about taking this shortcut but hesitate to take a position that conflicts with that of your friend. What should you do? In a professional relationship, your commitment to the organization takes precedence— unless, of course, it is asking you to do something morally wrong.[25]

Keep an Open Mind We often make decisions and then refuse to consider any other point of view that might lead us to question our beliefs. Many times our attitudes persist even in the presence of overwhelming evidence to the contrary. If you have been raised in a family or community that supports racist views, it may seem foreign to you when your colleagues at work openly accept and enjoy healthy relationships with people whose ethnicity is different from your own. Exposing yourself to new information and experiences beyond what you have been socialized to believe can be a valuable growth experience.

FIGURE 6.2 Serenity Prayer

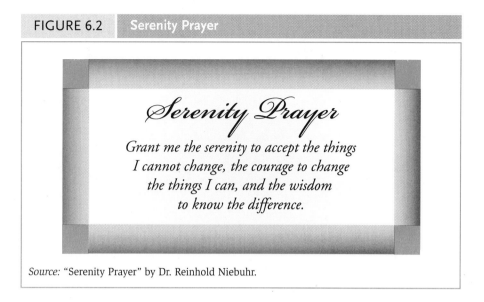

Serenity Prayer

Grant me the serenity to accept the things
I cannot change, the courage to change
the things I can, and the wisdom
to know the difference.

Source: "Serenity Prayer" by Dr. Reinhold Niebuhr.

In his book *The 100 Absolutely Unbreakable Laws of Business Success*, Brian Tracy suggests reflecting on the "Law of Flexibility." He said "You are only as free in life as the number of well-developed options you have available to you." The more thoroughly you open your mind to the options available to you, the more freedom you have.[26] This flexibility to see beyond what you thought was true and examine others' perspectives could be one of the most powerful tools you have to inspire the rest of your life.

Helping Others Change Their Attitudes

As the Serenity Prayer (Figure 6.2) expresses, you have a choice whether to accept circumstances or try to change them. Sometimes we *can* do more than just change our attitude—perhaps we can change a condition over which we have no absolute control but which we might be able to influence. For example, at some point you may want to help another person change his or her attitude about something. If you try to beg, plead, intimidate, or even threaten him or her into thinking differently, you probably will get nowhere. This process is similar to attempting to push a piece of yarn across the top of a table. When you *push* the yarn in the direction you want it to go, it gets all bent out of shape. However when you gently *pull* the yarn with your fingertips, it follows you wherever you want it to go. Two powerful techniques can help you pull people in the direction you want them to go:

1. Change the *conditions* that precede the behavior.

2. Change the *consequences* that follow the behavior.

Change the Conditions   If you want people to change their attitudes, identify the behaviors that represent the poor attitudes and alter the conditions that *precede* the behavior. Consider the following situation.

A new employee in a retail store is having a problem adjusting to her job. The manager needed her on the sales floor as soon as possible, so he rushed through her job training procedures without taking time to answer her questions. Now she finds there are many customers' questions she cannot answer, and she has trouble operating the computerized cash register. She wants to quit, and her negative attitudes are affecting her job performance and the way she handles her customers.

The manager could easily have prevented this employee's negative attitudes by answering all her questions *before* she was placed on the sales floor. Perhaps he could have asked an experienced salesperson to stay with her as she helped her first few customers. Above all, he could have displayed a caring, supportive attitude toward her.

Change the Consequences   Another way to help other people change their attitudes is to alter what happens *after* they exhibit the behavior you are attempting to change. A simple rule applies: When an experience is followed by positive consequences, the person is likely to repeat the behavior. When an experience is followed by negative consequences, the person will likely stop the behavior. For example, if you are a supervisor, and several of your employees are consistently late for work, you might provide some form of negative consequence each time they are tardy, such as a verbal reprimand or reduced pay. Keep in mind, however, that we tend to focus attention on the people who exhibit disruptive attitudes and to ignore the employees exhibiting the attitudes we want to encourage. Saying: "Thank you for being here on time. I really appreciate your commitment" can be an extremely effective reward for those who arrive at work on time. Behaviors rewarded will be repeated.

An attitude is nothing more than a personal thought process. We cannot control the thinking that takes place in someone else's mind, but we can sometimes influence it. And sometimes we can't do that either, so we have to set certain rules of behavior. Some organizations have come to the conclusion that behavior that offends or threatens others must stop. It may be impossible to stop someone from thinking prejudicial thoughts, but you can establish a zero tolerance policy regarding acts that demean or threaten others.[27]

SKILL DEVELOPMENT CHALLENGE

An important step in changing your attitudes is understanding them. To practice the skill of monitoring your current thought patterns, add four or five different endings to each of the following incomplete sentences. Work as rapidly as possible and don't worry about whether the ending is reasonable or significant; the object is to build awareness of your attitudes toward your life.[28]

I am very thankful for . . .

I am glad I'm not . . .

When I wake up in the morning, my first thoughts are . . .

My most common reaction to an annoying situation is . . .

Personal happiness to me means . . .

I often compare myself to . . .

Organizations' Efforts Toward Improving Employees' Attitudes

Most companies realize that an employee's attitude and performance cannot be separated. When employees have negative attitudes about their work, their job performance and productivity suffer. When Thomas Kuwatsch, vice president of the German information technology company Nutzwerk, discovered that employees' whining was cutting into productivity and costing the company an average of $17,600 a year, he formed the "two moans and you're out" policy. A clause in employees' contracts requires them to be in a good mood to keep their jobs. Everyone can complain, but employees must present a solution or better idea to overcome the problem they are complaining about.[29]

When employees have positive attitudes, job performance and productivity are likely to improve. One CEO of a software company has stated, "The way you get superior performance is to get people's passionate loyalty and belief. That means being flexible and giving your people what they need to do a great job."[30]

People who are asked what they most want from their job typically cite mutual respect among coworkers, interesting work, recognition for work well done, the chance to develop skills, and so forth. Of course, workers expect the pay to be competitive, but they want so much more. As author and management consultant Peter Drucker says, "To make a living is not enough. Work also has to make a life."[31] Organizations are finding creative ways to influence worker attitudes. The following companies made *Fortune* magazine's list of the 100 best companies to work for.[32]

At Mango's Tropical Café in Miami, Florida, dance classes help employees embrace the look and feel of the company's culture, which emphasizes fun and multicultural celebration. These classes also build friendships, trust, and teamwork.

■ Plante & Moran is an accounting firm with a human touch and a sense of humor. The company describes itself as "relatively jerk-free." Full-time employees get at least four weeks of paid vacation.

■ Baptist Health Care is a hospital that the competition tries to imitate. Top management maintains close contact with all employees, and employee-led initiatives have resulted in low turnover among registered nurses. Periodic open-forum meetings give employees a chance to voice concerns or make suggestions.

■ Adobe Systems, a successful Silicon Valley firm, strives to generate camaraderie among its employees. It schedules frequent all-hands meetings, job rotations, and Friday night parties. Perks include a fitness center with trainer, seasonal farmers' market, and basketball court.

What do these organizations have in common? Each has given thought to the attitudes that are important for a healthy work environment and has taken steps to shape these attitudes. Many organizations are attempting to improve employee attitudes and productivity by enhancing the quality of their employees' work life.

A Final Word

Viktor Frankl, a survivor of the Auschwitz concentration camp and author of *Man's Search for Meaning*, said, "The last of the human freedoms is to choose one's attitude in any given set of circumstances." Changing an attitude can be a challenge, but the process can also be an important step toward your continued growth and success.

LOOKING BACK: Reviewing the Concepts

■ Understand the impact of employee attitudes on the success of individuals as well as organizations.

Attitudes represent a powerful force in every organization. Employees' attitudes and performance cannot be separated. When employees display a positive attitude toward their work and coworkers, teamwork and productivity improve. When employees display a caring attitude toward their customers, the business is likely to enjoy a high degree of customer loyalty and repeat business. When employees display a serious attitude toward safety rules and regulations, fewer accidents are likely to occur.

■ List and explain the ways people acquire attitudes.

People acquire attitudes through early childhood socialization, peer and reference groups, rewards and punishment, role model identification, and cultural influences. However, attitudes are not set in stone. You always have the power to choose your attitude toward any situation.

■ Describe attitudes that employers value.

Employers hire and attempt to retain employees who have basic interpersonal skills, are self-motivated, accept change, are team players, are concerned about their health, value coworker diversity, and are honest.

■ Learn how to change your attitudes.

You can decide to change your attitudes by choosing to be happy, becoming an optimist, thinking for yourself without undue pressure from others, and keeping an open mind.

■ Learn how to help others change their attitudes.

You can help others change their attitudes by altering the conditions that lead to negative behaviors, such as by providing effective training so that the employee's job performance and personal satisfaction improve. You can also alter the consequences following people's behavior by providing positive consequences if you want them to have a positive attitude toward their behavior and repeat it, and negative consequences to deter them from participating in that behavior again.

■ Understand what adjustments organizations are making to develop positive employee attitudes.

Employers realize that money alone will not make employees happy. Organizations are taking steps to improve employee attitudes by enhancing the quality of their work life.

● Career Corner

Q: Two years ago I left a job I loved when the executives of an exciting new company offered me a position that seemed to have tremendous potential. I gave my two weeks' notice and jumped to the new employer. I worked day and night to help the new company be successful and enhance my climb to the top of it. Last week I was informed that it is declaring bankruptcy next month. I am choosing how I react to this devastating news and am trying not to panic, but I need advice on how to approach my former employer about returning to my old position. I still see some of my former colleagues socially, and they believe that there might be an opportunity to return to my old job. What can I do to enhance my chances at reentry?

A: You are not alone! Many workers grab new job opportunities when they believe the grass might be greener on the other side, only to discover they were better off in the first location. You were smart when you offered two weeks' notice before leaving your position. This considerate attitude toward your colleagues and customers will speak well for you during your reentry attempt. Determine what new skills you learned with the new organization and how those skills might be transferred to your former employer. Did you learn to effectively handle multiple priorities simultaneously, work faster, or take more risks? Point out why this new knowledge makes you even more valuable to your former employer. Who knows, they may reinstate you in a higher position than before!

Keep in mind that returning to your previous employer may not be your only choice. You could choose to look at this forced change as an opportunity to explore options you never considered before. Are there other employers in your field that might consider your experience an asset? Are your skills transferable to another career path? Keep an open mind as you examine your future.

Key Terms

attitudes	reference group
empathizer	role model
socialization	culture
peer group	cynicism

Applying What You Have Learned

1. Describe your attitudes concerning

   a. a teamwork environment

   b. health and wellness

   c. life and work

   d. learning new skills

   How do these attitudes affect you on a daily basis? Do you feel you have a positive attitude in most situations? Can you think of someone you have frequent contact with who displays negative attitudes toward these items? Do you find ways to avoid spending time with this person?

2. Identify an attitude held by a friend, coworker, or spouse that you would like to see changed. Do any conditions that precede this person's behavior fall under your control? If so, how could you change those conditions so the person might change his or her attitude? What positive consequences might you offer when the person behaves the way you want? What negative consequences might you impose when the person participates in the behavior you are attempting to stop?

3. For a period of one week, keep a diary or log of positive and negative events. Positive events might include the successful completion of a project, a compliment from a coworker, or just finding time for some leisure activities. Negative events might include forgetting an appointment, criticism from your boss, or simply looking in the mirror and seeing something you don't like. An unpleasant news story might also qualify as a negative event. At the end of one week, review your entries and determine what type of pattern exists. Also, reflect on the impact of these events. Did you quickly bounce back from the negative events, or did you dwell on them all week? Did the positive events enhance your optimism? Review the root causes of negative attitudes, and try to determine if any of these factors influence your reaction to negative or positive events.

Internet Insights

Every Friday, ABC News posts a new article called "Working Wounded," by Bob Rosner, author of the book with the same title. Each article discusses some aspect of the challenges people face in their life at work. Visit the website at *www.ABCNEWS.go.com* and access this week's "Working Wounded" article. Write a brief paper explaining your reaction to the comments. If time allows, go to *www.WorkingWounded.com* and read articles with titles that pique your interest. Report your findings to your classmates.

Role-Play Excercise

In this role-play excercise you will be attempting to change the attitudes of a friend who is a chronic underachiever. He has a great deal of potential, but he does things at work that result in self-sabotage. For example, he tends to procrastinate and often misses deadlines. When he does complete a project, his approach is to get by with the least amount of effort. When things don't go well at work, he tends to blame others. You will meet with another member of your class who will assume the role of your friend. Prior to the meeting, think about things you might say or do that would help your friend develop the attitudes that employers value today.

Case 6.1   Life Is Good at the Pike Place Fish Market

The popular books *Fish!, Fish! Tales,* and *Fish! Sticks,* mentioned at the beginning of this chapter, present a business philosophy that focuses on building employees' commitment to their employers and organizations. This philosophy is applicable to almost every organization because it is based on the idea that most people like working in happy places, so they are more likely to stay on the job and do a better job. While some people might argue that these "feel-good" attitudes are "soft skills" and do not affect the bottom line, a spokesperson for a very large organization said that the savings they experienced as a result of implementing the *Fish!* philosophy was in the millions of dollars because of employee retention.

The philosophy emphasizes four ways that companies can help employees and workers can help themselves.

- *Play.* A sense of playfulness makes a huge difference between those who perceive their jobs as no fun and those who have fun doing their jobs. When employees are having as much fun as they can at whatever they are doing, they generate a spirit of innovation and creativity.

- *Be there.* Don't daydream about what you could be doing and things you do not have. Make the most of where you are. Listen in depth to customers' and colleagues' concerns or ideas. When you really focus on a conversation and postpone other activities such as answering phone calls or processing paperwork, you avoid communicating indifference to the other person.

- *Make someone's day.* Delight customers instead of grudgingly doing the bare minimum. Do favors for others, even those who make you uncomfortable, and your job will become much more rewarding.

- *Choose your attitude.* People often add unnecessary stress to their lives because they stay upset with certain aspects of their job that they cannot control, rather than focusing on how they can make things better.

First Essex Bank chairman and CEO Leonard Wilson admits that *"Fish!* isn't going to make horrible, inexperienced employees into good employees. . . . But most workers can give an extra 10 to 40 percent. . . . *Fish!* is a way to get at an employee's 'pool of discretionary effort.' "[33]

Questions

1. Which of the four *Fish* principles do you believe can have the most dramatic effect on employees' productivity? Explain your answer.

2. What would you say to someone who sincerely believed that the *Fish* principles were ridiculous and frivolous?

3. Would you like to work for a *Fish* organization? Why or why not?

4. Identify workers and/or organizations that you believe have caught on to the powerful impact of this "attitude adjustment" program. How can you tell? What effect has it had on the individuals' and/or the organizations' success?

Case 6.2   An A-Mazing Way to Deal with Change

The new millennium was ushered in by a series of corporate scandals involving Enron, WorldCom, Tyco, and other large companies. In many cases, investors in these companies lost large amounts of money, and employees lost all or part of their pension funds. Also, several large companies have declared bankruptcy. United Airlines and U.S. Airways provide just two examples. Most of these firms' employees had defined-benefit pension plans that guaranteed payments to retirees based on a specific formula. When it became obvious that these organizations could no longer pay out these enormous sums of money in light of their financial woes, many handed off their pension obligations to the Pension Benefit Guaranty Corporation, the federal agency that was established to protect these individuals from losing their promised retirement funds. Now this agency has a deficit of more than $23 billion and faces an even larger deficit as more and more companies bail out of their pension fund obligations. Some organizations have seen the writing on the wall and have taken action to reduce or eliminate employees' pension funds so that they can remain competitive with organizations that do not offer such generous pensions.

When a company enters bankruptcy or goes out of business, employees usually lose their health care benefits. The loss of health care benefits and the loss of pension funds place an enormous burden on employees who no longer have jobs. Needless to say, most of these employees are feeling a deep sense of frustration and anger.

These employee attitudes are contagious. Workers in companies that have not yet been hit with such troubles face the fear that their organization is next. Perhaps they could benefit by reading the simple parable presented in Spencer Johnson's book *Who Moved My Cheese? An A-Mazing Way to Deal with Change in Your Work and in Your Life.* The four characters in the book, Sniff and Scurry (two little mice) and Hem and Haw (two little people the size of mice), live in a maze with lots of paths leading nowhere and some leading to rooms filled with cheese that could keep them happy for the rest of their lives. Each of the characters has a unique way of handling the depletion of their cheese supply in Cheese Station C. All four were initially very comfortable thinking that their cheese would always be there. Sniff and Scurry noticed that the cheese was rapidly diminishing and risked exploring the maze to discover a new source for their happiness. Hem and Haw kept doing their daily routine over and over again thinking the situation would improve. They did not acknowledge what was happening around them, and when the cheese was gone, they demanded compensation, declaring that the problem was not their fault. They waited for someone else to replace the cheese and continue to provide their security. They considered going out into the maze, but were afraid they could never find another source of cheese.[34]

Questions

1. *Who Moved My Cheese?* is the all-time best-selling book in *Amazon.com*'s history and is printed in forty-two languages. Why would organizations around the world buy millions of these books for their employees?

2. The book encourages readers to pay attention to what is happening around them, anticipate change, and look at the opportunities that exist outside their comfort zones. How does this reflect on those workers losing their pension funds?

3. One of the book's most powerful questions is "What would you do if you were not afraid?" As you look to your future and grasp the attitudes Spencer Johnson suggests, share your answer to that question with your classmates.

INTEGRATED RESOURCES

VIDEO: "Communicating Across Cultures at IDG"

CLASSROOM ACTIVITIES (*college.hmco.com/pic/reece10e*)

Attitudes Are Contagious
Helping Others Change Their Attitudes
Attitudes Necessary for Getting and Keeping a Job

business.college.hmco.com/students

ACE

Self-tests

7

MOTIVATING YOURSELF AND OTHERS

Chapter Preview

After studying this chapter, you will be able to

- Differentiate between internal and external motivators in the workplace.

- Explain the five characteristics of motives.

- Describe five of the most influential theories of motivation.

- List and describe contemporary motivation strategies.

- Identify motivating factors important to individuals from different generations.

- Describe selected self-motivation strategies.

Mary Cadagin was responsible for moving mortgage lender Fannie Mae's computer center to a new location twenty-five miles away. She asked more than 550 employees to do their regular jobs all week and then throw themselves into the moving project over thirteen consecutive weekends, pulling all-nighters on Friday evenings. The group had to shut down, move, and start up more than 300 business applications; unplug, wrap, and box 577 computer servers; lay more than 1.8 million feet of copper cable and 35 miles of fiber; and perform more than a million separate tasks to transfer the data. They did it flawlessly, without a single interruption to the company's business, and without even the promise of extra pay. How?

Each weekend project had a project manager who wore a red baseball cap, a badge of distinction for everyone who got one. Most of these individuals had never before held a leadership position. Cadagin empowered them by saying, "You own it. You run with it. Come back and tell me what you want to do." Each Friday at 5 p.m. the moving process started not with packing, but with eating. The more than 100 volunteers would dine together first. Between 9 p.m. and midnight, all the equipment was packed and moved. Snacks were served at midnight at the new location. At 8 a.m. Saturday morning, a full breakfast was served and work would continue, sometimes into Saturday night. If workers were too tired to drive home after completing their weekend project, the company paid for an overnight hotel stay. In short, Cadagin made the project fun by creating a sense of community and by being conspicuously visible throughout the weekends. "I couldn't ask them to work these hours and then just check in on them during the morning."

At the end of the thirteen weeks, she invited all the employees who participated in the project and their families to a picnic with face painting for children

Moving a large computer center requires not only hard work, but a spirit of teamwork by everyone involved in the project. Mary Cadagin, the person responsible for the move, asked more than 550 employees to do their regular jobs throughout the week and then help with the moving project over 13 consecutive weekends.

and opportunities for the "red hats" to take their turns in the dunk tank. Plus, she convinced the company to hand out bonuses to all employees involved in the relocation. Fannie Mae's CEO delivered the ultimate compliment when he said to Cadagin and her team, "You performed open-heart surgery on the company for 13 weeks in a row, and we didn't even know we were operated on."[1]

What motivated each of these workers to perform so well? Questions about what motivates anyone are not easily answered because everyone's needs differ so much. This chapter will help you gain some useful insight into understanding how your needs motivate you to take action and learn how to identify the needs of others.

The Complex Nature of Motivation

People are motivated by many different kinds of needs. They have basic needs for food, clothing, and shelter, but they also need acceptance, recognition, and self-esteem. Each individual experiences these needs in different ways and to varying degrees. To complicate matters more, people are motivated by different needs at different times in their lives. Adults, like children and adolescents, continue to develop and change in significant ways throughout life. Patterns of adult development have been described in such important books as *Passages* and *Pathfinders*, by Gail Sheehy, and *Seasons of a Man's Life*, by Daniel Levinson. No one approach to motivation works for all people or for the same person all the time.

Motivation Defined

People interact with each other in a variety of ways because they are driven by a variety of forces. **Motivation**, derived from the Latin word *movere*, meaning "to move," can be defined as the influences that account for the initiation, direction, intensity, and persistence of behavior. The study of motivation is complicated by the fact that the number of possible motives for human behavior seem endless. *Emotional* factors such as fear, anger, and love are some sources of motivation. Others may stem from *social* factors that are influenced by parents, teachers, friends, and television. And then there are the basic *biological* factors such as our need for food, water, or sleep.[2]

TOTAL PERSON INSIGHT	**STEPHEN R. COVEY**
	AUTHOR, *THE 7 HABITS OF HIGHLY EFFECTIVE PEOPLE*
	"Dependent people need others to get what they want. Independent people can get what they want through their own efforts. Interdependent people combine their own efforts with the efforts of others to achieve their greatest success."

Although the major focus of this chapter will be motivation in a work setting, it is important to realize that some people find meaning through the obsessions that consume their leisure time. To earn a living, Henry Sakaida helps operate a wholesale nursery in Rosemead, California, but his passion is World

War II aviation history. For the past twenty years he has arranged healing meetings between Japanese and American pilots who once shot at each other over the Pacific.[3] Tatsuo and Yukiko Ono operate a small business in Japan, but they get their greatest satisfaction from following the band The Rolling Stones. They have attended about three hundred Stones concerts held at major cities around the world.[4]

In a work setting, it is motivated employees who get the work done. Without them, most organizations would falter. Motivation is two dimensional; it can be internal or external.

Internal motivation comes from the satisfaction that occurs when work is meaningful and gives us a sense of purpose. Psychologist Frederick Herzberg has said that motivation comes from an internal stimulus resulting from job content, that is, what a worker actually does all day long. He suggests that organizations motivate their employees by enriching jobs so that workers are challenged, have an opportunity for achievement, and can experience personal growth.[5] These intrinsic rewards motivate some people more than money, trophies for outstanding performance, or other similar external rewards.

External rewards are rarely enough to motivate people on a continuing basis.

External motivation is an action taken by another person. It usually involves the anticipation of a reward of some kind. Typical external rewards in a work setting include money, feedback regarding performance, and awards. Some organizations are using **incentives** to encourage workers to develop good work habits and to repeat behavior that is beneficial to themselves and the organization. An incentive can take the form of additional money, time off from work, or some other type of reward.

External rewards are rarely enough to motivate people on a continuing basis. Ideally, an organization will provide an appropriate number of external rewards while permitting employees to experience the ongoing, internal satisfaction that comes from meaningful work.

The Motivation to Satisfy Basic Desires

Steven Reiss, professor of psychology and psychiatry at Ohio State University, conducted a major study to determine what *really* drives human behavior. He asked six thousand people from many stations in life which values were most significant in motivating their behavior and in contributing to their sense of happiness.[6] The results of his research showed that nearly everything we experience as meaningful can be traced to one of sixteen basic desires or to some combination of these desires (see Figure 7.1). Each of us has a different combination of the sixteen desires, a mix that can change with time and circumstances. The challenge is to determine which ones (the fundamental values) are most important and then live your life accordingly. You do not need to satisfy all sixteen desires, only the five or six that are most important to you.

Reiss and his research team found that most people cannot find *enduring* happiness by aiming to have more fun or pleasure. People who focus primarily on "feel-good" happiness (partying, drinking, etc.) discover that this source of satisfaction rarely lasts more than a few hours. It is "value-based" happiness that gives life meaning over the long run.[7]

FIGURE 7.1	The Sixteen Basic Desires in the Reiss Profile (Order of Presentation Not Significant)

DESIRE	DEFINITION
CURIOSITY	The desire for knowledge
ACCEPTANCE	The desire for inclusion
ORDER	The desire for organization
PHYSICAL ACTIVITY	The desire for exercise of muscles
HONOR	The desire to be loyal to one's parents and heritage
POWER	The desire to influence others
INDEPENDENCE	The desire for self-reliance
SOCIAL CONTACT	The desire for companionship
FAMILY	The desire to raise one's own children
STATUS	The desire for social standing
IDEALISM	The desire for social justice
VENGEANCE	The desire to get even
ROMANCE	The desire for sex and beauty
EATING	The desire to consume food
SAVING	The desire to collect things
TRANQUILITY	The desire for emotional calm

Source: Steven Reiss, *Who Am I?* (New York: Berkley Books, 2000), pp. 17–18.

Characteristics of Motives

Motives have been described as the "why" of human behavior. An understanding of the following five characteristics of motives can be helpful as you seek to understand the complex nature of motivation.[8]

Motives Are Individualistic People have different needs. What satisfies one person's needs, therefore, may not satisfy anyone else's. This variation in individual motives often leads to a breakdown in human relationships unless individuals take the time to understand the motives of others.

CRITICAL THINKING CHALLENGE

In Chapter 5 you were encouraged to identify and reflect on the values that are important in your life. Return to Table 5.1 and review the five-part values clarification process. Now examine each of the sixteen basic desires in Figure 7.1 and identify five or six that seem most important to you. Then apply the five-part valuing process to each of these desires. Do they accurately reflect factors that would motivate you at this point in your life? How might your desires change in the future?

Motives Change   As noted at the beginning of this chapter, motives change throughout our lives. What motivates us early in our careers may not motivate us later on.

Motives May Be Unconscious   In many cases, we are not fully aware of the inner needs and drives that influence our behavior. The desire to win the "Employee of the Month" award may be triggered by unconscious feelings of inadequacy or the desire for increased recognition.

Motives Are Often Inferred   We can observe the behavior of another person, but we can only infer (draw conclusions about) what motives caused that behavior. The motives underlying our own behavior and others' behavior are often difficult to understand.

Motives Are Hierarchical   Motives for behavior vary in levels of importance. When contradictory motives exist, the more important motive usually guides behavior. Workers often leave jobs that are secure to satisfy the need for work that is more challenging and rewarding.

Influential Motivational Theories

The work of various psychologists and social scientists has added greatly to the knowledge of what motivates people and how motivation works. The basic problem, as many leaders admit, is knowing how to apply that knowledge in

HUMAN RELATIONS IN ACTION | **Greatest Comeback in Sports History**

In 1998 Lance Armstrong returned to cycling after almost losing his life to testicular cancer. His goal at that point was to dominate the Tour de France, the world's most grueling biking competition. To fully appreciate the challenge facing Armstrong, you need to understand the immense physical endurance the Tour demands. Cyclists compete in the 2,000 mile race for over three weeks and spend nearly 90 hours on the bike. The Tour de France has been described as the equivalent of running 20 marathons in 20 days. Armstrong has won this event seven times in a row.

the workplace. Although many theories of motivation have emerged over the years, we will discuss four of the most influential.

Maslow's Hierarchy of Needs

According to Abraham Maslow, a noted psychologist, people tend to satisfy their needs in a particular order—a theory he calls the **hierarchy of needs**. Maslow's theory rests on three assumptions: (1) People have a number of needs that require some measure of satisfaction. (2) Only unsatisfied needs motivate behavior. (3) The needs of people are arranged in a hierarchy of prepotency, which means that as each lower-level need is satisfied, the need at the next level demands attention.[9] Basically, human beings are motivated to satisfy physiological needs first (food, clothing, shelter); then the need for safety and security; then social needs; then esteem needs; and, finally, self-actualization needs, or the need to realize their potential. Maslow's theory is illustrated in Figure 7.2.

Physiological Needs The needs for food, clothing, sleep, and shelter, or physiological needs, were described by Maslow as survival or lower-order needs. When the economy is strong and most people have jobs, these basic needs rarely dominate because they are reasonably well satisfied. But, needless to say, people who cannot ensure their own and their family's survival, or are homeless, place this basic need at the top of their priority list.

Safety and Security Needs Most people want order, predictability, and freedom from physical harm in their personal and professional lives and will be motivated to achieve these safety needs once their basic physiological needs are satisfied. At this level of the hierarchy, job security is very important. Until people are comfortable with these safety and security issues, higher-order motivators will generally not be effective.

Social or Belongingness Needs Whereas the first two types of needs deal with aspects of physical safety and survival, social or belongingness needs deal

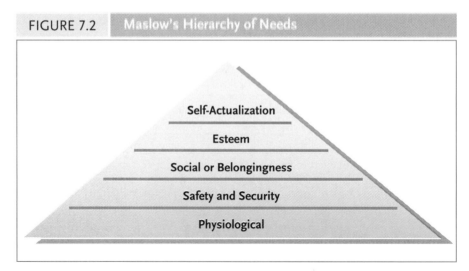

FIGURE 7.2 Maslow's Hierarchy of Needs

Self-Actualization
Esteem
Social or Belongingness
Safety and Security
Physiological

with emotional and mental well-being. Research has shown that needs for affection, for a sense of belonging, and for identification with a group are powerful. There are two major aspects of the need to belong: frequent, positive interactions with the same people and a framework of stable, long-term caring and concern.[10]

Esteem Needs People need respect and recognition from others as well as an inner sense of achievement and self-worth. Promotions, honors, and awards from outside sources tend to satisfy this need. Several esteem-building initiatives that build self-respect and self-confidence are discussed in Chapters 4 and 10.

Self-Actualization Needs The four needs just described motivate people by their *absence*—that is, when people feel a lack of food and shelter, security, social relationships, or esteem. Self-actualization needs, however, represent the need for growth, and they motivate people by their *presence*. Self-actualization is people fulfilling their potential or realizing their fullest capacities as human beings (see Table 7.1).

It is worth noting that Maslow's list of higher-level needs has been criticized because it does not specifically address some needs of the new generation of workers, such as the need for leisure time and the opportunity for self-actualization through family relationships. However, it teaches us one important lesson: A need that is satisfied will usually not motivate an individual. If you have food and shelter, you will not be motivated when someone offers you these things.

TABLE 7.1	Ways of Satisfying Individual Needs in the Work Situation
Need	**Organizational Conditions**
Physiological	Pay Breakfast or lunch programs Company services
Safety and security	Company benefits plans Pensions Seniority Pay
Social or belongingness	Coffee breaks Sports teams Company picnics and social events Work teams
Esteem	Recognition of work well done Responsibility Pay (as symbol of status) Prestigious office location and furnishings
Self-actualization	Challenge Autonomy

Source: Adapted from Judith Gordon, *A Diagnostic Approach to Organizational Behavior*, 3d ed. (Boston: Allyn & Bacon, 1991), p. 144.

Maslow's work is considered a classic in the field of management theory, and his original works have been republished in the book *Maslow on Management*.

Herzberg's Motivation-Maintenance (Two-Factor)Theory

Psychologist Frederick Herzberg proposes another motivation theory called the **motivation-maintenance theory**.[11] **Maintenance factors** represent the basic things people consider essential to any job, such as salaries, fringe benefits, working conditions, social relationships, supervision, and organizational policies and administration. We often take such things for granted as part of the job. These basic maintenance factors *do not* act as motivators, according to Herzberg; but if any of them is absent, the organizational climate that results can hurt employee morale and lower worker productivity. Health insurance, for example, generally does not motivate employees to be more productive, but the loss of it can cause workers to look for employment in another organization that provides the desired coverage.

Motivational factors are those elements that go above and beyond the basic maintenance factors. They include opportunities for recognition, advancement, or more responsibility. When these are present, they tend to motivate employees to improve their productivity. The workers may seek out new and creative ways to accomplish their organizations' goals as well as their personal goals. Herzberg's list of motivational factors parallels, to some degree, Maslow's hierarchy of needs (see Table 7.2).

Herzberg theorizes that if employees' motivational factors are not met, they may begin to ask for more maintenance factors, such as increased salaries and fringe benefits, better working conditions, or more liberal company policies regarding sick leave or vacation time. Critics of Herzberg's theory have pointed out that he assumes that most, if not all, individuals are motivated only by higher-order needs such as recognition or increased responsibility, and that they seek jobs that are challenging and meaningful. His theory does not acknowledge that

TABLE 7.2	Comparison of the Maslow and Herzberg Theories	
	Maslow	**Herzberg**
Motivational factors	Self-actualization	Work itself Achievement Responsibility
	Esteem needs	Recognition Advancement Status
Maintenance factors	Social or belongingness needs	Social network Supervision
	Safety and security needs	Company policy and administration
	Physiological needs	Job security Working conditions Salary

some people may prefer more routine, predictable work and may be motivated more by the security of a regular paycheck (a maintenance factor) than by the prospect of advancement. Nonetheless, Herzberg made an important contribution to motivation theory by emphasizing the importance of enriched work.

The Expectancy Theory

The **expectancy theory** is based on the assumption that motivational strength is determined by whether or not you *believe* you can be successful at a task. (This theory is an expansion of the self-efficacy concept detailed in Chapter 4.) If you really want something and believe that the probability of your success is high, then your motivation increases. *Perception* is an important element of this theory. Research conducted at the University of Kansas found a link between expectations and achievement in college. Students who wanted to complete college and believed they were capable of doing so earned higher grades and were less likely to drop out. In fact, aspirations combined with expectations predicted achievement better than standardized test scores.[12] This somewhat mysterious connection between what you expect in life and what you actually achieve is sometimes referred to as the **self-fulfilling prophecy**: If you can conceive it and believe it, you can achieve it.

McGregor's Theory X/Theory Y

Douglas McGregor, author of the classic book *The Human Side of Enterprise*, suggests that managers who are placed in charge of motivating their workers are essentially divided into two groups. Theory X managers maintain a pessimistic attitude toward their workers' potential. These managers believe that workers are basically lazy and have to be goaded into doing things with incentives such as pay or with punishment, that they have little or no ambition, that they prefer to avoid responsibility, and that they do only as much work as they have to in order to keep their jobs. Theory Y mangers, on the other hand, maintain an optimistic view of workers' ambition. These managers believe that their subordinates are creative people who want to work and do their best, are capable of self-direction, and can learn to both accept and seek responsibility if they are committed to the objectives of the organization. Often the expectancy theory kicks in and workers perform to their managers' pessimistic or optimistic expectations.

The Goal-Setting Theory

Successful people and successful organizations have one thing in common: They share the power of purpose. The more you focus on achieving a desired outcome, the greater your likelihood of success.[13] Your goals play a key role in bringing purpose to your life.

Motivation researchers indicate that goals tend to motivate people in four ways (see Figure 7.3). First, goals provide the power of purpose by directing your attention to a specific target. Second, they encourage you to make the effort to achieve something difficult. Third, reaching a goal requires sustained effort and therefore encourages persistence. Fourth, having a goal forces you to bridge the

FIGURE 7.3	A Model of How Goals Can Improve Performance

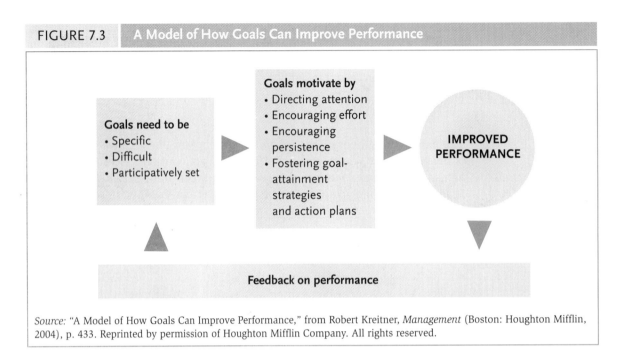

Goals need to be
- Specific
- Difficult
- Participatively set

Goals motivate by
- Directing attention
- Encouraging effort
- Encouraging persistence
- Fostering goal-attainment strategies and action plans

IMPROVED PERFORMANCE

Feedback on performance

Source: "A Model of How Goals Can Improve Performance," from Robert Kreitner, *Management* (Boston: Houghton Mifflin, 2004), p. 433. Reprinted by permission of Houghton Mifflin Company. All rights reserved.

gap between the dream and the reality; it fosters your creating a plan of action filled with strategies that will get you where you want to go.[14]

If your goal is easy to achieve and requires little effort, it may not serve as a motivator. Goals need to be difficult enough to challenge you but not impossible to reach. Goal setting is an excellent self-motivation strategy. Take a moment and review the goal-setting principles listed in Table 4.1.

Contemporary Employee Motivation Strategies

A healthy, mutually supportive relationship based on trust, openness, and respect can create a work climate in which employees want to give more of themselves. However, creating this type of organizational culture in the age of information may not be easy. How do you motivate employees who work from virtual offices? How do organizations experiencing major upheavals keep their employees' trust? The answers may have been provided by Jeffrey Pfeffer, a Stanford professor who has reported a strong connection between people-centered practices and an organization's higher profits and lower employee turnover. Organizations that recognize human wants, needs, passions, and aspirations and put people first understand that many of the following motivation strategies have merit even during times of great uncertainty.[15]

Motivation Through Job Design

Today's workers place a high value on jobs that provide rewards such as a sense of achievement, challenge, variety, and personal growth. It is possible to redesign existing jobs so they will have characteristics or outcomes that are intrinsically satisfying to employees. There are at least three design options.[16]

At the age of 14, Lynne Cox tackled her first open-water swim, three miles in the rough Pacific ocean of the California coast. After that successful swim she set more challenging goals that required greater strength and stamina.

Jacket cover, from *Swimming to Antarctica* by Lynne Cox, copyright © 2004 by Lynne Cox. Used by permission of Alfred A. Knopf, a division of Random House, Inc.

One of SPORTS ILLUSTRATED's Ten Best Books of the Year

"What emerges here is an athlete whose determination is so fierce that it seems almost exotic. She is fit. She is focused. She is Lance Armstrong with body fat." —*USA Today*

SWIMMING TO ANTARCTICA

Tales of a Long-Distance Swimmer

Job Rotation   **Job rotation** allows workers to move through a variety of jobs in a predefined way over a period of time. For example, a worker might attach a wheel assembly one week, inspect it the next, organize the parts for assembly during the third week, then return to the original assembly job the fourth week and begin the rotation again.

Job Enlargement   **Job enlargement** means expanding an employee's duties or responsibilities. When a job becomes stale, motivation can often be increased by encouraging employees to learn new skills or take on new responsibilities. In a bank setting, for example, a teller might develop expertise in the area of loan services or opening new accounts.

Job Enrichment   **Job enrichment** is an attempt to make jobs more desirable or satisfying, thereby triggering internal motivation. One approach assigns new and more difficult tasks to employees; another grants them additional authority. The Ritz-Carlton Hotel Co. has used this job enrichment strategy to improve customer service. When a customer has a problem, employees are encouraged to find a solution immediately. They have the discretion to spend up to $2,000 to fix a problem.[17]

Job rotation, job enlargement, and job enrichment appeal to Generation Y workers, who often do not value work for only external rewards. These workers are more apt to view work as a valuable learning experience that leads to something better.

Motivation Through Incentives

Incentives are often used to improve quality, reduce accidents, increase sales, improve attendance, and speed up production. They often focus on improving behaviors that will cut expenses and improve customer satisfaction. At Sysco Corporation, the Houston-based marketer of food service products, incentive pay for managers, drivers, and loaders depends on whether the right products get delivered at the right time, with no torn bags or dented cans.[18] We are seeing new incentive plans that erase the idea that everyone is motivated by the same thing, a "one-size-fits-all" approach. Incentives and rewards are discussed in more detail in Chapter 10.

Many companies are experimenting with programs that reward the development of new ideas. These programs, known as **intrapreneurship,** encourage employees to pursue their ideas at work, with the company providing the money, equipment, and time to do so. For example, 3M Company permits employees to spend 15 percent of company time experimenting with their own ideas. This practice resulted in the development of Post-it Notes.

Motivation Through Learning Opportunities

Learning opportunities, both on and off the job, can be a strong motivational force. Employees realize that education and training are critical to individual growth and opportunity. Rosabeth Moss Kanter says, "The chance to learn new skills or apply them in new arenas is an important motivator in a turbulent environment because it's oriented toward securing the future."[19] Of course, employees will be more motivated to participate in training programs if they perceive that such participation will lead to salary increases, advancement, or more meaningful work.

Many companies are using advanced communications technology to deliver instruction. Digital Equipment Corporation maintains its training curriculum catalog on the Internet, which enables employees to access self-paced courses from their personal computers.[20] Many other organizations provide tuition reimbursement for online courses offered by colleges and universities across the country.

Motivation Through Empowerment

Empowerment refers to those policies that share information, authority, and responsibility with the lowest ranks of the organization. When employees are empowered to make decisions for the good of the organization, they experience feelings of pride, self-expression, and ownership.

TechTarget, a Needham, Massachusetts, interactive media company, has embraced empowerment to a high degree. All of its 210 employees are free to set their own work schedules. There are no set policies mandating working hours or specifying the number of sick, personal, or vacation days. Managers set quarterly goals and timetables, but employees determine how to achieve them. In exchange for the flexibility, employees are expected to stay in contact with their managers. Greg Strakosch, founder and CEO, says the company's

Maria Mantz prepares to give the monthly financial report to employees at Development Counselors International (DCI). Andrew Levine, DCI's president, wants every employee to be knowledgeable in the area of company financial matters. Each month an employee is appointed to be chief financial officer (CFO) for a day. DCI provides a good example of the open-book management approach.

"open-leave" policy is credited with attracting and keeping a very talented and dedicated workforce.[21]

Although empowerment efforts are growing in popularity, this motivational strategy should not be viewed as a quick fix. Empowerment requires a long-term commitment of human and financial resources from top management down.

Motivation Through Others' Expectations

Earlier in this chapter you were introduced to the power of your own self-fulfilling prophecy: You will probably get whatever it is you expect. But there is another aspect of the expectancy theory: the power *others'* expectations can have on your motivation.

Research has confirmed that people tend to act in ways that are consistent with what others expect of them. In the classic study *Pygmalion in the Classroom*, Harvard University professors Robert Rosenthal and J. Sterling Livingston described the significant effect of teachers' expectations on students. They discovered that when teachers had high expectations for certain students who they believed had excellent intellectual ability and learning capacity, those students learned at a faster rate than others in the same group—even though the teachers did not consciously treat the higher-achieving students differently. These teachers had unintentionally communicated their high expectations to the students they *thought* possessed strong intellectual abilities.

The source of low expectations in the workplace is often a boss who perceives an employee as a weak performer and then treats the employee differently than high performers. The employee who thinks he or she is a weak performer in the eyes of the boss will often perform down to expectations.[22]

Motivating the Generations

In Chapter 5 we discussed the variety of historical events that influence the values of various generations (see Table 5.2). It is interesting to discover how those values translate into motivational factors for people in those same generation categories. This information may be helpful in discovering your own motivators, but gaining a greater understanding of these population segments may also be helpful as you learn how to motivate others in your personal and professional life. Figure 7.4 provides a brief summary of motivational factors for each generation.

FIGURE 7.4	Motivational Factors for the Generations
MATURES Born between 1928 and 1945	• They are often referred to as *loyalists*. • They want to build a legacy, both professionally and personally. • They want to be a part of the company's future. • Their view of feedback: No news is good news. • Rewards that are meaningful to them: The satisfaction of a job well done. • Their motivators: Money, public recognition, leadership opportunities, organizational loyalty, responsibility, accomplishment, control.
BABY BOOMERS Born between 1946 and 1964	• They are often referred to as the *optimists*. • They want to build an outstanding career. • They want to move up within the company and gain personal and financial responsibilities. • Their view of feedback: Performance review once a year, with a lot of documentation. • Rewards that are meaningful to them: Money, title, recognition, the corner office. • Their motivators: More money, public recognition, desire for subordinates, loyalty to self, promotion, peer recognition, control.
GENERATION X Born between 1965 and 1976	• They are often referred to as the *skeptics*. • They want to build a portable career. • They want to know exactly what they will be doing and whether they are on the right career path. • Their view of feedback: They want frequent comments on how they are doing. • Rewards that are meaningful to them: Freedom. • Their motivators: Doing good, meeting organizational goals, recognition from the boss, bonuses, and stock options.
GENERATION Y Born between 1977 and 1994	• They are often referred to as the *realists*. • They want to build a multifaceted career. • They want help seeing the future and the role they will play in it. • Their view of feedback: Whenever they want it, at the push of a button. • Rewards that are meaningful to them: Work that has meaning for them. • Their motivators: Time off, meeting personal goals, recognition from the boss, skills training, stock options, mentoring.

Source: Adapted from Peggy Blake Gleeson, "Managing and Motivating the Generations: Implications for the Student and the Employee." [cited on 28 December 2005]. Available from www.uwsp.edu/education/facets/links_resource/4413.pdf; INTERNET; "Motivating Generation Y," *Management Issues News.* [cited on 28 December 2005]. Available from www.management-issues.com; INTERNET.

Learning about the various generations helps you individualize your interactions with them, regardless of your generation. Whether you are a member of one of the older generations or of the younger generations, the majority of the work force of the future will include Generation X and Y workers. If you are one of them, manage them, or are managed by them, it will be critical to your career to adjust your human relations skills accordingly. Some generalizations may be helpful.

Generation X and Y workers

■ are more comfortable with diversity than previous generations are.

■ are self-reliant and seek fun and meaning in their work.

■ lived during an age of corporate downsizing, massive layoffs, government scandals, and merged families, so they are skeptical and often cynical about managers' motives and authenticity.

■ were often latchkey children, so they tend to be self-reliant. Give them a goal, and then set them free to accomplish it.

When working with Generation X and Y workers,

■ keep fun prevalent.

■ provide instruction and communication in multimedia. Talking-heads videos, routine memos, and scripted handbooks simply will not work. Use charts, photos, graphics, color, sound techno-gadgets, and interactive computer-based training.

■ coach them, don't lecture them. Make feedback regular and specific. Annual performance appraisals are too late and bore them. They need frequent rapid, specific feedback.

■ spend time with them. Read some of what they read. Watch some of what they watch.

■ show them respect, and they'll respect and perform for you.[23]

SKILL DEVELOPMENT CHALLENGE

Identify at least one friend or family member from each of the generations discussed previously. Visualize them working for you as you enter into a major project with a budget that allows no extra compensation for the additional work you will expect of them. List the ways you would motivate them to put forth their full efforts.

Now interview each of the people you identified and confirm whether your motivational techniques would work. Be prepared to share your insights with your classmates.

Self-Motivation Strategies

The material presented in this chapter explains how, why, when, and where motivation strategies work, and we have identified many organizations that do all they can to motivate their employees to stay on the job and to improve their productivity. But let's face it; some organizations just don't care if you are motivated or not, as long as you get your job done. If you are satisfied with your life and work, that's great! If you are yearning for a more exciting professional and/or personal life, guess what? It's up to you! The following self-motivation strategies can help you achieve your potential.

Nurture a Gritty Nature

What factors will contribute most to your future success? A series of recent studies indicate that the quality of **grit**, in the form of hard work and determination, is a major indicator of success. Intelligence accounts for only a fraction of the success formula. Grit has value for people at all levels of ability.[24]

Research conducted by University of Pennsylvania faculty members found that grit is the premier attribute for surviving the grueling first summer of training at West Point. Gritty people tend to be highly self-disciplined and focused on goal achievement. They also bring passion to their tasks. Lance Armstrong entered his first distance running race at age 10. He won, and within three years, he was winning swim meets and other forms of athletic competition. In his autobiography *It's Not About the Bike*, he says, "If it was a suffer-fest, I was good at it."[25]

How do you nurture grit? Self-discipline, an important part of grit, can be achieved by refraining from doing something. M. Scott Peck, author of the best-selling book *The Road Less Traveled*, told his readers that delaying gratification was "the only decent way to live." Early in life we are encouraged (or required by our parents) to complete our homework before watching television. Later in life we have to make hard decisions on our own and become self-disciplined. Should

"Oh, not bad. The light comes on, I press the bar, they write me a check. How about you?"

I stay with my diet or throw in the towel? Should I stay home and study for an exam or go drinking with friends? Should I add to my credit-card debt or refrain from buying that wide screen television? With a measure of self-discipline, we can learn to schedule the pain first (using Peck's words) and enjoy the pleasure later.[26]

Go Outside Your Comfort Zone.   Many people do not achieve their full potential because they are afraid to venture outside their "comfort zone." These individuals often earn less than they deserve, exert little effort to win a promotion to a more challenging position, and refuse assignments that might enhance their career. Some people stay in their comfort zone because they fear success. If someone says, "You can never do this," or, "It's never been done," consider accepting the challenge implicit in these statements.

Strive for Balance.   Self-motivation often decreases when we no longer have a sense of balance in our life. To achieve balance between your work and personal life, take time to reflect on what is most important to you, and then try to make the necessary adjustments. Employees at Miller & Associates, a Dallas wholesaler of kitchen equipment, complete annual "life-purpose" statements. Each person records the ten most satisfying experiences in his or her life, making note of those that carry special meaning. When David Rogers, a salesperson, finished his "life-purpose" statements, he realized that he wasn't taking time to do some of the things he most valued. He said, "I was so weighted toward work that it was getting in the way of work." Once he cut back on his hours, freeing up time for his social life, his sales actually increased.[27]

> *Self-motivation often decreases when we no longer have a sense of balance in our life.*

TOTAL	**JOAN BORYSENKO**
PERSON	AUTHOR, *MINDING THE BODY, MENDING THE MIND*
INSIGHT	"People who feel in control of life can withstand on enormous amount of change and thrive on it. People who feel helpless can hardly cope at all."

Take Action.   If you are feeling bored or trapped in a dead-end job, you can enhance your self-motivation by taking responsibility for the situation you are in, and then taking action to improve it. Taking personal responsibility for your current situation is not easy because change can be threatening. Don't just wait and hope that things get better. Do something!

- Instead of waiting to see what will happen, volunteer for a project or make a request.

- Have lunch with the person in your organization who is doing work that you find intriguing.

- Talk to your boss about the things you want to do.

- Follow up on an idea you have had for a long time.

- Read a book, attend a conference, or do something else that will help you grow and learn.[28]

● LOOKING BACK: Reviewing the Concepts

■ Differentiate between internal and external motivators in the workplace.

Motivation is a major component of human relations training because it provides a framework for understanding why people do the things they do. Internal motivation occurs when the task or duty performed is in itself a reward. External motivation is initiated by another person and usually is based on rewards or other forms of reinforcement for a job well done.

■ Explain the five characteristics of motives.

Different people are motivated by different things. Motives are individualistic and can change over the years. In many cases, people are not aware of the factors that motivate their behaviors. Because there is no valid measure of a person's motives, motives can only be inferred. Motives vary in strength and importance and are therefore hierarchical.

■ Describe five of the most influential theories of motivation.

Maslow's hierarchy of needs theory states that physiological needs will come first, followed by safety and security, social, esteem, and then self-actualization needs. According to Maslow, although any need can be a motivator, only higher order needs will motivate people over the long run.

Herzberg's motivation-maintenance theory contends that when motivational factors such as responsibility, recognition, and opportunity for advancement are not present, employees will demand improvement in maintenance factors such as higher salaries, more benefits, and better working conditions.

Expectancy theory is based on the assumption that personal expectations, as well as the expectations of others, have a powerful influence on a person's motivation. These expectations can become self-fulfilling prophecies. Managers can motivate employees by expressing belief in their abilities and talents.

McGregor's Theory X/Theory Y suggests that managers use two distinct motivational strategies when they attempt to motivate workers toward the goals of the organization. Theory X managers believe that people do not really want to work so they must be pushed, closely supervised, and prodded into doing things. Theory Y managers believe that people want to work and are willing to accept and seek responsibility if they are rewarded for doing so.

Goal-setting theory suggests that people become more focused and persistent if they establish specific, realistic goals in cooperation with their supervisors.

■ List and describe contemporary motivation strategies.

Contemporary organizations attempt to motivate their employees through positive expectations and job design modifications such as job rotation, job enlargement, and job enrichment. They are also discovering the effects of various incentives, intrapreneurship opportunities, additional training and empowerment.

■ Identify motivating factors important to individuals from different generations.

There are specific strategies that can be used to motivate workers from various age brackets such as the Matures, the Baby Boomers, Generation X, and Generation Y. Once you understand their motivating factors, you can individualize your interactions with them and enhance your interpersonal relations skills, regardless of your age.

■ Describe selected self-motivation strategies.

People must make their own plans to keep themselves motivated. They can nurture their grit, move beyond their comfort zone, strive for balance between their professional and personal lives, and take action.

Career Corner

Q: I love what I do, but I hate where I work. My workplace is very old, has no windows, and is very depressing. Besides, the two-hour commute is killing me! I've been with the company almost 6 months and hate to leave because the money and benefits are great, but I believe I can do my work from my home. When I asked my supervisor if she would consider allowing me to telecommute, she said her company tried that several years ago and it just didn't work.

A: For decades, managers have relied on the ability to walk past an employee's work area and *see* that the job is being done. Happily, that tradition has changed. Many managers have discovered that telecommuters are no more difficult to manage than in-house workers. Conduct your own research on the success of other organizations' telecommuting programs and learn about the sophisticated technology that will enhance your ability to fulfill your responsibilities to the organization. Succinctly present your findings to your supervisor. Remember to keep *her* needs in mind, not just yours. Employers know how difficult it can be to find and keep good workers, and they know that a happy worker is a productive worker. Suggest a 90-day trial period. If you or your employer is not satisfied with the arrangement, discontinue it. If you like the telecommuting arrangement and disagree with the decision to bring you back on site, take your skills elsewhere to an environment that will motivate you to do your best work.

Key Terms

motivation	expectancy theory
internal motivation	self-fulfilling prophecy
external motivation	job rotation
incentives	job enlargement
hierarchy of needs	job enrichment
motivation-maintenance theory	intrapreneurship
maintenance factors	empowerment
motivational factors	grit

Applying What You Have Learned

1. How much grit have you got? On a scale of one to five, rate how well the following statements describe you. In the first section, a five is *strongly agree* and a one is *strongly disagree*. In the second section, the scoring is reversed: One is *strongly agree* and five is *strongly disagree*. Total your score and divide the total by six. If you score over 3.5, consider yourself gritty.[29]

	Strongly Agree	Agree	Moderately Agree	Disagree	Strongly Disagree
I'm a hard worker.	5	4	3	2	1
Setbacks don't deter me.	5	4	3	2	1
I am now working on a project that may take years to finish.	5	4	3	2	1
I get interested in new pursuits every few months	1	2	3	4	5
People often tell me that I don't perform to my potential.	1	2	3	4	5
New ideas and new projects sometimes distract me from previous ones.	1	2	3	4	5

2. Prepare a list of all the things you wanted to accomplish during the past year, but didn't. Think of activities, responsibilities, and commitments, as well as personal and professional goals. Without making excuses for your behavior or blaming others, identify self-motivating strategies discussed in this chapter that you can implement to improve your chances of completing those tasks successfully.

3. Are you frustrated with any aspect of your personal or professional life right now? Write a major frustration on a piece of paper but do not put your name on it. Form a group of four or five class members who have completed the same task. Pass each other's papers randomly from group member to group member until your instructor says stop. One at a time, each group member can describe his or her ideas on how to overcome the frustration identified on the paper he or she is holding. At the conclusion of this exercise, describe how this "outsider's" viewpoint of your situation has influenced your thinking.

 Internet Insights

1. Visit *www.betterworkplacenow.com* and review the material presented. Click on the "insight and inspiration" tab. Which comments mean the most to you? Why?

2. Visit *www.greatplacetowork.com* and read the mission of the creators of this site. Then click on the various tabs at the top of the site. What factors make an organization a "great place to work?" Click on the "Best Companies List" and review the organizations that make up the list for the past year. Would you like to pursue job opportunities in one or more of the best places to work? If your answer is yes, explain your plan of action to get a job there. If your answer is no, why not? If location is an issue, what factors are holding you back from relocating?

 Role-Play Exercise

You just graduated from college and have accepted an entry-level job with a big-box electronics retail store that has tremendous career potential. You love your work, but hate your job because Lynn, your supervisor, does not seem to understand you. Lynn is highly educated, knows everything there is to know about all of the organization's products and services, and has three years of experience as a salesperson, but seems to know little about how to manage people. Lynn is about twenty years older than you are and sincerely believes you can meet your daily sales quota without any feedback as to how well you are doing. Your daily routine is highly restrictive, with two 15-minute breaks and a 30-minute lunch break that must be taken at specific points on the clock. Because you are new to the organization, you feel abandoned and have no idea if you are doing things right or not. You are beginning to feel worthless and to want to quit, but you want to build a career within this organization. Meet with one of your classmates who will play the role of Lynn, and discuss your concerns about the lack of feedback. Also discuss how the organization can make better use of your knowledge, skills, and abilities, which will in turn make Lynn (and you) look good to the executives in charge of promotions.

Case 7.1　Let the People Have the Power

As detailed in the opening vignette of this chapter, it appears Mary Cadagin at Fannie Mae had the right idea for effectively motivating workers to go beyond the call of duty: Give them the task that needs to be accomplished; give them the time, information, and resources to get the job done; and then let them do it. Jack Stack, president of Springfield Remanufacturing Company, did basically the same thing when he asked his workers to participate in financial and production decisions and thereby turned a struggling company with a devastating 89-to-1 debt-to-equity ratio into a $43 million enterprise with a debt-to-equity ratio of 1.8 to 1.[30]

Each year, Stack's employees study the numbers and determine what the greatest threat to SRC's success is. They then develop a plan to overcome the threat. If they achieve the desired results, each employee receives a share of the resulting profit through a year-end bonus that can exceed 18 percent of his or her pay. Employees meet weekly to review numbers and decide how to improve operations. Everyone understands that part of his or her job is to help prevent losses and increase productivity. "If we don't achieve a goal, we find out very quickly why we missed it. Everybody is looking through the numbers to see what the problem is."[31] If a department is having trouble, another department will send in reinforcements, and everybody understands why. They spontaneously help each other out, sometimes at great inconvenience. Even in tough times, SRC has never had a layoff. When it slightly missed its sales goal one year, 60 percent of the employees said they did not want their bonus. Obviously, money was *not* their only motivating factor.

Questions

1. What are the motivating factors at SRC? Where do they fit on Maslow's hierarchy of needs pyramid?

2. If you were an SRC employee, would these factors motivate you to hunt for another job or stay put? Explain.

3. In the months before the fall of the Enron Corporation, employees were led to believe that "all was well" with the company and were encouraged to continue to invest their time and money in its future. If Enron executives had implemented the motivational strategies exemplified at SRC, how might Enron's story have been altered? Explain your reasoning.

Case 7.2   What Drives Them?

At the early age of 9, Lynne Cox began training to become a long-distance swimmer. At age 14, she tackled her first open-water swim, three miles in the rough Pacific Ocean off the coast of California. At age 15, she swam across the English Channel in record time. Later she would participate in ambitious swims around the shark-infested Cape of Good Hope and across Alaska's Glacier Bay. The latter event helped prepare her for her big dream, a swim from Alaska to the Soviet Union across the Bering Strait. In her book *Swimming to Antarctica*, Cox says that long swims in very inhospitable bodies of water become vehicles for personal goals.[32]

Marla Runyan, a top distance runner, has competed on two Olympic teams and was the first American woman over the finish line in the 2002 New York City Marathon. Runyan, who is legally blind, says her tenacity to achieve was ignited early in life by the low expectations of her mother and her doctors. She was diagnosed with a retina-damaging disease when she was 8 years old. Runyan says, "I remember my Mom telling me what doctors thought I would and would not be able to do. It made me really angry, because they didn't think I was going to do anything." At that point she was set on proving them wrong.[33]

Cheri Blauwet, a wheelchair racer from Iowa, was 15 months old when she was paralyzed from the waist down in a farm accident. Throughout her life, her parents treated her no differently than they treated her siblings and other kids. She believes her disability has provided her with a unique way of seeing things that most people will never understand and is amazed at the low expectations strangers have of her abilities, even though she is a strong and capable Stanford Medical School student. As an adult, she has won marathons in Boston, New York, and Los Angeles. She says, "I've always been an inherent overachiever. I have a nagging dislike of defeat. Having to give up anything that is important is heart wrenching. And I can think of almost no time when I've had to do that."[34]

Questions

1. This chapter reveals that a person's *needs* serve as motivators toward achieving goals. What do you believe drives these women to achieve these extremes?

2. How did the power of expectations affect these women?

3. Do you have a similar driving force within you, personally or professionally? Explain.

INTEGRATED RESOURCES

VIDEOS: "Motivating the Sales Force at Wheelworks"
"Awards.com Becomes a Major Online Resource"
"Alternative Work Arrangements at Hewlett-Packard"

CLASSROOM ACTIVITIES (*college.hmco.com/pic/reece10e*)

Discovering Your Needs Questionnaire
Theory X or Theory Y?
Valuing Diversity Discussion

business.college.hmco.com/students

ACE

Self-tests

PART III

PERSONAL STRATEGIES FOR IMPROVING HUMAN RELATIONS

8   IMPROVING INTERPERSONAL RELATIONS
    WITH CONSTRUCTIVE SELF-DISCLOSURE

9   ACHIEVING EMOTIONAL BALANCE
    IN A CHAOTIC WORLD

10 BUILDING STRONGER RELATIONSHIPS
    WITH POSITIVE ENERGY

11 DEVELOPING A PROFESSIONAL PRESENCE

8

IMPROVING INTERPERSONAL RELATIONS WITH CONSTRUCTIVE SELF-DISCLOSURE

Chapter Preview

After studying this chapter, you will be able to

- Explain how constructive self-disclosure contributes to improved interpersonal relationships and teamwork.

- Understand the specific benefits you can gain from self-disclosure.

- Identify and explain the major elements of the Johari Window model.

- Explain the criteria for appropriate self-disclosure.

- Understand the barriers to constructive self-disclosure.

- Apply your knowledge and practice constructive self-disclosure.

Marsh & McLennan, the New York City financial-services giant, agreed to pay an $850 million settlement of civil fraud charges. The settlement agreement also required the company to publicly apologize to the firm's clients who were cheated by Marsh brokers. Big deal? Yes, when you consider that many corporations are willing to pay huge fines, but unwilling to acknowledge wrongdoing or apologize. With the intent of rebuilding its credibility, the Hardee's fast-food chain launched an ad campaign that directly addressed its biggest failures, which included poor service and some menu items that did not appeal to customers. One TV spot features Chief Executive Andrew Puzder acknowledging, in a confessional tone, that the company has not satisfied consumers in recent years.[1]

Pete Rose, the greatest singles hitter of all time, has struggled for years to repair his tarnished image. In his 1989 book *Pete Rose: My Story*, he claimed he had never bet on baseball. In his recent book *My Prison Without Bars*, he admitted that he did bet on baseball. Is it time for a contrite apology to his fans? Rose decided that a sincere apology was not possible: "I'm sure that I'm supposed to act all sorry or sad or guilty now that I've accepted that I've done something wrong. But, you see, I'm just not built that way."[2]

Before the rise of extreme partisanship in U.S. politics, presidents were sometimes willing to admit failure. After the invasion of Cuba was thwarted in the Bay of Pigs, President Kennedy told the nation he was "responsible" for the government's actions. When a Marine housing base was bombed in Lebanon in 1983, President Reagan told the nation that blame "properly rests here in this office with this president." More recently, in 1999, President Clinton grudgingly

Marsh & McLennan reached an $850 million settlement of civil fraud charges with the state of New York. In addition to the large fine, the pact requires an apology to the firm's clients.

took responsibility for his actions during the Monica Lewinsky sex scandal that led to impeachment charges. He was criticized for being "less than contrite." President Bush, during his second term, refused a reporter's invitation to acknowledge any mistakes in his handling of the issue of terrorism or planning for the invasion of Iraq.[3]

A sincere apology, one that comes from the heart, can deepen relationships at home and at work. However, these small acts of compassion are not common today. Expressing personal thoughts and feelings to a coworker, friends, or family members can be very difficult.

Self-Disclosure: An Introduction

As a general rule, relationships grow stronger when people are willing to reveal more about themselves and their work experiences. It is a surprising but true fact of life that two people can work together for many years and never really get to know each other. In many organizations, people are encouraged to hide their true feelings. The result is often a weakening of the communication process. Self-disclosure can lead to a more open and supportive environment in the workplace.

In some cases self-disclosure takes the form of an apology or of granting forgiveness to someone who apologizes to you. If you are a supervisor or manager, self-disclosure may take the form of constructive criticism of an employee whose performance is unsatisfactory. This chapter focuses on constructive self-disclosure and on conditions that encourage appropriate self-disclosure in a work setting.

Self-Disclosure Defined

Self-disclosure is the process of letting another person know what you think, feel, or want. It is one of the important ways you let yourself be known by others. Self-disclosure can improve interpersonal communication, resolve conflict, and strengthen interpersonal relationships.

It is important to note the difference between self-disclosure and self-description. **Self-description** involves disclosure of nonthreatening information, such as your age, your favorite food, or where you went to school. This is information that others could acquire in some way other than by your telling them. Self-disclosure, by contrast, usually involves some degree of risk. When you practice self-disclosure, you reveal private, personal information that cannot be acquired from another source. Examples include your feelings about being a member of a minority group, job satisfaction, and new policies and procedures.

The importance of self-disclosure, in contrast to self-description, is shown by the following situation. You work at a distribution center and are extremely conscious of safety. You take every precaution to avoid work-related accidents. But another employee has a much more casual attitude toward safety rules and often "forgets" to observe the proper procedures, endangering you and other workers. You can choose to disclose your feelings to this person or stay silent. Either way, your decision has consequences.

Benefits Gained from Self-Disclosure

Before we discuss self-disclosure in more detail, let us examine four basic benefits you gain from openly sharing what you think, feel, or want.

TOTAL	**ALBERT J. BERNSTEIN AND**
PERSON	**SYDNEY CRAFT ROZEN**
INSIGHT	AUTHORS, *SACRED BULL: THE INNER OBSTACLES THAT HOLD YOU BACK AT WORK AND HOW TO OVERCOME THEM*

"It's great when employees can read the subtle nuances of your behavior and figure out exactly what you require of them. But let's face it: Most people aren't mind readers. Even if they're smart, they may be oblivious to what's important to you—unless you spell it out for them."

1. *Increased accuracy in communication.* Self-disclosure often takes the guesswork out of the communication process. No one is a mind reader; if people conceal how they really feel, it is difficult for others to know how to respond to them appropriately. People who are frustrated by a heavy workload and loss of balance in their life, but mask their true feelings, may never see the problem resolved. The person who is in a position to solve this problem may be oblivious to what's important to you—unless you spell it out.

   > *Self-disclosure often takes the guesswork out of the communication process.*

   The accuracy of communication can often be improved if you report both facts and feelings. The other person then receives not only information but also an indication of how strongly you feel about the matter. For example, a department head might voice her concern about an increase in accidents this way: "Our accident rate is up 20 percent over last year, and to be honest, I feel terrible! Everyone must pay more attention to our safety procedures."

2. *Reduction of stress.* Sidney Jourard, a noted psychologist who wrote extensively about self-disclosure, states that too much emphasis on privacy and concealment of feelings creates stress within an individual. Too many people keep their thoughts and feelings bottled up inside, which can result in considerable inner tension. When stress indicators like blood pressure, perspiration, and breathing increase, our immune function declines. The amount of stress that builds within us depends on what aspects of ourselves we choose to conceal. If you compulsively think about a painful human relations problem but conceal your thoughts and feelings, the consequence will likely be more stress in your life.[4]

   Your supervisor asks you to work late to help complete a project your coworkers fumbled. You must put in overtime without extra pay and with little appreciation. If you do your usual good job, there is a good chance you will get more worked dumped on you. Do you discuss the problem with your boss or simply hide your feelings of bitterness?[5]

3. *Increased self-awareness*. Chapter 1 stated that self-awareness is one of the major components of emotional intelligence at work. Daniel Goleman, author of *Working with Emotional Intelligence*, defines **self-awareness** as the ability to recognize and understand your moods, emotions, and drives, as well as their effect on others.[6] Self-awareness is the foundation on which self-development is built. To plan an effective change in yourself, you must be in touch with how you behave, the factors that influence your behavior, and how your behavior affects others. A young Asian associate at a financial services firm learned from her supervisor that she was perceived as not being assertive enough in her dealings with clients. As she reflected on this feedback and listened to views expressed by her female peers, the associate became aware of how her cultural background influenced her communication with clients. This feedback motivated her to modify her communication style.[7]

The quality of feedback from others depends to a large degree on how much you practice self-disclosure. The sharing of thoughts and feelings with others often sets the stage for meaningful feedback (see Figure 8.1).

4. *Stronger relationships*. Another reward from self-disclosure is the strengthening of interpersonal relationships. When two people engage in an open, authentic dialogue, they often develop a high regard for each other's views. Often they discover they share common interests and concerns, and these serve as a foundation for a deeper relationship. John Powell, author of *Why Am I Afraid to Tell You Who I Am?* says this about the importance of openness: "Anyone who builds a relationship on less than openness and honesty is building on sand. Such a relationship will never stand the test of time, and neither party to the relationship will draw from it any noticeable benefits."[8]

In too many organizations, workers feel they must be careful about what they say and to whom they say it. David Stewart, organizational consultant, says people long for a work environment in which they can say what is on their mind in an honest and straightforward manner. They yearn for an authentic kind of interaction with their boss and coworkers.[9]

| FIGURE 8.1 | Self-Disclosure/Feedback/Self-Awareness Cycle |

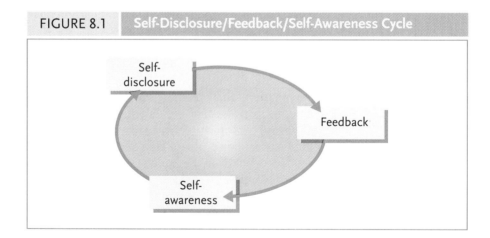

CRITICAL THINKING CHALLENGE

Throughout life there are occasions when we feel great frustration over an incident and some type of self-disclosure is an option for improving the situation. Reflect on some frustrating personal or work-related events that occurred in the past. Did you use self-disclosure to achieve some degree of personal satisfaction? If so, were your efforts successful or unsuccessful?

The Johari Window: A Model for Self-Understanding

A first step in understanding the process of self-disclosure is to look at the **Johari Window**, illustrated in Figure 8.2. The word *Johari* is a combination of the first names of the model's originators: Joseph Luft and Harry Ingham. This communication model takes into consideration that there is some information you know about yourself and other information you are not yet aware of. In addition, there is some information that others know about you and some they are not aware of. Your willingness or unwillingness to engage in self-disclosure, as well as to listen to feedback from others, has a great deal to do with your understanding of yourself and with others' understanding of you.[10]

FIGURE 8.2	Johari Window

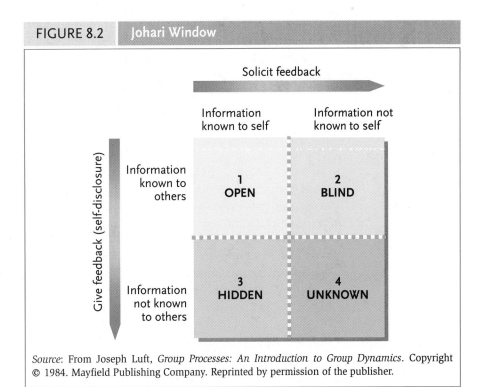

Source: From Joseph Luft, *Group Processes: An Introduction to Group Dynamics*. Copyright © 1984. Mayfield Publishing Company. Reprinted by permission of the publisher.

The Four Panes of the Johari Window

The Johari Window identifies four kinds of information about you that affect your communication with others. Think of the entire model as representing your total self as you relate to others. The Johari Window is divided into four panes, or areas, labeled (1) open, (2) blind, (3) hidden, and (4) unknown.[11]

Open Area   The **open area** of the Johari Window represents your "public" or "awareness" area. This section contains information about you that both you and others know and includes information that you do not mind admitting about yourself. As your relationship with another person matures, the open pane gets bigger, reflecting your desire to be known.

The open pane is generally viewed as the part of the relationship that influences effective interpersonal relations. Therefore, a productive interpersonal relationship is related to the amount of mutually held information. Building a relationship with another person involves working to enlarge the open area. As self-awareness and sharing of information and feelings increase, the open pane becomes larger.

Blind Area   The **blind area** consists of information about yourself that others know, but you are not aware of. Others may see you as aloof and stuffy, whereas you view yourself as open and friendly. Or you may view your performance at work as mediocre, and others see it as above average. You may consider your dress and grooming practices appropriate for work, but others feel your appearance is not suitable for such a setting. Information in the blind area is acquired when you learn about people's perceptions of you.

Building a relationship and improving interpersonal effectiveness often involve working to enlarge the open pane and reduce the size of the blind pane. This can be achieved as you become more self-disclosing and thereby encourage others to disclose more of their thoughts and feelings to you (see Figure 8.1). People are more likely to give feedback to a person who is open and willing to share appropriate personal information with them.

Hidden Area   The **hidden area** contains information about you that you know but others do not. This pane is made up of all those private feelings, needs, and past experiences that you prefer to keep to yourself. These could be incidents that occurred early in life or past work-related experiences you would rather not share.

Sometimes people spend too much effort building a wall of separation between their inner and outer lives. They conceal too much private information, leading others to ask, "Is this person the same on the inside as he presents himself on the outside?" If we perceive in others—or they in us—a lack of authenticity, human relations problems are more likely to occur. It's very difficult to mask who we are because the people we work with are usually adept at discerning our thoughts, values, and beliefs.[12]

Unknown Area   The **unknown area** of the Johari Window is made up of things unknown to you and others. Because you, and others, can never be known completely, this area never completely disappears. The unknown may represent such factors as unrecognized talents, unconscious motives, or early childhood memories that influence your behavior but are not fully understood. Many people have abilities that remain unexplored throughout their lives. A person capable of rising to the position of department manager may remain a receptionist throughout his or her career because the potential for advancement is unrecognized. You may possess the talent to become an artist or musician but never discover it.

Marshall Goldsmith, one of America's preeminent executive coaches, was hired to work with a very successful employee who treated direct reports and colleagues like "gravel in a driveway." Goldsmith says, "They were the pebbles; he was the SUV." Although this person was delivering outstanding results for the company, he was offending many of the employees he worked with. During the first meeting with Mike (not his real name), Goldsmith asked, "How do you treat people at home?" Mike insisted he was a great husband and father. He said, "I'm a warrior on Wall Street but a pussycat at home." Goldsmith suggested they call his wife and ask her how she viewed his behavior at home. When she finally stopped laughing at her husband's assessment, she confirmed that Mike was a jerk at home, too. His two sons also agreed with their mother. Once Mike realized how he was perceived by family members and coworkers, he made a commitment to change. Within a year his treatment of people scores on a standardized instrument improved dramatically—and so did his income.[13]

Some of the unknown information that is below the surface of awareness can be made public with the aid of open communication. Input from others (teacher, mentor, or supervisor) can reduce the size of the unknown pane and increase the size of the open area.

The four panes of the Johari Window are interrelated. As you change the size of one pane, others are affected. At the beginning of a relationship, the open area is likely to be somewhat small. When you start a new job, for example, your relationship with your supervisor and other workers may involve a minimum of open communication. As time passes and you develop a more open relationship with coworkers, the open area should grow larger.

Self-Disclosure/Feedback Styles

Our relationship with others is influenced by two communication processes over which we have control. We can consciously make an effort to self-disclose our thoughts, ideas, and feelings when such action would improve the relationship. And we can also act to increase the amount of feedback from others. Figure 8.3a represents a self-disclosure/feedback style that reflects minimum use of self-disclosure and feedback processes. This style represents an impersonal approach to interpersonal relations, one that involves minimal sharing of information. Figure 8.3b represents a self-disclosure/feedback style that reflects considerable use of self-disclosure and feedback. Candor, openness, and mutual respect are characteristics of this style.

You can take positive steps to develop a larger open window (Figure 8.3b) by displaying a receptive attitude when others attempt to give you feedback. Openness to feedback from supervisors and coworkers, as opposed to defensiveness,

| FIGURE 8.3 | Johari Window at the Beginning of a Relationship (*left*) and After a Closer Relationship Has Developed (*right*) |

(a) Beginning of relationship   (b) A closer relationship

Source: From Joseph Luft, *Group Processes: An Introduction to Group Dynamics*. Copyright © 1984. Mayfield Publishing Company. Reprinted by permission of the publisher.

is an important key to success in the workplace. If you become defensive, this behavior is likely to cut off the flow of information you need to be more effective in your job. You can also actively solicit feedback from your supervisor and coworkers so that they will feel comfortable in giving it to you.

360-Degree Feedback   Many organizations are using an assessment strategy known as **360-degree feedback**. With this approach, employees are rated by persons who have had opportunities to observe their performance. The person who completes the feedback form may be the immediate boss, coworkers, team members, and, in some cases, even customers, clients, or patients. The feedback is generally anonymous and often provides valuable insights regarding a worker's talents and shortcomings.

Although 360-degree feedback programs are often successful, some poorly planned and implemented programs result in heightened tensions and low morale. Some rating forms look too much like a report card. The multirater instrument should give raters an opportunity to designate the areas most in need of development. In an ideal situation, the employee being reviewed will receive a feedback summary report and help developing a plan for growth in areas that need improvement.[14]

Appropriate Self-Disclosure

At the beginning of this chapter, we stated that the primary goal of self-disclosure should be to build stronger relations. Self-disclosure is also a condition for emotional health, according to Sidney Jourard. These goals (strong relationships and good emotional health) can be achieved if you learn how to disclose in constructive ways. Appropriate self-disclosure is a skill that anyone can learn. However, developing this skill often means changing attitudes and behaviors that have taken shape over a lifetime.

In the search for criteria for developing appropriate self-disclosure, many factors must be considered. How much information should be disclosed? How intimate should the information be? Who is the most appropriate person with whom to share information? Under what conditions should the disclosures be made? In this section we examine several criteria that will help you develop your self-disclosure skills.

Use Self-Disclosure to Repair Damaged Relationships

Many relationships at work and in our personal life are unnecessarily strained. The strain often exists because people refuse to talk about real or imagined problems. Self-disclosure can be an excellent method of repairing a damaged relationship. The business manager for a large hospital and the physician in charge of the emergency room maintained a feud for two months because neither person was willing to sit down and openly discuss the problem. The problem began when a member of the physician's staff sent some incomplete medical records to the business office for processing. The business manager called the doctor and accused her staff of incompetence. As soon as he spoke the words, he was sorry. He had overreacted. The doctor in charge of the emergency room, anxious to defend her department, responded angrily with very strong language. She later regretted her lack of self-control. After several weeks, the business manager visited the emergency room and said, "Look, I'm sorry for what I said to you. You and your staff provide outstanding service to our patients, and I should not have reacted to the problem with such anger. Please accept my apology." The

Many workers personalize their work area with art, family pictures, awards and other items. These things often tell us what is important to that person. Larkin Teasley, CEO of Golden State Mutual Life Insurance Company, displays art that represents the triumph of artists over poverty and discrimination. These artists had to overcome many obstacles in order to be successful.

TOTAL	**BEVERLY ENGEL**
PERSON	AUTHOR, *THE POWER OF APOLOGY*
INSIGHT	"Almost like magic, apology has the power to repair harm, mend relationships, soothe wounds and heal broken hearts."

business manager and the doctor shook hands, and each returned to work feeling relieved that the problem was behind them.

> *Even in cases where your intention was not to upset or hurt someone, the apology must come from your heart.*

The Art of Apologizing   If your actions have caused hurt feelings, anger, or deep-seated ill will, an apology is in order. A sincere apology can have a tremendous amount of healing power for both the receiver and the giver. In addition, it can set the stage for improved communications in the future. Many people avoid apologizing because they feel awkward about admitting they were wrong. If you decide to apologize to someone, the best approach is to meet with the injured party in private and own up to the wrongdoing. In a private setting, feelings can be exchanged with relative comfort. An effective apology will communicate the three Rs: Regret, Responsibility, and Remedy.[15]

- *Regret*. The regret that you feel must be communicated sincerely. Even in cases where your intention was not to upset or hurt someone, the apology must come from your heart.

- *Responsibility*. Do not make excuses or blame others for what you did. Don't say, "I'm sorry about what happened, but you shouldn't have . . ." You must accept total responsibility for your actions.

- *Remedy*. A meaningful apology should include a commitment that you will not repeat the behavior. It might also include an offer of restitution.

The Art of Forgiveness   If someone you work with, a friend, or a family member offers a sincere apology, be quick to forgive. Forgiveness is almost never easy, especially when you feel you have been wronged. But forgiveness is the only way to break the bonds of blame and bitterness. To forgive means to give up resentment and anger. D. Patrick Miller, author of *A Little Book of Forgiveness,* says: "To carry an anger against anyone is to poison your own heart, administering more toxin every time you replay in your mind the injury done to you." He also says forgiveness provides healing and liberates your energy and your creativity.[16]

When you convey an apology to someone or forgive another person, remember that you reveal a great deal through nonverbal messages. The emotion in your voice, as well as your eye contact, gestures, and body posture, will communicate a great deal about your inner thoughts.

Present Constructive Criticism with Care

Constructive criticism is a form of self-disclosure that helps another person look at his or her own behavior without putting that individual on the defensive.

"Let's offer an apology, but without expressing contrition, regret or responsibility."

© Mark Litzler.

Constructive criticism is not the same as blaming. Blaming people for mistakes will seldom improve the situation.

Many people are very sensitive and are easily upset when they receive criticism. However, giving criticism effectively is a skill that can be mastered through learning and practice. Here are two effective methods for giving constructive criticism. First, avoid starting your message with "You," such as "You didn't complete your monthly inventory report" or "You never take our customer service policies seriously." For better results, replace "You-statements" with "I-statements." Say, "I am concerned that you have not completed your monthly inventory report." Another way to avoid defensiveness is to request a specific change in the future instead of pointing out something negative in the past. Instead of saying, "You did not have authorization to order office supplies," try saying, "In the future, please obtain authorization before ordering office supplies."[17]

Discuss Disturbing Situations As They Happen

You should share reactions to a work-related problem or issue as soon after the incident as possible. It is often difficult to recapture a feeling once it has passed, and you may distort the incident if you let too much time go by. Your memory is not infallible. The person who erred is also likely to forget details about the situation.

If something really bothers you do not delay expressing your feelings. Clear the air as soon as possible so you can enjoy greater peace of mind. Some people maintain the burden of hurt feelings and resentment for days, weeks, even years. The avoidance of self-disclosure usually has a negative effect on a person's mental and physical health as well as on job performance.

Accurately Describe Your Feelings and Emotions

It has been said that one of the most important outcomes of self-disclosure is the possibility for others to become acquainted with the "real" you. When you accurately describe your feelings and emotions, others get to know you better. This kind of honesty takes courage because of the risk involved. When you tell another person how you feel, you are putting a great amount of faith in that person. You are trusting the other person not to ridicule or embarrass you for the feelings you express.[18]

Experiencing feelings and emotions is a part of being human.

Too often, people view verbalizing feelings and emotions in a work setting as inappropriate. But emotions are an integral part of human behavior. People should not be expected to turn off their feelings the moment they arrive at work. Experiencing feelings and emotions is a part of being human. If we don't know each other, we can't be close to each other.[19]

What is the best way to report emotions and feelings? Some examples may be helpful. Let's suppose you expected to be chosen to supervise an important project, but the assignment was given to another worker. At a meeting with your boss, you might make the following statement: "For several weeks I've been looking forward to heading up this project. I guess I didn't realize that anyone else was being considered. Now I feel not only disappointed but also embarrassed."

Or suppose a coworker constantly borrows equipment and supplies but usually fails to return them. You might say: "Thanks for taking a few minutes to meet with me. I'm the type of person who likes to keep busy, but lately I've spent a lot of time retrieving tools and supplies you've borrowed. I've experienced a great deal of frustration and decided I should tell you how I feel."

As you report your feelings, be sure the other person realizes that your feelings are temporary and capable of change. You might say, "At this point I feel very frustrated, but I am sure we can solve the problem." Expressing anger can be especially difficult. This special challenge is discussed in Chapter 9.

Select the Right Time and Place

Remarks that otherwise might be offered and accepted in a positive way can be rendered ineffective not because of what we say but because of when and where we say it.[20] When possible, select a time when you feel the other person is not preoccupied and will be able to give you his or her full attention. Also, select a setting free of distractions. Telephone calls or unannounced visitors can ruin an opportunity for meaningful dialogue. If there is no suitable place at work to hold the discussion, consider meeting the person for lunch away from work or talking with the person after work at some appropriate location. If necessary, make an appointment with the person to ensure that time is reserved for your meeting.

Sharing Secrets in the Workplace Can Be Treacherous

Monica Lewinsky decided to share a secret with her friend Linda Tripp. Within a few weeks, millions of people would learn about her relationship with the president of the United States. In recent years, keeping secrets seems to be losing favor as openness becomes the mantra of modern America. More and more people are willing to talk about their love life, mental health problems, or rocky marriages. Information that was once exchanged only between the very closest of friends and lovers is sometimes shared with complete strangers. William Rawlins, professor of communication at Purdue University, says there is a new kind of workplace friendship that can be treacherous. People thrown together in the same department sometimes begin to share intimacies as if they have had a long, trusting relationship. Rawlins notes, "We want those work friendships to live up to the ideals we associate with other friendships, but sometimes they don't."

Avoid Overwhelming Others with Your Self-Disclosure

Although you should be open, do not go too far too fast. Many strong relationships are built slowly. The abrupt disclosure of highly emotional or intimate information may actually distance you from the other person, who may find your behavior threatening. Unrestricted "truth" can create a great deal of anxiety, particularly in an organization where people must work closely together. Dr. Joyce Brothers says we must balance the inclination to be open and honest with the need to be protective of each other's feelings. Disclosure in such areas as mental illness, domestic violence, fertility problems, or drug abuse is usually off limits at work. To be safe, it is also best to avoid expressing strong political or religious beliefs.[21]

Buddha gave some good advice about what to say and not say to others. The founder of Buddhism recommended that a person ask three vital questions before saying anything to another person: (1) Is the statement *true*? (2) Is the statement *necessary*? (3) Is the statement *kind*? If a statement falls short on any of these counts, Buddha advised that we say nothing.[22] His recommendations establish a high standard for anyone who engages in self-disclosure.

Barriers to Self-Disclosure in an Organizational Setting

At this point you might be thinking, "If self-disclosure is such a positive force in building stronger human relationships, why do people avoid it so often? Why do so many people conceal their thoughts and feelings? Why are candor and openness so uncommon in many organizations?" To answer these questions, let's examine some of the barriers that prevent people from self-disclosing.

Lack of Trust

Trust exists when we firmly rely on the integrity, ability, or character of a person or organization. Although trust is intangible, it is at the core of all meaningful relationships.[23]

TERRY MIZRAHI

PRESIDENT, NATIONAL ASSOCIATION OF SOCIAL WORKERS

"Trust is the core of all meaningful relationships. Without trust there can be no giving, no bonding, no risk taking."

Trust is a complex emotion that combines three components: caring, competency, and commitment. Consider the relationship between a doctor and her patient. Trust builds when the patient decides that the doctor is competent (capable of diagnosing the health problem), caring (concerned about the patient's health) and committed (willing to find a solution to the medical problem).[24] Trust between a salesperson and a customer is built upon the same three components. Customers want to do business with a salesperson who can accurately diagnose their needs, prescribe the right product, and provide excellent service after the sale.

Toyota Motor Corporation trusts ordinary workers to run its production lines better. The company respects the problem solving skills of every employee.

When the trust level in an organization is low, the consequences are a culture of insecurity, high turnover, marginal loyalty, and often damaged customer relations.[25] Unfortunately, in a work environment characterized by rapid change and uncertainty caused by frequent layoffs, trust has greatly declined in many organizations. The recent wave of business scandals has also undermined employee trust at many companies.

Lack of trust is the most common—and the most serious—barrier to self-disclosure.

Lack of trust is the most common—and the most serious—barrier to self-disclosure. Without trust, people usually fear revealing their thoughts and feelings because the perceived risks of self-disclosure are too high. When trust is present, people no longer feel as vulnerable in the presence of another person, and communication flows more freely.[26]

Jack Gibb, in his book *Trust: A New View of Personal and Organizational Development*, points out that the trust level is the thermometer of individual and group health. When trust is present, people function naturally and openly. Without it, they devote their energies to masking their true feelings, hiding thoughts, and avoiding opportunities for personal growth.[27]

Many people spend part of their time building trust and part of their time destroying trust. Table 8.1 compares behaviors that build trust with behaviors that destroy it. Essentially, the way to build trust is to be trustworthy all the time.

Fear/Distrust Cycle Jack Gibb states that the normal fears people bring to a new job are magnified when they encounter tight controls, veiled threats, and impersonal behavior. This climate sets the stage for what he describes as the "fear/distrust cycle" (see Figure 8.4).[28] The cycle begins with the management philosophy that people are basically lacking in motivation and cannot be trusted (discussed in Chapter 7 as Theory X). To bring about maximum production, management tries to maintain tight control over employees by initiating a series of strict rules and regulations. As management increases the controls, workers often become more defensive and resentful. The spirit of teamwork diminishes, and everyone in the organization begins talking in terms of "we" versus "they."

TABLE 8.1	How Trust Can Be Built and Destroyed
Building Trust	**Destroying Trust**
■ Openly share information.	■ Withhold information.
■ Admit your mistakes.	■ Cover up mistakes.
■ Network with coworkers.	■ Keep your distance from coworkers.
■ Display competence.	■ Display incompetence.
■ Be honest all the time.	■ Be honest only some of the time.
■ Be clear in your convictions.	■ Avoid commitment.
■ Be true to your values.	■ Ignore your values.

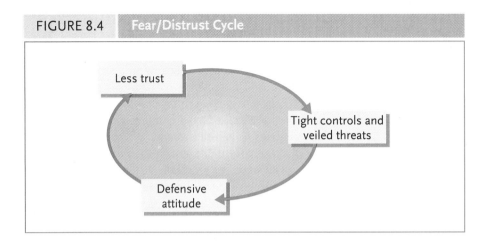

FIGURE 8.4 Fear/Distrust Cycle

Less trust → Tight controls and veiled threats → Defensive attitude → (cycle)

Role Relationships Versus Interpersonal Relationships

Self-disclosure is more likely to take place within an organization when people feel comfortable stepping outside their assigned roles and displaying openness and tolerance for the feelings of others. In our society, role expectations are often clearly specified for people engaged in various occupations. For example, some people see the supervisor's role as an impersonal one. Supervisors are supposed to enforce policies, maintain high production, and avoid getting too close to the people they supervise. The advice given to some new supervisors is "Don't try to be a nice guy, or people will take advantage of you." Yet often the most effective supervisors are those who are approachable, display a sense of humor, and take time to listen to employee problems.

Some newly appointed supervisors may deliberately try to build barriers between themselves and subordinates. They draw a sharp distinction between **role relationships** and **interpersonal relationships**. They are too impersonal and aloof, thinking that this is appropriate "role" behavior. Employees usually respond to these actions by becoming defensive or less trusting.

SKILL DEVELOPMENT CHALLENGE

You have worked in the graphic design department for almost five years. About six months ago your boss, who had been your mentor, retired and was replaced by someone who has very poor interpersonal relationship skills. Often, his attempts at communication with staff members tend to create a negative emotional wake. He frequently says, "If I were you . . ." or "You don't get it," accompanied by negative facial expressions. Sometimes he exaggerates by saying, "You always do this" or "Never once have you . . ." You have decided to meet with him and describe how uncomfortable you feel when he talks to you in such a demeaning way. On a piece of paper, write your opening statement, which should include examples of the behavior or situation you want to change. Be sure to describe the emotions that surface when he says something inappropriate. Once the statement is completed, practice saying it out loud.[29]

Roles are inescapable, but they need not contribute to the depersonalization of relationships. Each role is played by a person. Others should be able to get to know that person regardless of the role the individual has been assigned.

Practice Self-Disclosure

Many people carry around an assortment of hurt feelings, angry thoughts, and frustration that drains them of the energy they need to cope with life's daily struggles. Although self-disclosure provides a way to get rid of this burden, some people continue through life imprisoned by negative thoughts and feelings. If you avoid disclosing your thoughts and feelings, you make it harder for others to know the real you. You will recall from the beginning of this chapter that self-disclosure involves revealing personal information that cannot be acquired from other sources. This type of information can often improve the quality of your relationships with others.

Could you benefit by telling others more about your thoughts, wants, feelings, and beliefs? To answer this question, complete Figure 8.5, which will give you an indication of your self-disclosure style. If you tend to agree with most of these items, consider making a conscientious effort to do more self-disclosing.

FIGURE 8.5	Self-Disclosure Indicator

Instructions: Read each statement and then place a checkmark (✔) in the appropriate space.

	YES	NO
1. In most cases I avoid sharing personal thoughts and feelings with others.		
2. My relationships with others tend to be quite formal.		
3. I would not be comfortable discussing personal problems at work.		
4. I tend to avoid discussing my concerns even when feelings of frustration build inside me.		
5. I tend to avoid giving praise or criticism to others.		
6. I tend to believe that familiarity breeds contempt.		
7. I find it difficult to apologize.		
8. I find it difficult to forgive the wrongdoer.		

Becoming a more open person is not difficult if you are willing to practice.

Becoming a more open person is not difficult if you are willing to practice. If you want to improve in this area, begin by taking small steps. You might want to start with a nonthreatening confrontation with a friend or neighbor. Pick someone with whom you have had a recent minor problem. Tell this person as honestly as possible how you feel about the issue or problem. Keep in mind that your objective is not simply to relate something that is bothering you but also to develop a stronger relationship with this person.

As you gain confidence, move to more challenging encounters. Maybe you feel your work is not appreciated by your employer. Why not tell this person how you feel? If you are a supervisor and one of the people you supervise seems to be taking advantage of you, why not talk to this person openly about your thoughts? With practice you will begin to feel comfortable with self-disclosure, and you will find it rewarding to get your feelings out in the open. As you become a more open person, the people you contact will be more likely to open up and share more thoughts, ideas, and feelings with you. Everyone wins!

● LOOKING BACK: Reviewing the Concepts

■ Explain how constructive self-disclosure contributes to improved interpersonal relationships and teamwork.

Open communication is an important key to personal growth and job satisfaction. Self-disclosure—the process of letting another person know what you think, feel, or want—improves communication. Most people want and need opportunities for meaningful dialogue with coworkers and the person who supervises their work.

■ Understand the specific benefits you can gain from self-disclosure.

Constructive self-disclosure can pave the way for increased accuracy in communication, reduction of stress, increased self-awareness, and stronger interpersonal relationships.

■ Identify and explain the major elements of the Johari Window model.

The Johari Window helps you conceptualize four kinds of information areas involved in communication: The open area, what you and others know about you; the blind area, what others know about you that you do not know about yourself; the hidden area, what you know but others do not; and the unknown area, what neither you nor others know.

■ Explain the criteria for appropriate self-disclosure.

Always approach self-disclosure with the desire to improve your relationship with the other person. Describe your feelings and emotions accurately, and avoid making judgments about the other person. Use self-disclosure to repair damaged relationships. It is helpful to understand the art of apologizing and the art of forgiveness.

■ Understand the barriers to constructive self-disclosure.

A climate of trust serves as a foundation for self-disclosure. In the absence of trust, people usually avoid revealing their thoughts and feelings to others. Self-disclosure is more likely to take place within an organization when people feel comfortable stepping outside their assigned roles and displaying sensitivity to the feelings of others.

■ Apply your knowledge and practice constructive self-disclosure.

As with learning any new skill, you can improve your ability to disclose your thoughts and feelings by starting with less threatening disclosures and proceeding slowly to more challenging situations.

Career Corner

Q: I am nearing my first employment anniversary, and my supervisor will soon complete my first performance appraisal. Prior to meeting with my boss, I will be completing a self-evaluation form. She gave me a copy of the form and said, "Be as objective as possible." Well, I am not sure how to approach this assignment. Can you give me some guidance?

A: In an ideal situation, you would have been given feedback on your performance throughout the past year. Effective supervisors document strengths and problem areas over time rather than "save them up" for the annual performance evaluation. Prior to completing the self-evaluation, reflect on your accomplishments for the time you have been employed. You should also review your job description. One of the best ways to approach self-evaluation is to prepare a three-part report. Part one includes major activities that consume most of your time. Part two includes a description of major accomplishments. The third part of your report might be a list of "discussion" topics such as your ideas for improving the way work gets done. Use your self-evaluation as an opportunity to improve communication with your boss. Once you decide what approach you want to use, meet briefly with your supervisor and make sure she is comfortable with your plan.

Key Terms

self-disclosure	unknown area
self-description	360-degree feedback
self-awareness	constructive criticism
Johari Window	trust
open area	role relationships
blind area	interpersonal relationships
hidden area	

Applying What You Have Learned

1. To learn more about your approach to self-disclosure, complete each of the following sentences. Once you have completed them all, reflect on your

written responses. Can you identify any changes in your approach to self-disclosure that would improve communications with others? Are there any self-disclosure skills that you need to practice?

   a. "For me, the major barrier to self-disclosure is . . ."

   b. "To establish a more mutually trusting relationship with others, I need to . . ."

   c. "In order to receive more feedback from others, I need to . . ."

   d. "In situations where I should apologize for something or voice forgiveness, I tend to . . ."

2. On Friday afternoon a coworker visits your office and requests a favor. She wants you to review a proposal she will give to her boss on Monday morning at 10:00 a.m. You agree to study the proposal sometime over the weekend and give her feedback on Monday before her meeting. You put a photocopy of the proposal in your briefcase and take it home. Over the weekend you get busy and forget to review the proposal. In fact, you are so busy that you never open your briefcase. On Monday morning you make a call on a customer before reporting to the office. While sitting in the customer's office, you open your briefcase and see the report. It is too late to study the report and give feedback to your coworker. Which of the following actions would you take?

   a. Try to forget the incident and avoid feeling guilty. After all, you did not intentionally avoid your obligation.

   b. Call the person's boss and explain the circumstances. Confess that you simply forgot to read the report.

   c. Meet with your coworker as soon as possible and offer a sincere apology for failing to read the report and provide the feedback.

   Provide a rationale for your choice.

3. Constructive self-disclosure is based on a foundation of trust. When the trust level is low, open and honest communication is unlikely to occur. We inspire trust by what we say and what we do. Some behaviors that inspire trust are listed below. Rate yourself with this scale: U = Usually; S = Sometimes; I = Infrequently. After you finish the self-assessment, reflect on your ability to inspire trust, and think about ways to improve yourself in this area.

	U	S	I
I disclose my thoughts and feelings when appropriate.	☐	☐	☐
I admit my mistakes.	☐	☐	☐
Others know that I keep confidences.	☐	☐	☐
I keep my promises and commitments.	☐	☐	☐
I avoid distortion of information when communicating with others.	☐	☐	☐

Internet Insights

What is the best way for a supervisor to get feedback on his or her performance? One approach is to gather your staff in a meeting room and ask, "Who loves me? Show of hands!" To obtain truly anonymous feedback on your performance, the Internet is a good bet. Several companies offer web-based 360-degree review services. Visit the online clearinghouse HR Guide (*www.hr-guide.com*) and review the available resources for 360-degree feedback. Prepare a brief summary of your findings.

Role-Play Exercise

To prepare for this role-play activity, review the second exercise in this chapter's Applying What You Have Learned. You have decided to take action c, which involves a sincere apology. For the purpose of this role play, you will assume the role of Lonnie Caban. The coworker who requested your help is Tyler Siverman. In order to be well prepared for the role play, read the text material that describes the use of self-disclosure to repair damaged relationships. Keep in mind that when you apologize to someone you reveal a great deal through nonverbal messages. The emotion in your voice, as well as your eye contact, gestures, and body posture, will communicate a great deal about your inner thoughts.

Case 8.1   The Art of Giving Criticism

Large numbers of employees feel uncomfortable giving negative feedback to people they work with. Robert A. Baron, chair of the management department at Rensselaer Polytechnic Institute in Troy, New York, says, "Everybody is reluctant to give negative feedback, so all they do is bite their tongue until they can't stand it anymore." If someone is doing something that interferes with your work, causes you discomfort, or puts you in danger, do not remain silent. When you allow someone to do something you do not want, you become part of the problem. By remaining quiet, you allow the behavior to continue.

We live in a culture that encourages outspokenness, but the disclosure of thoughts and feelings must be handled with care. How something is said can be more important than what was said. Robert Genua, author of Managing *Your Mouth*, says that the most important thing is to pause before you speak and think about what you are going to say. If you are highly critical of someone's suggestion and express your views with strong sarcasm, the people who work with you may not remember that you happen to be right. However, they will remember your insensitive behavior. Genua says, "People who choose their words carefully come across as well-mannered, polished and refined."

Although some people are too direct in giving feedback and may actually be perceived as threatening, others make passive statements and fail to solve the problem. When giving negative feedback, you should look the person in the eye and be straightforward in expressing your thoughts and feelings. If someone is taking credit for your suggestions and ideas and has ignored your protests, you might say, "I want you to stop taking credit for my ideas. If you do not stop, I will ask our department head to schedule a meeting for the three of us so we can discuss the problem." To leave some things unchallenged can have negative results. Your reputation is formed not only by what you stand for but by what you won't stand for.

If you are a supervisor, the major reason you give negative feedback is to improve performance. Robert Baron has researched how bosses criticize employees and says some criticize too much and others criticize too little. Some give negative feedback for the wrong reasons, such as to reinforce their sense of power or to get revenge. To improve performance, you want to avoid comments that will make the other person angry or defensive. When it comes to giving criticism, do it with sensitivity.[30] Avoid the temptation to blame or condemn the person for mistakes made.

Questions

1. Do you agree that speaking out at work is generally beneficial to you and your employer? Explain your answer.

2. Why are many people reluctant to give negative feedback to another person? What are some of the reasons some people are afraid to speak out?

3. If a coworker openly criticizes your work in a meeting and says things that are not true, what should your immediate response be? Should you make contact with this person after the meeting and try to resolve the problem? Explain your answer.

Case 8.2 360-Degree Feedback Uncovers Blind Spots

One of the more controversial employee-development practices has been the introduction of an assessment approach known as 360-degree feedback. As noted earlier in this chapter, organizations that have adopted this assessment strategy believe employees will benefit from feedback collected from several different sources. This means an employee may be evaluated by peers, subordinates, a supervisor, and sometimes even customers. Each review typically enlists the opinions of eight to twelve people.

Feedback usually comes in the form of a completed questionnaire or inventory. This feedback—generally anonymous—usually provides valuable insights regarding one's talents and shortcomings. An executive at Ameritech Corp. learned that his habit of making points by stabbing at a person with his index finger, thumb upright, was threatening to some subordinates. A written anonymous comment from an employee said, "Don't make your hand into a gun and point at people. . . . It's very intimidating." The executive's reaction: "I wish someone had told me this thirty years ago."

A major goal of 360-degree feedback is to increase self-awareness. Some people simply do not know themselves well enough. In companies that incorporate peer reviews in their 360-degree feedback effort, coworkers deliver performance reviews of one another. Tenneco Automotive Inc. uses peer reviews to reduce injury rates at its seventy-four plants. Hourly workers share twice-a-week peer evaluations, and the findings are used for solving safety problems.

Peer appraisals have become quite common at companies that maintain a leaner, less hierarchical organization structure and rely more on teams. Although some employees pull their punches to avoid hurting a coworker's feelings, others deliver criticism with candor. One goal of peer reviews is to give members an opportunity to disclose feelings of frustration and to comment on others' behaviors that bother them. Another goal is to give group members a chance to boost one another's self-esteem by praising good performance.[31]

Questions

1. Today 360-degree feedback has been introduced into most *Fortune* 100 companies, and it continues to spread among smaller companies. Do you feel that multisource feedback is superior to feedback from a single source such as your supervisor? Explain.

2. Would you feel comfortable giving anonymous performance reviews to coworkers? To your supervisor?

3. Multisource feedback evolved over the past two decades as a development tool—a way to help people develop new skills and overcome weaknesses. Today, a few companies use feedback data to make decisions regarding pay raises and promotions. Do you see any risks involved in using the feedback data for major human resource decisions?

INTEGRATED RESOURCES

CLASSROOM ACTIVITIES (*college.hmco.com/pic/reece10e*)

My Johari Window/Adjusting the Panes
The Perfect Work Environment
Building Trust

business.college.hmco.com/students

ACE

Self-tests

9

ACHIEVING EMOTIONAL BALANCE IN A CHAOTIC WORLD

Chapter Preview

After studying this chapter, you will be able to

- Describe how emotions influence our thinking and behavior.

- Understand the factors that contribute to emotional balance.

- Explain the critical role of emotions in the workplace.

- Describe the major factors that influence our emotional development.

- Learn how to deal with your anger and the anger of others.

- Understand the factors that contribute to workplace violence.

- Identify and explain the most common emotional styles.

- Describe strategies for achieving emotional control.

Sports provide a showcase for just about every type of emotion. Pick up the morning paper and you see a picture of Phil Mickelson jumping high in the air after making his final putt and winning the prestigious PGA Championship. Mickelson had been waiting a long time for a big win, and this happy moment was cheered by his many fans. On another day, you might see a display of anger as NASCAR driver Robby Gordon throws his helmet at the car driven by Michael Waltrip. Gordon was upset because he believed that Waltrip had deliberately caused the crash that eliminated Gordon from the race. And sometimes fear surfaces in sports. After a hard hit, a football player lies motionless on the field. The fans, many of whom fear the worse, suddenly become very quiet.

In recent years, fans have displayed a lack of emotional control at many sporting events. A White Sox fan rushed the field and tackled an umpire. A right fielder with the Texas Rangers was hit in the back of the head by a spectator's cell phone. Some of the more disrespectful fans are college students. Some of these fans are inclined to use coarse trash talk and infantile behavior. At University of Wisconsin football games, fans frequently douse officials with beer and throw eggs at visitors' buses. An Ohio State football fan, after attending a game at Madison, said, "For the first time ever, I was fearful for my safety."[1]

The world of sports, like life itself, introduces us to many different emotions. We witness hugs, tantrums, back slaps, and, yes, an occasional punch in the nose.

Anger, fear, love, joy, jealousy, grief, and other emotions can influence our behavior at work and in our personal world. To the extent that we can become

Phil Mickelson jumps high in the air after making his final putt and winning the Master's Golf Championship. He had waited several years for this big win.

more aware of our emotions and assess their influence on our daily lives, we have the opportunity to achieve a new level of self-understanding. That greater awareness can help us avoid inappropriate behavior.

Emotions—An Introduction

An **emotion** is a strong, temporary feeling that is positive or negative. Emotional experiences tend to alter the thought processes by directing attention toward some things and away from others. Emotions energize our thoughts and behaviors.[2]

Throughout each day our feelings are activated by a variety of events (see Figure 9.1). You might feel a sense of joy after learning that a coworker has just given birth to a new baby. You might feel overpowering grief after learning that your supervisor was killed in an auto accident. Angry feelings may surface when you discover that someone borrowed a tool without your permission. Once your feelings have been activated, your mind interprets the event. In some cases, the feelings trigger irrational thinking: "No one who works here can be trusted!" In other cases, you may engage in a rational thinking process: "Perhaps the person who borrowed the tool needed it to help a customer with an emergency repair." The important point to remember is that we can choose how we behave. We can gain control over our emotions.

Achieving Emotional Balance—A Daily Challenge

The need to discover ways to achieve emotional balance has never been greater. To be successful in these complex times, we need to be able to think and feel simultaneously. People make choices dictated primarily by either their heads (reason) or their hearts (feelings). The thinking function helps us see issues logically; the feeling function helps us be caring and human.[3] Many organizations are spawning fear, confusion, anger, and sadness because the leaders lack emotional balance.

The basic emotions that drive us—such as fear, love, grief, greed, joy, and anger—have scarcely changed over the years. However, we are now seeing enormous differences in the expression of emotions. Today, people are much more

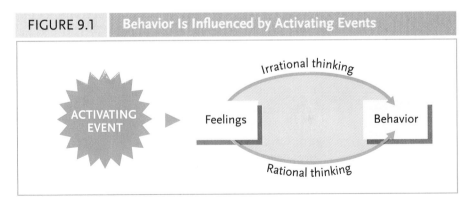

FIGURE 9.1 | Behavior Is Influenced by Activating Events

likely to engage in aggressive driving, misbehave at public events, or become abusive when they are unhappy with service. In the workplace many people experience emotional pain because of disagreeable bosses.

Emotional Intelligence

Daniel Goleman, author of several popular books on emotional intelligence, challenges the traditional view of the relationship between IQ and success. He says there are widespread exceptions to the rule that IQ predicts success: "At best, IQ contributes about 20 percent to the factors that determine life success, which leaves 80 percent to other forces.[4] **Emotional intelligence** can be described as the ability to monitor and control one's emotions and behavior at work and in social settings. Whereas standard intelligence (IQ) deals with thinking and reasoning, emotional intelligence (EQ) deals more broadly with building social relationships and controlling one's emotions. Several studies indicate that EQ can be increased through a combination of awareness and training.[5] The focus of Goleman's research is the human characteristics that make up what he describes as *emotional competence.* The emotional competence framework is made up of two dimensions.[6]

Personal Competence This term refers to the competencies that determine how we manage ourselves. Recognizing one's emotions and their effects, keeping disruptive emotions and impulses in check, and maintaining standards of honesty and integrity represent a few of the competencies in this category.

Social Competence This refers to the competencies that determine how we handle relationships. Sensing others' feelings and perspectives, listening openly and sending convincing messages, and negotiating and resolving disagreements represent some of the competencies in this category.

Although IQ tends to be stable throughout life, emotional competence is learnable and tends to increase throughout our life span. The emotional competencies that really matter for work can be learned.

Emotional Expression

We sometimes suffer from a lack of emotional balance because we learn to inhibit the expression of certain emotions and to overemphasize the expression of others. Some families, for example, discourage the expression of love and affection. Some people are taught from an early age to avoid expressing anger. Others learn that a public display of grief (crying, for example) is a sign of weakness. If as a child you were strongly encouraged to avoid the expression of anger, fear, love, or some other emotion, you may repress or block these feelings as an adult.[7]

Emotional imbalance also develops if we become fixated on a single emotion. The high incidence of violent crime in America has motivated some people to become almost totally infused with the emotion of fear. One writer noted that people who are preoccupied with fear may be intensifying the problem:

> "We have a habit of keeping ourselves overwhelmed, through the news media, with bad and scary things that have happened all over the world each day; and the chronic pattern of worrying about which of these bad things might happen to us in the future."[8]

To focus on one emotion to the exclusion of others creates a serious imbalance within us.

The Emotional Factor at Work

Emotions play a critical role in the success of every organization, yet many people in key decision-making positions—leaders with outstanding technical skills—fail to understand the important role emotions play in a work setting. In part, the problem can be traced to leadership training that emphasizes that "doing business" is a purely rational or logical process. Some leaders learn to value only those things that can be arranged, analyzed, and defined. One consultant put the problem into proper perspective when he said, "We are still trying to do business as if it requires only a meeting of the minds instead of a meeting of the hearts."[9]

Tim Sanders, former chief solutions officer at Yahoo! says, "How we are perceived as human beings is becoming increasingly important in the new

TOTAL PERSON INSIGHT	**JAMES C. GEORGES**
	CHIEF EXECUTIVE OFFICER, *THE PAR GROUP*
	"All of our technology is underutilized and will remain so until we put the emotion of doing business onto parity with the logical and rational aspects of performance improvement."

economy." He notes that compassion is an important key to long-term personal success. This is the human ability to reach out with warmth through eye contact, physical touch, or words. It is a quality machines can never possess.[10]

Relationship Strategy Emotional undercurrents are present in almost every area of every organization. Most banks, hospitals, retail firms, hotels, and restaurants realize that they need a relationship strategy—a plan for establishing, building, and maintaining quality relationships with customers. Cosco Systems, for example, measures itself by the quality of its relationships with customers. Salespeople achieve their bonuses based in large part on customer satisfaction instead of on gross sales or profit.[11]

Emotional labor, which taxes the mind, is often more difficult to handle than physical labor, which strains the body.

Frontline employees, those persons responsible for delivering quality service and building relationships, engage in "emotional labor," and those who have frequent contact with the public often find the work very stressful.[12] *Emotional labor*, which taxes the mind, is often more difficult to handle than physical labor, which strains the body. For this reason, frontline employees need the support of leaders who are both caring and competent.

At Umpqua Bank, every element of the culture is focused on great customer service. Here we see a customer and his friend relaxing at a Umpqua branch bank in Portland, Oregon.

> **CRITICAL THINKING CHALLENGE**
>
> Emotional undercurrents are present in almost every area of work and every aspect of our personal lives. Recall a situation at work or at school when the leadership displayed emotional blindness. What are some of the reasons the important role of emotions was not taken into consideration?

Factors That Influence Our Emotions

The starting point in achieving greater emotional control is to determine the source of emotional difficulties. Why do we sometimes display indifference when the expression of compassion would be more appropriate? Why is it so easy to put down a friend or coworker and so hard to recognize that person's accomplishments? Why do we sometimes worry about events that will never happen? To answer these and other questions, it is necessary to study the factors that influence our emotional development.

Temperament

Temperament refers to a person's individual style of expressing needs and emotions; it is biological and genetically based. It reflects heredity's contribution to the beginning of an individual's personality.[13] Researchers have found that certain temperamental characteristics are apparent in children at birth and remain somewhat stable over time. For example, the traits associated with extroversion and introversion (see Chapter 3) can be observed when a baby is born. Of course, many events take place between infancy and adulthood to alter or shape a person's temperament. Personality at every age reflects the interplay of temperament and of environmental influences, such as parenting.[14]

TOTAL PERSON INSIGHT	**DANIEL BROWN** CLINICAL PROFESSOR, *HARVARD MEDICAL SCHOOL* "An emotion has at least three necessary components: the felt bodily experience, the cognition or thought, and the expressive reaction."

Unconscious Influences

The **unconscious mind** is a vast storehouse of forgotten memories, desires, ideas, and frustrations, according to William Menninger, founder of the famed Menninger Foundation.[15] He noted that the unconscious mind can have a great influence on behavior. It contains memories of past experiences as well as memories of feelings associated with past experiences. The unconscious is active, continuously influencing conscious decision-making processes.

Although people cannot remember many of the important events of the early years of their lives, these incidents do influence their behavior as adults. Joan Borysenko offers this example:

> Inside me there is a seven-year-old who is still hurting from her humiliation at summer camp. Her anguish is reawakened every time I find myself in the presence of an authority figure who acts in a controlling manner. At those moments, my intellect is prone to desert me, and I am liable to break down and cry with the same desolation and helplessness I felt when I was seven.[16]

This example reminds us that childhood wounds can cause us to experience emotions out of proportion to a current situation. Also, we often relive the experience in a context very different from the one we experienced as a child. A worker who is strongly reprimanded by an angry supervisor may experience the same feelings that surfaced when he was scolded by his mother for breaking an expensive vase.

Transactional Analysis   A promising breakthrough in understanding the influence of the unconscious came many years ago with the development of the **Transactional Analysis** (TA) theory by Eric Berne. After years of study, Berne concluded that, from the day of birth, the brain acts like a two-track stereo tape recorder. One track records events, and the other records the feelings associated with those events.

To illustrate how feelings associated with early childhood experiences can surface later in life, picture in your mind's eye a 3-year-old walking around his mother's sewing room. He picks up a pair of sharp scissors and begins walking toward the staircase. The mother spots the child and cries, "Tommy, drop those scissors! Do you want to kill yourself?" Tommy's tape recorder records both the event (walking with scissors) and the emotions (fear and guilt). Ten years later, Tommy is taking an art class and his teacher says, "Tommy, bring me a pair of scissors." As he begins to walk across the room, his mind is flooded by the feelings of fear and guilt attached to that earlier childhood event.

The practical applications of Transactional Analysis were discussed in such books as *I'm OK—You're OK,* written by Thomas Harris; *Staying OK,* by Amy Bjork Harris and Thomas Harris; and *Born to Win,* by Muriel James and Dorothy Jongeward. TA concepts have been incorporated into many corporate training programs.

Cultural Conditioning

A professor at Dartmouth College said, "Culture is what we see and hear so often that we call it reality. Out of culture comes behavior."[17] Culture helps shape just about every aspect of our behavior and our mental processes. Culture is frequently associated with a particular country; but actually, most countries are multicultural. African Americans, Hispanic Americans, Asian Americans, and American Indians represent a few of the subcultures within the United States.[18]

The rate of interpersonal violence in the United States is higher than in other industrialized countries. Domestic abuse is the leading cause of injury to women in this country. The United States Justice Department estimates that one in four women have been involved in abusive relationships. Many people, both men and women, are victims of verbal abuse, which may take the form of insults or swearing.[19]

Too much violence makes it difficult for us to achieve emotional balance. People who have experienced violence, or the threat of violence, express high levels of fear and distress. As life becomes a constant state of tension and anxiety, their ability to build and maintain good relationships with others decreases. How do we rise above negative cultural conditioning? To achieve this goal, we must find ways to let go of the things we cannot control. For many people, forgiveness, or an attitude of acceptance, is a valued tool for staying balanced.[20]

Thus far we have established two important points regarding the role of emotions in our life:

1. *It is important that we remain open to the full range of emotions that influence our thinking and behavior.* To deny our feelings or attempt to repress them is not a healthy way to handle emotions. Shakti Gawain, a pioneer in the field of personal growth, says, "Our feelings are an important part of the life force that is constantly moving through us. If we don't allow ourselves to fully experience our emotions, we stop the natural flow of that life force.[21]

2. *Emotional undercurrents are present in every aspect of our work, and separating our mental and emotional energies at work is very difficult because they are so closely intertwined.*[22] We live in a society where many people are openly suspicious of emotions, so it is not surprising that in many work settings employees are encouraged to express their thoughts but not their feelings.

Coping with Your Anger and the Anger of Others

Anger in the workplace is clearly on the rise.

Anger may be defined as the thoughts, feelings, physical reactions, and actions that result from unacceptable behavior by others. Anger is almost always a response to perceived injustice, and may dissolve with a deeper understanding of the cause. Anger in the workplace is clearly on the rise. In a survey conducted by Marlin Company, a national workplace communication company, 52 percent of respondents said their colleagues need help managing anger. The authors of *Anger Kills* say that about 20 percent of the general population has levels of hostility high enough to be dangerous to their health.[23]

Managing Your Anger

Learning to deal with their own anger and the anger of other people is one of the most sophisticated and mature skills people are ever required to learn. Intense anger takes control of people and distorts their perceptions, which is why angry people often make poor decisions.[24]

Dr. Art Ulene, author of *Really Fit Really Fast*, says the first step in anger management is to monitor your anger. How often do you get angry each day? What

| HUMAN RELATIONS IN ACTION | Emotional Eating |

Dr. Phillip McGraw, author of *The Ultimate Weight Solution*, knows a great deal about what it takes to lose weight and maintain that loss. Many people use food to deal with emotional demands such as anxiety, loneliness, worry, or depression. Food gives us the perception of relief. He says,

"When you stop medicating feelings with food—which is an absolute must in order to get healthy—you need to have other ways to deal with emotions." The key is to substitute exercise, meditation, rational thinking, or something else for that caloric quick fix.

are the causes of irritation in your life? How upsetting is each episode of anger? How well do you manage each episode? Ulene suggests using a diary or journal to record this information. This self-monitoring activity will help you determine the impact of anger in your life. Record not only the source of the irritation, but the feelings that surfaced when you became angry. Also record the behaviors you displayed when angry. Ulene says that people who monitor their behavior carefully see positive results: "Without even trying, their behavior begins to change in ways that are usually desirable."[25]

What makes you angry? The anger journal will help you identify your most common anger triggers. You may find that irritations and annoyances such as traffic delays, interruptions, or loud noise are very irritating. You may discover that your anger is frequently connected to disappointment in someone or to some annoying event.

Intense anger often takes the form of rage.

Intense anger often takes the form of rage. In addition to road rage, air rage, and customer rage, we are witnessing more incidents of "workplace rage." Workplace rage can take the form of yelling, verbal abuse, and physical violence. It is more likely to occur when workers are stressed by long hours, unrealistic deadlines, cramped quarters, excessive e-mail, lack of recognition, bullying incidents, or some combination of these factors.

Effective Ways to Express Your Anger

Buddha said, "You will not be punished for your anger, you will be punished by your anger." Buddhist teachings tell us that patience is the best antidote to aggression.[26] Intense anger that is suppressed will linger and become a disruptive force in your life unless you can find a positive way to get rid of it. Expressing feelings of anger can be therapeutic, but many people are unsure about the best way to self-disclose this emotion. To express anger in ways that will improve the chances that the other person will receive and respond to your message, consider these suggestions:

1. *Avoid reacting in a manner that could be seen as emotionally unstable.* If others see you as reacting irrationally, you will lose your ability to influence them.[27] Failure to maintain your emotional control can damage your image.

Did you hear me? Anger control has been a challenge for Bobby Knight. Here we see the Texas Tech coach yelling at an official during a game against Baylor University.

2. *Do not make accusations or attempt to fix blame.* It would be acceptable to begin the conversation by saying, "I felt humiliated at the staff meeting this morning." It would not be appropriate to say, "Your comments at the morning staff meeting were mean spirited and made me feel humiliated." The latter statement invites a defensive response.[28]

3. *Express your feelings in a timely manner.* The intensity of anger can actually increase with time. Also, important information needed by you or the person who provoked your anger may be forgotten or distorted with the passing of time.

4. *Be specific as you describe the factors that triggered your anger, and be clear about the resolution you are seeking.* The direct approach, in most cases, works best.

In some cases the person who triggers your anger may be someone you cannot confront without placing your job in jeopardy. For example, one of your best customers may constantly complain about the service he receives. You know he receives outstanding service, and you feel anger building inside you each time he complains. But any display of anger may result in loss of his business. In this situation you rely on your rational thinking power and say to yourself, "This part of my work is very distasteful, but I can stay calm each time he complains."

TOTAL	**PEMA CHÖDRÖN**
PERSON	AUTHOR AND BUDDHIST TEACHER
INSIGHT	"We can suppress anger or act it out, either way making things worse for ourselves and others. Or we can practice patience: wait, experience the anger and investigate its nature."

How to Handle Other People's Anger

Dealing with other people's anger may be the most difficult human relations challenge we face. The following skills can be learned and applied to any situation where anger threatens to damage a relationship.

1. *Recognize and accept the other person's anger.* The simple recognition of the intense feelings of someone who is angry does a lot to defuse the situation.[29] In a calm voice you might say, "I can see that you are very angry," or "It's obvious that you are angry."

2. *Encourage the angry person to vent his or her feelings.* By asking questions and listening carefully to the response, you can encourage the person to discuss the cause of the anger openly. Try using an open-ended question to encourage self-disclosure: "What have I done to upset you?" or "Can you tell me why you are so angry?"

3. *Do not respond to an angry person with your own anger.* To express your own anger or become defensive will only create another barrier to emotional healing. When you respond to the angry person, keep your voice tone soft. Keep in mind the old biblical injunction, "A soft answer turns away wrath."[30]

4. *Give the angry person feedback.* After venting feelings and discussing specific details, the angry person will expect a response. Briefly paraphrase what seems to be the major concern of the angry person, and express a desire to find ways to solve the problem. If you are at fault, accept the blame for your actions and express a sincere apology.

Violence in the Workplace

Doug Williams, an employee at a Lockheed Martin airplane parts plant in Meridian, Mississippi, left a meeting, went out to his car, and came back with several guns. He then shot six coworkers to death and wounded eight others before committing suicide. Although workplace homicides are not very common, violence at work is a problem. The Bureau of Labor statistics reports that in 2002 (the latest year for which data are available), U.S. employees at work were the victims of 18,104 injuries from assault and 609 homicides.[31] Research conducted by Pinkerton, a security-service firm, identified workplace violence as the number one security concern of security officials who participated in the study.[32] Many workers are less productive because they fear workplace violence.

Violence in the workplace is often triggered by loss of a job, conflict between the employee and management, or a personal tragedy, such as divorce or separation. Abusive behavior by supervisors and managers is widespread, according to Columbia University psychologist Harvey Hornstein. In his book *Brutal Bosses and Their Prey*, Hornstein says the abusive behavior takes the form of verbal and physical threats, lying, deviousness, and sexual harassment.[33] A rigid, autocratic, impersonal work environment also appears to foster violence. **Workplace violence** encompasses a wide range of behaviors, including hostile remarks, intimidation of another employee by stalking, physical assaults, and threatening phone calls.

Employee Sabotage

Employee sabotage is a problem that is causing nightmares throughout corporate America. It is often described as employee misconduct tinged with an edge of revenge. Employee sabotage may involve deliberate nonperformance, financial fraud, slander, destruction of equipment, arson, or some other act that damages the organization or the careers of people within the organization. Computer crimes have become a common form of sabotage. Computer sabotage by ex-workers is rising.[34]

Sabotage is committed most often by employees who have unresolved grievances, want to advance by making others look less qualified, or want to get even for real or imagined mistreatment. Today, many employees are acting out their anger, rather than discussing it.[35]

Preventing Workplace Violence

The National Safe Workplace Institute estimates that incidents of workplace violence cost employers and others several billion dollars each year. This figure does not, of course, reflect the human suffering caused by acts of violence. Although violence cannot be eliminated, some steps can help curb violent behavior in the workplace.

1. *Use hiring procedures that screen out unstable persons.* In-depth interviews, drug testing, and background checks can help identify signs of a troubled past.

2. *Develop a strategy for responding to incidents before they actually occur.* Establish policies that make it clear that workplace violence incidents will not be tolerated. Every organization should establish a strong expectation of workplace civility. After the Meridian shootings, Lockheed Martin formed a task force on workplace violence. One outcome of this action is a zero-tolerance policy (violators can be fired) for hostile or intimidating speech or actions.[36]

3. *If someone must be demoted, fired, or laid off, do it in a way that does not demoralize the employee.* Some rigid, authoritarian companies handle such personnel actions in a very dehumanizing manner.

4. ***Provide out-placement services for laid-off or terminated employees.*** These services may include development of job-search skills, retraining, or, in cases where the employee is displaying signs of aggression, counseling.

5. ***Establish a systematic way to deal with disgruntled employees.*** Federal Express Corp. developed the Guaranteed Fair Treatment program to provide a forum for employees who feel they have been treated unfairly. (Chapter 13 covers conflict resolution programs in more detail.)

As the workplace gets leaner, it need not become meaner.

6. ***Provide supervisors and managers with training that will help them prevent workplace violence and deal effectively with violence if it does occur.*** Workplace violence is a growing problem in America, but it is not a problem without solutions. As the workplace gets leaner, it need not become meaner.

Emotional Styles

A good starting point for achieving emotional control is to examine your current emotional style. How do you deal with emotions? Your style started taking shape before birth and evolved over a period of many years. As an adult, you are likely to favor one of four different emotional styles when confronted with events that trigger your emotions.

Suppressing Your Emotions

Some people have learned to suppress their feelings as much as possible. They have developed intellectual strategies that enable them to avoid dealing directly with emotional reactions to a situation. In response to the loss of a loved one, a person may avoid the experience of grief and mourning by taking on new responsibilities at work. This is not, of course, a healthy way to deal with grief.

Hale Dwoskin, author of *The Sedona Method*, says suppression is "keeping a lid on our emotions, pushing them back down, denying them, repressing them, and pretending they don't exist."[37] He says habitual suppression is unhealthy and unproductive. Dwoskin says an alternative to inappropriate suppression and expression is releasing emotions, an approach he calls the Sedona Method (see Figure 9.2).

To continually suppress feelings, hide fears, swallow annoyances, and avoid displaying anger is not healthy. If suppressing your feelings becomes a habit, you create opportunities for mental and physical health problems to develop.

Capitulating to Your Emotions

People who display this emotional style see themselves as the helpless victims of feelings over which they have no control. By responding to emotion in this manner, one can assign responsibility for the "problem" to external causes,

FIGURE 9.2 | The Sedona Method

Hale Dwoskin, author of *The Sedona Method* and CEO of Sedona Training Associates *(www.sedonapress.com)*, developed a unique program for making positive changes in your life. He encourages everyone to let go of or release their unwanted emotions. A brief introduction to the process of releasing follows.

Step 1: Focus on an issue you would like to feel better about. You may be experiencing guilt or fear. Allow yourself to feel whatever you are feeling at this moment.
Step 2: Ask yourself one of the following questions:
  • Could I let this feeling go?
  • Could I allow this feeling to be here?
  • Could I welcome this feeling?

Each of these questions points you to the experience of letting go.

Step 3: Ask yourself this basic question: Would I? Am I willing to let go?
Step 4: Ask yourself this simpler question: When?

Dwoskin suggests repeating these four steps as often as needed to feel free of a particular feeling.

Source: Hale Dwoskin, *The Sedona Method* (Sedona, Ariz. Sedona Press 2003), pp. 36–44.

such as other people or unavoidable events. For example, Paula, a busy office manager, is frustrated because her brother-in-law and his wife frequently show up unannounced on weekends and expect a big meal. Paula has a tight schedule during the week, and she looks forward to quiet weekends with her family. She is aware of the anger that builds within her, but tends to blame others (family members) for these feelings. Paula would rather endure feelings of helplessness than find a positive solution to this problem. People who capitulate to their emotions are often overly concerned about the attitudes and opinions of others.[38]

Overexpressing Your Emotions

In a work setting, we need to be seen as responsible and predictable. One of the quickest ways to lose the respect and confidence of the people you work with is to frequently display a lack of emotional control. Frequent use of foul and vulgar language, flared tempers, raised voices, and teary eyes are still regarded as unacceptable behavior by most coworkers and supervisors.

One acceptable way to cope with fear, anger, grief, or jealousy is to sit down with pen and paper and write a letter to the person who triggered these emotions. Don't worry about grammar, spelling, or punctuation—just put all your thoughts on paper. Write until you have nothing more to say. Then destroy the letter. Once you let go of your toxic feelings, you will be ready to deal constructively with whatever caused you to become upset.[39] Another approach is to express your feelings through daily journal entries. Studies indicate that a significant emotional uplift and healing effect can result from spending as little as 5 to 10 minutes a day writing about whatever issues or problems are getting you down.[40]

Accommodating Your Emotions

At the beginning of this chapter we said an emotion can be thought of as a feeling that influences our thinking and behavior. Accommodation means you are willing to recognize, accept, and experience emotions and to attempt to react in ways appropriate to the situation. This style achieves an integration of one's feelings and the thinking process. People who display the accommodation style have adopted the "think before you act" point of view. Let's assume that as you are presenting a new project proposal at a team meeting, someone interrupts you and strongly criticizes your ideas. The criticism seems to be directed more at you than at your proposal. Anger starts building inside you, but before responding to the assailant, you pause and quickly engage in some rational thinking. During the few seconds of silence, you make a mental review of the merits of your proposal and consider the other person's motives for making a personal attack. You decide the person's comments do not warrant a response at this point. Then you continue with your presentation, without a hint of frustration in your voice. If your proposal has merit, the other members of the group will probably speak on your behalf.

Do we always rely on just one of these four emotional styles? Of course not. Your response to news that a coworker is getting a divorce may be very different from your response to a demeaning comment made by your boss. You may have found appropriate ways to deal with your grief but have not yet learned to cope with the fear of making a team presentation. Dealing with our emotions is a very complex process.

SKILL DEVELOPMENT CHALLENGE

Anger builds when we perceive an injustice. Take time to remember a few occasions when someone's behavior triggered a torrent of anger in you. With pen and paper (not your computer), start writing about the reasons for your anger. Keep writing until your feelings become more focused and the reasons for your anger more clear. Keep writing until the anger is fully voiced.

Gender Differences in Emotional Style

Men often complain that women are too emotional. Women often complain that men are too rational and too insensitive to the emotions of others. Although these complaints are not valid in all cases, they can help us understand gender differences in emotional styles.[41] In many families, males are encouraged to hide their feelings, to appear strong and stable. Participation in team sports and work may reinforce this early conditioning. Many women say that men do not take their emotional needs seriously enough and do not respond with support and understanding. Joan Borysenko suggests that men take time to comfort a woman who wants to talk about an important problem and to validate her right to feel her emotions. An appropriate male response in this situation might be nothing more than a sincere acknowledgment of the problem: "Gee, Susan, I can see that you are really upset. Let's talk about the problem." Borysenko suggests that women keep in mind that many men find it difficult to talk about emotions and to display emotions. For example, many men still cling to the notion that crying is not a manly thing to do. A good relationship does not require both people to have the same emotional style, but it does require each person to respect the other person's style.[42]

Strategies for Achieving Emotional Control

Each day we wake up with a certain amount of mental, emotional, and physical energy that we can spend throughout the day. If we allow our "difficult" emotions to deplete our energy, we have no energy to change our life or to give to others.[43] The good news is that we can learn to discipline the mind and banish afflicting thoughts that create needless frustration and waste energy. In this, the final part of the chapter, we share with you some practical suggestions for achieving greater control of the emotions that affect your life.

Identifying Your Emotional Patterns

We could often predict or anticipate our response to various emotions if we would take the time to study our emotional patterns—to take a running inventory of circumstances that touch off jealousy, fear, anger, or some other emotion. Journal entries can help you discover emotional patterns. Record not only your conscious feelings, such as anxiety or guilt, but feelings in your body, such as a knot in your stomach or muscle tension.

If you don't feel comfortable with journal writing, consider setting aside some quiet time to reflect on your emotional patterns. A period of quiet reflection will help you focus your thoughts and impressions. Becoming a skilled observer

© KING FEATURES SYNDICATE.

Becoming a skilled observer of your own emotions is one of the best ways to achieve greater emotional control.

of your own emotions is one of the best ways to achieve greater emotional control.

In addition to journal writing and quiet reflection, there is one more way to discover emotional patterns. At the end of the day, construct a chart of your emotional landscape. Make a chart (see Table 9.1) of the range of emotions you experienced and expressed during the day.[44] Your first entry might be "I woke up at 6:00 a.m. and immediately felt _____." The final entry might be "I left the office at 5:30 p.m. with a feeling of _____." What emotions surfaced throughout your workday? Resentment? Creative joy? Anxiety? Boredom? Contentment? Anger? Reflect on the completed chart and try to determine which patterns need to be changed. For example, you might discover that driving in heavy traffic is a major energy drain. Repeat this process over a period of several days in order to identify your unique emotional patterns.

Fine-Tuning Your Emotional Style

Once you have completed the process of self-examination and have identified some emotional patterns you want to change, it is time to consider ways to fine-tune your emotional style. Bringing about discipline within your mind can help you live a fuller, more satisfying life. Here are four things you can begin doing today.

TABLE 9.1	Charting Your Emotional Landscape	
Time	**Circumstance**	**Emotion**
6:00 a.m.	Alarm goes off. Mind is flooded by thoughts of all the things that must be done during the day.	Anxiety
7:10 a.m.	Depart for work. Heavy traffic interferes with plan to arrive at work early.	Anger and helplessness
8:00 a.m.	Thirty-minute staff meeting scheduled by the boss lasts fifty minutes. No agenda is provided. Entire meeting seems a waste of time.	Anger and frustration
9:35 a.m.	Finally start work on creative project.	Contentment
10:15 a.m.	Progress on project interrupted when coworker enters office, sits down, and starts sharing gossip about another coworker.	Anger and resentment
11:20 a.m.	Progress is made on creative project.	Contentment
1:45 p.m.	Creative project is complete and ready for review.	Joy and contentment
2:50 p.m.	Give project to boss for review. She says she will not be able to provide any feedback until morning. This delay will cause scheduling problems.	Frustration
4:00 p.m.	Attend health insurance update seminar sponsored by human resources department. No major changes are discussed.	Boredom
5:40 p.m.	Give up on a search for a missing document, turn off computer, and walk to parking lot.	Relief and fatigue

GERARD EGAN

AUTHOR, *YOU AND ME*

"It's unfortunate that we're never really taught how to show emotion in ways that help our relationships. Instead, we're usually told what we should not do. However, too little emotion can make our lives seem empty and boring, while too much emotion, poorly expressed, fills our interpersonal lives with conflict and grief. Within reason, some kind of balance in the expression of emotion seems to be called for."

■ *Take responsibility for your emotions.* How you view your emotional difficulties will have a major influence on how you deal with them. If your frustration is triggered by thoughts such as "I can never make my boss happy" or "Things always go wrong in my life," you may never achieve a comfortable emotional state. By shifting the blame to other people and events, you cannot achieve emotional control.

■ *Put your problems into proper perspective.* Why do some people seem to be at peace with themselves most of the time while others seem to be in a perpetual state of anxiety? People who engage in unproductive obsessing are unable or unwilling to look at problems realistically and practically, and they view each disappointment as a major catastrophe. To avoid needless misery, anxiety, and emotional upsets, use an "emotional thermometer" with a scale of 0 to 100. Zero means that everything is going well, and 100 denotes something life-threatening or truly catastrophic. Whenever you feel upset, ask yourself to come up with a logical number on the emotional thermometer. If a problem surfaces that is merely troublesome but not terrible, and you give it 60 points, you are no doubt over reacting. This mental exercise will help you avoid mislabeling a problem and feeling upset as a result.[45]

■ *Take steps to move beyond negative emotions such as envy, anger, jealousy, or hatred.* Some people are upset about things that happened many years ago. Some even nurse grudges against people who have been dead for years. The sad thing is that the negative feelings remain long after we can achieve any positive learning from them.[46] Studies of divorce, for example, indicate that anger and bitterness can linger a long time. Distress seems to peak one year after the divorce, and many people report that it takes at least two years to move past the anger.[47] When negative emotions dominate one's life, whatever the reason, therapy or counseling may provide relief. Learning to release unwanted patterns of behavior is very important.

■ *Give your feelings some exercise.* Several prominent authors in the field of human relations have emphasized the importance of giving our feelings some exercise. Leo Buscaglia, author of *Loving Each Other*, says, "Exercise feelings. Feelings have meaning only as they are expressed in action."[48] Sam Keen, author of *Fire in the Belly,* said, "Make a habit of identifying your feelings and expressing them in some appropriate way."[49] If you have offended someone, how about sending that person a note expressing regret? If someone you work with has given extra effort, why not praise that person's work? Make a decision to cultivate positive mental states like kindness and compassion. A sincere feeling of empathy, for example, will deepen your connection to others.

Every day of our personal and work life we face some difficult decisions. One option is to take only actions that feel good at the moment. In some cases, this means ignoring the feelings of customers, patients, coworkers, and supervisors. Another option is to behave in a manner that is acceptable to the people around you. If you choose this option, you will have to make some sacrifices. You may have to be warm and generous when the feelings inside you say, "Be cold and selfish." You may have to avoid an argument when your feelings are insisting, "I'm right and the other person is wrong!" To achieve a positive emotional state often requires restructuring our ways of feeling, thinking, and behaving.

● LOOKING BACK: Reviewing the Concepts

■ Describe how emotions influence our thinking and behavior.

We carry inside us a vast array of emotions that can help us cope with our environment. An emotion can be thought of as a feeling that influences our thinking and behavior. Feelings are activated by a variety of events. Angry feelings may surface when another employee borrows something without your permission. Feelings of grief will very likely follow the loss of a close friend.

■ Understand the factors that contribute to emotional balance.

The need to discover ways to achieve emotional balance has never been greater. We sometimes suffer from a lack of emotional balance because we learn to inhibit the expression of certain emotions and to overemphasize the expression of others. The study of emotional intelligence has helped us discover ways to achieve emotional balance.

■ Explain the critical role of emotions in the workplace.

Emotions play a critical role in the success of every organization. Emotional undercurrents are present in almost every area of the organization, and they influence employee morale, customer loyalty, and productivity.

■ Describe the major factors that influence our emotional development.

Our emotional development is influenced by temperament (the biological shaper of personality), our unconscious mind, and cultural conditioning. These influences contribute to the development of our emotional intelligence. Throughout the long process of emotional development, we learn different ways to express our emotions.

■ Learn how to deal with your anger and the anger of others.

Appropriate expressions of anger contribute to improved interpersonal relations, help us reduce anxiety, and give us an outlet for unhealthy stress. We must also learn how to handle other people's anger. It takes a great deal of effort to learn how to deal with our own anger and the anger of others.

■ Understand the factors that contribute to workplace violence.

Workplace violence encompasses a wide range of activities, including homicides, hostile remarks, physical assaults, and sabotage directed toward the employer or other workers. Although violence cannot be eliminated, steps can be taken to curb violent employee behavior in the workplace.

■ Identify and explain the most common emotional styles.

To achieve emotional balance, we need to start with an examination of our current emotional style. When confronted by strong feelings, we are likely to display one of four different emotional styles: suppressing emotions, capitulating to them, overexpressing them, or accommodating them. Researchers suggest that there are gender differences in emotional style.

■ Describe strategies for achieving emotional control.

Emotional control is an important dimension of emotional style. The starting point in developing emotional control is to identify your current emotional patterns. One way to do this is to record your anger experiences in a diary or journal. Additional ways to identify emotional patterns include setting aside time for quiet reflection and developing a chart of your emotional landscape.

● Career Corner

Q: When I started working for this company, I was never put in a situation where it was necessary to make presentations to others. After receiving a promotion to department head, I was expected to make monthly reports to my staff. I never feel comfortable in the role of group presenter. Hours before the monthly meeting I start feeling tense, and by the time the meeting begins I am gripped by fear. Two weeks ago, my boss asked me to make a presentation to senior management. Shortly before the meeting I started experiencing chest pain, sweating, and trembling. I told my boss I was sick and went home. Why am I so frightened of speaking to a group? Should I seek professional help?

A: It appears that you may have developed a social phobia. Social phobias are fears of situations in which the person can be watched by others. Phobias of various types are quite common—they currently afflict over 11 million Americans. Your problem could be serious, and you might consider seeking help from a qualified therapist. Psychotherapy can result in greater self-understanding and self-expression. Throughout the treatment you will learn new ways to cope with your problem. It is encouraging to note that about 80 percent of psychotherapy patients benefit from treatment.

Key Terms

emotion   Transactional Analysis
emotional intelligence   anger
temperament   workplace violence
unconscious mind

Applying What You Have Learned

1. Recall the last time you were angry at another person or were a victim of a situation that made you angry. For example, perhaps a housemate or roommate refused to pay her share of the grocery bill, or your manager accused you of wrongdoing without knowing all the facts. Then answer the following questions:

   a. Did you express your anger verbally? Physically?

   b. Did you suppress any of your anger? Explain.

   c. What results did you experience from the way you handled this situation? Describe both positive and negative results.

   d. If you could relive the situation, would you do anything differently? Explain.

2. To learn more about the way you handle anger, record your anger responses in a journal for a period of five days. When anger surfaces, record as many details as possible. What triggered your anger? How intense was the anger? How long did your angry feelings last? Did you express them to anyone? At the end of the five days, study your entries and try to determine whether any patterns exist. If you find this activity helpful, consider keeping a journal for a longer period of time.

3. To learn more about how emotions influence your thinking and behavior, complete each of the following sentences. Once you have completed them all, reflect on your written responses. Can you identify any changes you would like to make in your emotional style?

   a. "When someone makes me angry, I usually . . ."

   b. "The most common worry in my life is . . ."

   c. "When I feel compassion for someone, my response is to . . ."

   d. "My response to feelings of grief is . . ."

   e. "When I am jealous of someone, my response is to . . ."

 Internet Insights

Many people have an anger management problem. Although anger is a natural human emotion, the mismanagement of anger can result in serious inter-personal relations problems. Help with anger management is as close as your computer. The American Psychological Association has a webpage on "Controlling Anger—Before It Controls You." The address is *www.apa.org/pubinfo/anger.html*.

Visit this site and prepare a written summary of the information presented. If you wish to study anger management in greater detail, visit *www.angermgmt.com* or *www.angermgt.com*.

 Role-Play Exercise

You are currently manager of a bank branch that employs twenty-six people. About three weeks ago you learned that one of your employees, Wesla Perez, needed time off to spend with a parent who was very ill. You approved the time off without hesitation. Soon, you learned that the parent (mother) had died. On Monday morning Wesla will return to work. You plan to meet with Wesla and express your condolences. In this role-play exercise, a member of your class will play the role of Wesla Perez. The name you will use during the role-play is Evony Hillison.

Case 9.1   Romance at Work

Romance at work has become more common in recent years, but some relationships do have unintended consequences. Harry Stonecipher, Boeing Company's former president and CEO, lost his job when the board of directors learned (from an anonymous message) about his consensual extramarital affair with a female executive. Consensual romances at work are not unlawful and are tolerated far more today than they were in the past. So why did Stonecipher lose his job? Boeing's code of conduct prohibits behavior that may embarrass the company.

Today, men and women often work alongside each other in almost equal numbers, sharing long hours and job pressures. Although romance at work is more acceptable today, it is still viewed as a major productivity disrupter by many consultants, human-resource professionals, and executives. The president of a consulting business tells of a female employee in her office who broke off a relationship with a fellow worker. The spurned man began stalking the woman, who discussed her fears and anger openly with other employees. They, in turn, spent time on the job trying to advise and comfort her. Other critics of romance at work say companies should be concerned when relationships create conflicts of interest and lower job performance. The use of pet names, kissing, and hand-holding can be distracting to other workers.

Although critics of romance at work make some valid points, the truth is corporate America is getting more comfortable with love in the workplace. In fact, 67 percent of the respondents to a 2003 survey on romance at work by the American Management Association said they approved of dating by coworkers. Dennis Powers, author of *The Office Romance*, feels that companies need to lighten up in their attitudes about romance at work. He says that most of these romances have no detrimental effect on the workplace or on workers. However, he does feel that supervisors need to know how to ease conflict when a failed romance invades the workplace.[50]

Questions

1. Is an office romance likely to affect the productivity of the two workers involved? Is it likely to affect the people who work with them?

2. Should organizations establish policies that prevent dating a coworker? A supervisor? Explain your answer.

3. Can you think of a situation where employment of married couples would create problems for a firm? Explain your answer.

Case 9.2   Coping with Grief

Grief over losing a loved one is one of the most difficult personal problems to discuss at work. Many of the estimated 4 million workers who are bereaved each year keep their grief a secret on the job. Bill Foote, CEO of USG Corporation, is an exception. Foote was promoted to the top position at USG one month before his wife, an accomplished attorney and the mother of three young daughters, died of breast cancer. Talking about his grief at work was not easy. He finally decided that hiding it would violate the leadership principles that guided him each day. He believes that building teamwork requires being open and honest about weaknesses as well as strengths.

Foote opened his first speech as CEO to 150 USG managers by talking about his loss and the spiritual lessons he had learned. Life is precious and fleeting, he told the group; live in the moment, and simplify your days to make time for what really matters. At one point he paused, struggling to contain his emotion. Some crusty USG veterans wiped away tears. The response to Foote's presentation was strengthened commitment to the new CEO and a renewed sense of the corporate value placed on family. One senior executive said the thinking among the managers after the presentation was clear: "If we have to go through a few walls for this guy, we're going to do it."

Dealing with grief at work can be very difficult, especially when the work environment is cold and indifferent to a grieving employee. Deborah DeVito met her brother's flight at the Albuquerque airport and walked with him to the baggage claim area. Suddenly he grew dizzy, then incoherent. A few hours later he was dead. The shock of his death was overwhelming, and DeVito struggled at work. She took five days off to arrange and attend her brother's funeral. When she requested an additional day to attend a memorial service for her brother, her boss denied her request. He then scolded her for missing an important teleconference. Once Ms. DeVito returned to work she felt "ready to explode" with grief.

Unsympathetic bosses often prolong the grieving process. An environmental specialist missed his father's funeral because he was working overseas. Depressed, he requested family leave to recover and set his mother's affairs in order. His boss refused to approve the request. His work soon deteriorated, and after a few months he was forced to resign.

Psychologists note that grieving is unpredictable and takes varying amounts of time. Unresolved grief can result in depression and lost productivity. Workplace grief, according to research conducted by the Grief Recovery Institute, costs U.S. businesses about $75 billion a year in reduced productivity, increased errors, and accidents. Sources of grief range from miscarriages to divorce. Managers and coworkers often do not know how to respond to grief. Workplace attitudes toward grief, in many organizations, seem to be stuck in the workplace practices common during the industrial age.[51]

Questions

1. Work/life specialists say that employers have much to gain from responding to grief with care and compassion. Do you agree?

2. Pitney Bowes provides its employees with a copy of a book entitled *One More Star in Heaven Now*. It describes how to help both bereaved employees and coworkers who may not know what to say to them. Is this a good use of company resources? Explain.

3. What information presented in this chapter would be helpful to someone who is trying to cope with the emotion of grief?

INTEGRATED RESOURCES

CLASSROOM ACTIVITIES (*college.hmco.com/pic/reece10e*)

The Bright Light of Hindsight
Accelerated Learning
Journal Entry: Emotional Control Inventory

business.college.hmco.com/students

ACE

Self-tests

10

BUILDING STRONGER RELATIONSHIPS WITH POSITIVE ENERGY

Chapter Preview

After studying this chapter, you will be able to

- Describe how positive energy contributes to improved interpersonal relationships.

- Create awareness of the strong need people have for encouragement and positive feedback.

- Understand how to use positive reinforcement to improve relationships and reward behavior.

- Describe the major barriers to the use of positive reinforcement.

- Explain how to reward individual and team performance.

The muted cry of frustration surfaced on page five of Mike Trippani's performance evaluation. In the self-appraisal section, he voiced concern that he might not be able to advance in the company. Someone else had recently become director of the Network Operations Center (NOC) where Trippani worked. Arunas Chesonis, CEO of PaeTec Communications, reviewed the performance evaluation form and then decided to visit with Trippani. "What is this crap?" Chesonis asked him. "You're one of the keys to future growth. You have a future here." It was just the message Trippani needed. A personal visit from the CEO proved to be a powerful form of recognition.

Visits from the CEO are not uncommon at PaeTec, a fast growing communications company located near Rochester, New York (paetec.com). Everything at PaeTec revolves around respect for the employee. Chesonis realizes that modest forms of recognition often have the greatest impact. He writes short thank-you notes, sends e-mail, and sticks his head through the door to say thanks for a job well done. He wants everyone in the organization, regardless of position, to relate to one another as equals. PaeTec Communications is also a company that honors family life. Every effort is made to reduce the barriers between work and home.

The core team that founded PaeTec realized from day one that when you put employees first, the customer wins. Worker contentment is an important key to excellence in customer service. The founders created an organizational culture (see Figure 10.1) that emphasizes cooperation, information sharing, and mutual respect.

Most of the over 1,000 employees realize that they are working at a unique place where an unusual kind of goodwill flows down from the top and then rises back up from the bottom.[1]

Arunas Chesonis, CEO of PaeTec Communications, knows that happiness pays. Chesonis is seen here talking to his employees. He realizes that even modest forms of recognition can have a great deal of impact. He enjoys writing short thank-you notes to deserving employees.

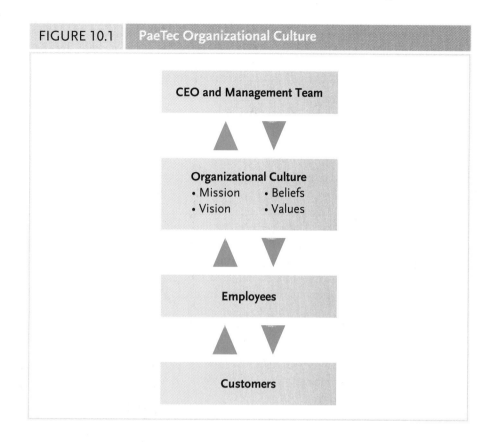

FIGURE 10.1 PaeTec Organizational Culture

This chapter discusses the impact of positive energy on both individual and group behavior. **Energy** can be defined as the capacity for work, or the force that helps us do things with vitality and intensity. The chapter examines the importance of encouragement, the power of positive feedback, various types of positive reinforcement, and the reasons why many people have difficulty expressing positive thoughts and feelings. A section of the chapter is devoted to awards and incentive programs that a variety of organizations use.

How Positive Energy Contributes to Improved Interpersonal Relationships

It is positive energy that helps us cope with disappointments, uncertainty, and work that is physically and mentally demanding.

Throughout periods of great uncertainty and turbulence, negative energy can become a powerful force. Many people go to work everyday wondering if they will be the next victim of a merger, buyout, downsizing effort, or business closing. Some wonder if they will be able to cope with rapid technological changes. Stressful working conditions caused by rising productivity demands and long hours can also be the source of negative energy. In a negative, stressful work climate, these pressures often result in physical fatigue, decreased optimism, and lower morale. A positive work climate is more likely to instill workers with positive energy, which results in greater strength of will, increased optimism, and higher employee productivity.

It is positive energy that helps us cope with disappointments, uncertainty, and work that is physically and mentally demanding. In the presence of positive energy people feel uplifted, encouraged, and empowered. Positive energy helps us remain balanced in a work environment that is increasingly characterized by change and uncertainty.

Energy: An Important Force in Our Lives

Judith Orloff, author of *Positive Energy* and pioneer in the field of energy psychiatry, says *energy* is a term with many intriguing dimensions. In basic terms, it is the "get-up-and-go," the stamina that gets you through the day. Energy comes to us from food, exercise, sleep, and subtle forces that penetrate and surround our bodies. Envision energy as having one of two qualities: either positive or negative. Positive energy is supportive, loving, and nurturing. Negative energy is fearful, judgmental, and depleting. How you respond to people and places determines, to a large degree, your energy level. Dr. Orloff makes an interesting observation regarding the impact of relationships on our energy level: "Each millisecond of our relationships is governed by a give and take of energy. Some people make us more electric or at ease. Others suck the life right out of us."[2]

Actions and Events That Create Positive Energy

In the age of information, organizations need to discover creative ways to generate positive energy. Progressive companies find ways to frequently encourage, recognize, and reward employees. Consider the following examples:

"THEY SAVE ALL OF THEIR ENERGY FOR QUITTING TIME."

©2006. Reprinted courtesy of Bunny Hoest and *Parade* Magazine.

■ Great Plains Software puts people first, and the result is a very low turnover rate of 5 percent—far below the information technology industry average, which ranges from 18 to 25 percent. The company gives employees ownership at every level and provides a wide range of personal development opportunities. Employees praise the company's commitment to work/life balance.[3]

■ Stew Leonard's is a highly successful supermarket that offers groceries and an entertaining shopping experience. Roy Snider is the supermarket chain's official pep rally cheerleader. His title is Director of Wow, and he's responsible for boosting employee morale and building team spirit. Stop at Stew Leonard's and you might see Snider dancing with a customer or singing happy birthday to an employee.[4]

This is a very small sample of actions and events that can generate positive energy. Throughout the remainder of this chapter we will discuss how basic courtesy, positive written communication, encouragement, and various forms of positive reinforcement can be used to "accentuate the positive."

Our Need for Positive Experiences

Psychologist William James believed that the craving to be appreciated is a basic principle of human nature.

How strong is the need for positive experiences in our life? Psychologist William James believed that the craving to be appreciated is a basic principle of human nature. Mark Twain, the noted author, answered the question by saying he could live for three weeks on a compliment. Twain was willing to admit openly what most people feel inside. Many of us have a deep desire for personal recognition in one form or another but almost never verbalize these thoughts.

Few people have the strength of ego to maintain high self-esteem without encouragement and positive feedback from others. We often are not certain we have performed well until some other person tells us. Kenneth Blanchard and Spencer Johnson, authors of *The One Minute Manager*, stress the importance of "catching people doing things right" and engaging in "one minute praisings."[5] Without positive experiences, we often suffer from an energy deficit.

Support from Maslow

The hierarchy of needs developed by Abraham Maslow (discussed in Chapter 7) provides additional support for positive experiences. In part, the need for security (a second-level need) is satisfied by positive feedback from a supervisor, manager, coworker, or friend. You are likely to feel more secure when someone recognizes your accomplishments. A feeling of belonging (a third-level need) can be satisfied by actions that communicate the message "You are part of the team." Maslow states that as each lower-level need is satisfied, the need at the next level demands attention. It would seem to be almost impossible to satisfy the esteem needs (fourth level) without positive feedback and reinforcement. A person's level of self-esteem may diminish in a work environment where accomplishments receive little or no recognition.

Support from Skinner

The research of B. F. Skinner at Harvard University has contributed to our understanding of reinforcement as a factor influencing the behavior of people in a work setting. Skinner maintained that any living organism will tend to repeat a particular behavior if that behavior is accompanied or followed by a reinforcer. A **reinforcer** is any stimulus that follows a response and increases the probability that the response will occur again.[6] Skinner also demonstrated that the timing of reinforcement has an important effect on behavior change. He discovered that if the delay between a response (behavior) and its reinforcement is too great, a change in behavior is less likely to take place.

Support from Berne

In Chapter 9, you were given a brief introduction to Transactional Analysis (TA), a theory of communication developed by Eric Berne. TA is a simplified explanation of how people communicate. Berne's research also provided evidence that most people have a strong need for recognition, or "strokes."

The word *stroking* is used to describe the various forms of recognition one person gives another. Strokes help satisfy the need to be appreciated. A **physical stroke** may be a pat on the back or a smile that communicates approval. **Verbal strokes** include words of praise and expressions of gratitude.

Berne said that stroking is necessary for physical and mental health. He believed, as do others, that infants who are deprived of physical strokes (hugs, caresses, and kisses) begin to lose their will to live. As people grow into adulthood, they are willing to substitute verbal stroking for physical stroking. Adults still need and want physical stroking, but they will settle for words of praise, positive feedback, awards, and other forms of recognition.

TOTAL	**JACK CANFIELD**
PERSON	AUTHOR, *THE SUCCESS PRINCIPLES*
INSIGHT	"Successful people speak words of inclusion rather than words of separation, words of acceptance rather than words of rejection, and words of tolerance rather than words of prejudice."

Positive Reinforcement—Creating Positive Energy

In recent years, researchers have quantified the cost of negativity in the workplace, and the results are quite shocking. Negative, or "actively disengaged," workers cost the U.S. economy between $250 and $300 billion a year according to the Gallup International Research and Education Center. The costs associated with negativity are even higher when you add on the expenses associated with employee turnover, absenteeism, fraud, and workplace injuries.[7] The good news is that organizations such as PaeTec Communications, Great Plains Software, and Stew Leonard's have found ways to neutralize and even reverse damaging negativity.

Bob Nelson, author of *1001 Ways to Reward Employees*, provides us with numerous ways to provide praise, recognition, and rewards. If you are not sure what to say or do, check out this important book.

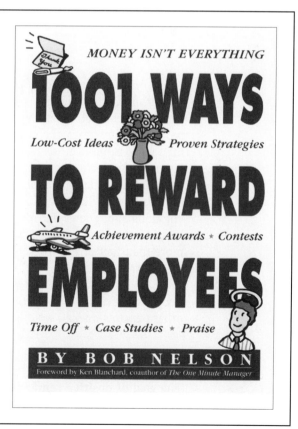

FIGURE 10.2 | How Full Is Your Bucket?

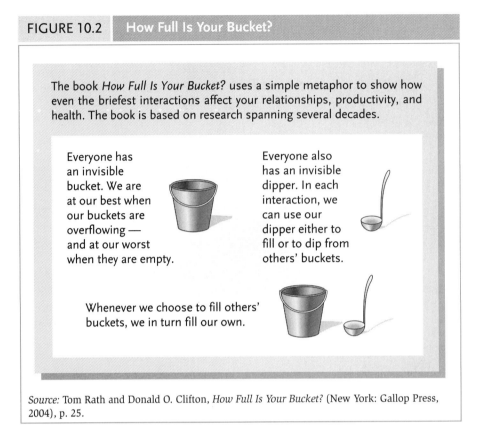

The book *How Full Is Your Bucket?* uses a simple metaphor to show how even the briefest interactions affect your relationships, productivity, and health. The book is based on research spanning several decades.

Everyone has an invisible bucket. We are at our best when our buckets are overflowing — and at our worst when they are empty.

Everyone also has an invisible dipper. In each interaction, we can use our dipper either to fill or to dip from others' buckets.

Whenever we choose to fill others' buckets, we in turn fill our own.

Source: Tom Rath and Donald O. Clifton, *How Full Is Your Bucket?* (New York: Gallop Press, 2004), p. 25.

A brief book entitled *How Full Is Your Bucket?* (*www.bucketbook.com*), written by Gallup Practice Leaders Tom Rath and Donald Clifton, provides a simple yet compelling strategy for reducing negativity in the workplace. After more than fifty years of comprehensive psychological and workplace research, they were inspired to develop the Theory of the Dipper and the Bucket (see Figure 10.2). According to Rath and Clifton, each of us has an invisible bucket. It is constantly being emptied or filled, depending on what others say or do to us. When our bucket is full, we feel great. A full bucket increases our positive emotions and renews our energy. When it is empty, we feel awful: There are a lot of empty buckets in today's work force. Survey after survey has found that more than half of the workers in America say they do not feel appreciated in their current jobs.[8]

Each of us also has an invisible dipper. We can use that dipper to fill other people's buckets or our own bucket. When we use that dipper to dip from another person's bucket, we diminish that person and ourselves.

Positive Reinforcement Defined

The goal of **positive reinforcement** is to encourage productive behaviors. At PaeTec Communications, information sharing between both individuals and departments is a major key to the company's success. Arunas Chesonis, CEO, sets an example for every employee by sharing financial information, acquisition plans, profits, and other information usually discussed only in the boardroom. He answers e-mails from every employee and expects everyone else to do the same. He rewards information sharing with personal thank-you notes, e-mails, and visits. This pattern is followed in other important areas such as customer service and honoring family life.

Positive reinforcement has never been more important than it is today. Large numbers of workers at all levels of organizations encounter energy-draining experiences at work and in their personal lives. Positive energy is an important form of life enrichment. As we will see in the remaining pages of this chapter, positive reinforcement is an easy to use, inexpensive, and effective way to generate positive energy in the workplace.[9]

CRITICAL THINKING CHALLENGE

Throughout life we form habits that can have a major impact on our ability to develop positive relationships with others. Take a few minutes and reflect on the dipper and bucket metaphor. Do you find it easy or difficult to fill someone else's bucket? Your own bucket? Do you frequently dip from others' buckets?

The Power of Praise

As we have noted, today's workplace is characterized by a recognition deficit. Millions of workers are seeking an answer to the same question: How well am I doing? Praise, in its many forms, can help answer this question.

Giving praise is one of the easiest and most powerful ways to make an employee feel important and needed. A person who receives praise knows that his or her work is not being taken for granted. When handled correctly, praise can be an effective reinforcement strategy that ensures repetition of desired behaviors. The authors of *The One Minute Manager*, a book that has sold more than 12 million copies, point out that praising others need not take a great deal of time. The key is to pay attention to what others are doing and try not to miss an opportunity to use praise to generate positive energy. Table 10.1 provides some excellent tips on planning and delivering praise.

Courtesy Can Be Contagious

The poet Alfred Tennyson once said, "The greater the man, the greater the courtesy." Courtesy means being considerate of others in small ways, showing respect for what others revere, and treating everyone, regardless of position, with consideration. In today's fast-paced world, the impact of courtesy can easily be overlooked. Rudeness flourishes in our society, so it is not surprising that common courtesies are sometimes forgotten. Someone arrives late for an important meeting, but does not see the need to apologize or even explain why he is late. You schedule an important meeting with a coworker, and suddenly

TABLE 10.1	One-Minute Praisings

The one-minute praising works well, say authors Kenneth Blanchard and Spencer Johnson, when you

1. Tell people up front that you are going to let them know how they are doing.
2. Praise people immediately.
3. Tell them what they did right—be specific.
4. Tell them how good you feel about what they did right and how it helps the organization and others who work there.
5. Stop for a moment of silence to let them feel how good you feel.
6. Encourage them to do more of the same.
7. Shake hands or touch people in a way that makes it clear that you support their success in the organization.

Source: The One Minute Manager by Kenneth Blanchard, PhD, and Spencer Johnson, MD. Copyright © 1981, 1982 by the Blanchard Family Partnership and Candle Communications Corporation, Inc. Reprinted by permission of HarperCollins Publishers, Inc.

she is talking to a friend on her cell phone. Common courtesy dictates that you turn off interruptive devices.

Saying "thank you" to someone who has been helpful to you is another important courtesy. Most people respond positively to notes and letters that express appreciation. (See Figure 10.3). Unfortunately, this positive gesture is used all too infrequently. Handwritten notes are especially rare today.

Active Listening

As discussed in Chapter 2, everyone feels a sense of personal value when speaking with a good listener. Active listening can be a powerful reinforcer. Active listening is the process of sending back to the speaker what you as a listener think the speaker meant in terms of both content and feelings.

People long for more authentic interactions with coworkers or bosses who are good listeners. *Dialogue* as a specific practice is being implemented in a number of progressive organizations. A *dialogue group* is a meeting where everyone agrees to be especially aware of what they say, how well they listen, and how well they give feedback to others. This training activity is designed to promote self-reflection and increased self-awareness.[10]

Pride as a Source of Positive Energy

Pride is the emotional high that follows performance and success. This definition was developed by Jon Katzenbach, author of *Why Pride Matters More Than Money*. He notes that the power of pride is obvious when you observe the high-performing work forces at Southwest Airlines, Marriott, the U.S. Marine

FIGURE 10.3	Congratulatory Letter Reinforcing Desirable Behavior

Infra-Dynamics, Inc.

Binghamton Houston Palo Alto

May 19, 2007

Ms. Patty Rodriguez, Manager
Process Control Division
Plant Number Five
126 James Avenue
Binghamton, NY 13901

Dear Patty:

Once again it gives me great pleasure to recognize you and your staff
for outstanding performance in the area of safety. You folks have
maintained a perfect record throughout the past twelve months.

Congratulations to you and all your employees for your contributions
to this important job responsibility. All of us here at the home office
are proud of you. Keep up the good work!

Sincerely,

Ralph Plazio
Vice President
Production and Quality Control

RP:br

Corps, and Microsoft. "Pride is a natural by-product of the successes of those organizations," says Katzenbach.[11]

Southwest Airlines Company was founded by Herb Kelleher (now retired). Over the years, he developed a culture that other airlines envy. By almost every measure of efficiency in the airline industry, Southwest is at the top of the charts. Kelleher's dedication to his employees was a major reason for the success of this company. The high level of employee moral at Southwest supports excellence in customer service.

Katzenbach notes that pride-builders can be found at all levels of the organization. They often get involved in the everyday problems of their employees. Roy Pelaez leads a work force of 426 people who clean airplanes for Delta Airlines and Southwest Airlines. Many of his staff are recent immigrants, so he brought in an English-language teacher to tutor employees twice a week on their own time. He scheduled Friday citizenship classes to help employees become

U.S. citizens. To help single mothers, Pelaez arranged for certified babysitters subsidized by government programs.[12]

Barriers to Positive Reinforcement

The material in this chapter is based on two indisputable facts about human nature. First, people want to know how well they are doing and if their efforts are satisfactory. Second, they appreciate recognition for their accomplishments. Performance feedback, encouragement, and positive reinforcement can satisfy these important human needs. People often say they prefer negative feedback to no feedback at all. "Don't leave me in the dark" is a common plea (spoken or unspoken) of most people.

SKILL DEVELOPMENT CHALLENGE

Chances are you owe somebody a thank-you note. Think about the events of the past six months. Has someone given time and effort to assist you with a problem? Make a list of at least three people who deserve a thank-you note. Pick one, write that person a note of appreciation, and mail it today.

Preoccupation with Self

One of the major obstacles to providing positive reinforcement is preoccupation with self. The term **narcissism** is often used to describe this human condition. Narcissism is a Freudian term alluding to the mythical youth who wore himself out trying to kiss his own reflection in a pool of water.

Deepak Chopra, author of *The Seven Spiritual Laws of Success,* encourages everyone to practice the "Law of Giving." This law states that you must give in order to receive. If you want attention and appreciation, you must learn to give attention and appreciation. If you want joy in your life, give joy to others. He says the easiest way to get what you want is to help others get what they want.[13] Put another way, when you do good for another person, you do good for yourself.

The publication of *Random Acts of Kindness* and many people's acceptance of its central theme may have signaled a movement away

> *If you want attention and appreciation, you must learn to give attention and appreciation.*

TOTAL	**MALCOLM BOYD**
PERSON	EPISCOPAL PRIEST; AUTHOR, *VOLUNTEERING THANKS*
INSIGHT	"Feeling grateful is good for us. Gratitude is the opposite of the qualities of self-centeredness, indifference, and arrogance. Expressing gratitude affords each of us unique opportunities to reach out in love and share happiness. Saying thank you is a very positive thing to do."

from self-preoccupation. Random acts of kindness are those little things that we do for others that have no payback. They involve giving freely, purely, for no reason.[14] Here are some examples from the book:

■ Send a letter to a teacher you once had letting him or her know about the difference he or she made in your life.

■ Write a card thanking a service person for his or her care and leave it with your tip.

Misconceptions About Positive Reinforcement

Some people fail to use positive reinforcement because they have misconceptions about this human relations strategy. One misconception is that people will respond to positive feedback by demanding tangible evidence of appreciation. "Tell people they are doing a good job and they will ask for a raise" seems to be the attitude of some managers. Actually, just the opposite response will surface more often than not. In the absence of intangible rewards (such as praise), workers may demand greater tangible rewards.

A few managers seem to feel they will lose some of their power or control if they praise workers. Yet if managers rely on power alone to get the job done, any success they achieve will no doubt be short-lived.

The "Too Busy" Syndrome

Ken Blanchard, noted author and consultant, says, "We're often too busy or too stressed to remember that the recognition we crave, others crave as well."[15] When you are under a great deal of pressure to get your work done, and you are struggling to achieve some degree of work/life balance, it's easy to postpone sending a thank-you note or contacting someone simply for the purpose of saying, "Thank you."

The key to solving this problem is planning. A consciously planned positive reinforcement program will ensure that recognition for work well done is not overlooked. One approach might be to set aside a few minutes each day to work on performance feedback and positive reinforcement activities (see Table 10.1).

Failing to Identify Commendable Actions

There are numerous opportunities to recognize the people you work with. By exercising just a little creativity, you can discover many actions that deserve to be commended.

Assume you are the manager of a large auto dealership. One of the key people within your organization is the service manager. This person schedules work to be performed on customers' cars, handles customer complaints, supervises the technicians, and performs a host of other duties. If you want to give your service manager performance feedback and positive recognition, what types of behavior can you praise? Table 10.2 lists some examples.

TABLE 10.2	Job Performance Behaviors to Be Reinforced

1. Performance Related to Interpersonal Relations
   a. Demonstrates empathy for customer needs and problems
   b. Is able to handle customer complaints effectively
   c. Is able to keep all employees well informed
   d. Cooperates with supervisory personnel in other departments
   e. Recognizes the accomplishments of employees
   f. Exhibits effective supervision of employees

2. Personal Characteristics
   a. Is honest in dealings with people throughout the organization
   b. Is punctual
   c. Does not violate policies and procedures
   d. Maintains emotional stability
   e. Maintains a neat appearance
   f. Is alert to new ways to do the job better

3. Management Skills
   a. Avoids waste in the use of supplies and materials
   b. Maintains accurate records
   c. Spends time on short- and long-range planning
   d. Takes steps to prevent accidents
   e. Delegates authority and responsibility
   f. Maintains quality-control standards

Not Knowing What to Say or Do

Bob Nelson, author of *1001 Ways to Reward Employees,* reminds us that we can provide encouragement, praise, recognition, and rewards in a variety of ways. He encourages us to use thoughtful, personal kinds of recognition that signify true appreciation.[16] Many words and phrases can communicate approval. Here are several examples:

- "Good thinking!"
- "Excellent idea."
- "Thank you."
- "Keep up the good work."

Rich DeVos, cofounder of Amway Corporation, says there are several phrases that can be used every day to enrich your life and the lives of other people. Here are six of his favorites:[17]

- "I'm wrong."
- "I'm sorry."
- "I need you."
- "Thank you."
- "I'm proud of you."
- "I love you."

And you can give recognition to others through some type of action. Here are some activities that show approval:

- Sending an employee to a workshop or seminar that covers a topic he or she is interested in

- Asking for advice

- Asking someone to demonstrate the correct performance or procedure for others

- Displaying another person's work, or discussing another person's ideas

- Recognizing someone's work at a staff meeting

It should not be surprising that some people view praise or recognition with some degree of apprehension. This is especially true in a work environment where the level of trust is low. Positive reinforcement must be sincere. Tim Sanders, one of America's most compassionate business leaders, says, "People hold you in the highest esteem when they realize you have no expectations that you will receive anything in return for what you are willing to give."[18]

Rewarding Individual and Team Performance

In recent years we have seen expanded use of positive reinforcement strategies in the workplace. In the past we viewed positive reinforcement as the responsibility of supervisors and managers. This view was much too narrow. As shown in Figure 10.4, everyone in the organization has opportunities to recognize the accomplishments of others. Persons in supervisory and management positions can benefit from positive reinforcement initiated by subordinates.

Employees can also be encouraged to recognize the accomplishments of coworkers. In some cases, praise from a respected colleague is more important than praise from the boss. This is especially true when employees work together on a team.

The concept of teamwork and the growing popularity of various types of teams are changing the way companies structure their reward systems. If a work force is reorganized into self-directed work teams (discussed in Chapter 12), it makes sense to consider various types of team recognition plans. Such plans often emphasize the recognition of group performance rather than the recognition of individual performance.

Incentive Programs

Every year organizations spend billions of dollars for incentives and awards given to their employees. This money is spent on color TVs, vacation trips, rings, plaques, pins, certificates, stock options, merit pay, cash bonuses, and a

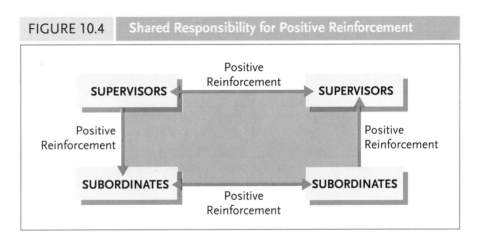

FIGURE 10.4 **Shared Responsibility for Positive Reinforcement**

host of other items. An **incentive program** is a planned activity designed to motivate employees to achieve an organizational objective.[19] The objective may be increasing quality, improving sales, ensuring safety, decreasing absenteeism, fostering teamwork, rewarding participation in wellness programs, or improving customer service.

One of the most widespread developments in recent years has been the introduction of innovative incentive plans that reward increased productivity, improved quality, improved customer service, lower operating costs, or some combination of these factors. These plans include cash and noncash awards. The most common noncash awards include merchandise, travel opportunities, and recognition in the form of a plaque, trophy, pin, or letter of commendation. Noncash awards offer some advantages over cash awards, particularly "memory value." A weekend at a luxury hotel, valued at $500, is likely to make a more lasting impression on the recipient than a $500 cash bonus. Noncash awards also have "trophy value." A high-quality gold pen or leather attaché case can be displayed and admired like a trophy.[20] Despite these advantages, many companies find that cash awards are needed to get employees to exert continuous effort. Table 10.3 provides a brief description of common incentive programs involving cash payments.

Criticisms of Incentive Programs

Although the vast majority of U.S. companies use some type of incentive program based on cash or noncash rewards, the practice is not without its critics. One of the foremost critics of incentive programs is Alfie Kohn, author of *No Contest: The Case Against Competition* and *Punished by Rewards: The Trouble*

TABLE 10.3	Common Incentive Programs Involving Cash Payments
Type of Program	**Description**
Gain sharing	Managers and employees develop methods of increasing productivity, improving quality, and/or cutting costs. When a unit betters a predetermined performance objective, the resulting financial gains are divided according to a formula.
Profit sharing	Each employee receives a share of the company's profits, paid in cash or put in a retirement fund.
Production incentives	Employees receive payments based on how well they perform in relation to established standards. In a factory setting, for example, the rewards are often based on piecework. For each acceptable piece they produce, workers receive a specific payment.
Pay for knowledge	Workers are paid for the skills they master or tasks they perform. This plan is often used by companies that want employees to be able to perform more than one job.
Suggestion program	Employees who suggest ways to improve company operations receive a monetary award. The amount of the award is based on the estimated value of resulting increases in efficiency or cost cutting.

There is no firm basis for the assumption that paying people more will encourage them to do better work or even, in the long run, more work.

with Gold Stars, Incentive Plans, A's, Praise, and Other Bribes. Kohn states that reward systems often fail for these reasons:

1. *Pay is not an effective motivator.* Citing research by Frederick Herzberg and others, Kohn argues, "There is no firm basis for the assumption that paying people more will encourage them to do better work or even, in the long run, more work."[21]

2. *Rewards can punish.* Employees may view the reward as a form of manipulation: "Do this and you will get that." Kohn further notes that, in the mind of the employee, failing to receive a reward one has expected is indistinguishable from being punished.[22]

3. *Rewards can damage relationships.* A reward system that forces people to compete for awards or recognition may undermine cooperation and teamwork. In addition to damaged interpersonal relationships, the reward plan may result in loss of self-esteem. Kohn says, "For each person who wins, there are many others who carry with them the feeling of having lost."[23]

4. *Rewards may mask real problems.* In some cases incentives treat the symptom, not the problem.[24] For example, a firm that gives merchandise awards or cash incentives may reduce absenteeism but fail to cure the real problem—which could be poor working conditions or poor supervision.

Although these criticisms have a great deal of merit, the fact remains that large numbers of organizations have achieved positive results with *carefully developed* incentive programs. It is possible to design programs that will have long-range benefits for both the organization and the individual employee. A well-designed program gives employees a specific, achievable goal and an adequate reward for reaching it. Also, incentive programs structured with employee input usually work best.[25]

Reexamining Our Ideas About Productivity

We need to continuously reexamine our ideas about what actions and events increase employee productivity. Many firms take the position that if employees work more hours, they will be more productive. Therefore, overtime pay is used to reward some employees who work extra hours. Critics of this approach say that employees perform optimally for six or seven hours, but then the fatigue factor surfaces. Critics of overtime (voluntary and required) also point out the need for employees to have a life outside work.[26]

Will the employee who is rewarded for working faster be more productive? Critics of this approach note that slower, intuitive thinking is often more effective in solving problems. Also, they note that a greater number of complex, creative ideas result from a slower thought process.[27]

As a nation, we have progressed from a society of farmers to a society of factory workers to a society of knowledge workers. And now, according to Daniel Pink, author of *A Whole New Mind,* we are progressing yet again—to a society of creators and empathizers. He says the information age is giving way to a new world in which creative abilities and high touch abilities mark the fault line between who gets ahead and who falls behind.[28] What type of organizational culture will bring out the best in these future employees?

The Critical Importance of Environment

Positive energy flourishes in a supportive environment. Within the organization, there should be respect for each person, regardless of job title, duties performed, or earnings. The prevailing climate within the organization should also be positive. People must feel good about the organization, its leadership, and other employees. Positive energy comes naturally in a positive work environment. But positive energy will almost never flourish in a negative work environment.

LOOKING BACK: Reviewing the Concepts

■ Describe how positive energy contributes to improved interpersonal relationships.

Positive energy can have a major influence on employee morale and productivity. Encouragement, positive feedback, and other types of practices that create positive energy are important factors in improving interpersonal relationships.

■ Create awareness of the strong need people have for encouragement and positive feedback.

People usually feel good when their accomplishments are recognized and become upset when they are ignored. Positive reinforcement, when used correctly to reward accomplishments, is a powerful motivator. Everyone needs to receive personal recognition for work done well.

■ Understand how to use positive reinforcement to improve relationships and reward behavior.

Although many studies indicate that recognition of their accomplishments is important to employees, often more so than monetary rewards and job security, many people seem unable or unwilling to reward a job well done. Praise, pride, courtesy, active listening, written thank-you notes, incentives, and awards can be used to instill positive energy.

■ Describe the major barriers to the use of positive reinforcement.

Preoccupation with self is a major obstacle to providing reinforcement to others. Self-centered persons are likely to overlook the accomplishments of others. Some people say a busy schedule does not allow them time to give recognition to others, and some people have difficulty identifying commendable actions. These and other barriers tend to minimize the use of positive reinforcement.

■ Explain how to reward individual and team performance.

Individual and team performance are often rewarded through the use of incentive programs. Some of the most common incentive programs involving cash payments are gain sharing, profit sharing, production incentives, pay for knowledge, and suggestion programs. Employee stock options have also been popular in recent years.

Career Corner

Q: Is "kissing up" to the boss an acceptable behavior today? I have heard that this practice can make a difference in today's competitive workplace.

A: Performance is what matters most, but it would be a mistake to disregard the impact of flattery on your boss. Complimenting your supervisor on how he or she conducted a business meeting or solved a major problem may enhance your career. Employees with good people skills—which include building rapport with the boss—are the ones most likely to advance. The primary rule to follow when praising your boss is *Don't fake it*. Don't give a compliment unless you genuinely believe it is deserved. To offer endless, insincere flattery will backfire. And don't forget to praise the accomplishments of your coworkers. The people you work with can often help or hinder your move up the ladder.

Key Terms

energy	positive reinforcement
reinforcer	pride
physical stroke	narcissism
verbal strokes	incentive program

Applying What You Have Learned

1. Assume you are currently the owner of a small company with about one hundred employees. In recent years, rising premiums for employee health insurance have reduced profits. To encourage your employees to maintain a healthy lifestyle (which will reduce medical insurance claims), you are considering two options:

   Option A: Add a $25 monthly surcharge to the health insurance premiums of employees who smoke. Establish healthy ranges for weight, cholesterol, and blood pressure, and assess small fines when employees fail to meet prescribed guidelines.

   Option B: Provide a cash reward of $200 for any employee who quits smoking. Establish healthy ranges for weight, cholesterol, and blood pressure, and award small cash or merchandise incentives to employees who meet prescribed guidelines.

   List the advantages and disadvantages of each proposal. Then select the proposal you feel will be most effective. Justify your choice.

2. Organizations are continually searching for ways to reward various employee behaviors. Pretend you are currently working at an upscale retail clothing store and the manager asks you to help her design an incentive

plan that would result in improved sales of clothing and accessories. She asks you to review and comment on the following options:

a. Employee-of-the-month awards for highest sales. (A special plaque would be used to recognize each monthly winner.)

b. Commission on sales. All employees would be given a 5 percent commission on all sales. Each salesperson would receive an hourly wage plus the commission.

c. Time off. Employees who achieve sales goals established by management could earn up to four hours of paid time off each week.

d. Prizes. Employees who achieve weekly sales goals established by management would be eligible for prizes such as sports or theater tickets, dinner at a nice restaurant, gift certificates, or merchandise sold by the store.

Rank these four options by assigning "1" to your first choice, "2" to your second choice, "3" to your third choice, and "4" to your fourth choice. Provide a written rationale for your first choice.

3. The authors of *Random Acts of Kindness* tell us that the little things we do for others can have big payoffs. These acts give us an outward focus that helps us move away from self-preoccupation. Plan and initiate at least two acts of kindness during the next week, and then reflect on the experience. What impact did the act have on the other person? How did you feel about this experience?

 Internet Insights

Organizations spend billions of dollars on incentives and awards designed to motivate employees to achieve a specific objective. The Internet provides information on this topic. Using your search engine, type in the following keywords: *incentive programs, production incentives,* and *employee suggestion programs.* Review the resources (such as books, articles, and training programs) that are available, paying special attention to incentive programs that would appeal to you as a worker. Describe resources you would recommend to someone who would like to develop an effective incentive program. Also, visit the Society of Incentive and Travel Executives webpage (*www.SITE-intl.org*) for additional information. Prepare a written summary of your findings.

 Role-Play Exercise

Peggy Klaus, author of *Brag! The Art of Tooting Your Own Horn Without Blowing It,* says, "You have to let the people above you know what you are doing, what skills you're developing, which goals you're achieving." She says, "Don't make them guess." Self-promotion has become more important today because many careers are being buffeted by downsizing, mergers, and business closings. For the purpose of this role play, assume the role of Britten Higgins, a full-time employee in the computer electronics department of Best Buy. You have heard rumors that your department manager may be promoted. You hope to move up within the Best Buy organization, and advancing to department head would be an important first step. You have decided to meet with your manager and discuss two things: (1) your interest in becoming department head and (2) your accomplishments and the steps you have taken to prepare for advancement. Feel free to ad-lib the information you present during the role play.[29]

Case 10.1	Incentives: The Good, the Bad, and the Ugly

Frequent recognition of accomplishments ranks high as a worker preference in most industries. Thus recognition in the form of incentives can be an effective motivator. The Society of Incentive and Travel Executives has conducted research to determine the relationship among incentives, motivation, and performance in the workplace. The findings indicate that incentive programs aimed at individuals increased performance 27 percent and incentive programs aimed at teams increased performance by 45 percent.

Banks constitute one industry that has used incentives to achieve a variety of goals. Most of these programs are designed to improve customer service. Bank of America gives employees on-the-spot awards, such as small cash bonuses and gift certificates, when managers see them providing excellent service to customers. Bank One rewards good customer service with small cash bonuses and gives employees certificates and plaques they can display in their offices.

As health insurance costs increase, organizations are searching for better ways to help employees get healthy and stay healthy. L.L. Bean has given cash awards to employees whose families take prenatal classes, and Quad/Graphics printing company has given cash awards to employees who quit smoking. Other companies have given cash awards to families that adopt an exercise program, lower their cholesterol, or wear seat belts.

Of course, there is a dark side to some incentive programs. Competition for an award can sometimes undermine cooperation and teamwork. In some cases employees will abandon good work practices in order to "win" a contest. In the field of personal selling, for example, a salesperson might attempt to sell a product that the customer really does not need. And sometimes a reward will mask real problems. Cash rewards to reduce absenteeism may fail to solve the real problem, which is poor working conditions.

The ugly side of incentives surfaced during recent corporate scandals when stock options became the symbol of a compensation system gone haywire. Employees were given the opportunity to buy stock at a low price with the option to sell it later at a higher price. However, a parade of big companies, such as Enron, Xerox, Computer Associates, and Adelphia Communications, improperly inflated earnings (cooked the books) to achieve an increase in their stock price. Greed motivated many executives to engage in these unethical practices.[30]

Questions

1. Is money the best incentive to use when you want to encourage an employee to give better customer service or adopt a healthy habit? What other types of incentives might be just as effective or more effective?

2. Should employees at various levels of the organization be involved in the design and implementation of incentive programs?

3. Many of America's largest corporations are allocating shares to employee stock options, and experts expect this trend to continue. Do you support this practice? Would you like to work for a company that offers its employees stock options?

Case 10.2 — Does Pride Matter More Than Money?

Paetec Communications, introduced at the beginning of the chapter, wants its employees to engage in exceptional efforts to make customers happy. Arunas Chesonis, CEO of Paetec, realizes that high morale among his employees is an important key to good customer service. He wants each employee to feel a sense of pride in the company, so he makes every effort to recognize work done well. Rewards range from a personal note to a cruise vacation.

Jon R. Katzenbach, author of *Why Pride Matters More Than Money*, says employee pride is what drives high-performing organizations like Southwest Airlines, SAS Institute, the U.S. Marine Corps, and the Container Store. He offers the following tool kit for those who want to become effective pride builders.

- *Personalize the workplace.* This means get involved in the everyday problems of your employees. Managers at some Marriott hotels work with employees from several different countries. These workers often need help learning the English language, preparing to become American citizens, and finding affordable child-care services. Marriott realizes that any problem that affects employees will eventually affect their on-the-job performance.

- *Always have your compass set on pride, not money.* There is no doubt that financial rewards can help an organization attract and retain good people. However, monetary incentives motivate only a narrow set of behaviors and place an emphasis on self-interest that may not be in the best interests of the company. In recent years, monetary rewards have proven to be a risky source of motivation. Compensation programs can be manipulated by clever employees to their advantage.

- *Localize as much as possible.* "Don't wait for your organization or its leaders to instill pride," says Katzenbach. The best pride builders are quick to spot and recognize the small achievements that will instill pride in their people.

- *Make your messages simple and direct.* A pride building program should not be built on needless complexity. In some cases, a good story about an employee who went the extra mile to help a customer solve a problem can stir up feelings of pride.[31]

Questions

1. Some human resource department employees voice concerns when supervisors or team leaders get involved with the everyday problems of their workers. What are your thoughts regarding this issue?

2. Some leaders in business and industry say that worker pride is the byproduct of achievement. Do you agree? What factors constitute achievement at your local McDonald's restaurant? Your local community hospital?

3. Do you agree that pride building can be localized throughout the organization?

INTEGRATED RESOURCES

VIDEO: "Awards.com Becomes a Major Online Resource"

CLASSROOM ACTIVITIES (*college.hmco.com/pic/reece10e*)

The Power of Positive Reinforcement
No Thanks!
Incentive Plans Effectiveness Ranking

business.college.hmco.com/students

ACE
Self-tests

11

DEVELOPING A PROFESSIONAL PRESENCE

Chapter Preview

After studying this chapter, you will be able to

- Explain the importance of professional presence.

- Discuss the factors that contribute to a favorable first impression.

- Define *image* and describe the factors that form the image you project to others.

- List and discuss factors that influence your choice of clothing for work.

- Understand how manners contribute to improved interpersonal relations in the workplace.

What do Macintosh computers and BMW motorcycles have in common? Each is a consumer product with a cult following. These brands have become a form of self-expression for those who own them. They have achieved brand personality through unique design and performance attributes. The Macintosh brand seems to communicate youthful, independent, and creative qualities. BMW motorcycles have a loyal following of riders who feel these bikes are superior in quality, performance, and design. A brand is more than the product. The best brands build an emotional connection with the consumer.[1]

Why introduce the concept of brands in a book devoted to human relations? Because branding can play a crucial role in your career success. The authors of *Be Your Own Brand: A Breakthrough Formula for Standing Out from the Crowd* say branding can have a significant impact on your relationships, career, and life.[2] Developing a strong personal brand involves all the little ways in which you express your feelings about yourself and present yourself to others.

Dave Olsen, chief coffee guru with Starbucks, was once asked to describe the most important factor contributing to the company's success. Was it the coffee? The employees working behind the counter? The design of the stores? Olsen thought about the question for a while and then said, "Everything matters." When it comes to developing your own personal brand, everything matters.[3]

Professional Presence—An Introduction

There are many personal and professional benefits to be gained from a study of the concepts in this chapter. You will acquire new insights regarding ways to communicate positive impressions during job interviews, business contacts,

BMW motorcycles have a lot in common with Lexus automobiles, Starbucks coffee, and Craftsman tools. Each is a *brand* that receives the highest quality ratings and consistently lives up to expectations.

and social contacts made away from work. You will also learn how to shape an image that will help you achieve your fullest potential in the career of your choice. Image is a major component of brand development.

This is not a chapter about ways to make positive impressions with superficial behavior and quick-fix techniques. We do not discuss the "power look" or the "power lunch." The material in this chapter will not help you become a more entertaining conversationalist or win new customers by pretending to be interested in their hobbies or families. Stephen Covey, author of *The 7 Habits of Highly Effective People*, says that the ability to build effective, long-term relationships is based on character strength, not quick-fix techniques. He notes that outward attitude and behavior changes do very little good in the long run *unless* they are based on solid principles governing human effectiveness. These principles include service (making a contribution), integrity and honesty (which serve as a foundation of trust), human dignity (every person has worth), and fairness.[4]

Professional Presence—A Definition

We are indebted to Susan Bixler, author of *Professional Presence*, for giving us a better understanding of what it means to possess professional presence. **Professional presence** is a dynamic blend of poise, self-confidence, control, and style that empowers us to be able to command respect in any situation.[5] Once acquired, it permits us to project a confidence that others can quickly perceive the first time they meet us. Obviously, to *project* this confidence, you need to *feel* confident.

Bixler points out that, in many cases, the credentials we present during a job interview or when we are being considered for a promotion are not very different from those of other persons being considered. It is our professional presence that permits us to rise above the crowd. Debra Benton, a career consultant, says, "Any boss with a choice of two people with equal qualifications will choose the one with style as well as substance."[6]

The Importance of Making a Good First Impression

As organizations experience increased competition for clients, patients, or customers, they are giving new attention to the old adage "First impressions are lasting ones." Research indicates that initial impressions do indeed tend to linger. Therefore, a positive first impression can be thought of as the first step in building a long-term relationship.

Of course, it is not just first contacts with clients, patients, customers, and others that are important. Positive impressions should be the objective of every contact. Many organizations have learned that in the age of information, high tech without high touch is not a winning formula.

The Primacy Effect The development of professional presence begins with a full appreciation of the power of first impressions. The tendency to form and retain impressions quickly at the time of an initial meeting illustrates what

The development of professional presence begins with a full appreciation of the power of first impressions.

social psychologists call a **primacy effect** in the way people perceive one another. The general principle is that initial information tends to carry more weight than information received later. First impressions establish the mental framework within which a person is viewed, and information acquired later is often ignored or reinterpreted to coincide with this framework.[7]

Ann Demarais and Valerie White, founders of First Impressions, Inc. (*www.firstimpressionsconsulting.com*), note that in a first impression others see only a very small sample of you, a tiny percentage of your life. But to them, that small sample represents 100 percent of what they know of you. And they will weigh initial information much more heavily than later information.[8]

The First Few Seconds   Malcolm Gladwell (*www.gladwell.com*), a best-selling author, learned a great deal about the power of first impressions a few years ago when he let his close-cropped hair grow wild. His life changed immediately. He got far more speeding tickets and was routinely pulled out of airport security lines for special attention. People he met knew nothing about him except that he had shaggy hair, but they were ready to think the worst.[9]

Gladwell was inspired to try to understand what happens beneath the surface of rapidly made decisions. His findings later appeared in *Blink: The Power of Thinking Without Thinking*. He says most of us would like to think our decision making is the result of rational deliberation, but in reality most decisions are made subconsciously in a split second.[10]

TOTAL	**SUSAN BIXLER AND NANCY NIX-RICE**
PERSON	AUTHORS, *THE NEW PROFESSIONAL IMAGE*
INSIGHT	"Books are judged by their covers, houses are appraised by their curb appeal, and people are initially evaluated on how they choose to dress and behave. In a perfect world this is not fair, moral, or just. What's inside should count a great deal more. And eventually it usually does, but not right away. In the meantime, a lot of opportunities can be lost."

Most people assess another person very quickly and then settle on a general perception of that individual. It is very difficult for us to reverse that first impression. Paula rushed into a restaurant for a quick lunch—she had to get back to her office for a 1:30 p.m. appointment. At the entrance of the main dining area was a sign reading "Please Wait to Be Seated." A few feet away, the hostess was discussing a popular movie with one of the waitresses. The hostess made eye contact with Paula but continued to visit with the waitress. In this situation, Paula immediately formed a negative impression of the hostess, even though no words were exchanged. She quickly left the restaurant. Unfortunately, the hostess may not have been fully aware of the negative impression she communicated to the customer.

CRITICAL THINKING CHALLENGE

The authors of *First Impressions* say that making a good first impression means making the person you meet feel positive toward you. When you have contact with someone, do you think about how the other person is feeling during the initial contact, or do you stay focused on yourself?

Assumptions Versus Facts   The impression you form of another person during the initial contact is made up of both assumptions and facts. Most people tend to rely more heavily on **assumptions** during the initial meeting. If a job applicant sits slumped in the chair, head bowed and shoulders slack, you might assume the person is not very interested in the position. If the postal clerk fails to make eye contact during the transaction and does not express appreciation for your purchase, you may assume this person treats everyone with indifference. Needless to say, the impression you form of another person during the initial contact can be misleading. The briefer the encounter with a new acquaintance, the greater the chance that misinformation will enter into your perception of the other person. The authors of a popular book on first impressions state that "depending on assumptions is a one-way ticket to big surprises and perhaps disappointments."[11]

Where Is Your Emotional Focus?   Making a good first impression means making the person you meet feel positive about you. When you make contact with someone, it is not uncommon to focus on yourself. You talk to someone at a party or a meeting, and you think about how you feel—whether you are comfortable, bored, nervous, intimidated, and so on. But do you think about the impression you are making on the other person? Do you think about how the other person is feeling during the initial contact? The authors of *First Impressions—What You Don't Know About How Others See You* say that focusing on how the other person feels is the secret to making a positive first impression.[12]

Cultural Influence

Cultural influences, often formed during the early years of our life, lead us to have impressions of some people even before we meet them. People often develop stereotypes of entire groups. Although differences between cultures are often subtle, they can lead to uncomfortable situations. We need to realize that the Korean shopkeeper is being polite, not hostile, when he puts change on the counter and not in your hand. Some Asian students do not speak up in class out of respect for the teacher, not boredom.[13]

Many American companies are attempting to create a new kind of workplace where cultural and ethnic differences are treated as assets, not annoyances. Recently, Walt Disney, known for its squeaky-clean dress and grooming standards, announced it was loosening grooming rules for workers at its theme parks. Under the new policy, male workers can wear braids provided they are above the collar and neatly tied close to the scalp in straight rows. Female workers at Disney have been able to braid their hair for years.[14]

Norine Dresser, author of *Multiculture Manners—New Rules of Etiquette for a Changing Society*, notes that it is becoming more difficult for organizations to develop policies that do not offend one ethnic group or another. She argues that it is the collective duty of the mainstream to learn the customs and practices of established minority groups as well as the ways of the latest arrivals from other countries.[15]

The Image You Project

Image is a term used to describe how other people feel about you. In every business or social setting, your behaviors and appearance communicate a mental picture that others observe and remember. This picture determines how they react to you.

Think of image as a tool that can reveal your inherent qualities, your competence, your attitude, and your leadership potential. If you wish to communicate your professional capabilities and create your own brand, begin by scrutinizing your attitudes; only then can you invest the time and energy needed to refine and enhance your personal image.

In many respects, the image you project is very much like a picture puzzle, as illustrated in Figure 11.1. It is formed by a variety of factors, including manners, self-confidence, voice quality, versatility [(see Chapter 3), integrity (see Chapter 5),] entrance and carriage, facial expression, surface language, competence, positive attitude, and handshake. Each of these image-shaping components is under your control, though some are harder to develop than others. As you reflect on the image you want to project, remember that a strong personal brand is built from the inside out.

Surface Language

As noted earlier, we base opinions about other people on both facts and assumptions. Unfortunately, assumptions often carry a great deal of weight. Many of the assumptions we develop regarding other people are based on **surface language**, a pattern of immediate impressions conveyed by what we *see*—in other words, by appearance. The clothing you wear, your hairstyle,

FIGURE 11.1   Major Factors That Form Your Image

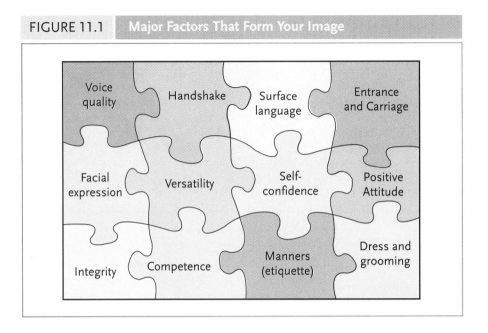

the fragrances you use, and the jewelry you display all combine to make a statement about you to others.

According to many writers familiar with image formation, clothing is particularly important. Although a more relaxed dress code has evolved in some employment areas, people judge your appearance long before they judge your talents. It would be a mistake not to take your career wardrobe seriously. Bixler suggests that those making career wardrobe decisions should keep in mind that three things haven't changed:[16]

A good rule to follow is to dress for the job you want, not the job you have.

1. *If you want the job, you have to look the part.* Establish personal dress and grooming standards appropriate for the organization where you wish to work. Before you apply for a job, try to find out what the workers there are wearing. If in doubt, dress conservatively. Casual dress can convey indifference.

2. *If you want the promotion, you have to look promotable.* A good rule to follow is to dress for the job you want, not the job you have. If you are currently a bank teller and want to become a branch manager, identify the successful branch managers and emulate their manner of dress.

3. *If you want respect, you have to dress as well as or better than your industry standards.* One would expect to find conservative dress standards in banking, insurance, accounting, and law, and more casual dress standards in advertising, sports entertainment, and agriculture. Spend time researching the dress and grooming standards in the industry in which you hope to find a job.

Selecting Your Career Apparel

Millions of American workers wear a uniform especially designed for a particular job. The judges on the U.S. Supreme Court and the technicians at the local Midas Muffler and Brake shop have one thing in common—both groups wear a special uniform to work. Companies that have initiated extensive career apparel programs rely on uniforms to project an image of consistent quality, good service, and uniqueness.

Enterprise Rent-A-Car, the nation's largest recruiter of college students, requires its 52,000 workers to follow conservative dress and grooming policies. Men, for example, follow twenty-six rules that include no beards (unless medically necessary) and dress shirts with coordinated ties. Female employees follow thirty dress code guidelines, including one for skirt length (skirts must not be shorter than two inches above the knee) and one for mandatory stockings. Why does Enterprise choreograph how its employees look? The company maintains that its personal appearance and grooming standards give it a marketing advantage.[17]

The uniforms worn by United Parcel Service employees, airport screeners, and the employees at your local restaurant might be classified as special-design **career apparel**. In addition to special-design uniforms, there is another type of career apparel, somewhat less predictable, worn by large numbers of people in the labor force. Here are two examples:

Many American workers wear a uniform that is especially designed for a particular job. This airport security officer wears a uniform that communicates authority. It complements the serious nature of his work.

- A male bank loan officer would be appropriately dressed in a tailored gray or blue suit, white shirt, and tie. This same person dressed in a colorful blazer, sport shirt, and plaid slacks would be seen as too casual in most bank settings.

- A technician employed by an auto dealership that sells new cars would be appropriately dressed in matching gray, tan, or blue shirt and pants. The technician would be inappropriately dressed in jeans and a T-shirt.

Many organizations seek advice about career apparel from image consultants who have received certification from the Association of Image Consultants International (*www.aici.org*) or Global Protocol, Inc. (*www.globalprotocol.com*). The demand for etiquette and protocol consultants has increased in recent years.[18]

Wardrobe Engineering

The term **wardrobe engineering** was first used by John Molloy, author of *Dress for Success*, to describe how clothing and accessories can be used to create a certain image. This concept was later refined by several other noted image consultants in hundreds of books and articles on dress and grooming. Although these authors are not in complete agreement on every aspect of dress, they do agree on the four basic points presented in Table 11.1. Use this information as a guide. Although you should consider the dress and grooming standards of others in your field, don't give in to blind conformity. As noted by one consultant, "Effective packaging is an individual matter based on the person's circumstances, age, weight, height, coloring, and objectives."[19]

TABLE 11.1	Factors Influencing Your Choice of Clothing for Work

Dress codes are undergoing changes, and this complicates the selection of clothing for work. Use the four factors described here for guidance.

1. *Products and services offered.* In some cases the organization's products and services more or less dictate a certain type of dress. For example, a receptionist employed by a well-established law firm is likely to wear clothing that is conservative, modest, and in good taste. These same dress standards would apply to a pharmaceutical sales representative who calls on medical doctors.

2. *Type of person served.* Research indicates that first impressions created by dress and grooming are greatly influenced by unconscious expectations. Throughout life we become acquainted with real estate salespeople, nurses, police officers, and others employed in a wide range of occupations. We form mental images of the apparel common to each of these occupations. When we encounter someone whose appearance does not conform to our past experiences, we often feel uncomfortable.

3. *Desired image projected by the organization.* Some companies establish dress codes that help shape the image they project to the public. Walt Disney Company, for example, maintains a strict dress and grooming code for all its theme-park employees. They are considered "cast members" and must adhere to dress and grooming standards that complement the image projected by Disney theme parks.

4. *Geographic region.* Dress in the South and Southwest tends to be more casual than dress in the Northeast. Climate is another factor that influences the clothing people wear at work.

The Business Casual Look

The term **business casual** is used to describe the movement toward dress standards that emphasize greater comfort and individuality. Business casual is clothing that allows you to feel comfortable at work but looks neat and professional. It usually means slacks, khaki pants, collared long-sleeved shirts and blouses, and shoes with socks or hosiery. It usually does not include jeans, T-shirts, shorts, sneakers, or sandals.[20]

Some companies are relaxing dress codes and allowing workers to dress casually. Although no precise definition of business casual exists, the following casual-dress guidelines are typical.

1. *Wear dressier business clothing when meeting with customers or clients.* You should avoid creating inconsistencies between your message and your appearance. Workers at ProVox Technologies Corporation, based in Roanoke, Virginia, keep company-designed ProVox shirts and khakis in the office for client visits.[21]

2. *Respect the boundary between work and leisure clothing.* Victoria's Secret once sold body-hugging spandex tube tops as workplace wear. Anne Fisher of *Fortune* magazine's "Ask Annie" career advice column says, "As a rule, people should avoid wearing anything that shows so much skin that it distracts other people from their work." How about body piercing, tattoos, orange hair (or other colors not found in nature), three-day stubble, no socks, micro-mini skirts, or rubber flip-flops? In some

"Is it casual casual or expensive casual?"

cases, you will be guided by company policy. At Ford Motor Company, "non-offensive" tattoos are permitted and body piecing is acceptable if it does not pose safety risks. Subway Restaurants permit "discrete" tattoos, but body piercing is limited to one piercing per ear.[22] Of course, some dress-code violations fall into the "unwritten" category. If you wear a nose ring to work, you may be sending the wrong message to the person responsible for your next promotion.

3. *Wear clothing that is clean and neat and that fits well.* Casual dress codes tend to emphasize the importance of this guideline.

Do not let "dress-down" influences rob you of common sense. You don't get a second chance to make a good first impression, so select your casual clothing with care. If you have to ask yourself, "Is this clothing acceptable?" you probably shouldn't wear it to work.

Your Facial Expression

Facial expressions are the cues most people rely on in initial interactions.

After your overall appearance, your face is the most visible part of you. Facial expressions are the cues most people rely on in initial interactions. They provide the clues by which others read your mood and personality.

Studies conducted in nonverbal communication show that facial expressions strongly influence people's reactions to each other. The expression on your face can quickly trigger a positive or negative reaction from those you meet. How you rate in the "good-looks" department is not nearly as important as your ability to communicate positive impressions with a pleasant smile and eye contact.

If you want to identify the inner feelings of another person, watch the individual's facial expressions closely. A frown may tell you "something is wrong." A pleasant smile generally communicates "things are OK." Everyone has encountered a "look of surprise" or a "look that could kill." These facial expressions usually reflect inner emotions more accurately than words. The smile is the most recognizable signal in the world. People everywhere tend to trust a smiling face.[23]

Your Entrance and Carriage

The way you enter someone's office or a business meeting can influence the image you project, says Susan Bixler. She notes that "your entrance and the way you carry yourself will set the stage for everything that comes afterward."[24] A nervous or apologetic entrance may ruin your chances of getting a job, closing a sale, or getting the raise you have earned. If you feel apprehensive, try not to let it show in your body language. Hold your head up, avoid slumping forward, and try to project self-assurance. To get off to the right start and make a favorable impression, follow these words of advice from Bixler: "The person who has confidence in himself or herself indicates this by a strong stride, a friendly smile, good posture, and a genuine sense of energy. This is a very effective way to set the stage for a productive meeting. When you ask for respect visually, you get it."[25] Bixler says the key to making a successful entrance is simply believing—and projecting—that you have a reason to be there and have something important to present or discuss.

Your Voice Quality and Speech Habits

The tone of your voice, the rate of speed at which you speak (tempo), the volume of your speech, your ability to pronounce words clearly (diction), and your speech habits contribute greatly to the image you project. Consider these real-world examples:

- Regina Tell, court reporter at a liability trial involving Merck & Company's painkiller Vioxx, said the rapid speech patterns of the attorneys was "killing her." She reported that they spoke at a rate of over 300 words a minute, or more than 100 words a minute faster than average people speak.[26]

- Kristy Pinand, a youthful-looking 23-year-old, routinely used "teen speak" when talking to colleagues and clients. Words such as "cool" and "like" were frequently part of her speech pattern. With feedback from her supervisor, she was able to correct the problem.[27]

- A senior project manager at a major financial-service company was surprised when his boss blamed his thick Brooklyn accent for his stalled advancement in the company. Despite his MBA, the project manager was speaking too fast and skipping many consonants. His frequent use of "deez" and "doze" created the impression that he was poorly educated and inarticulate.[28]

A conscious effort to improve your voice begins with awareness. A tape or video recording of your conversations will help you identify problem areas. If you hear a voice that is too monotone, too nasal, too high-pitched, too weak, too insincere, or too loud, you can target the problem for improvement. With practice and the use of a tape recorder, you can change your voice quality and speech habits.

If you routinely receive requests to repeat yourself, the problem may be your accent, or something as simple as your breathing. You may not be breathing correctly, leaving your words soft and inaudible. If you are looking for professional help, consider working with a voice coach or a speech pathologist. You may also want to join Toastmasters International, a professional organization dedicated to effective personal and public communication.

Your Handshake

When two people first meet, a handshake is usually the only physical contact between them. A handshake is a friendly and professional way to greet someone or to take leave, regardless of gender. The handshake can communicate warmth, genuine concern for the other person, and strength. It can also communicate aloofness, indifference, and weakness. The message you send the other party through your handshake depends on a combination of the following factors:

1. *Degree of firmness.* Generally speaking, a firm (but not viselike) grip communicates a caring attitude, whereas a weak grip communicates indifference.

2. *Degree of dryness of hands.* A moist, clammy palm is unpleasant to feel and can communicate the impression that you are nervous. People who have this problem often remove the moisture with a clean handkerchief.

3. *Duration of grip.* There are no specific guidelines for the ideal duration of a grip. Nevertheless, by extending the handshake just a little, you can often communicate a greater degree of interest in and concern for the other person.

4. *Depth of interlock.* A full, deep grip is more likely to convey friendship to the other person. Position your hand to make complete contact with the other person's hand. Once you have connected, close your thumb over the back of the other person's hand and give a slight squeeze.[29]

5. *Eye contact during handshake.* Visual communication can increase the positive impact of your handshake. Maintaining eye contact throughout the handshaking process is important when two people greet each other.[30]

Most individuals have shaken hands with hundreds of people but have little idea whether they are creating positive or negative impressions. It is a good idea to obtain this information from those coworkers or friends who are willing to provide you with candid feedback. Like all other human relations skills, the handshake can be improved with practice.

SKILL DEVELOPMENT CHALLENGE

Four years ago, you completed a two-year culinary arts program at Morgan Community College. Soon after graduation, you assumed the duties of assistant chef at a local country club. One of your primary duties was to plan the luncheon menu, which included several types of salads and sandwiches. Today you are preparing to open a small restaurant that will focus on fresh, high quality breakfast and lunch meals. The restaurant will be located in the financial district and cater mostly to employees who work for various financial services firms. Using information presented in Table 11.1 and other material in this chapter, prepare a dress and grooming code for the waitstaff.

Etiquette for a Changing World

Why are so many etiquette guides crowding bookstore shelves? And why are many organizations hiring consultants to conduct classes on etiquette guidelines? Well, one reason is that we need advice on how to avoid annoying other

HUMAN RELATIONS
IN ACTION

Handyman Etiquette

Andy Bell, founder of Handyman Matters Franchising Corporation, manages 100 franchises in 37 states. He has implemented strict initial contact guidelines for all of his technicians. Technicians must take two steps back after ringing a doorbell and wear a clean, neat uniform (collared shirt and slacks) with identifying logo. When the homeowner comes to the door, the technician immediately presents a business card. Handyman technicians receive training in all areas of in-home conduct.

people and what to do if they annoy us. In today's fast-paced, often tense, work environment, we have to work a little harder to maintain a climate of fairness, kindness, and mutual respect.[31]

Etiquette (sometimes called *manners or protocol*) is a set of traditions based on kindness, efficiency, and logic.[32] Letitia Baldrige, author and etiquette consultant, says, "It's consideration and kindness and thinking about somebody other than oneself."[33] Sometimes we need new etiquette guidelines to deal with our changing world. Today smoking at work is usually prohibited or restricted to a certain area. Meetings often begin with the announcement "Please silence your cell phones and beepers." And the nearly universal use of e-mail has spawned hundreds of articles on e-mail etiquette (see Chapter 2). A diverse work force has created many new challenges in the area of protocol.

Although it is not possible to do a complete review of the rules of etiquette, we will discuss those that are particularly important in an organizational setting.

Dining Etiquette   Job interviews and business meetings are frequently conducted at breakfast, lunch, or dinner, so be aware of your table manners. To illustrate decisions you might need to make during a business meal, let's eavesdrop on Tom Reed, a job candidate having a meal with several employees of the company he wants to work for. After introductions, the bread is passed to Tom. He places a roll on the small bread-and-butter plate to the right of his dinner plate. Soon, he picks up the roll, takes a bite, and returns it to the plate. Midway through the meal, Tom rises from his chair, places his napkin on the table, and says, "Excuse me; I need to make a potty run." So far, Tom has made four etiquette blunders: The bread-and-butter plate he used belongs to the person seated on his right; his own is to the left of his dinner plate. When eating a roll, he should break off one piece at a time and butter the piece as he is ready to eat it. The napkin should have been placed on his chair, indicating his plan to return. (When departing for good, leave it to the left of your plate.) And finally, the words *potty run* are too casual for a business meal. A simple statement such as, "Please excuse me; I'll be back in just a moment," would be adequate.

There are some additional table manners to keep in mind. Do not begin eating until the people around you have their plates. If you have not been served, however, encourage others to go ahead. To prevent awkward moments during the meal, avoid ordering food that is not easily controlled, such as ribs, spaghetti, chicken with bones, or lobster.

How would you like to be seated next to three people who are talking on their cell phones? If you receive a call at a restaurant, take the call outside the dining area. It's rude to inflict your conversation on people seated near you.

Meeting Etiquette Business meetings should start and end on time, so recognize the importance of punctuality. Anne Marie Sabath, owner of a firm that provides etiquette training for business employees, says, "We teach people that if you're early, you're on time, and if you're on time, in reality, you're late." Showing up late for any meeting will be viewed as rudeness by coworkers, your boss, and your clients. Do not feel obligated to comment on each item on the agenda. Yes, sometimes silence is golden. In most cases, you should not bring up a topic unless it is related to an agenda item. If you are in charge of the meeting, end it by summarizing key points, reviewing the decisions made, and recapping the responsibilities assigned to individuals during the meeting. Always start and end the meeting on a positive note.[34]

Cell Phone Etiquette New technologies often bring new annoyances, and the cell phone is no exception. *Cell phone contempt* surfaces in offices, restaurants, houses of worship, and many other places. Cell phone etiquette is based on a few simple guidelines. First, it's not acceptable to use your cell phone at business meetings, in elevators, or at restaurants. If you receive a call at a restaurant, take the call outside the dining area. When making or receiving a call, talk in a normal speaking voice. Too often cell phone users talk louder than normal because they feel the need to compensate for the size of small phones. Try to confine your calls to private areas; it's rude to inflict your conversation on people near you.[35] Finally, if a coworker or friend insists

Cell phone contempt surfaces in offices, restaurants, houses of worship, and many other places.

on "staying connected" at all times and you find this behavior annoying, confront the person. However, choose your words carefully. If a coworker takes a call at a meeting, for example, you might say, "When you answer your cell phone it makes the group feel unimportant and as if we don't have your full attention."[36]

Conversational Etiquette When you establish new relationships, avoid calling people by their first name too soon. Never assume that work-related associates prefer to be addressed informally by their first names. Use titles of respect—Ms., Mr., Professor, or Dr.—until the relationship is established. Too much familiarity will irritate some people. When the other person says, "Call me Ruth" or "Call me John," it is alright to begin using the person's first name.

A conversation that includes obscene language can create problems in the workplace. Although the rules about what constitutes profanity have changed over the years, inappropriate use of foul language in front of a customer, a client, or, in many cases, a coworker is a breach of etiquette. An obscenity implies lack of respect for your audience. Also, certain language taboos carry moral and spiritual significance in most cultures. Obscene language is often cited by persons who file sexual harassment charges.[37]

Networking Etiquette Networking—making contact with people at meetings, social events, or other venues—is an effective job search method. Networking is also important to salespeople searching for prospects and to professionals (accountants, lawyers, consultants, etc.) who need to build a client base.

When you meet people at an event, tell them your name and what you do. Avoid talking negatively about any aspect of your current job or your life. In some cases you will need to make a date to call or meet with the new contact later. After the event, study your contacts and follow up.

Send a *written* thank-you note if someone has been helpful to you or generous with his or her time. You might also consider sending a newspaper or magazine article as an "information brief," since one goal of networking is information exchange.[38]

TOTAL	**JUDITH MARTIN**
PERSON	AUTHOR
INSIGHT	"In a society as ridden as ours with expensive status symbols, where every purchase is considered a social statement, there is no easier or cheaper way to distinguish oneself than by the practice of gentle manners."

We have given you a brief introduction to several areas of etiquette. This information will be extremely helpful as you develop a strong personal brand. Remember that good etiquette is based on consideration for the other person. If you genuinely respect other people, you will have an easier time developing your personal approach to business manners. You will probably also agree with most of the etiquette "rules" we have been discussing. Nancy Austin, coauthor of *A Passion for Excellence*, says, "Real manners—a keen interest in and a regard for somebody else, a certain kindness and at-ease quality that add real value—can't be faked or finessed."[39] Real manners come from the heart.

Incivility—The Ultimate Career Killer

Civility in our society is under siege. In recent years we have witnessed an increase in coarse, rude, and obnoxious behavior. Unfortunately, some of the most outrageous behavior by athletes, coaches, politicians, and business leaders has been rewarded with wealth and influence.

As noted in Chapter 1, civility is the sum of the many sacrifices we are called upon to make for the sake of living together. At work, it may involve refilling the copier paper tray after using the machine or making a new pot of coffee after you take the last cup. It may mean turning down your radio so workers nearby are not disturbed or sending a thank-you note to someone who has helped you complete a difficult project. Small gestures, such as saying "Please" and "Thank you" or opening doors for others, make ourselves and others more content. Learning to discipline your passions so as to avoid obnoxious behavior will demonstrate also your maturity and self-control.

Professional Presence at the Job Interview

Professional presence has special meaning when you are preparing for a job interview. In most cases you are competing against several other applicants, so you can't afford to make a mistake. A common mistake among job applicants is failure to acquire background information on the employer. Without this information, it's difficult to prepare questions to ask during the interview, and decisions about what to wear will be more difficult.

Keep in mind that regardless of the dress code of the organization, it's always appropriate to dress conservatively. If you arrive for an interview wearing torn jeans and a T-shirt, the person conducting the interview may think you are not serious about the job. The expectation of most employers is that the job applicant will be well groomed and dressed appropriately.

One of the most important objectives of a job interview is to communicate the image that you are someone who is conscientious, so be prepared. If possible, visit the place of business before your interview. Observe the people already working there; then dress one step up in terms of professional appearance. What's most important is that you show that you care enough to make a good impression.

LOOKING BACK: Reviewing the Concepts

■ Explain the importance of professional presence.

Professional presence is a dynamic blend of poise, self-confidence, control, and style. Once acquired, it permits you to be perceived as self-assured and competent. These qualities are quickly perceived the first time someone meets you.

■ Discuss the factors that contribute to a favorable first impression.

People tend to form impressions of others quickly at the time they first meet them, and these first impressions tend to be preserved. The impression you form of another person during the initial contact is made up of assumptions and facts. Assumptions are often based on perceptions of surface language—the pattern of immediate impressions conveyed by appearance. Your verbal messages also influence the impression you make on others.

■ Define *image* and describe the factors that form the image you project to others.

Image is a term used to describe how other people feel about you. In every business or social setting, your behaviors and appearance communicate a picture that others observe and remember. This picture determines how they react to you. Image is formed by a variety of factors, including manners, self-confidence, voice quality, versatility, integrity, entrance and carriage, facial expression, surface language, competence, positive attitude, and handshake.

■ List and discuss factors that influence your choice of clothing for work.

Image consultants contend that discrimination on the basis of appearance is a fact of life. Clothing is an important part of the image you communicate to others. Four factors tend to influence your choice of clothing for work: (1) the products or services offered by the organization, (2) the type of person served, (3) the desired image projected by the organization, and (4) the region where you work.

■ Understand how manners contribute to improved interpersonal relations in the workplace.

Manners, sometimes called etiquette or protocol, are traditions based on kindness, efficiency, and logic. Dining, meeting, cell phone, conversational, and networking etiquette are all important in the workplace.

Career Corner

Q: In the near future I will begin my job search, and I want to work for a company that will respect my individuality. Some companies are enforcing strict dress and grooming codes and other policies that, in my opinion, infringe on the rights of their employees. How far can an employer go in dictating my lifestyle?

A: This is a good question, but one for which there is no easy answer. For example, most people feel they have a right to wear the fragrance of their choice, but many fragrances contain allergy-producing ingredients. In some employment settings, you will find "nonfragrance" zones. Secondhand smoke is another major issue in the workplace because most research indicates that it can be harmful to the health of workers. Rules regarding body piercings, hair length, and the type of clothing that can be worn to work have also caused controversy. There is no doubt that many companies are trying to find a balance between their interests and the rights of workers. Enterprise Rent-A-Car has placed restrictions on the length of an employee's hair and established over twenty-five dress code guidelines for its employees. The company believes employee appearance is crucial to its success. The best advice I can give you is to become familiar with the employer's expectations *before* you accept a job. The company has a responsibility to explain its personnel policies to prospective employees, but sometimes this information is not covered until after a person is hired.

Key Terms

professional presence	surface language
primacy effect	career apparel
assumptions	wardrobe engineering
cultural influences	business casual
image	etiquette

Applying What We Have Learned

1. Many people complain that interrupting has become a major annoyance. You begin speaking and someone finishes your sentence. Marilyn Vos Savant, author of the "Ask Marilyn" column, recommends a technique that can stop interrupters. When someone interrupts you, stop speaking abruptly and say "What?" This will highlight the interruption, and the person who interrupts you will be forced to repeat himself or herself too, which is an unpleasant experience. Repeat this method, if necessary, until the offender lets you complete your sentences. Marilyn Vos Savant says you should save this method for *chronic* interrupters.[40]

2. The first step toward improving your voice is to hear yourself as others do. Listen to several recordings of your voice on a dictation machine, tape recorder, or VCR, and then complete the following rating form. Place a checkmark in the appropriate space for each quality.

Quality	Major Strength	Strength	Weakness	Major Weakness
Projects confidence	_____	_____	_____	_____
Projects enthusiasm	_____	_____	_____	_____
Speaking rate is not too fast or too slow	_____	_____	_____	_____
Projects optimism	_____	_____	_____	_____
Voice is not too loud or too soft	_____	_____	_____	_____
Projects sincerity	_____	_____	_____	_____

3. You have assumed the duties of sales manager at a new Lexus automobile dealership that is sheduled to open in three weeks. You will hire and train all salespeople. What types of career apparel would you recommend to members of your sales team? What grooming standards would you recommend?

 Internet Insights

Throughout the past few years we have seen an increase in the number of etiquette consulting and training companies. These firms will help you develop and initiate dress codes and conduct etiquette-training programs for employees. Contact two of the companies listed below and review the services offered. Then prepare a written summary of your findings. Also, contact the Association of Image Consultants International (*www.aici.org*) and Global Protocol, Inc. (*www.globalprotocol.com*), to determine what services are offered to members.

Patricia Stephenson & Associates
West Palm Beach, FL
etiquettepro.com

The Protocol School of Washington
McLean, VA
info@psow.com

Brody Communications
Elkins Park, PA
info@brodycommunications.com

Eticon Inc.
Columbia, SC
eticon@eticon.com

 Role-Play Exercise

After spending eight years working for a well-established kitchen design firm, you established your own company. Whitehall Design Kitchens is the area's premier kitchen design studio. You have partnered with the industry's finest artisans and suppliers and can offer exotic veneers, gourmet appliances, unique hand carvings, and modern cabinetry to people who want their kitchen to be an extension of their image and lifestyle. You cater to an upscale clientele who appreciate quality, beauty, and fine craftsmanship. At the present time you employ five design consultants. The newest member of your design team, Dera Corian, is a talented designer who recently completed the Certified Kitchen Design (CKD) professional designation. She has excellent design skills, but often she does not project the upscale image of Whitehall Design Kitchens. Although she is well paid, Dera likes to shop at discount clothing stores, always searching for a great bargain. Very often her clothing and accessories communicate a "thrift store" image that clashes with the upscale image of Whitehall Design Kitchens. You have decided to meet with Dera and try to encourage her to adopt a wardrobe that is more appropriate for the clientele she serves. You will meet with another class member who will assume the role of Dera Corian.

Case 11.1   The Importance of Class

The words *magnetism*, *charisma*, and *class* are used to describe persons who are admired and respected. These special individuals are also memorable. Some say class and charm are fading fast from the American scene, replaced by bad behavior displayed by professional athletes, movie stars, radio and TV commentators, and politicians. Many sports fans mourn the retirement of John Elway, Michael Jordan, and Wayne Gretzky, who were gracious in victory and gracious in defeat.

Arthur Ashe was the first African-American male to win the U.S. Open and Wimbledon tennis tournaments and the first African-American on the U.S. Davis Cup team. He was also the first African-American male ranked number one in the tennis world. He displayed a unique combination of grace and class. His life was marked by personal modesty, civility, and generosity. Ashe led an exemplary family and professional life until his untimely death from AIDS contracted after heart bypass surgery. The late Payne Stewart, killed in the bizarre crash of a Learjet, is remembered as a vicious competitor and a classy hero to many golf fans. Cellist Yo-Yo Ma and talk-show host Oprah Winfrey display magnetism and charm. The late Peter Jennings, popular news anchor, was described as the "voice of civility."

The authors of *Make Yourself Memorable* say that memorable people have style. They describe the four interlocking elements of style as *look*, *conduct*, *speech*, and *presentation*. Ann Landers, the late advice columnist, used to say that if you had class, success would follow. She described some of the elements of class:[41]

- Class never tries to build itself up by tearing others down.

- Class never makes excuses.

- Class knows that good manners are nothing more than a series of small, inconsequential sacrifices.

- Class is comfortable in its own skin. It never puts on airs.

- Class is real. It can't be faked.

Questions

1. Some social critics say that too many people these days are rude, crude, and inconsiderate of others. Do you agree? Explain.

2. Make a list of prominent people who in your opinion have class. Also, make a list of friends or coworkers who have class. What personal qualities displayed by these individuals do you most admire?

3. Ann Landers says that if you have class, nothing else matters. Do you agree?

4. If you want to become a more memorable person—someone with class—what type of self-improvement program would you undertake? Explain. If you decided to develop a strong personal brand, would class be a major component of your brand?

Case 11.2   Do You Want to Be Your Own Brand?

About twenty years ago Toyota Motor Company decided to develop a line of luxury automobiles that would compete with Mercedes Benz, BMW, Cadillac, and Lincoln. After several years of research and development, the Lexus brand was born. Today, Lexus cars are recognized by automobile writers and consumers as the best mass-produced luxury cars. They stand for quality.

Branding, a concept that has been used in the field of marketing for over fifty years, has recently surfaced as a personal development strategy. Using the principles of successful brand development, many people are positioning themselves to stand for something—to say something important about themselves that will affect how others perceive them. The authors of *Be Your Own Brand* note that the concept of brand in business has a well-defined meaning: "A brand is a perception or emotion, maintained by a buyer or a prospective buyer, describing the experience related to doing business with an organization or consuming its products or services."[42] In a personal context, you can think of it this way: "Your brand is a perception or emotion, maintained by somebody other than you, that describes the total experience of having a relationship with you."[43]

The key to understanding the concept of personal and business branding is understanding the nature and needs of a relationship. L. L. Bean has become a major force in outdoor and casual clothing by implementing business practices that build customer loyalty and repeat business. In addition to selling quality products, this company works hard to build a trusting relationship with its customers.

Personal brand development begins with self-management practices that help you create and strengthen relationships with other people. Early in his career, Jerry Seinfeld decided he would never use profanity in his comedy routines. This personal decision forced him to use more creativity, and he became a stronger comedian. Jeff Bezos, founder of Amazon.com, recalls an early life experience that changed the way he viewed relationships. He made a comment to his grandmother that hurt her feelings. Later his grandfather met with him privately and said, "You'll learn one day that it's much harder to be kind than clever."[44] This insight has helped Bezos in his professional life.

To develop a distinctive brand that will help you in your interactions with others may require making some changes in your life. To become distinctive, you must stand for something. What you stand for relates to your values. Thus a strong personal brand is generally built from the inside out. But to some extent you can also decide what type of image you want these values to project. This may require changes in your manners, dress, voice quality, facial expression, posture or behaviors that reflect your integrity.

Questions

1. Given this brief introduction to brand development, would you consider taking steps to develop a distinctive personal brand? Explain your answer.

2. Experts in personal brand development say that employees should align their values with their employer's values. Do you agree with this recommendation?

3. Association of Image Consultants International says its members help clients achieve authenticity, credibility, and self-confidence. Would you consider hiring a personal consultant to help you grow in these areas? Explain.

4. If you decide to develop a personal brand, what changes will you make in your life?

INTEGRATED RESOURCES

CLASSROOM ACTIVITIES (*college.hmco.com/pic/reece10e*)

First Impressions
The Job Interview
Your Voice!

ACE

Self-tests

business.college.hmco.com/students

PART IV

IF WE ALL WORK TOGETHER . . .

12 TEAM BUILDING:
A LEADERSHIP STRATEGY

13 RESOLVING CONFLICT AND
DEALING WITH DIFFICULT PEOPLE

12

TEAM BUILDING: A LEADERSHIP STRATEGY

Chapter Preview

After studying this chapter, you will be able to

■ Explain the importance of teamwork in an organizational setting.

■ Identify and explain common types of work teams.

■ List the characteristics of an effective work team.

■ Explain the behavioral science principles that support team building.

■ Describe the team-building skills that leaders need.

■ Describe the team-member skills that employees need.

Mount Everest, the highest elevation in the world, offers the ultimate challenge to climbers. Many gifted climbers have attempted to reach the top of this 29,028 feet high mountain, but most have failed. During one thirty-year period, seven climbing expeditions from England confronted Mount Everest and braved its dangers, but failed to make it to the top. Finally, in 1953 two English climbers, Edmund Hillary and Tenzing Norgay, set foot on the highest point on the planet.

Although Hillary and Norgay became instant legends, the person who planned and led the successful expedition was the unsung hero of Mount Everest. John Hunt was, by modern-day assessment criteria, a talented professional manager. He organized a team of climbers, Sherpas, porters, and yaks that would carefully move up the mountain, shuttling supplies to ever higher camps. The expedition was provided with the proper equipment and the correct amount of rations. Hunt also gave the human element careful attention. Later, he would say that Everest demands an "unusual degree of selflessness and patience." He recognized that the desire to reach the top must be both individual and collective. When Hillary and Norgay stood atop Everest, five miles in the sky, they represented every member of the expeditionary team.[1]

The focus of this chapter is team-building leadership strategies, so it is important to understand the difference between leadership and management. **Leadership** is the process of inspiring, influencing, and guiding employees to participate in a common effort.[2] Stephen Covey, in his book *The 8th Habit*, says, "Leadership is communicating people's worth and potential so clearly that they come to see it in themselves only."[3] Leaders are made, not born. Leadership is a series of skills that can be acquired through study and practice.

Edmund Hillary, John Hunt, and Tenzing Norgay (left to right) take a last look at Mount Everest before leaving Katmandu, Nepal. A great deal of credit for the successful expedition was given to John Hunt, a talented professional manager.

| FIGURE 12.1 | **Five Practices of Exemplary Leadership** |

The Leadership Challege is considered to be the definitive field guide on leadership. There are over a million copies in print in fifteen languages. The authors have devised the following five practices of exemplary leadership.

Model the Way. Leaders must model the behavior they expect from others.

Inspire a Shared Vision. The leader's dream or vision is the force that invents the future. It is the employees' belief in and enthusiasm for the vision that motivates them to give their best.

Challenge the Process. Leaders do not accept the status quo. They search for opportunities to innovate, grow, and improve processes.

Enable Others to Act. Effective leaders make people feel confident, strong, and capable of taking action.

Encourage the Heart. Through good times and bad, leaders encourage the heart of their employees to carry on and do their best.

Source: James M. Kouzes and Barry Z. Posner, *The Leadership Challenge*, 3rd ed. (San Francisco, Calif. Jossey-Bass, 2002), pp. 13–20.

Thanks to the efforts of James Kouzes and Barry Posner, we know a great deal about the practices of exemplary leaders. Kouzes and Posner have summarized and reported on many years of research on this topic in *The Leadership Challenge*, a best-selling book.[4] After a lengthy study of the dynamic process of leadership, they found that the most effective leaders engage in five practices of exemplary leadership (see Figure 12.1).

Management is the process of coordinating people and other resources to achieve the goals of the organization. Most managers focus on four kinds of resources: material, human, financial, and informational.[5] John Hunt was able to conquer Mount Everest by combining effective leadership and management skills.

Leadership Challenges in a Changing Workplace

The New Economy is characterized by rapid change and demand for increased productivity. As the pace of change quickens and the pressure to work harder increases, the result is greater employee stress and tension. How can a supervisor motivate employees who are tired and frustrated? Some of the most important leadership strategies, such as building trust, empowering employees, and developing the spirit of teamwork, can take many months, even years, to implement. How do managers respond to leaders at the top of the organization who want changes implemented overnight?

Diversity has also become a more prominent characteristic of today's work force. We have seen increased participation in the labor force by women and minorities. Supervising a multicultural and multilingual work force can be very challenging. We have also seen greater use of part-time or temporary workers, who may have less commitment to the organization.

Team Building: An Introduction

Most organizations today are trying to develop the spirit of teamwork, and many organizations have organized their workers into teams. When a person assumes the duties of team supervision, the individual's title is likely to be "team leader" or "team facilitator." The changing role of this new breed of leader is discussed in this chapter. In addition, we discuss ways in which you can become an effective team member.

Can the element of teamwork make a difference between the successful and unsuccessful operation of an organization? Yes, there is evidence that a leadership style that emphasizes **team building** is positively associated with high productivity and profitability. Problems in interpersonal relations are also less common where teamwork is evident. Teamwork ensures not only that a job gets done but also that it gets done efficiently and harmoniously.

There is also evidence that team building can have a positive influence on the physical and psychological well-being of everyone involved. When employees are working together as a team, the leader and members often experience higher levels of job satisfaction and less stress.

Another positive outcome of teamwork is an increase in synergy. **Synergy** is the interaction of two or more parts to produce a greater result than the sum of the parts taken individually.[6] Mathematically speaking, synergy suggests that two plus two equals five. Teamwork synergy is especially important at a time when organizations need creative solutions to complex problems.

Teamwork Doesn't Come Naturally

Many organizations are working hard to get all employees to pull together as a team. Teamwork at a hospital, for example, may begin with acceptance of a common vision, such as providing outstanding health care services. The only way to make this vision a reality is to obtain the commitment and cooperation of every employee. This will require meaningful employee participation in planning, solving problems, and developing ways to improve health care.

Most jobs today require ongoing interaction between coworkers and managers. The spirit of teamwork helps cement these interpersonal relationships. However, working together as a team does not come naturally. Some people value individualism over teamwork. Team skills tend to lag far behind technical skills. The good news is that teamwork does flourish under strong leadership.

The Transition to Team-Based Structures

One of the most popular workplace initiatives today is the development of organizations that are structured around teams. Teams have become popular because they have proven to be effective in such areas as cost reduction, developing innovative new products, and improving quality. This section focuses on two of the most common types of teams: self-managed and cross-functional.

Self-Managed Teams   **Self-managed teams** assume responsibility for traditional management tasks as part of their regular work routine. Examples

Employees formerly concerned only with their own jobs suddenly become accountable for the work of the total team.

include decisions about production quotas, quality standards, and interviewing applicants for team positions. A typical self-managed team usually has five to fifteen members who are responsible for producing a well-defined product (such as an automobile) or service (such as processing an insurance claim). Team members usually rotate among the various jobs and acquire the knowledge and skills to perform each job. Each member eventually can perform every job required to complete the entire team task. Employees formerly concerned only with their own jobs suddenly become accountable for the work of the total team.[7] One advantage of this approach is that it reduces the amount of time workers spend on dull and repetitive duties.

The General Electric aircraft-engine assembly facility in Durham, North Carolina, has more than 200 employees who build jet engines, the size of a large automobile. The engines are assembled by nine self-managed teams. Team members make a wide range of decisions, such as job assignments, how to improve the manufacturing process, vacation schedules, and the assignment of overtime. If a team member slacks off, members deal with the problem. Team members are also responsible for quality control.[8]

United Airlines employees pick up team-building ideas at "Pit Crew U." This pit crew training experience is intended to reinforce the importance of such things as teamwork, preparedness, and safety.

Cross-Functional Teams   **Cross-functional teams** are task groups staffed with a mix of specialists focused on a common objective.[9] These teams are often temporary units with members from different departments and job levels. The teams are often involved in developing new work procedures or products, devising work reforms, or introducing new technology in an organization. Team members often provide a link among separate functions, such as production, distribution, finance, and customer service. Cross-functional teams often make major decisions that directly influence quality and productivity improvements.

Hypertherm Incorporated, a metal-cutting equipment maker based in Hanover, New Hampshire, has developed cross-functional teams for each of its five product lines. Team members represent engineering, marketing, production, and sales. Salespeople and marketers know customers best, so they make an important contribution to new product development. During the hiring process, every effort is made to screen out persons who would not be effective team players.[10]

■ Teams Take Time to Develop

Although we are seeing greater use of teams, this approach to employee participation is by no means a quick fix. In the case of self-managed teams, it can sometimes take one or two years for members to learn all the tasks they will perform as they rotate from job to job. It also takes time for a team to mature to the point where it is comfortable making decisions in such areas as work scheduling, hiring, training, and problem solving.

As teams become more popular, we need to increase our understanding of factors that contribute to team effectiveness. If you have ever enjoyed the experience of being part of a great team, then you probably discovered the following determinants of team effectiveness.[11]

People-Related Factors   The team is characterized by mutual trust and respect. Team members know the power of reflection and silence when agenda topics are being discussed. Members listen to each other and welcome a diversity of ideas and viewpoints.

HUMAN RELATIONS IN ACTION

Marine Corps Built upon Real Teams

U.S. Marines at all levels must be prepared to make decisions in response to fast-changing situations without consulting the chain of command. Even the lowly privates know they're expected to take whatever initiative is necessary to complete a mission. After Marines complete boot camp, they enter infantry school. Each Marine rotates through all the positions in a fire team—leader, machine gunner, assistant machine gunner, and rifleman. All the Marines learn when and how to shift the leadership role. By the time the team is ready for duty, it is truly a self-managed team. Each member is prepared to fill every position.

Organization-Related Factors   Team development is supported by management personnel at every level. They are interested in outcomes and provide rewards and recognition of accomplishments.

Task-Related Factors   Each team has clear objectives and project plans. They are given autonomy and assignments that are professionally challenging.

Basic Beliefs About Teamwork

One approach to the study of leadership is examining the careers of successful leaders who demonstrated their ability to develop teamwork. For instance, coach Dean Smith became a legend in college basketball. During his 36-year tenure at the University of North Carolina, his teams won 879 games. He recruited players from high schools all over the country—players accustomed to being the stars of their high school teams. He then worked hard to encourage this group of superstars to place "team before the individual."[12] Books such as *My American Journey* by Colin Powell and *Leadership* by Rudolph Giuliani provide us with gems of wisdom regarding effective leadership.

A second approach to the study of leadership is reviewing the findings of scholars who have identified the characteristics of successful leaders. What do successful leaders have in common? See, in the sections that follow, how Douglas McGregor, Robert Blake, Jane S. Mouton, and Jay Hall have answered this question.

McGregor's Influence

In the late 1950s, a book by Douglas McGregor entitled *The Human Side of Enterprise* presented convincing arguments that management had been ignoring certain important facts about people. The author said that managers often failed to recognize the potential for growth of most workers and their desire for fulfillment. McGregor emphasized that "unity of purpose" is the main distinguishing characteristic of many productive work teams. When a work group shares common goals and a common commitment, it accomplishes more than it would without them.

In *The Human Side of Enterprise,* McGregor discusses several characteristics of an effective work team.[13]

1. The atmosphere of the workplace tends to be informal, comfortable, relaxed. There are no obvious tensions. It is a working environment in which people are involved and interested.

2. There is a lot of discussion about work-related issues. Virtually everyone participates, but contributions remain pertinent to the task of the group. The members listen to one another.

3. The tasks or objectives of the group are well understood and accepted by the members.

4. There is disagreement. The group is comfortable with this and shows no signs of having to avoid conflict.

5. People freely express their feelings as well as their ideas, both on the problem and on the group's operation. There is little avoidance, and there are few "hidden agendas."

McGregor's views on the characteristics of effective work teams represent "classic" thinking. His thoughts continue to have merit today.

TOTAL	**GENERAL COLIN POWELL (RET.)**
PERSON	UNITED STATES ARMY
INSIGHT	"The day soldiers stop bringing you their problems is the day you have stopped leading them. They have either lost confidence that you can help them or concluded that you do not care. Either case is a failure of leadership."

■ The Leadership Grid®

In the early 1960s, Robert Blake and Jane Mouton authored a popular book entitled *The Managerial Grid* (*www.gridinternational.com*). The **Leadership Grid®** (formerly called the Managerial Grid®) is a model based on two important leadership-style dimensions: concern for people and concern for production.[14] Where work is physical, concern for production may take the form of number of units assembled per hour or time needed to meet a certain production schedule. In an office setting, concern for production may take the form of document preparation volume and accuracy. Concern for people can be reflected in the way a supervisor views work and safety conditions, compensation, recognition for a job well done, and awareness of employees' need to be treated with respect. The Grid helps clarify how these two dimensions are related and establishes a uniform language for communication about leadership styles and patterns. Although there are many possible leadership styles within the Grid, five encompass the most important differences among managers. Blake and Mouton developed descriptive names for each.[15]

- *Impoverished management.* People with the **impoverished management** orientation might be classified as "inactive" managers. They display little concern for people or production.

- *Country club management.* Low concern for production and high concern for people characterize the **country club management** orientation. These managers take steps to prevent unhappiness and dissension.

- *Authority-compliance management.* The **authority-compliance management** style is task-oriented, placing much attention on getting the job done. Managers with this orientation display concern for production, not people.

- *Middle-of-the-road management.* Managers with a **middle-of-the-road management** style display moderate concern for both people and production. They see a limited amount of participative management as practical.

■ *Team management*. The **team management** style is a proactive style of management. Persons with this orientation display a high concern for both people and production.

Blake and Mouton devoted more than thirty years to the study of the team-building leadership style. They maintain that this style is the one most positively associated with productivity and profitability, career success and satisfaction, and physical and mental health. The term *one best style* is used by the authors to describe this orientation. This style, they state, achieves production through a high degree of shared responsibility coupled with high participation, involvement, and commitment—all of which are hallmarks of teamwork.[16]

Hall's Contributions

Jay Hall, founder of Teleometrics International Inc. (*www.teleometrics.com*), a national consulting firm, completed a large-scale research project that supports the work of Blake and Mouton.[17] He studied several thousand managers—their personalities and management styles and patterns. In his book *The Competence Process,* he reports that high-achieving managers had a deep interest in both people and productivity and relied heavily on the participative approach. Low and moderate achievers, by contrast, avoided involving their subordinates in planning and decision making.

Hall says the values that supervisors and managers hold dear flow from their basic convictions about the worth of the people who perform the work in an organization.[18] Participative management practices are more likely to be fostered in an organization where supervisory-management personnel project confidence in the potentialities of subordinates than in organizations where they do not.

CRITICAL THINKING CHALLENGE

Reflect on your work experience and experiences in high school or college. Recall situations when you felt like a member of an effective team. What did the supervisor, manager, teacher, or coach do to develop the spirit of teamwork? Once you have reviewed the behaviors of these team leaders, assign each person one of the five leadership styles developed by Blake and Mouton.

Behavioral Science Principles Supporting Team Building

In almost every field of study there are a few universal principles (sometimes called fundamentals) that are supported by research evidence. Principles can be thought of as general guidelines that are true regardless of time, place, or situation. In the field of human relations there are several principles—based on the behavioral sciences—that support the team-building leadership style. Blake and Mouton have developed a list of these principles and have applied them to the art of leadership.[19]

1. *Shared participation in problem solving and decision making is basic to growth, development, and contribution.* When people are encouraged to participate in making decisions that affect them, they develop an identity and a sense of control over their destiny.

2. *Mutual trust and respect undergird productive human relationships.* Research consistently shows that employee commitment is directly linked to trust in the supervisor or manager. Trust is a catalyst. When trust exists within an organization, a spirit of teamwork is more likely to exist.

3. *Open communication supports mutual understanding.* Everyone has a need to communicate. People are naturally curious and interested in what is happening within the organization. Price Pritchett said it best: "Communication breathes the first spark of life into teamwork, and communication keeps teamwork alive."[20]

4. *Conflict resolution by direct problem-solving confrontation promotes personal health.* A primary goal of team building is to provide a natural forum for conflict resolution. Conflict can drain people of the energy they need to perform their regular duties.

5. *Responsibility for one's own actions stimulates initiative.* As humans grow and mature, they become less dependent on others and seek more control over their own lives. Generally adults tend to develop a deep psychological need to be viewed by others as self-directing.

Team-Building Skills for Leaders

This section discusses ways that supervisory-management personnel can become team builders. Later in this chapter, you will see how employees can contribute to the team-building process.

TOTAL	**MICHAEL CROM**
PERSON	VICE PRESIDENT, DALE CARNEGIE & ASSOCIATES, INC.
INSIGHT	"Life is good when trust is present. Life hurts when trust disappears. We understand this at a level so deep it is indistinguishable from our very being."

The wide range of types of supervisory-management positions may cause you to ask, Do people in these positions have much in common? Will team-building strategies work in most situations? The answer to both questions is yes. A great majority of successful supervisory-management personnel share certain behavior characteristics. Two of the most important dimensions of supervisory leadership—consideration and structure—have been identified in research studies conducted by Edwin Fleishman at Ohio State University[21] and validated by several additional studies. By making a matrix out of these two independent dimensions of leadership, the researchers identified four styles of leadership (see Figure 12.2).

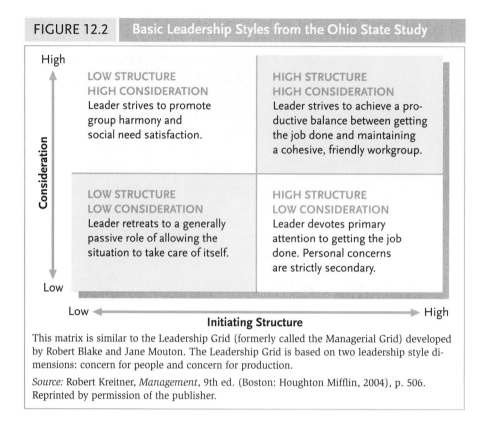

FIGURE 12.2 | Basic Leadership Styles from the Ohio State Study

This matrix is similar to the Leadership Grid (formerly called the Managerial Grid) developed by Robert Blake and Jane Mouton. The Leadership Grid is based on two leadership style dimensions: concern for people and concern for production.

Source: Robert Kreitner, *Management,* 9th ed. (Boston: Houghton Mifflin, 2004), p. 506. Reprinted by permission of the publisher.

Consideration

The dimension of **consideration** reflects the extent to which a supervisor's or manager's relationships with subordinates are characterized by mutual trust, respect for the employees, consideration of their feelings, and a certain warmth in interpersonal relationships. When consideration is present, the supervisor-subordinate relationship is characterized by a climate of good rapport and two-way communication. Consideration is the equivalent of "concern for people" on the Leadership Grid and *social competence,* a concept introduced in Chapter 9.

Structure

The dimension of **structure** reflects the extent to which a supervisor is likely to define and direct his or her role and the roles of subordinates toward goal attainment. Managers who incorporate structure into their leadership style actively direct group activities by planning, setting goals, communicating information, scheduling, and evaluating performance. People who work under the direction of a highly structured supervisor know what is expected of them. Structure is the equivalent of "concern for production" on the Leadership Grid.

It is interesting to note that the dimensions of consideration and structure are independent of each other. A supervisor may be well qualified in one area but lack competence in the other. Anyone who assumes a leadership role can consciously work to develop competence in both areas.

Improving Consideration Skills

Brian Tracy says that effective leaders are guided by the *law of empathy*: "Leaders are sensitive to and aware of the needs, feelings, and motivations of those they lead."[22] This is good advice for anyone who wants to become an outstanding leader. To improve the dimension of consideration, one should adopt the following practices.

Recognize Accomplishments When individual achievements are overlooked, supervisors miss a valuable opportunity to boost employee self-confidence and build morale. As noted in Chapter 10, people need recognition for good work, regardless of the duties they perform or the positions they hold. Of course, recognition should be contingent on performance. When recognition is given for mediocre performance, the supervisor is reinforcing a behavior that is not desirable.

Provide for Early and Frequent Success According to an old saying, "Nothing succeeds like success." A supervisor should provide each employee with as many opportunities to succeed as possible. The foundation for accomplishment begins with a carefully planned orientation and training program. Supervisors and managers should review job duties and responsibilities, organizational policies and procedures, and any other pertinent information with their employees early in the relationship. Successful leaders are successful teachers. No worker should have to rely on gossip or the advice of a perennially dissatisfied employee for answers to important questions.

> *A supervisor should provide each employee with as many opportunities to succeed as possible.*

Take a Personal Interest in Each Employee Everyone likes to be treated as an individual. Taking a personal interest means learning the names of spouses and children, finding out what employees do during their leisure time, asking about their families, and acknowledging birthdays. The more you learn about the "whole person," the better you will be able to help employees balance their work lives with the rest of their lives. Some supervisors keep a record of significant information about each of their workers (see Figure 12.3). This record is especially helpful for supervisors who are in charge of a large number of employees and find it difficult to remember important facts about each person.

> *Therefore, efforts to improve the communication process represent a good use of the supervisor's time and energy.*

Establish a Climate of Open Communication To establish a climate of open communication, the leader must be available and approachable. Employees should feel comfortable talking about their fears, frustrations, and aspirations. Communication is closely linked to employee morale—and morale is directly linked to productivity. Therefore, efforts to improve the communication process represent a good use of the supervisor's time and energy.

Discover Individual Employee Values Today's lean, flatter organizations offer employees fewer opportunities for promotion, smaller

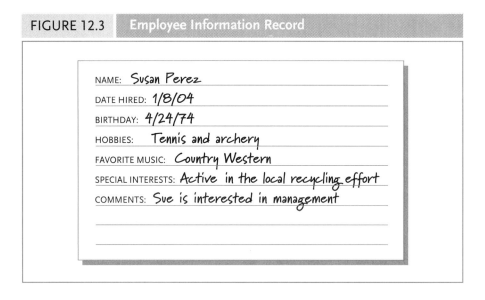

FIGURE 12.3 Employee Information Record

NAME: Susan Perez
DATE HIRED: 1/8/04
BIRTHDAY: 4/24/74
HOBBIES: Tennis and archery
FAVORITE MUSIC: Country Western
SPECIAL INTERESTS: Active in the local recycling effort
COMMENTS: Sue is interested in management

raises, and less job security. As a result, many workers no longer feel secure or identify with the company. Supervisors should encourage employees to explore their values and determine if there is a match between what matters most to them and the work they are doing. If a value conflict turns up, the supervisor may be able to redesign the job or give an employee a new assignment.[23] Supervisors should also attempt to find out whether there are any conflicts between the employee's job and personal life. Many employees view their family and personal life as their primary source of satisfaction. The employee who feels pressured to work excessive overtime or travel a great deal may experience a major value conflict. Supervisors who are able to meet the needs of employees who have work/life conflicts embrace an important leadership fundamental: Live by your values, and encourage others to live by theirs.[24]

Improving Structure Skills

The supervisor who incorporates structure into his or her leadership style plays an active role in directing group activities. The team builder gives the group direction, establishes performance standards, and maintains individual and group accountability. The following practices can be used to develop the dimension of structure.

Communicate Your Expectations   Members of the group or team must possess a clear idea of what needs to be accomplished. The law of expectations, according to Brian Tracy, states, "Whatever you expect, with confidence, becomes your own self-fulfilling prophecy."[25] Leaders must effectively formulate their expectations and then communicate them with conviction.

Bob Hughes, a consultant in the area of team building, suggests establishing baseline performance data so progress can be assessed.[26] In an office that processes lease applications, where accuracy and speed are critically important, the baseline data might include the number of error-free lease applications the

team processes in one day. In an ideal situation, team members will be involved in setting goals and will help determine how best to achieve the goals. Setting and reaching goals can provide individuals and teams with a sense of accomplishment. Specific goals are more likely to motivate us than general goals. The goal-setting process is described in Chapter 4.

Provide Specific Feedback Often   Feedback should be relevant to the task performed by the employee and should be given soon after performance. Feedback is especially critical when an employee is just learning a new job. The supervisor should point out improvements in performance, no matter how small, and always reinforce the behavior she or he wants repeated. The most relevant feedback in a self-managed work team usually comes from coworkers because team members are accountable to one another. Some self-managed work teams design their own performance appraisal system.

Deal with Performance Problems Immediately   As a supervisor, you must deal quickly with the person who does not measure up to your standards of performance. When members of the group are not held accountable for doing their share of the work or for making mistakes, group morale may suffer. Other members of the group will quickly observe the poor performance and wonder why you are not taking corrective action.

> *A person can make a mistake and still be a valuable employee.*

To achieve the best results, focus feedback on the situation, issue, or behavior, not on the employee. A person can make a mistake and still be a valuable employee. Correct the person in a way that does not create anger and resentment. Avoid demoralizing the person or impairing his or her self-confidence.[27]

Coaching for Peak Performance   When performance problems surface, leaders must assume the role of coach. **Coaching** is an interpersonal process between the supervisor and the employee in which the leader helps the employee improve in a specific area. The coaching process involves four steps. *Step one* involves documentation of the performance problem. *Step two* involves getting the employee to recognize and agree that there is a need to improve performance in a specific area. Supervisors should never assume the employee sees the problem in the same way they do. *Step three* involves exploring options. At this point it is often best to let the employee suggest ways to improve performance. *Step four* involves getting a commitment from the employee to take action.[28]

SKILL DEVELOPMENT CHALLENGE

Assume you are the manager of the record-keeping department at a credit union. Three of the employees are responsible for sorting and listing checks and keeping personal and commercial accounts up-to-date. A fourth employee handles all inquiries concerning overdrafts and other problems related to customer accounts. List four specific behaviors you could develop that would contribute to the supervisory-management quality described as *consideration* and four behaviors that would contribute to the quality described as *structure*.

Situational Leadership

The **Situational Leadership Model**, developed by Paul Hersey and his colleagues at the Center for Leadership Studies *(www.situational.com)*, offers an alternative to the Leadership Grid. **Situational leadership** is based on the theory that the most successful leadership occurs when the leader's style matches the situation. Situational leadership theory emphasizes the need for flexibility.[29]

Paul Hersey says that the primary behaviors displayed by effective managers in the Situational Leadership Model can be described as *task behavior* and *relationship behavior*. Task behavior, as Hersey describes it in his book *The Situational Leader*, is very similar to the "concern for production" dimension of the Leadership Grid. And relationship behavior is very similar to the "concern for people" dimension. In essence, the situational leader and the person who uses the Leadership Grid model rely on the same two dimensions of leadership.[30]

What is the major difference between these two leadership models? Hersey says that, when attempting to influence others, you must (1) diagnose the readiness level of the follower for a specific task and (2) provide the appropriate leadership style for that situation. In other words, given the specific situation, you must decide how much task behavior and how much relationship behavior to display. Readiness is defined as the extent to which an employee has the ability and willingness to accomplish a specific task. If an employee has the experience and skill to perform a certain task or activity, this information will influence the leader's style. But the leader must also consider the employee's confidence level, commitment, and motivation to accomplish the task or activity. Hersey reminds us that readiness levels often vary greatly among members of the work group.[31]

TOTAL	**DANIEL GOLEMAN**
PERSON	AUTHOR, *WORKING WITH EMOTIONAL INTELLIGENCE*
INSIGHT	"The most effective leaders are alike in one crucial way: They all have a high degree of what has come to be known as *emotional intelligence*."

Additional Leadership Qualities

In addition to consideration and structure skills, leaders need some additional qualities (see Figure 12.4). One of these is character. As noted in Chapter 5, character is composed of personal standards of behavior, including honesty, integrity, and moral strength. Effective leadership is characterized by honesty, truthfulness, and straight dealing with every person.[32] Without character it is impossible to build a trusting relationship with the people you lead.

A second important quality is emotional intelligence, a concept that was discussed in Chapter 9. Emotional intelligence is a much more powerful predictor of leadership success than IQ because it gives you the ability to monitor your own and others' emotions and deal with them effectively.[33] For example, a leader with high emotional intelligence is more likely to detect friction and eliminate conflict among team members. This leader is also more flexible, and therefore better able to use situational leadership.

Character and emotional intelligence are leadership qualities that can be developed. Leaders create themselves—they are not born. One very important key to growth in both of these areas is self-awareness. Without self-awareness we may behave in ways that are potentially ineffective.[34]

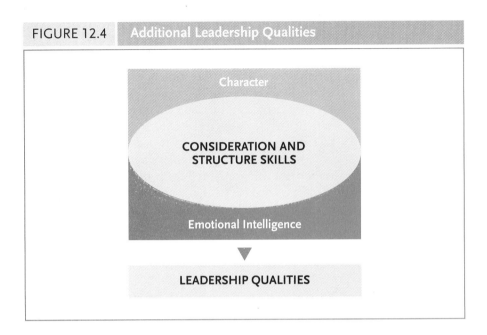

FIGURE 12.4   Additional Leadership Qualities

Character

CONSIDERATION AND STRUCTURE SKILLS

Emotional Intelligence

▼

LEADERSHIP QUALITIES

Teamwork: The Employee's Role

Each member should assume an active part in helping the work unit achieve its mission. This means that every member of the work group can and should be a team member and a team builder. These dual roles are achieved when employees assume greater responsibility for the success of the work unit. Today's most valued employees are those who are willing to assume leadership responsibilities.

Employees as Leaders

In traditional organizations there were leaders and followers, and the followers were not expected to develop leadership skills. Today, some of the most effective leaders are helping their work team members develop leadership skills so that the team's success will not ride on one person. At a time when most organizations are attempting to compete in a complex, ever changing global market, there is real merit in establishing a diversity of leadership within the work group. If we are willing to expand our definition of leadership, we can see leaders everywhere.[35]

- The quiet "worker bee" frequently serves as a leader when the issue is how to get the work done during a crisis situation.

- The "corporate counselor," who informally guides coworkers through stressful problems by merely listening, is an emotional leader.

- The rigid "rule follower" keeps our creativity from becoming irresponsible.

Will the "employees as leaders" approach catch on? J. Oliver Crom, CEO of Dale Carnegie & Associates, Inc., is optimistic. He says that leadership skills are needed at all levels of the organization and adds that "Every employee is a leader" might well be today's business slogan.[36]

Becoming a Valued Team Member

Throughout your working life, your success is very likely to depend on your ability to be an effective team member. Here are some tips on how to become a respected team member in any organizational setting.[37]

1. *Avoid becoming part of a clique or subgroup within the team.* As a member of a clique you are very likely to lose the trust and respect of other team members.

2. *Avoid any action that might sabotage the team.* By engaging in frequent criticism of other team members, gossip, or other unconstructive behaviors, you undermine team efforts.

TOTAL PERSON INSIGHT	**JOHN C. MAXWELL** AUTHOR, *THE 17 ESSENTIAL QUALITIES OF A TEAM PLAYER* "Great challenges require great teamwork, and the quality most needed among teammates amid the pressure of a difficult challenge is collaboration. . . . Each person brings something to the table that adds value to the relationship and synergy to the team."

3. *Keep in mind that effective team membership depends on honest, open communication among team members.* Use the fundamentals of constructive self-disclosure discussed in Chapter 8.

4. *As a team member, do not feel the need to submerge your own strong beliefs, creative solutions, and ideas.* If the team members are about to make a decision that in your opinion is not "right," do not hesitate to speak up and express your views.

Teamwork can be a very satisfying experience. It can generate positive energy and contribute to a sense of optimism about the future. As a team member you have the opportunity to assume a very important leadership role.

Managing the Relationship with Your Boss

The idea that you should manage the relationship with your boss may sound a little unusual at first. But it makes a lot of sense when you consider the advantages of assuming this responsibility. When the subordinate and the boss are both working to maintain a good relationship, conflict is less likely to surface. The boss-subordinate relationship is not like the one between parent and child—the burden for managing the relationship should not and cannot fall entirely on the one in authority.

When you take time to manage the relationship with your boss, he or she will become more effective in performing his or her job. In many cases, managers are no more effective than the combined competence of the people they supervise. Some employees do not realize how much their boss needs assistance and support from them.

How do you go about managing your boss? Here are some general considerations.

Assess Your Own Strengths   The boss represents only one-half of the relationship. The development of an effective working relationship also requires reflecting on your own strengths, weaknesses, work habits, communication style, and needs. What personal characteristics might impede or facilitate working with your boss? The most effective team players assume the responsibility for self-assessment and adjustment. It is a burden they gladly accept.

Develop an Understanding of Your Boss   Become familiar with this person's strengths, weaknesses, work habits, communication style, and needs. Spend time studying your boss. In some cases, the direct approach is best. Ask your boss, "How would you like me to work with you?" Try to determine his or her goals and expectations. What is the person trying to accomplish? Does your boss enjoy casual meetings to discuss business matters or formal meetings with written agendas?

Flex Your Communication Style   In terms of communication style, is your boss supportive, emotive, reflective, or director? Once you have answered this question, begin thinking of how to flex your style in ways that will build rapport and avoid unnecessary stress. Remember, style flexing is a temporary effort to act in harmony with another person's preferred communication style (see Chapter 3).

Be Frank and Candid   Suppose that to avoid conflict you almost never disagree with your boss—even when the boss is obviously wrong. Are you making a contribution to his or her growth and development? Obviously not. At times you must be your own person and say what is on your mind. The information you share with your boss may in fact contribute to his or her success. Chapter 8 provides some excellent tips on how to effectively self-disclose your thoughts and feelings.

As organizations become flatter, with fewer layers of management and more projects carried out by teams, collaboration has become more important. Effective team members are those who collaborate actively with their leader and other members of the team.

HUMAN RELATIONS IN ACTION | **Tips for Young Managers**

Wanted: A new breed of boss who can provide strong leadership, handle technology, inspire teamwork, and cope with uncertainty. The person who fits this description may be quite young and inexperienced. Many of today's leaders are no longer molded solely by seniority and experience. Here are some tips for the young manager:

■ Keep in mind that watching your own bosses in action is not enough to teach you to be one.

■ Never assume that others are motivated by the same things you are.
■ Don't ask for suggestions or opinions that you are not seriously prepared to consider.
■ Give before you take. Approach relationships (with your employees, your boss, customers) with what you have to offer, not with what you want.
■ Reach out to people with more age and experience.

LOOKING BACK: Reviewing the Concepts

■ Explain the importance of teamwork in an organizational setting.

Teamwork ensures not only that a job gets done, but also that it gets done efficiently. Therefore, successful teamwork can often make the difference between the profitable and the unprofitable operation of an organization. The team-building leadership style is effective because it is suited to the needs of most of today's employees.

■ Identify and explain common types of work teams.

Many companies are forming specific types of teams. Two of the most common are self-managed teams and cross-functional teams. Self-managed teams assume responsibility for traditional management tasks as part of their regular work routine. Team members are responsible for producing a well-defined product or service. They usually rotate among the various jobs and acquire the knowledge and skills to perform each one. Cross-functional teams are task groups staffed with a mix of specialists focused on a common objective. These teams are often temporary units with members from different departments.

■ List the characteristics of an effective work team.

An effective work team tends to be informal and relaxed, with no obvious tensions. People are involved, interested, and eager to participate in solving work-related problems. An effective work group also has clearly understood goals and objectives.

■ Explain the behavioral science principles that support team building.

One way to learn about teams is to study leaders who promote teamwork and scholars who discuss it; examples are McGregor, Blake and Mouton, and Hall. We reviewed a series of behavioral science principles developed by these noted scholars.

■ Describe the team-building skills that leaders need.

Two important dimensions of supervisory leadership contribute to team building. One of these dimensions, *consideration*, reflects the extent to which a supervisor maintains relationships with employees that are characterized by mutual trust, respect, and rapport. The other dimension, *structure*, reflects the extent to which a supervisor is likely to direct group activities through planning, goal setting, communication, scheduling, and evaluating. The Leadership Grid® and the Situational Leadership Model help clarify these two dimensions of leadership. Effective leaders must also develop the qualities of character and emotional intelligence.

■ Describe the team-member skills that employees need.

Members of an effective work group should assume effective leadership and membership roles. Each team member helps the group achieve its mission. Everyone assumes the role of team member and team builder. Employees are in a unique position to give guidance and support to their supervisor or manager. Most bosses need this assistance and support to achieve success.

Career Corner

Q: I work for a company that frequently uses cross-functional teams to complete certain projects. Whenever I serve on one of these teams, I feel frustrated. I want to get a promotion, but team assignments seem to hide my talents. How can I make the best of my next team assignment?

A: If your company is having success with these teams, the best way to get the attention of top management is to be an effective team member. When you get your next team assignment, make a quick study of how the group is working together and note any problems that could prevent the team from reaching its goals. Your visibility will increase if you find ways to enhance team performance. You might share important information with team members or offer to help team members develop some specific skills. In most cases it's possible to help your teammates grow while developing yourself.

Key Terms

leadership	authority-compliance management
management	middle-of-the-road management
team building	team management
synergy	consideration
self-managed teams	structure
cross-functional teams	coaching
Leadership Grid®	Situational Leadership Model
impoverished management	situational leadership
country club management	

Applying What You Have Learned

1. Business publications such as the *Wall Street Journal, Fortune, Business Week,* and *Fast Company* frequently feature articles describing problem bosses. Managers with high-tech backgrounds (computer science, electrical engineering, mathematics, etc.) sometimes create employee frustration through insensitive or vindictive behavior. These so-called nerd managers are often more focused on technology than on people. They have high IQs but rank low in emotional intelligence, and they lack people skills. The result is often high employee turnover. Let's assume that you are working for a small business and the owner is often described by employees as the "nerd boss from hell." What steps might you take to influence your boss, who seems to spend all his time obsessing about technology and ignoring the needs of his employees? Review the material featured in this chapter, and then develop a plan that would help your boss develop a strong team-building leadership style.[38]

2. There is increasing pressure on organizations to allow employees' personal problems to be brought to the attention of the supervisor or manager.

Personal problems that can disrupt people's lives include dealing with a teenager on drugs, coping with the needs of a sick parent, losing a babysitter, or getting a divorce. Schedule an interview with two persons who hold supervisory-management positions and ask these questions:

a. Do you assume the role of mentor and counselor when an employee brings a personal problem to your attention?

b. Should you give the person with a serious problem some special consideration, such as time off, less demanding work, or professional help that is paid for by the company?

3. The skills needed to be an effective leader can be developed by anyone who is willing to invest the time and energy. It is possible to practice important leadership skills before you assume the duties of a supervisor or manager. Review the various ways to improve consideration and structure skills discussed in this chapter, and then begin searching for opportunities to practice these skills. Here are some opportunities for practice:

a. Volunteer assignments in your community

b. Group assignments at work, at college, or at place of worship

c. Involvement in political, professional, or social activities

 Internet Insights

1. Many companies provide Internet access for employees and allow them to work in virtual teams. Members may work at headquarters, in satellite offices, on the road, and from home. Virtual team members may never meet one another face to face because they communicate via e-mail, conference calls, and other methods. Web-based tools have been designed to help teams work together more effectively. Visit the following websites and review their services. Then prepare a brief written report on your findings.[39]

Website	Purpose
GroupVine *www.groupvine.com*	Lets you create members-only discussion boards so that a team can post audio files, comments, documents, or pictures concerning a project.
WebOffice *weboffice.com*	WebOffice Workgroup combines asynchronous tools such as document sharing and calendaring with real-time web meeting technology.
ScheduleOnline *www.scheduleonline.com*	A group calendar that lets users schedule events, invite people to meetings, and reserve physical resources such as conference rooms or equipment.

2. Several websites provide workers with an opportunity to post complaints about their boss, employer, or coworker. Visit the following websites and prepare a brief written report on your findings.

www.corporatesuicidewatch.com is designed to call attention to employers who are committing "corporate suicide" because their leaders are not taking care of their employees.

www.badbossology.com will help you with difficult boss problems. It offers free access to hundreds of articles on solving problems with difficult bosses.

 Role-Play Exercise

You are currently a computer technician employed by Tech Doctors, Inc. The company provides a wide range of services including computer system setup, PC and server repairs and upgrades, virus and spyware removal, data recovery services, and Internet security. The company was founded by Evony Leeson about five years ago. You are one of five technicians who make service calls and occasionally work in the repair center when needed. You like your work, but feel a sense of frustration when fellow employees fail to give their best efforts. The owner is very effective in solving technical problems, but often displays poor people skills. He simply does not pay attention to employees, to what they are doing, and to how they are feeling. He knows almost nothing about their hobbies, family status, or personal concerns. There are times when you feel like quitting, but you like solving technical problems and helping customers with their computer needs. You have decided to meet with Evony and provide some suggestions on how to become a more effective leader. Use the name Deaven Wilcox during the role play.

Case 12.1   Coaching to Improve Human Performance

Coaching has been defined as an interpersonal process between a manager and an employee; the purpose is to improve the employee's performance in a *specific* area. Coaching focuses on patterns of behavior such as arriving late for work after being told that tardiness is not acceptable, or violating safety rules after being reminded that safety is very important. The coaching process should help the employee recognize the need to improve performance and to make a commitment to improving performance. Coaching has become a very popular business initiative used to maximize employee productivity and morale.

Managers who develop a leadership style that combines structure and consideration behaviors possess the basic skills for being effective coaches. Coaching involves four steps.

Step One: Carefully document performance problems by collecting factual information. In some cases the best approach may be to observe and assess performance during actual job performance. A sales manager might accompany a salesperson during an actual sales call.

Step Two: Meet with the employee and try to get the person to recognize and agree that there is a need to improve performance in a specific area. Employees often do not see the problem in the same way as the manager views it.

Step Three: Involve the employee in the process of exploring solutions. The employee is often in the best position to suggest ways to improve performance.

Step Four: Get a commitment from the employee to take action. This step may involve development of a contract (verbal or written) that clarifies the coaching goals, approaches, and outcomes.

Throughout the coaching process the manager must use empathic listening (introduced in Chapter 2). This will ensure full understanding of the conditions and dynamics that led to the performance breakdown. At the conclusion of the coaching meeting, thank the employee briefly and describe his or her important role in the organization.[40]

Questions

1. Can the four-step coaching process be used with a group of employees? Explain.

2. Experts say the most critical aspect of coaching is getting an employee to recognize a need for performance improvement. Do you agree? Explain.

3. It has been said that through coaching we empower the employee—we allow the person to see and act on the capability and commitment that he or she already possesses. Do you believe this is true? Explain.

4. If you were preparing a manager to become a successful coach, what suggestions would you give this person? Can you think of some factors that would serve as barriers to effective coaching?

Case 12.2 Can You Become a Leader?

The number of career opportunities in supervision and management continues to be quite high. Persons working in the fields of health care, retailing, manufacturing, and many other employment areas will be given an opportunity to move up to a leadership position. What qualities do you need to achieve success? What sacrifices might be needed if you accept a promotion to the position of supervisor or manager? One way to prepare for a leadership position is to study the wisdom that can be gleaned from the writings of respected leaders. Consider these examples.

- Rudolph Giuliani says he spent his entire life thinking about being a leader. This may explain how he became a successful federal prosecutor and an effective two-term mayor of New York City, a city many people thought ungovernable. In his book *Leadership* he describes what it was like to guide the recovery of New York City after the horror of the World Trade Center attack. The book also describes what he thinks it takes to be a leader during "normal" times. Giuliani feels that holding people accountable is very important. He scheduled morning meetings with top aides to keep them focused on specific problem areas. He recommends staying true to your core values, promising *only* what you can deliver, and not being a bully.[41]

■ Colin Powell, secretary of state during George W. Bush's first-term, has been described as a leader who scores very high in emotional intelligence because he has the intuitive ability to connect with others. Powell has been guided by several "laws of power." Here are two of them.[42]

Dare to be the skunk. He says, "Every organization should tolerate rebels who tell the emperor he has no clothes." In other words, let your employees know it's OK to disagree with you.

Come up for air. Powell demands excellence from his staff, but he also insists they put balance in their life. He sets a good example by spending as much time as possible with his wife and children.

■ Joe Torre, manager of the New York Yankees, may be a model for today's corporate leaders. He will always be remembered as the leader of the team that won four World Series in five years. One of his management principles is "Every employee must feel useful." Today, every employee is important, or he or she wouldn't be on the payroll. The mailroom clerk and the person who cleans the hospital rooms should never feel they are not important. Another Torre management principle is "Manage against the cycle." When things get tense, Torre grows outwardly calmer.[43]

It's not difficult to find articles on bully bosses, supervisors who never give praise for work well done, or leaders who push too hard for increases in productivity. Yet there are many great leaders who can teach us a lot about effective leadership.

Questions

1. Select the two leadership qualities described above that you feel are most important. Provide a rationale for each selection.

2. If you needed a mentor to help you achieve success in a leadership position, which of these three persons would you select? Explain your choice.

INTEGRATED RESOURCES

VIDEOS: "Mary Guerrero-Pelzel, Contractor"
        "Team Decision Making"

CLASSROOM ACTIVITIES (*college.hmco.com/pic/reece10e*)

  Dream Team
  Pieces of the Puzzle
  Valuing Diversity

business.college.hmco.com/students

ACE

Self-tests

13

RESOLVING CONFLICT AND DEALING WITH DIFFICULT PEOPLE

Chapter Preview

After studying this chapter, you will be able to

- List and describe some of the major causes of conflict in the work setting.

- Utilize assertiveness skills in conflict situations.

- Understand when and how to implement effective negotiation skills.

- Identify key elements of the conflict resolution process.

- Discuss contemporary challenges facing labor unions.

If you are a die-hard hockey fan, you will probably always remember the 2004–2005 season. The season was canceled because the National Hockey League and the NHL Players Association could not settle an ongoing labor dispute, and for the first time since 1919, the Stanley Cup was not awarded.

The NHL became the first professional sports league in North America to cancel an entire season because of a labor conflict. The conflict over economic issues began when the owners of the NHL's 30 professional teams locked out the 700 members of the players' union when their collective-bargaining agreement expired. Negotiations spanned a ten-month period before an agreement could be reached. During that time teams lost an estimated $2 billion in revenue from tickets, media, sponsorships, and concessions, while players lost approximately $1 billion in salaries. Team office personnel and stadium attendants were laid off, and Canadian government agencies that owned the stadiums lost rental income. The Canadian government estimated that the country's gross domestic product was reduced by $170 million Canadian dollars as a result of the cancelled season.[1]

The lost NHL season and the lost revenue associated with the conflict are a reminder of how difficult and expensive it can be when conflicts cannot be effectively resolved. While disputes within most organizations are not of this magnitude, companies pay a high price for conflict. Often productivity drops, work relationships suffer, and energy is wasted as workers become increasingly angry, stressed and defensive.[2] It is estimated that managers spend about 20 percent of their time resolving disputes among staff members.[3] This chapter offers workers and managers alike specific guidelines for effectively and productively resolving a variety of conflicts.

Joe Louis Arena in Detroit, home of the Detroit Red Wings, is shown empty. The National Hockey League became the first professional sports league in North America to cancel an entire season. There were no winners in this conflict.

A New View of Conflict

Most standard dictionaries define **conflict** as a clash between incompatible people, ideas, or interests. These conflicts are almost always perceived as negative experiences in our society. But when we view conflict as a negative experience, we may be hurting our chances of dealing with it effectively. In reality, conflicts can serve as opportunities for personal growth if we develop and use positive, constructive conflict resolution skills.[4]

Much of our growth and social progress comes from the opportunities we have to discover creative solutions to conflicts that surface in our lives. Dudley Weeks, professor of conflict resolution at American University, says conflict can provide additional ways of thinking about the *source* of conflict and open up possibilities for improving a relationship.[5] When people work together to resolve conflicts, their solutions are often far more creative than they would be if only one person addressed the problem. Creative conflict resolution can shake people out of their mental ruts and give them a new point of view.

> *Much of our growth and social progress comes from the opportunities we have to discover creative solutions to conflicts that surface in our lives.*

Too much agreement is not always healthy in an organization. Employees who are anxious to be viewed as "team players" may not voice concerns even when they have doubts about a decision being made. Four years before the first flight of space shuttle Challenger, some NASA engineers discovered problems with the O-ring seals, but these concerns were disregarded. Howard Schwartz, in his book *Narcissistic Process and Corporate Decay,* described the Challenger disaster as a tragic example of the "exportation of conflict."[6] Meaningful conflict can be the key to producing healthy, successful organizations because conflict is necessary for effective problem solving and for effective interpersonal relationships.[7] As Mark Twain once said, "It were not best that we should all think alike; it is difference of opinion that makes horse races."[8] The problem isn't with disagreements, but with how they are resolved.

Finding the Root Causes of Conflict

If left unattended, weeds can take over a garden and choke all the healthy plants. When inexperienced gardeners cut weeds off at the surface instead of digging down to find the roots, the weeds tend to come back twice as strong. Conflicts among people at work often follow the same pattern. Unless the root of the conflict is addressed, the conflict is likely to recur. If the root cause appears to stimulate *constructive* conflict, it can be allowed to continue. However, as soon as the symptoms of *destructive* conflict become apparent, steps need to be taken to correct the problem that is triggering it.[9] This segment of the chapter discusses the most common causes of conflicts in the workplace.

> *Unless the root of the conflict is addressed, the conflict is likely to recur.*

Organizational Change Organizational change is one of the seven root causes of conflict. In most organizations there is tension between opposing forces for stability (maintain the status quo) and change. If management wants to shift more health care costs onto workers, tension may surface. With too much stability, the organization may lose its competitive position in the marketplace. With too much change, the mission blurs and employee anxiety develops.[10]

Ineffective Communication A major source of personal conflict is the misunderstanding that results from ineffective communication. In Chapter 2 we discussed the various filters that messages must pass through before effective communication can occur. In the work setting, where many different people work closely together, communication breakdowns are inevitable.

Often it is necessary to determine if the conflict is due to a misunderstanding or a true disagreement. If the cause is a *misunderstanding*, you may need to explain your position again or provide more details or examples to help the other person understand. If a *disagreement* exists, one or both parties have to be persuaded to change their position on the issue. Those involved in the conflict can attempt to explain their position over and over again, but until someone changes, the root problem will persist.[11] This issue is discussed in greater detail later in this chapter.

Value and Culture Clashes In Chapter 5 you read that differences in values can cause conflicts between generations, among men and women, and among people with different value priorities. Today's diverse work force reflects a kaleidoscope of cultures, each with its own unique qualities. The individual bearers of these different cultural traditions could easily come into conflict with one another. The issues may be as simple as one person's desire to dress in ethnic fashion and a supervisor's insistence on strict adherence to the company dress code, or as complex as work ethics.

Work Policies and Practices   Interpersonal conflicts can develop when an organization has unreasonable or confusing rules, regulations, and performance standards. The conflicts often surface when managers fail to tune in to employees' perceptions that various policies are unfair. Managers need to address the source of conflict rather than suppress it. Conflict also surfaces when some workers refuse to comply with the rules and neglect their fair share of the workload.

Adversarial Management   Under adversarial management, supervisors may view their employees and even other managers with suspicion and distrust and treat them as "the enemy." Employees usually lack respect for adversarial managers, resenting their authoritarian style and resisting their suggestions for change. This atmosphere makes cooperation and teamwork difficult.

Competition for Scarce Resources   It would be difficult to find an organization, public or private, that is not involved in downsizing or cost cutting. The result is often destructive competition for scarce resources such as updated computerized equipment, administrative support personnel, travel dollars, salary increases, or annual bonuses. When budgets and cost-cutting efforts are not clearly explained, workers may suspect coworkers or supervisors of devious tactics.

Personality Clashes   There is no doubt about it: Some people just don't like each other. They may have differing communication styles, temperaments, or attitudes. They may not be able to identify exactly what it is they dislike about the other person, but the bottom line is that conflicts will arise when these people have to work together. Even people who get along well with each other

---

HUMAN RELATIONS IN ACTION | **Fire the Client?**

Lisa Zwick knew that her client, the CEO of an Internet start-up company, was a problem. He was irritable and extremely hard to work with. When he called her California home at 5:00 a.m. one Monday morning from his New York City hotel room and asked her to order a limousine for him, she refused and took the issue to her boss. With his support, Lisa fired the client, telling him, "This isn't working out for several reasons; but most of all, you're a jerk!" Many firms are concluding that firing cantankerous clients can be a good business decision. One company fired a client who was bringing in $1 million a year, or 20 percent of the company's revenue, for making nasty, digging comments about employees. The owner of the company believed that if the irritating client was going to drive her employees crazy, the relationship wasn't worth it. Her respected employees replaced the lost business and have since doubled revenue to $10 million.

in the beginning stages of a work relationship may begin to clash after working together for many years.

Resolving Conflict Assertively

Conflict is often uncomfortable whether it is in a personal or professional setting. People sometimes get hurt and become defensive because they feel they are under attack personally. Because we have to work or live with certain people every day, it is best to avoid harming these ongoing relationships. But many people don't know how to participate in and manage conflict in a positive way. Many professionals advise going directly to the offending person and calmly discussing his or her irritating behavior, rather than complaining to others.[12] Figure 13.1, "Dealing with People You Can't Stand," offers specific strategies you might use. By taking those steps to change *your* behavior, you might facilitate a powerful change in theirs. Keep in mind that some people are unaware of the impact of their behavior, and if you draw their attention to it, they may change it.

Whereas these strategies may be comfortable for some people, such a direct approach may be very uncomfortable for many others. People who attempt to avoid conflict by simply ignoring things that bother them are exhibiting **nonassertive behavior**. Nonassertive people often give in to the demands of others, and their passive approach makes them less likely to make their needs known. If you fail to take a firm position when such action is appropriate, customers, coworkers, and supervisors may take advantage of you, and management may question your abilities.

Assertive behavior, on the other hand, provides you the opportunity to stand up for your rights and express your thoughts and feelings in a direct, appropriate way that does not violate the rights of others. It is a matter of getting the other person to understand your viewpoint.[13] People who exhibit appropriate assertive behavior skills are able to handle their conflicts with greater ease and assurance while maintaining good interpersonal relations.

Some people do not understand the distinction between being aggressive and being assertive. **Aggressive behavior** involves expressing your thoughts and feelings and defending your rights in a way that *violates* the rights of others. Aggressive people may interrupt, talk fast, ignore others, and use sarcasm or other forms of verbal abuse to maintain control.

Table 13.1 may give you a clearer understanding of how nonassertive, assertive, and aggressive individuals respond when confronted with conflict situations.

How to Become More Assertive

Entire books have been written that describe how to improve your assertiveness skills. Several years ago the American Management Association (*www.amanet.org*) began offering skill development seminars that focus on assertiveness training, including Assertiveness Training for the New or Prospective Manager and Assertiveness Training for Women in Business.[14] Enrollees have the opportunity to achieve greater credibility by learning how to handle tough

FIGURE 13.1	Dealing with People You Can't Stand

THE BULLY ▶ Bullies find ways to manipulate or control others. They are pushy, ruthless, loud, and forceful and tend to intimidate you with in-your-face arguments. They assume that the end justifies the means.

Strategy: Keep your cool. Immediately respond calmly and professionally to let the bully know you are not a target: "When you're ready to speak to me with respect, I'll be ready to discuss this matter." Walk away from a ranting bully. Ask the bully to fully explain what he or she is trying to say or do, and then paraphrase your understanding of the bully's real intentions.

THE BACKSTABBER ▶ They present themselves as your friend but do everything in their power to sabotage your relationships with your supervisors, coworkers, and clients. They use tactics such as withholding information from you and then suggesting to others that you are incompetent, witless, and worthy of demotion.

Strategy: Once you've discovered your saboteur, tell key people that the person is, in fact, not a friend, which takes power from the backstabber and reveals the smear campaign.

THE WHINER ▶ They wallow in their woe, whine incessantly about the injustices that surround them, and carry the weight of the world on their shoulders.

Strategy: Listen and write down their main points. Interrupt and get specifics so you can identify and focus on possible solutions. If they remain in "it's hopeless" mode, walk away saying, "Let me know when you want to talk about a solution."

THE JERK ▶ They tend to be self-centered, arrogant, manipulative, and goal-oriented. They trust no one and refuse to collaborate with others. They may take pot-shots at you during meetings, but avoid one-on-one confrontations. They lack empathy, but can be great sweet-talkers to the boss.

Strategy: They do not respond to normal pleas to change their behavior, so just back off. Do not take their bait, limit your contact with them, avoid conflict when possible, and always be on guard.

THE KNOW-IT-ALL ▶ They will tell you what they know, but they won't bother listening to your "clearly inferior" ideas. Often they really don't know much, but they don't let that get in the way. They exaggerate, brag, and mislead.

Strategy: Acknowledge their expertise, but be prepared with your facts. Use "I" statements, such as "From what I've read and experienced . . ."

THE NEBBISH ▶ When faced with a crucial decision, they keep putting it off until it's too late and the decision makes itself, or they say yes to everything but follow through on nothing.

Strategy: Help them feel comfortable and safe in their rare decisions to move forward, and stay in touch until the decision is implemented. Arrange deadlines and describe the consequences that will result when they complete the tasks and what will happen if they don't.

THE EXPLODERS ▶ They throw tantrums that can escalate quickly. When they blow their tops, they are unable to stop. When the smoke clears and the dust settles, the cycle begins again.

Strategy: When an explosion begins, assertively repeat the individual's name to get his or her attention, or repeat a neutral comment such as "Stop!" Calmly address what they said in their first few sentences, which usually reveals the real problem. Give them time to regain self-control. Suggest they take time out to cool down, and then listen to their problems in private.

Source: Adapted from Rick Brinkman and Rick Kirschner, *Dealing with People You Can't Stand* (New York: McGraw-Hill, 1994); Don Wallace and Scott McMurray, "How to Disagree (without being disagreeable)," *Fast Company*, November 1995, p. 146; Kris Maher, "The Jungle," *Wall Street Journal*, April 15, 2003, p. B8; Jared Sandberg, "Sabotage 101: The Sinister Art of Back-Stabbing," *Wall Street Journal*, February 11, 2004, p. B1.

TABLE 13.1	Behaviors Exhibited by Assertive, Aggressive, and Nonassertive Persons		
	Assertive Person	**Aggressive Person**	**Nonassertive Person**
In conflict situations	Communicates directly	Dominates	Avoids the conflict
In decision-making situations	Chooses for self	Chooses for self and others	Allows others to choose
In situations expressing feelings	Is open, direct, honest, while allowing others to express their feelings	Expresses feelings in a threatening manner; puts down, inhibits others	Holds true feelings inside
In group meeting situations	Uses direct, clear "I" statements: "I believe that . . ."	Uses clear but demeaning "you" statements: "You should have known better . . ."	Uses indirect, unclear statements: "Would you mind if . . . ?"

situations with composure and confidence. Whether you choose to read the books or participate in assertiveness training, know that you can communicate your wants, dislikes, and feelings in a clear, direct manner without threatening or attacking others. Here are three practical guidelines that will help you develop your assertiveness skills.

In the beginning, take small steps. Being assertive may be difficult at first, so start with something that is easy. You might decline the invitation to keep the minutes at the weekly staff meeting if you feel others should assume this duty from time to time. If you are tired of eating lunch at Joe's Diner (the choice of a coworker), suggest a restaurant that you would prefer. If someone insists on keeping the temperature at a cool 67 degrees and you are tired of being cold all the time, approach the person and voice your opinion. Asking that your desires be considered is not necessarily a bad thing.

Use communication skills that enhance assertiveness. A confident tone of voice, eye contact, firm gestures, and good posture create nonverbal messages that say, "I'm serious about this request." Using "I" messages can be especially helpful in cases where you want to assert yourself in a nonthreatening manner. If you approach the person who wants the thermostat set at 67 degrees and say, "You need to be more considerate of others," the person is likely to become defensive. However, if you say, "I feel uncomfortable when the temperature is so cool," you will start the conversation on a more positive note.

Be soft on people and hard on the problem. The goal of conflict resolution is to solve the problem but avoid doing harm to the relationship. Of course, relationships tend to become entangled with the problem, so there is a tendency to treat the people and the problem as one. Your coworker Terry is turning in projects late every week, and you are feeling a great deal of frustration each time it happens. You must communicate to Terry that each missed deadline creates serious problems for you. Practice using tact, diplomacy, and patience as you keep the discussion focused on the problem, not on Terry's personality traits.

CRITICAL THINKING CHALLENGE

List the various conflicts you witnessed among workers within an organization in which you worked as an employee or volunteer. Carefully examine each conflict scenario and go beyond the generally perceived cause for the disagreements. Determine if there was a "root" cause. What did you discover?

Learn to Negotiate Effectively

In the past, the responsibility for negotiating an effective resolution to conflicts was often given to supervisors, department heads, team leaders, shop stewards, mediators, and other individuals with established authority and responsibility. Today, many companies have organized workers into teams and are empowering those workers to solve their own problems whenever possible. This means that every employee needs to learn how to effectively negotiate satisfactory resolutions to conflicts. Danny Ertel, author and consultant in the area of negotiations, says, "Every company today exists in a complex web of relationships, and the shape of that web is formed, one thread at a time, through negotiations,"[15] Team assignments, compensation, promotions, and work assignments are just a few of the areas where you can apply negotiation skills.

Think Win/Win

There are basically three ways to approach negotiations: win/lose, lose/lose, and win/win. When you use the **win/lose approach**, you are attempting to reach your goals at the expense of the other party's. For example, a manager can say, "Do as I say or find a job somewhere else!" The manager wins; the employee loses. Although this approach may end the conflict on a short-term basis, it doesn't usually address the underlying cause of the problem. It may simply sow the seeds of another conflict because the "losers" feel frustrated. (This strategy may be effective in those rare instances when it is more important to get the job done than it is to maintain good human relations among the work force.)

When the **lose/lose approach** is used to settle a dispute, each side must give in to the other. If the sacrifices are too great, both parties may feel that too much has been given. This strategy can be applied when there is little time to find a solution through effective negotiation techniques, or when negotiations are at a standstill and no progress is being made. Union-management disputes, for example, often fall into the lose/lose trap when neither side is willing to

Soon after celebrating their 15th wedding anniversary Elaine and Michael Honig decided to get a divorce. As joint owners of the successful Honig Vineyard, the divorce could have created serious problems. However, they decided to remain friends as well as business partners after the divorce.

yield. In these cases an arbitrator, a neutral third party, may be called in to impose solutions on the disputing parties.

In general, the win/lose and lose/lose approaches to negotiating create a "we versus they" attitude among the people involved in the conflict, rather than a "we versus the problem" approach. "We versus they" (or "my way versus your way") means that participants focus on whose solution is superior, instead of working together to find a solution that is acceptable to all. Each person tends to see the issue from his or her viewpoint only and does not approach the negotiations in terms of reaching the goal.

The basic purpose of the **win/win approach** to negotiating is to fix the problem—not the blame! Don't think hurt; think help. Negotiating a win/win solution to a conflict is not a debate where you are attempting to prove the other side wrong; instead, you are engaging in a dialogue where each side attempts to get the other side to understand its concerns and both sides then work toward a mutually satisfying solution. Your negotiations will go better when you shift your emphasis from a tactical approach of how to counter the other person's every comment to discovering a creative solution that simple haggling obscures.[16]

Perhaps the most vital skill in effective negotiations is listening. When you concentrate on learning common interests, not differences,

The basic purpose of the win/win approach to negotiating is to fix the problem—not the blame!

FIGURE 13.2

Rob Walker reviewed several of the best-selling books on negotiation, including *Getting to Yes, You Can Negotiate Anything, The Negotiation Tool Kit,* and *The Power of Nice.* He discovered a few basic negotiating tips that recur in these popular advice books:

- Stay rationally focused on the issue being negotiated.

- Exhaustive preparation is more important than aggressive argument.

- Think through your alternatives.

- The more options you feel you have, the better a negotiating position you'll be in.

- Spend less time talking and more time listening and asking good questions. Sometimes silence is your best response.

- Let the other side make the first offer. If you're underestimating yourself, you might make a needlessly weak opening move.

Source: Rob Walker, "Take It or Leave It: The Only Guide to Negotiating You Will Ever Need," *Inc.,* August 2003, p. 81.

the nature of the negotiations changes from a battle to win to a discussion of how to meet the objectives of everyone involved in the dispute (see Figure 13.2).

Beware of Defensive Behaviors

Effective negotiations are often slowed or sidetracked completely by defensive behaviors that surface when people are in conflict with each other. When one person in a conflict situation becomes defensive, others may mirror this behavior. In a short time, progress is slowed because people stop listening and begin thinking about how they can defend themselves against the other person's comments.

We often become defensive when we feel our needs are being ignored. Kurt Salzinger, Executive Director for Science at the American Psychological Association, reminds us that conflicts are often caused by unfulfilled needs for

HUMAN RELATIONS IN ACTION

Parable of the Orange

Two people each want an orange, but negotiations drag on without a solution. Finally, they agree to split it in half. But it turns out that one person simply wanted the juice, and the other person wanted only the rind. In this case, haggling obscured the solution. If they had engaged in a true dialogue, each side could have gotten what it wanted.

things such as dignity, security, identity, recognition, or justice. He says, "Conflict is often exacerbated as much by the process of the relationship as it is by the issues."[17] Determining the other person's needs requires careful listening and respect for views that differ from your own. If you feel you are trapped in a win/lose negotiation and can hear yourself or the other person becoming defensive, do everything in your power to refocus the discussion toward fixing the problem rather than defending your position.

Know That Negotiating Styles Vary

Depending on personality, assertiveness skills, and past experiences in dealing with conflict in the workplace, individuals naturally develop their own negotiating styles. But negotiating is a skill, and people can learn how and when to adapt their style to deal effectively with conflict situations.

Robert Maddux suggests that there are five different behavioral styles that can be used during a conflict situation. These styles are based on the combination of two factors: assertiveness and cooperation (see Figure 13.3). He takes the position that different styles may be appropriate in different situations.

| FIGURE 13.3 | Behavioral Styles for Conflict Situations |

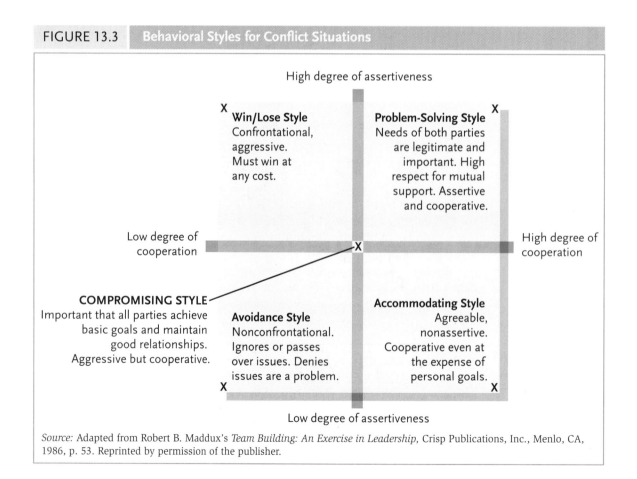

Source: Adapted from Robert B. Maddux's *Team Building: An Exercise in Leadership,* Crisp Publications, Inc., Menlo, CA, 1986, p. 53. Reprinted by permission of the publisher.

TOTAL	**ROGER FISHER AND WILLIAM URY**
PERSON	AUTHORS, *GETTING TO YES*
INSIGHT	"Any method of negotiation may be fairly judged by three criteria: It should produce a wise agreement if agreement is possible. It should be efficient. And it should improve or at least not damage the relationship between the parties."

Avoidance Style (Uncooperative/Nonassertive)   This style is appropriate when the conflict is too minor or too great to resolve. Any attempt to resolve the conflict might result in damaging a relationship or simply wasting time and energy. Avoidance might take the form of diplomatically sidestepping an issue or postponing your response until a more appropriate time.

Accommodating Style (Cooperative/Nonassertive)   This style is appropriate when resolving the conflict is not worth risking damage to the relationship or general disharmony. Individuals who use this approach relinquish their own concerns to satisfy the concerns of someone else. Accommodating might take the form of selfless generosity or blind obedience to another's point of view.

Win/Lose Style (Uncooperative/Aggressive)   This style may be appropriate when the conflict involves "survival of the fittest," when you must prove your superior position, or when your opinion is the most ethically or professionally correct. This power-oriented position allows you to use whatever means seem appropriate when it is time to stand up for your rights.

Problem-Solving Style (Assertive/Cooperative)   This style is appropriate when all parties openly discuss the issues and a mutually beneficial solution can be found without anyone making a major concession. Problem solvers attempt to uncover underlying issues that may be at the root of the problem and then focus the discussion toward achieving the most desirable outcome. They seek to replace conflict with collaboration.

Compromising Style (Moderately Aggressive/Moderately Cooperative)   This style is appropriate when no one person or idea is perfect, when there is more than one good way to do something, or when you must give to get what you want. Compromise attempts to find mutually acceptable solutions to the conflict that partially satisfy both sides. Never use this style when unethical activities are the cause of the conflict.

SKILL DEVELOPMENT CHALLENGE

Identify an instance when you were in a conflict with another person. How was the conflict resolved? How would the conflict resolution have changed had you *intentionally* implemented your avoidance style, your accommodating style, your win/lose style, your problem-solving style, and your compromising style? What does this tell you about your potential conflict resolution skills?

Conflict Resolution Process

The **conflict resolution process** consists of five steps that can be used at work and in your personal life. To apply the five steps requires understanding and acceptance of everything we have discussed up to this point in the chapter: application of assertiveness skills, understanding how to deal with various types of difficult people, support for the win/win approach to conflict resolution, and learning how to negotiate.

Step One: Decide Whether You Have a Misunderstanding or a True Disagreement

David Stiebel, author of *When Talking Makes Things Worse!*, says a misunderstanding is a failure to accurately understand the other person's point. A disagreement, in contrast, is a failure to agree that would persist despite the most accurate understanding. In a true disagreement, people want more than your explanation and further details; they want to change your mind.[18] When we fail to realize the distinction between these two possibilities, a great deal of time and energy may be wasted. Consider the following conflict situation.

As Sarah entered the driveway of her home, she could hardly wait to share the news with her husband Paul. Late that afternoon she had met with her boss and learned she was the number-one candidate for a newly created administrative position. Sarah entered the house and immediately told Paul about the promotion opportunity. In a matter of seconds, it became apparent that he was not happy about the promotion. He said, "We don't need the extra money, and you do not need the headaches that come with an administrative position." Expecting a positive response, Sarah was very disappointed. In the heat of anger, Sarah and Paul both said things they would later regret.

If Sarah and Paul had asked each other a few questions, this conflict might have been avoided. Prior to arriving home, Sarah had already weighed the pros and cons of the new position and decided it was not a good career move; however, she wanted her husband's

> *A misunderstanding is a failure to accurately understand the other person's point. A disagreement, in contrast, is a failure to agree that would persist despite the most accurate understanding.*

input before making the final decision. This conflict was not a true disagreement, in which one person tries to change the other person's mind; it was a misunderstanding that was the result of incomplete information. If Sarah and Paul had fully understood each other's position, it would have become clear that a true disagreement did not exist.

Step Two: Define the Problem and Collect the Facts

The saying "A problem well defined is a problem half solved" is not far from the truth. It is surprising how difficult this step can be. Everyone involved needs to focus on the real cause of the conflict, not on what has happened as a result of it. At this stage, it is helpful to have everyone write a one- or two-sentence definition of the problem. When everyone is allowed to define the problem, the real cause of the conflict will often surface.

As you begin collecting information about the conflict, it may be necessary to separate facts from opinions or perceptions. Ask questions that focus on who is involved in the conflict, what happened, when, where, and why. What policies and procedures were involved?

Conflict resolution in the age of information offers us new challenges. As we are faced with information overload, we may be tempted to use the information we already have rather than search for the new information needed to guide a decision.[19]

Step Three: Clarify Perceptions

Your perception is your interpretation of the facts surrounding the situations you encounter. Perceptions can have a tremendous influence on your behavior. In a conflict situation, it is therefore very important that you clarify all parties' perceptions of the problem. You can do this by attempting to see the situation as others see it. Take the case of Laura, a sales representative who was repeatedly passed over for a promotion even though her sales numbers were among the best in the department.

Over a period of time Laura became convinced that she was the victim of gender discrimination. She filed charges with the Equal Employment Opportunity Commission (EEOC), and a hearing was scheduled. When Laura's boss was given a chance to explain his actions, he described Laura as someone who was very dedicated to her family. He said, "It's my view that she would be unhappy in a sales management position because she would have to work longer hours and travel more." He did not see his actions as being discriminatory. Laura explained that she valued the time she spent with her husband and children but achieving a management position was an important career goal. Laura's and her boss's perceptions of the same situation were totally different.

Step Four: Generate Options for Mutual Gain

Once the basic problem has been defined, the facts surrounding it have been brought out, and everyone is operating with the same perceptions, everyone involved in the conflict should focus on generating options that will fix the problem. Some people, however, do not consider generating options to be part of the conflict resolution process. Rather than broadening the options for mutual gain, some individuals want to quickly build support for a single solution. The authors of the best-selling book *Getting to Yes* say, "In a dispute, people usually believe that they know the right answer—their view should prevail. They become trapped in their own point of view."[20] This is where brainstorming can be helpful. **Brainstorming** is a process that encourages all those involved in the conflict to generate a wide variety of ideas and possibilities that will lead to the desired results. No one should be allowed to evaluate, judge, or rule out any proposed solution. Each person is encouraged to tap his or her creative energies without fear of ridicule or criticism. Once all options are on the table, you will need to eliminate those that will not lead to the desired results and settle on the most appropriate ones.

Step Five: Implement Options with Integrity

The final step in the conflict resolution process involves finalizing an agreement that offers win/win benefits to those in conflict. Sometimes, as the conflict resolution process comes to a conclusion, one or more parties in the conflict may be tempted to win an advantage that weakens the relationship. This might involve hiding information or using pressure tactics that violate the win/win spirit and weaken the relationship. Even the best conflict solutions can fail unless all conflict partners serve as "caretakers" of the agreement and the relationship.[21]

Establish timetables for implementing the solutions, and provide a plan to evaluate their effectiveness. On a regular basis, make a point to discuss with others how things are going to be sure that old conflict patterns do not resurface. Conflict resolution agreements must be realistic and effective enough to survive as the challenges of the future confront them. Avoid the temptation to implement quick-fix solutions that may prove to be unsatisfactory in a few weeks.[22]

Alternative Dispute Resolution

At times, you and your coworkers or employer may not be able to reach a satisfactory resolution to your conflicts. You may believe you have been fired without cause, sexually harassed, discriminated against, overlooked for a promotion, or unfairly disciplined. Your only recourse may be to ignore the situation or take your employer to court. Ignoring the situation does not make it go away, and court battles can take years and can be extremely expensive. In some instances, you may have a legitimate complaint but not a legal claim. To help keep valued employees content and out of court, many oganizations have created formal Alternative Dispute Resolution programs, or ADRs. A Cornell University study discovered that over 80 percent of large employers nationwide operate internal ADRs, and all federal departments are required to offer ADR options.[23]

These programs usually involve any or all of the following: an open door policy that allows you to talk confidentially with upper management personnel, a toll-free hot line where employees can air grievances and get general advice, a peer review panel that investigates and attempts to resolve the problem,

a third-party mediator who listens to arguments and attempts to forge a mutually acceptable solution, or an arbitrator who imposes a final and binding solution to the problem.[24]

FedEx developed the Guaranteed Fair Treatment (GFT) process. Employees who believe they have been treated unfairly can appeal a manager's decision through the GFT. Each week the CEO and two top officers of the company personally hear appeals that have worked their way through the system. Cases that have merit are turned over to a panel of five employees, three of whom are picked by the appealing employee, for a final and binding decision.[25]

The Role of Labor Unions in Conflict Resolution

Since the 1930s, labor unions have had the authority to negotiate disputes between union members and management. This arrangement serves as an equalizing factor that allows organized workers the power necessary to challenge managers' decisions. Most management–labor union disputes escalate when the employment contracts that establish the workers' wages, benefits, and working conditions expire and need to be renegotiated. The overwhelming majority of employment contracts are settled through **collective bargaining**, a process that defines the rights and privileges of both sides involved in the conflict and establishes the terms of employment and length of the contract (usually from three to five years). However, if labor and management cannot settle their differences, they may submit their disputes to one of the following:

- **Mediation**—A neutral third party listens to both sides and suggests solutions. It carries no binding authority. Both parties are free to reject or accept the mediator's decision.

- **Voluntary arbitration**—Both sides willingly submit their disagreements to a neutral party. The arbitrator's decision must be accepted by both sides.

- **Compulsory arbitration**—When the government decides that the labor-management dispute threatens national health and safety or will damage an entire industry, it can appoint an arbitrator who dictates a solution that is binding on both sides and can be enforced in a court of law.

When collective bargaining, mediation, and arbitration are not enough to settle disputes, union leaders may recommend and members may vote to go on strike against their employers. A strike generally results in a lose/lose situation in which workers lose paychecks, employers lose sales, customers lose products or services, and communities lose economic stability.

However, some organizations are choosing the option of a **virtual strike**, in which only labor and management suffer. During a virtual strike, worker wages and management salaries go into an escrowed account held by a third party. Neither side gets paid unless they settle their dispute within a certain period of time. Production goes on, and customers and suppliers experience no change. This option eliminates the pressure the public can play in a strike and thus frees the two sides to focus on settling their differences. It is especially viable when disputes disrupt essential public services such as schools, hospitals, police protection, and firefighting.[26]

Contemporary Issues Facing Labor Unions

Only 12.5 percent of workers in America are members of a labor union and thus protected by collective bargaining. This is down from 33 percent in the 1950s.[27] Although many organizations have adopted conflict resolution policies similar to unions' collective-bargaining process, most employees have few choices beyond quitting their jobs and moving on to a friendlier employer if they cannot settle disputes with their current employer.

The future of labor unions and the protection they provide workers seems to depend on union organizers' ability to attract new members. As workers lose jobs to cheaper offshore workers and take on a larger proportion of their health insurance premiums, thus lowering their take-home pay, it would seem logical that union membership might begin to climb. At the same time, anti-union employers such as Wal-Mart, FedEx, and McDonalds actively strive to keep their workers happy and productive so that they do not perceive a need for

Yale University has a troubled labor history. Yale employees who are members of the Hotel Employees and Restaurant Employees (HERE) union have mounted several strikes over the years. Other Yale service workers have also been involved in disputes with the administration.

what unions have to offer them.[28] Organizations often hire expensive anti-union consulting and legal firms to fend off union attempts to be sanctioned through the long and involved process established by the National Labor Relations Board (NLRB). But there is an alternative that is becoming popular in the global union movement. The "card-check neutrality" process allows union representatives to gather signatures from employees, expressing their desire to join a union. If it is able to get signed cards from a majority of eligible workers, the union is authorized to negotiate the employees' next labor contract. Companies organized via the card-check process include Marriott, Freightliner, Cingular, and Rite-Aid.[29]

Labor unions are striving for survival, but they may thrive in the next millennium if they take direct action to address the following needs of the work force.

- Adopt a global mentality: Acknowledge that offshore workers under contract to American-based companies may be eligible for union representation, too, and adjust policies and decisions accordingly.

- Encourage organizations to save money by sending low-wage jobs offshore and then using the additional revenue to create good, higher-paying jobs and fund the necessary re-training for workers who live in the United States.

- Reduce the inequities between executives' million-dollar salaries and climbing corporate profits and employees' declining compensation (in real dollars).

■ Provide affordable health care at reasonable rates through whatever avenue is effective, including, but not limited to, socialized medicine.

■ Provide membership and corresponding benefits to temporary and contract workers.

● LOOKING BACK: Reviewing the Concepts

■ List and describe some of the major causes of conflict in the work setting.

Conflicts among people at work happen every day and can arise because of changes within the organization, poor communication, values and culture clashes, confusing work policies and practices, competition for scarce resources, or adversarial management. Often, however, conflicts come from coworkers who refuse to carry their fair share of the workload or have a difficult personality. While unresolved conflicts can have a negative effect on an organization's productivity, a difference of opinion sometimes has a positive effect by forcing team members toward creative and innovative solutions to problems.

■ Utilize assertiveness skills in conflict situations.

Assertiveness skills are necessary when you want to maintain your rights during a conflict with someone else, but want to avoid being overly aggressive, which means interfering with others' rights. Begin building assertiveness skills by tackling relatively minor issues first until you gain the confidence to take on those who try to take away your power. Use "I" statements rather than "you" statements so that the other person does not become defensive. Focus on fixing the problem rather than attacking the other person.

■ Understand when and how to implement effective negotiation skills.

You can vastly improve your human relations skills when dealing with difficult people by learning when and how to intentionally implement Robert Maddux's five negotiating styles: avoidance style, accommodating style, win/lose style, problem-solving style, and compromising style.

■ Identify key elements of the conflict resolution process.

When employees cannot solve their conflicts in an informal manner, many organizations create solutions through a conflict resolution process. The five-step conflict resolution process is described in this chapter. Often, an Alternative Dispute Resolution (ADR) program can resolve conflicts that might otherwise lead to legal action.

■ Discuss contemporary challenges facing labor unions.

Labor leaders and business owners are finding new ways to cooperate with each other rather than negotiating with a nonproductive "us versus them" attitude. They are finding that flexibility and innovation are far more effective than old adversarial styles. If labor and management cannot settle their differences, they may submit their disputes to mediation, voluntary arbitration, or compulsory arbitration. Labor unions today must be more responsive to balancing the inequities between executives' salaries and employees' wages, controlling health care costs, retaining "good" high-paying jobs, containing the competition for jobs from cheap offshore laborers, and adjusting to management's trend of hiring temporary and part-time workers as opposed to full-time workers.

● Career Corner

Q: The old adage "Fool me once, shame on you. Fool me twice, shame on me!" has become a reality in my career search. Last year I accepted a position with an ad agency where the owners did not disclose they were married to each other until after I was on the job. I quit after nine months when I discovered they expected me to lie to clients about the size of the agency. I accepted my next job with an event-production company, even though the hiring supervisor made disparaging remarks about the person who had previously held my position. It is now obvious that this supervisor acts condescendingly toward everyone, including me. I should have recognized the clues that indicated I was heading into these bad-boss environments. How can I avoid falling into another bad situation now that I am once again looking for a job?

A: Many applicants ignore warning signs about their prospective supervisors, yet the type of person you will be working with is one of the most important factors you should consider when job hunting. Prepare a list of ideal traits you would want in your next supervisor and a second list of what bothers you most about your current one, and then quiz present and past employees about your prospective boss while keeping your itemized lists in mind. Ask them and your interviewer direct questions such as "Who was your employee of the year and why was that employee selected?" "Give me an example of how an employee's unethical conduct is handled." "During a recent crisis within the organization, who was the 'hero' and why?" "What is your employee retention rate?" If your stomach aches throughout an interview, talk about your feelings with a friend so that you can separate bad-boss anxiety from normal interview jitters. Don't let financial pressure dictate whether you take any job. Good luck!

● Key Terms

conflict	conflict resolution process
nonassertive behavior	brainstorming
assertive behavior	collective bargaining
aggressive behavior	mediation
win/lose approach	voluntary arbitration
lose/lose approach	compulsory arbitration
win/win approach	virtual strike

● Applying What You Have Learned

1. Has there been someone in your life (now or in the past) that you just can't (or couldn't) stand? Explain the behaviors this person exhibits that get on your nerves. Carefully examine Figure 13.1, determine which category fits the person best, and then describe what you might do to help this person change his or her behavior. Be specific.

2. Describe a conflict that is disrupting human relations at school, home, or work. It might involve academic requirements at school, distribution of responsibilities at home, or hurt feelings at work. Identify all the people involved in the conflict, and decide who should be involved in the conflict resolution process. Design a conflict resolution plan by following the steps given in this chapter. Implement your plan and report the results of this conflict resolution process to other class members.

3. To develop your assertiveness skills, find a partner who will join you for a practice session. The partner should assume the role of a friend, family member, or coworker who is doing something that causes you a great deal of frustration. (The problem can be real or imaginary.) Communicate your dislikes and feelings in a clear, direct manner without threatening or attacking. Then ask your partner to critique your assertiveness skills. Participate in several of these practice sessions until you feel confident that you have improved your assertiveness skills.

 Internet Insights

1. Go to *www.adr.org* to view the website of the American Arbitration Association to discover the current arbitration cases they are handling. Also visit *www.adr.org/International* to view the related website of the International Center for Dispute Resolution. List the services the ICDR provides. When might you utilize their services?

2. Go to *www.work911.com*, click on "Dealing with Difficult People—It's About Skill," and read the excerpts from *The Complete Idiot's Guide to Handling Difficult Employees*. What information did you find helpful?

 Role-Play Exercise

Assume the role of a business manager for a large hospital. About three weeks ago you received some incomplete medical records from Ashley Carver, the physician in charge of the emergency room. With a red pen, you marked the areas that were incomplete and sent the forms back to the doctor. You attached a terse note that requested the forms be returned within twenty-four hours. Three days passed without a reply, and your anger increased each day. Finally, you sent the doctor an e-mail that basically accused Dr. Carver of incompetence in the area of medical record keeping. The doctor phoned you immediately and said the entire emergency room staff had been extremely busy and did not have a moment to spare. You replied that timely and accurate record keeping is the responsibility of every physician employed by the hospital. Unfortunately, your tone of voice and your selection of words were totally inappropriate. Basically, you treated Dr. Carver like a child who had misbehaved, and the doctor hung up on you. You immediately felt like a fool and regretted your behavior. The next day, the completed forms were returned to you. You have decided to meet with Dr. Carver. Your goal is to repair the damaged relationship and set the stage for effective communications in the future. Prior to meeting with another class member who will assume the role of Dr. Carver, review the information on the art of apologizing in Chapter 8 and information in this chapter on resolving conflicts.

Case 13.1   The Global Union Movement

The focus of Union Network International (UNI), a coalition of 900 unions with 15 million members around the world, is to create global agreements that will affect a targeted list of 100 multinational organizations and all their subsidiaries worldwide. The agreements will cover labor standards, the right to organize, and human rights issues. Although many of the targeted organizations have their headquarters in Europe, UNI is also planning activities to encourage Arkansas-based Wal-Mart to change its anti-union policies in North America and to help organize Wal-Mart workers in other parts of the world.

With union membership in the United States at an all-time low, U.S. labor leaders are reaching out to their global counterparts with the slogan "Workers of the world unite." An international approach to combating anti-union campaigns might be extremely effective. This solidarity is already having an effect in the United States as multinational companies in Europe sign global agreements that have a direct impact on their U.S. subsidiaries. UNI realizes that it can accomplish much more by beginning its campaigns in countries such as Germany, where boards of companies are required to have union members, rather than in the United States. Some of the agreements allow unions to use the card-check neutrality process: If 51 percent of the company's employees sign cards saying they want the union to represent them, the union wins representation.

The Communications Workers of America (CWA) is working in conjunction with UNI because it has workers who need union protection in all parts of the world—including war zones. They are attempting to organize workers in India, where many members' jobs are being sent. However, some employers are moving communications jobs to China to avoid union organization. China poses a huge challenge for the labor movement because the country does not allow workers to organize. Union members recognize that there will always be some jobs that are sent to China, but hope that by organizing workers in other countries, they can raise labor standards globally. Yvette Herrera, senior director of education and communications for the CWA, said, "It's not going to be a level playing field, but anytime you can increase the voice of workers and raise their wages and benefits, it helps everyone."[30]

Questions

1. What are the pros and cons of UNI's tactics to confirm union agreements with companies in Europe who have subsidiaries in other countries, including the United States?

2. The global labor movement is in its infancy. How successful the unions' international tactics will be remains to be seen. Gary Glaser, a partner in the New York office of law firm Seyfarth Shaw, says that the best way for an organization to avoid the global labor movement is to make sure that all of their employees, regardless of their worldwide location, are getting benefits and wages that are competitive in the industry.[31] Who do you think will win this battle: the unions or the employers?

3. What impact will China's position against the global labor movement have? Will the workers in the sweatshops of China have any rights to a better working environment? How?

Case 13.2   Couples Combat

A growing body of research indicates that there is no such thing as a compatible couple. Most couples, whether they are happy or unhappy, tend to argue about the same things: money, expectations as to who should do what around the house, work obligations, kids, insufficient separation from extended family members, and differing leisure activities such as a golf game or family outing, or vacation with or without the kids. As a result, marriage therapists are now attempting to help spouses manage, accept, and even honor their discord rather than trying to resolve the irresolvable.[32]

In his book *Don't You Dare Get Married Until You Read This!*, Corey Donaldson says that the majority of issues that cause marital conflict exist before the wedding, but couples are not willing to ask or answer tough questions: Can physical violence by a mate be justified? What will we do if our child is born with a disability? Are you uncomfortable with women in high-paying jobs? Are you comfortable with my religious observance? My family? My desire for wealth?[33]

Of course asking the right premarital questions does not guarantee a relationship free from conflicts: They will and do occur in even the most solid marriages. Some experts suggest that bickering can be good for relationships. It may be one of the keys to a strong marriage because open conflict improves communication and allows each partner to vent his or her frustrations. But you need to learn how to argue effectively. Dr. Phil McGraw suggests several ways you can make your arguments as constructive as possible.[34]

■ Decide what you want before you start an argument. Avoid simply complaining; ask for what you want.

■ Keep it relevant. Focus on what you are arguing about. If you stray, the argument will resurface again until the real issue is addressed.

- Make it possible for your partner to retreat with dignity. Avoid calling each other names that linger beyond the argument. Show your partner courtesy and respect, even if he or she is wrong.

- Know when to say when. If you have to give up too much of your life to maintain the relationship, maybe it's not worth it.

Keep in mind that if your objective in an argument is to win, the other person has to lose. This win/lose mind-set will only perpetuate the conflict.[35]

Questions

1. Have you had a conflict at home that had an effect on your work? Explain.

2. How might the premarital questions suggested in this case impact marital relations? What other questions need to be answered?

3. Recall your most recent conflict with your significant other. Did you follow Dr. Phil's suggestions? What was the outcome?

INTEGRATED RESOURCES

VIDEOS: "Interpersonal Communication—Video Cases"
    "Managing Equality"
    "Informal Organization Structure"

CLASSROOM ACTIVITIES (*college.hmco.com/pic/reece10e*)

    "Win as Much as You" Game
    Divorce Mediation
    Assertiveness/Cooperation Scenarios and Discussion

business.college.hmco.com/students

ACE

Self-tests

PART V

SPECIAL CHALLENGES IN HUMAN RELATIONS

14 RESPONDING TO PERSONAL AND WORK-RELATED STRESS

15 VALUING WORK FORCE DIVERSITY

16 THE CHANGING ROLES OF MEN AND WOMEN

14

RESPONDING TO PERSONAL AND WORK-RELATED STRESS

Chapter Preview

After studying this chapter, you will be able to

- Understand the major personal and work-related causes of stress.

- Recognize the warning signs of too much stress.

- Learn how to identify and implement effective stress management strategies.

- Identify stress-related psychological disorders and therapy options.

More than one-third of the work force consists of parents with children, the majority of whom are school age. Most of these parents have work schedules that do not allow them to be home when their children return from school at the end of the day, which leaves these children unsupervised an estimated 20–25 hours a week. These working parents often worry about their children during the afterschool hours, and this worry can have a profound effect on the parents' well-being and performance on the job. Research indicates that parents who have concerns about their children's afterschool arrangements report that they are more frequently interrupted, distracted, and drained of energy at work by nonwork issues; make significantly more errors; turn down more requests to work extra hours; miss more meetings and deadlines at work because of nonwork issues; and rate their productivity and the quality of their work significantly lower than do those employees free of this stress. Stress of this nature can result in up to five days of missed work per year per employee.[1]

It is estimated that workers' stress causes employers to lose approximately $200 billion annually in absenteeism, sub par performance, tardiness, and workers' compensation claims related to stress.[2] Employees and employers alike are asking the same question: Whose problem is it? Should employers implement programs that help reduce employees' stress, or should employees take responsibility for creating a reduced-stress lifestyle?

Most organizations are searching for ways to wring more productivity from a smaller number of employees. Job cuts are an ongoing strategy to improve profits and stay competitive.[3] This downsizing often results in a work force that is unsettled and insecure. Tensions build as people work longer hours and then try to cram their family time and social activities into their dwindling leisure

"I still say we're stretched dangerously thin."

time. You may or may not work for an organization that recognizes the negative effects of stress and offers stress-reduction strategies to its employees. Since this variable exists, consider taking personal responsibility for controlling your stress. This chapter will help you examine the most common sources of stress and discover effective ways to respond to personal and work-life stressors.

The Stress Factor in Your Life

Stress is the behavioral adjustment to change that affects you physically and psychologically. It is the process by which you mobilize energy for coping with change and challenges. Stress can come from your environment, your body, or your mind.[4] Environmental stress at work may be caused by noise, safety concerns, windowless settings, long hours, or unrealistic deadlines. Some bodily stress can be attributed to poorly designed workstations that produce eye strain, shoulder tension, or lower-back discomfort. But the stress that comes from our minds is the most common type of stress.

However, a great deal of the mental stress we encounter every day is caused by our negative thinking and faulty reasoning.

There can be positive aspects of mental stress. Stress *can* be a powerful stimulus for growth if it motivates you to do your best work. It can build within you the energy and desire needed to perform effectively. It can also promote greater awareness and help you focus on getting tasks completed quickly and efficiently. However, a great deal of the mental stress we encounter every day is caused by our negative thinking and faulty reasoning. For example, someone with large house payments and a great deal of personal debt may begin to worry excessively about the possibility of a layoff; the individual who lacks self-confidence may fear each technology change that is introduced at work; workers in organizations being merged may mentally anguish over who will be laid off next.

Responding to Stress

Stress consists of three elements: the event or thought (stressor) that triggers stress; your perception of it; and your response to it.[5] In his book *Stress for Success*, James Loehr suggests that as you are exposed to new stressors, you should try to respond in ways that help you establish mental, physical, and emotional balance.[6] Unfortunately, most of us do not take the time to train our minds and bodies so that we build our capacity to handle the stress in our lives.

TOTAL	**PRICE PRITCHETT AND RON POUND**
PERSON	AUTHORS, *THE STRESS OF ORGANIZATIONAL CHANGE*
INSIGHT	"Most people seem to agree that these are high pressure times. Employees complain of being burned out. Used up. Overloaded. Too many of us are just plain tired, overdosed on change, sick of ambiguity and uncertainty."

The authors of *The Stress of Organizational Change* note that much of the stress we are feeling these days is self-induced. Many of us resist change and hang on to old habits and beliefs.

Our natural response to stress is as old as life itself—adapted by almost all species as a means of coping with threats to survival. When faced with an unexpected or possibly threatening situation, human beings—like animals—instinctively react with the **fight or flight syndrome**: Adrenaline pours into the bloodstream, heart rate and blood pressure increase, breathing accelerates, and muscles tighten. The body is poised to fight or run. Ironically, the same instincts that helped our ancestors survive are the ones causing us physical and mental health problems today.

The human response to stress is not easily explained. Repeated or prolonged stress can trigger complex physiological reactions that may involve several hundred chemical changes in the brain and body.[7] Everyone reacts differently to stress, so there is no single best way to manage it. You must train yourself to respond effectively to the stressors in your personal and professional life so that you will not only survive, but thrive. The first step is to understand what might cause you to become stressed.

> *Repeated or prolonged stress can trigger complex physiological reactions that may involve several hundred chemical changes in the brain and body.*

Major Causes of Stress

A study by the National Institute for Occupational Safety and Health found that half the working people in the United States view job stress as a major problem in their lives.[8] Some say the pace at work is so dizzying that it takes them hours to finally relax after the workday ends. Most of us can benefit from learning how to pinpoint the sources of stress in our life. If we can anticipate the stressors, we may be able to respond to them in a more effective manner.

Change

Changes in the workplace come in many forms, including the need to do a job faster, to master advanced technology, or to take on a new work assignment. Consider employees who have been accustomed to working alone and now must work with a team, or employees who have held jobs that required little contact with the public and now must spend a great deal of time with clients, patients, or customers. When companies restructure in an attempt to meet demands of the marketplace, they often do not take into consideration the life demands of the employees. Many companies offer flexible work schedules, but many others do little or nothing to help employees balance jobs with personal and family life.

As we look to the future, there are two realities to keep in mind. First, management personnel above you are trying to cope with their own high-pressure responsibilities, so you are not likely to get much emotional handholding from them. Second, the pace of change is not likely to slow down. The authors of *The Stress of Organizational Change* say the secret to coping with high-velocity change is *surrender*: "Surrendering to change does the most to eliminate the stress. It creates the opportunity for break*through* rather than break*down*." They note that much of the pressure we are feeling these days is self-induced stress. Resisting change, or hanging on to old habits and beliefs, requires the investment of a great deal of emotional energy.[9] Surrendering to change demands a higher level of adaptability to our ever-changing workplace.

Technostress

The rapid introduction of new technologies requires workers to quickly learn new techniques to keep up with the demands of employers, customers, suppliers, and communication in general. Today's plugged-in worker is trying to answer an important question: When is technology a help, and when does it become an intrusion on peace of mind and personal life?

There is no doubt that information technology, in its many forms, is now one of the great stressors in our lives. Craig Brod, a consultant specializing in stress reduction, was one of the first people to use the term *technostress* to describe this source of stress. **Technostress** is the inability to cope with computer and related technologies in a healthy manner. It may take several forms.[10]

Tether Anxiety The authors of *Dot.Calm—The Search for Sanity in a Wired World* say the never-ending sea of information and our desire to access it result in a wireless tether. Our work is always with us through technology, and it is constantly demanding our immediate attention and response.[11] Many companies provide their employees with laptop computers, personal digital assistants (PDAs) cell phones, pagers, and other types of wireless technology. These employees are often too accessible and are unable to create a balanced, sane personal life.

Monitoring Anxiety In order to assess employees' productivity, companies are developing new ways to monitor their work. Managers, in some cases, can track performance division by division, employee by employee, with startling precision.[12] Software can track every keystroke and mouseclick. Video surveillance cameras, generally established for security purposes, monitor the worker's every movement. Even workers who travel outside the office may be tracked through global positioning satellite technology.

Internet Addiction Many Internet users become addicted to computer use in the same way that some people become addicted to gambling or alcohol. Research suggests that as many as 6 to 10 percent of the 189 million U.S. Internet users have a dependency on the Internet. Problems associated with Internet addiction include the adoption of a machinelike mind-set that reflects the characteristics of the computer itself; withdrawal from relationships with coworkers, family members, and friends; depression and irritability when not at the computer; and health issues due to a bad diet and the lack of sleep and exercise.[13]

Information Overload It is easy to experience sensory overload as you sort through the hundreds of messages that come to you daily by means of the Internet, e-mail, pagers, commercial advertising, and many other sources.

Information overload is a major source of stress in today's workforce. Hundreds of messages and reports compete for attention. Information overload creates anxiety and it crowds out the quiet moments needed for a balanced life.

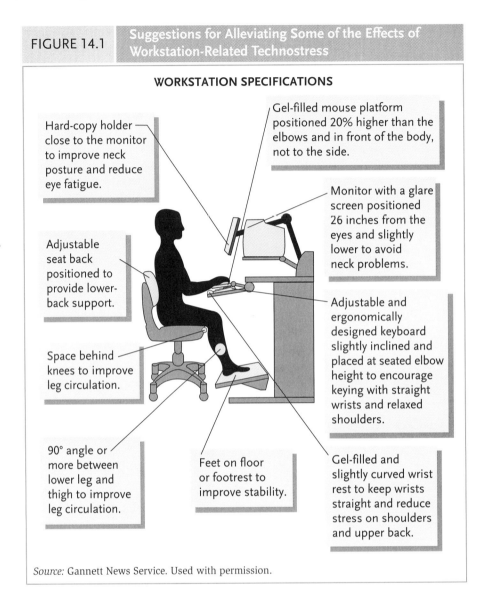

FIGURE 14.1 **Suggestions for Alleviating Some of the Effects of Workstation-Related Technostress**

WORKSTATION SPECIFICATIONS

Hard-copy holder close to the monitor to improve neck posture and reduce eye fatigue.

Gel-filled mouse platform positioned 20% higher than the elbows and in front of the body, not to the side.

Monitor with a glare screen positioned 26 inches from the eyes and slightly lower to avoid neck problems.

Adjustable seat back positioned to provide lower-back support.

Adjustable and ergonomically designed keyboard slightly inclined and placed at seated elbow height to encourage keying with straight wrists and relaxed shoulders.

Space behind knees to improve leg circulation.

90° angle or more between lower leg and thigh to improve leg circulation.

Feet on floor or footrest to improve stability.

Gel-filled and slightly curved wrist rest to keep wrists straight and reduce stress on shoulders and upper back.

Source: Gannett News Service. Used with permission.

Data smog, the term that David Shenk uses to describe the information-dense society we live in, is a problem because it crowds out quiet moments, obstructs much needed contemplation, and often leaves us feeling confused.[14] In an age where information is viewed as a valuable commodity, we have too much of it!

The Computer Workstation Many employees spend the majority of their time at work sitting at a computer workstation, which may or may not be properly designed for long-term comfort. To keep up with the increasing demands at the office, many continue their work in front of their home computers. Telecommuters and home-based business workers often spend countless hours at their workstations, too, but they often resist spending their personal income to buy professionally designed office furniture and equipment. They may sit in

| FIGURE 14.2 | Contribution to Workspace Distractions Overall |

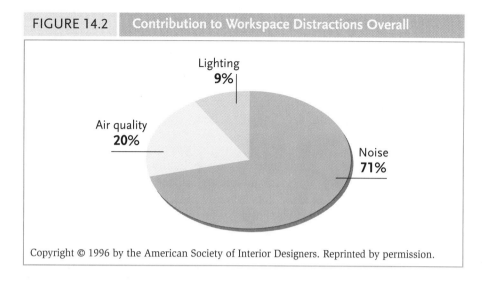

Copyright © 1996 by the American Society of Interior Designers. Reprinted by permission.

a cast-off chair with little support, in front of an antique desk, and stare at a poorly positioned monitor. Or perhaps they are hunched over a laptop on the couch or at the kitchen table. Poorly designed computer workstations at the office and in the home can produce major stress when they cause carpal tunnel syndrome (a repetitive stress wrist injury), back pain, spine and neck problems, aching shoulders, sore elbows, and eyestrain. Experts in **ergonomics**—techniques for adapting the work environment to the human body—say that anyone spending hours in front of a computer should get the right equipment and use it properly.[15] Figure 14.1 presents some pointers that might help alleviate some of the effects of workstation-related stress.

Noise Pollution

Noise is unwanted sound such as the roar of traffic, your neighbor's loud music, or the loud voice of the person who occupies the cubicle nearby. It can increase your stress level without your conscious awareness. It is the uncontrollability of noise, rather than its intensity, that often is the greatest irritant. The noise you can't shut off is likely to have a negative effect on your emotional well being. Persistent exposure to noise can cause headaches, sleep disturbances, anxiety, and depression. Research indicates that noise affects people more than any other work area pollutant.[16] See Figure 14.2.

SKILL DEVELOPMENT CHALLENGE

Troubleshoot your computer workstation at home or at work. Evaluate the lighting, noise infiltration, air quality, seating, monitor and keyboard placement, and work surface. Identify ways you could improve it and how those improvements might reduce your stress level.

Long Hours/Irregular Schedules

Do employees in America work longer hours today than in the past? Are more people addicted to work? Do more workers feel frazzled today? Finding answers to these questions is not easy because researchers often reach different conclusions. Some of the most important conclusions that do appear to have sufficient support follow.

- Workers in America spend more hours on the job over the course of a year than employees in any other developed nation do, and many do not take full advantage of the vacation time allotted them by their employers. A recent study indicated that they are likely to give back 421 million employer-paid vacation days a year, compared to the majority of French and Japanese workers who take three- to four-week vacations each year, and German workers who take twelve weeks. According to the Travel Industry Association, American workers' average length of vacation time spent away from home is only four days a year.[17]

- In recent years, a growing number of workers call workloads excessive and say that they are bothered by increased pressure on the job. Many of the companies that have slashed their payroll now spread the same amount of work over fewer people. Years of multitasking and workaholism have left workers across the American economic and geographic spectrum feeling exhausted.[18]

- The New Economy, sometimes referred to as the 24/7 economy, is a non-stop "We never close" economy. Companies increasingly need employees who can work flexible schedules. Evening shifts, rotating shifts, 12-hour workdays, and weekend work often add stress to workers' lives.

Incompetent Leaders

Organizations often promote individuals into supervisory positions when they exhibit extraordinary talents in a specific technical field. The most talented electrician becomes maintenance supervisor. The most efficient surgical nurse is promoted to nursing supervisor. The top salesperson is made sales manager. But technical superstars may be poor supervisors. And studies indicate that incompetent supervisors are a major source of stress in the workplace.[19] They

TOTAL	**CAROL S. PEARSON**
PERSON	EDITOR, *THE INNER EDGE*
INSIGHT	"Our lives are complex, but we are not helpless to do something about the stress we feel. In fact, we often choose to intentionally overcrowd our schedules as a means of avoiding difficult feelings and choices. Then something forces us to slow down. We must listen to our hearts and bodies, and face a dawning awareness: My job, my spouse, my lifestyle—something—is not right for me."

tend to ignore employee ideas and concerns, withhold information from employees, and fail to clarify roles and responsibilities. Incompetent leaders may set unrealistic deadlines and then blame employees for not meeting them.

Work and Family Transitions

In our fast-moving world, most of us have learned that certain transitions are inevitable. A **transition** can be defined as the experience of being forced to give up something and face a change. Author Edith Weiner states, "People are now in a constant state of transitioning. It is difficult for anyone to say with any degree of certainty where he or she will be maritally, professionally, financially or geographically five years from now."[20]

When a single person marries or a married couple divorces, the transition can be extremely stressful and can affect job performance. A new baby and the challenge of child care can cause stress in working mothers and fathers. As double-income parents attempt to meet the needs of the family, they often feel guilty about the time spent away from their children.

> **CRITICAL THINKING CHALLENGE**
>
> How would having your stress under control help your interpersonal relationships at work? At home?

Warning Signals of Too Much Stress

In today's stress-filled world, it makes sense to become familiar with the signals that indicate you are experiencing too much stress in your life. Table 14.1 offers information regarding physical, emotional, and relational symptoms that may need your attention. When these symptoms persist, you are at risk for serious health problems because stress can exhaust your immune system, making you more vulnerable to colds, flu, fatigue, and infections. Recent research demonstrates that 90 percent of illnesses are stress related.[21]

Stress Management Strategies

Ideally, we should do everything in our power to eliminate those elements that cause us stress—change, technostress, noise pollution, long hours/irregular schedules, incompetent leaders, and work/family transitions—but this is not generally a realistic option. We can try to reduce them, but eliminating them is often not possible. We can, however, learn ways to manage our reactions to the stressors in our daily lives and minimize their negative impact.

There is no one-size-fits-all way to reduce stress. Some believe that quick fixes such as smoking, alcohol, or food binges will reduce their stress, but these strategies have no staying power and will cease working over time.[22] You

TABLE 14.1	Symptoms of Stress

Physical symptoms may result from or be exacerbated by stress.

Sleep disturbances
Back, shoulder, or neck pain
Tension or migraine headaches
Upset or acid stomach, cramps, heartburn, gas, irritable bowel syndrome
Constipation, diarrhea
Weight gain or loss, eating disorders
Hair loss
Muscle tension
Fatigue
High blood pressure
Irregular heartbeat, palpitations
Asthma or shortness of breath
Chest pain
Sweaty palms or hands
Cold hands or feet
Skin problems (hives, eczema, psoriasis, itching)
Periodontal disease, jaw pain
Reproductive problems
Immune system suppression: more colds, flu, and infections
Growth inhibition

Emotional symptoms can affect your performance at work, your physical health, or your relationships with others.

Nervousness, anxiety
Depression, moodiness
"Butterflies"
Irritability, frustration
Memory problems
Lack of concentration
Trouble thinking clearly
Feeling out of control
Substance abuse
Phobias
Overreactions

Relational symptoms are antisocial behaviors displayed in stressful situations and can cause the rapid deterioration of relationships with family, friends, coworkers, or even strangers.

Increased arguments
Isolation from social activities
Road rage
Domestic or workplace violence
Conflict with coworkers or employers
Frequent job changes
Overreactions

Source: Sheila Hutman, Jaelline Jaffe, Robert Segal, Heather Larson, Lisa F. Dumke, "Stress: Signs and Symptoms, Causes and Effects," *Helpguide: Expert, Non-Commercial Information on Mental Health & Lifelong Wellness.* [cited on 11 February 2006]. Available from *www.helpguide.org/mental/stress_signs.htm*; INTERNET.

have to become aware of what calms you best. Do not wait until you are feeling stressed before you employ stress management techniques; make them part of your daily routine. Space does not permit an in-depth presentation of all stress management strategies, but we will describe those that are widely used today.

Everyone should make the effort to put stressful situations into proper perspective and deal with them accordingly. Once you become aware of what creates a stressful response in you (stress is very individualized), begin looking for stress management strategies that will help you cope with the stressful situations. Space does not permit an in-depth presentation of all stress management strategies, but we will describe those that are widely used today. You will be pleased to discover that many of these strategies require only a small investment of your time.

Sleep

Perhaps one of the most effective strategies for managing the negative aspects of stress is getting enough quality sleep. Growth hormones and repair enzymes are released and various chemical restoration processes occur during sleep. (This explains why children need considerably more sleep than adults.) In order to train your body so that you can deepen your capacity to handle stress, follow these guidelines to improve your sleep recovery periods:

■ Develop a sleep ritual: Go to bed and get up at the same time as often as possible.

■ Mentally wind down before going to bed. Avoid stressful activities.

■ Avoid central nervous system stimulants such as caffeine, chocolate, alcohol, or nicotine near bedtime.

■ Keep your bedroom cool, well ventilated, and dark.[23]

Many workers get less than the recommended amount of sleep (7 to 8 hours) at night and therefore experience daytime drowsiness. This problem is so widespread that many employers encourage employees to take a short nap. Most employees are more productive and less apt to make fatigue-induced errors after waking from a short nap.[24]

Exercise

Study after study has proven that exercise, for most people, is the number one treatment for stress and tension. Exercise designed to reduce stress is not necessarily strenuous and may include aerobics exercise such as walking, swimming, low-impact aerobics, tennis, or jogging. Even gentle exercise such as yoga or tai chi will help you manage your daily stress load.

Unfortunately, about 70 percent of Americans do not exercise regularly, and nearly 40 percent are not active at all. A study published in the *New England Journal of Medicine* indicates that by age 18 or 19, a majority of American females engage in virtually no regular exercise outside of their schools' physical education classes.[25] Too many people, men and women, fail to take advantage of the physical and mental benefits of exercise. These

This Google employee is enjoying a swim in the jet-powered lap pool located on campus. Exercise can act as a buffer against stress, so stressful events have less of a negative impact on your helath.

benefits include lower cholesterol, weight loss, increased mental alertness, and a stronger heart. Before you begin a strenuous physical exercise program, check with your doctor to be sure it is appropriate for you.

Deep Breathing

When you participate in deep breathing exercises you are forced to focus on the present moment rather than those things that are causing you stress. In his book *Breathe Smart: The Secret to Happiness, Health, and Long Life*, Aaron Hoopes describes three techniques that can effectively calm your body.[26]

Complete Cycle Breathing Start and end your day with three rounds of a complete cycle of breathing: Inhale, then pause while gently holding the breath in; exhale, then pause while holding the breath out. When you pause with your breath in, it creates a moment of stillness in which the whole body is focused on processing oxygen. When you suspend breathing out for a moment, it allows the body to use all the oxygen remaining in your lungs. Normally, we take fourteen to nineteen breaths a minute while at rest. The goal of deep breathing programs is to lower that rate to under ten.[27]

Abdominal Breathing Press your abdominal muscles out and down as you inhale, which creates a vacuum that pulls the lungs down, allowing them to expand beyond the typical shallow breath that uses only the top third of the lungs. As you exhale, pull the abdominal muscles up and in so that the lungs empty from the bottom up, which clears the stale air out of your body and brings in fresh oxygen.

Reverse Abdominal Breathing   As you inhale, pull your abdominal muscles in and up to fill the upper chest, like blowing up a balloon. As you exhale, push your abs down and out. Normal abdominal breathing is relaxing and should be done daily. Reverse abdominal breathing is more energetic and should be done less often.

Meditation

Once the fight or flight reaction was fully understood, researchers began searching for a way humans could proactively *respond* to rather than simply *react* to this innate condition. A real breakthrough came when Herbert Benson at Harvard Medical School discovered a simple series of steps that lead toward effective **meditation**, a relaxation technique that slows your pulse, respiration, and brain-wave activity and lowers your blood pressure. Meditation is sometimes called the smart person's bubble bath.[28]

Scientific studies show that meditation can have a profound stress-reducing effect because it trains and conditions the mind in the same way exercise trains and conditions the body. Richard Davidson's research at the University of Wisconsin in Madison suggests that through regular meditation, the brain is reoriented from a stressful fight or flight mode to one of acceptance, a shift that increases contentment with the realities of life. The process effectively deactivates the frontal areas of the brain, where sensory information is received and processed. Meditation allows people to quietly and intentionally detach from their emotional reactions so that they can respond appropriately.

It allows them to peacefully observe their stress-producing thoughts and then choose to release them.[29]

Most meditation techniques involve these elements:

1. Sit or lie down in a comfortable, quiet place where you are not likely to be disturbed.

2. Intentionally relax the muscles of your body from your toes to your head.

3. Focus on the sound of each breath, using the abdominal breathing techniques mentioned earlier.

4. Train yourself to think about the calm and peaceful present. Mentally place past and potential future stressful events into this calm place. Fully and calmly accept these realities, thus robbing the innate fight or flight reaction of its power. Acknowledge your thoughts, realize which ones do not serve you, and then mentally release them.

To receive the full benefits of meditation, many people find it helpful to be trained by an expert in the field. Meditation classes and facilities are available in schools, hospitals, prisons, law firms, government buildings, airports, and corporate offices throughout the civilized world. Companies such as AOL, Raytheon, and Nortel Networks offer their employees meditation classes because they acknowledge the possibility that employees who participate will experience sharpened intuition, steely concentration, and plummeting stress levels. They recognize the power in the statement "Don't just do something—sit there!"[30]

Don't just do something—sit there!

In addition to meditation, there are other stress management activities that can be used during brief pauses in your day. Table 14.2 provides some examples.

Laugh and Have Fun

Laughter is a gentle exercise of the body, a form of "inner jogging." When you laugh, your immune system is given a boost, stress-related hormones such as cortisol are reduced, and your respiratory function is improved.[31] Having fun while you are on the job does not exclude being serious about your work and caring about doing a good job, but being serious and caring is

---

TABLE 14.2	5-Minute Stress Busters

- Take 5 minutes to identify and challenge unreasonable or distorted ideas that precipitated your stress. Replace them with ideas that are more realistic and positive.
- Take a 5-minute stress-release walk outdoors: Contact with nature is especially beneficial.
- Enjoy stress relief with a gentle 5-minute neck and shoulder massage.
- Spend 5 minutes visualizing yourself relaxing at your favorite vacation spot.
- Take a 5-minute nap after lunch.
- Spend 5 minutes listening to a recording featuring your favorite comedian.

very different from being humorless and solemn. It is possible for people to have fun at work without being silly or inappropriate.

Some people are not funny, and not everyone needs to be able to tell a funny story. The goal is to create a fun-loving atmosphere that helps reduce stress levels. When asked how they infused fun into the workplace, employers said:

> "I'm pretty task-oriented and serious most of the time. One time I did dress up for Halloween, and my employees were all completely shocked. That was a real stretch for me. Most of the time I just let them have their fun, without judging or squelching it."

> "Every month we had client reports due, and most of us dreaded the solitary extra-hours work that the tasks required. So we started planning to stay late one night each month. We went to a deli for snacks and then held a work party. We were all on our own computers in our own offices, but we took regular breaks, helped each other, enjoyed our meals together, and had some laughs in the after-work casual environment."

> "We had been working so hard and had nailed all of our goals for the quarter. I called my team into my office and presented them with movie tickets—for the two o'clock show, that day! It was great. We took off as a group and felt like kids, playing hooky from school. It was so spontaneous, and they loved it."[32]

Some people have lost touch with what is fun for them. Ann McGee-Cooper, author of *You Don't Have to Go Home from Work Exhausted*, recommends making a list of things that are fun for you and then estimating the time they take.[33] This exercise may help you realize that there is plenty of time for fun things in your life. A walk in the park will require only twenty minutes, and reading the comics takes only five minutes out of your day.

Solitude

Those who are constantly in touch with others can benefit from the therapeutic effect of solitude.

Although some people feel uncomfortable when alone, many others feel "over-connected" because of the need to constantly respond to telephones, e-mails, and pagers. Those who are constantly in touch with others can benefit from the therapeutic effect of solitude. Solitude can be viewed as an emotional breather, a restorer of energy, and a form of rest similar to sleep. Ester Buchholz, author of *The Call of Solitude*, says alone-time is a great protector of the self and the human spirit. She also notes that solitude is often required for the unconscious to process and unravel problems.[34] To experience the benefits of solitude, get up twenty minutes earlier in the morning. Use this time for meditation, journal writing, or just sitting in silence. Enjoy this period of solitude free from the current pressures and demands on your life.

Resilience

Resilience means being capable of bouncing back when you are confronted with stressful situations. At 3M's headquarters in Maplewood, Minnesota, over

7,000 employees have completed a "Resilience at Work" training program that covers such diverse topics as financial planning, time management, and parenting. These topics represent those factors in a person's life that could cause stress if they got out of control. Participants are taught to determine what issues are within their control and how to deal with them when they get out of control.

In many cases, planning ahead is all that is needed to begin the process of taking control of your life. Creating a realistic family budget that leads toward effective financial planning can provide resilience when unexpected, uncontrollable expenses occur. Rework the budget accordingly, and move forward with the new one. If your time management is chaotic, try controlling your schedule by building in fifteen minutes of cushion time that allow you to recover your composure before each appointment. If the kids are out of control and driving you crazy, arrange the appropriate child-care arrangements at least one evening a month (preferably one a week) so that you can get away and recharge your parenting batteries.

Many people create their own stress. They may want more leisure time, but they also want that new SUV or flat screen HDTV, so they take on a second job. As they engage in stressful multitasking, put in long days, and use words such as "obsessed" and "overwhelmed," they often begin to think that busyness is a measure of their status. They live in a permanent state of perceived emergency that causes toxins to build up inside them.[35] Programs like the one at 3M help employees realize they can be in control of their lives—and thereby their stress—by making different decisions.

TOTAL PERSON INSIGHT	**JACOB NEEDLEMAN**
	AUTHOR, *TIME AND THE SOUL*
	"Culturally and individually, somewhere in our history, we chose to make material possessions important, not realizing that we would pay for all these things— consumer goods, improvements, technology—at the cost of our time."

Coping with Psychological Disorders

In the ideal scenario, when a stressful situation ends, hormonal signals switch off the fight or flight response, and the body returns to normal. Unfortunately, stress does not always let up. If you are under stress day after day and year after year, your hormonal response never shuts down. This can have a hazardous, even lethal, effect on your body and mental health.[36]

Once every ten years, the National Institute of Health (NIH) conducts a national study to assess mental illness in America. The findings of the most recent study, published in 2005, indicate that mental illness, in its many forms, affects one-quarter of the U.S. population.[37] In the final pages of this chapter, we will briefly examine three common psychological disorders and discuss therapy options.

Anxiety

Anxiety is a condition in which intense feelings of apprehension are long-standing and usually disruptive. Millions of Americans struggle with unwanted anxiety, and the cost in terms of suffering and lost productivity is very high. For most people, anxious feelings surface from time to time, but they are neither long-standing nor disruptive. If you have ever been tense before taking an exam or making an oral presentation, you have some idea of what anxiety feels like.[38]

Anxiety becomes a *disorder* only when it persists and prevents you from leading a normal life. Psychiatrists have found that there are several different anxiety disorders. *A phobia*, an irrational fear of a specific object or situation, represents one type of anxiety. Claustrophobia (fear of confined spaces) and agoraphobia (fear of crowds and public places) are two of the many phobias that can have a disruptive effect on a person's daily life.[39]

What is the best treatment for anxiety? Many anxious states are caused by stress, so consider using the stress management methods described in this chapter. Various methods of relaxation, for example, can lessen the severity of anxiety symptoms. However, when self-help methods do not bring the desired results, seek professional help. (See Figure 14.3.)[40]

FIGURE 14.3	Getting Professional Help

Anxiety Disorders Association of America www.adaa.org	► The mission of the ADAA is to promote the prevention, treatment, and cure of anxiety disorders and to improve the lives of all people who suffer from them.
Depression and Bipolar Support Alliance www.dbsalliance.org	► This organization runs local support groups around the country for people coping with depression and bipolar disorder.
National Alliance for the Mentally Ill www.nami.org	► NAMI offers support groups and courses to help people with psychiatric disorders, as well as family members living with and caring for the mentally ill.
The Therapy Directory http://therapists.psychology today.com/rms/prof_search.php	► *Psychology Today* magazine maintains a searchable database people can use to find a therapist in their area.
The Mental Health Association www.depressionscreening.org	► The Mental Health Association offers a free depression-screening test, which may help identify depressive symptoms and determine whether a further evaluation by a medical or mental health professional is necessary.
Online Clinics www.onlineclinics.com	► Online Clinics was created to serve clinics, clinicians, and patients who want to find quality health care services online.

Source: Adapted from Leila Abbound, "Mental Illness Said to Affect One-Quarter of Americans," *Wall Street Journal,* June 6, 2005.

Depression

Depression is a mood disorder. Nearly 19 million American adults suffer from it. This psychological disorder costs U.S. businesses nearly $70 billion annually in lost productivity, medical expenditures, and other related expenses. People of all ages can experience depression, but it primarily impacts workers in their most productive years: the 20s through 40s.[41]

When depression seriously affects a person's productivity on the job or interpersonal relationships, psychiatrists consider that individual to have a depression. Symptoms such as withdrawal, overwhelming sadness, or hopelessness may persist for weeks or months.[42] The exact cause of depression is not clear, but it can be triggered by a stressful event such as job loss, divorce, or death of a loved one.

In most cases depression is a treatable disorder, but it often requires a variety of approaches. Research shows that exercise can help improve mood and alleviate clinical depression.[43] Many people who are battling depression rely on either antidepressant medications or psychotherapy. When patients stop taking antidepressants, they suffer a high risk of relapse in the year after they stop. People completing psychotherapy, usually described as cognitive-behavior therapy, relapse less frequently.[44] To learn more about these two options, see Figure 14.3.

Burnout

Burnout is a gradually intensifying pattern of physical, psychological, and behavioral dysfunction that evolves in response to a continuous flow of stressors.[45] When you experience burnout, you feel that your energy fuel tank is operating on empty. Just as the engine of a car literally stops running without fuel and oil, a complete mental or physical breakdown can result from burnout. The most common symptoms of burnout include the following:

■ Increased detachment from coworkers, customers, or clients

■ Increased tardiness, absenteeism, cynicism, and moodiness

■ Increased disorientation: forgetfulness, low concentration

■ Increased personal problems: drug or alcohol abuse, decreased social contacts, marital discord

All individuals experience one or two of these symptoms from time to time. But a person experiencing burnout exhibits these behaviors with increasing frequency and intensity. Those who burn out are usually successful, motivated, and committed to their work, but they often hold high-level positions in which there is little feedback from those who might offer a calming perspective to stressful events.

The report *Employee Burnout: America's Newest Epidemic* suggests that if you feel you are nearing burnout, take action immediately—at home *and* at work—before it's too late.[46]

1. Stop trying to do everything: When someone asks you to take on another task, always ask for its priority and a deadline.

2. Clarify your value priorities. If you had just one year to live, what tasks would you stop doing? What would you do instead?

3. Make time to participate in as many stress management techniques as possible.

Therapy Options

Many organizations offer various **employee assistance programs** (EAPs) aimed at overcoming anxiety, depression, burnout, alcohol abuse, and drug abuse. These programs are designed to address the negative effects of psychological disorders before employees become dysfunctional.

In addition to EAPs, millions of people choose to participate in one or more relevant **twelve-step programs** for help with drug and alcohol addiction, eating disorders, and gambling addiction. All twelve-step programs rely on the same fundamentals:

- *Working the steps.* This means admitting the problem, recognizing that life has become unmanageable, and turning life over to a higher power.

- *Attending meetings.* Meetings of twelve-step programs are held in convenient locations throughout communities across the country. Members describe their own problems and listen to others who have experienced similar problems. In most cases, members form strong support groups.

Web-based counseling is growing in popularity. Some licensed therapists give their clients a choice of face-to-face counseling or online counseling. In addition, there are thousands of support groups organized around various psychological disorders and moderated by therapists—some are licensed, some are not. Web-based therapy may be risky. There is often no guarantee that the self-proclaimed therapist is legitimate or licensed to practice in your state and no online therapist can promise confidentiality.[47]

LOOKING BACK: Reviewing the Concepts

- Understand the major personal and work-related causes of stress.

When individuals cannot adequately respond or successfully adapt to change, stress is usually the result. Technostress, the inability to cope with technology in a healthy manner, is a significant threat to individuals and organizations. Noise pollution, irregular schedules, and incompetent leaders, as well as work and family transitions such as marriage, divorce, or relocation, may add to the stress of today's workers.

- Recognize the warning signs of too much stress.

Some stress in life can have a positive effect as it helps keep people motivated and excited. Therefore, the goal is not to eliminate stress, but to learn how to manage various stressors and reduce their negative effects on the body and the mind. It makes sense to become familiar with the signals that indicate there is too much stress in your life.

- Learn how to identify and implement effective stress management strategies.

You are more likely to handle the ever increasing stress of today's demands when you maintain a sleep routine and exercise program, practice the relaxing effects of deep breathing and meditation, laugh and have fun, seek out moments of solitude, and learn how to physically and mentally recover once the stress is reduced or ended.

- Identify stress-related psychological disorders and therapy options.

When stress becomes persistent and overwhelming, it can lead to debilitating psychological disorders such as anxiety, depression, and burnout. While self-management techniques sometimes help, there may come a time when medication and one-on-one or group therapy with a licensed therapist is necessary. Employee assistance programs at work and community-based twelve-step programs may offer additional support.

● Career Corner

Q: I work for a large company and have a terrific job. Because of downsizing, all of us in the office are working 60-hour weeks to get the work done. I take work home and do the work four people used to do. By the end of the week my mind is numb, my productivity is down, and I am exhausted. This not only is hard on my family but is bad for the company. It seems that if the work can't be handled during a normal workweek, then we need to hire more people to do the job. What do you suggest?

A: If you can get another job that is less stressful, then consider starting a job search. However, if you feel lucky to have your job, then let your boss know that you need help. Talk with your colleagues to find out if they share your concerns, conduct your own research on the impact that unrelenting stress has on worker productivity, and then report your findings to your employer. There is ample evidence that working on too many projects at one time (multitasking) actually reduces worker effectiveness. Explain that on-the-job productivity is enhanced when you are able to shift your focus by going home, being with your family, or socializing. Then, do not accept unreasonable amounts of work that force you to take that work home. If this results in threats of termination, keep in mind that a job that is causing you to burnout is not worth it.

● Key Terms

stress	resilience
fight or flight syndrome	anxiety
technostress	depression
ergonomics	burnout
transition	employee assistance programs
meditation	twelve-step programs

● Applying What You Have Learned

1. Determine what circumstances are causing the most stress in your life. For example, are you trying to work too many hours while going to school? Are you experiencing parental or peer pressure? Do you feel burdened with things you cannot control? Then answer the following questions:

   a. What aspects of the situation are under your control?

   b. Are there any aspects of the situation that are out of your control? Explain.

   c. What steps can you take to help eliminate the stress?

   d. What individual stress management strategies could you use to counteract the effects of this stress?

2. Consider the following company-sponsored stress management programs. List them in order from most beneficial to you to least beneficial. Explain your reasoning.

   a. Access to on-site exercise facilities or company-sponsored health club membership

   b. A workshop on stress management sponsored by the company

   c. A cafeteria where healthy, nutritionally balanced foods are served

   d. Access to a soundproof audiovisual room for viewing relaxing videotapes, listening to soothing music, or taking a nap

3. Stress often increases as we struggle with time management. How well do you manage your time? Take a few minutes and answer each question below. Then spend time developing a time management program that meets your individual needs.

   a. Do you develop a daily "to do" list that indicates the activities you hope to work on?

   b. Do you maintain a planning calendar—a single place to record daily appointments, deadlines, and tasks?

   c. Do you have a series of personal and professional goals that guide you in setting priorities for use of your time?

   d. Have you learned to say no to proliferating requests for your participation in team activities, projects, social activities, and so on, that may complicate your life?

4. Try a one-day "news fast." Do not read, watch, or listen to any news for a day and see how you feel.

Internet Insights

1. Go to *Monster.com*, the online jobs database, and enter *fun* or *humor* into the search box. Are there any organizations in your area that promote a "fun" working environment? Search East Coast (example: New York City),

West Coast (example: San Diego), and Midwest (example: Kansas City) locations. Which region exhibits more fun opportunities than the others? What semantics are used to describe the fun working environment?

2. Go to *www.netaddiction.com/resources/internet_addiction_test.htm* and take the twenty-question Internet Addiction Test. Determine your score and then do as the test's creator suggests when it comes to time to evaluate your responses to specific questions.

 Role-Play Exercise

Assume you are the spouse of Leslie, a call-center customer-service representative. Leslie routinely comes home from work stressed out and in a surly mood. Each representative at the center handles up to 120 calls per day and faces more frequent personal attacks than workers in most other occupations, with little or no opportunity to respond. The management of the organization is inflexible when it comes to accommodating its customers' needs, so the call-center personnel have little power to make the customers happy. Many times they are forced to refuse the customers' requests and respond, "It's corporate policy." Leslie has become irritable, impatient, and emotionally unavailable to you and your three elementary-school-aged children. The job pays better than any other opportunities in the area, and your family has become dependent on Leslie's income. Upon returning home from work today, Leslie walked past you and the kids, went into your bedroom, closed the door, turned on the TV, and began rapidly consuming a six-pack of beer. You've had enough! Rather than escalate the stress by mentioning the divorce option, you have decided to try to talk with Leslie about reducing the stress in your lives. Role-play this discussion with one of your classmates, who will play the role of Leslie.

Case 14.1 Vacation Starvation

In many families similar to those mentioned in the opening vignette of this chapter, working parents are forced to "burn" their vacation days as they attempt to coordinate their work and personal schedules. Others juggle part-time or temporary jobs that offer no paid vacation days. Some may be forced to use their vacation days when an illness consumes their allotted paid sick days. Still others don't take their vacation days because their workload does not allow an interruption or they fear being laid off when employers discover they can get along without the worker.

One study of workers who did not take all of their allowed vacation days found that 13 percent did so because they got money back for unused days, 12 percent said it was because they had to schedule a vacation in advance, and 10 percent said they were simply too busy at work to get away. Other people cannot take a break from work even when they are on vacation. They carry their laptops and PDAs to the beach, mountain retreat, or family reunion.

Bryson Koehler, a director of international services at a hotel company, went with his extended family on a vacation and camped out in the corner of his parents' bathroom, since that was the only place his BlackBerry and wireless laptop connection received signals. When the family went biking, he surreptitiously planted his laptop, cell phone, and BlackBerry in the bicycle trailer carrying his 9-month-old son, leaving them with their power on to collect messages during the ride. His wife, upset by his persistent connectedness, "accidentally" switched the cell phone from ring to vibrate and booked their next vacation onboard a cruise ship where Internet charges were $3 a minute.[48]

You need to take vacations from the stress your work life places on your personal life and leisure time. Yes, the e-mails pile up and the problems that weren't taken care of while you were away await you upon your return. Colleagues who have to pick up the slack while you are gone may be irritable, but only until their vacation time comes around and you reciprocate. But this down time provides a physical and mental rejuvenation that allows you to return to work with a renewed spirit, relaxed and ready to take on the next challenge. According to a study by Xylo, a workplace consulting firm, 94 percent of working adults say time away from work makes them better employees. Seventy percent said it makes them feel a lot more productive. Another study found that regular vacations lower the risk of death by almost 20 percent for men and cut the risk of heart attacks among women by nearly 50 percent.[49]

Questions

1. If you were an employer, would you require your workers to take all of their vacation days? Why or why not?

2. How long has it been since your last vacation? When is your next vacation? Will you actually "get away from it all," or will you work at another job or on projects at home? Discuss with your classmates the ramifications of your plans on your mental and physical health.

3. Standard stress relievers such as medications and vacations can help, but what do you do to relax when you can't leave your desk? Some workers are training themselves to withdraw for what you might call an inner vacation.[50] Can you go virtually to your favorite vacation spot without leaving your desk? Explain.

Case 14.2 Drugs on Campus

It is estimated that 1.6 million incoming college freshmen experience episodes of depression and that approximately 20 percent of the nation's student population take antidepressants at some point in their college years. College health officials know that students, some on their own without parental guidance for the first time in their lives, live with academic pressure, experience frequent romantic rollercoasters, eat too much junk food, and get too little sleep. To help students cope with the pressures associated with college life, many campuses conduct screenings for depression, eating disorders, anxiety, and alcohol abuse. They create public service ads and posters aimed at increasing students' awareness of these potentially debilitating psychological disorders.

To help defray the costs of these on-campus programs, some college administrators are accepting the financial sponsorship of drug companies that offer programs meant to raise students' awareness of depression and the drugs that can treat it. Wyeth (maker of the antidepressant Effexor) created a 90-minute forum called "Depression in College: Real World, Real Life, Real Issues." Wyeth joined with Pfizer Inc. (maker of the antidepressant Zoloft), Glaxo (maker of the antidepressant Paxil), and Eli Lilly & Co. (maker of the antidepressant Prozac) to help underwrite the National Depression Screening Day.

Glaxo offered an online self-test to raise awareness of *general anxiety disorder*. Some of the questions on the self-test were: "Do you worry excessively?" "Are you anxious a lot of the time?" "Do you have trouble sleeping?" "Does anxiety ever interfere with your family or social life?" "Do you avoid giving speeches?" "Does criticism frighten you?" If participants answered yes to any or all of these questions, they were advised that they might be candidates for antidepressant drugs and encouraged to contact their physicians.

While drugs like Paxil, Prozac, Zoloft, and Effexor are helping millions of people live more productive lives, critics believe that there is an inherent problem in having the producers of such drugs presenting on-campus forums and issuing online diagnoses of depression or anxiety. They believe these programs run the risk of misdiagnosis and unnecessary prescriptions. While they agree that it is important to recognize the danger signs of psychological disorders, they encourage those who participate in these programs to question: Who doesn't feel tense, tired, or irritable at some time? They suggest better self-test questions might be: "Is there something wrong with me, or is there something wrong with my academic or career choices?" "Do my efforts give me satisfaction?" "Do I feel valued by my friends and colleagues?" "Do I receive recognition for a task well done?" If the answer to these is no, maybe the self-test participants should take action, not drugs.[51]

Questions

1. Does it bother you that drug companies have a role in educating college students about the warning signs and possible medicinal solutions to psychological disorders? Explain your reasoning.

2. What is meant by the statement that "maybe self-test participants should take action, not drugs"?

3. Are there alternatives to drug therapy for psychological disorders that college students might implement to help them with the stress of college life? What are they?

INTEGRATED RESOURCES

CLASSROOM ACTIVITIES (*college.hmco.com/pic/reece10e*)

The NWNL Workplace Stress Test
Eustress and Distress
Inner Jogging Journal Entry

business.college.hmco.com/students

ACE

Self-tests

15

VALUING WORK FORCE DIVERSITY

Chapter Preview

After studying this chapter, you will be able to

- Define the primary and secondary dimensions of diversity.

- Discuss how prejudiced attitudes are formed.

- Develop an awareness of the various forms of discrimination in the workplace.

- Understand why organizations are striving to develop organizational cultures that value diversity.

- Identify ways in which individuals and organizations can enhance work force diversity.

- Discuss the current status of affirmative action programs.

A growing number of companies realize that they need a work force that reflects the changing demographics of their customers. Diversity is not simply a matter of doing the right thing; it is a business imperative. PepsiCo Incorporated used to have a reputation as a mostly white-male fraternity, but things have changed. People of color now hold 17 percent of the management jobs at midlevel and above, and women hold nearly 30 percent. Steve Reinemune, CEO of PepsiCo, is leading the diversity initiative. He believes that diversity promotes innovation and better decision making. New products inspired by employees include a wasabi-flavored snack aimed at Asian-Americans; guacamole-flavored Doritos chips aimed at Hispanics, and Mountain Dew Code Red, which appeals to African Americans.[1]

Harley-Davidson, the Milwaukee-based motorcycle maker, concluded many years ago that its sales would falter unless it expanded beyond its traditional white male customers. To attract people of color and women, the company needed employees who reflected the customer base they wanted to attract. Over the past decade, Harley-Davidson has worked hard to attract both women and minority managers.[2]

Work Force Diversity

America has always served as host to a kaleidoscope of the world's cultures, and the diversity movement is likely to continue. Growing minority and immigrant populations will contribute to increased racial and ethnic diversity. The American work force is becoming more racially and ethnically diverse, increasingly female, and increasingly older.[3] Foreign-born population trends are presented in Figure 15.1.

Eastman Kodak Company has worked hard to increase minority representation at all levels. The company realizes that fostering diversity in their workplace in an important business practice.

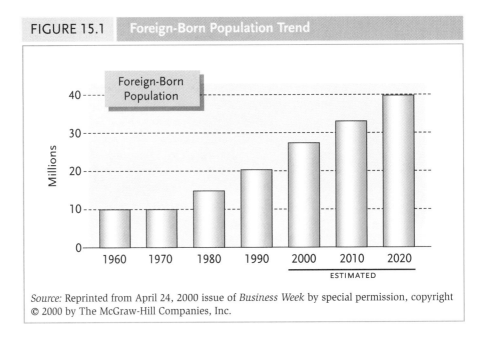

FIGURE 15.1   Foreign-Born Population Trend

Source: Reprinted from April 24, 2000 issue of *Business Week* by special permission, copyright © 2000 by The McGraw-Hill Companies, Inc.

> *In the past, most U.S. organizations attempted to assimilate everyone into one "American" way of doing things.*

In the past, most U.S. organizations attempted to assimilate everyone into one "American" way of doing things. Labor unions were formed so that everyone would be treated the same. The women's rights movement began when women wanted to be treated just like men in the workplace. The emphasis now, however, is on **valuing diversity**, which means appreciating everyone's uniqueness, respecting differences, and encouraging every worker to make his or her full contribution to the organization. Organizations that foster the full participation of all workers will enjoy the sharpest competitive edge in the expanding global marketplace.

Dimensions of Diversity

There are primary and secondary dimensions of diversity. The **primary dimensions** are core characteristics of each individual that cannot be changed: age, race, gender, physical and mental abilities, and sexual orientation (see Figure 15.2). Together they form an individual's self-image and the filters through which each person views the rest of the world. These inborn elements are interdependent; no one dimension stands alone. Each exerts an important influence throughout life. Marilyn Loden and Judy Rosener describe individual primary dimensions in their book *Workforce America!* They say, "Like the interlocking segments of a sphere, they represent the core of our individual identities."[4]

The greater the number of primary differences between people, the more difficult it is to establish trust and mutual respect. When we add the secondary dimensions of diversity to the mix, effective human relations become even more difficult. The **secondary dimensions** of diversity are elements that can

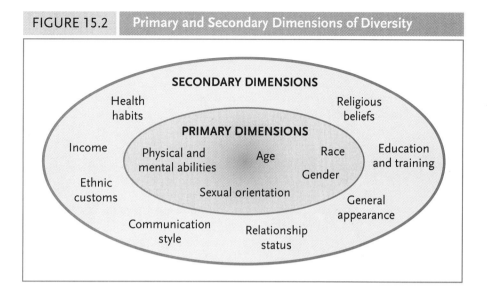

FIGURE 15.2   **Primary and Secondary Dimensions of Diversity**

be changed or at least modified. They include a person's health habits, religious beliefs, education and training, general appearance, relationship status, ethnic customs, communication style, and income (see Figure 15.2). These factors all add a layer of complexity to the way we see ourselves and others. The blend of secondary and primary dimensions adds depth to each person and helps shape his or her values, priorities, and perceptions throughout life.[5]

Each of us enters the work force with a unique perspective shaped by these dimensions and our own past experiences. Building effective human relationships is possible only when we learn to accept and value the differences in others. Without this acceptance, both primary and secondary dimensions of diversity can become roadblocks to further cooperation and understanding.

Prejudiced Attitudes

Prejudice is a premature judgment or opinion that is formed without examination of the facts. Throughout life we often prejudge people in light of their primary and secondary dimensions. Rather than treat others as unique individuals, prejudiced people tend to think in terms of **stereotypes**—perceptions, beliefs, and expectations about members of some group. In most cases, a stereotype involves the false assumption that all members of a group share the same characteristics.

TOTAL	**J.T. "TED" CHILDS, JR.**
PERSON	VICE PRESIDENT, IBM GLOBAL WORKFORCE DIVERSITY
INSIGHT	"No matter who you are, you're going to have to work with people who are different from you. You're going to have to sell to people who are different from you, and buy from people who are different from you, and manage people who are different from you."

HUMAN RELATIONS IN ACTION

Tools for Tolerance: Personal

■ Attend a play, listen to music, or go to a dance performance by artists whose race or ethnicity is different from your own.

■ Visit a local senior citizens center and collect oral histories. Donate large-print reading materials and books on tape. Offer to help with a craft project.

■ Take a conversation course in another language that is spoken in your community.

■ Sign the Declaration of Tolerance (see Figure 15.3).

■ Speak up when you hear slurs. Let people know that biased speech is always unacceptable.

The most common and powerful stereotypes focus on observable personal attributes such as age, gender, and ethnicity.[6]

Prejudiced attitudes and the resulting stereotypes are more likely to change when we take time to learn more about specific members of a particular group.

FIGURE 15.3   Declaration of Tolerance

Declaration of Tolerance

Tolerance is a personal decision that comes from a belief that every person is a treasure. I believe that America's diversity is its strength. I also recognize that ignorance, insensitivity, and bigotry can turn that diversity into a source of prejudice and discrimination.

To help keep diversity a well-spring of strength and make this country a better place for all, I pledge to have respect for people whose abilities, beliefs, cultures, race, sexual identity or other characteristics are different from my own.

To fulfill this pledge, I will . . .

• examine my own biases and work to overcome them,

• set a positive example for my family and friends,

• work for tolerance in my own community, and

• speak out against hate and injustice.

_____

Signature

Please sign and mail a copy to:
National Campaign for Tolerance,
400 Washington Avenue
Montgomery, AL 36104.

Source: Adapted from "101 Tools For Tolerance: Simple Ideas for Promoting Equity and Celebrating Diversity." Copyright © 2000, Southern Poverty Law Center, Montgomery, Alabama. *101 Tools for Tolerance* is available free from the SPLC. For more information, visit *www.splcenter.org* or send a fax to (334) 264-7310. Reprinted by permission of Southern Poverty Law Center.

For example, twenty years ago, women were often viewed as indecisive, passive, and too emotional to succeed in leadership positions. As the work force became increasingly female, men and women began working together and learning that leadership ability might *not* be gender-related. Now that women occupy a greater proportion of management and executive positions, stereotypes formed by prejudiced attitudes are contradicted by facts.

How Prejudicial Attitudes Are Formed and Retained

Three major factors contribute to the development of prejudice: childhood experiences, ethnocentrism, and economic conditions.

Childhood Experiences   Today's views toward others are filtered through the experiences and feelings of childhood. Children watch how their family members, friends, teachers, and other authority figures respond to different racial, ethnic, and religious groups. As a result, they form attitudes that may last a lifetime, unless new information replaces the old perceptions. Prejudicial attitudes are not unalterable. Whatever prejudice is learned during childhood can be unlearned later in life.[7]

TOTAL	**SHERYLN CHEW**
PERSON	CREATOR, THE PURPLE BAMBOO ORCHESTRA
INSIGHT	"To bring Chinese music to an African American church, it means that when we leave Chinatown we are promoting our culture. If we stay in Chinatown, we're only preserving it. If you're going to promote cultural understanding, it has to be to all people of all walks of life."

Ethnocentrism   The tendency to regard our own culture or nation as better or more "correct" than others is called **ethnocentrism**. The word is derived from *ethnic*, meaning a group united by similar customs, characteristics, race, or other common factors, and *center*. **Ethnicity** refers to the condition of being culturally rather than physically distinctive.[8] When ethnocentrism is present, the standards and values of our own culture are being used as a yardstick to measure the worth of other cultures.

In their book *Valuing Diversity*, Lewis Brown Griggs and Lente-Louise Louw compare ethnocentrism in an organization to icebergs floating in an ocean. We can see the tips of icebergs above the water level, just as we can see our diverse coworkers' skin color, gender, mannerisms, and job-related talents and hear the words they use and their accents. These are basically "surface" aspects of a person that others can easily learn through observation. However, just as the enormous breadth of an iceberg's base lies beneath the water's surface, so does the childhood conditioning of people from different cultures. As icebergs increase in number and drift too close together, they are likely to clash at their base even though there is no visible contact at the water's surface.[9] As organizations increase the diversity of their work force, the potential for clashes resulting from deep-seated cultural conditioning and prejudiced attitudes also increases.

Economic Factors   When the economy goes through a recession or depression, and housing, jobs, and other necessities become scarce, people's prejudices against other groups often increase. If enough prejudice is built up against a particular group, members of that group may be barred from competing for jobs. The recent backlash against immigrants can be traced, in part, to a fear that the new arrivals will take jobs that would otherwise be available to American workers. Prejudice based on economic factors has its roots in people's basic survival needs, and, as a result, it is very hard to eliminate.

Rising income and wealth inequality in America is viewed by many as a serious barrier to racial harmony. Ronald Walters, University of Maryland political scientist, says, "You can only have meaningful racial reconciliation when people of roughly equal socioeconomic status can reach across the divide of race."[10] The gap in well-being between whites and nonwhites barely changed throughout the booming 1990s and remains huge. The racial divide in wealth (value of all assets) and income shows no sign of narrowing.[11]

CRITICAL THINKING CHALLENGE

In an ideal world, everyone would be free of prejudiced attitudes and would avoid thinking in terms of stereotypes. However, childhood experiences can shape attitudes that are difficult to change. Do you carry any prejudices that are obvious carryovers from your childhood or adolescence? Are you doing anything to overcome these prejudices? Explain.

The Many Forms of Discrimination

Discrimination is behavior based on prejudiced attitudes. If, as an employer, you believe that overweight people tend to be lazy, that is a prejudiced attitude. If you refuse to hire someone simply because that person is overweight, you are engaging in discrimination.

Discrimination is behavior based on prejudiced attitudes.

Individuals or groups that are discriminated against are denied equal treatment and opportunities afforded to the dominant group. They may be denied employment, promotion, training, or other job-related privileges on the basis of race, lifestyle, gender, or other characteristics that have little or nothing to do with their qualifications for a job.

Gender

Discrimination based on gender has been, and continues to be, the focus of much attention. The traditional roles women have held in society have undergone tremendous changes in the past few decades. Women enter the work force not only to supplement family income but also to pursue careers in previously all-male professions. Men have also been examining the roles assigned them by society and are discovering new options for themselves. Most companies have recognized that discrimination based on gender is a reality and are taking steps to deal with the problem. Chapter 16 is devoted to an in-depth discussion of overcoming gender bias in organizations.

■ Age

Oscar-winner Paul Newman climbs into a race car every chance he gets, even though he is in his 80s. He was proud to be co-driver of one of the cars that competed in the 2005 Rolex 24-hour endurance race held at Daytona International Speedway.[12] The people who make up today's work force are working longer and living longer. Meaningful employment is a source of well-being for many of these workers. Yet, many workers over 50 face discrimination based on age.

There is the widespread perception that older workers are unable or unwilling to adapt to accelerating change.[13] This stereotypical notion exists in spite of studies indicating that workers 55 and over are productive, cost-effective employees who can be trained in new technologies as easily as younger people. Because of prejudice, workers over 50 take nearly twice as long to find a new job as do younger people.[14] Many must accept positions that pay considerably less than their previous job.

According to recent reports from the Equal Employment Opportunity Commission (EEOC), age discrimination is on the rise. As companies search for ways to cut costs, they often find creative ways to get rid of older workers (see Table 15.1) and replace them with younger workers who earn less. The rise in age discrimination complaints is also due to our aging work force. By 2015, workers 55 and older will make up nearly 20 percent of the work force.[15]

Some companies have discovered that employees in their 50s and 60s have valuable knowledge and experience and are taking steps to retain these older workers. They realize the value of senior staff members passing along "institutional memory," giving the new generation of employees the advantage of learning from the past so that they can effectively direct the future of the organization. Often those who are nearing retirement serve as mentors who can offer guidance and advice unclouded by personal ambition.[16] At Home Depot, older employees serve as a powerful draw to young shoppers needing help with home improvement projects. West Pac Banking Corporation, a large financial-services company, recently recruited 950 workers over 45 as financial planners. Older clients prefer advisers with experience. Many progressive companies are taking steps to retain older workers. These retention tools include phased

---

TABLE 15.1	Age-Related Discriminatory Practices

Many organizations have fostered cultures of age bias. This bias is expressed in a variety of age-related discriminatory practices:

■ Cutting off older workers from job-related training and career development opportunities

■ Excluding older workers from important activities

■ Favoring younger job applicants over older, better-qualified candidates

■ Forcing older workers out of the work force with negative performance evaluations

■ Pressuring older workers to accept financial incentives and retire early

Source: Sheldon Steinhauser, "Age Bias: Is Your Corporate Culture in Need of an Overhaul?" *HR Magazine,* July 1998.

© King Features Syndicate

retirement, portable jobs for people who want to live in warmer climates in the winter, and part-time projects for retirees.[17]

Race

Few areas are more sensitive and engender more passion than issues surrounding race. **Race** denotes a category of people who are perceived as distinctive on the basis of certain biologically inherited traits such as skin color or hair texture.[18] Because people cannot change these inherited traits, they can easily become victims of discrimination.

Throughout American history we have seen attempts to place people in racial categories and judge them as racial symbols rather than as unique individuals. During World War II, many Japanese Americans of Japanese ancestry were confined in concentration camps because they were considered a security threat, merely because of their racial heritage. Until the mid-1960s, some African Americans were not allowed to drink from public water fountains, to sit anywhere but in the rear of public transportation, or to attend public schools established for white children only. Because of the war on terrorism, today's "racial" targets often include immigrants from Pakistan, Iraq, and other Middle Eastern countries, as well as their American-born children.

There is as much genetic variability between two people from the same "racial group" as there is between two people from any two different "racial" groups.

The Myth of Race Critics of racial categories view them as social inventions that intensify and reinforce racist beliefs and actions. They believe that one way to break down racial barriers and promote a race-free consciousness is to get rid of traditional racial categories (see Table 15.2). A growing number of geneticists and social scientists reject the view that "racial" differences have an objective or scientific foundation.[19] The American Anthropological Association (AAA) has taken the official position that "race" has no scientific justification in human biology. The AAA position is that "There is as much genetic variability between two people from the same 'racial group' as there is between two people from any two different 'racial' groups."[20]

It is important to keep in mind that some race categories include people who vary greatly in terms of ethnicity. The Asian label includes a wide range of groups, such as Vietnamese, Filipinos, Chinese, and Koreans, with distinct histories and languages. The

TABLE 15.2	Traditional Nonwhite Race Categories
African American	Persons who descended from peoples of African origin. The term *Black* is often used to describe persons of African ancestry.
Hispanic	This is the broadest term used to encompass Spanish-speaking peoples in both American hemispheres. The widely used term *Latino* is generally restricted to persons of Latin American descent.
Asian	The term *Asian* is preferred over *Oriental* for persons of East, Southeast, and South Asian ancestry, such as Chinese, Koreans, Japanese, Indonesians, and Filipinos.
Native American	This term refers to peoples indigenous to America. However, the term *Indian* is sometimes used as a term of pride and respect by Native Americans.

Source: American Heritage Dictionary, 4th ed. (Boston: Houghton Mifflin, 2000), pp. 105, 189–190, 832, 1171.

label "African American" does not take into consideration the enormous linguistic, physical, and cultural diversity of the peoples of Africa.[21]

Since interracial relationships are now much more common than they were before, millions of Americans are of mixed races that do not fit the usual general categories. Golf champion Tiger Woods (his father is African American and his mother is from Thailand) is proud of his multiracial background. He joins a growing number of Americans who believe that identities can evolve, that people needn't be locked into the identities bestowed on them at birth. As a result, respondents to U.S. census forms are now provided the opportunity to check one or more boxes from sixty-three racial options.[22]

Race as Social Identity Although races are not scientifically defensible, they are "real" socially, politically, and psychologically. Race and racism affect our own self-perception and how we are treated by others. Groups that are working to build ethnic pride, such as Native Americans, oppose efforts to get rid of the traditional racial categories, which they consider part of a positive identity. Many feel that this system of racial categories is necessary to create minority voting districts and to administer an array of federal laws and programs designed to ensure that minorities get equal housing, education, health care, and employment opportunities.[23] That is why the federal government has assured the public that the agencies responsible for enforcement of nondiscriminatory housing laws, employment laws, and so forth will break down the many census report categories in ways that allow them to enforce the current laws.

Religion

Discrimination based on a person's religious preference has been an issue throughout history. Christianity is the most commonly practiced religion in the United Sates, and Judaism is the second.[24] During the 1930s, however, many Christian Americans considered Jews a separate "race" and treated them accordingly. Religion has always had the power to fracture and divide people of faith. Members of various denominations often lack tolerance for beliefs that differ from their own.

Wheaton College, an evangelical Protestant college in Illinois, was very pleased to have Assistant Professor Joshua Hochschild teach students about medieval Roman Catholic thinkers. But when the popular teacher converted to Catholicism, the college fired him. Associate Professor Susan Anderson of Appalachian State University was a faculty candidate at Baylor University several years ago. Baylor is the largest Baptist university in the world. The president asked her how she would integrate the Bible into her accounting classes. He also asked her why she was a member of the Methodist faith. Although the department faculty voted to extend her a job offer, the decision was vetoed by Baylor's administration. Religious colleges are increasingly "hiring for mission," even at the cost of eliminating more academically qualified candidates.[25]

Today the headlines document the pervasive discrimination of Muslims in the workplace. They are often ridiculed for their daily prayer routine. Misunderstandings seem to occur frequently over relatively minor issues such as Muslim women's right to wear head scarves and Muslim men's right to maintain facial hair. With more than 5 million Muslims in America, Islam is expected to soon surpass Judaism and become the second most practiced religion in the United States. The EEOC has reported an increase in discrimination complaints brought by Muslims, Arabs, Middle Easterners, South Asians, and Sikhs. Even those who are American born but are perceived to be members of these groups because of physical features can become victims of this type of discrimination.

Joshua Hochschild had to leave his assistant professorship at Wheaton College after he converted to Catholicism. Wheaton College is an evangelical Protestant college based in Wheaton, Illinois.

Disability

The Americans with Disabilities Act (ADA) sets forth requirements for businesses with fifteen or more employees. It bans discrimination against workers and customers with disabilities and requires employers to make "reasonable accommodations" so that the disabled can access and work in the workplace. It covers a wide range of disabilities, including mental impairments, AIDS, alcoholism, visual impairments, and physical impairments that require use of a wheelchair (visit *www.adata.org*). Although legal protection is in place, the employment rate for people with disabilities age 21 to 64 is only 38 percent.[26]

Disabled people who want to work face several problems. Many of the jobs performed by people with disabilities are being outsourced abroad. Doug Schalk lost his position as a call-center customer representative at Vanguard Car Rental USA Incorporated when it transferred his job to India. Many of the low-paying service-sector jobs often filled by those with disabilities do not provide adequate health benefits to meet the needs of disabled workers.[27] Some employers are simply unwilling to hire people who are blind or use a wheelchair and to accommodate their needs with ramps, power doors, Braille signage, and voice-activated technology. They fail to see that these adjustments might serve as a gateway to valuable, hard-working employees, a new customer base, and an economic opportunity.

The good news is that several companies are setting a good example with major programs to accommodate both employees and customers with disabilities (see Table 15.3). In addition, many corporate diversity training programs include sessions on disability awareness and employment.

TABLE 15.3	Enabling Those with Disabilities
Company	**Type of Assistance**
Crestar Bank	Provides voice-activated technology for disabled customer service representatives. Makes special services available to customers with disabilities.
Honeywell	Participates in Able to Work program, a consortium of 22 companies that find ways to employ disabled persons. Uses its high-tech innovations to assist employees with disabilities.
Johnson & Johnson	Has established a comprehensive disability management program that tailors work assignments to employees returning to work after an injury.
Caterpillar	Serves as a model of high-tech accessibility for the disabled; sponsors Special Olympics.
America OnLine	Has agreed to work with the National Federation of the Blind to ensure that AOL content is largely accessible to the blind.

Sources: John Williams, "The List—Enabling Those with Disabilities," *Business Week,* March 6, 2000, p. 8; "The New Work Force," *Business Week,* March 20, 2000, pp. 64–74; and Douglas M. Towns, "What Internet Companies Must Know About the Americans with Disabilities Act." [cited on 23 February 2006]. Available from www.gigalaw.com; INTERNET.

Sexual Orientation

Discrimination based on a person's sexual orientation is motivated by *homophobia*, an aversion to homosexuals. Not long ago, gays and lesbians went to great lengths to keep their sexuality a secret. But today many gays and lesbians are "coming out of the closet" to demand their rights as members of society. Indeed, many young people entering the work force who are used to the relative tolerance of college campuses refuse to hide their orientation once they are in the workplace.

Gay rights activists are working hard to create awareness that discrimination based on sexual orientation is no less serious than discrimination based on age, gender, race, or disability. Activists are also working to rid the workplace of

The National Sports Center for the Disabled's mission is to positively impact the lives of people with any physical or mental challenge. Today, the NSCD is one of the largest outdoor therapeutic recreational agencies in the world. Thousands of lessons are provided each year.

What kind of people take blind kids mountain climbing?
The same ones who take paraplegics sailing and amputees horseback riding.

THE NATIONAL SPORTS CENTER FOR THE DISABLED

To participate, volunteer, or help financially, visit www.nscd.org

HUMAN RELATIONS IN ACTION

Meeting Someone with a Disability

Here are a few suggestions for making a good impression. If the person . . .

. . . is in a wheelchair. Sit down, if possible. Try to chat eye to eye. Don't touch the wheelchair. It is considered within the boundaries of an individual's personal space.

. . . has a speech impediment. Be patient, actively listen, and resist the urge to finish his or her sentences.

. . . is accompanied by a guide dog. Never pet or play with a guide dog; you will distract the animal from its job.

. . . has a hearing loss. People who are deaf depend on facial expressions and gestures for communication cues. Speak clearly and slowly. Speak directly to the person, not to an interpreter or assistant if one is present.

antigay behaviors such as offensive jokes, derogatory names, or remarks about gays. An atmosphere in which gays and lesbians are comfortable about being themselves is usually more productive than an atmosphere in which they waste their time and energy maintaining alternate, and false, personalities.

In recent years we have witnessed several workplace trends favorable to gay and lesbian employees. More than 80 percent of *Fortune* 500 companies include sexual orientation in their antidiscrimination policies, and some companies have established lesbian and gay employee associations that provide a point of contact for previously invisible employees. Also, a majority of the nations top 500 companies now extend medical benefits to same-sex partners. Some major companies such as American Express and J. P. Morgan & Company are targeting recruiting efforts at gay and lesbian college students.[28]

Many state and local governments have passed laws that help protect gays and lesbians from discrimination and violence. Policies aimed at preventing verbal and physical harassment of homosexual students have been adopted by many public schools and colleges. In some cases, these initiatives have generated considerable controversy. Some religious and conservative groups have actively opposed these violence-prevention efforts, believing that they promote homosexuality.[29]

Subtle Forms of Discrimination

A person who feels he or she has been the victim of discrimination based on gender, age, race, abilities, or sexual orientation can take legal action by filing a complaint with his or her state's office of the Equal Employment Opportunity Commission. However, while state and federal laws protect individuals from discrimination based on these issues, they do not specifically protect workers from the more subtle forms of discrimination. For example, those who graduated from an Ivy League college may treat coworkers who graduated from state-funded colleges as inferior. Overweight employees might experience degrading remarks from coworkers. Those who speak with a distinct regional accent may hear snickers behind their back at work. People who do not value differences often equate a difference with a deficiency.

In its valuing diversity training program, Kaiser Permanente identifies twenty concrete examples of human differences that might cause discrimination among its workers. The list includes the standard diversity issues, but it also identifies characteristics such as education, politics, personal history, and socioeconomic status.[30] Since there are no laws regarding these issues, employees need to understand the negative impact of these subtle forms of discrimination and take responsibility for creating an atmosphere where they are not tolerated.

What Can You Do?

What should you do if you discover you are the target of some form of subtle, unprotected discrimination because you are different from others at work? If you want to stay in the organization, you will need to determine whether the "difference" is something you can change—your weight, the way you dress, your manner of speaking. If the difference is something you cannot or choose not to change, you may need to address the situation directly. Review the assertiveness skills you studied in Chapter 13. Your assertiveness may help change other people's attitudes and in turn alter their discriminatory behaviors. Another powerful method of eliminating subtle discrimination is to compensate for it by excelling in your work. Become an expert on the job, and work to increase your skills and your value to the organization. As your colleagues gain respect for your talents, they will likely change their attitudes toward you. But if your future appears blocked, investigate other workplaces where management may be more open to diversity. The important point is that you should refuse to allow discrimination to limit your personal and professional success.

The Economics of Valuing Diversity

The new millennium has brought a strong shift away from the traditional pattern of treating everyone the same and toward valuing diversity in a work setting. This means that a company intends to make full use of the ideas, talents, experiences, and perspectives of all employees at all levels of the organization. Joe Watson, a recruiter of minorities, believes that if you want to satisfy clients and customers from diverse backgrounds, you need a diverse mix of employees who are more likely to understand them. People from various cultural and ethnic backgrounds can offer different perspectives and stimulate creativity. "This type of inclusion," says Watson, "isn't about joining hands and singing 'Kumbaya.' This is about improving corporate performance."[31]

The price tag for not helping employees learn to respect and value each other is enormous.

A study conducted by the Society for Human Resource Management revealed diversity initiatives within organizations can affect an organization's bottom line by reducing costs associated with turnover, absenteeism, and low productivity. In addition, efforts to value workers' and customers' diversity reduce complaints and litigation and improve the organization's public image.[32] Organizations that pursue diversity and make it part of their culture usually outperform companies that are less committed to diversity.

The price tag for *not* helping employees learn to respect and value each other is enormous. Many highly skilled and talented employees will leave an organization that does not value diversity. A comment, gesture, or joke delivered without malice but received as an insult will create tension among workers and customers alike. Valuable time will be wasted clarifying miscommunication and misunderstandings. Recognizing the value of diversity and managing it as an asset can help eliminate these negative effects.

TOTAL PERSON INSIGHT	**LEWIS BROWN GRIGGS AND LENTE-LOUISE LOUW**
	AUTHORS, *VALUING DIVERSITY: NEW TOOLS FOR A NEW REALITY*
	"More and more, organizations can remain competitive only if they can recognize and obtain the best talent; value the diverse perspectives that come with talent born of different cultures, races, and genders; nurture and train that talent; and create an atmosphere that values its workforce."

Managing Diversity

Managing diversity is the process of creating an organizational culture where the primary and secondary dimensions of diversity are respected. This process can be a challenge now that the work force is composed of so many different nationalities. Managers at some Marriott Hotels work with employees from thirty different countries. The employees who are part of the Toyota Formula 1 race team represent twenty-seven nationalities. Even some small retail stores have become a kind of United Nations. The Kroger supermarket in Durham, North Carolina, has employees from ten countries. The issue is further complicated when an organization's diverse work force is in global satellite offices separated by thousands of miles. Microsoft's research unit, for example, is staffed by 700 multinational scientists and engineers working in six laboratories on three continents.[33]

What Individuals Can Do

People tend to hang on to their prejudices and stereotypes. If certain white people believe people of color are inferior, they are likely to notice any incident in which a person of color makes a mistake. But when a person of color exhibits competence and sound decision-making abilities, these same white people may not notice, or they may attribute the positive results to other circumstances. You cannot totally eliminate prejudices that have been deeply held and developed over a long time. But you can take steps to change those attitudes and behaviors that may have a negative impact on your employer's efforts to enhance diversity.

Learn to look critically and honestly at the particular myths and preconceived ideas you have been conditioned to believe about others.

1. *Learn to look critically and honestly at the particular myths and preconceived ideas you have been conditioned to believe about others.* Contact among people of different races, cultures, and lifestyles can break down prejudice when people join together for a common task. The more contact there is among culturally diverse individuals, the more likely it will be that stereotypes based on myths and inaccurate generalizations will not survive.

2. *Develop a sensitivity to differences.* Do not allow gender-based, racist, or antigay jokes or comments in your presence. If English is not a person's native language, be aware that this person might interpret your messages differently from what you intended. When in doubt as to the appropriate behavior, ask questions. "I would like to open the door for you because you are in a wheelchair, but I'm not sure whether that would offend you. What would you like me to do?"

3. *Develop your own diversity awareness program.* The starting point might be creation of a "diversity profile" of your friends, coworkers, and acquaintances. How much diversity do these individuals have in terms of race? Ethnicity? Religion? Assess the cultural diversity reflected in the music you listen to and the books you read. Visit an ethnic restaurant and try to learn about more than the food. Study Islam, Buddhism, and other faiths that may be different from your own.[34]

SKILL DEVELOPMENT CHALLENGE

Career success often depends on your ability to work effectively with people who differ from you in age, gender, race, physical traits, sexual orientation, and other dimensions of diversity. Assume that you have decided to develop your own diversity awareness program. What activities would you include? Be specific.

What Organizations Can Do

A well-planned and well-executed diversity program can promote understanding and defuse tensions between employees who differ in age, race, gender, religious beliefs, and other characteristics. Programs that are poorly developed and poorly executed often backfire, especially in organizations where bias and distrust have festered for years. A comprehensive diversity program has three

FIGURE 15.4	Three Pillars of Diversity

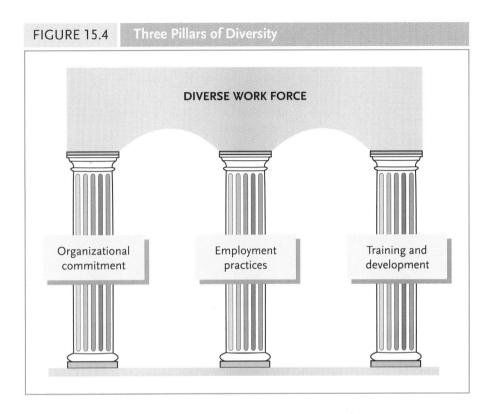

pillars:[35] organizational commitment, employment practices, and training and development (see Figure 15.4).

Organizational Commitment   Catalyst, a research and advisory group, conducted a survey of 106 global companies to determine why these companies use diversity strategies as part of their overall business plan. Nearly 90 percent said their diversity program was designed to help them gain a competitive advantage.[36] When the objective of the diversity initiative is to achieve a stronger competitive position, the commitment is usually quite strong.

Companies that see diversity programs as a quick-fix *event*—a one-day workshop that promotes the advantages of a diverse work force—often create greater, not less, divisiveness among workers. Companies that see diversity programs as a *process* know that the key to a successful diversity program is long-term commitment.

At Consolidated Edison, responsibility for diversity extends to the entire management team. Each of the 2,100 officers and managers is reviewed and compensated in part for their success in hiring, promoting, and retaining minorities. PepsiCo, the soft drink maker, links bonuses to diversity performance. Both of these companies made "America's 50 Best Companies for Minorities" list published by *Fortune*.[37]

Coca-Cola Company has been a strong backer of civil rights, but it has not always been a model for diversity in corporate America. Former black employees sued the company, alleging vast discrepancies in pay, promotions, and performance evaluations. Reporting on the lawsuit, *Business Week* said, "The cola giant needs a cultural overhaul. Just as Texaco needed to scrub its 'oil rig' culture clean of racism, Coke needs to scrap the insular environment that ex-employees say is dominated by good ol' boys. . . ." After paying $192.5 million to settle a race discrimination class action lawsuit in 2000, the company took steps to strengthen its diversity program. In 2002, Coca-Cola made the *Fortune* list of best companies for minorities.[38]

> *To achieve work force diversity, organizations need to design a plan that actively recruits men and women of different ethnicities, family situations, disabilities, and sexual orientations. Diversity should not be limited to race and gender.*

Employment Practices   To achieve work force diversity, organizations need to design a plan that actively recruits men and women of different ethnicities, family situations, disabilities, and sexual orientations. Diversity should not be limited to race and gender. One approach is to make a special effort to plug into networks that are often ignored by corporate recruiters. Many communities have established groups such as the Center for Independent Living for those with limited abilities, the Family Service League for displaced homemakers and single parents, and Parents, Families, and Friends of Lesbians and Gays. All of these groups can help identify employees.

Organizations must also foster a climate for retention. Newly hired people who are different from the majority must often contend with an atmosphere of tension, instability, and distrust and may soon lose the desire to do their best work. Subtle biases often alienate these employees and create unnecessary stress. An organization that makes every effort to make *all* employees comfortable will reduce this stress and thus benefit from low turnover and high individual and team performance levels.

Training and Development   To develop a culture that values and enhances diversity, organizations need training programs that give managers and employees the tools they need to work more effectively with one another regardless of their backgrounds. These programs can also reduce an organization's liability for discrimination.

Lockheed Martin Corporation launched an educational awareness program called "Diversity Dialogue: Building an Inclusive Workplace." Managers receive training on how to lead diversity discussions. This effort recognizes that employees need to talk about diversity just as they might spend time talking about how to improve quality. Managers are also introduced to Lockheed's new Diversity Maturity Model, which measures the company's progress in creating an inclusive environment.[39]

Done well, diversity training programs can promote harmony, reduce conflict, and help give the organization a competitive advantage. Training programs that are poorly designed and delivered by incompetent trainers, however, can end up alienating and offending employees. Participants should learn specific behaviors that will not be condoned and the basic rules of civil behavior. We may not be able to stop people from bringing their prejudices to work, but they can learn to act as though they have none.

Affirmative Action: Yesterday and Today

The Civil Rights Act of 1964 marked the beginning of antidiscrimination employment legislation. In an attempt to make up for past discrimination in the workplace, most organizations are required to take affirmative (positive) action to include women and racial minorities in the work force (see Table 15.4). Various laws have been passed to expand the list of *protected* individuals beyond women and racial minorities. The updated list includes those who share the following characteristics:

- Sex/gender (women, including those who are pregnant)
- Racial or ethnic origin (not limited to those of color)
- Religion (special beliefs and practices: e.g., attire, holidays)
- Age (individuals over 40)
- Individuals with disabilities (physical or mental)
- Sexual orientation (some state and city laws, not federal laws)
- Military experience (Vietnam-era veterans)
- Marital status (same-gender couples; some state laws, not federal laws)

Affirmative action plans (AAPs) are the formal documents that employers compile annually for submission to various enforcement agencies, including the EEOC. The documents clarify the organizations' efforts to actively seek out, employ, and develop the talents of individuals from the various protected classes. The affirmative action programs that fulfill the AAPs of many organizations include the following:[40]

1. Active recruitment of women and minorities

2. Elimination of prejudicial questions on employment application forms

TABLE 15.4	Organizations Subject to Affirmative Action Rules and Regulations
■ All private employers of 15 or more people who are employed 20 or more weeks per year
■ All educational institutions public and private
■ State and local governments
■ Public and private employment agencies
■ Labor unions with 15 or more members
■ Joint labor/management committees for apprenticeships and training

Source: From *Human Resource Management* with West Group Product Booklet, 10th edition, by Mathis/Jackson, © 2003. Reprinted with permission of South-Western, a division of Thomson Learning: www.thomsonrights.com, fax 800-730-2215.

Tools for Tolerance: Community

- Frequent minority-owned businesses and get to know the proprietors.
- Start a language bank of volunteer interpreters for all foreign languages used in your community.
- Host a "multicultural extravaganza" such as a food fair or an art, fashion, and talent show.

- Bring people of diverse faiths together for retreats, workshops, or potluck dinners. Be welcoming to agnostics and atheists, too.
- Participate in a blood drive or clean up a local stream. Identify issues that reach across racial, ethnic, and other divisions and forge alliances for tackling them.

3. Establishment of specific goals and timetables for minority hiring

4. Validation of employment testing procedures

Affirmative action allowed a tremendous influx of diverse individuals through the front door of thousands of schools and organizations. Many were able to work their way into advanced, top-level positions. At the same time, however, affirmative action reinforced the historical view that the members of protected groups are not qualified for various positions and therefore need assistance just to get a job.

The Affirmative Action Debate   Many people say it is time to rethink affirmative action or even eliminate it. Recent political and legal interpretations of affirmative action have stimulated a nationwide debate over the merits of any program that grants preferential treatment to specific groups. The following are common arguments voiced by those who want to end preferential policies:[41]

- *Preferences are discriminatory.* They tend to discriminate against those who are not members of the "right" race or gender, such as white men. Preferential policies often give a leg up to those who have suffered no harm, while holding back those who have done no wrong.

- *Preferences do not make sense, given changing demographics.* The population eligible for affirmative action continues to grow several times faster than the "unprotected" population. Hugh Davis Graham, author of *Collision Course,* believes the future of affirmative action programs is threatened because of the explosive growth in the number of people immigrating to the United States. Recent immigrants are eligible for affirmative action programs originally designed to empower minorities.[42]

Those who say affirmative action causes companies to hire and promote less qualified people fail to realize that the hiring process usually goes beyond the abilities, knowledge, and skills of the job candidate and includes additional merit-based factors, such as education and experience. When these factors are included in the hiring process, recipients of affirmative action are less likely to feel stigmatized. The way people react to a preferential selection procedure will often depend on how well it is structured and implemented.[43]

The concept of affirmative action and the means for implementing it will continue to be challenged in the courts for years to come. A recent Supreme Court ruling (*Grutter v. Bollinger*) states that an employer can legally give preferential treatment to applicants based on their race when the intent is to create a diverse workplace environment. However, if the hiring process resembles a quota system, which involves reserving a specific number of positions for protected class members, it will likely be considered illegal.

● LOOKING BACK: Reviewing the Concepts

■ Define the primary and secondary dimensions of diversity.

Primary dimensions of diversity include gender, age, race, physical and mental abilities, and sexual orientation. Secondary dimensions include health habits, religious beliefs, ethnic customs, communication style, relationship status, income, general appearance, and education and training.

■ Discuss how prejudiced attitudes are formed.

Prejudice is an attitude based partly on observation of others' differences and partly on ignorance, fear, and cultural conditioning. Prejudiced people tend to see others as stereotypes rather than as individuals. Prejudicial attitudes are formed through the effects of childhood experiences, ethnocentrism, and economic factors.

■ Develop an awareness of the various forms of discrimination in the workplace.

Discrimination is behavior based on prejudicial attitudes. Groups protected by law from discrimination in the workplace include people who share characteristics such as gender, age, race, abilities, religion, and sexual orientation. More subtle discrimination can arise when individuals have different appearances or educational backgrounds. These subtle forms of discrimination may not be illegal, but they are disruptive to a productive work force.

■ Understand why organizations are striving to develop organizational cultures that value diversity.

The issue of valuing diversity is an economic one for most organizations. The work force will soon be made up of a minority of white men and a majority of women, people of color, and immigrants. To remain competitive, organizations must value the contributions of all of their diverse workers and make full use of their ideas and talents. Only then will they be able to understand their equally diverse customers' needs. Valuing diversity is not just a nice idea, but a business imperative.

■ Identify ways in which individuals and organizations can enhance work force diversity.

Individuals can enhance diversity by letting go of their stereotypes and learning to critically and honestly evaluate their prejudiced attitudes as they work and socialize with people who are different. They will need to develop sensitivity to differences and their own personal diversity awareness programs. Organizations must commit to valuing individual differences and implementing effective employment practices that respect and enhance diversity. Their diversity training programs should be an ongoing process rather than a one-time event. They need to seek out, employ, and develop employees from diverse backgrounds.

■ Discuss the current status of affirmative action programs.

Affirmative action guidelines have helped bring fairness in hiring and promotion to many organizations. Today, however, some people believe these guidelines are discriminatory because they allow preferential treatment for the people they were designed to protect. These preferences may no longer make sense, critics say, given the changing demographics of today's work force.

● Career Corner

Q: I am a call-center technician for a global computer manufacturer whose headquarters is in Simi Valley, California. My office is in New Delhi. We take calls from customers all over the world who are asking for help solving their computer problems. Although we have been trained to use simple semantics as we try to assess callers' situations and offer them advice accordingly, some customers get irritated and verbally abusive when they realize English is my second language. My supervisor says that handling customers' discriminatory behaviors is part of my job. I am the sole supporter of my family and must keep this job, as it is one of the best opportunities in New Delhi. Should I expect my employer to protect me from this verbal abuse, or is there a better way to handle these callers?

A: Your employers have a vested interest in keeping their customers *and* employees happy. Discriminatory behavior in any form can have a major effect on their competitive advantage in the global marketplace. Rest assured; they want to solve this problem. Talk with them and ask for training that will help you handle callers who may be making judgments about your competence before you are allowed to exhibit your knowledge and expertise.

● Key Terms

valuing diversity	ethnicity
primary dimensions	discrimination
secondary dimensions	race
prejudice	managing diversity
stereotypes	affirmative action plans
ethnocentrism	

● Applying What You Have Learned

1. The "managing diversity" movement has raised the discussion of equal employment opportunity and affirmative action to a higher level. Consider the following comments by R. Roosevelt Thomas, Jr., which appeared in a *Harvard Business Review* article entitled "From Affirmative Action to Affirming Diversity":

   > Managers usually see affirmative action and equal employment opportunity as centering on minorities and women, with very little to offer white males. The diversity I'm talking about includes race, gender, creed, and ethnicity but also age, background, education, function, and personality differences. The objective is not to assimilate minorities and women into a dominant white male culture but to create a dominant heterogeneous culture.[44]

   What does "dominant heterogeneous culture" mean to you? Consider your former or current workplace. How would the atmosphere at work be different if Roosevelt got his wish? Be specific.

2. For one week, keep a diary that records every instance in which you see actions or hear comments that reflect outmoded, negative stereotypes. For instance, watch a movie, and observe whether the villains are all of a particular race or ethnic group. As you read textbooks from other courses you are taking, notice whether the pictures and examples reflect any stereotypes. Listen to your friends' conversations, and notice any time they make unfair judgments about others based on stereotypes. Finally, reflect on your own attitudes and perceptions. Do you engage in stereotyping?

   Share your experiences with class members, and discuss what steps you can take to help rid the environment of negative stereotyping.

3. Meet with someone who is a member of a racial or ethnic group different from your own, and attempt to build a relationship by discussing the things that are important to each of you. As you get to know this person, become aware of his or her beliefs and attitudes. Try not to be diverted by accent, grammar, or personal appearance; rather, really listen to the person's thoughts and ideas. Search for things you and your new acquaintance have in common, and do not dwell on your differences.

▣ Internet Insights

1. Before, during, and after the terrorist attacks and the war in Iraq, Muslims became victims of discrimination throughout the world merely because of their religious beliefs and stereotyped physical appearance. Some people from other cultures and religions were afraid to be in their presence, and some Muslims were verbally, if not physically, abused by those who could not see beyond the terrorist stereotype. Just as Americans discriminated against the Japanese before, during, and after World War II, Muslims will probably face the same behaviors in the years to come—unless individuals take the responsibility to learn more about their culture. Visit the Muslim Public Affairs Council website at *www.mpac.org,* the Muslim American Society at

www.masnet.org, or *Islam101.com,* an introductory guide for non-Muslims. What did you learn that would help you visit with someone who displays a bias against Muslims in your presence?

2. Go to the website of the National Organization on Disability at *www.nod.org.* The NOD is dedicated to closing the employment gap that exists between people with disabilities and those without, and thereby helping to strengthen the nation's work force. It brings opportunities for employers to tap into new sources of creativity, to find loyal employees, and to expand work force and consumer diversity. Click on the Economic Participation icon, and then on Featured Articles. Read the article of your choice and share the information you learn with your classmates.

 Role-Play Exercise

You are currently supervising six skilled tool and die makers. Until recently the work group was working as a productive team and was free of any serious interpersonal relationship problems. Then the work climate began to change. One day Kira Purcell, the most experienced employee, hung a small poster in the work area. The poster featured a biblical quotation that spoke to the evils of homesexual relationships. The headline at the top of the poster read "The Homosexual Plague." One day, during lunch break, the poster disappeared. Someone in the group apparently removed it. Purcell complained that removal of the poster was no different from stealing tools from her work area. Purcell was upset and the next day replaced the poster with one that featured another biblical quotation with the headline "moral perversity." You explained the problem to the owner of the company, and he suggested that you meet with Purcell and request that no more posters be displayed in the work area. You will meet with another class member who will assume the role of Kira Purcell. Try to convince your role-play partner that these posters are inappropriate in a work setting.

Case 15.1   Quality Education Through Enhanced Diversity

For decades universities have sought to admit students from different cultures and social backgrounds. Educators contend that academic discussion is most beneficial and has the most lasting social benefits when it draws on different experiences and perspectives. Various affirmative action programs have been developed to assure such diversity through admissions policies that create preferential treatment of minority applicants.

In an effort to create a diverse undergraduate student body at the University of Michigan, admissions standards were revised so that black, Hispanic, and Native American applicants could effectively compete with white students, including Asian and Arab applicants. The protected students automatically received 20 points on the 150-point "selection index" that assigned a numerical value to each of several factors of an applicants' history, including 110 points for academic achievement. As a result, a minority student with a GPA of 3.0 and an ACT score of 18 would be accepted into undergraduate programs, but a white student with a GPA of 3.6 and an ACT score of 21 would be rejected. The University of Michigan said it did not have a quota system but did have admission policies designed to ensure that each class included a "critical mass" of minorities. Two white applicants with outstanding GPAs and ACT scores were denied admission, and they filed a lawsuit (*Gratz v. Bollinger*) charging reverse discrimination. In a companion case (*Grutter v. Bollinger*), the university was sued by a white student who was denied admission to its law school.

After a variety of appeals in the Michigan courts, the Supreme Court agreed to hear both cases at the same time and thereby attempt to clarify the confusion regarding affirmative action legislation. It decided in favor of the two white undergraduate students. The Court ruled that the university's undergraduate admissions process resembled a quota system because it unfairly rewarded or penalized an applicant because of their race. The Court said that schools can implement affirmative action programs that consider an applicant's race for the purpose of creating a diverse student body but prohibits them from using a strict formulaic approach that leads to racial quotas. The Court upheld the law school's right as well as responsibility to use race as a factor among many in order to pursue the educational benefit of diversity while training the nation's future lawyers. In her opinion, Justice Sandra Day O'Connor wrote that attaining a diverse student body is "at the heart of the law school's proper institutional mission."[45]

Questions

1. Most people agree that a diverse classroom population can create a rich learning environment that will enhance the education of all students. The lingering question seems to be how a university can establish a diverse student population without developing admissions quotas for various races? List your suggestions.

2. Will *any* black, Hispanic, or Native American student in a college class bring their culture's perspective to the discussion? Does it matter if these students attended an impoverished inner-city high school or a chic prep school? Should this issue be incorporated into an admissions policy at a university?

3. Studies show that university affirmative action policies have improved racial diversity not only in the classrooms but also later in life, in business and in the professions.[46] In what ways might affirmative action programs at the university level affect the dynamics of interracial interactions in the work force?

Case 15.2   The Baggage of Bigotry

Bigots are people who are strongly partial to their own group, religion, race, lifestyle, and so on and intolerant of those who differ from them. Bigotry, prejudiced attitudes expressed through intolerant behaviors, has long been a part of American history, as witnessed by slavery, anti-gay hate crimes, anti-Semitism, and terrorist stereotyping. Bigoted ideas do not arise spontaneously; they are learned. If they are learned, they can be changed.

The "No Place for Hate" campaign in the Houston, Texas, schools was designed to help young people respect diversity. The hope is that if children learn this lesson early enough, they will reject bigotry for life and thereby rid the world of this historical baggage. Jordan's Queen Rania attended an English school in her native Kuwait that had children from Europe, Africa, the Far East, and the United States. She acknowledges that her interactions with the children from various cultures helped her realize that those things that make everyone similar far outweigh those things that make them different. At the end of the day, everyone wants the same thing out of life.

Research shows that prejudiced attitudes are fluid and that when we become conscious of our bigotry, we can take active and successful steps to combat it. In experiments, researchers have discovered that as people become consciously aware of their prejudices, they feel guilty and try harder to rid themselves of them. Once you become aware of your bigoted tendencies, feel guilty about them, and have the desire to overcome them, the cure is meaningful contact with and knowledge about different cultures.

Today it is easy to obtain information about different countries and cultures through the Internet, TV news, and journalists' reports from various regions of the world. As neighborhoods are integrated with various cultures from around the world, people learn to live with and respect their neighbors' traditions. Biases change when members of racially mixed groups cooperate to accomplish shared goals.[47]

Questions

1. Do any of your family members exhibit bigotry? If so, where do you believe those attitudes originated? Do you share the same beliefs? Why or why not?

2. Do bigots come in only one color? Explain your reasoning.

3. Is racial profiling a form of bigotry? Explain your reasoning.

4. What would the workplace be like if we could end bigotry? What would the world be like? Where do we start this process?

INTEGRATED RESOURCES

VIDEOS: "Mary Guerrero-Pelzel, Contractor"
"Diversity at the New England Aquarium"
"Hewlett-Packard Leverages Global Diversity"

CLASSROOM ACTIVITIES (*college.hmco.com/pic/reece10e*)

Real World Diversity Issues
Global Opportunities Discussion
A World Apart Journal Entry

business.college.hmco.com/students

ACE

Self-tests

16

THE CHANGING ROLES OF MEN AND WOMEN

Chapter Preview

After studying this chapter, you will be able to

- Describe how the traditional roles of men and women are changing.

- Understand problems facing women and men as a result of gender bias in organizations.

- Discuss ways to cope with gender-biased behaviors.

- Explain the forms of sexual harassment and learn how to avoid being a victim or perpetrator of them.

After graduating from high school, Andrea Rush completed a nursing degree and accepted a job at a local hospital. Soon she began to feel uncomfortable with the organization of the hospital and the way nurses were treated. She began thinking about changes she would make if she were in charge of the hospital. This desire to be in charge motivated Rush to pursue a master's degree in business administration while working long nursing shifts on the weekends to help pay the bills. After completing her internship at a trucking company, Rush began thinking about being her own boss. Fortunately for her, the trucking industry was being deregulated, and for the first time, entrepreneurs could enter the business with a small investment.[1]

Rush Trucking was started on a shoestring with three trucks—one new and two used. During the early days she divided her time between managing the business, making sales calls on potential customers, and helping maintain the trucks. Today Rush Trucking, based in Wayne, Michigan, makes 1,400 shipments daily with 1,000 trucks. The business generates over $100 million in revenue.[2] Andrea Rush, and more than 6.2 million other women business owners, view entrepreneurship as the next frontier.

Most women start their own business because their female perspective was not valued in the workplace or their positions did not offer the flexibility needed to manage a home and raise children. Many men face similar challenges

Andrea Rush, owner of Rush Trucking, became an entrepreneur after interning at a Michigan-based trucking company. Rush liked the idea of being her own boss. She is part Mohawk and sits on the board of the Native American Business Alliance.

as they realize that long hours at work and inflexible work schedules create serious barriers to a healthy marriage and responsible fatherhood.[3]

Women and men often face injustices due to gender stereotyping in the workplace. Throughout this chapter we will examine these and other gender issues that create human relations problems at work and at home.

Traditional Roles Are Changing

All cultures promote one set of behaviors for boys and a separate set for girls. Children generally learn their socially acceptable roles by the time they are 5 years old, but these roles are often continually reinforced throughout the life cycle by teachers, parents, authority figures, and the media. These traditional roles can be harmful to both men and women. For instance, the expectation that men should be aggressive and unemotional stifles their sensitivity and creativity. The assumption that women are emotional and weak hinders them in reaching leadership positions. Although men and women will always be different, their roles can and should be more nearly equal.

Gender bias (also known as **sexism**) is discrimination on the basis of gender. When employers base employment, promotion, job-assignment, and compensation decisions on a person's gender, human relations and productivity suffer. Gender bias is no longer a female-only issue, and many organizations are making the necessary adjustments.

Changes in the Role of Women

In the past, children were more likely to see their mothers as homemakers and their fathers as breadwinners. This has dramatically changed, with women joining the work force in record numbers. The women's movement that began in the 1960s with Betty Friedan's book *The Feminine Mystique* has helped women make tremendous strides toward equality with men in the workplace.[4] Figure 16.1 summarizes several important changes in women's lives since the 1960s. In the mid-1960s, about 40 percent of women worked outside the home. Today, over 60 percent of all women work, and 76 percent of the women between 25 and 54 work. The number of dual-income families has doubled since 1950. In addition, women receive more than 55 percent of both the bachelor's and the master's degrees awarded by U.S. colleges. Women are rapidly closing the MD and PhD gap and make up almost half of law school graduating classes.[5]

The impact of women in the workplace has been described as the "revolution that won't quit." As more and more women spend time and money on their education and postpone marriage and motherhood, we will no doubt see women's participation in the work force increase even more. Many women receive important financial and intrinsic rewards from their work, but they also face many challenges. Those who choose to have children must decide if and when to leave the work force and for how long. Women who leave their jobs to start a family wonder if their education and skills will be obsolete by the time they return to work. There is the very real possibility that during these women's absence, the types of jobs they were trained for will disappear.

FIGURE 16.1	Women's Lives: Four Decades of Change

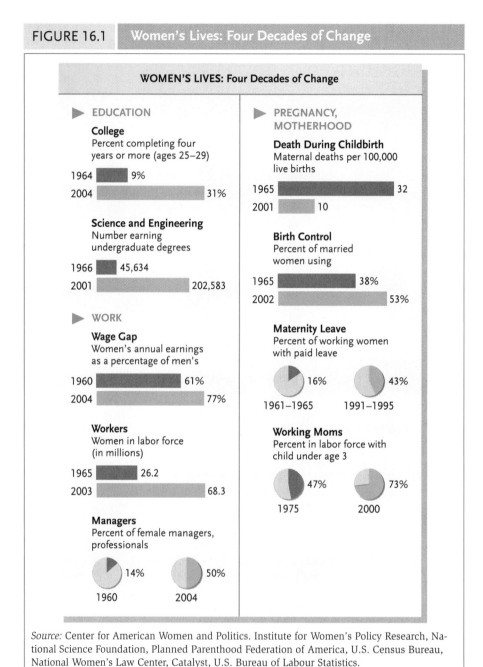

Source: Center for American Women and Politics. Institute for Women's Policy Research, National Science Foundation, Planned Parenthood Federation of America, U.S. Census Bureau, National Women's Law Center, Catalyst, U.S. Bureau of Labour Statistics.

When new mothers return to work, they often find it difficult to find jobs with schedules that are flexible enough to allow for the demands of a family. They actively seek out organizations that are not only female-friendly in hiring and promotion, but also family-friendly in their employment practices. It has been more than thirty years since the National Organization for Women (NOW) was formed to fight business policies and behaviors that discriminate against women, and there is reason for women to celebrate their progress. Women are now more likely than men to hold managerial and professional jobs, reflecting a twenty-five-year pattern of gains in education and job status. However, women still lag behind men at the higher levels of the organization. They hold only 12 percent of the top-level jobs at the 500 largest U.S. companies.[6]

Women have made significant gains in a wide range of traditionally male-dominated areas such as finance, marketing, law, medicine, and computer technology. However, some problem areas persist. Studies indicate that men continue to dominate craft, repair, and construction jobs, whereas women hold only 2 percent of these skilled trade jobs.

Achieving success in the new millennium will require women to take risks that could lead to failure in their personal as well as their professional lives. Yet many women today are impelled by fearless confidence that they can achieve anything they choose. They embrace these risks as opportunities for success, recognition, and financial security.

TOTAL	**SHOSHANA ZUBOFF**
PERSON	PROFESSOR, HARVARD BUSINESS SCHOOL
INSIGHT	"Highly trained women leaving work aren't opting out. Torn up by conflicts between motherly love, inflexible career structures, and substandard child care, they're being 'squeezed out' of organizations that have quietly but determinedly resisted their presence by not adapting to their needs."

Changes in the Role of Men

Many boys have been conditioned from their early years to be competitors and to win. They have been urged to be aggressive, to learn teamwork, to select traditional male pastimes such as sports and cars, and to enter a masculine profession such as sales, automotive repair, management, engineering, or law. A boy was taught to withstand physical pain and to push his body to the limits. Above all, he was not to act like a girl, to take up interests that were considered feminine, or to show any tendencies that could be considered homosexual. A girl could be a tomboy, but a boy could not be a "sissy." Whereas a woman's worth was measured in terms of her physical attractiveness, a man's was measured by his ability to compete and achieve his goals. This traditional man's world attached great value to independence and autonomy and less value to relationships and connection. If women have been viewed as "sex objects," perhaps men have been seen as "success objects." Robert Bly, author of *Iron John*, says its time for men to question the images of manhood conveyed by popular culture:

> We are living at an important and fruitful moment now, for it is clear to men that the images of adult manhood given by the popular culture are worn out; a man can no longer depend on them. By the time a man is thirty-five he knows that the images of the right man, the tough man, the true man which he received in high school do not work in life.[7]

A man is under constant pressure to prove himself and keep moving up the ladder.

The men of the twenty-first century are discovering that the strong, unemotional, in-control image supported by previous generations is not healthy or realistic.

The Burden of Stress Psychologists have become increasingly aware that we have neglected the stress associated with being male throughout the generations. The 1950s "organization man" assumed the role of breadwinner—a role accompanied by a great deal of self-imposed as well as societal stress. The pressure to achieve in the workplace was intense, but he was still expected to be the head of the household at home. His male identity often revolved around being the sole provider of the family's income because the woman's place was in the home. Men were reluctant to leave a bad job because they feared losing their family's only paycheck. The 1980s baby boomer men were likely to equate success with high income, movement up the career ladder, and the accumulation of material things such as a nice home and a nice car. Long hours at work often meant that men were emotionally and physically absent from friends and family members, which resulted in a great deal of guilt.[8]

The men of the twenty-first century are discovering that the strong, unemotional, in-control image supported by previous generations is not healthy or even realistic. Many have learned to define the kind of life they want to lead, rather than being restricted to traditional gender-role stereotypes.

Where Is the Balance? As men reexamine their role in society, they face conflicting role messages, even as women entering the work force do. Both men

Many men are reexamining their professional and personal lives. This working mother is saying goodbye to her young child. Dad is taking charge!

and women often discover that the joy of parenting can be just as satisfying as the achievement of career goals. But such feelings are confusing. Men and women alike are often expected to maintain aggressive attitudes toward their careers while being attentive husbands or wives and fathers or mothers. Those who were brought up in homes with a single parent who struggled to make ends meet have had few role models from whom to learn how to balance career and family life. Is it any wonder they feel frustrated?

CRITICAL THINKING CHALLENGE

1. Do members of your immediate family hold traditional gender roles? If so, have any of these roles undergone changes during the past decade? In what way?

2. Before marriage, each partner should understand the other partner's expectations with regard to careers, family responsibilities, and priorities. What are your expectations of your spouse (if you are married), or what do you imagine they would be (if you are not)?

Problems Facing Women in Organizations

When women pursue careers, they often face three major challenges: the wage gap, the glass ceiling, and balancing career and family. Many employers are making changes that will accommodate the needs of the growing number of working women and mothers, but more needs to be done.

The Wage Gap

The gap between women's and men's earnings has been shrinking since the 1980s, yet wage inequality continues. (See Figure 16.2.) Data collected by the Institute for Women's Policy Research indicates that a white woman earns

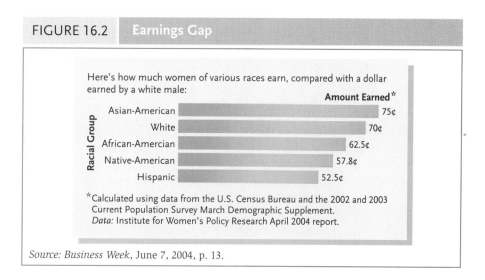

FIGURE 16.2 | **Earnings Gap**

Here's how much women of various races earn, compared with a dollar earned by a white male:

Racial Group	Amount Earned*
Asian-American	75¢
White	70¢
African-Amercian	62.5¢
Native-American	57.8¢
Hispanic	52.5¢

*Calculated using data from the U.S. Census Bureau and the 2002 and 2003 Current Population Survey March Demographic Supplement.
Data: Institute for Women's Policy Research April 2004 report.

Source: Business Week, June 7, 2004, p. 13.

about 70 cents for every dollar earned by a white man. The inequity is even more serious for minorities: 63 cents for black women and 53 cents for Hispanic women.[9] These figures are somewhat misleading because research data does not compare similar jobs held by men and women; it lumps together all jobs that women hold and all jobs that men hold.

Although discrimination is partly to blame for wage disparities, other factors also contribute to this problem. Today, women are more committed to building a career, but many still take time off to have children. This works against them, since continuous work experience tends to increase both productivity and pay in many employment settings.[10]

Research indicates that some women are willing to accept lower pay than men, and women are less apt to haggle when offered a starting salary or a pay raise. Women, as well as men, need to acquire as much information as possible about their value in the open market and use their negotiation skills to achieve equity in compensation.[11]

The Glass Ceiling

There is a condition in the workplace that gives women a view of top management jobs but blocks their ascent. It is often referred to as the **glass ceiling**. Catalyst, a women's advocacy group that has studied women in business since 1962, has documented widespread limits on career advancement to the highest levels of our nation's largest corporations. Nearly all of the *Fortune* 500 companies have male CEOs. Although we are seeing some positive change at the middle-management ranks, women are still being held back by some widely held misconceptions. Top male executives say the major barrier for women is a lack of significant general management and line experience and less time in the "pipeline." Women in senior management positions say the *real* problems are (1) preconceptions of women held by men and (2) exclusion of women from informal networks of communication.[12]

More top-level positions are available to women today than at any other time in history. However, many women do not take advantage of these opportunities because they have been socially conditioned to first satisfy the needs of their family members: husbands, children, elderly parents, and others. Women who pursue top-level positions must often cope with jobs structured to accommodate the lives of men with wives who do not have full-time careers. They also must cope with the social pressure to fulfill more traditional "feminine" roles.[13]

Why should we be concerned about the dominance of men in top leadership positions? Cultures that are totally masculine often lack compassion and give rise to rigid, intolerant practices, since they lack the intuitive, empathic qualities more common among women. In some cases, a highly competitive masculine culture encourages greed and corruption. The male-dominated hierarchy at Enron and WorldCom, for example, fostered unethical practices on a grand scale.

Macho leadership styles can also alienate women. The idea is not to push men off the stage, but to get more women on the stage with them. In an ideal situation, women and men will share the stage and create a culture where everyone is able to express the full range of his or her talents.[14]

TOTAL	**DEBRA E. MEYERSON AND JOYCE K. FLETCHER**
PERSON	PROFESSORS, CENTER FOR GENDER IN ORGANIZATIONS,
INSIGHT	SIMMONS GRADUATE SCHOOL OF MANAGEMENT

"We believe that it is time for new metaphors to capture the subtle, systemic forms of discrimination that still linger. It's not the ceiling that's holding women back; it's the whole structure of the organizations in which we work: the foundation, the beams, the walls, the very air."

▮ Balancing Career and Family Choices

Women today know that they will probably be working for pay for part or all of their adult lives. This expectation is quite a departure from previous generations, when most women assumed the responsibilities of wife and mother. The challenge of performing multiple roles, however, can be stressful and tiring. A majority of the women in two-income families not only contribute significantly to their family's income, but also do most of their family's household chores. Lily Tomlin once said, "If I'd known what it was like to have it all, I would have settled for a lot less."[15] Many women in America no doubt share this thought.

As we look for ways to help women balance career and family, we should not overlook the rewards that are experienced by women who work. Many women who hold both work and family roles treasure the friendships they develop at work and enjoy the intellectual challenges that work provides. Yet a large number of women who try to balance work and family roles say "work is no haven." They feel frustrated because many long-standing work and family problems remain unresolved. These include a lack of quality, affordable child care, inflexible work schedules, and time management problems.[16]

The "Mommy Track" and Other Options   Over a decade ago, Felice Schwartz, founder of Catalyst, wrote an essay entitled "Management Women and the New

HUMAN RELATIONS IN ACTION

Discovering the Hidden Barriers

In the past, the women's movement used strong rhetoric and legal action to drive out overt discrimination. Today most of the barriers that exist are hidden—or at least not fully understood. One author said, "Even the women who feel its impact are often hard-pressed to know what hit them." And even companies that sincerely want to increase the number of women managers and executives create barriers unintentionally.

A large retail company based in Europe could not figure out why it had so few women in senior positions and had such a high turnover rate among women in its middle-management ranks. A consultant hired to study the problem quickly identified an important inequity for women. The company culture emphasized an informal approach to conducting business. People were casual about setting deadlines. Meetings were routinely canceled and often ran late. Managers were expected to be available at all times to attend delayed or emergency meetings. This way of conducting business created problems for women, who typically had to bear a disproportionate amount of responsibility for home and family; they had more demands on their time outside the office.

Facts of Life." She stated that companies needed to provide women with more flexibility, not force them to choose between work and family. She believed that women are far more inclined than men to give a high priority to raising children. Critics of the essay said Schwartz was encouraging companies to create a "mommy track" for women who wanted a career *and* children. Schwartz responded that women who opted to make raising children their highest priority had to accept the fact that this emphasis would have some impact on their careers, at least temporarily.[17] Several years later Judith Warner wrote *Perfect Madness—Motherhood in the Age of Anxiety* and arrived at the same conclusions. Mothers who try to achieve work/family balance (I'm a great mom and a great worker) often feel a sense of frustration as they try to "do it all."[18]

Many women want to expand their life choices but are uncertain about the options available. If you are a woman who wants both career and family, then consider the following:[19]

- Choose a career that will give you the gift of time. Some careers provide more flexibility and are more forgiving of interruptions such as parental leave.

- Choose a partner who supports your goal of having a career and family.

- Choose an employer who has given work/life balance a high priority. Be prepared for some disappointments, because many corporate leaders are still unwilling to respond to work/life issues.

- Be prepared to use your negotiation skills to push for policies and practices that are favorable to employees with children. If your employer does not provide job-protected leave or flexible work schedules, use your assertiveness skills to press for policy changes.

"MOM, WHAT'S MULTITASKING?"

©2006. Reprinted courtesy of Bunny Hoest and *Parade* Magazine.

Problems Facing Men in Organizations

Many men are beginning to realize that they have been as rigidly stereotyped in their role as women have been in theirs. Men encounter resistance from their family, coworkers, and friends when they attempt to break out of their stereotypes. The changes a man makes to alter traditional masculine role characteristics can be threatening to others and can cause serious problems in his relationships. Yet the stress men are under today to conform to the expectations of society often leads to heart disease and other health problems. Many wonder if upholding the male image is worth the price.

Men Working with Women

Male attitudes toward female ambitions have changed over the years. One reason for this change is the dramatic increase of female college classmates. Men have learned that they will be competing with these smart and ambitious women in the workplace. They are also learning that women can be excellent coworkers, team members, and leaders. Those men who are secure in their talents and abilities welcome the opportunity to work beside equally self-assured women. Those men who are threatened by powerful, talented women need an attitude adjustment.

Balancing Career and Family Choices

Henry David Thoreau observed that "the mass of men lead lives of quiet desperation." Does this dire observation apply to men who are pursuing careers and assuming family roles today? The answer is a qualified yes. Men, like women, now have more choices regarding marriage and family life and face many barriers to achieving work/life balance.

- The long-term trend toward wage equality gives families more choices regarding who should assume the roles of breadwinner, child-care provider, and housekeeper. One wife in four now outearns her husband. Because of their upbringing, most men are often ill suited to staying at home with their children while their wives become the breadwinners.[20]

- Men often seek a "package deal" in life that includes four elements: marriage, fatherhood, employment, and homeownership—not necessarily in that order. Yet these goals often conflict. Many men express the desire to be closer to their children than their traditional fathers were to them, but they get caught in the traditional cycle of working long hours to pay for a nice home for the wife and kids.[21] Unfortunately, men are often reluctant to talk openly about personal pressures created by these work/family conflicts, and the cycle continues.

- Working fathers who want to take paternity leave, or time off to help raise their children, often suffer discrimination in the workplace. Women who choose these options are generally seen in a more positive light. Many men still feel that taking parental leave will unofficially penalize them.[22] Just as women struggle with this issue, men must also step forward and encourage employers to commit to family-friendly workplace policies and practices.

■ Men are less likely than women to adopt a healthy lifestyle and seek health care when it is needed. As a result, they lead in each of the ten leading causes of death and have a life span that is 5.8 years shorter than that of their female counterparts.[23]

During life's most stressful transitions, such as divorce or loss of a job, men often spend more time reflecting on things they value in life.

During life's most stressful transitions, such as divorce or loss of a job, men often spend more time reflecting on things they value in life. Those who feel that their male identity is dependent on what is accomplished at work and that success is measured by the size of their paycheck sometimes reestablish their priorities. In a *Wall Street Journal* article entitled "Who's the New Guy at Dinner? It's Dad . . . ," one dad explains his transition following the loss of his managerial job at AOL. He says he told his young twin daughters, "I'm going to find a new job doing something I love that makes people happy." When he was hired as a fifth-grade teacher, his children were thrilled, and so was he. He can now spend more time with his children.[24]

Challenges and Opportunities for Working Men and Women

As men and women struggle with their career and family choices, many progressive organizations are gearing up to meet the needs of their employees in the twenty-first century. They are recognizing the demands placed on working parents and are attempting to address the problems associated with quality child care. At the same time, they realize they must provide flexible work schedules that adjust to the changing roles of men and women.

The Challenge of Child Care

The need for affordable, quality child care has never been greater. Mothers and fathers alike face forced overtime and unpredictable hours as their employers attempt to cut costs while improving productivity. At the same time, many day-care providers shut their doors at 6 p.m. and on weekends. Workers who cannot balance the demands of work with available child care are often disciplined or fired.

Some companies provide on-site day-care centers and find this fringe benefit a strong factor in retaining valuable employees who are also parents. The subsidized on-site day-care center at Genentech, a San Francisco biotech firm, offers classrooms, outdoor playgrounds, and a staff of seventy who care for employees' children 6 weeks to 5 years old. Judy Heyboer, senior vice president of human resources, explains, "Our employees work really hard when they are here because they don't have to worry that their home life is out of control." Once every three months, the center stays open until 10:00 p.m. for "Date Night." Employees of the company are encouraged to take their spouses out for the evening while their children enjoy a slumber-party atmosphere complete with pajamas, pizza, and games.[25]

The Family and Medical Leave Act

The Family and Medical Leave Act (FMLA) guarantees continuation of any paid health benefits, plus a return to the same or an equivalent job, for employees (men as well as women) who take up to twelve weeks' unpaid time off—all at once or intermittently—so that they can care for themselves or an ailing family member such as a parent, child, or spouse during a serious health condition, or for childbirth or adoption. (Some states are considering providing financial compensation during part or all of the employee's time off.)

To qualify, you must work for an employer with fifty or more employees and at a location with at least fifty employees within seventy-five miles.

Your employer can deny leave if you haven't worked there for at least twelve months and for at least 1,250 hours during the past year. You also may be ineligible for protection if you are among your employer's top 10 percent of employees, based on pay.

The FLMA also prohibits employers' retaliation against leave takers; however, some employers are attempting to get around the intent of the law. For example, they provide unfavorable performance appraisals because work was not completed in a timely manner. Some attempt to reduce or refuse to award year-end bonuses or annual raises because the person was absent due to a family medical emergency.

To protect yourself against this subtle discrimination, train your temporary replacement before you leave so that your responsibilities are covered; if it's feasible, establish a telecommuting arrangement; and invite coworkers to in-home meetings to stay on top of changing events at work. If all else fails and you feel you have a legitimate family leave dispute, contact the Wage and Hour Division of the United States Department of Labor (*www.wageandhour.dol.gov*).

SKILL DEVELOPMENT CHALLENGE

Being able to determine whether an organization is a good "fit" for you and your family's needs is an important skill to develop. Consider the organizations in your area that might be considered "family friendly." Describe the benefits working mothers receive. Do these benefits apply to working fathers, too? If you are choosing to be child-free, what benefits are important to you as you strive to balance your work/life? Explain.

Keep in mind, however, the resentment that may build among child-free employees who see employees with children receiving special treatment. Child-free workers are often asked to work overtime, the night shift, or weekends while their coworkers who are parents arrive late or leave early to accommodate the needs of their children. To prevent this potential human relations problem, employers should considering offering flexible schedules to all employees. See Figure 16.3.

Flexible Work Schedule Opportunities

Men and women who are concerned about balancing personal and work lives say that flexible work schedules rank very high on the list of desired benefits. As a result, many organizations allow various scheduling options so that they can recruit and retain the top talent in the labor market.

FIGURE 16.3   A Two-Way Street

To make flexible scheduling more fair for working parents and child-free employees alike, some employers are:

- Allowing all employees to apply for flexible schedules
- Requiring proposals that outline how the flexible schedule will impact work that must be completed in a timely manner
- Evaluating flexible setups regularly
- Making scheduling a team responsibility
- Cross training workers so that they can take over their coworkers' responsibilities when necessary

Source: Adapted from Sue Shellenbarger, "A Two-Way Street," *Wall Street Journal*, November 17, 2005, p. D1.

Flextime   **Flextime** typically includes a core time when all employees work, usually between 9:00 a.m. and 3:30 p.m. Employees can determine their own arrival and departure times within certain limits, which may mean arriving at 7 a.m. or leaving at 5:30 p.m. (see Figure 16.4). Today about 30 percent of all workers enjoy flexible schedules, compared to 15 percent in 1991.[26]

Compressed Workweek   Typically, a **compressed workweek** consists of four 10-hour days—for example, Monday through Thursday, or Thursday through Sunday. Employees may be given the opportunity to adjust their work schedules to fit their lifestyle. One of the newest compressed workweek schedules, often called the 9/80, is growing in popularity. Employees work one extra hour each day for nine days, a total of eighty hours in two weeks, and receive a three-day weekend every other week.[27]

FIGURE 16.4   Flextime in Action

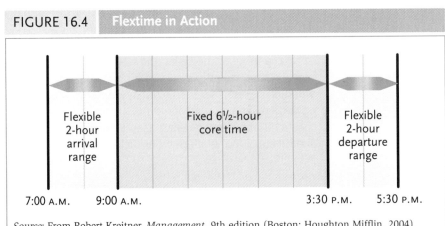

| Flexible 2-hour arrival range | Fixed 6½-hour core time | Flexible 2-hour departure range |

7:00 A.M.   9:00 A.M.   3:30 P.M.   5:30 P.M.

Source: From Robert Kreitner, *Management*, 9th edition (Boston: Houghton Mifflin, 2004). Reprinted by permission of Houghton Mifflin Company. All rights reserved.

Job Sharing   With **job sharing**, two employees share the responsibilities of one job. For example, one employee might work the mornings and the other works the afternoons. In some cases, each job sharer works two days alone and one day overlapping with the other person. This means the job is fully covered and each job sharer knows what the other is doing.[28] Job sharing is growing in popularity.

Telecommuting   The availability of powerful home-office computer and communication technologies, the large-scale use of temporary workers due to massive downsizing, and the demands of workers who want to blend work and family have fueled an increase in **telecommuting**—employees working at home at a personal computer linked to their employer's computer. At Sun Microsystems nearly 50 percent of the employees can work from home, cafes, or drop-in centers.[29]

Telecommuting was once the primary domain of lower-level and technical employees, but today it is increasingly moving into the senior management ranks. Pathlore, a Columbus, Ohio, provider of corporate training services, employs 150 workers. Eighty-three employees telecommute full-time, and four of seven senior executives work in locations as far apart as New York and California.[30]

How to Cope with Gender-Biased Behavior

Traditional attitudes, beliefs, and practices are not changed easily. If you are a man or woman breaking into a nontraditional role, you may encounter resistance. In addition, you may be confused about how to act or may be overly sensitive about the way others treat you. As a result, if you are choosing a new role for yourself, you may have to adopt new behaviors and be prepared to confront some of the very real obstacles you will encounter.

Sexual Harassment in the Workplace

One of the most sensitive problems between men and women in organizations is **sexual harassment**, unwelcome verbal or physical behavior that affects a person's job performance or work environment. Employers have a legal and moral responsibility to prevent sexual harassment, which can occur from men harassing women, women harassing men, or same-sex harassment. As men and women work together on teams, more employers are becoming acutely aware of the increased potential for misinterpreted comments and actions between the genders. When sexual harassment is present in the workplace, the cost of increased absenteeism, staff turnover, low morale, and low productivity can be high.

Forms of Sexual Harassment   Under the law, sexual harassment may take one of two forms. The first is **quid pro quo** (something for something), which occurs when a person in a supervisory or managerial position threatens the job security or a potential promotion of a subordinate worker who refuses to submit to sexual advances. These kinds of threats are absolutely prohibited, and employers are liable for damages under the Fair Employment Practices section of the Civil Rights Act.

One of the most sensitive problems between men and women in organizations is sexual harassment, unwelcome verbal or physical behavior that affects a person's job performance or work environment.

Pregnancy Discrimination

Discrimination against pregnant women in the work force has become the fastest growing category of charges filed with the EEOC. The birthrate and the number of working new moms are down, yet pregnancy-discrimination settlements are at an all-time high. In 2003, the EEOC and state and local agencies collected $12.4 million from charges of pregnancy discrimination, as opposed to the $3.7 million collected in 1992.

The charges are coming from women in entry-level jobs as well as executives. Pregnant women claim they have been unfairly fired, denied promotions, and in some cases urged to terminate pregnancies in order to keep their jobs. Well-known employers that have faced pregnancy-discrimination lawsuits include Wal-Mart, Hooters, and Cincinnati Bell. Several factors may be behind this trend.

■ More pregnant women are staying in the workplace rather than quitting their jobs as in previous generations.

■ Pregnancy is expensive for employers. Fewer employees are doing more work, so a pending maternity leave might mean they must hire replacement workers. Also, health insurance that covers pregnancies is expensive.

■ Stereotypes about pregnant women persist. Mounting research indicates that men and women alike view pregnant women as less competent. Some feel that when women become pregnant they are putting their personal lives ahead of work.

■ Employers are making honest mistakes or are confused by conflicting laws. Many states have protections for pregnant women that go beyond the federal law, which allows for twelve weeks of unpaid leave. Some state laws allow some paid time off through employee payroll taxes.

These behaviors can take the form of comments of a personal or sexual nature, unwanted touching and feeling, or demands for sexual favors.

The second form of sexual harassment involves the existence of a **hostile work environment**. Supreme Court decisions have held that sexual harassment exists if a "reasonable person" believes that the behavior is sufficiently severe or pervasive to create an abusive working environment, even if the victim does not get fired or held back from a promotion. A hostile work environment exists when supervisors, coworkers, vendors, or customers use sexual innuendo, tell sexually oriented jokes, display sexually explicit photos in the work area, discuss sexual exploits, and so on. Unlike quid pro quo harassment, hostile work environment claims tend to fall in a gray area: What is offensive to one person may not be offensive to another. The bottom line is that most kinds of sexually explicit language, conduct, and behavior are inappropriate in the workplace, regardless of whether such conduct constitutes sexual harassment within the legal meaning of the term.

How to Deal with Sexual Harassment

Ever since Professor Anita Hill accused Supreme Court nominee Judge Clarence Thomas of lewd and overbearing conduct toward her, the country has been trying to determine the difference between innocent comments and sexual harassment. The key word is *unwelcome*. Victims of sexual harassment need to tell the harasser, in no uncertain terms, that his or her behavior is inappropriate. Meanwhile, victims should record the occurrence in a journal that includes the date and details of the incident. They should also talk with coworkers, who can provide emotional support and help verify instances of harassment. Chances are, if one person is being harassed, others are as well. If the harasser continues the behavior, the victim should go to a higher authority, such as the harasser's supervisor or the organization's human resources division. Under the law, companies are legally liable if they do not immediately investigate the situation and take action to eliminate the offensive behaviors. These actions can include reprimand, suspension, or dismissal of the harasser.

The Supreme Court has recently given employees and employers help in understanding the legal aspects of sexual harassment. The court handed down two landmark rulings that included the following guidelines.[31]

- Companies can be held liable for a supervisor's sexually harassing behavior, even if the offense was never reported to management.

- An employer can be liable when a supervisor threatens to punish a worker for resisting sexual demands—even if such threats aren't carried out.

The court also offered employers advice on how to avoid costly legal fees. A company can deflect sexual harassment charges by developing a zero-tolerance policy on harassment, communicating it to employees, and making sure victims can report abuses without fear of retaliation. If the employer can show that an employee failed to use internal procedures for reporting abusive behavior, the company will be protected in a court of law.

Discrimination against pregnant women in the work place is a major problem. Stereotypes about pregnant women persist. Every employer needs to be aware of state and federal laws that relate to pregnancy discrimination.

Although the courtroom doors are open for individuals to protect themselves from unwanted behavior, pressing a sexual harassment charge is a lengthy, expensive, and psychologically draining experience. Before you file charges, be sure you have used all the remedies available to you through your employer.

Learn to Understand and Respect Gender Differences

As mentioned in Chapter 2, gender bias often acts as a filter that interferes with effective communication between men and women. In recent years, popular books such as *You Just Don't Understand: Women and Men in Conversation* by Deborah Tannen and *Men Are from Mars, Women Are from Venus* by John Gray have heightened awareness of the differences between women's and men's communication styles. These differences, according to Tannen, are due to linguistic style. **Linguistic style** refers to a person's speaking pattern and includes such characteristics as directness or indirectness, pacing and pausing, word choice, and the use of such elements as jokes, figures of speech, stories, questions, and apologies. Linguistic style is a series of culturally learned signals that we use to communicate what we mean.[32] Communication experts and psychologists have made the following generalizations concerning gender-specific communication patterns:

- Men tend to be more direct in their conversation, whereas women are more apt to emphasize politeness.

- Men tend to dominate discussions during meetings and are more likely to interrupt.

- Women prefer to work out solutions with another person; men prefer to work out their problems by themselves.

- Men tend to speak in a steady flow, free of pauses, interrupting each other to take turns. Women tend to speak with frequent pauses, which are used for turn taking.

- Male-style humor tends to focus on banter, the exchange of witty, often teasing remarks. A woman's style is often based on anecdotes in which the speaker is more likely to mock herself than she is to make fun of another person.

- Women are likely to downplay their certainty; men are likely to minimize their doubts.[33]

Does linguistic style really make a difference? Let's assume that two employees, Mary and John, are being considered for promotion to a management position. The person who must make the decision wants someone who displays a high degree of self-confidence. If John is regularly displaying the "male" communication patterns described above, he may be viewed as the more confident candidate. But if the person making the promotion decision is searching for someone who is sensitive, an attentive listener, and a consensus builder, Mary may win the promotion. We know that people in positions of power tend to re-ward linguistic styles similar to their own, so the candidate (male or female) with the greatest versatility may get the promotion.[34] You will recall that in Chapter 3 we defined *versatility* as acting in ways that earn social acceptance.

A Few Words of Caution

Differences do exist: Men are somewhat more competitive, assertive, and task-focused, and most women are more sensitive, cooperative, and people-focused than most men. However, our stereotypes about men and women are often too strong and too inflexible.[35] When we place too much emphasis on the ways in which women and men differ, we stop viewing them as individuals. As noted in Chapter 3, it is tempting to put a label on someone and then assume the la-bel tells you everything you need to know about that person.

Once you understand the concept that men and women communicate in different ways, you can begin to flex your style. Refer to Table 16.1 for more specific suggestions on how to communicate better with the opposite gender. Keep in mind, however, that an overextension of a strength *can* become a weakness. It is interesting to note that some men who have worked with women on a regular basis for many years and have successfully adjusted their

TABLE 16.1	Workplace Tips for Avoiding Gender-Specific Language Barriers

Men can . . .

■ think about women as fellow employees rather than sexual objects.

■ recognize that, within their gender group, women are as unique as men.

■ communicate with women based on their individuality, rather than on the characteristics of a stereo-typed group.

■ use general humor, not sexual humor.

■ remember that even when intentions are good, the impact of your communication may be bad.

■ follow this rule: When in doubt, do not make the statement or act out the thought.

Women can . . .

■ stay calm when expressing feelings to avoid being labeled as overemotional.

■ express feelings verbally rather than nonverbally. Men are not always good at reading behavior.

■ avoid male bashing.

■ use general humor, not self-effacing humor.

■ say what needs to be said concisely, without excessive apologies or disclaimers.

■ recognize that a man may not understand the impact of his sexually related comment. When some-thing is offensive, say something right away.

Source: From "Working Toward a Truce in the Battle of the Sexes." Anita Bruzzese, *Gannett News Service,* August 9, 1994, p. B1.

communication style accordingly may find it difficult to communicate in a male environment. The same may be true for women who have worked for years in a male environment. They may find it difficult to transfer into a new work setting that is dominated by women.

TOTAL	**ALICE SARGEANT**
PERSON	AUTHOR, *THE ANDROGYNOUS MANAGER*
INSIGHT	"Men and women should learn from one another without abandoning successful traits they already possess. Men can learn to be more collaborative and intuitive, yet remain result-oriented. Women need not give up being nurturing in order to learn to be comfortable with power and conflict."

Men and women have so much to learn from each other. NYU psychologist Carol Gilligan offers this metaphor: "One can think of the oboe and the clarinet as different, yet when they play together, there is a sound that's not either one of them, but it doesn't dissolve the identity of either instrument."[36]

Learn New Organization Etiquette

As women enter into upper levels of management and men begin to work in support positions, the ways in which men and women deal with each other change subtly. Does this change require new rules of etiquette? In some cases, yes. The following guidelines may help you understand how to act in these new situations:

1. When a woman visits a man's office, he should rise from his desk to greet her. When a man enters a woman's office, she should rise from her desk.

2. Whoever has a free hand (could be a small woman) should help anyone carrying too heavy a load (could be a large man).

3. Women resent being "go-fers." Meeting participants should not expect a woman to take notes, answer the phone, or type material. Men and women should rotate such clerical duties. A woman should not leap to serve coffee when it is time for a break.

4. Whoever arrives first at a door should open it, and whoever stands in the front row in the elevator should get off first.

5. Whoever extends an invitation to lunch or dinner should in most cases pay the tab.

6. Training materials, memos, and so on should be written in gender-free language. Clerical and secretarial personnel should not be referred to only as "she" or "her" and management personnel only as "he" or "him."

The new etiquette provides a means to overcome old stereotypes and traditional ways of setting men and women apart solely on the basis of gender. By practicing these points of etiquette and adopting a positive, helpful attitude toward each other, men and women can help ease the transition from traditional to nontraditional roles. Women and men both will be winners.

● LOOKING BACK: Reviewing the Concepts

■ Describe how the traditional roles of men and women are changing.

The traditional roles assigned to both genders limit their opportunities to choose careers and lifestyles best suited to their abilities and true interests. Many men and women are breaking out of these traditional roles. Over the past few decades, women have entered the job world in increasing numbers and in professions previously considered all male. As a result, men and women have a wider range of choices regarding marriage and children than ever before. Organizations are beginning to offer their employees options such as job sharing, flextime, and telecommuting so that they can better handle the demands of work and family.

■ Understand problems facing women and men as a result of gender bias in organizations.

Women are still subject to a wage gap, earning less than men receive for similar work, but the gap is narrowing. Moreover, the glass ceiling gives women a view of top-level jobs, but blocks their ascent. They are making progress, however, in the mid-management ranks. The real problems seem to be the preconceptions men have of women and the exclusion of women from the informal networks of communication. Men are working to dispel the myth that men must always be in control, emotionally unexpressive, logical, and achievement oriented. They realize that the rigid male role has had adverse effects on their relationships with their families. Many men are choosing more personally rewarding careers that allow time for family responsibilities even if they must sacrifice some material gain to do so.

■ Discuss ways to cope with gender-biased behaviors.

Methods of coping with gender-biased behaviors include understanding remedies available through the organization's sexual harassment policy, learning how to effectively communicate with the opposite gender, and observing the new rules of etiquette in the workplace.

■ Explain the forms of sexual harassment and learn how to avoid being a victim or perpetrator of them.

Sexual harassment may be a problem for men as well as women. It may take two forms: quid pro quo, a threat to job security or promotion if sexual favors are not granted, or sexually explicit language, photos, or innuendo that create a hostile work environment. Most organizations have developed guidelines to help employees avoid harassment or fight it when it occurs.

● **Career Corner**

Q: I just graduated from college and have accepted my dream job with a medium-size company that seems to have a healthy balance of men and women throughout all levels of the organization. I want to position myself for advancement, but am not quite sure how to go about it.

A: Start building a network early on with the women as well as the men at work and in your community with whom you share common professional interests. Initially, you will probably be working long hours and you might find it difficult to attend workshops or evening networking events. Consider these events part of your career strategy and make time for them. When you are networking, show that you have a well-balanced life, the initiative to take on new roles, and the ability to handle whatever you are given. Remember to talk about what you can do, not about what you are unable to do because you are too busy. Success at work depends on your relationships with colleagues and managers and how you handle them.

● **Key Terms**

gender bias (sexism)   telecommuting
glass ceiling   sexual harassment
flextime   quid pro quo
compressed workweek   hostile work environment
job sharing   linguistic style

● **Applying What You Have Learned**

1. The following situations represent either quid pro quo or hostile environment forms of sexual harassment in the workplace. Identify the form represented by each situation, and explain your reasoning. Describe the actions you might take if you were the potential victim in each incident.

   a. Julie thinks David is very handsome. She often stares at him when she thinks he is not looking. David is aware of Julie's staring and is very uncomfortable but is too shy and embarrassed to say anything to her.

   b. While sitting at her desk, Karen receives the following electronic message from her boss on her computer screen: "Can we discuss your possible promotion over dinner this evening?"

   c. At a convention reception, one of Joan's most important clients invites her out for cocktails and dinner. She politely declines. He announces loudly, "She won't go out to dinner with me, and I'm her best customer!" Under his breath he says, "Honey, if you want my business, you'd better cooperate." Joan's boss insists she go to dinner with the client.

2. On a sheet of paper, list and explain the various choices you would make when attempting to balance your career and family responsibilities. For ex-

ample, will marriage be a part of your future? Will you have children? When? How will you provide care for these children while you and your spouse are at work? Would you prefer home-based work? Which flextime options would you consider valuable? Do you want to work for someone else or own your own business?

3. Over a period of one week analyze your verbal and nonverbal communications with people who are of the opposite gender. Try to determine if any linguistic style differences are apparent during conversations. If you discover style differences, try to determine if they serve as a barrier to effective communication.

 Internet Insights

1. As men and women struggle with interpreting their changing roles at work and at home, they need all the information and support they can find. Professional organizations such as the National Association of Female Executives, *www.nafe.com*, the Families and Work Institute, *www.familiesandwork.org*, and At-Home Dad, *www.athomedad.com*, offer tremendous support. Visit any or all of these sites and discover the support and advice they offer.

2. Those who would like to examine various flexible work-schedule options can visit *www.workoptions.com*, *www.workfamily.com*, or *www.gilgordon.com*. Write an analysis of how the information available on these sites might help individuals make an educated decision about their personal and professional life choices.

 Role-Play Exercise

At your employer's request, you have been working late for the past few weeks on a project that will take another three months to complete. Over the past several weeks you have been stalked by a former boyfriend who was once employed by your company. He frequently parks next to your car in the garage area. This usually happens when you work late and the garage area is nearly deserted. You have complained to the police, but they have not been very responsive. You are nervous and distracted each time you discover you will have to work late. On two occasions you have refused to work beyond your scheduled 5 p.m. departure time and have been disciplined because of it. You know your organization has limited personnel, but you have requested that you work only during daylight hours. You feel your employer has created a hostile work environment by not accommodating your needs, even though the organization has a sexual harassment policy in place that clearly states that it is responsible for taking appropriate corrective action following a severely offensive event. Select a class member to play the role of your supervisor and role-play your discussion.

Case 16.1   Salomon Smith Barney Learns the Hard Way

In her book *Tales from the Boom-Boom Room, Women vs. Wall Street,* author Susan Antilla detailed the landmark sexual harassment and discrimination lawsuit against the brokerage firm Salomon Smith Barney (recently re-named Citigroup Global Markets). Before the lawsuit was settled, women working at a Smith Barney brokerage office in Garden City, New York, were exposed to triple-X-rated sexual harassment, including strippers brought into the office to celebrate male brokers' birthdays, pornographic videotapes played in the office, simulated phone sex on speaker phones during work hours, and lewd, threatening, and humiliating comments. In addition to this hostile work environment, women were paid lower base salaries than their male equivalents, had clients and commissions taken away, and were often demoted following maternity leave. They were refused access to the study materials that helped their male brokers earn their licenses and, as a result, were eight times less likely to make broker status than the men in the firm. The 1,950 women of Salomon Smith Barney banded together and filed a class action sexual harassment suit against their employer and won. To this day, no one but the firm knows how much cash the women received, but it is estimated that Smith Barney paid in the hundreds of millions of dollars to settle the case.

Tameron Keyes, a broker in the Los Angeles branch of Shearson Lehman Brothers (now owned by Smith Barney), complained about her hostile work environment and was granted a transfer to their Beverly Hills office. There, she was forced to sit in a broker "bullpen" for five years even though empty offices were available. The firm interfered with her attempts to collaborate with other brokers, refused to provide financial assistance for marketing, held her to a higher production standard than her male counterparts, and gave her no accounts from departing brokers. An arbitration panel agreed that Keyes was subjected to a sexually hostile work environment. As a result, she was entitled to compensation because of the "disruption of her career by the work environment" and was awarded $3.2 million for economic losses, emotional distress, and punitive damages.

Morgan Stanley averted a potentially embarrassing sexual-discrimination trial by agreeing to pay $54 million to settle claims from dozens of women who accused the firm of systematically denying them promotions and pay increases. Twelve million dollars went to the former saleswoman whose repeated complaints of discrimination prompted the class action suit, and approximately $40 million went to about 100 current and former female employees. The remaining $2 million was placed in a fund that will be used to enhance antidiscrimination training at the firm.[37]

Questions

1. It took many years and millions of dollars in legal fees—let alone cash settlements—to reach these workplace adjustments. Was it worth it? Would you have the personal fortitude to pursue legal action if you were a victim of sexual harassment or discrimination? Explain.

2. As part of the settlement Salomon Smith Barney agreed to:

■ hire and retain qualified women and minorities as brokers, analysts, and investment bankers

■ link managers' compensation to women's success at the firm

■ dramatically increase the percentage of female branch managers, brokers, and broker trainees

■ put all employees on notice that the firm would not tolerate sexual harassment of any kind

Do you believe this list of concessions is complete? Explain.

3. Are there viable alternatives to legal action? Explain.

Case 16.2 Creating a Balance

A new, young generation of baby boomers, the "40-somethings," are taking over the leadership of many of the nation's companies. Most of them have survived heavy travel requirements, round-the-clock shifts, and forced overtime that allowed little time or energy for their families. They had to conscientiously juggle their work and family duties and are now taking steps to help their employees do the same. This is producing a subtle yet profound change in the way organizations are run in this country.

■ Charter Communications CEO Jerald Kent says, "The biggest way to illustrate the importance of balancing work and family is to believe in it and do it yourself."

■ Guerra DeBerry Coody, a San Antonio marketing firm, provides its employees with on-site child care. Partner Tess Coody says that the perk helps attract and retain star performers and that turnover is almost nonexistent.

■ Michael Critelli, CEO of Pitney Bowes and father of three, conducted a dozen focus groups on life-balance issues among the company's thirty thousand employees.

■ Eddie Bauer Inc. offers an annual "Balance Day" to all of its 5,500 full-time employees nationwide. The extra day off each year allows workers time to find balance in their lives and do whatever they want.

■ BP–Amoco provides $1,500 a year for expenses related to employees' unscheduled business trips—even if it means flying Grandma in to take care of the children.

Arthur Emlen, professor emeritus at Portland State University and a researcher for the Oregon Child Care Research Partnership says that the lives of working parents are interdependent triangles of support: work, family, and child care. Those who reach a successful balance have discovered that they must create flexibility in at least one of these areas to make up for the rigidity in the others—for example, a flexible work environment such as those just listed above, a supportive partner or stay-at-home spouse, or flexible child-care facilities or extended-family caregivers such as grandparents. One family found a unique solution when they enrolled their children in a school that operates until 6:00 p.m. year round and allows students to learn at their own pace, so that they can take vacations at their families' convenience. Individuals must be creative in learning ways to make work/life adjustments.[38]

Questions

1. As you strive to keep a healthy balance between your professional and personal life, which of the three dimensions of support—work, family, or child care—do you project will be the most flexible? Explain your answer.

2. Most experts agree that the creation of work/life employee benefits will, in the long run, benefit the organizations that participate as well as the children of the future. Do you agree? Why?

3. From the foregoing list of organizations that are making work/life adjustments, which benefits would apply to only those workers who have children? Do you believe these benefits would cause resentment among workers who do not have children? Explain.

INTEGRATED RESOURCES

VIDEOS: "Mary Guerrero-Pelzel, Contactractor"
          "Managing Equality"

CLASSROOM ACTIVITIES (*college.hmco.com/pic/reece10e*)

  Is This Sexual Harassment, or Not?
  Gender-Neutral Constitutions
  Gender-Biased Comments/Discussion

business.college.hmco.com/students

ACE

Self-tests

PART VI

YOU CAN PLAN
FOR SUCCESS

17 A LIFE PLAN FOR EFFECTIVE
HUMAN RELATIONS

17

A LIFE PLAN FOR EFFECTIVE HUMAN RELATIONS

Chapter Preview

After studying this chapter, you will be able to

- Define success by standards that are compatible with your needs and values.

- Learn how to cope with the forces that influence work/life balance.

- Discuss the meaning of *right livelihood*.

- Describe four nonfinancial resources that can enrich your life.

- Provide guidelines for developing a healthy lifestyle.

- Develop a plan for making needed changes in your life.

I t seems like only yesterday that job seekers were searching for employment with companies that offered the promise of a big paycheck. Job security was not the most important element of the compensation package. Then came September 11, the tech crash, Enron, layoffs, and concerns about Social Security. Now long-term benefits such as health insurance and retirement plans are very important to soon-to-be college graduates. Universum, a research and consulting firm, conducted a survey of 29,046 undergraduates in all fields of study and discovered a changing pattern of job expectations. The CEO of Universum, reflecting on the research findings, said, "This generation is really trying to take their future in their own hands, and do something about it."[1]

This generation is also giving greater attention to work/life balance. In fact, this employer attribute is usually the most important element of the compensation package. Many of today's job seekers have grown up in homes where one or both parents worked long hours and were often cut off from family life. They are questioning a lifestyle that is characterized by long hours at work, infrequent vacations, and loss of leisure time. Many observers of the American scene say you can have a good job or a life, but not both. Maybe this new generation of workers will prove these skeptics wrong.

Achieving Balance in a Chaotic World

In this chapter we help you construct a life plan that will enhance your relationships with people in your personal life and in your work life. This plan will also help you better manage the relationship you have with yourself. We discuss the meaning of success and suggest ways to cope with major disappointments that will surface in your work life. You will learn how to avoid being trapped by a lifestyle that offers financial rewards but little else. This chapter also helps you define your relationship with money and describes four nonfinancial resources that give meaning to life. Finally, you will learn how to develop the mental and physical fitness needed to keep up in today's frantic, fast-paced world.

Redefining Our Work Lives

In Chapter 1 we noted that the labor market has become a place of churning dislocation caused by the heavy volume of mergers, acquisitions, business closings, bankruptcies, and downsizings. General Motors and Ford Motor Company recently added an exclamation point to this dire development when they announced plans to shed 60,000 workers.[2] We also noted that changing work patterns have created new opportunities and new challenges. For example, the demand for temporary workers has increased.

It is important to visualize a future filled with sharp detours and several redefinitions of our work lives. Tom Peters, noted author and consultant, was one of the first observers to recognize that a typical career path is no longer linear and is not always upward. He says, "It's more like a maze, full of hidden turns, zigs and zags that go in all sorts of directions—even backwards sometimes, when that makes sense."[3] The dream of finding job security and knowing that we have "arrived" is obsolete.

Stella Ogiale is a self-styled socio-capitalist. With a small loan from her sister, a small amount of birthday money, and earnings from a night job at UPS, she founded Chesterfield Health Services. Her company provides home care to mentally or physically disabled patients.

Toward a New Definition of Success

Most of us have been conditioned to define success in narrow terms. Too frequently we judge our own success, and the success of others, by what is accomplished at work. Successful people are described as those who have a "good job," "make good money," or have "reached the top" in their field. We sometimes describe the person who has held the same job for many years as successful. We do not stop to consider that such a person may find work boring and completely devoid of personal rewards.

From early childhood on many people are taught to equate success with pay increases and promotions. Too often, unfortunately, people who try to achieve these career goals are forced to give up everything else that gives purpose and meaning to their lives. Po Bronson, author of *What Should I Do with My Life?* says more people need to search for work they are passionate about. His best-selling book profiles fifty-five people who struggled to find their calling. One of the persons he interviewed was Ann Miyhares, a Cuban-American who made her family proud by becoming a senior vice president at a bank, but lost their respect when she exchanged her banking career for that of a social worker.[4]

From early childhood on many people are taught to equate success with pay increases and promotions.

TOTAL	**RALPH FIENNES**
PERSON	ACTOR
INSIGHT	"I call people successful not because they have money or their business is doing well but because, as human beings, they have a fully developed sense of being alive and engaged in a lifetime task of collaboration with other human beings—their mothers and fathers, their family, their friends, their loved ones, the friends who are dying, the friends who are being born."

The Need for New Models of Success

In recent years, a growing number of people are angry, disillusioned, and frustrated because they have had to abruptly change their career plans. They gave their best efforts to an employer for ten, fifteen, or twenty years, and then the company eliminated their jobs. For years the firm said, "Take care of business and we'll take care of you," but then the situation changed. Under pressure from new global competition, hostile takeovers, and the need to restructure, companies started getting rid of experienced workers. The unwritten and unspoken contract between the company and the employee was broken. Many of the people who lost their jobs during the past decade were once told that if they had ambition and worked tirelessly to achieve their career goals, success would be their reward. But the "reward" for many people has been loss of a job, loss of self-esteem, and increased anxiety about the future.

We should certainly feel sympathy for persons who have lost their jobs and watched their dreams dissolve. But there is another group of people who also merit our concern. These are the persons who still have a job (the survivors), but must work harder and give up leisure time and quality time with friends and family.

It is inspiring to look at a different way of living. When Jeff Soderberg founded Software Technology Group, a technology consulting business based in Salt Lake City, he created a new model of success. His company provides employees with plenty of time to have a life. He doesn't believe there is a correlation between time spent at work and success. He refuses to hire workaholics, and in an industry where 80-hour workweeks are common, he tells new hires, "We expect a 40-hour workweek." Soderberg sets a good example by frequently taking time off during the week to enjoy rock climbing in the nearby canyons.[5]

One-Dimensional Model   The traditional success model defined success almost exclusively in terms of work life. The model emphasized working long hours, reaching work-related goals, and meeting standards often set by others.

The old model of success required us to be "one-dimensional" people for whom work is the single dimension. In the life of such a person, everything that has meaning seems to be connected to the job. When a person defines himself or herself by a job and then loses that job, what does that person have left? Of course, the loss of a job encourages some people to search for meaning beyond their work.

"It's come to my attention, Wycliff, that you're actually planning a life outside the office."

TOTAL	**CHERYL SHAVERS**
PERSON	SENIOR MANAGER, INTEL CORPORATION
INSIGHT	"We don't like to think of ourselves as slaves to money, prestige or power, but in fact many only feel worthy by attaining these things. When we allow 'things' to have power over us to the extent that we lose ourselves, our values, our ability to choose, we become slaves."

Loss of Leisure Time

Throughout history Americans have burdened themselves with a very demanding work ethic. They spend more time on the job than employees in any other industrialized nation. What's more, downsizing efforts have left fewer people to do the same amount of work, so many people are working even harder. Most of these workers yearn for more leisure time.

U.S. workers not only work long hours, but they spend less time on vacation than do workers in most other industrialized countries. A typical American worker averages about 13 vacation days a year, *including* public holidays. By comparison, workers in Germany, France, and Italy take 35 and 40 vacation days each year.[6] In addition, American workers, equipped with cell phones, pagers, and PalmPilots, are often too accessible during their vacations. There is a growing sense, matched by growing reality, that our work is always with us, demanding our attention.[7]

Some of America's best-managed companies realize the negative consequences of long hours on the job and loss of leisure time. The director of human resource strategy and planning for Merck and Company says, "You can't build an effective company on a foundation of broken homes and strained personal relationships." A senior executive at Price Waterhouse says, "We want the people who work for our firm to have lives outside Price Waterhouse—people with real lives are well rounded, and well-rounded people are creative thinkers."[8]

Developing Your Own Life Plan

The goal of this chapter is to help you develop a life plan for effective relationships with yourself and others. The information presented thus far has, we hope, stimulated your thinking about the need for a life plan. We have noted that personal life can seldom be separated from work life. The two are very much intertwined. We have also suggested that it is important for you to develop your own definition of success. Too frequently people allow others (parents, teachers, counselors, a spouse) to define success for them. Finally, as you

CRITICAL THINKING CHALLENGE

For most people true success is a combination of achievements. These achievements might relate to such things as leisure time, earnings, job status, health, or relationships. On a piece of paper, describe your personal definition of success.

Jack Canfield, author of *The Success Principles,* has described 64 fundamentals of success in his best-selling book. These timeless principles have been used by successful men and women throughout history.

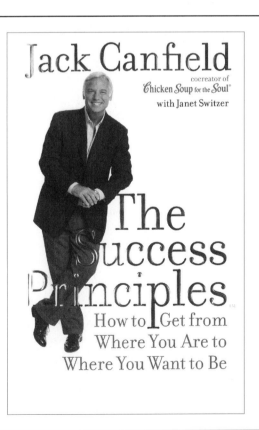

begin work on your life plan, keep in mind the following advice from Jack Canfield, author of *The Success Principles:*

> If you want to be successful, you have to take 100% responsibility for everything that you experience in your life. This includes the level of your achievements, the results you produce, the quality of your relationships, the state of your health and physical fitness, your income, your debts, your feelings—everything![9]

Because work is such an important part of life, we now move to a discussion of items that will help you in your career planning. We discuss the concept of "right livelihood."

Toward Right Livelihood

At age 45 Vera Shanley closed her lucrative medical practice in Atlanta and moved to a small farm near Hillsborough, North Carolina. She had a busy practice and good friends, but she was working sixty to eighty hours a week and thinking about passions that needed to be explored. Now she travels to Third World countries as a volunteer with Interplast, a nonprofit agency that performs free facial reconstructive surgeries on needy people. When she is back home, she works several hours a day as a potter and raises tomatoes and flowers.[10]

Vera Shanley, like many other people, has been searching for "right livelihood." The concept of right livelihood is described in the core teachings of Buddhism. In recent years, the concept has been described by Michael Phillips in his book *The Seven Laws of Money* and by Marsha Sinetar in her book *Do What You Love . . . The Money Will Follow*. **Right livelihood** is work consciously chosen, done with full awareness and care, and leading to enlightenment. Barbara Sher, contributor to *New Age* magazine, says right livelihood means that you wake up in the morning and spend all day working at something you really want to do.[11]

For Stephen Lyons, the search for right livelihood began when he fell on hard times—divorce, unemployment, and bankruptcy. He came from a family of blue-collar tradesmen, none of whom had attended college. He trained as an electrician and had steady work until a recession created large-scale unemployment in the San Francisco area. Finally, he convinced a small college that he could repair their cranky air-conditioning system and ended up with a job and the opportunity to earn a business degree at the school. With more education, he felt confident to start a business installing home solar-power systems. Creating renewable energy has turned out to be a form of right livelihood for Lyons.[12]

There are three characteristics to right livelihood: choice, emphasis on more than money, and personal growth.

Right Livelihood Is Based on Conscious Choice

Marsha Sinetar says, "When the powerful quality of conscious choice is present in our work, we can be enormously productive."[13] She points out that many people have learned to act on what others say, value, and expect and thus find conscious choice very difficult:

> It takes courage to act on what we value and to willingly accept the consequences of our choices. Being able to choose means not allow-

ing fear to inhibit or control us, even though our choices may require us to act against our fears or against the wishes of those we love and admire.[14]

To make the best choices, you must first figure out what you like to do, as well as what you are good at doing. What you like doing most is often not obvious. It may take some real effort to discover what really motivates you. Students often get help from career counselors or explore a career option during a summer internship. If you are employed, consider joining a temporary project team. A team assignment provides an opportunity to work with persons who perform very different types of duties. You might also consider reassignment within your organization.

Right Livelihood Places Money in a Secondary Position

People who embrace right livelihood accept that money and security are not the primary rewards in life. Michael Phillips explains that "right livelihood has within itself its own rewards; it deepens the person who practices it."[15] For example, people who work in the social services usually do not earn large amounts of money, but many receive a great deal of personal satisfaction from their work. You may need to trade some income for self-expression, mental rewards, or some other form of personal satisfaction. Vera Shanley may not make much money as a potter, but the work provides enormous personal satisfaction.

Many people who once viewed success in terms of wealth, material possessions, and status are realizing that something is missing from their lives. They do not *feel* successful. They once felt pressured to "have it all" but now feel disappointed that their achievements have not brought them real happiness.

Right Livelihood Recognizes That Work Is a Vehicle for Personal Growth

Most of us spend from 40 to 60 hours each week at work. Ideally, we should not have to squelch our real abilities, ignore our personal goals, and forget our need for stimulation and personal growth during the time we spend at work.[16] Most employees know intuitively that work should fulfill their need for self-expression and personal growth, but this message has not been embraced by many leaders. Too few organizations truly empower workers and give them a sense of purpose. When employees feel that the company's success is their own success, they will be more enthusiastic about their work.

Most employees know intuitively that work should fulfill their need for self-expression and personal growth, but this message has not been embraced by many leaders.

The search for right livelihood should begin with a thoughtful review of your values. The values clarification process (see Table 5.1) should be completed *before* you interview for a job. Mark Buzek, a graduate of Ohio State University, decided not to take a job that would require frequent relocation and excessive travel. Although he is not married, he has strong ties with his parents, two sisters, and a brother in Ohio. Staying close to family members is an important value in his life.[17]

When a job fails to fulfill your expectations, consider changing jobs, changing assignments, or changing careers. If the job isn't right for you, your body and your mind will begin sending you messages.

When you begin feeling that something is lacking, try to answer these basic questions: What is making me feel this way? What, exactly, about my current position is unpleasant? Choosing a satisfying career and lifestyle requires understanding what contributes to your job satisfaction. Self-exploration and continual evaluation of your needs, goals, and job satisfaction are important. Don't wait for a crisis (layoff) to clear your vision.[18]

TOTAL	**PAMELA YORK KLAINER**
PERSON	FOUNDER, *POWER AND MONEY LLC*
INSIGHT	"Plain talk about our experiences with money remains the last taboo to break in our society. . . . Part of becoming an effective, happy person is making old money messages current and bringing hidden money messages out into the open."

Defining Your Relationship with Money

Money is a compelling force in the lives of most people. It often influences the selection of a career and the commitment we make to achieve success in that career. Sometimes we struggle to achieve a certain economic goal only to discover that once we got what we wanted it didn't fulfill us in the way we had hoped. Money does not create or sustain happiness. Happiness comes from social relationships, enjoyable work, fulfillment, a sense that life has meaning, and membership in civic and other groups.[19]

Many people struggle with money management decisions and seem unable to plan for the future. The personal savings rate in America is at a record low, and the household debt burden is at a record high. After many years of decline, our savings rate is down to about 1 percent of our income, the world's lowest. Many people are ill prepared to cope with the financial drain that comes with loss of one's job or a serious health problem that is not covered by medical insurance. We are also a nation of hyperconsumers, "living way beyond our means and seemingly helpless to save ourselves," according to Geoffrey Colvin, senior editor of *Fortune* magazine.[20]

True Prosperity The way we choose to earn, save, and spend our money determines, in large measure, the quality of our lives. For example, if you think that having *more* money is going to produce happiness or peace of mind, will you ever earn enough? Shakti Gawain, author of *Creating True Prosperity*, says that more money does not necessarily bring greater freedom, fewer problems, or security. Rather, "prosperity is the experience of having plenty of what we truly need and want in life, material and otherwise." Gawain says, "The key point to understand is that prosperity is an *internal* experience, not an *external* state, and it is an experience that is not tied to having a certain amount of money."[21] Many of us go through life unconscious of our own real needs and desires. We must learn to predict more accurately what will give us lasting pleasure instead of short-term pleasure.[22] How do we do this? Steven Reiss (see Chapter 7) says that nearly everything we experience as meaningful can be traced to one of sixteen basic desires or to some combination of those desires (see Figure 7.1). Now would be a good time to revisit this list of basic desires and identify the five or six that seem most important to you. This review may help you understand your relationship with money.

Mature Money Management   Many people do not have a mature relationship with money. They spend everything they earn and more, and then have bouts of financial anxiety. People who are deep in debt often experience symptoms of depression. Money issues continue to be the number one cause of divorce in the United States. Space does not permit a comprehensive examination of money management, but here are some important suggestions from Jonathan Clements, an expert on financial planning.[23]

- ▪ *Develop a personal financial plan.* With a financial plan, you are more likely to achieve your financial goals. Without a plan, you are likely to follow a haphazard approach to management of your finances. A key element of your plan is determining where your income is going. With a simple record-keeping system, you can determine how much you spend each month on food, housing, clothing, transportation, and other things. Search for spending patterns you may want to change.

- ▪ *Spend less than you earn.* Most people who spend more than they earn are buying things they do not really need. They need to get off the earn-and-spend treadmill. One way to spend less than you earn is to establish spending guidelines. For example, plan to save at least 10 percent of your pretax income every year for retirement. (Ten percent is the minimum recommended by most financial planners.)

- ▪ *Maintain a cash cushion.* If you lost your job today, how long could you live on your current cash reserves? Financial consultants suggest that cash reserves should be equal to the amount you earn during a two- or three-month period.

HUMAN RELATIONS IN ACTION

Plan to Win the Lottery?

Chances are, you won't win the lottery anytime soon. You can, however, build a large fund with a regular savings plan. A mixture of the following three things can produce amazing results:

- ▪ A small amount of money
- ▪ An average rate of return
- ▪ A period of time for your investment to grow

Steve Moore of the Cato Institute and Tom Kelly of the Savers and Investors Foundation provide a simple illustration of the stunning results that can be achieved. If your parents placed $1,000 in a mutual fund in 1950, and the money was allowed to grow at the stock market's average rate of return, they would now have more than $218,000. This is a reminder that fortunes can be made even by low-wage earners who save regularly during their working years.

Many people do not think about financial compatibility before or after marriage. When couples talk about financial issues and problems, the result is usually less conflict and smarter financial decisions. David Bach, author of several books on financial planning, helps couples achieve financial compatibility. He has the partners start by writing down what's most important to each of them—their five top values. They are also instructed to write down what the purpose of money is. He says, "Smart financial planning is more than a matter of numbers; it involves values first and stuff second."[24]

Com-Corp Industries, a manufacturing plant based in Cleveland, Ohio, sees personal money management skills as one key to reducing conflict in the workplace. Employees who cannot live within their means are often under great stress and are more likely to experience interpersonal problems at work and at home. The company provides employees with classes on such subjects as developing a household budget and wise use of credit.[25]

TOTAL	**JULIE CONNELLY**
PERSON	CONTRIBUTING EDITOR, *FORTUNE*
INSIGHT	"Keep in mind that there is no harder work than thinking—really thinking—about who you are and what you want out of life. Figuring out where your goals and your skills match up is a painful, time-consuming process."

Defining Your Nonfinancial Resources

If you become totally focused on your financial resources, then chances are you have ignored your **nonfinancial resources.** And it is often the nonfinancial resources that make the biggest contribution to a happy and fulfilling life. A strong argument can be made that the real wealth in life comes in the form of good health, peace of mind, time spent with family and friends, learning (which develops the mind), and healthy spirituality. Paul Hwoschinsky, author of *True Wealth*, makes this observation about nonfinancial resources: "If you are clear about who you are, and clear about what you want to do, and bring your financial and nonfinancial resources together, it's extraordinary what can happen. I encourage people to really honor their total resources, and magical things happen. New options occur."[26]

If you focus most or all of your attention on work and you suffer a major work-related disappointment, then the result is likely to be feelings of depression and despair. Thoughts such as "Now I have lost everything" can surface when you fail to get a promotion, find out that you were not selected to be a member of a special project team, or learn that your job has been eliminated. But if you fully understand the power of your nonfinancial resources, then work-related disappointments are easier to cope with. The starting point is to realize that *most* of your resources are nonfinancial. During periods of great uncertainty, it is especially important that you think about your nonfinancial assets and consider ways to enhance them. We briefly discuss four nonfinancial resources that can enrich your life: physical and mental health, education and training (intellectual growth), leisure time (time for family, socializing, recreation), and healthy spirituality (see Figure 17.1).

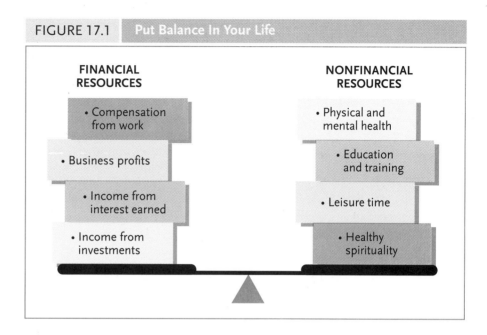

FIGURE 17.1 | Put Balance In Your Life

Physical and Mental Health Is the statement "Health means wealth" just a worn-out cliché, or is this slogan a message of inspiration for people who want to get more out of life? If good health is such an important nonfinancial asset, then why are so many people flirting with self-destruction by eating the wrong foods, drinking too much, exercising too little, and generally choosing unhealthy lifestyles? The answer to the second question may be lack of awareness of the benefits of physical fitness. Here are a few benefits of a modest excercise program.[27]

- There is an interrelationship between health and outlook on life. For example, when the physical body is fit, toned, and strong, this condition has a positive effect on the mind. We are more likely to experience higher levels of self-esteem, feel a greater sense of self-confidence, and have a more positive outlook on life.

- Regular exercise and a healthy diet produce greater mental clarity, a higher energy level, and a more youthful appearance. Even low-intensity exercise such as walking can result in weight loss and reduction in the death rate from coronary artery disease and stroke.

Increasingly, incentives are being used to encourage employee participation in some type of health promotion program. A study conducted by Hewitt Associates found that half of the 960 large companies surveyed believe that employees who make a reasonable effort to manage their health should be rewarded.[28]

Education and Training (Intellectual Growth) The New Economy thrives on a well-educated and well-trained work force. It rewards workers who take personal responsibility for their learning. The need to continually update, train, and develop yourself has never been greater. Here are some tips on how to acquire the skills and abilities you need:

■ *Think of yourself as a unique brand.* In Chapter 11 we noted that branding can play a crucial role in your career success. Developing a strong personal brand requires giving attention to several things, one of which is staying competent. To do this you must build your strengths and try to overcome your weaknesses. The authors of *What Every Successful Woman Knows* say, "Build your brand and toot your own horn—a lot."[29]

■ *Be selective in what you learn.* Learning often requires large amounts of time and energy, so consider carefully what knowledge or skill will generate the most improvement.

■ *Take advantage of various learning pathways.* It helps to think of your job as a learning resource. Take full advantage of instructional programs offered by your employer. Volunteer for team assignments that will provide new learning opportunities. Peter Senge, author of *The Fifth Discipline*, says the fundamental learning unit in any organization is a team.[30] And look outside the company at community college classes or programs offered by Toastmasters, Dale Carnegie, or other organizations.

Dr. Vera Shanley began the search for right livelihood while working long hours at her medical practice in Atlanta. Today she travels the world as a volunteer with Interplast, a nonprofit group that performs free facial reconstructive surgeries on people in Third World countries. When she is home, Shanley works as a potter.

In his best-selling book *The Art of Happiness,* the Dalai Lama says the role of learning and education in achieving happiness is widely overlooked. He notes that numerous surveys have conclusively found that higher levels of education have a positive correlation with better health and a longer life, and even protect us from feelings of depression.[31]

Leisure Time   Leisure time can provide an opportunity to relax, get rid of work-related stress, get some exercise, spend time with family and friends, or simply read a good book. Many people cherish leisure time, but experience schedule creep. *Schedule creep* is the tendency of work to expand beyond the normal work schedule and replace available leisure time. It often surfaces in small symptoms—an extra hour on two here, a weekend worked there.[32]

If you are working for a workaholic, someone who may have given up all or most of his or her leisure time, you may be pressured to work at the same pace. If your boss is constantly trying to meet impossible deadlines and deal with last-minute rushes, you may feel the need to give up time for recreation or family. If this happens, try to identify the consequences of being overworked. Look at the situation from all points of view. If you refuse to work longer hours, what will be the consequences for your relationship with the boss, your relationship with other employees, your future with the organization?[33] You have choices, but they may be difficult ones. If it looks as though the pressure to work longer hours will never end, you may want to begin searching for another job.

Is it worth taking some risks to protect the leisure time you now have? Should you increase the amount of leisure time available in your life? Consider the following benefits of leisure time:

■ As we noted previously in this text, maintaining social connections with friends and family can be good for your health. A growing number of studies show that if you have strong and fulfilling relationships, you may live longer, decrease your chances of becoming sick, and cope more successfully when illness strikes.[34] Time spent with friends and family can be a powerful source of mental and physical renewal.

■ One of the best ways to feel satisfied about your work is to get away from it when you begin to feel worn out. People who take time off from work often return with new ideas, a stronger focus, and increased energy. When you discover that end-of-the-week exhaustion is still hanging around Monday morning, it's time to take some vacation or personal days.[35]

■ A growing body of research indicates that the American trend toward skipping vacations is hazardous. People who skip vacations have a higher risk of death from heart disease and other serious health problems.[36] You need time away from work to relax, renew your creative powers, and reduce your level of stress.

■ Find some quiet time for yourself each day. You might use it to meditate, take the dog for a walk, or just sit quietly. Use this time to nourish yourself and bring balance to your life.

If you want more leisure time, then you must establish your priorities and set your goals. This may mean saying no to endless requests to work overtime or rejecting a promotion. Sometimes you must pull back from the endless demands of work and "get a life."

Healthy Spirituality A discussion of nonfinancial resources would not be complete without an introduction to healthy spirituality. To become a "whole" or "total" person requires movement beyond the concrete, material aspects of life to the spiritual side of the human experience. Healthy spirituality can bring a higher degree of harmony, wholeness, and meaning to our lives and move us beyond self-centeredness.

Spirituality can be defined as an inner attitude that emphasizes energy, creative choice, and a powerful force for living. It involves opening our hearts and cultivating our capacity to experience reverence and gratitude. It frees us to become positive, caring human beings.[37]

Spirituality encompasses faith, which can be described as what your heart tells you is true when your mind cannot prove it. For some people, faith exists within the framework of a formal religion; for others it rests on a series of personal beliefs such as "Give others the same consideration, regard, kindness, and gentleness that you would like them to accord you."[38] A special report entitled *Spirituality 2005,* published by *Newsweek,* indicates that 24 percent of those polled describe themselves as spiritual but not religious; 55 percent described themselves as religious and spiritual.[39]

> *An understanding of the many aspects of spirituality can give us an expanded vision of what it means to be human.*

An understanding of the many aspects of spirituality can give us an expanded vision of what it means to be human. Although spirituality is often associated with religion, it should be viewed in broader terms. Robert Coles, of Harvard Medical School, likes a definition of spirituality given to him by an eleven-year-old girl:

I think you're spiritual if you can escape from yourself a little and think of what's good for everyone, not just you, and if you can reach out and be a good person—I mean live like a good person. You're not spiritual if you just talk spiritual and there's no action. You're a fake if that's what you do.[40]

The words of this young girl remind us that one dimension of spirituality involves showing concern and compassion for others. Thomas Moore, author of the best selling book *Care of the Soul,* says, "To be spiritual means to mature to a point beyond limited self-interest and anxiety about self."[41] Healthy spirituality involves acts of generosity, sharing, and kindness.

TOTAL PERSON INSIGHT	**THE DALAI LAMA** COAUTHOR, *THE ART OF HAPPINESS* "Spirituality I take to be concerned with those qualities of human spirit—such as love and compassion, patience, tolerance, forgiveness, contentment, a sense of responsibility, a sense of harmony—which bring happiness to both self and others."

In many ways, large and small, work can be made more spiritual. The philosophy of Worthington Industries is expressed in a single sentence: "We treat our customers, employees, investors and suppliers as we would like to be treated."[42] Allied Holdings Inc., Herr Foods Inc., and many other campanies have hired chaplains to provide needed support and counseling to their employees.[43] Lotus Development Corporation formed a "soul" committee to examine the company's management practices and values. The company wants to find ways to make the work environment as humane as possible.[44] Many companies, large and small, feel that healthy spirituality can enhance the ethical dimensions of the business.

Will the growing interest in healthy spirituality influence education? We are already seeing changes in some professional education programs. More than fifty medical schools across the United States have incorporated spirituality into their coursework. One objective of these programs is to develop medical students' empathy for patients.[45]

Many activities can be considered spiritual. Visiting an art gallery, listening to a concert, or walking near the ocean can stimulate healthy spirituality. Table 17.1 describes some ways to begin your journey to healthy spirituality.

Healthy spirituality can often serve as a stabilizing force in our lives. As noted in Chapter 14, the various twelve-step programs (Alcoholics Anonymous is one example) emphasize the need for a spiritual connection. "Working the steps" means, among other things, turning life over to a higher power. This spiritual connection seems to give hope to persons who feel a sense of loneliness and isolation.

For many people, a commitment to a specific religion is an important dimension of spirituality. Active membership in a religious group provides an opportunity to clarify spiritual values and achieve spiritual direction. It also provides social connections—an extended family that you can depend on for social support.[46]

TABLE 17.1	Ways to Achieve Healthy Spirituality

As interest in healthy spirituality grows, people are searching for ways to become more spiritual. The following spiritual practices draw our focus away from ourselves and the anxieties in our lives.

■ **Meditation**   Oprah Winfrey described the powerful influence of meditation this way: "There is no greater source of strength and power for me in my life now than going still, being quiet and recognizing what real power is." (See Chapter 14 for a step-by-step guide to meditation.)

■ **Prayer**   Dr. Larry Dossey, physician and author of numerous books on the role of spirituality in medicine, says prayer can be a powerful force in our lives. Prayer groups have been established at many organizations.

■ **Spiritual Reading**   In addition to sacred readings, consider *Healing and the Mind* by Bill Moyers, *The Soul of a Business* by Tom Chappell, and *The Hungry Spirit* by Charles Handy.

■ **Time with Nature**   Spiritual contemplation during a walk in the woods or a visit to a quiet lake can help us balance mind, body, and spirit.

Sources: David Elkins and Amanda Druckman, "Four Great Ways to Begin Your Spiritual Journey," *Psychology Today*, September/ October 1999, p. 46; Larry Dossey, M.D., "Can We Change the World?" *The Inner Edge*, June/July 2000, pp. 22–23.

AUTHOR, UNKNOWN

"Don't get crispy fried in business. The insidious suction of achievement could leave you with no soul."

Developing a Healthy Lifestyle

Earlier in this chapter we noted that a healthy lifestyle can provide a higher energy level, a greater sense of self-confidence, and generally a more positive outlook on life. People who maintain good health usually have more endurance, spend less time feeling tired or ill, and miss less work than persons who are not healthy. Good health is receiving greater attention today because many Americans are investing more time and energy in their work. They are being asked to work longer hours and do more in less time. Good health can help combat stress and tension at work and at home.

The first step toward adopting a healthy lifestyle is to become well informed—to read, study, and learn what can be done to maintain your current level of health or improve your health. In this section we offer guidelines that form the framework for a good diet and a good exercise program.

Guidelines for a Healthy Diet

Eating the right foods can improve your health, boost your energy level, and in some cases extend your life. The link between health and diet is quite clear. We will review several important dietary guidelines.

Maintain a Diet That Is Balanced and Varied Recently the U.S. Department of Agriculture (USDA) published the MyPyramid, an individualized approach to improving diet and lifestyle (see Figure 17.2). A new USDA website (*www.mypyramid.gov*) allows consumers to enter their age, sex, and activity level and get back a tailored personal diet. For example, here are the daily recommendations for a 30-year-old female who gets less than 30 minutes of exercise a day:

Grains	6 ounces
Vegetables	2.5 cups
Fruits	1.5 cups
Milk	3 cups
Meat & Beans	5 ounces
Oils	5 teaspoons

This customized plan is based on an estimated requirement of 1,800 calories a day. Everyone should monitor their body weight to determine if they need to adjust calorie intake.[47]

FIGURE 17.2	U.S. Department of Agriculture's MyPyramid

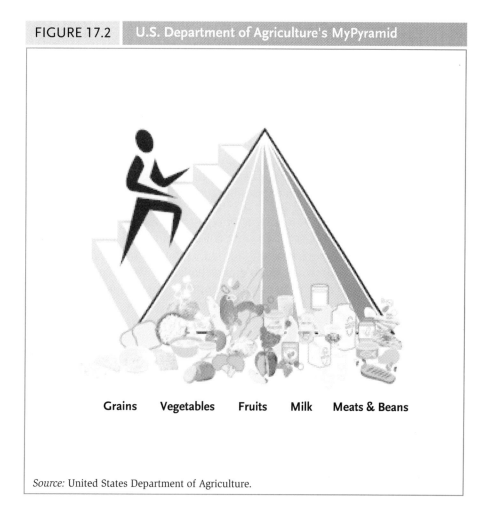

Grains   Vegetables   Fruits   Milk   Meats & Beans

Source: United States Department of Agriculture.

Eating a variety of foods is important because you need more than forty different nutrients for good health: vitamins and minerals, amino acids (from proteins), essential fatty acids (from fats and oils), and sources of energy (calories from carbohydrates, fats, and proteins). The number of servings you need each day depends on your total calorie intake. The type of foods you eat is also very important. Whole grains should be substituted for refined grains, and dark greens such as broccoli and kale represent a preferred vegetable food group. These foods help reduce the risk of developing diabetes and heart disease and help with weight maintenance.

Reduce Calorie Intake Over 65 percent of Americans are overweight and these added pounds increase the risk of heart disease, cancer, and diabetes. Inactivity combined with diets high in calories, salt, and fats will soon be the number one cause of preventable deaths. Americans are putting on extra pounds much earlier and faster than they did in previous generations. Control of weight is fundamentally simple—*calories in versus calories out*. If you eat

100 more calories a day than you burn, you gain about 1 pound in a month, or about 10 pounds in a year.[48]

Cut Down on Fatty Foods The foods that are popular with many Americans are relatively high in fat, especially saturated fat, which contributes to high blood cholesterol levels. Many restaurant foods are high in fat because it gives menu items the flavor people often seek when eating out. Heart disease and certain kinds of cancer are byproducts of foods that contain highly saturated fats. Avoid foods that include partially hydrogenated oils—better known as *trans fats*. These artery-clogging fats can be very harmful to your health. Although diet is the most important factor in lowering cholesterol, exercise can help.

Eat Foods with Adequate Starch and Fiber Foods high in starch, such as breads made with whole grains, dry beans and peas, and potatoes, contain many essential nutrients. Many starches also add dietary fiber to your diet. A growing number of scientists believe that high-fiber diets can help reduce the odds of getting cancer of the colon. Some cereals and most fruits and vegetables are good sources of fiber.

Avoid Too Much Sodium A common byproduct of excess sodium is high blood pressure. In the United States, where sodium-rich diets are very common, the average person consumes about 5,000 milligrams of sodium each day, more than twice the amount the American Dietetic Association recommends.[49] Table 17.2 includes some examples of foods that are low in sodium and saturated fats.

If You Drink Alcohol, Do So in Moderation Alcoholic beverages are high in calories and low in nutrients and cause serious health risks when used in excess. Excessive alcohol consumption has been linked to liver damage, certain types of cancer, and high blood pressure.

With the help of these healthy diet guidelines, you can develop your own plan for achieving a healthful diet. Keep in mind that good nutrition is a bal-

TABLE 17.2	Low-Fat Snack Choices		
	Saturated Fat (grams)	Sodium (milligrams)	Calories
Quaker Lightly Salted Rice Cakes	0	15	35
Barbara's Rite Lite Rounds (crackers)	0	200	70
Healthy Choice Microwave Popcorn	1.5	140	100
Mariani Sweetened Dried Cranberries	0	0	100

Note: Read labels carefully. Be sure to notice the portion sizes and be realistic about what you actually consume.

Source: University of California, *Berkeley Wellness Letter*, May 2001, p. 6; The Quaker Oats Company, Chicago, Ill. Barbara's Bakery, Petaluma, Calif. Mariani Packing Company, Vacaville, Calif.

ancing act. You want to select foods with enough vitamins, minerals, protein, and fiber but avoid too much fat and sodium. You want to consume enough calories to maintain the energy level required in your life but avoid weight gain.

Improving Your Physical Fitness

With regard to exercise, people often choose one of two extreme positions. Some adopt the point of view that only high-intensity activities (running, high-impact aerobics) increase physical fitness. These people believe in the "no-pain, no-gain" fitness approach. The other extreme position is to become a "couch potato" and avoid all forms of exercise. Both positions should be avoided.

Physical fitness can be defined as the ability to perform daily tasks vigorously and have enough energy left over to enjoy leisure activities. It is the ability to endure difficult and stressful experiences and still carry on. Physical fitness, which involves the performance of the lungs, heart, and muscles, can also have a positive influence on mental alertness and emotional stability. Research indicates that even a moderate level of physical activity can have a surprisingly broad array of health benefits on virtually every major organ system in the body.[50] For most people, a program that involves regular physical activity at least three or four times a week and includes sustained physical exertion for 30 to 35 minutes during each activity period is adequate.[51] This modest investment of time and energy will give you a longer and healthier life.

To achieve lifesaving benefits from exercise, start slowly with an aerobic fitness activity you feel you will enjoy. Walking, swimming, running, low-impact aerobics, and jogging are aerobic exercise. When we engage in aerobic exercise, the body is required to improve its ability to handle oxygen.[52] These exercises strengthen the heart, burn up calories, increase stamina, and help release tension.

SKILL DEVELOPMENT CHALLENGE

A major purpose of this chapter is to help you create a plan for effective relationships with yourself and others. Take time to reflect on your life and identify the specific behaviors that you want to develop. List these behaviors on a piece of paper and then describe when and how you will develop these behaviors.

If you are younger than 35 and in good health, you probably do not need to see a doctor before beginning an exercise program. If you are older than 35 and have been inactive for several years, consult your doctor before engaging in vigorous exercise.[53]

Planning for Changes in Your Life

Throughout this book we have emphasized the concept that you can control your own behavior. In fact, during these turbulent times changes in your behavior may be one of the few things under your control. What are some behaviors you can adopt (or alter) that will make an important positive change in your life? Once you have identified these behaviors, you can set goals and do what is necessary to achieve them.

At the end of Chapter 1 you were encouraged to complete the Human Relations Abilities Assessment (HRAA) Form that is on the website (*college .hmco.com/pic/reece10e*) (see Application Exercise 1 in Chapter 1) and in the Classroom Activities Manual. If you completed this instrument, then you no doubt gained awareness of your strengths and a better understanding of the abilities you want to improve. Now would be a good time to complete the instrument a second time and determine if your *Xs* have moved to the right on the various scales. Completion of the HRAA Form will help you identify the behaviors you want to change.

The Power of Habits

Before we discuss specific goal-setting methods, let us take a look at the powerful influence of habits. Some habits, like taking a long walk three or four times a week, can have a positive influence on our well-being. Simply saying "Thank you" when someone does a favor or pays a compliment can be a habit. Other habits, such as smoking, never saying no to requests for your time, feeling jealous, or constantly engaging in self-criticism, are negative forces in our lives. Stephen Covey, author of *The 7 Habits of Highly Effective People*, makes this observation: "Habits are powerful factors in our lives. Because they are consistent, often unconscious patterns, they constantly, daily, express our character and produce our effectiveness . . . or ineffectiveness."[54]

Breaking deeply embedded habits, such as impatience, procrastination, or criticism of others, can take a tremendous amount of effort. The influences supporting the habit, the actual root causes, are often repressed in the subconscious mind and forgotten.[55] How do you break a negative habit or form a positive habit? The process involves five steps.

Motivation   Once you are aware of the need to change, you must develop the willingness or desire to change. After making a major commitment to change, you must find ways to maintain your motivation. The key to staying motivated is to develop a mind-set powerful enough that you feel compelled to act on your desire to change.

Knowledge   Once you clearly understand the benefits of breaking a habit or forming a new one, you must acquire the knowledge you need to change. Seek information, ask for advice, or learn from the experiences of others. This may involve finding a mentor, joining a group, or gathering sufficient material and teaching yourself.

Practice   Information is only as useful as you make it. This means that to change your behavior you must *practice* what you have learned. If you are a shy person, does this mean you need to volunteer to make a speech in front of several hundred people? The answer is no. Although there is always the rare individual who makes a major change seemingly overnight, most people find that the best and surest way to develop a new behavior is to do so gradually.

Feedback   Whenever you can, seek feedback as you attempt to change a habit. Dieters lose more weight if they attend counseling sessions and weigh-ins. People who want to improve their public speaking skills benefit from practice followed by feedback from a teacher or coach. Everyone has blind spots, particularly when trying something new.

Reinforcement   When you see yourself exhibiting the type of behavior you have been working to develop—or when someone mentions that you have changed—reward yourself! The rewards can be simple, inexpensive ones—treating yourself to a movie, a bouquet of flowers, a favorite meal, or a special event. This type of reinforcement is vital when you are trying to improve old behaviors or develop new ones.

The Goal-Setting Process

Goals should be an integral part of your plan to break old habits or form new ones. You will need an assortment of goals that address the different needs of your life. After a period of serious reflection, you may be facing many goal-setting possibilities. Where do you begin? We hope that reading the previous chapters in this book, completing the HRAA Form, and reviewing the material in this chapter will help you narrow the possibilities.

The goal-setting process was described in Chapter 4. The major principles of goal setting are outlined in Table 4.1. These time-tested principles can help you achieve any realistic goal.

The Choice Is Yours

Are you ready to develop a life plan for effective human relations? We hope the answer is yes. One of the positive aspects of personal planning is that you are making your own choices. You decide what kind of person you want to be and then set your own standards and goals. The results can mean not only career advancement and financial benefits, but also the development of strong, satisfying relationships with others. These relationships may be the key to future opportunities, and you in turn may be able to help others reach their goals.

In the opening chapter of this text, we talked about the total person approach to human relations. By now, we hope you realize that you are someone special! You have a unique combination of talents, attitudes, values, goals, needs, and motivation—all in a state of development. You can decide to tap your potential to become a successful, productive human being, however *you* understand those terms. We hope this book helps you to develop your human relations skills and to become what you want to be. You can turn the theories, concepts, and guidelines presented here into a plan of action for your own life and career. We wish you the best!

● LOOKING BACK: Reviewing the Concepts

- Define success by standards that are compatible with your needs and values.

The traditional definitions of success that most of us know are too confining. They describe success almost entirely in terms of measurable job achievements. These definitions leave out the intangible successes to be had in private and professional life. Many people today are discovering that true success is a combination of achievements.

- Learn how to cope with the forces that influence work/life balance.

The labor market has become a place of great uncertainty due to the heavy volume of mergers, acquisitions, business closings, and downsizing. There is increasing pressure to work harder, work longer hours, and give up more leisure time. Learning how to cope with the forces that influence work/life balance has never been more challenging.

- Discuss the meaning of *right livelihood*.

Achieving right livelihood is a very important dimension of success. Right livelihood is work consciously chosen and done with full awareness and care that leads to enlightenment. Right livelihood recognizes that work is a vehicle for self-expression, and places money in a secondary position.

- Describe four nonfinancial resources that can enrich your life.

A person's nonfinancial resources often make the biggest contribution to a happy and fulfilling life. Each of us has four nonfinancial resources that can enrich our lives: physical and mental health, education and training (intellectual growth), leisure time (time for family, socializing, recreation), and healthy spirituality.

- Provide guidelines for developing a healthy lifestyle.

Many Americans are working to achieve healthy lifestyles. Healthy lifestyles can give us a higher energy level, greater sense of self-confidence, and generally a more positive outlook. People who maintain good health usually have more endurance, spend less time feeling tired or ill, and miss less work than those who are not physically fit.

- Develop a plan for making needed changes in your life.

Planning for changes in your life often requires breaking negative habits or forming positive habits. The process of breaking habits and forming new ones involves five steps: motivation, knowledge, practice, feedback, and reinforcement. Goal setting is also an integral part of a successful plan to make changes. Chapter 4 deals with goal setting in detail.

Key Terms

right livelihood   spirituality
nonfinancial resources   physical fitness

Applying What You Have Learned

1. In recent years, it has become popular for organizations to develop a mission statement or a statement of values that reflects their philosophy and objectives. Biogen's values statement provides one example (see Chapter 5). Prepare a personal mission statement that reflects your goals and aspirations for a successful life. Your mission statement should cover the roles of financial and nonfinancial resources in your life.

2. Throughout this chapter you were encouraged to take control of your life and establish your own definition of success. This chapter has a strong "all development is self-development" theme. Can we really control our own destinies? Can we always make our own choices? Mike Hernacki, author of the book *The Ultimate Secret of Getting Absolutely Everything You Want*, says yes:

   > To get what you want, you must recognize something that at first may be difficult, even painful to look at. You must recognize that *you alone* are the source of all the conditions and situations in your life. You must recognize that whatever your world looks like right now, you alone have caused it to look that way. The state of your health, your finances, your personal relationships, your professional life—all of it is your doing, yours and no one else's.[56]

   Do you agree with this viewpoint? Take a position in favor of or in opposition to Hernacki's statement. Prepare a short one- or two-paragraph statement that expresses your views.

3. There are many ways to deepen and extend your spirituality. One way is to begin placing a higher value on silence, tranquillity, and reflection. If your life is extremely busy, you may not be taking time for thought or reflection. If you are accustomed to living in the presence of noise throughout the day, quiet times may make you feel uncomfortable at first. Over a period of one week, set aside a few minutes each day for your own choice of meditation, prayer, contemplation, or reflection. Try to find a quiet place for this activity. At the end of the week, assess the benefits of this activity, and consider the merits of making it part of your daily routine.[57]

Internet Insights

1. At some point in your life, full-time employment will become less appealing. You will begin thinking about part-time work that will give you time to pursue a personal interest, start a family, become an independent consultant,

earn a degree, or simply enjoy more leisure time. Several Internet sites can help you acquire information:

Name	URL	Services
Aquent	*www.aquentpartners.com*	Helps find work for health care, finance, marketing, and other areas
Manpower	*www.manpower.com*	Finds assignments in a wide variety of fields
Monster	*www.monster.com*	Lists several contract jobs and includes a ten-question quiz on whether "flex work" is for you

Visit two of these websites and study the job opportunities. Prepare a written summary of your findings.

2. Visit *www.mypyramid.gov* and request a personalized MyPyramid health plan. Simply key in your age, gender, and physical activity level. Review the recommendations you receive and compare these to your current diet and exercise level.

 Role-Play Exercise

Ambry Waller, one of your closest friends, used to go fishing quite often, and he loved to hike in the mountains. After getting married, his life changed dramatically. He and his wife purchased a new home, and soon they were raising a family. Once the bills started piling up, he abandoned his leisure-time activities and started working long hours at his job. He eagerly volunteered for overtime in order to increase his earnings. As the years passed, Ambry and his wife adopted many trappings of middle-class life: a big house, two cars, a huge flat screen TV in the family room, and a motorboat that sits idle for most of the year. One afternoon, you meet Ambry for a beer at a local bar. The conversation quickly turns serious as Ambry describes his frustration: "I love my wife and children, but I am so tired of working long hours and worrying about my financial obligations. My credit-card debt is now over $7,000."

In this role-play activity, you will meet with another class member who will assume the role of Ambry Waller. Your goal is to help Ambry identify some ways he can achieve greater work/life balance. Your name for this role play will be Corey Cell.

Case 17.1   Toward Right Livelihood

When Mary Lou Quinlan entered the field of advertising, she set the goal of someday running a major advertising agency. After twenty years of climbing the ladder, she became chief executive officer of N. W. Ayer. Later, she would make a decision that surprised many of her friends and colleagues. Here, in her own words, is what happened:

> In achieving that goal, I became "successful," but I wasn't happy. So I said two words that I had never said before: 'I quit.' Then I took a chance on starting a completely new career.[58]

Quinlan didn't make a hasty decision after leaving her corporate position. She took a five-week sabbatical before deciding to become an entrepreneur. Again, in her own words, here is what happened:

> I got a piece of paper and divided it in half. On the left side, I wrote down what I love to do and what I'm good at, and on the right side, I wrote down what I don't like to do and what I stink at. Unfortunately, what I don't like to do and what I stink at were my job description as CEO.[59]

Quinlan loved to write, she loved public speaking, and she wanted to write a book. She also enjoyed meeting and working with women, and felt they were often neglected as consumers. With these thoughts in mind, she founded Just Ask a Woman, a firm that helps companies market with women, not to them. She based her new company on the premise that women want to be listened to. Quinlan also wrote a book entitled *Just Ask a Woman,* which focuses on what women want and how they make purchases. Just Ask a Woman has become a leading consultancy on women today.[60]

Questions

1. Mary Lou Quinlan says the decision to seek right livelihood should begin with conversations with family members and friends who love you. Ask questions such as "How do you think I'm doing?" and "How do you see me right now?" Do you agree with her advice? Explain.

2. Right livelihood is based on conscious choice, places money in a secondary position, and recognizes that work is a vehicle for personal growth. Which of these three characteristics would be most difficult for you to accept and implement in your life?

3. In your opinion, does the concept of right livelihood seem realistic? Is right livelihood an option for everyone or only a select few? Explain.

INTEGRATED RESOURCES

VIDEO: "Alternative Work Arrangements at Hewlett-Packard"

CLASSROOM ACTIVITIES (*college.hmco.com/pic/reece10e*)

Right Livelihood
How Do YOU Spell Success?
Break a Habit

business.college.hmco.com/students

ACE

Self-tests

NOTES

Chapter 1

1. Jim Carlton, "In Quest for Steady Work, a Man Traces States Decline," *Wall Street Journal*, July 30, 2003, p. A1.
2. Edward M. Hallowell, *Connect* (New York: Pantheon Books, 1999), pp. 1–14.
3. John Seely Brown and Paul Duguid, *The Social Life of Information* (Boston: Harvard Business School Press, 2000), pp. 2–13.
4. Ronald Alsop, "How to Get Hired," *Wall Street Journal*, September 22, 2004; Marshall Goldsmith, "Nice Guys Can Finish First," *Fast Company*, November 2004, p. 123.
5. Joann S. Lublin, "Mergers Often Trigger Anxiety, Lower Morale," *Wall Street Journal*, January 16, 2001, pp. B1, B4; Daniel Roth, "How to Cut Pay, Lay Off 8,000 People, and Still Have Workers Who Love You," *Fortune*, February 4, 2002, pp. 63–68.
6. Sabrina Jones, "How We'll Work," *The News & Observer*, January 2, 2000, p. 3E; Ron Zemke, "Free Agent Nation," *Training*, January 2002, p. 18; Mike Brewster, "The Freelance Conundrum," *Inc.*, December 2004, p. 38.
7. Jeffrey Pfeffer, *The Human Equation* (Boston: Harvard Business School Press, 1998), pp. 293.
8. Chris Lee, "The Death of Civility," *Training*, July 1999, pp. 24–30.
9. Stephen L. Carter, *Civility* (New York: Basic Books, 1998), p. 11.
10. Jeff Pettit, "Team Communication: It's in the Cards," *Training & Development*, January 1997, p. 12.
11. Robert Guy Matthews, "Recovery Bypasses Many Americans," *Wall Street Journal*, August 31, 2005, p. A2.
12. Lauren Storck, "The Rich Make Us Sick," *Psychology Today*, September/October 1999, p. 2; "Helping America's Working Poor," *Business Week*, July 17, 2000, p. 164. "Barely Staying Afloat," *The New York Times*, May 10, 2006, p. A22.
13. Casey Selix, "Employers Push Resilience as a Key Skill for Workers," *San Jose Mercury News*, March 4, 2001, p. 1PC; Harry Wessel, "New Fringe Benefit: Dieting," *The News & Observer*, January 25, 2004, p. 12E.
14. Robert Kreitner, *Management*, 9th ed. (Boston: Houghton Mifflin, 2004), p. 304.
15. Allan A. Kennedy, interview by, in "The Culture Wars," *Inc.*, 20th Anniversary Issue, 1999, pp. 107–108.
16. Anita Raghavan, Kathryn Kranhold, and Alexei Barrionuevo, "How Enron Bosses Created a Culture of Pushing Limits," *Wall Street Journal*, August 26, 2002, p. B1.
17. Suein L. Hwang, "Workers' Slogans Find New Home This Side of the Great Wall," *Wall Street Journal*, October 16, 2002, p. B1.
18. Sue Shellenbarger, "Along with Benefits and Pay, Employees Seek Friends on the Job, "*Wall Street Journal*, February 20, 2002, p. B1.
19. "Great Expectations," *Fast Company*, November 1999, p. 224.
20. Betsy Jacobson and Beverly Kaye, "Balancing Act," *Training & Development*, February 1993, p. 26.
21. Sue Shellenbarger, "Job Candidates Prepare to Sacrifice Some Frills and Balance—For Now," *Wall Street Journal*, November 21, 2001, p. B1; Stephanie Armour, "Workers Put Family First Despite Slow Economy, Jobless Fears," *USA Today*, June 6, 2002, p. 38.
22. Rochelle Sharpe, "Labor Letter," *Wall Street Journal*, September 13, 1994, p. 1.
23. Alan Farnham, "The Man Who Changed Work Forever," *Fortune*, July 21, 1997, p. 114.
24. George F. Will, "A Faster Mousetrap," *New York Times Book Review*, June 15, 1997, p. 8; "Scientific Management," *Training*, December 1999, p. 33.
25. Bradley J. Rieger, "Lessons in Productivity and People," *Training & Development*, October 1995, pp. 56–58.
26. For a detailed examination of the Hawthorne criticisms and the legacy of the Hawthorne research, see David A. Whitsett and Lyle Yorks, *From Management Theory to Business Sense* (New York: American Management Association, 1983).
27. Jim Collins, "The Classics," *Inc.*, December 1996, p. 55.
28. Thomas J. Peters and Robert H. Waterman, Jr., *In Search of Excellence: Lessons from America's Best-Run Companies* (New York: Harper & Row, 1982), p. 14; Tom Peters, "Tom Peters' True Confessions," *Fast Company*, December 2001, p. 80.
29. Stephen R. Covey, *The Seven Habits of Highly Effective People* (New York: Simon & Schuster, 1989), pp. 66–67.
30. Richard Koonce, "Emotional IQ, A New Secret of Success," *Training & Development*, February 1996, p. 19; Cary Cherniss and Daniel Goleman, eds., *The Emotionally Intelligent Workplace* (San Francisco: Jossey-Bass, 2001), pp. 13–26.
31. Denis Waitley, *Empires of the Mind* (New York: Morrow, 1995), p. 133.
32. Michael Crom, "Building Trust in the Workplace," *The Leader*, October 1998, p. 6; Ron Zemke, "Can You Manage Trust?" *Training*, February 2000, pp. 76–83.
33. Harold H. Bloomfield and Robert K. Cooper, *The Power of 5* (Emmaus, Pa.: Rodale Press, 1995), p. 61.
34. Jack Canfield, *The Success Principles* (New York: Harper Collins, 2005), pp. 3–18.
35. Malcolm Flescher, "World Wide Winner—The UPS Story," *Selling Power*, November/December 2001, p. 58.
36. Thomas Petzinger, Jr., "The Front Lines," *Wall Street Journal*, May 21, 1999, p. B1; Robert Kreitner, *Management*, 9th ed. (Boston: Houghton Mifflin, 2004), p. 99.
37. Thomas Petzinger, Jr., "The Front Lines," *Wall Street Journal*, May 21, 1999, p. B1; Lucy McCauley, "Relaunch!"

Fast Company, July 2000, pp. 97–108; Liz Stevens, "In the Race, America Has the Most Rats," *The News and Observer*, November 21, 1999, p. E3; Julie Gordon, "Teaching Selling Skills to the Financial World," *Denver Business Journal*, November 3, 2000, p. 10B.

38. Stephanie Armour, "Workers Put Family First Despite Slow Economy, Jobless Fears," *USA Today*, June 6, 2002, p. 3B; "Working Mother 100 Best Companies." [cited 14 June 2006]. Available from www.workingmother.com; INTERNET.

Chapter 2

1. Jean P. Fisher, "Surgical Tools Cleaned Improperly," *The News & Observer*, January 7, 2005, p. B1; Jonathan B. Cox and Andrea Weigl, "Health Execs Admit PR Was Inadequate," *The News & Observer*, July 10, 2005, p. A1; Sarah Avery, "Experts' Answers Iffy; Case Has No Parallel," *The News & Observer*, July 10, 2005, p. A1.

2. David Shenk, *Data Smog—Surviving the Information Glut* (San Francisco: Harper Edge, 1997), p. 54.

3. John Stewart and Gary D'Angelo, *Together—Communicating Interpersonally* (New York: Random House, 1988), p. 5.

4. For more information on the components of communication, see Scot Ober, *Contemporary Business Communication*, 5th ed. (Boston: Houghton Mifflin, 2003), pp. 5–9.

5. Suein L. Hwang, "It Was a Wombat for the Meatware, But It Was a Good Sell," *Wall Street Journal*, May 15, 2002, p. B1.

6. "Memos from Hell," *Fortune*, February 3, 1997, p. 120.

7. Cai Shaoyao, "Cyberlingo—A Jargon Not for General Use," *Shanghai Star*, January 6, 2005. [cited 26 October 2005]. Available from http://app1.chinadaily.com.cn/star/2005/0206/vo2–3.html; INTERNET; Julie Martin, "Cyberlingo! BRB? ROTFL? LOL? It's Greek to Me." [cited 26 October 2005]. Available from www.goodchatting.com/articles/archives/000006.php; INTERNET.

8. Matthew McKay, Martha Davis, and Patrick Fanning, *Messages: The Communication Skills Book* (Oakland, Calif.: New Harbinger, 1995), p. 108.

9. Deborah Tannen, *You Just Don't Understand: Men and Women in Conversation* (New York: Ballantine Books, 1990), pp. 24–25, 85.

10. Peter F. Drucker, quoted by Bill Moyers in *A World of Ideas* (Garden City, N.Y.: Doubleday, 1990).

11. Phyllis Mindell, "The Body Language of Power," *Executive Female*, May/June 1996, p. 48.

12. Don Clark, "Communication and Leadership," July 17, 2005, pp. 9, 10. [cited 27 October 2005]. Available from www.nwlink.com/donclark/leader/leadcom.html; INTERNET.

13. Ibid., p. 7.

14. William B. Gudykunst, Stella Ting-Toomey, Sandra Sudweeks, and Lea Stewart, *Building Bridges: Interpersonal Skills for a Changing World* (Boston: Houghton Mifflin, 1995), pp. 315–316.

15. Clark, "Communication and Leadership," p. 8.

16. "Sssh! Listen Up! *High Gain Inc. Newsletter*, June 2003, p. 3.

17. Ibid., p. 4.

18. Susan Scott, *Fierce Conversations: Achieving Success at Work and in Life, One Conversation at a Time* (New York: Viking, 2002), pp. 156–157.

19. Michael Toms, "Dialogue—the Art of Thinking Together—Sparks Spirit of 'Aliveness' in Organizations," *The Inner Edge*, August/September 1998, p. 462.

20. Stephen R. Covey, *The Seven Habits of Highly Effective People* (New York: Simon & Schuster, 1989), pp. 240–241.

21. C. Glenn Pearce, "Learning How to Listen Empathically," *Supervisory Management*, September 1991, p. 11.

22. Robert Epstein, "Waiting," *Psychology Today*, September/October 2001, p. 5.

23. Jared Sandberg, "Ruthless Rumors and the Managers Who Enable Them," *Wall Street Journal*, October 29, 2003, p. B1.

24. Tammy Galvin, "Nothing Ventured," *Training*, February 2004, p. 4.

25. Karen Carney, "How to Keep Staff in a Boom Economy," *Inc.*, November 1998, p. 110.

26. Robert Kreitner, *Management*, 9th ed. (Boston: Houghton Mifflin, 2004), p. 403.

27. Suzy Wetlaufer, "The Business Case Against Revolution," *Harvard Business Review*, February 2001, p. 119.

28. Matthew Boyle, "What We Learned," *Fortune*, December 24, 2001, p. 179.

29. Jonathan B. Cox, "To Blog or Not to Blog," *The News & Observer*, August 21, 2005, p. E1.

30. "Etiquette with Office Gadgets," *Training*, January 1999, p. 24.

31. Marina Krakovsky, "Caveat Sender—The Pitfalls of E-mail," *Psychology Today*, March/April 2004, pp. 15–16.

32. Matthew Holohan, "How to Use E-mail Responsibly at Work." [cited 21 June 2000]. Available from ehow.com/Center/catIndex/o,1004,1016,00.html; INTERNET.

33. This exercise is based on information taken from Scott, *Fierce Conversations*, pp. 117–118.

34. Jonathan B. Cox and Andrea Weigl, "Duke, Patients Poles Apart over Fluid Mix-up," *The News & Observer*, July 10, 2005, p. A1; Victor J. Dzau, "Learning from the Hydraulic Fluid Incident," *The News & Observer*, July 15, 2005, p. A19; "Report: Surgical Tools at Hospitals Were Washed in Hydraulic Fluid, Not Detergent," *San Diego Tribune*, June 13, 2005. [cited 4 November 2005]. Available from www.symtym.com/index.php/symtym/comments/lube_job; INTERNET; Jean P. Fisher, "Surgical Tools Cleaned Improperly." [cited 4 November 2005]. Available from www.newsobserver.com/new/health_science/story/2581297p-8376237c.html; INTERNET; Jeff Molter, "Duke Provides Additional Information to Patients Exposed to Hydraulic Fluid," August 4, 2005. [cited 4 November 2005]. Available from www.dukemednews.org/news/article.php?id = 9189; INTERNET; Sarah Avery, "New Firm to Track Duke Patients," *The News & Observer*, August 26, 2005, p. B1.

35. Ibid.

36. Ann David, Joseph Pereira, and William M. Bulkeley, " Security Concerns Bring New Focus on Body Language," *Wall Street Journal*, August 15, 2002, p. A1, A6; "The Power of Body Language," Course Archive. [cited 6 January 2003]. Available from www.presentersuniversity.com/courses/show_archive.cfm?RecordID 539; INTERNET.

Chapter 3

1. Camille Wright Miller, "Mirroring Others Helps You Connect with Them," *The Roanoke Times*, August 24, 2005.
2. Douglas A. Bernstein, Louis A. Penner, Alison Clarke-Stewart, and Edward J. Roy, *Psychology*, 6th ed. (Boston: Houghton Mifflin, 2003), p. 518.
3. Robert Bolton and Dorothy Grover Bolton, *People Styles at Work* (New York: AMACOM, 1996), p. 10.
4. For more information concerning training programs offered by Wilson Learning Corporation, visit their website at www.wilsonlearning.com.
5. Tony Alessandra, *Behavioral Profiles: Participant Workbook* (San Diego: Pfeiffer & Company, 1994), p. 12.
6. Bolton and Bolton, *People Styles at Work*, pp. ix–x.
7. Bolton and Bolton, *People Styles at Work*, p. x.
8. Robert J. Sternberg, *Thinking Styles* (New York: Cambridge University Press, 1997), p. 8.
9. Bolton and Bolton, *People Styles at Work*, p. x.
10. Susan Foster, "What's Your Client's Style?" *Selling*, December 1998.
11. David W. Johnson, *Reaching Out—Interpersonal Effectiveness and Self-Actualization* (Englewood Cliffs, N.J.: Prentice-Hall, 1981), pp. 43–44. The dominance factor was described in an early book by William M. Marston, *The Emotions of Normal People* (New York: Harcourt, 1928). Research conducted by Rolfe La Forge and Robert F. Suczek resulted in the development of the Interpersonal Check List (ICL), which features a dominant-submissive scale. A person who receives a high score on the ICL tends to lead, persuade, and control others. The Interpersonal Identity Profile, developed by David W. Merrill and James W. Taylor, features a factor called "assertiveness." Persons classified as high in assertiveness tend to have strong opinions, make quick decisions, and be directive when dealing with people. Persons classified as low in assertiveness tend to voice moderate opinions, make thoughtful decisions, and be supportive when dealing with others.
12. Christopher Caggiano, "Psychopath," *Inc.*, July 1998, pp. 77–85.
13. American Management Association, *Catalog of Seminars* (New York: American Management Association, 2002), p. 33.
14. The research conducted by La Forge and Suczek resulted in identification of the hostile/loving continuum, which is similar to the sociability continuum. Their Interpersonal Check List features this scale. L. L. Thurstone and T. G. Thurstone developed the Thurstone Temperament Schedule, which provides an assessment of a "sociable" factor. Persons with high scores in this area enjoy the company of others and make friends easily. The Interpersonal Identity Profile developed by Merrill and Taylor contains an objectivity continuum. A person with low objectivity is seen as attention seeking, involved with the feelings of others, informal, and casual in social relationships. A person who is high in objectivity tends to be indifferent toward the feelings of others. This person is formal in social relationships.
15. "On the Human Side," *Time*, February 19, 1979, p. 75.
16. Bolton and Bolton, *People Styles at Work*, p. 87.
17. Ibid.
18. "Ask Dr. E," *Psychology Today*, January/February 2000, p. 28.
19. David W. Merrill and Roger H. Reid, *Personality Styles and Effective Performance* (Radnor, Pa.: Chilton Book, 1981), p. 88.
20. Wilson Learning Corporation, *Growth Through Versatility* (Eden Prairie, Minn.: Wilson Learning Corporation), p. 4.
21. "Versatility: The Key to Sales Performance" (Edina, Minn.: Wilson Learning Worldwide, 2004), pp. 1–4.
22. Bob Reeves, "It Takes All Types," *Lincoln Star*, May 24, 1994, p. 11.
23. Gary A. Williams and Robert B. Miller, "Changing the Way You Persuade," *Harvard Business Review*, May 2002, pp. 65–67.
24. Stuart Atkins, *The Name of Your Game* (Beverly Hills, Calif.: Ellis & Stewart, 1981), pp. 49–50.
25. Ibid., p. 51.
26. Chris Lee, "What's Your Style?" *Training*, May 1991, p. 28.
27. Michael Kaplan, "How to Overcome Your Strengths," *Fast Company*, May 1999, p. 225.
28. Robert Kreitner, *Management*, 8th ed. (Boston: Houghton Mifflin, 2001), p. 293; "The Best Managers," *Business Week*, January 13, 2003, p. 72.

Chapter 4

1. Shoshana Zuboff, "Only the Brave Surrender," *Fast Company*, October 2004, p. 121.
2. "Struggling with Low Self-Esteem," Go Ask Alice! June 6, 1997. [cited 9 November 2005]. Available from www.goaskalice.columbia.edu/1202.html; INTERNET.
3. David E. Shapiro, "Pumping Up Your Attitude," *Psychology Today*, May/June 1997, p. 14.
4. Douglas A. Bernstein, Louis A. Penner, Alison Clarke-Stewart, and Edward J. Roy, *Psychology*, 6th ed. (Boston: Houghton Mifflin, 2003), pp. 534–535; Richard Laliberte, "Self-Esteem Workshop," *Self*, May 1994, p. 201.
5. Nathaniel Branden, *The Six Pillars of Self-Esteem* (New York: Bantam, 1994), p. 7.
6. Robert Reasoner, "The True Meaning of Self-Esteem," National Association for Self-Esteem, Normal, Il. [cited April 30, 2003]. Available from INTERNET.
7. Phillip C. McGraw, *Self Matters* (New York: Simon & Schuster, 2001), pp. 69–70.
8. Sharon Begley, "Follow Your Intuition: The Unconscious You May Be the Wiser Half," *Wall Street Journal*, August 30, 2002, p. B1; Sharon Begley, "How Do I Love Thee? Let Me Count the Ways—and Other Bad Ideas," *Wall Street Journal*, September 6, 2002, p. B1.
9. Bernstein et al., Psychology, pp. 432–467.
10. Marilyn Elias, "Short Attention Span Linked to TV," *USA Today*, April 5, 2004, p. A1; Lyric Wallwork Winik, "The Toll of Video Violence," *Parade*, July 22, 2004, p. 15.
11. Bernstein et al., *Psychology*, pp. 467–471.
12. Ibid., 471.
13. Emmett Miller, *The Healing Power of Happiness* (Emmaus, Pa.: Rodale Press, 1989), pp. 12–13.
14. Lacey Beckmann, "One More Thing Money Can't Buy," *Psychology Today*, November/December, 2002, p. 16.

15. Amy Saltzman, *Downshifting* (New York: HarperCollins, 1990), pp. 15–16.

16. Miller, *The Healing Power of Happiness*, pp. 12–13.

17. McGraw, *Self Matters*, p. 73.

18. Reasoner, "The True Meaning."

19. Arthur H. Goldsmith, Jonathan R. Veum, and William Darity, Jr., "The Impact of Psychological and Human Capital on Wages," *Economic Inquiry*, October 1997, p. 817.

20. Hyrum W. Smith, *The 10 Natural Laws of Successful Time and Life Management* (New York: Warner Books, 1994), p. 178.

21. Don Miguel Ruiz, *The Four Agreements* (San Rafael, Calif.: Amber-Allen Publishing, 1997), pp. 47–61.

22. James J. Messina and Constance M. Messina, *The SEA's Program Model of Self-Esteem* [cited 9 November 2005]. Available from www.coping.org/selfesteem/model.htm.

23. Branden, *The Six Pillars of Self-Esteem*, p. 33.

24. Matthew McKay and Patrick Fanning, *Self-Esteem*, 2d ed. (Oakland, Calif.: New Harbinger, 1992), p. 42.

25. McGraw, *Self Matters*, pp. 209–212.

26. Arnold A. Lazarus and Clifford N. Lazarus, *The 60-Second Shrink* (San Luis Obispo, Calif.: Impact Publishers, 1997), p. 40.

27. Marcus Buckingham and Donald O. Clifton, *Now, Discover Your Strengths* (New York: Free Press, 2001), p. 8.

28. Ibid., pp. 28–35.

29. Ibid., pp. 28–31.

30. Nanette Byrnes, "Start Search," *Business Week*, October 10, 2005, p. 74.

31. Chip R. Bell, "Making Mentoring a Way of Life," *Training*, October 1996, p. 138; Lin Standke, review of *Managers as Mentors: Building Partnerships for Learning*, by Chip R. Bell, *Training*, April 1997, pp. 64–65.

32. Fiona Haley and Christine Canabou, interviews by, "The Mentors' Mentors," *Fast Company*, October 2003, p. 59.

33. Hal Lancaster, "It's Harder, but You Still Can Rise Up from the Mail Room," *Wall Street Journal*, June 18, 1996, p. B1.

34. Ginger Adams and Tena B. Crews, "Telementoring: A Viable Tool," *Journal of Applied Research for Business Education*, vol. 2, no. 3, 2004, pp. 1–4.

35. Hal Lancaster, "It's Harder, but You Still Can Rise Up from the Mail Room," *Wall Street Journal*, June 18, 1996, p. B1.

36. Gottlieb, "The Radical Road to Self-Esteem," p. 101.

37. Stan Goldberg, "The 10 Rules of Change," *Psychology Today*, September/October 2002, pp. 38–44.

38. Andrew Weil, "Images of Healing," *Dr. Andrew Weil's Self Healing*, November 2003, p. 3; Amy Dockser Marcus, "Heart Surgeons Try Using the Power of Suggestion," *Wall Street Journal*, February 20, 2004, p. D1.

39. James Bauman, "The Gold Medal," *Psychology Today*, May/June 2000, pp. 62–68.

40. See McGraw, *Self Matters*, for comprehensive coverage of how internal dialogue influences our self-concept.

41. McKay and Fanning, *Self-Esteem*, p. 42.

42. Julie Morgenstern, "Fire Your Inner Critic," *O The Oprah Magazine*, August 2004, pp. 75–77.

43. Herb Kindler, "Working to Change Old Habits," *Working Smart*, May 1992, p. 8.

44. McGraw, *Self Matters*, pp. 204–205.

45. Roy J. Blitzer, Colleen Petersen, and Linda Rogers, "How to Build Self-Esteem," *Training & Development*, February 1993, pp. 58–60.

46. Messina and Messina, *The SEA's Program Model of Self-Esteem*, p. 9.

47. Haley and Canabou, "The Mentors' Mentors," p. 60.

48. Cheryl Hall, "Mentoring as Critical as Ever, but Companies Are Ignoring It," *San Jose Mercury News*, February 11, 2001, p. PC1.

49. Haley and Canabou, "The Mentors' Mentors," pp. 59–66.

50. Frank Jossi, "Mentoring in Changing Times," *Training*, August 1997, p. 52.

51. Jennifer Reingold, "Want to Grow as a Leader? Get a Mentor!" *Fast Company*, January 2001, p. 58.

52. Dave Longaberger, *Longaberger: An American Success Story* (New York: Harper Business, 2001), p. 8.

53. "David Longaberger Sets the Standard for Success," *Selling*, May 2000, p. 8; Steve Williford and Dave Longaberger, *The Longaberger Story: And How We Did It* (Lincoln-Bradley Publishing, 1991); *Dave Longaberger: An American Success Story* (New York: Harper Business, 2001); P. Kelly Smith, "Entrepreneurial Expert Tami Longaberger: What She Learned from Her Father About Business and Life," April 16, 2001. [cited 8 January 2003]. Available from www.entrepreneur.com/Your_Business/YB_SegArticle/0,4621,288626,00.html; INTERNET.

Chapter 5

1. Troy McMullen, "Private Properties," *Wall Street Journal*, September 23, 2005, p. W10; Cassell Bryuan-Low, "WorldCom's Auditors Took Shortcuts," *Wall Street Journal*, July 23, 2003, p. C9.

2. Kees Cools, "Ebbers Rex," *Wall Street Journal*, March 22, 2005, p. A22.

3. Jaren Sandberg, "Office Sticky Fingers Can Turn the Rest of Us into Joe Fridays," *Wall Street Journal*, November 19, 2005, p. B1.

4. David Gergen, "Candidates with Character," *U.S. News & World Report*, September 27, 1999, p. 68.

5. Patrick Smith, "You Have a Job, but How About a Life?" *Business Week*, November 16, 1998, p. 30.

6. Nathaniel Branden, *Self-Esteem at Work* (San Francisco: Jossey-Bass, 1998), p. 35.

7. Stephen R. Covey, *The Seven Habits of Highly Effective People* (New York: Simon & Schuster, 1989), p. 92.

8. Hyrum W. Smith, *The 10 Natural Laws of Successful Time and Life Management* (New York: Warner Books, 1994), pp. 14–15.

9. J. David McCracken and Ana E. Falcon-Emmanuelli, "A Theoretical Basis for Work Values Research in Vocational Education" *Journal of Vocational and Technical Education*, April 1994, p. 4.

10. Sue Shellenbarger, "Some Top Executives Are Finding a Balance Between Job and Home," *Wall Street Journal*, April 23, 1997, p. B1.

11. Katharine Mieszkowski, "FitzGerald Family Values," *Fast Company*, April 1998, p. 194.

12. Rebecca Ganzel, "Book Reviews," *Training*, June 2000, pp. 76–77.

13. Jack Canfield, *The Success Principles* (New York: HarperCollins, 2005), pp. 20–29.

14. Jeffrey Zaslow, "The Latest Generation Gap:Boomers Are Often Unfairly Lumped Together," *Wall Street Journal*, July 8, 2004, p. D1; Shirley Holt, "Generation Gaps in the Workplace," *The Roanoke Times*, March 27, 2005, pp. 1, 3.

15. Katherine Paterson, "Family Values," *New York Times Book Review*, October 15, 1995, p. 32.

16. Toms, "Investing in Character," *The Inner Edge*, June/July 2000, pp. 5–8.

17. Chris Lee and Ron Zemke, "The Search for Spirit in the Workplace," *Training*, June 1993, p. 21.

18. Sonia L. Nazario, "School Teachers Say It's Wrongheaded to Try to Teach Students What's Right," *Wall Street Journal*, April 6, 1990, p. B1; Steve Rosen, "Battle Against Corporate Swindlers Hits the Classroom," *Springfield Newsleader*, January 21, 2003, p. C1.

19. Character Counts! National Office at www. charactercounts.org. [cited 12 January 2003]. Available from www.charactercounts.org; INTERNET.

20. Linda Formichelli, "Programming Behavior," *Psychology Today*, January/February 2001, p. 10.

21. Morris Massey, *The People Puzzle* (Reston, Va.: Reston Publishing, 1979).

22. O. C. Ferrell, John Fraedrich, and Linda Ferrell, *Business Ethics*, 5th ed. (Boston: Houghton Mifflin, 2002), pp. 123–135.

23. Neal Donald Walsch, *Conversations with God, Book 1 Guidebook* (Charlottesville, Va.: Hampton Roads, 1997), p. 71.

24. John Hollon, "Drucker Knew Best," *Workforce Management*, November 21, 2005, p. 58.

25. Sue Shellenbarger, "In Cataclysmic Times, Workers Need Room to Rethink Priorities," *Wall Street Journal*, September 19, 2001, p. B1.

26. Toddi Gutner, "A Balancing Act for GenX Women," *Business Week*, January 21, 2002, p. 82.

27. John Beebe, "Conscience, Integrity and Character," *The Inner Edge*, June/July 2000, pp. 9–11.

28. "Making Sense of Ethics." [cited 13 January 2003]. Available from www.josephsoninstitute.org/ MED/ MED-1makingsense.htm; INTERNET.

29. "Workers Cut Ethical Corners, Survey Finds," *Wall Street Journal*, March 10, 1995, p. A2.

30. Price Pritchett, *The Ethics of Excellence* (Dallas, Tex: Pritchett & Associates, n.d.), p. 28.

31. "CyberSource® Joins with Association of Certified Fraud Examiners to Support 2002 National Fraud Awareness Week," July 29, 2002. [cited 13 January 2003]. Available from www.cybersource.com/news_and_events/view.xml? page_id=949; INTERNET.

32. "Making Sense of Ethics."

33. Ed Emde, "Employee Values Are Changing Course," *Workforce*, March 1998, p. 84. [cited 18 November 2005]. Available from www.workforce.com/archive/ article/21/97/39.php?ht=values%20values; INTERNET.

34. Jerry Useem, "Welcome to the New Company Town," *Fortune*, January 10, 2000, pp. 62–70.

35. Susan Scherreik, "A Conscience Doesn't Have to Make You Poor," *Business Week*, May 1, 2000, pp. 204–206.

36. Andy Pasztor and Jonathan Karp, "How an Air Force Official's Help for a Daughter Led to Disgrace," *Wall Street Journal*, December 9, 2004, p. A1, A10.

37. Ken Belson, "WorldCom's Audacious Failure and Its Toll on an Industry," *New York Times*, January 28, 2005, p. B1.

38. Gregory L. White and Amy Merrick, "Exide Unit Pleads Guilty to Charges over Battery Flaws," *Wall Street Journal*, March 26, 2001, p. B9.

39. Nancy D. Holt, "Workspaces," *Wall Street Journal*, December 2, 2004, p. B4; "Code of Ethics." [cited 27 October 2005]. Available from www.simmons.com; INTERNET.

40. Bob Filipczak, "The Soul of the Hog," *Training*, February 1996, pp. 38–42.

41. Kathryn Cates Moore, "Taking the High Road," *Journal Star*, April 28, 2001, p. B1.

42. Andrew Stark, "What's the Matter with Business Ethics?" *Harvard Business Review*, May/June 1993, p. 38.

43. "Tom Chappell—Minister of Commerce," *Business Ethics*, January/February 1994, p. 17.

44. Ferrell, Fraedrich, and Ferrell, *Business Ethics*, pp. 182–183.

45. Patrick M. Lencioni, "Make Your Values Mean Something," *Harvard Business Review*, July 2002, pp. 5–9.

46. Joshua Hyatt, "How to Hire Employees," *Inc.*, March 1990, p. 2.

47. Anne Fisher, "How Can You Be Sure We're Not Hiring a Bunch of Shady Liars?" *Fortune*, May 26, 2003, p. 180.

48. Jennifer Merritt, "Welcome to Ethics 101," *Business Week*, October 18, 2004, p. 90; Ronald Alsop, "Right and Wrong," *Wall Street Journal*, September 17, 2003, p. R9.

49. Richard Lacayo and Amanda Ripley, "Persons of the Year," *Time*, December 31, 2002, pp. 32–33.

50. Paula Dwyer and Dan Carney, with Amy Borrus and Lorraine Woellert in Washington and Christopher Palmeri in Los Angeles, "Year of the Whistleblower," *Business Week*, December 16, 2002, pp. 107–108; Michael Orey, "WorldCom-Inspired 'Whistle-Blower' Law Has Weaknesses," *Wall Street Journal*, October 1, 2002, p. B1.

51. Dwyer and Carney, "Year of the Whistleblower," p. 108.

52. Sarah Jay, "Corruption Issues: A View from Shanghai," *International Business Ethics Institute*, vol. 1, no. 1, November 1, 1997. [cited 27 November, 2005]. Available from www.business-ethics.org/newsdetail.asp? newsid=31; INTERNET.

53. Chris Hill and Toby Hanlon, "26 Simple Ways to Change How You Feel," *Prevention*, August 1993, p. 126.

54. Sue Shellenbarger, "How and Why We Lie at the Office: From Pilfered Pens to Padded Accounts," *Wall Street Journal*, March 24, 2005, B1; Jared Dandberg, "Hard to Rein in Office Pilfering," *The News & Observer*, November 23, 2003, p. E12; Jared Sandberg, "Office Sticky Fingers Can Turn the Rest of Us into Joe Fridays," *The News & Observer*, November 19, 2003, p. B1.

55. Deborah Solomon, "For Financial Whistle-Blowers, New Shield Is an Imperfect One," *Wall Street Journal*, October 4, 2004, p. A1.

56. "Fraud Busters: Eight Who Made a Difference," Taxpayers Against Fraud, [cited 30 November 2005]. Available from www.taf.org/whistleblowerbios.pdf; INTERNET;

"Company to Pay in Kickback Case," *The News & Observer*, July 31, 2004, p. D6; Deborah Solomon and Kara Scannell, "Whistle-Blower Provision Cited," *Wall Street Journal*, November 15, 2004, p. B4; "The False Claims Act/History." [cited 30 November 2005]. Available from www.quitamhelp.com/statis/fase_claims/history.html; INTERNET; "Qui Tam Basics." [cited 30 November 2005]. Available from www.quitamhelp.com/statis/fase-claims/history.html; INTERNET; Solomon "For Financial Whistle-Blowers, New Shield Is an Imperfect One."

Chapter 6

1. Rob Walker, "Hook, Line, & Sinker," *Inc.*, August 2002, p. 86.
2. Ibid., p. 88.
3. Ibid., p. 87.
4. Douglas A. Bernstein, Louis A. Penner, Alison Clarke-Stewart, and Edward J. Roy, *Psychology*, 6th ed. (Boston: Houghton Mifflin, 2003), p. 660.
5. Harry E. Chambers, *The Bad Attitude Survival Guide* (Reading, Mass.: Addison-Wesley, 1998), pp. 17–37.
6. John Hollon, "The Cult of Welch," *Workforce Management*, October 10, 2005, p. 74.
7. Daniel H. Pink, *A Whole New Mind* (New York: Riverhead Books, 2005), pp. 48–63.
8. Laura Landro, "Compassion 101: Teaching M.D.s to Be Nicer," *Wall Street Journal*, September 28, 2005, p. D1.
9. Pink, *A Whole New Mind*, p. 154.
10. Jerome Kagan, *Psychology: An Introduction* (New York: Harcourt Brace Jovanovich, 1984), p. 548.
11. William F. Schoell and Joseph P. Guiltinan, *Marketing*, 5th ed. (Boston: Allyn & Bacon, 1992), pp. 166–167; William M. Pride and O. C. Ferrell, *Marketing* (Boston: Houghton Mifflin, 2000), p. 211.
12. Joan Hamilton, "Net Work: At Icarian, It's All Work and Some Play," *Business Week E.BIZ*, April 3, 2000, p. EB116.
13. Nicholas Varchaver, "Who's the King of Delaware?" *Fortune*, May 13, 2002, pp. 124–128.
14. Thomas E. Ricks, "New Marines Illustrate Growing Gap Between Military and Society," *Wall Street Journal*, July 27, 1995, p. A1.
15. Kellye Whitney, "New-Hire Failure Linked to Interpersonal Skills," *Chief Learning Officer Magazine*. [cited 5 October 2005]. Available from www.clomedia.com; INTERNET.
16. Nathaniel Branden, *Self-Esteem at Work* (San Francisco: Jossey-Bass, 1998), pp. 94–97; "Adjusting an Attitude," *San Jose Mercury News*, August 20, 1997, p. G6.
17. His Holiness the Dalai Lama and Howard C. Cutler, *The Art of Happiness* (New York: Riverhead Books, 1998), pp. 16–17.
18. Michael Crom, "Live Enthusiastically and You'll Live Successfully," *Training*, April 1999, p. 6.
19. Dalai Lama and Cutler, *The Art of Happiness*, p. 22.
20. Ibid., p. 23.
21. Patricia Sellers, "Now Bounce Back!" *Fortune*, May 1, 1995, p. 57.
22. Martin Seligman, *Learned Optimism* (New York: Knopf, 2001), p. 4.

23. Redford Williams and Virginia Williams, *Anger Kills* (New York: Harper Perennial, 1993), p. 12.
24. Bob Wall, *Working Relationships* (Palo Alto, Calif.: Davies-Black, 1999), pp. 11–12.
25. Ibid., p. 17.
26. Brian Tracy, *The 100 Absolutely Unbreakable Laws of Business Success* (San Francisco: Berrett-Koehler 2000), pp. 67–70.
27. Branden, *Self-Esteem at Work*, pp. 111–112.
28. Harry E. Chambers, *The Bad Attitude Survival Guide* (Reading, Mass.: Addison-Wesley, 1998), pp. 6–7.
29. Weekly online news from *Workforce Week Management* distributed to subscribers November 29, 2005.
30. Hamilton, "Net Work," p. EB117.
31. Quoted in Nancy W. Collins, Susan K. Gilbert, and Susan Nycum, *Women Leading: Making Tough Choices on the Fast Track* (Lexington, Mass.: Stephen Greene Press, 1988), p. 1.
32. "100 Best Companies to Work For," *Fortune*, January 20, 2003, pp. 128–152.
33. Dave Murphy, "Going to School with 'FISH,' Happy Employees Can Save Companies More than a Few Fins," *San Francisco Chronicle*, April 21, 2002, pp. J1–2; Stephen C. Lundin, Harry Paul, and John Christensen, *Fish!* (Hyperion, 2000); Stephen C. Lundin, John Christensen, Harry Paul, with Philip Strand, *Fish! Tales* (Hyperion, 2001); Walker, "Hook, Line, & Sinker," pp. 85–88.
34. George F. Will, "The Perils of Bad Promises," *The Washington Post*, January 16, 2005 p. B7; Associated Press, "Fed Pension Agency Could See $71 Billion Deficit," June 9, 2005. [cited 9 December 2005]. Available from www.msnbc.msn.com; INTERNET; Associated Press, "Verizon Ends Manager Pension Contributions." [cited 7 December 2005]. Available from www.abcnews.go.com; INTERNET; "Dr. Spencer Johnson." [cited 7 December 2005]. Available from www.spencerjohnsonpartners.com; INTERNET; Spencer Johnson, *Who Moved My Cheese?* (New York: G. P. Putnam's Sons), 1998.

Chapter 7

1. John A. Byrne, "How to Lead Now," *Fast Company*, August 2003, p. 62. [cited 26 December 2005]. Available from www.fastcompany.com/magazine; INTERNET.
2. Douglas A. Bernstein, Louis A. Penner, Alison Clarke-Stewart, and Edward J. Roy, *Psychology*, 6th ed. (Boston: Houghton Mifflin, 2003), pp. 381–382.
3. M. G. Lord, "Raison McÊtre," *New York Times Book Review*, August 18, 2002, p. 13.
4. Jim Carlton, "Wild Horses, Couldn't Drag Them Away from Stones Shows," *Wall Street Journal*, November 22, 2002, p. A1.
5. Robert Kreitner, *Management*, 7th ed. (Boston: Houghton Mifflin, 1998), pp. 156–157.
6. Data were collected by use of the Reiss Profile, a standardized psychological test used to measure sixteen desires.
7. Steven Reiss, "Secrets of Happiness," *Psychology Today*, January/February 2001, pp. 50–56. To learn more about the Reiss Profile, see *Who Am I: The 16 Basic Desires That Motivate Our Happiness and Define Our Personalities* (New York: Berkley Books, 2000).

8. Cynthia Berryman-Fink, *The Managers' Desk Reference* (New York: AMACOM, 1989), pp. 156–157.

9. Robert Kreitner, *Management*, 8th ed. (Boston: Houghton Mifflin, 2001), pp. 395–396.

10. "Belonging Satisfies Basic Human Need," *The Menninger Letter*, August 1995, p. 6.

11. Frederick Herzberg, Bernard Mausner, and Barbara Black Snyderman, *The Motivation to Work* (New York: Wiley, 1959).

12. C. R. Snyder, "Hope Helps," *Psychology Today*, November/December 1999, p. 20.

13. Richard Barrett, "The Power of Purpose," *The Inner Edge*, August/September 1999, p. 20.

14. Kreitner, *Management*, 8th ed., p. 403.

15. Ibid., p. 403; Ron Zemke, "Toxic Energy Dumps," *Training*, January 2001, p. 18.

16. Berryman-Fink, *The Manager's Desk Reference*, pp. 156–157.

17. "Management Glossary." [cited 27 December 2005]. Available from www.management.about.com; INTERNET; Brigitte Blobel, "If You Have Class, Then You Are Just as Good as Your Guests," *Audi Magazine*, December 2001, pp. 72–75.

18. Michelle Conlin, "Now It's Getting Personal," *Business Week*, December 16, 2002, pp. 90–92.

19. Rosabeth Moss Kanter, "The New Managerial Work," *Harvard Business Review*, November/December 1989, p. 91.

20. Leslie Overmyer-Day and George Benson, "Training Success Stories," *Training & Development*, June 1996, p. 27.

21. Patrick J. Sauer, "Open-Door Management," *Inc.*, June 2003, p. 44.

22. Janice Love, review of *The Set-Up-to-Fail Syndrome*, by Jean-Francois Manzoni and Jean-Louis Barsoux, *Training*, April 2003, p. 49; Sharon Begley, "Expectations May Alter Outcomes Far More Than We Realize," *Wall Street Journal*, November 7, 2003, p. B1.

23. Ibid.; Ann C. Humphries, "Motivating Generation X." [cited 27 December 2005]. Available from www.christianwomentoday.com/workplace/genx; INTERNET.

24. Peter Doskoch, "The Winning Edge," *Psychology Today*, November/December 2005, pp. 42–45.

25. Ibid., pp. 46–47.

26. M. Scott Peck, *The Road Less Traveled* (New York: Simon & Schuster, 1978), pp. 18–20; Christine B. Whelan, "The Road Is Heavily Traveled Now," *Wall Street Journal*, October 7, 2005, p. W13.

27. G. Pascal Zachary, "The New Search for Meaning in 'Meaningless' Work," *Wall Street Journal*, January 9, 1997, p. B1.

28. Robin A. Sheerer, *No More Blue Mondays* (Palo Alto, Calif.: Davies-Black Publishing, 1999).

29. Doskoch, "The Winning Edge," p. 50.

30. Bo Burlingham, "For Going Naked," *Inc.*, April 2004, p. 124.

31. Jack Stack's *The Great Game of Business* (New York: Currency Books, 1992) p. 124.

32. Lynne Cox, *Swimming to Antarctica*, Editors' Pick, Mercedes, Winter 2004, p. 72; "The Barnes & Noble Review," accessed March 24, 2004 at www.barnesandnoble.com.

33. Doskoch, "The Winning Edge," p. 49.

34. Ryan Underwood, "No Brakes," *Fast Company*, September 2004, p. 112.

Chapter 8

1. Ian McDonald, "March, Spitzer Settle with $850 Million, an Apology to Clients," *Wall Street Journal*, February 1, 2005, p. C1; Stephanie Kang, "Hardee's Fesses Up to Shortcomings," *Wall Street Journal*, June 24, 2003, p. B4.

2. Daniel Henninger, "Pete Rose Isn't the Only One in Pete Roseland," *Wall Street Journal*, January 9, 2004, p. A10; "Charlie's Hustle," *Wall Street Journal*, January 7, 2004, p. A12.

3. Jeanne Cummings, "Bush Enters a Political Quandary as He Faces Calls for an Apology," *Wall Street Journal*, April 15, 2004, p. A6.

4. Martha Beck, "True Confessions," *O The Oprah Magazine*, June 2002, pp. 183–184.

5. Aviva Patz, "Go Ahead—Get Mad," *Health & Healing*, June 2003, pp. 95–97.

6. Daniel Goleman, "What Makes a Leader?" *Harvard Business Review*, November/December 1998, p. 95.

7. Cary Cherniss and Daniel Goleman, *The Emotionally Intelligent Workplace* (San Francisco: Jossey-Bass, 2001), p. 258.

8. John Powell, *Why Am I Afraid to Tell You Who I Am?* (Chicago: Argus Communications, 1969), p. 77.

9. David Stewart, "Talk at Work: Do You Dialogue?" *Health & Healing*, Vol. 5, Number 6, 2002, p. 2.

10. Roy M. Berko, Andrew D. Wolvin, and Darlyn R. Wolvin, *Communicating* (Boston: Houghton Mifflin, 1995), p. 46.

11. *Communication Concepts—The Johari Window* (New York: J. C. Penney Company, Consumer Affairs Department, 1979).

12. Parker J. Palmer, "Life on the Mobius Strip," *Inner Edge*, August/September 2000, pp. 22–23.

13. Marshall Goldsmith, "How to Learn the Truth About Yourself," *Fast Company*, October 2003, p. 127.

14. Maury A. Peiper, "Getting 360 Feedback Right," *Harvard Business Review*, January 2001, pp. 3–7; William C. Byham, "Fixing the Instrument," *Training*, July 2004, p. 50.

15. Beverly Engel, "Making Amends," *Psychology Today*, July/August 2002, pp. 40–42.

16. Sharon Nelton, "The Power of Forgiveness," *Nation's Business*, June 1995, p. 41.

17. Lazarus and Lazarus, *The 60-Second Shrink* (San Luis Obispo, Calif.: Impact, 1997), pp. 76–79.

18. John R. Diekman, *Human Connections* (Englewood Cliffs, N.J.: Prentice-Hall, 1985), p. 63.

19. Bob Wall, *Working Relationships* (Palo Alto, Calif.: Davies-Black, 1999), p. 166.

20. Hendrie Weisinger and Norman Lobsenz, *Nobody's Perfect—How to Give Criticism and Get Results* (Los Angeles: Stratford Press, 1981), p. 39.

21. Joyce Brothers, "The Most Important People We Know . . . Our Friends," *Parade Magazine*, February 16, 1997, pp. 4–6; Sue Shellenbarger, "Ovulating? Depressed? The Latest Rules on What Not to Talk About at Work," *Wall Street Journal*, July 21, 2005, p. D1.

22. Mark Matousek, "The Cat Is on the Roof," *Common Boundary*, January/February 1997, p. 64.

23. *The American Heritage Dictionary of the English Language*, 3d ed. (Boston: Houghton Mifflin, 1992), p. 1920.

24. Blaine Hartford, "Trust Your Surgeon? Mate? Friends? Colleagues? What Makes Up a Feeling of Trust?" *Health & Healing*, June 2000, p. 36.

25. Ron Zemke, "Can You Manage Trust?" *Training*, February 2000, p. 78; Ron Zemke, "A Matter of Trust," *Training*, December 2002, p. 12.

26. Aubrey C. Daniels, *Bringing Out the Best in People* (New York: McGraw-Hill, 1994), p. 41.

27. Jack R. Gibb, *Trust: A New View of Personal and Organizational Development* (Los Angeles: Guild of Tutors Press, 1978), p. 29.

28. Ibid., p. 192.

29. Susan Scott, *Fierce Conversations* (New York: Viking, 2002), pp. 198–201, 254.

30. Derek Reveron, "Employee Criticism: Do It with Sensitivity," *San Jose Mercury News*, July 12, 1992, p. PC1; "How to Sidestep Verbal Pitfalls," *San Jose Mercury News*, January 31, 1993, p. PC2; "Speaking Out Counts at Work," *San Jose Mercury News*, December 20, 1992, p. PC1.

31. Mary Scott, "Interview with Howard Schultz," *Business Ethics*, November/December 1995, p. 28; Kate Berry, "Starbucks Opens First Stores in Miami, Hoping to Woo Lovers of Cuban Coffee," *Wall Street Journal*, March 31, 1997, p. A9; Jennifer Reese, "Starbucks—Inside the Coffee Cult," *Fortune*, December 9, 1996, pp. 190–198; Coates, "Don't Tie 360-Degree Feedback to Pay," pp. 68–78; "Work Week," *Wall Street Journal*, March 7, 2000, p. A1.

Chapter 9

1. Rose Palazzolo, "The Crowd Goes Wild," *Psychology Today*, July/August 2003, p. 14; Mark Yost, "Dis, Boom, Bah," *Wall Street Journal*, December 26, 2003, p. W9.

2. Douglas A. Bernstein, Louis A. Penner, Alison Clarke-Stewart, and Edward J. Roy, *Psychology*, 6th ed. (Boston: Houghton Mifflin, 2003), pp. 412–413.

3. Carol S. Pearson, "The Emotional Side of Workplace Success," *The Inner Edge*, December 1998/January 1999, p. 3.

4. Daniel Goleman, *Emotional Intelligence* (New York: Bantam Books, 1995), p. 34.

5. Robert Kreitner, *Management*, 9th ed. (Boston: Houghton Mifflin, 2004), p. 504.

6. Daniel Goleman, *Working with Emotional Intelligence* (New York: Bantam Books, 1998), pp. 24–28.

7. John Selby, *Conscious Healing* (New York: Bantam Books, 1989), p. 32.

8. Ibid.

9. James Georges, "The Not-So-Stupid Americans," *Training*, July 1994, p. 90.

10. Tim Sanders, *Love Is the Killer App* (New York: Crown Business, 2002), pp. 17–18.

11. Ibid., p. 23.

12. Ron Zemke, "Contact! Training Employees to Meet the Public," *Service Solutions* (Minneapolis: Lakewood Books, 1990), pp. 20–23.

13. Bernstein et al., *Psychology*, p. 454.

14. Ibid.

15. William C. Menninger and Harry Levinson, *Human Understanding in Industry* (Chicago: Science Research Associates, 1956), p. 29.

16. Joan Borysenko, *Guilt Is the Teacher, Love Is the Lesson* (New York: Warner Books, 1990), p. 70.

17. Donella H. Meadows, "We Are, to Our Harm, What We Watch," *Roanoke Times & World-News*, October 16, 1994, p. G3.

18. Bernstein et al., *Psychology*, p. 22.

19. Rachel Zimmerman, "Study Finds Violence Takes 1.6 Million Lives a Year," *Wall Street Journal*, October 3, 2002, p. D5; Kimberley Shearer Palmer, "Young Women Turn Wrong Way to Escape Abusive Boyfriends," *USA Today*, September 10, 2001, p. A17.

20. James R. Dykes, "A Precious Balance," *Integrative Health Care*, February 2004, p. 4.

21. Shakti Gawain, *The Path of Transformation* (Mill Valley, Calif.: Nataraj Publishing, 1993), p. 96.

22. Ibid.

23. Harold H. Bloomfield and Robert K. Cooper, *The Power of 5* (Emmaus, Pa.: Rodale Press, 1995), p. 334; Redford Williams and Virginia Williams, *Anger Kills* (New York: HarperCollins, 1993), p. 3; Jared Sandberg, "The Upside of Anger: Some Use It as a Shield Against Work, Others," *Wall Street Journal*, October 11, 2005, p. B1; Martha Beck, "Impotent Rage," O *The Oprah Magazine*, October 2004, p. 205.

24. Kimes Gustin, *Anger, Rage, and Resentment* (West Caldwell, N.J.: St. Ives' Press, 1994), p. 1.

25. Art Ulene, *Really Fit Really Fast* (Encino, Calif.: HealthPoints, 1996), pp. 170–174.

26. Pemna Chödrön, "The Answer to Anger and Other Strong Emotions," *Shambhala Sun*, March 2005, p. 32.

27. Susan Bixler, *Professional Presence* (New York: G. P. Putnam's Sons, 1991), pp. 190–191.

28. Rolland S. Parker, *Emotional Common Sense* (New York: Barnes & Noble Books, 1973), pp. 80–81.

29. Gustin, *Anger, Rage, and Resentment*, p. 37.

30. Les Giblin, *How to Have Confidence and Power in Dealing with People* (Englewood Cliffs, N.J.: Prentice-Hall 1956), p. 37.

31. Anne Fisher, "How to Prevent Violence at Work," *Fortune*, February 21, 2005, p. 42.

32. Kevin Dobbs, "The Lucrative Menace of Workplace Violence," *Training*, March 2000, p. 55; Albert R. Karr, "Work Week," *Wall Street Journal*, April 4, 2000, p. A1.

33. Kenneth Labich, "Psycho Bosses from Hell," *Fortune*, March 18, 1996, p. 123.

34. Jennifer J. Laabs, "Employee Sabotage: Don't Be the Target," *Workforce*, July 1999, pp. 32–42; Michelle Conlin and Alex Salkever, "Revenge of the Downsized Nerds," *Business Week*, July 30, 2001, p. 40.

35. Laabs, "Employee Sabotage," pp. 32–42.

36. Fisher, "How to Prevent Violence at Work," p. 42.

37. Hale Dwoskin, *The Sedona Method* (Sedona Ariz.: Sedona Press, 2003), p. 30.

38. Walton C. Boshear and Karl G. Albrecht, *Understanding People: Models and Concepts* (San Diego: University Associates, 1977), pp. 41–46.

39. Chris Hill and Toby Hanlon, "Twenty-Six Simple Ways to Change How You Feel," *Prevention*, August 1993, p. 63.
40. Bloomfield and Cooper, *The Power of 5*, p. 368.
41. Joan Borysenko, *Minding the Body, Mending the Mind*, (New York: Bantam Books, 1987), pp. 164–165.
42. Ibid.
43. Don Miguel Ruiz, *The Four Agreements* (San Rafael, Calif.: Amber-Allen Publishing, 1997), p. 111.
44. Sam Keen, *Fire in the Belly—On Being a Man* (New York: Bantam Books, 1991), p. 242.
45. Arnold A. Lazarus and Clifford N. Lazarus, *The 60-Second Shrink* (San Luis Obispo, Calif.: Impact, 1997), pp. 10–11.
46. Borysenko, *Minding the Body, Mending the Mind*, p. 169.
47. Ellen Safier, "Our Experts Answer Your Questions," *Menninger Letter*, May 1993, p. 8.
48. Leo F. Buscaglia, *Loving Each Other* (Thorofare, N.J.: Slack, 1984), p. 160.
49. Keen, *Fire in the Belly*, p. 242.
50. Carol Hymowitz and Joann S. Lubin, "Many Companies Look the Other Way at Employee Affairs," *Wall Street Journal*, March 8, 2005, p. B1; Aleksandra Todorova, "Romancing a Colleague," *The News & Observer*, February 27, 2005, p. E9; Carol Hymowitz, "Managing Your Career," *Wall Street Journal*, November 18, 1997, p. B1; Hal Lancaster, "Managing Your Career," *Wall Street Journal*, September 23, 1997, p. B1; Jennifer J. Salopek, "You Don't Have to Play Cupid, Exactly," *Training & Development*, December 1998, p. 60.
51. Jeffrey Zaslow, "Putting a Price Tag on Grief," *Wall Street Journal*, November 20, 2002, p. D1; Sue Shellenbarger, "A Workplace Can Seem Cold and Indifferent to a Grieving Employee," *Wall Street Journal*, January 12, 1999, p. B1; Sue Shellenbarger, "An Anguishing Flaw in Many Benefit Plans: Bereavement Leaves," *Wall Street Journal*, February 23, 2000, p. B1.

Chapter 10

1. David Dorsey, "Happiness Pays," *Inc.*, February 2004, pp. 89–94.
2. Judith Orloff, "Accessing Sacred Energy," *Spirituality & Health*, May/June 2004, pp. 48–51; Judith Orloff, *Positive Energy* (New York: Harmony Books, 2004), pp. 1–15, 288.
3. Sarah Boehle, "From Humble Roots," *Training*, October 2000, pp. 106–113.
4. Robert Levering and Milton Moskowitz, "100 Best Companies to Work For," *Fortune*, January 20, 2003, p. 152.
5. Kenneth Blanchard and Spencer Johnson, *The One Minute Manager* (New York: Morrow, 1982), p. 43.
6. Douglas A. Bernstein, Louis A. Penner, Alison Clarke-Stewart, and Edward J. Roy, *Psychology*, 6th ed. (Boston: Houghton Mifflin, 2003), p. 197.
7. Tom Rath and Donald O. Clifton, *How Full Is Your Bucket?* (New York: Gallup Press, 2004), pp. 31–33.
8. Holly Dolezalek, "Don't Go," *Training*, July/August 2003, p. 52; Rath and Clifton, *How Full Is Your Bucket?* pp. 39–40.
9. For a comprehensive introduction to positive reinforcement, see Aubrey C. Daniels, *Other People's Habits—How to Use Positive Reinforcement to Bring Out the Best in People Around You* (New York: McGraw-Hill, 2001).
10. David Stewart, "Talk at Work: Do You Dialogue?" *Health & Healing*, Vol. 5, No. 6, 2002, p. 2.
11. Jon R. Katzenbach, *Why Pride Matters More Than Money* (New York: Crown Business, 2003), pp. 23–24.
12. John A. Byrne, "How to Lead Now," *Fast Company*, August 2003, pp. 62–70.
13. Deepak Chopra, *The Seven Spiritual Laws of Success* (San Rafael, Calif.: Amber-Allen, 1994), pp. 30–31.
14. *Random Acts of Kindness* (Berkeley, Calif.: Conari Press, 1993), pp. 1, 54, 68, 91.
15. Bob Nelson, *1001 Ways to Reward Employees* (New York: Workman, 1994), p. ix.
16. Ibid., p. xv.
17. "Rich DeVos Remarks—Delta Pi Epsilon Distinguished Lecturer," *Delta Pi Epsilon Journal*, Fall 1995, pp. 221–223.
18. Tim Sanders, *Love Is The Killer App* (New York: Crown Business, 2002), p. 39.
19. "How to Run an Incentive Program," *Incentive*, July 1990, p. 2.
20. Susan Sonnesyn Brooks, "Noncash Ways to Compensate Employees," *HR Magazine*, April 1994, p. 39.
21. Alfie Kohn, "Why Incentive Plans Cannot Work," *Harvard Business Review*, September/October 1993, p. 58.
22. Ibid.
23. Ibid., pp. 58–59.
24. Ibid., pp. 61–62.
25. Dave Murphy, "If You Want Gold, Give Them a Goal," *San Francisco Chronicle*, April 14, p. J1; Jeff Barbian, "Golden Carrots," *Training*, July 2002, p. 18.
26. Cedric B. Johnson, "When Working Harder Is Not Smarter," *The Inner Edge*, April/May 2000, pp. 18–21.
27. Ibid., p. 19.
28. Daniel H. Pink, *A Whole New Mind* (New York: Riverhead Books, 2005), pp. 48–53.
29. Anne Fisher, "Show off, Without Being a Blowhard," *Fortune*, March 8, 2004, p. 68.
30. David Wessel, "Why the Bad Guys of the Boardroom Emerged en Masse," *Wall Street Journal*, June 20, 2002, pp. A1, A6; Crayton Harrison, "Happy Customers Are Loyal, Banks Find," *San Jose Mercury News*, January 29, 2001, p. PC1; Barbian, "Golden Carrots," p. 18.
31. John A. Byrne, "How to Lead Now," *Fast Company*, August 2003, pp. 62–70; Katzenbach, *Why Pride Matters More Than Money*, pp. 13–19, 47–67; Dorsey, "Happiness Pays," pp. 89–94.

Chapter 11

1. Daniel Akst, "Totally Devoted," *Wall Street Journal*, June 16, 2004, p. D8. Michael R. Solomon, Greg W. Marshall, and Elnora W. Stuart, *Marketing*, 4th ed. (Upper Saddle River, N.J.: Prentice Hall, 2006), pp. 275–279.
2. Heather Johnson, "A Brand-New You," *Training*, August 2002, p. 14.
3. Gerry Khermouch, "What Makes a Boffo Brand," *The Business Week*, Spring 2002, p. 20.
4. Stephen R. Covey, *The 7 Habits of Highly Effective People* (New York: Simon & Schuster, 1989), pp. 22, 34.
5. Susan Bixler, *Professional Presence* (New York: G. P. Putnam's Sons, 1991), p. 16.

6. "Author: Success Pivots on First Impressions," *San Jose Mercury News*, November 8, 1992, p. PC2.

7. Douglas A. Bernstein, Alison Clarke-Stewart, Louis A. Pence, Edward J. Roy, and Christopher D. Wickens, *Psychology*, 5th ed. (Boston: Houghton Mifflin, 2000), pp. 226–227.

8. Ann Demarais and Valerie White, *First Impressions* (New York: Bantam Books, 2004), p. 16.

9. Gordon Anders, "Hey, Not So Fast," *Wall Street Journal*, January 11, 2005, p. D9.

10. Danielle Sacks, "The Accidental Guru," *Fast Company*, January 2005, pp. 69–70.

11. Leonard Zunin and Natalie Zunin, *Contact—The First Four Minutes* (New York: Ballantine Books, 1972), p. 17.

12. Demarais and White, *First Impressions*, pp. 22–23.

13. Clyde Haberman, "No Offense," *New York Times Book Review*, February 18, 1996, p. 11.

14. "Disney Restyles Grooming Rules," *San Jose Mercury News*, July 12, 2003, p. B1.

15. Haberman, "No Offense," p. 11.

16. Bixler, *Professional Presence*, p. 141.

17. Suein L. Hwang, "Enterprise Takes Idea of Dressed for Success to a New Extreme," *Wall Street Journal*, November 20, 2002, p. B1.

18. GPA Licensee Certification/Train-the-Trainer," [cited 16 January 2006]. Available from www.globalprotocol.com; INTERNET.

19. Dave Knesel, "Image Consulting—A Well-Dressed Step up the Corporate Ladder," *Pace*, July/August 1981, p. 74.

20. Cora Daniels, "The Man in the Tan Khaki Pants," *Fortune*, May 1, 2000, p. 338.

21. Megan Schnabel and Amy Kane, "Toss the Tie, Lose the Suit—The Casual Look Is In," *The Roanoke Times*, September 5, 1999, pp. B1, B2; Gene Bedell, *3 Steps to Yes* (New York: Crown Business, 2000), p. 143.

22. Anne Fisher, "Ask Annie," *Fortune*, May 15, 2000, p. 504; Frederic M. Biddle, "Work Week," *Wall Street Journal*, February 15, 2000; Mielikki Org, "The Tattooed Executive," *Wall Street Journal*, August 28, 2003, p. D1.

23. Deborah Blum, "Face It!" *Psychology Today*, September/October 1998, pp. 34, 69.

24. Susan Bixler, *The Professional Image* (New York: Perigee Books, 1984), p. 217.

25. Ibid., p. 219.

26. Heather Won Tesoriers, "At Vioxx Trial, Fast Talkers Challenge Court Stenographer," *Wall Street Journal*, October 25, 2005, p. B1.

27. Joann S. Lublin, "To Win Advancement, You Need to Clean Up Any Bad Speech Habits," *Wall Street Journal*, October 5, 2004, p. B1.

28. Ibid.

29. Lydia Ramsey, "You Never Get a 2nd Chance," *Selling*, October 2003, p. 3.

30. Adapted from Zunin and Zunin, *Contact*, pp. 102–108; "Handshake 101," *Training & Development*, November 1995, p. 71.

31. Cynthia Crossen, "Etiquette for Americans Today," *Wall Street Journal*, December 28, 2001, p. W13.

32. Barbara Pachter and Mary Brody, *Complete Business Etiquette Handbook* (Englewood Cliffs, N.J.: Prentice-Hall, 1995), p. 3.

33. Amy Gamerman, "Lunch with Letitia: Our Reporter Minds Her Manners," *Wall Street Journal*, March 3, 1994, p. A14.

34. Ann Marie Sabath, "Meeting Etiquette: Agendas and More," *DECA Dimensions*, January/February 1994, p. 8; "Is Etiquette a Core Value?" *Inc.*, May 2004, p. 22.

35. Leila Jason, "Are There Rules of Etiquette for Cell-phone Use?" *Wall Street Journal*, September 10, 2001, p. R16; Dana May Casperson, "Tactfully Respond to Cell Phone Intrusion," *Selling*, April 2005, p. 5.

36. Dana May Casperson, "Break Those Bad Cell-phone Habits," *Selling*, January 2002, p. 9.

37. Gene Veith, "Curse of the Foul Mouth," *Wall Street Journal*, January 24, 2003, p. D1; Tara Parker-Pope and Kyle Pope, "When #@%&@ Is—and Isn't—Appropriate," *Wall Street Journal Sunday*, featured in *The News & Observer*, January 21, 2001, p. D4.

38. Barbara Moses, *Career Intelligence* (San Francisco: Berrett-Koehler, 1997), p. 175.

39. Nancy K. Austin, "What Do America Online and Dennis Rodman Have in Common?" *Inc.*, July 1997, p. 54.

40. Marilyn Vos Savant, "Ask Marilyn," *Parade*, May 30, 2002, p. 19.

41. Stephanie G. Sherman, *Make Yourself Memorable* (New York: American Management Association, 1996), pp. 3–4; "People in the News," *U.S. News & World Report*, November 8, 1999, p. 12; Ann Landers, "If You've Got Class, Nothing Else Matters," *The News & Observer*, July 11, 1998, p. E2; Carlin Flora, "The Superpowers," *Psychology Today*, May/June 2005, pp. 40–50.

42. David McNally and Karl D. Speak, *Be Your Own Brand* (San Francisco: Berrett-Koehler, 2002), p. 4.

43. Ibid.

44. "The Right Words at the Right Time," *O The Oprah Magazine*, May 2002, p. 202.

Chapter 12

1. Michael Useem and Jerry Useem, "The Board That "Conquered Everest," *Fortune*, October 27, 2003, pp. 73–74. Professor Michael Useem and *Fortune* writer Jerry Useem, with Paul Asel of Upward Bound, are authors of *Nine Original Accounts of How Business Leaders Reached Their Summits*.

2. Robert Kreitner, *Management*, 9th ed. (Boston: Houghton Mifflin, 2004), p. 503.

3. "Stephen Covey Talks About the 8th Habit: Effective Is No Longer Enough," *Training*, February 2005, pp. 17–19.

4. James M. Kouzes and Barry Z. Posner, *The Leadership Challenge*, 3d ed. (San Francisco, Calif.: Jossey-Bass, 2002), pp. 3–12.

5. William M. Pride, Robert J. Hughes, and Jack R. Kapoor, *Business*, 8th ed. (Boston: Houghton Mifflin, 2005), p. 198.

6. "Synergy: Or, We're All in This Together," *Training*, September 1985, pp. 64, 65.

7. Kreitner, *Management*, pp. 447–448.

8. Paul Roberts, "Live from Your Office! It's . . . ," *Fast Company*, October 1999, p. 180, Vicki Lee Parker,

"Durham Plant Is GE's 'Go-To,'" *The News & Observer*, April 22, 2004, p. D1.

9. Kreitner, *Management*, pp. 482–483.

10. Scott Thurm, "Teamwork Raises Everyone's Game," *Wall Street Journal*, November 7, 2005, p. B8.

11. Kreitner, *Management*, pp. 485–486; David Stewart, "True Teamwork," *Health & Healing*, Vol. 6, No 1, 2003, p. 2.

12. Gene Hoffman, "Beware the Superstars Syndrome," *San Jose Mercury News*, April 2, 2000, p. E2.

13. Adapted from a list in Douglas McGregor, *The Human Side of Enterprise* (New York: McGraw-Hill, 1960), pp. 232–235.

14. The Leadership Grid® from *Leadership Dilemmas—Grid Solutions* by Robert R. Blake and Anne Adams McCanse (formerly of the Manager Grid Figure by Robert R. Blake and Jane S. Mouton.) Gulf Publishing Company, p. 29. Copyright ©1991 by Scientific Methods, Inc. Reprinted by permission.

15. Text list of Blake/Mouton descriptive names for leadership styles in grid. From *The New Managerial Grid*, by Robert R. Blake and Jane Srygley Mouton. Houston: Gulf Publishing Company. Copyright ©1978, p. 11. Reprinted by permission of Scientific Methods. Scientific Methods now operates as Grid International, Inc. For information regarding Grid International see "A Proud Legacy of Success" at www.gridinternational.com.

16. Robert R. Blake and Jane Srygley Mouton, "How to Choose a Leadership Style," *Training & Development*, February 1982, pp. 41–42.

17. Reported in Ron Zemke, "What Are High-Achieving Managers Really Like?" *Training/HRD*, February 1979, pp. 35–36. For current information on Teleometrics International see "Who We Are" at www.teleometrics.com.

18. Jay Hall, *The Competence Connection* (The Woodlands, Tex.: Woodstead Press, 1988), p. 77.

19. Material by *Training Magazine*. Copyright 1998 Bill Communications. Reproduced with permission of Bill Communications, via Copyright Clearance Center.

20. Price Pritchett, *Teamwork—The Team Member Handbook* (Dallas, Tex.: Pritchett & Associates Inc., 1992), p. 2.

21. These two dimensions can be measured by the *Leadership Opinion Questionnaire* developed by Edwin A. Fleishman and available from Pearson Performance Solutions (www.pearsonps.com).

22. Brian Tracy, *The 100 Absolutely Unbreakable Laws of Business Success* (San Francisco: Berrett-Koehler, 2000), pp. 138–139.

23. "Making a Nickel Do a Dime's Work," *Training*, April 1994, p. 12.

24. Sue Shellenbarger, "Enter the New Hero: A Boss Who Knows You Have a Life," *Wall Street Journal*, May 8, 1996, p. B1.

25. Tracy, *The 100 Absolutely Unbreakable Laws of Business Success*, pp. 19–20.

26. "Tips for Teams," *Training*, February 1994, p. 14.

27. David G. Baldwin, "How to Win the Blame Game," *Harvard Business Review*, July/August 2001, pp. 1–7 (Reprint RO107C).

28. Kenneth R. Phillips, "The Achilles' Heel of Coaching," *Training & Development*, March 1998, p. 41; Anne Fisher,

"In Praise of Micromanaging," *Fortune*, August 23, 2004, p. 40.

29. Kreitner, *Management*, p. 508.

30. Paul Hersey, *The Situational Leader* (Escondido, Calif.: Center for Leadership Studies, 1984), pp. 29, 30. To obtain current information on the Situational Leadership Model, visit www.situational.com.

31. Ibid., pp. 29–45.

32. Tracy, *The 100 Absolutely Unbreakable Laws of Business Success*, p. 121.

33. Cary Cherniss and Daniel Goleman, *The Emotionally Intelligent Workplace* (San Francisco: Jossey-Bass, 2001), pp. 22–23.

34. Will Schutz, *The Human Element* (San Francisco: Jossey-Bass, 1994), pp. 237–238.

35. Margaret Kaeter, "The Leaders Among Us," *Business Ethics*, July/August 1994, p. 46.

36. J. Oliver Crom, "Every Employee a Leader: Part One," *The Leader*, April 1997, p. 6.

37. Peter Koestenbaum, *Leadership—The Inner Side of Greatness* (San Francisco: Jossey-Bass, 1991), pp. 179–183.

38. Michaele Weissman, "Nerd Alert!" *Wall Street Journal*, May 14, 2001, p. R14; Peter Frost and Sandra Robinson, "The Toxic Handler: Organizational Hero—and Casualty," *Harvard Business Review*, July/August 1999, pp. 97–106.

39. Eleena de Lisser, "Firms with Virtual Environments Appeal to Workers," *Wall Street Journal*, October 5, 1999, p. B2; Gina Imperato, "Real Tools for Virtual Teams," *Fast Company*, July 2000, p. 382.

40. Phillips, "The Achilles' Heel of Coaching," pp. 41–44.

41. Clyde Haberman, "Kinder and Gentler, but Still Rudy," *New York Times Book Review*, October 13, 2002, p. 11.

42. Oren Harari, "Open Doors Behind," *Modern Maturity*, January/February 2002, pp. 49–50.

43. Jerry Useem, "A Manager for All Seasons," *Fortune*, April 30, 2001, pp. 66–72.

Chapter 13

1. Kevin Allen, "NHL Wiped Out," *USA Today*, February 17, 2005, p. C1; Paul D. Staudohar, "The Hockey Lockout of 2004–05," *Monthly Labor Review*, December 2005, pp. 23–29.

2. Cheryl Shavers, "Some Positive Steps That You Can Take to Resolve Conflicts," *San Jose Mercury News*, March 21, 1999, p. E3.

3. Anne Fisher, "Which One Should I Fire? . . . Is My Voice Mail Monitored? . . . and Other Queries," *Fortune*, November 25, 1996, p. 173.

4. Dudley Weeks, *The Eight Essential Steps to Conflict Resolution* (New York: G. P. Putnam's Sons, 1992), p. 7.

5. Ibid., pp. 7–8.

6. Adam Hanft, "The Joy of Conflict," *Inc.*, August 2005, p. 112; Adam Hanft, "Down with Bossocracy" *Inc.*, April 2004, p. 126.

7. Susan M. Heathfield, "Fight for What's Right: Ten Tips to Encourage Meaningful Conflict." [cited 7 February 2006]. Available from www.about.com; INTERNET.

8. Don Wallace and Scott McMurray, "How to Disagree (Without Being Disagreeable)," *Fast Company*, November 1995, p. 146.

9. Robert Kreitner, *Management*, 9th ed. (Boston: Houghton Mifflin, 2004), pp. 544–546.

10. Ibid., pp. 529–530.

11. David Stiebel, "The Myth of Hidden Harmony," *Training*, March 1997, p. 114.

12. Carol Kleiman, "How to Deal with a Co-worker Who's Getting on Your Nerves," *San Jose Mercury News*, October 3, 1999, p. PC1.

13. "Assertiveness: More Than a Forceful Attitude," *Supervisory Management*, February 1994, p. 3.

14. American Management Association, *Catalog of Seminars* (New York: American Management Association). [cited 1 January 2006]. Available from www.amanet.org; INTERNET.

15. Danny Ertel, "Turning Negotiation into a Corporate Capability." *Harvard Business Review*, May/June 1999, p. 3.

16. Rob Walker, "Take It or Leave It: The Only Guide to Negotiating You Will Ever Need," *Inc.*, August 2003, pp. 65–77.

17. Kurt Salzinger, "Psychology on the Front Lines," *Psychology Today*, May/June 2002, p. 34.

18. David Stiebel, *When Talking Makes Things Worse!* (Dallas: Whitehall & Nolton, 1997), p. 17.

19. Roger Fisher and Alan Sharp, *Getting It Done* (New York: Harper Business, 1998), pp. 81–83.

20. Roger Fisher and William Ury, *Getting to Yes* (New York: Penguin Books, 1981), p. 59.

21. Weeks, *The Eight Essential Steps to Conflict Resolution*, p. 228.

22. Ibid., p. 223.

23. University of North Texas-Dallas: Alternative Dispute Resolution Certificate Brochure, updated 25 March 2002. [cited 22 February 2003]. Available from www.unt.edu/unt-dallas/brochures/adresd.htm; INTERNET.

24. Toddi Gutner, "When It's Time to Do Battle with Your Company," *Business Week*, February 10, 1997, pp. 130–131.

25. Interview with Robert Wehrman, vice president, FedEx Services, August 19, 2000.

26. Roberta J. Burnette, "Walking Out on Wages," *Workforce Management*, August 2005, pp. 12–23.

27. Bureau of Labor Statistics, "Union Members Summary," news release, January 20, 2006. [cited 28 January 2006]. Available from www.bls.gov/news.release/union2.nr0.htm; INTERNET.

28. Andy Meisler, "A High-Stakes Union Fight: Who Will Fold First?" *Workforce Management*, January 2004, p. 28.

29. Ibid., p. 38.

30. Jessica Marquez, "U.S. Unions Act Globally, Benefit Locally," *Workforce Management*, January 30, 2006, p. 333; Andrew Bibby, "The Wal-Martization of the World, UNI, Global Response," March 2005. [cited 8 February 2006]. Available from www.global-unions.org; INTERNET; Andrew Bibby, "UNI Supports CWA Campaign on Safety for Media Workers in War Zones," April 5, 2004. [cited 8 February 2006]. Available from www.global-unions.org; INTERNET.

31. Marquez, "U.S. Unions Act Globally, Benefit Locally," p. 334.

32. Hilary Stout, "The Key to a Lasting Marriage: Combat," *Wall Street Journal*, November 4, 2004, p. D1.

33. Jeffrey, Zaslow, "Ready to Pop the Question? Hold Off Until You've Done the Interrogation," *Wall Street Journal*, February 6, 2003, p. D1.

34. Phillip C. McGraw, "Couples Combat: The Great American Pastime," *O The Oprah Magazine,* August 2002, p. 43.

35. Ibid.; "How To," *Training & Development*, April 1998, p. 10; Jeffrey Zaslow, "Divorce Makes a Comeback," *Wall Street Journal*, January 14, 2003, pp. D1, D10; Zaslow, "Ready to Pop the Question?" p. D1.

Chapter 14

1. Anne Marie-Chaker, "Stressed Parents Report On-the-Job Problems," *Wall Street Journal*, March 23, 2004, p. D2; "Community, Families & Work Program: PASS Report." [cited 9 February 2006]. Available from www.bcfwp.org; INTERNET.

2. Michelle Conlin, "Meditation," *Business Week*, August 30, 2004, p. 137.

3. Michelle Conlin, "The Big Squeeze on Workers," *Business Week*, May 13, 2002, pp. 96–97.

4. Arnold A. Lazarus and Clifford N. Lazarus, *The 60-Second Shrink* (San Luis Obispo, Calif.: Impact, 1997), pp. 86–87; Howard I. Glazer, *Getting in Touch with Stress Management* (American Telephone and Telegraph, 1988), p. 2.

5. Richard Laliberte, "Lighten Up," *New Choices*, June 2001, p. 65.

6. James E. Loehr, *Stress for Success* (New York: Times Books, 1997), p. 4.

7. Harold H. Bloomfield and Robert K. Cooper, *The Power of 5* (Emmaus, Pa.: Rodale Press, 1995), p. 18.

8. Cora Daniels, "The Last Taboo," *Fortune*, October 28, 2002, p. 138.

9. Price Pritchett and Ron Pound, *The Stress of Organizational Change* (Dallas, Tex.: Pritchett, 2005), pp. 3–8.

10. Craig Brod, *Technostress: The Human Cost of the Computer Revolution* (Reading, Mass.: Addison-Wesley, 1984), p. 16.

11. Jane Bozarth, "In Print," *Training*, August 2001, p. 60.

12. Carol Hymowitz, "Can Workplace Stress Get Worse?" *Wall Street Journal*, January 16, 2001, p. B1.

13. Brod, *Technostress*, p. 17; "Factsheet: Internet Addiction." [cited 10 February 2006]. Available from www.childnet-int.org/downloads/factsheet_addiction.pdf; INTERNET.

14. David Shenk, *Data Smog—Surviving the Information Glut* (San Francisco: HarperEdge, 1997), p. 31.

15. Karin Rives, "Home Workers Feel the Pain," *The News & Observer*, July 18, 2004, p. E1; Albert R. Karr, "An Ergo-Unfriendly Home Office Can Hurt You," *Wall Street Journal*, September 30, 2003, p. D6.

16. "Sound Bites," *UC Berkeley Wellness Letter*, September 2004, pp. 6–7; Jane Spencer, "Behind the Music: IPods and Hearing Loss," *Wall Street Journal*, January 10, 2006, p. D1.

17. Sue Shellenbarger, "The American Way of Work (More!) May Be Easing Up," *Wall Street Journal*, January 19, 2000, p. B1; Amy Joyce, "At the Breaking Point, Passing up Vacation, *Washington Post*, May 22, 2005, p. F6;

"Ethic Creates a Nation of Workaholics," *Daily Press*, September 6, 2004, p. A7.

18. Sonja Steptoe, "Ready, Set, Relax!" *Time*, October 27, 2003, pp 38–41; Sue Shellenbarger, "Are Saner Workloads the Unexpected Key to More Productivity?" *Wall Street Journal*, March 10, 2000, p. B1.

19. Kenneth Labich, "Psycho Bosses from Hell," *Fortune*, March 18, 1996, p. 123; Vanessa Ho, "Companies Get the Message That Happy Workers Help Bottom Line," *Roanoke Times & WorldNews*, November 13, 1995, p. E6.

20. Edith Weiner, "The Fast Approaching Future," *Retail Issues Letter*, July 1994, p. 3.

21. Art Ulene, *Really Fit Really Fast* (Encino. Calif.: Health-Points, 1996), pp. 56–58.

22. John Carpi, "Stress: It's Worse Than You Think," *Psychology Today*. [cited 16 February 2006]. Available from www.psychologytoday.com; INTERNET.

23. Loehr, *Stress for Success*, pp. 179, 183; Eilene Zimmerman, "Sleep Less, Feel Better," *Sales & Marketing Management*, June 2004, p. 49.

24. "Nappers of the World, Lie Down and Be Counted," *Training*, May 2000, p. 24; Donald D. Hensrud, "The Mayo Clinic Doctor," *Fortune*, April 2, 2001, p. 202.

25. Robert Tomsho, "Exercise Levels Drop for Teenage Women," *Wall Street Journal*, September 5, 2002, p. D3; "What's News," *Wall Street Journal*, April 8, 2002, p. A1.

26. Jennifer Derryberry, "The Joy of Breathing," *Spirituality & Health*, July/August 2004, pp. 78–79.

27. Robert J. Davis, "Breathing and Hypertension," *Wall Street Journal*, April 27, 2004, p. D4.

28. Joel Stein, "Just Say Om," *Time*, August 4, 2003, p. 50.

29. Ibid., pp. 47–56; Richard J. Davidson et al., "Alterations in Brain and Immune Function Produced by Mindfulness Meditation, *Psychosomatic Medicine*, received for publication December 2002. [cited 16 February 2006]. Available from www.psychosomaticmedicine.org; INTERNET; "Mindfulness Meditation," *Spirituality & Health*, March/April 2004, p. 74; Michelle Conlin, "Meditation," *Business Week*, August 30, 2004, pp. 136–137.

30. Conlin, "Meditation," pp. 136–137.

31. Megan Satosus, "No Fun of Any Kind," *CIO Magazine*, May 2, 2005. [cited 16 February 2006.] Available from www.cio.com; INTERNET.

32. Beverly Kaye and Sharon Jordan-Evans, "Ain't We Got Fun?" *Fast Company, Talent & Careers Resource Center*. [cited 16 February 2006]. Available from www.fastcompany.com; INTERNET.

33. Ann McGee-Cooper, *You Don't Have to Go Home from Work Exhausted* (New York: Bantam Books, 1992), pp. 52–53.

34. Ester Buchholz, "The Call of Solitude," *Psychology Today*, January/February 1998, pp. 50–54.

35. Kim Wright Wiley, "Reaching Your Peak," *Selling Power*, March 2004, pp. 56–61.

36. Sheila Hutman Jaelline Jaffe, Robert Segal, Heather Larson, and Lisa Dumke, "Stress: Signs and Symptoms, Causes and Effects." [cited 11 February 2006]. Available from www.helpguide.org/mental/stress_signs.htm; INTERNET.

37. Leila Abbound, "Mental Illness Said to Affect One-Quarter of Americans," *Wall Street Journal*, June 7, 2005, p. D1.

38. Douglas A. Bernstein, Louis A. Penner, Alison Clark-Stewart, and Edward J. Roy, *Psychology*, 6th ed. (Boston: Houghton Mifflin, 2003), pp. 565–569.

39. Charles B. Clayman, *Family Medical Guide* (New York: Random House, 1994), p. 325.

40. Ibid., p. 325.

41. Paul Raeburn, "Mental Health: Better Benefits Won't Break the Bank," *Business Week*, December 17, 2001, p. 100; Elyse Tanouye, "Mental Illness: A Rising Workplace Cost," *Wall Street Journal,* June 13, 2001, p. B1.

42. Clayman, *Family Medical Guide*, pp. 321–322.

43. John Swartzberg, "Speaking of Wellness," *UC Berkeley Wellness Letter*, November 2002, p. 3.

44. Sharon Begley, "New Hope for Battling Depression Relapses," *Wall Street Journal*, January 6, 2004, p. D1.

45. Bernstein, *et al.*, *Psychology*, p. 495.

46. *Employee Burnout: America's Newest Epidemic* (Minneapolis, Minn.: Northwestern National Life Insurance Co., 1991), p. 17.

47. Rebecca Segall, "Online Shrinks: The Inside Story," *Psychology Today*, May/June 2000, pp. 38–43; Joshua Rosenbaum, "The Typing Cure," *Wall Street Journal*, September 16, 2002, p. R10.

48. Jared Sandberg, "Workaholics Use Fibs, Subterfuge to Stay Connected on Vacation," *Wall Street Journal*, August 25, 2004, p. B1.

49. Ibid.; Amy Joyce, "At the Breaking Point Passing Up Vacation"; Nadine Heintz, "Breaking Away," *Inc.*, October 2004, p. 44; Karin Rives, "Vacation Starvation," *The News & Observer*, June 22, 2003, pp. E1, E12.

50. Sue Shellenbarger, "Taking an 'Inner Vacation': How to Relax When You're Chained to Your Desk," *Wall Street Journal*, October 9, 2003, p. D1.

51. Paul Glader, "From the Maker of Effexor: Campus Forums on Depression," *Wall Street Journal*, October 10, 2002, pp. B1–B3; Suein L. Hwang, "Feeling Blah at Work? It May Be Your Job, Not Your Prescription," *Wall Street Journal*, September 18, 2002, p. B1; Rosenbaum, "The Typing Cure," p. R10; Raeburn, "Mental Health," p. 110.

Chapter 15

1. Carol Hymowitz, "The New Diversity," *Wall Street Journal*, November 14, 2005, pp. R1–R3.

2. Ibid.

3. Robert Kreitner, *Management*, 9th ed. (Boston: Houghton Mifflin, 2004), pp. 78–79.

4. Marilyn Loden and Judy B. Rosener, *Workforce America!* (Homewood, Ill.: Business One Irwin, 1991), pp. 114–115.

5. Ibid., p. 21.

6. Douglas A. Bernstein, Louis A. Penner, Alison Clarke-Stewart, and Edward J. Roy, *Psychology*, 6th ed. (Boston: Houghton Mifflin, 2003), p. 666.

7. D. Stanley Eitzen and Maxine Baca Zinn, *In Conflict and Order* (Boston: Allyn & Bacon, 2001), p. 237.

8. Ibid.

9. Lewis Brown Griggs and Lente-Louise Louw, *Valuing Diversity* (New York: McGraw-Hill, 1995), pp. 3–4, 150–151.

10. Ibid., p. 151.

11. Yochi J. Dreazen, "U.S. Racial Wealth Gap Remains Huge," *Wall Street Journal*, March 14, 2000, p. A2.

12. Mike Harris, "Newman Going Strong," *The News & Observer*, February 5, 2005, p. C8.

13. Sue Shellenbarger, "Baby Boomers Already Are Getting Agitated over Age-Bias Issues," *Wall Street Journal*, May 30, 2001, p. B1.

14. Anne Fisher, "Finally! A Ray of Hope for Job Seekers over 50," *Fortune*, December 10, 2001, p. 278.

15. Darren Dahl, "A New Wrinkle on Age Bias," *Inc.*, July 2005, p. 36; Kathy Chen, "Age-Discrimination Complaints Rose 8.7% in 2001 amid Overall Increase in Claims," *Wall Street Journal*, February 25, 2002, p. B13.

16. Richard Hadden and Bill Catlette, *Contented Cows Give Better Milk*. [cited 14 November 2005]. Available from www.contentedcows.com; INTERNET.

17. Sue Shellenbarger, "Gray Is Good: Employers Make Efforts to Retain Older, Experienced Workers," *Wall Street Journal*, December 1, 2005 p. D1. Peter Coy, "Surprise! The Graying of the Workforce Is Better News Than You Think," *Business Week*, June 27, 2005, p. 78.

18. Craig Calhoun, Donald Light, and Suzanne Keller, *Sociology*, 6th ed. (New York: McGraw-Hill, 1994), p. 241.

19. Nicholas D. Kristof, "Is Race Real?" *New York Times*, July 11, 2003; Robert S. Boynton, "Color Us Invisible," *New York Times Book Review*, August 17, 1997, p. 13.

20. Stephen Magagini, "A Race Free Consciousness," *The News & Observer*, November 23, 1997, pp. A25–A26.

21. Carol Mukhopadhyay and Rosemary C. Henze, "How Real Is Race? Using Anthropology to Make Sense of Human Diversity," *Phi Delta Kappan*, May 2003, p. 675.

22. John McWhorter, "We're Not Ready to Think Outside the Box on Race," *Wall Street Journal*, March 28, 2002, p. A20; G. Pascal Zachary, "A Mixed Future," *Wall Street Journal*, January 1, 2000, p. R43. A recent book entitled *One Drop of Blood—The American Misadventure of Race* by Scott L. Malcomson provides an excellent review of America's separatist history.

23. Mukhopadhyay and Henze, "How Real Is Race? pp. 673–676.

24. Robert Kreitner, *Management*, 8th ed. (Boston: Houghton Mifflin, 2001), p. 117.

25. Daniel Golden, "A Test of Faith," *Wall Street Journal*, January 7, 2006, p. A1; "Narrow-Minded or Protecting One's Mission?" *Wall Street Journal*, January 16, 2006, p. A15.

26. Kris Maher, "Disabled Face Scarcer Jobs, Data Show," *Wall Street Journal*, October 5, 2005, p. D1.

27. Ibid.

28. Sue Shellenbarger, "A Mid Gay Marriage Debate: Companies Offer More Benefits to Same-Sex Couples," *Wall Street Journal*, March 18, 2004, p. D1; Barbara Rose, "Policies to Accommodate Gays Draw Scrutiny," *The News & Observer*, July 3, 2005, p. E12; Rachel Emma Silverman, "Wall Street, a New Push to Recruit Gay Students," *Wall Street Journal*, February 9, 2000, p. B1.

29. Robert Tomsho, "School & Efforts to Protect Gays Face Opposition," *Wall Street Journal*, February 20, 2003, p. B1.

30. Michael L. Wheeler, *Diversity: Business Rationale and Strategies* (New York: The Conference Board, 1995), p. 9.

31. Chuck Salter, "Diversity Without the Excuses," *Fast Company*, September 2002, p. 44.

32. Jessica Marquez, "Survey Says Diversity Contributes to the Bottom Line," *Workforce Management*, November 18, 2005. [cited 23 February 2006]. Available from www.workforce.com; INTERNET.

33. Fay Hansen, "Microsoft R & D Seeks Global Tech Talent, Not Bargains," *Workforce Management*, July 2005, p. 39; Kreitner, *Management*, p. 80; "Toyota's Charge Toward the Pinnacle of the Sport," *Canadian Grand Prix Program 2002*, p. 54; Robin Townsley Arcus, "World Market," *The Urban Hiker*, October 2000, p. 34.

34. *101 Tools for Tolerance* (Montgomery, Ala.: Southern Poverty Law Center), pp. 4–7.

35. Gail Johnson, "Time to Broaden Diversity," *Training*, September 2004, p. 16; Adapted from Leone E. Wynter, "Do Diversity Programs Make a Difference?" *Wall Street Journal*, December 4, 1996, p. B1.

36. "Time to Diversify," *Sales & Marketing Management*, May 2002, p. 62.

37. Jonathan Hickman, "America's 50 Best Companies for Minorities," *Fortune*, July 8, 2002, pp. 110–120.

38. Ibid., p. 118; Dean Foust, "Coke: Say Good-Bye to the Good Ol' Boy Culture," *Business Week*, May 29, 2000, p. 58.

39. Gail Johnson, "Lockheed Martin Corporation—Focusing on People Development," *Training*, March 2005, pp. 39–40.

40. Kreitner, *Management*, pp. 334–335.

41. Terry Eastland, "Endgame for Affirmative Action," *Wall Street Journal*, March 28, 1996, p. A15; John J. Miller, "Out of One Set of Preferences, Many . . . and Many New Debates," *New York Times Book Review*, March 27, 2002, p. A16; Roger Pilon, "The Complexities of Unfair Discrimination," *Wall Street Journal*, December 13, 2002, p. A17.

42. Miller, "Out of One Set of Preferences," p. A16.

43. Roger O. Crockett, "How to Narrow the Great Divide," *Business Week*, July 14, 2003, p. 104; Sharon S. Brehm, Saul M. Kassin, and Steven Fein, *Social Psychology*, 5th ed. (Boston: Houghton Mifflin, 2002), pp. 478–480.

44. R. Roosevelt Thomas, Jr., "From Affirmative Action to Affirming Diversity," *Harvard Business Review*, March/April 1990, p. 114.

45. "The Court's Social Agenda," *Wall Street Journal*, December 3, 2002, p. A22; Ward Connerly and Edward Blum, "Do the Right Thing," *Wall Street Journal*, December 4, 2002, p. A18; Ronald Dworkin, "Keeping on Course with Affirmative Action," *The News & Observer*, April 22, 2001, p. A31; Robert L. Mathis and John H. Jackson, *Human Resource Management*, 10th ed. (Manson, Ohio: Thomson South-Western, 2003), pp. 144–146; Daniel Golden, "Buying Your Way into College," *Wall Street Journal*, March 12, 2003, p. D1; Adam Wolfsen, "What Makes a Difference," *Wall Street Journal*, February 26, 2003, p. D10.

46. Dworkin, "Keeping on Course with Affirmative Action," p. A31.

47. Elizabeth Schulte, "Can We End Bigotry Through Education?" *Socialist Worker*, July 20, 2001, p. 9; "Bush Marks Black History Month with Call to End Bigotry," [cited 25 February 2006]. Available from www.eyewitnessnewstv.

com/global/story; INTERNET; Robert Epstein, "In Her Own Words," *Psychology Today*, May/June 2002, pp. 40–42.

Chapter 16

1. Nadine Heintzk, "For Rolling Up Her Sleeves," *Inc.*, April 2004, pp. 128–129.
2. Ibid.
3. Sue Shellenbarger, "Move Over, Mom: Research Suggests Dad's Role Sometimes Matters More," *Wall Street Journal*, June 12, 2003, p. D1.
4. Wendy Kaminer, "Sexual Politics, Continued," *New York Times Book Review*, March 23, 1997, p. 12.
5. Michelle Conlin, "The New Gender Gap," *Business Week*, May 26, 2003, pp. 75–82.
6. Sue Shellenbarger, "Number of Women Managers Rises," *Wall Street Journal*, September 30, 2003, p. D1.
7. Robert Bly, *Iron John* (Reading, Mass.: Addison-Wesley, 1990), p. iv.
8. Sue Shellenbarger, "For Harried Workers in the 21st Century, Six Trends to Watch," *Wall Street Journal*, December 29, 1999, p. B1.
9. Bonnie Erbe, "Pay Equity, Corporate Style," *Working Woman*, February 2000, p. 22.
10. "A Salary Gap Remains Between Genders, Census Results Indicate," *Wall Street Journal*, March 25, 2003, p. D1; Charles J. Whalen, "Closing the Pay Gap," *Business Week*, August 28, 2000, p. 38.
11. Gene Koretz, "She's a Woman, Offer Her Less," *Business Week*, May 7, 2001, p. 34.
12. Gale Duff-Bloom, "Women in Retailing—Is There a Glass Ceiling?" *Retailing Issues Letter*, Center for Retailing Studies, Texas A&M University, May 1996, pp. 1–4; Margaret Hefferman, "The Female CEO," *Fast Company*, August 2002, pp. 60–61.
13. Anna Fels, "Do Women Lack Ambition," *Harvard Business Review*, April 2004, pp. 7–8.
14. "The Emancipated Organization," *Harvard Business Review*, September 2002, pp. 1–3 (Reprint F0209B). (This article features an interview with Kim Campbell, Canada's first female prime minister.)
15. "Women Taking Care of Business," *Roanoke Times & World-News*, May 13, 1995, p. A16.
16. Sally Harris, "Research Finds Work Not 'Haven' from Home," *Spectrum*, February 21, 2003, p. 1.
17. Tony Schwartz, "While the Balance of Power Has Already Begun to Shift, Most Male CEOs Still Don't Fully Get It," *Fast Company*, December 1999, pp. 362–366.
18. Judith S. Nulevitz, "The Mommy Trap," *New York Times Book Review*, February 20, 2005, pp. 1, 12–13.
19. Sylvia Ann Hewlett, "Executive Women and the Myth of Having It All," *Harvard Business Review*, April 2002, pp. 5–11; Margaret Heffernan, "The Female CEO," *Fast Company*, August 2002, pp. 58–66.
20. Dorothy Foltz-Gray, "Bread Winning Wives," *Health*, October 2003, pp. 103–107; Sue Shellenbarger, "As Moms Earn More, More Dads Stay Home: How to Make the Switch Work," *Wall Street Journal*, February 20, 2003, p. D1.
21. "Today's Dads: Same Old Parenting Trap," *Business Week*, October 14, 2002, p. 167. (This article summarizes the views of Nicholas Townsend, author of *The Package Deal*, a book about the many life/work conflicts men face.)
22. Jeffrey Winters, "The Daddy Track," *Psychology Today*, September/October 2001, p. 17.
23. David Gremillion, "Men's Health Needs a Heartfelt Change," *The News & Observer*, June 17, 2001, p. A31.
24. Jeffrey Zaslow, "Who's the New Guy at Dinner? It's Dad; Laid-Off Fathers Face Tough Job at Home," *Wall Street Journal*, October 2, 2002, p. D1.
25. "Corporate Lullaby: You Two Go Out: The Boss Will Babysit," *Fortune*, January 24, 2000, p. 152.
26. Sue Shellenbarger, "Bob's Mobile Office and Day-Care Center," *Wall Street Journal*, December 26, 2002, p. D1.
27. Kathy Bergen, "Compressed Workweek Pays Off—On 10th Day," *Roanoke Times & World-News*, March 30, 1997, p. B2.
28. Carol Kleiman, "Get Two Workers for the Price of One!" *The News & Observer*, February 26, 2003, p. E14.
29. Michelle Conlin, "The Easiest Commute of All," *Business Week*, December 12, 2005, pp. 78–80.
30. Kris Maher, "Corner Office Shift: Telecommuting Rises in Executive Ranks," *Wall Street Journal*, September 21, 2004, p. B1.
31. Susan B. Garland, "Finally, a Corporate Tip Sheet on Sexual Harassment," *Business Week*, July 13, 1998, p. 39.
32. Deborah Tannen, "The Power of Talk: Who Gets Heard and Why," *Harvard Business Review*, September/October 1995, pp. 129–140.
33. Jayne Tear, "They Just Don't Understand Gender Dynamics," *Wall Street Journal*, November 20, 1995, p. A14; Dianna Booker, "The Gender Gap in Communication," *Training Dimensions* (West Des Moines, Ia.: American Media Incorporated, Fall 1994), p. 1; Jennifer J. Laabs, "Kinney Narrows the Gender Gap," *Personnel Journal*, August 1994, pp. 83–85; Scot Ober, *Contemporary Business Communication*, 5th ed. (Boston: Houghton Mifflin, 2003), pp. 58–59.
34. Tannen, "The Power of Talk," p. 146.
35. Sharon S. Brehm, Saul M. Kassin, and Steven Fein, *Social Psychology*, 5th ed. (Boston: Houghton Mifflin, 2002), pp. 154–156.
36. Anastasi Toufexis, "Coming from a Different Place," *Time*, Fall 1990, p. 66.
37. Kate Kelly and Colleen DeBaise, "Morgan Stanley Settles Bias Suit for $54 Million," *Wall Street Journal*, July 13, 2004, p. A1; Randall Smith, "Salomon Is Told to Pay Broker $3.2 Million," *Wall Street Journal*, December 17, 2002, p. C1; Jodi Kantor, "Tales from the Boom-Boom Room," *New York Times Book Review*, December 22, 2002, p. 7; Mary Stowell and Linda Friedman, "What Women Gained at Salomon Smith Barney," *Business Week*, December 23, 2002, p. 15.
38. Nadine Heintz, "Can I Bring the Kids?" *Inc.*, June 2004, p. 40; Carol Kleiman, "More Companies Are Recognizing That Single Workers Have Lives, Too," *San Jose Mercury News*, May 3, 1998, p. PC1; Sue Shellenbarger, "New Research Helps Families to Assess Flaws in Work Plans," *Wall Street Journal*, May 12, 1999, p. B1; Sue Shellenbarger, "Family-Friendly CEOs Are Changing Cultures at More Workplaces," *Wall Street Journal*, September 15, 1999,

p. B1; Sue Shellenbarger, "Taking On Employers over Family Issues Can Scare Even Victors," *Wall Street Journal*, October 14, 1998, p. B1.

Chapter 17

1. Sue Shellenbarger, "Avoiding the Next Enron: Today's Crop of Soon-to-Be Grads Seeks Job Security," *Wall Street Journal*, February 16, 2006, p. D1.
2. Jeffrey McCraken and Joseph B. White, "Ford Will Shed 28% of Workers in North America," *Wall Street Journal*, January 24, 2006, p. A1.
3. Robert M. Strozier, "The Job of Your Dreams," *New Choices*, April 1998, p. 25.
4. Po Bronson, *What Should I Do with My Life?* (New York: Random House, 2002), p. 365; Patricia Kitchen, "Seeking Your Calling," *The Record*, March 9, 2003, p. D1.
5. Ethan Watters, "Come Here, Work, and Get Out of Here, You Don't Live Here. You Live Someplace Else," *Inc.*, October 30, 2001, pp. 56–61.
6. Diane Brady, "Rethinking the Rat Race," *Business Week*, August 26, 2002, pp. 142–143.
7. Jane Bozarth, "In Print," *Training*, August 2001, p. 60. (This article reviews *Dot. Calm—The Search for Sanity in a Wired World*, a book written by Debra A. Dinnocenzo and Richard B. Swegan.)
8. Sue Shellenbarger, "Keeping Your Career a Manageable Part of Your Life," *Wall Street Journal*, April 12, 1995, p. B1; "Career vs. Family: Companies Respond," *Fortune*, April 28, 1997, p. 22.
9. Jack Canfield, *The Success Principles* (New York: Harper Collins, 2005), p. 3.
10. Mary E. Miller, "The Best Use of Her Time," *The News & Observer*, March 9, 2003, p. D1; Susan Broili, "Potter Exchanges Money for Tranquility," *Chapel Hill Herald*, July 23, 2004, p. 1.
11. Yvonne V. Chabrier, "Focus on Work," *New Age*, 1998, p. 95.
12. Bronson, *What Should I Do with My Life?* pp. 68–72.
13. Marsha Sinetar, *Do What You Love . . . The Money Will Follow* (New York: Dell, 1987), p. 11.
14. Ibid., pp. 11–12.
15. Michael Phillips, *The Seven Laws of Money* (Menlo Park, Calif.: Word Wheel and Random House, 1997), p. 9.
16. Sinetar, *Do What You Love*, pp. 14–15.
17. Sue Shellenbarger, "New Job Hunters Ask Recruiters, Is There a Life After Work?" *Wall Street Journal*, January 29, 1997, p. B1.
18. Carole Kanchier, "Dare to Change Your Job and Your Life in 7 Steps" *Psychology Today*, March/April 2000, pp. 64–67.
19. Suze Orman, "The Pursuit of Cold, Hard Happiness," *O The Oprah Magazine*, March 2004, pp. 54–56; Sharon Begley, "Wealth and Happiness Don't Necessarily Go Hand in Hand," *Wall Street Journal*, August 13, 2004, p. B1.
20. Geoffrey Colvin, "We're a Nation Helpless to Save Ourselves," *Fortune*, April 18, 2005, p. 52.
21. Shakti Gawain, *Creating True Prosperity* (Novato, Calif.: New World Library, 1997), p. 7.
22. Carlin Flora, "Happy Hour," *Psychology Today*, January/February 2005, p. 48.
23. Jonathan Clements, "If You Didn't Save 10% of Your Income This Year, You're Spending Too Much," *Wall Street Journal*, December 22, 2004, p. D1; Jonathan Clements, "Rich, Successful—and Miserable: New Research Probes Midlife Angst," *Wall Street Journal*, October 5, 2005, p. D1.
24. Toddi Gutner, "Talk Now, Retire Happily Later," *Business Week*, April 2, 2001, p. 92.
25. Teri Lammers Prior, "If I Were President . . . ," *Inc.*, April 1995, pp. 56–60.
26. Michael Toms, "Money: The Third Side of the Coin" (interview with Joe Dominguez and Vicki Robin), *New Dimensions*, May/June 1991, p. 7.
27. Susan Smith Jones, "Choose to Be Healthy and Celebrate Life," *New Realities*, September/October 1988, pp. 17–19.
28. Jean P. Fisher, "Healthy Habits Pay Off, Literally," *The News & Observer*, May 16, 2004, p. E1.
29. Toddi Gutner, "A 12-Step Program to Gaining Power," *Business Week*, December 24, 2001, p. 88.
30. Ron Zemke, "Why Organizations Still Aren't Learning," *Training*, September 1999, p. 43.
31. His Holiness the Dalai Lama and Howard C. Cutler, *The Art of Happiness* (New York: Riverhead Books, 1998), pp. 227–228.
32. Sue Shellenbarger, "Working 9 to 2: Taking Steps to Make Part-Time Job Setups More Palatable," *Wall Street Journal*, February 17, 2005, p. D1.
33. Jay T. Knippen, Thad B. Green, and Kurt Sutton, "Asking Not to Be Overworked," *Supervisory Management*, February 1992, p. 6.
34. Art Ulene, *Really Fit Really Fast* (Encino, Calif.: Health-Points, 1996), pp. 198–199.
35. Marilyn Chase, "Weighing the Benefits of Mental-Health Days Against Guilt Feelings," *Wall Street Journal*, September 9, 1996, B1.
36. Sue Shellenbarger, "Slackers, Rejoice: Research Touts the Benefits of Skipping Out on Work," *Wall Street Journal*, March 27, 2003, p. D1.
37. Leo Booth, "When God Becomes a Drug," *Common Boundary*, September/October 1991, p. 30; David N. Elkins, "Spirituality," *Psychology Today*, September/October, 1999, pp. 45–48.
38. Harold H. Bloomfield and Robert K. Cooper, *The Power of 5* (Emmaus, Pa.: Rodale Press, 1995), p. 484.
39. Jerry Adler, "In Search of the Spiritual," *Newsweek*, August 29/September 5, 2005, pp. 47–55.
40. "Making the Spiritual Connection," *Lears*, December 1989, p. 72.
41. Thomas Moore, "Will We Take the Moral Values Challenge?" *Spirituality & Health*, January/February 2005, pp. 10–11.
42. Robert Bolton and Dorothy Grover Bolton, *People Styles at Work* (New York: AMACOM, 1996), pp. 110–111.
43. Rachel Emma Silverman, "More Chaplains Take Ministering into the Workplace," *Wall Street Journal*, November 27, 2001, p. B1.
44. G. Paul Zachary, "The New Search for Meaning in Meaningless Work," *Wall Street Journal*, January 9, 1997, p. B1.

45. Daniel H. Pink, A Whole New Mind (New York: River-head Books, 2005), p. 52.

46. Kevin Helliker, "Body and Spirit: Why Attending Religious Services May Benefit Health,"*Wall Street Journal*, May 3, 2005, p. D1.

47. Sara Schaefer Munoz, "The Food Pyramid Gets Personalized," *Wall Street Journal*, April 20, 2005, p. D1; "Johanns Reveals USDA's Steps to a Healthier You." [cited 24 February 2006]. Available from www.mypyramid.gov; INTERNET.

48. Paul Raeburn, "Why We're So Fat," *Business Week*, October 21, 2002, pp. 112–114; Sara Schaefer Munoz, "New U.S. Diet Guide Focuses on Calories, Exercise," *Wall Street Journal* January 12, 2005, p. D4; Nancie Hellmich, "Obesity on Track as No. 1 Killer," *USA Today*, March 10, 2004, p. A1.

49. Cassandra Wrightson, "Snacks Worth Their Salt," *Health*, June 2001, p. 52.

50. Ulene, *Really Fit Really Fast*, pp. 20–21; Robert Langreth, "Every Little Bit Helps," *Wall Street Journal*, May 1, 2000, p. R5. Tara Parker-Pope, "Health Matters," *Wall Street Journal*, August 9, 2004, p. R5.

51. John Swartzberg, "Exercise: It's Not Just Physical," *UC Berkeley Wellness Letter*, November 2002, p. 3.

52. Robert A. Gleser, *The Healthmark Program for Life* (New York: McGraw-Hill, 1988), p. 147.

53. *Fitness Fundamentals* (Washington, D.C.: Department of Health and Human Services, 1988), p. 2.

54. Stephen R. Covey, *The Seven Habits of Highly Effective People* (New York: Simon & Schuster, 1989), p. 46.

55. James Fadiman, *Be All That You Are* (Seattle: Westlake Press, 1986), p. 25.

56. Mike Hernacki, *The Ultimate Secret of Getting Absolutely Everything You Want* (New York: Berkley Books, 1988), p. 35.

57. Adapted from Bloomfield and Cooper, *The Power of 5*, pp. 492–493.

58. Mary Lou Quinlan, "Just Ask a Women," *Fast Company*, July 2003, p. 50.

59. Ibid.

60. Just Ask a Woman Brand Consultants, Content Creators, Problem Solvers." [cited on 1 March 2006]. Available from www.justaskawoman.com; INTERNET.

CREDITS

Career Corner Credits

Chapter 1: Louis S. Richman, "How to get Ahead in America," *Fortune,* May 16, 1994, pp. 46-54; Ronald Henkoff, "Winning the New Career Game,: *Fortune,* July 12, 1993, pp. 46-49.

Chapter 2: Joann S. Lublin, "You Blew the Interview, but You Can Correct Some of the Blunders," *Wall Street Journal,* December 5, 2000, p. B1; Anne Faircloth, "How to Recover from a Firing," *Fortune,* December 7, 1998, p. 239; Chris Serres, "They Want to Get Inside Your Head," *News & Observer,* May 6, 2001, p 1E; "Ask Annie; Knowing When It's Time to Quit, and False Promises," *Fortune,* February 7, 2000, p. 210.

Chapter 3: Barry L. Reece and Gerald L. Manning, *Supervision and Leadership in Action* (New York: Glencoe, 1990); Camille Wright Miller, "Working It Out," *Roanoke Times & World-News,* July 17, 1994, p. F-3.

Chapter 4: www.goaskalice.columbia.edu/1202.html, accessed 11/9/2005.

Chapter 5: Hal Lancaster, "You Have Your Values, How Do You Identify Your Employer's?" *Wall Street Journal,* April 8, 1997. p.B1. Sue Shellenbarger, "How to Find Out if You're going to Hate A New Job Before You Agree to Take It," *Wall Street Journal,* June 13, 2002, p.D1. Camille Wright Miller, "Do Soul-Searching Before You Accept Job," *The Roanoke Times,* June 9, 2004, p. B2.

Chapter 6: Joann S. Lublin, " Getting Your Company to Take You Back After a Dot-Com fling," *Wall Street Journal,* June 5, 2001. p. BI.

Chapter 7: Carol Kleiman, "The Move to Telecommuting," *San Jose Mercury News,* April 16, 2000, p. PC1; Carol Kleiman, "Work/Life Programs Now Essential, Not a Frill, Consulting Firm Says," *San Jose Mercury News,* April 2, 2000, p. PC1.

Chapter 8: Excerpt adapted from Camille Wright Miller, "Self-Evaluation Painful, But It's Valuable," *The Roanoke Times,* November 16, 2003, p. B1.

Chapter 9: Glen O. Gabbard, "Are All Psychotherapies Equally Effective?" *Menninger Letter,* January 1995, pp. 1-2; "Fact About: Anxiety Disorders," published by Carrier Foundation, Belle Mead, N. J.

Chapter 10: Mitchell Schnurman, "Kissing Up: It Works. . . . But Only If You Mean It," *Roanoke Times & World-News,* September 28, 1993, p. E1.

Chapter 11: "How Much Can Employer Dictate Your Lifestyle?" *San Jose Mercury News,* May 2, 1993, pp. 1 PC and 2 PC; Susan Barciela, "Looks and Dress Still Count, Though the Lawyers Might Argue," *Roanoke Times & World-News,* June 19, 1993, p. D2; Susan Bixler, "Your Professional Presence," *Training Dimensions,* Vol. 9, No. 1, 1994, p.1.

Chapter 12: Timothy D. Schellhardt, "To Be a Star Among Equals, Be a Team Player," *Wall Street Journal,* April 20, 1994, p. B1.

Chapter 13: Excerpt adapted from Joann S. Lublin, "Before You Say Yes, Look for the Signs of a Bad Boss Ahead," in the *Wall Street Journal,* November 29, 2005, p. B1.

Chapter 14: Based on Ann Landers, "Maybe It's Time to Change Jobs," *Roanoke Times & World-News,* September 1994; Camille Wright Miller, "'Prime' Is Performance, Attitude Issue," *The Roanoke Times,* September 22, 1996, p. B2.

Chapter 16: Adapted from Perri Capell, "Strategies for Advancement," *Wall Street Journal,* October 31, 2005, p. R2.

Critical Thinking Challenge Credits

Chapter 1
p. 10: Adapted from Marshall Goldsmith, "Nice Guys Can Finish First," *Fast Company,* November 2004, p. 123.

Chapter 2
p. 42: Susan Scott, *Fierce Conversations* (New York: Viking, 2002), pp. 156-157. Chapter 7 is entitled "Let Silence Do the Heavy Lifting."

Chapter 4
p. 90: Oprah Winfrey, "You Are the Dream," *O, The Oprah Magazine,* March 2001, p. 39.

Chapter 5
p. 112: Adapted from Jack Canfield, *The Success Principles* (New York: Harper Collins, 2005), pp. 32-33.

Total Person Insight Credits

Chapter 1
p. 6: Harry E. Chambers, *The Bad Attitude Survival Guide* (Reading, Mass.: Addison-Wesley, 1998), p.1; p. 10: Anne Fisher, "Success Secret: A High Emotional IQ," *Fortune,* October 26, 1998, p. 293; p. 12: William Raspberry, "Topmost Priority: Jobs," *Washington Post,* (n.d.), 1977; p. 15: James Baughman quote from Frank Rose, "A New Age for Business?" *Fortune,* October 8, 1990, p. 162.

Chapter 2
p. 30: Eric Maisel, *20 Communication Tips @ Work,* Novato, CA: New World Library, 2001, pp. 12-13

Chapter 3
p. 59: Excerpt adapted from David W. Merrill and Roger H. Reid, *Personal Styles and Effective Performance* (Radnor, PA:

Chilton Book Company 1981) p. 1; p. 75: Alan Horowitz, "How to Be a Winner," *Selling Power*, November/ December 2004, p. 80.

Chapter 4
p. 90: Don Miguel Ruiz, *The Four Agreements,* San Rafael, CA: Amber-Allen Publishing, 1997, p. 12; p. 93: Fran Cox and Louis Cox, *A Conscious Life* (Berkeley, Calif.: Conari Press, 1996), p. 12.

Chapter 5
p. 110: Roy Chitwood, "Still Trying to Slip Past Gatekeepers? Forget it!" *Value-Added Selling* 21, December 26, 2003, p. 1.; p. 118: William J. Bennet, "Educating for National Leadership: A 20 Year Anniversary Seminar," *Imprimis,* November 2002, p.4; p. 119: Dan Rice and Craig Dreilinger, "Rights and Wrongs of Ethics Training," *Training & Development,* May 1990, p. 105; p. 123: www.josephsoninstitute.org, 7/12/01.

Chapter 6
p. 135: Price Pritchett, *New Work Habits for the Next Millennium* (Dallas, Tex.: EPS Solutions, 1999), p. 2; p. 143: His Holiness The Dalai Lama and Howard C. Cutler, *The Art of Happiness* (New York: Riverhead Books, 1998), p. 37.

Chapter 7
p. 156: Stephen R. Covey, *The 7 Habits of Highly Effective People,* Franklin Covey Company, Salt Lake City, Utah, August 1990, p. 185; p. 171: Joan Borysenko, *Minding the Body, Mending the Mind,* New York: Bantam New Age Books, 1987, p.22.

Chapter 8
p. 183: Albert J. Bernstein and Sydney Craft Rozen, "Why Don't They Get It?" *Executive Female,* March/April 1995, p. 33; p. 190: Beverly Engel, " Making Amends" *Psychology Today*, July/August 2002, p. 40; p. 195: Terry Mizrahi, President, National Association of Social Workers, "How Can you Learn to Trust Again?" *Psychology Today.*

Chapter 9
p. 208: James Georges, The Not-So-Stupid Americans," *Training,* July 1994, p. 90; p. 210: Daniel Goleman, ed., *Healing Emotions* (Boston: Shambhala Publications, Inc., 1997), p. 84; p. 215: Pema Chodron, "The Answers to Anger and Other Strong Emotions," *Shambhala Sun*, March 2005, p. 32.; p. 222: Gerard Egan, *You and Me* (Monterey, Calif.: Brooks/Cole, 1977), p. 73.

Chapter 10
p. 235: Jack Canfield, *The Success Principles* (New York: Harper Collins, 2005), p. 343; p. 240: Malcolm Boyd, "Volunteering Thanks," *Modern Maturity,* May/June 1997, p. 72.

Chapter 11
p. 255: Susan Bixler and Nancy Nix-Rice, *The New Professional Image* (Holbrook, Mass.: Adams Media Corporation , 1997), p. 3; p. 267: Judith Martin, "Low Income Is Not Low-Class," *Roanoke Times & World-News,* March 13, 1988, p. E 10. p. 291: Daniel Goleman, "What Makes a Leader?" *Harvard Business Review*, November/December, 1998, p. 94.

Chapter 12
p. 283: Oren Harari, *The Leadership Secrets of Colin Powell,* New York: McGraw-Hill, 2002, p. 256; p. 285: Michael Crom, "Building Trust in the Workplace," *The Leader,* October 1998, p.6; p. 293: John C. Maxwell, *The 17 Essential Qualities of a*

Team Player, Nashville, TN: Thomas Nelson Publishers 2002, pp. 13-14.

Chapter 13
p. 313: Roger Fisher and William Ury, *Getting to Yes* (New York: Penguin Books, 1981), p.4.

Chapter 14
p. 330: Price Pritchett and Ron Pound, *The Stress of Organizational Change* (Dallas: Pritchett, LP, 2005); p. 336: Carol S. Pearson, "Breaking Out of the Time Bind," *The Inner Edge,* December 1999/January 2000, p.3; p. 344: Michael Toms, "In Search of Time: An Interview with Jacob Needleman," *The Inner Edge,* December 1999/January 2000, p. 7.

Chapter 15
p. 357: Keith H. Hammonds, "Difference Is Power," *Fast Company,* July 2000, p. 260; p. 361: Vernon E. Jordan, Jr., "Look Outward, Black America," *Wall Street Journal,* October 27, 1995, p. A14; p. 359: "A Beautiful Voice and Cultural Bridge," *CBS News*, January 29, 2006, accessed at www.cbsnews.com/stories/2006/01/28/Sunday on January 29, 2006; p. 369: Lewis Brown Griggs and Lente-Louise Louw, *Valuing Diversity: New Tools for a New Reality* (New York: McGraw-Hill, Inc., 1995), p.9.

Chapter 16
p. 385: Shoshana Zuboff, "Career Taxidermy," *Fast Company*, June 2004, p. 103; p. 389: Debra E. Meyerson and Joyce K. Fletcher, "A Modest Manifesto for Shattering the Glass Ceiling," *Harvard Business Review,* January/February 2000, p. 136; p. 400: Alice Sargeant, *The Androgynous Manager,* New York American Management Association, 1983, p. 37.

Chapter 17
p. 411: Ralph Fiennes, "Success – An Owner's Guide," *O, the Oprah Magazine,* September 2001, p. 51; p. 412: Cheryl Shavers, "Set a Pace That Lets You Enjoy the Fruits of Your Labor," *San Jose Mercury News,* October 19, 1997, p. 30; p. 416: Polly LaBarre, "Money Therapy 101," *Fast Company*, February 2002, pp. 116-119. p. 422: "Teaching Tolerance, Spring 2005, p. 28. p. 418: Julie Connelly, "How to Choose Your Next Career," *Fortune,* February 6, 1995, p. 45; p. 424: Patricia Sellers, "Don't Call Me Slacker!" *Fortune,* December 12, 1994, p. 196.

Human Relations in Action
Chapter 1
p. 7: Excerpt adapted from Ronald Alsop, "Back on Top," Wall Street Journal, July 21, 2005, p. A.1; p. 16: Adapted from Ryan Underwood, "A Field Guide to the Gurus," *Fast Company*, November 2004, p. 104.

Chapter 2
p. 33: Suein L. Hwang, "It Was a Wombat for the Meatware, But It Was a Good Sell," *Wall Street Journal,* May 15, 2002, p. B1; p. 40: Excerpt adapted from "Ask Annie," *Fortune,* July 19, 1999. Copyright © 1999 Time Inc. All rights reserved.; p. 46: Adapted from "The 10 Commandments of E-MAIL," *Harvard Communications Update,* Vol. 2, No. 3, March 1999, pp. 7-8; Carolyn Kleiner, "Online Buffs Hit or Miss on Manners," *U. S. News and World Report,* March 22, 1999, p. 60; "Etiquette with Office Gadgets," *Training,* January 1999, p. 24;

p. 49: "Telephone Tips," *The Office Professional,* see www
.hardatwork.com; INTERNET. p. 48: Amy Joyce, "Freddie Mac
opens up to employees," *The News & Observer,* June 22, 2003.

Chapter 3

p. 69: Christopher Caggiano, "Psychopath," *Inc.,* July 1998,
p. 83; p. 74: Greg Hitt, "Spin Doctors Prescribe Dose of Self-
Deprecation for Howard Dean" (Yeeeaaah!) *Wall Street Journal,* January 23, 2004, p. B1; p. 77: Patricia Sellers, "Yep,
He's Gone," *Fortune,* July 20, 1998, p. 32.

Chapter 4

p. 86: www.es.emory.edu/mfp/efficacynotgiveup.html Accessed November 17, 2000; p. 96: "Best Practice -- > Mentoring," *Training,* March 2005, p. 70.

Chapter 5

p. 117: Leah Nathans Spiro, "Ethics and Anderson Didn't Add
Up," *Wall Street Journal,* March 20, 2003, p. D8; p. 120: Dennis
T. Jaffe and Cynthia P. Scott, "How to Link Personal Values
with Team Values," *Training & Development,* March 1998, pp.
24-26; p. 129: Adapted from Kris Maher, "Wanted: Ethical Employer," *Wall Street Journal,* July 9, 2002, p. B1. (This article includes "A Job Seeker's Ethics Audit," by Linda K. Trevino.)

Chapter 6

p. 138 (Fairmont): "At Your Service," *Fast Company,* October
2004, p. 81; p. 138 (Starbucks): Andy Serwer, "Starbucks Hot
to Go," *Fortune,* January 26, 2004, p. 68; p. 143: Tom Butler-
Bowdon, *50 Success Classics* (London: Nicholas Brealey,
2004), pp. 168-171.

Chapter 7

p. 159: Michael Specter, "The Long Ride," *The New Yorker,*
July 15, 2002, pp. 48-58; p. 172: "Management Theory? Management Madness," *Psychology Today,* March/April 1997, pp.
58-62.

Chapter 8

p. 193: Cynthia Crossen, "In This Tell-All Era. Secrets, Secrets
Just Aren't What They Used to Be," *Wall Street Journal,*
March 31, 1998, p. A-1; Bob Wall, *Working Relationships* (Palo
Alto, Calif.: Davies-Black Publishing, 1999), pp. 166-167.

Chapter 9

p. 208: Daniel Goleman, *Working with Emotional Intelligence*
(New York: Bantam Books, 1998), p. 23; p. 213: Phillip C.
McGraw, "Even If You've Failed at Every Diet, You Can Suc-
ceed Now," *O, The Oprah Magazine,* August 2004, pp. 46-48.

Chapter 10

p. 233: Justine Willis Toms, "A Baby Step Toward Better
Community," *New Dimensions,* May/June 1999, p. 2.

Chapter 11

p. 257: "Your Future Together May Be a Self-fulfilling
Prophecy," *Spirituality & Health,* March/April 2005, p. 19.
p. 265: Gwendolyn Bounds, Handyman Etiquette: Stay Calm,
Avert Eyes," *Wall Street Journal,* May 10, 2005, p. B1.

Chapter 12

p. 281: David H. Freeman, "Corps Value," *Inc.,* April 1998,
pp. 54-65; Jon R. Katzenback and Jason A. Santamaria, "Firing Up the Front Line," *Harvard Business Review,* May/June
1999, pp. 107-117. p. 298: Dimitry Elias Legger, "Help! I'm
the New Boss," *Fortune,* May 29, 2000, p. 281.

Chapter 13

p. 304: Adapted from Alex Taylor III, "How to Fix Detroit,"
Fortune, October 31, 2005, p. 36. p. 311: Rob Walker, "Take It
or Leave It: The Only Guide to Negotiating You Will Ever
Need," *Inc.,* August 2003, p. 77; p. 305: Excerpt abridged
from "More Firms, Siding with Employees, Bid Bad Clients
Farewell" *Wall Street Journal* (1889-1959) [STAFF PRO-
DUCED COPY ONLY] by Sue Shellenbarger. Copyright 2000
by Dow Jones & Co. Inc. Reproduced with permission of Dow
Jones & Co. Inc. in the format Textbook via Copyright Clear-
ance Center, p. B1.

Chapter 14

p. 341: "Doing Well by Doing Good," *Wellness Letter, University of California, Berkeley.*

Chapter 15

p. 358: "Tools for Tolerance: Personal," adapted from *101
Tools for Tolerance: Simple Ideas for Promoting Equity and
Celebrating Diversity.* Copyright © 2000, Southern Poverty
Law Center, Montgomery, AL. Reprinted by permission of
Southern Poverty Law Center. *101 Tools for Tolerance* is avail-
able free from the SPLC. For more information, visit
www.splcenter.org or send a fax to (334) 264-7310.; p. 367:
"When Meeting Someone with a Disability." Adapted from
"Communication Solutions." Used by permission of Progres-
sive Business Publications. p. 368: "Tools for Tolerance: Workplace," adapted from *101 Tools for Tolerance: Simple Ideas for
Promoting Equity and Celebrating Diversity.* Copyright © 2000,
Southern Poverty Law Center, Montgomery, AL. Reprinted by
permission of Southern Poverty Law Center. *101 Tools for
Tolerance* is available free from the SPLC. For more information, visit www.splcenter.org or send a fax to (334) 264-
7310.; p. 374: "Tools for Tolerance: Community," adapted
from *101 Tools for Tolerance: Simple Ideas for Promoting Equity and Celebrating Diversity.* Copyright © 2000, Southern
Poverty Law Center, Montgomery, AL. Reprinted by permission of Southern Poverty Law Center. *101 Tools for Tolerance*
is available free from the SPLC. For more information, visit
www.splcenter.org or send a fax to (334) 264-7310.

Chapter 16

p. 389: Debra E. Meyerson and Joyce K. Fletcher, "A Modest
Manifesto for Shattering the Glass Ceiling," *Harvard Business
Review,* January/February 2000, p. 127; p. 393: Aaron Bern-
stein, Ronald Grover, and Cliff Edwards, "Making Family
Leave Family Friendly," *Business Week,* September 30, 2002,
p. 44; Sue Shellenbarger, "Shaky Job Market Makes Family
Leave Riskier Business," *Wall Street Journal,* August 22, 2001,
p. D1; Sue Shellenbarger "A Downside of Taking Family
Leave: Getting Fired While You Are Gone," *Wall Street Jour-
nal,* January 25, 2003, p. D1; and "The Incredible Shrinking
Family Leave: Pressed Bosses Are Cutting Into Time Off,"
Wall Street Journal, October 17, 2002, p. D1. p. 396:
Stephanie Armour, "Pregnant workers report growing dis-
crimination," *USA Today,* February 17, 2005, p. 1B.

Chapter 17

p. 417: "Who Wants to Be a Millionaire?" *San Jose Mercury
News,* Weekly Tip.

Photo Credits

Chapter 1
p. 3: Marcio Jose Sanchez / AP-Wide World Photos. p. 12: Chris Mueller / Redux Pictures. p. 20: Tim Shaffer / © Reuters / Corbis.

Chapter 2
p. 28: Photo by Pailin Wedel / © *The News and Observer*. p. 33: © Money Sharma / Corbis. p. 41: © Royalty-Free / Corbis.

Chapter 3
p. 59: Jeff Christiansen / SIPA. p. 70: © P.A. News / Corbis Kipa. p. 74: AP-Wide World Photos.

Chapter 4
p. 88: William F. Campbell / Time & Life Pictures / Getty Images. p. 95: Courtesy The Gallup Organization. p. 97: Photo by George Skene / © McClatchy-Tribune Information Services.

Chapter 5
p. 109: Stephen Chernin / Getty Images. p. 123: Duke Photography. p. 124: Gregory Heisler / Time & Life Pictures / Getty Images.

Chapter 6
p. 133: AP-Wide World Photos. p. 136: *Jacket design* by Coudal Partners, copyright © 2005 by Daniel H. Pink, from A WHOLE NEW MIND by Daniel H. Pink. Used by permission of Riverhead Books, an imprint of Penguin Group (USA) Inc. p. 147: Jeff Greenberg / Photo Edit, Inc.

Chapter 7
p. 155: © Rob Crandall / The Image Works. p. 165: Jacket Cover, from SWIMMING TO ANTARCTICA by Lynne Cox, copyright © 2004 by Lynne Cox. Used by permission of Alfred A. Knopf, a division of Random House, Inc. p. 167: © 2006 Scott Houston.

Chapter 8
p. 181: Myrna Suarez / Getty Images. p. 189: © Michael Justice / Michael Justice Photography / Mercury Pictures. p. 194: Junko Kimura / Getty Images.

Chapter 9
p. 205: AP-Wide World Photos. p. 209: © John W. Clark. p. 214: AP-Wide World Photos.

Chapter 10
p. 230: Courtesy PAETEC COMMUNICATIONS. p. 235 Copyright © 1994. Used by permission of Workman Publishing Company, New York. All Rights Reserved.

Chapter 11
p. 253: © Joe Fox / Alamy. p. 259: Joyce Naitchayan / AFP / Getty Images. p. 266: Ingram Publishing / Getty Images.

Chapter 12
p. 277: AP-Wide World Photos. p. 280: Photo by Wayne Slezak, Courtesy United Airlines. p. 289: Courtesy Center for Creative Leadership.

Chapter 13
p. 302: Paul Sancya / AP-Wide World Photos. p. 310: © Timothy Archibald. p. 317: Courtesy American Arbitration Association. p. 319: Steve Miller / AP-Wide World Photos.

Chapter 14
p. 331: Used with full permission of PRITCHETT, LP. All Rights are Reserved. p. 333: Wide Group / Iconica Collection / Getty Images. p. 340: Eros Hoagland / Redux.

Chapter 15
p. 355: © Bob Daemmrich / The Image Works. p. 365: Jeff Hutchens / Getty Images. p. 366: Courtesy National Sports Center for the Disabled.

Chapter 16
p. 382: © Joe Vaughn / Vaughn Media, Inc. p. 386: Betsie Van Der Meer / Getty Images. p. 396: Jon Feingersh / © zefa / Corbis.

Chapter 17
p. 410: © Philip Newton. p. 413: Book cover from THE SUCCESS PRINCIPLES (TM) by JACK CANFIELD and JANET SWITZER, COPYRIGHT © 2005 BY JACK CANFIELD. Reprinted by permission of HarperCollins Publishers. p. 420: photo by Chris Seward / © *The News and Observer*.

NAME INDEX

Adelphia Communications, 109, 249
Adobe Systems, 148
Allied Holdings Inc., 423
Aloz, Larry, 105
Alyn, Kimberly, 75
Amazon.com, 65
American Academy of Pediatrics, 115
American Anthropological Association, 362
American Arbitration Association, 322
American Express, 367
American Management Association, 61, 306
American Psychiatric Association, 115
American Psychological Association, 225, 311
American Society for Training and Development, 137
American University, 303
America Online, 342, 365
Ameritech Corp., 202
Amway Corporation, 242
Anderson, Susan, 364
Antilla, Susan, 404
Appalachian State University, 364
Arizona State University, 341
Armstrong, Lance, 159, 170
Armstrong, Neil, 68
Arnold & Porter, 25
Arthur Anderson, 117
Ashe, Arthur, 272
Association of Certified Fraud Examiners, 118
Association of Image Consultants International, 271
Astaire, Fred, 86
AT&T, 105
At-Home Dad, 403
Atkins, Stuart, 78
Austin, Nancy, 267–268
Automatic Elevator, 28

Bach, David, 418
Baldridge, Letitia, 265
Ballmer, Steve, 59, 82
Bandura, Albert, 86
Bank of America, 249
Bank One, 249
Baptist Health Care, 148
Baron, Robert A., 201, 202
Baughman, James, 15

Bauman, Alan, 45
Baylor University, 364
Bell, Andy, 265
Bell, Chip, 95
Benjamin, Maria, 12
Bennett, William J., 118
Bennis, Warren, 95
Benson, Herbert, 341
Benton, Debra, 254
Bernard, Betsy, 105
Berne, Eric, 16, 211, 234
Bernstein, Albert J., 183
Better Communications, 32
Bezos, Jeff, 65, 273
Biogen, 120, 431
Bixler, Susan, 254, 255, 258, 262
Blake, Robert, 283–284
Blanchard, Kenneth, 233–234, 238, 241
Blauwet, Cheri, 176–177
Bly, Robert, 385
BMS Software, 119
BMW, 253
Boeing Company, 121, 131, 226
Bolles, Richard, 22
Born Information Services Inc., 45
Borysenko, Joan, 171, 211, 220
Boyd, Malcolm, 240
BP–Amoco, 405
Brabeck, Peter, 45
Branden, Nathaniel, 85–86, 92
Branson, Richard, 65
Brod, Craig, 332
Bronson, Po, 410
Brothers, Dr. Joyce, 68, 193
Brown, Daniel, 210
Buchholz, Ester, 343
Buckingham, Marcus, 94
Buddha, 193, 213
Bureau of Labor Statistics, 6, 215
Burke, Edmund, 123
Buscaglia, Leo, 222–223
Business Ethics, 120
Business Week, 82, 120
Buzek, Mark, 415

Cadagin, Mary, 155–156, 175
Canfield, Jack, 22–23, 112, 235, 414
Carrey, Jim, 65
Carter, Jimmy, 68
Carter, Stephen L., 7
Catalyst, 116, 371, 388, 389

Caterpillar, 365
Cato Institute, 417
Center for Corporate Ethics, 114
Center for Creative Leadership, 289
Center for Gender in Organizations, 389
Center for Independent Living, 372
Center for Leadership Studies, 290–291
Center for Public Integrity, 128
Challenger space shuttle, 303
Chambers, Harry E., 6
Chappell, Tom, 122, 423
Character Counts Coalition, 114
Character Education Partnership, 114
Charter Communications, 405
ChartHouse Learning, 133
Cheney, Dick, 66
Chesonis, Arunas, 230, 236–237, 250
Chesterfield Health Services, 410
Chew, Sheryln, 359
Childs, J. T. "Ted," Jr., 357
Chitwood, Roy, 110
Chödrön, Pema, 215
Chopra, Deepak, 240
Christensen, John, 133
Chrysler Corporation, 10
Cialdini, Robert, 341
Cigna, 130
Cincinnati Bell, 396
Cingular, 319
Citigroup Corporation, 25
Ciulla, Joanne, 112
Clements, Jonathan, 417
Clifton, Donald, 94, 236
Clinton, Bill, 181–182
Coca-Cola Company, 371–372
Coles, Robert, 422
Columbia University, 216
Colvin, Geoffrey, 416
Com-Corp Industries, 418
Communications Workers of America (CWA), 323
Computer Associates, 249
Connelly, Julie, 418
Consolidated Edison, 371
Container Store, 250
Coody, Tess, 405
Cooper, Cynthia, 124
Cornell University, 316, 341
Cosco Systems, 209

Costner, Kevin, 69
Covey, Stephen, 18, 42, 110, 114, 156, 254, 277, 428
Cox, Fran, 93
Cox, Louis, 93
Cox, Lynne, 165, 176
Crestar Bank, 365
Critelli, Michael, 405
Crom, J. Oliver, 292
Crom, Michael, 143, 285
Cutler, Howard C., 143

Dalai Lama, 142, 143, 421, 422
Dale Carnegie & Associates, Inc., 285, 292
Dale Carnegie Training, 143
Dartmouth College, 7, 211
Davidson, Richard, 341
Dean, Howard, 74
Delphi, 304
Demarais, Ann, 255
DeVito, Deborah, 227
DeVos, Rich, 242
Digital Equipment Corporation, 166
Disney, Walt, 86
Dole, Bob, 66
Donaldson, Corey, 324
Donovan, Mary Ellen, 85
Dossey, Dr. Larry, 423
Dreilinger, Craig, 119
Dresden Basket Company, 106
Dresser, Norine, 257
Drucker, Peter, 35, 116, 147
Duke University, 123
Duke University Health System, 28, 52–53
Dunlap, Al "Chainsaw," 77
DuPont Company, 25
Dwoskin, Hale, 217, 218

eBay, 11
Ebbers, Bernard, 109, 121
Eddie Bauer, 405
Edison, Thomas, 86
Egan, Gerard, 222
Einstein, Albert, 68, 86
Eli Lilly & Co., 352
Elway, John, 272
Emlen, Arthur, 405
Engel, Beverly, 190
Enron Corporation, 11, 32, 109, 122, 124, 152, 249
Enterprise Rent-A-Car, 259, 270
EPS Solutions, 135
Equal Employment Opportunity Commission (EEOC), 315, 361, 364, 367, 396
Ertel, Danny, 309
Exide Technologies, 121

Fairmont Hotels, 138
Families and Work Institute, 403
Family Service League, 372
Fannie Mae, 155–156, 175
Fast Company magazine, 16
Federal Express Corp., 217, 317, 318
Federal Home Loan Mortgage Corporation (Freddie Mac), 48
Fiennes, Ralph, 411
First Impressions, Inc., 255
Fisher, Anne, 40, 261
Fisher, Roger, 313
Fisher College of Business, 123
FitzGerald, Maura, 112
FitzGerald Communications, Inc., 112
Flatow, Ira, 91
Fleishman, Edwin, 285
Fletcher, Joyce K., 389
Foote, Bill, 227
Ford Motor Company, 262, 409
Fortune magazine, 4, 22, 23, 40, 77, 139, 147, 416
Frank, Small & Associates, 126
Frankl, Viktor, 148
Freightliner, 319
Friedan, Betty, 383

Gallup Organization, 94, 235
Gates, Bill, 59, 68, 82
Gawain, Shakti, 212, 416
Gecis, 33
Genentech, 392
General Electric, 15, 135, 280
General Mills, 96
General Motors, 409
Genua, Robert, 201
Georges, James C., 208
Gerstein, Dr. Joseph, 130
Gibb, Jack, 195
Gilligan, Carol, 400
Giuliani, Rudolph, 282, 299
Gladwell, Malcolm, 255
Glaxo, 352
Global Protocol, Inc., 271
Goldberg, Rich, 69
Goldsmith, Marshall, 187
Goleman, Daniel, 10, 18, 184, 207, 291
Gordon, Robby, 205
Graham, Hugh Davis, 374
Gray, John, 398
Great Plains Software, 233
Greenspan, Alan, 68
Gretzky, Wayne, 272
Grief Recovery Institute, 228
Griggs, Lewis Brown, 359, 369
Guerra DeBerry Coody, 405

Hall, Edward, 36–37
Hall, Jay, 284
Handy, Charles, 423

Handyman Matters Franchising Corporation, 265
Hardee's, 181
Harley-Davidson, 23, 121–122, 355
Harp, Fred, 3
Harris, Amy Bjork, 211
Harris, Thomas, 211
Harvard Business Review, 377
Harvard Business School, 385
Harvard Medical School, 210, 341, 422
Hernacki, Mike, 431
Herrera, Yvette, 323
Herr Foods Inc., 423
Hersey, Paul, 290–291
Herzberg, Frederick, 16, 157, 162–163
Hewitt Associates, 419
Hewlett Packard, 39
Heyboer, Judy, 392
Hill, Anita, 397
Hillary, Edmund, 277
Hochschild, Joshua, 364, 365
Hock, Dee, 105
Home Depot, 361
Honeywell, 365
Honig Vineyard, 310
Hoopes, Aaron, 340–341
Hooters, 396
Hornstein, Harvey, 216
Hotel Employees and Restaurant Employees Union, 319
Hughes, Bob, 288
Hunt, John, 277
Hwoschinsky, Paul, 418
Hypertherm Incorporated, 281

Iacocca, Lee, 10
IBM, 47
IBM Global Workforce Diversity, 357
Icarian Inc., 139
ImClone, 109
Ingham, Harry, 185
Instill Corporation, 105
Institute for Global Ethics, 114
Institute for Women's Policy Research, 387–388
Intel Corporation, 412
International Business Ethics Institute, 126
International Centre for Dispute Resolution (ICDR), 317
International Listening Association, 40
Interplast, 414

James, Muriel, 211
James, William, 233
Jennings, Peter, 272
Jensen, Paul, 126
Johnson, David W., 60
Johnson, Ken, 39

Johnson, Spencer, 143, 152–153, 233–234, 238
Johnson & Johnson, 365
Jongeward, Dorothy, 211
Jordan, Michael, 272
Josephson Institute of Ethics, 114, 128
Jourard, Sidney, 183, 188
J.P. Morgan & Company, 367
J. Rolfe Davis Insurance Company, 9
Jung, Carl, 58
Just Ask a Woman, 433

Kaiser Permanente, 368
Kanter, Rosabeth Moss, 166
Katzenbach, Jon, 238–239, 250
Keen, Sam, 223
Kelleher, Herb, 239
Kelly, Tom, 417
Kennedy, John F., 181
Kent, Jerald, 405
Keyes, Tameron, 404
King, Larry, 65
Klainer, Pamela York, 416
Klaus, Peggy, 248
Knight, Bobby, 214
Koehler, Bryson, 351
Kohn, Alfie, 244–245
Kouzes, James, 278
Kuralt, Charles, 68
Kuwatsch, Thomas, 147

Landers, Ann, 272
Lay, Beth, 97
Lay, Kenneth, 124
Leadership Institute at the University of Southern California, 95
Leno, Jay, 65
Letterman, David, 65
Levinson, Daniel, 156
Lewinsky, Monica, 193
Lichtenberg, Ronna, 105
Lickona, Thomas, 114
Livingston, J. Sterling, 167
L.L. Bean, 249, 273
Lockheed Martin Corporation, 215, 216, 372
Loden, Marilyn, 356
Loehr, James, 330
Lombardi, Vince, 86
Longaberger, Dave, 106–107
Longaberger, Tami, 107
Lotus Development Corporation, 423
Louw, Lente-Louise, 359, 369
Luft, Joseph, 185
Lyons, Stephen, 414

Macintosh, 253
Maddux, Robert, 312
Maisel, Eric, 30
Mango's Tropical Café, 147

Marlin Company, 212
Marriott, 250, 319
Marsh & McLennan, 181
Martin, Judith, 267
Maslow, Abraham, 16, 160–162, 234
Maxs Sacks International, 110
Maxwell, John C., 293
Mayo, Elton, 15
MBNA, 23
McDonalds, 318
McGee-Cooper, Ann, 343
McGraw, Phillip, 90, 93, 213, 324–325
McGregor, Douglas, 16, 163, 282–283
Melohn, Thomas, 122
Menninger, William, 210
Menninger Foundation, 210
Merrill, David W., 59
Merritt, Doug, 139
Meyerson, Debra E., 389
Mickelson, Phil, 205
Microsoft, 59, 82
Miller, Camille Wright, 57
Miller, D. Patrick, 190
Miller, Emmett, 89
Miller, Robert "Steve," 304
Miller & Associates, 171
Miyhares, Ann, 410
Mizrahi, Terry, 195
Molloy, John, 260
Moore, Mary Tyler, 69
Moore, Steve, 417
Moore, Thomas, 422
Morgan Stanley, 404
Mount Everest, 277
Moussaoui, Zacarias, 124
Mouton, Jane, 283–284
Moyers, Bill, 423
Mueller, Robert, 124
Mulcahy, Anne, 111–112
Muldoon, Paul, 105
Murphy, Tim, 105
Muslim American Society, 377
Muslim Public Affairs Council, 377

National Association for Self-Esteem, 86
National Association of Female Executives, 403
National Association of Social Workers, 195
National Federation of the Blind, 365
National Hockey League, 302
National Institute for Occupational Safety and Health, 331
National Institute of Health (NIH), 344
National Labor Relations Board (NLRB), 319
National Organization for Women (NOW), 384
National Organization on Disability, 378

National Safe Workplace Institute, 216
National Sports Center for the Disabled, 366
National Whistleblower Center, 125
Needleman, Jacob, 344
Nelson, Bob, 235, 242
Nestlé, 45
New Dimensions magazine, 233
New England Journal of Medicine, 339
Newman, Paul, 361
Newsweek, 422
Nix-Rice, Nancy, 255
Nordstrom, 23
Norgay, Tenzing, 277
Nortel Networks, 342
North American Tool & Die, Inc., 122
Nutzwerk, 147

Occupational Safety and Health Administration (OSHA), 124–125, 130
O'Donnell, Rosie, 65
Ogiale, Stella, 410
Ohio State University, 157, 285
Olsen, Dave, 253
Ono, Tatsuo, 157
Ono, Yukiko, 157
Oracle, 3
Oregon Child Care Research Partnership, 405
Orloff, Judith, 232
Ouchi, William, 16

Paetec Communications, 230, 236–237, 250
Parents, Families, and Friends of Lesbians and Gays, 372
Par Group, The, 208
Paterson, Katherine, 113
Pathlore, 395
Pearson, Carol S., 336
Peck, M. Scott, 170–171
Pelaez, Roy, 239
PeopleSoft, 3
Pepsico Incorporated, 355, 371
Peters, Tom, 16, 66, 409
Petzinger, Thomas, Jr., 24
Pfeffer, Jeffrey, 164
Pfizer Inc., 352
Phillips, Bob, 75
Phillips, Michael, 414, 415
Pike Place Fish Market, 133, 151
Pinand, Kristy, 263
Pink, Daniel, 136, 245
Pinkerton, 215–216
Pitney Bowes, 405
Plante & Moran, 148
Posner, Barry, 278
Pound, Ron, 330
Powell, Colin, 282, 283, 300

Powell, John, 184
Power and Money LLC, 416
Powers, Dennis, 226
Price Waterhouse, 413
Princess Diana, 69, 70
Princeton University, 105
Pritchett, Price, 135, 285, 330
ProVox Technologies Corporation, 261
Purple Bamboo Orchestra, 359
Puzder, Andrew, 181

Quad/Graphics, 249
Quinlan, Mary Lou, 432–433

Raspberry, William, 12
Rath, Tom, 236
Rawlins, William, 193
Raytheon, 342
Reagan, Ronald, 181
Reid, Roger H., 59
Reinemune, Steve, 355
Reiss, Steven, 157–158, 416–417
Rensselaer Polytechnic Institute, 201
Rice, Dan, 119
Richman, Louis S., 22
Rite Aid, 109, 319
Ritz-Carlton Hotel Co., 165
Roberts, Julia, 68
Roby, Brett, 131
Rocky Mountain, David, 88
Rogers, Carl, 16
Rogers, David, 171
Rose, Pete, 181
Rosener, Judy, 356
Rosenthal, Robert, 167
Rosner, Bob, 150
Rowley, Coleen, 124
Rozen, Sydney Craft, 183
Ruiz, Don Miguel, 90, 92
Runyan, Marla, 176
Rush, Andrea, 382
Rush Trucking, 382
Ryan, Meg, 69

Sabath, Anne Marie, 266
Sakaida, Henry, 156–157
Sales & Marketing Executives International, 137
Salomon Smith Barney, 404
Saltzman, Amy, 89
Salzinger, Kurt, 311–312
Sanders, Tim, 208–209, 243
Sanford, Tschirhart, 85
Sarbanes-Oxley law, 130
Sargeant, Alice, 400
SAS Institute, 23, 250
Savers and Investors Foundation, 417
Schalk, Doug, 364
Schering-Plough, 130
Scherreik, Susan, 120

Schultz, Howard, 138
Schwartz, Felice, 389–390
Schwartz, Howard, 303
Scott, Susan, 40
Seinfeld, Jerry, 273
Self-Esteem Seekers Anonymous, 104
Seligman, Martin, 143
Sellers, Patricia, 77
Senge, Peter, 420
Sennett, Richard, 110
Shanley, Vera, 414, 415, 420
Shavers, Cheryl, 412
Shearson Lehman Brothers, 404
Sheehy, Gail, 156
Sheindlin, Judge Judith, 68
Shenk, David, 334
Sher, Barbara, 414
Siemens Westinghouse Power Generation, 97
Simmons Bedding Company, 121
Simon, Paul, 69
Simpson, Al, 110
Sinetar, Marsha, 414–415
60 Minutes, 66
Skinner, B. F., 234
Smith, Hyrum, 110
Snider, Roy, 233
Society for Human Resource Management, 369
Society of Incentive and Travel Executives, 248, 249
Soderberg, Jeff, 411
Soeca, 131
Software Technology Group, 411
Sony Corporation, 3
Southwest Airlines Company, 23, 239, 250
Springfield Remanufacturing Company, 175–176
Stack, Jack, 175–176
Starbucks, 138, 253
Stewart, David, 184
Stewart, Martha, 66
Stewart, Payne, 272
Stew Leonard's, 233
Stiebel, David, 314
Stonecipher, Harry, 226
Strakosch, Greg, 166–167
Streep, Meryl, 69
Subway Restaurants, 262
Sullivan, Scott, 109
Sunbeam Corporation, 77
Sun Microsystems, 395
Swanson Russell Associates, 122
Sysco Corporation, 166

Tan, Kevin, 126
Tannen, Deborah, 398
TAP Pharmaceuticals, 130
Taylor, Frederick W., 14–15

Teasley, Larkin, 189
TechTarget, 166–167
Teleometrics International Inc., 284
Tell, Regina, 263
Templeton, John, 114
Tenneco Automotive Inc., 203
Tennyson, Alfred, 237
Thomas, Clarence, 397
Thomas, R. Roosevelt, Jr., 377
Thoreau, Henry David, 391
3M Corporation, 9, 166, 343–344
Tilling, Mack, 105
Time magazine, 124
Toffler, Barbara, 117
Tomlin, Lily, 389
Toms, Justine Willis, 233
Torre, Joe, 300
Toyota Motor Company, 273
Tracy, Brian, 112, 145, 287, 288
Travel Industry Association, 336
Trippani, Mike, 230
Twain, Mark, 233, 303
Tyco International, 109, 152

Ulene, Dr. Art, 212–213
United Airlines, 280
United Parcel Service, 24, 259
United States Justice Department, 212
University of Maryland, 360
University of Michigan, 378–379
University of North Carolina, 282
University of Pennsylvania, 170
University of Wisconsin, 341
Universum, 409
Ury, William, 313
U.S. Department of Agriculture, 424
USG Corporation, 227
U.S. Marines, 139, 250, 281
U.S. Olympic Training Center, 98

Vanguard Car Rental USA Incorporated, 364
Victoria's Secret, 261
Virgin Atlantic Airways, 65
Visa International, 105
Vos Savant, Marilyn, 270

Wagner, Aly, 133
Wallace, Mike, 66
Wall Street Journal, 392
Wal-Mart, 318, 323, 396
Walsch, Neal Donald, 116
Walt Disney, 256–257
Walters, Ronald, 360
Waltrip, Michael, 205
Warm Thoughts Communications, 69
Warner, Judith, 390
Waterman, Robert, 16
Watkins, Sherron, 124
Watson, Joe, 368–369

Weeks, Dudley, 303
Wegman's Food Markets, 12
Weiner, Edith, 337
Welch, Jack, 135
West Pac Banking Corporation, 361
West Point, 170
Wheaton College, 364, 365
White, Valerie, 255
Williams, Doug, 215
Wilson, Leonard, 152
Wilson Learning Corporation,
    58, 75

Winfrey, Oprah, 80, 90, 272, 423
Winnebago Industries, 45
Woodruff, Christy, 97
Woods, Tiger, 363
Working Mother magazine, 25
WorldCom Incorporated, 33, 109, 121,
    124, 152
Worthington Industries, 423
Wyeth, 352

Xerox Corporation, 249
Xylo, 351

Yahoo!, 208
Yale University, 319
Yokoyama, John, 133
Yo-Yo Ma, 272

Xerox Corporation, 111

Zuboff, Shoshana, 85, 105, 385
Zwick, Lisa, 305

SUBJECT INDEX

Able to Work program, 365
Acceptance, 158
Accommodating style, 219, 312, 313
Accomplishments, recognizing, 287
Accuracy
  in communication process, 183
  in describing emotions, 192
Actions
  self-motivation and, 171
  taking responsibility for, 285
  in value clarification, 111
Active listening, 40, 238
Adolescence
  attitude formation in, 137
  self-esteem in, 87–89
Adulthood, self-esteem in, 89–90
Affirmative action, 373–375, 377
  debate over, 374–375
  in higher education, 378–379
  organizations subject to, 373
Age discrimination, 361–362, 373
Aggressive behavior, 306, 308. *See also*
  Anger; Workplace violence
Agoraphobia, 345
Alcohol
  abuse, 346, 347
  moderate use of, 426
Alternative Dispute Resolution pro-
  grams (ADRs), 316–317
Americans with Disabilities Act (ADA),
  364
Androgynous Manager, The (Sargeant),
  400
Anger
  defined, 212
  effective expression of, 213–215
  handling other people's, 215
  learning to manage, 212–213,
    225–226
  in workplace, 212, 213
  See also Workplace violence
Anger Kills (Williams, Williams), 212
Annoying People (Alyn, Phillips), 75
Anthropology, 9
Anxiety, 332–333, 345
Apologizing, 181–182, 190
Appearance, 257–258. *See also* Profes-
  sional presence
Arbitration, 318, 322
Arrogance, 141

Art of Happiness, The (Dalai Lama),
  142, 143, 421, 422
Assertive behavior
  defined, 306, 308
  for discrimination, 368
  guidelines for developing, 306–309
"Assertiveness Training for Managers,"
  61
Assumptions, in first impressions, 256,
  257
Attitude changes, 142–146
  changing conditions, 145–146
  changing consequences, 146
  choosing happiness, 142–143
  embracing optimism, 143–144
  helping others with, 145–146
  keeping an open mind, 144–145
  thinking for yourself, 144
Attitudes
  as communication filter, 34
  defined, 134
  formation of, 137–139
  image and, 257
  importance of empathy, 136
  powerful influence of, 135
  prejudiced, 357–360
  root causes of negative, 134–135
  valued by employers, 139–142
  See also Employee attitudes
Authority-compliance management,
  283
Avoidance style, 312, 313

Baby Boomers
  motivators for, 168
  values of, 113
Bad Attitude Survival Guide, The
  (Chambers), 6
Balance. *See* Life plan; Work/life bal-
  ance
Behavior
  breaking habits, 428–429
  defensive, avoiding, 311–312
  emotions and, 206–207
  impact of self-esteem on, 90–92
  See also Attitudes; Employee
    behavior
Behavioral sciences, 9, 284–285
Behavior profiling, 53–54
Belongingness needs, 160–161, 234

*Be Your Own Brand: A Breakthrough
  Formula for Standing Out from the
  Crowd* (McNally, Speak), 253, 273
Bigotry, 379–380
Blind area, of Johari Window, 185, 186
*Blink: The Power of Thinking Without
  Thinking* (Gladwell), 255
Blogs, 47
Body language, 35–37
Body piercings, 261–262
Book of Virtues, The (Bennett), 118
Born to Win (James, Jongeward), 211
Bosses. *See* Leadership; Management
*Brag! The Art of Tooting Your Own
  Horn Without Blowing It* (Klaus),
  248
Brainstorming, 316
Branding, 253, 273, 420
*Breathe Smart: The Secret to Happiness,
  Health, and Long Life* (Hoopes),
  340–341
Breathing techniques, for managing
  stress, 340–341
Brutal Bosses and Their Prey (Horn-
  stein), 216
Built to Last (Collins), 16
Burnout, 346–347
Business casual look, 261–262

Call of Solitude, The (Buchholz), 343
Capitulation, of emotions, 217–218
Career apparel
  business casual look, 261–262
  guidelines for selecting, 258,
    259–260
  for job interviews, 258, 268
  vs. leisure clothing, 261–262
  See also Professional presence
Career corner
  avoiding bad-boss environments, 321
  burnout concerns, 348
  completing self-evaluations, 199
  dealing with discrimination, 376
  determining employer values, 127
  dress codes, 269–270
  enhancing team performance, 296
  fear of public speaking, 224
  personal phone calls, 80
  positioning for advancement, 402
  praising your boss, 247

Career corner (*continued*)
  preparing for a career, 22, 40
  relaunching career, 50, 103
  returning to previous employer,
     149–150
  telecommuting, 173
Career Ethic Inventory, 122
Care of the Soul (Moore), 422
Cell phone etiquette, 266–267
Change
  coping strategies, 143, 152–153
  goal-setting and, 97
  of motives, 159
  openness to, 141
  organizational, and conflict, 304–306
  stress and, 331, 332
  surrendering to, 332
  See also Attitude changes
Character
  decline of, 110
  education, 114
  importance of, 110
  for leadership, 291–292
  See also Values
Charisma, 272
Child care challenge, 392–393, 405
Child-free employees, 393
Childhood
  impact on emotional balance, 211
  prejudiced attitudes and, 359
  self-esteem in, 87
Choice
  in life planning, 429
  in right livelihood, 414–415
  in value clarification, 111
Civility (Carter), 7
Civil Rights Act, 373, 395
Class, importance of, 272
Claustrophobia, 345
Cliques, avoiding, 293
Clothing. *See* Career apparel
Coaching, 95, 290, 298–299
Codes of ethics, 122
Collective bargaining, 318
Collision Course (Graham), 374
Comfort zone, going outside, 171
Commitments, keeping, 110
Communication
  basic process for, 29–31
  climate of open, 287
  direct vs. indirect, 33
  in high-tech world, 29
  impersonal vs. interpersonal, 29–30
  importance of, 5–8, 17
  improving personal, 38–42
  increasing accuracy in, 183
  ineffective, and conflict, 304
  listening skills in, 39–42
  in organizations, 42–45
  responsibility in effective, 37–38

sender, message, receiver, feedback
     loop in, 30–31
  sending clear messages, 38–39
  silence in, 42
  in team building, 285
  in value clarification, 111
  See also Organizational communica-
     tion
Communication filters, 31–38
  attitudes, 34
  emotions, 34
  gender differences, 35
  language and cultural barriers, 32–33
  nonverbal messages, 35–37
  role expectations, 34–35
  semantics, 32
Communication style bias, 9, 59–60
Communication styles, 60–74
  basic concepts supporting, 58–59
  defined, 57–58, 71
  director style, 66–68, 73
  dominance continuum, 60–62
  emotive style, 65–66, 73
  excess zone, 72
  gender differences in, 398–400
  intensity zones, 71–72
  Jung's psychological types, 58
  as preferences, 58, 60
  reflective style, 68, 73
  sociability continuum, 62–65
  stability of, 58, 75
  strength/weakness paradox, 78–79
  style flexing, 59, 75–78, 294
  supportive style, 68–70, 73
  tips for identifying, 72–73
  variations within, 71–72
  versatility in, 74–78
Compassion, 208–209
Competence Process, The (Hall), 284
Compressed workweek, 394
Compromising style, 312, 313
Compulsory arbitration, 318
Computer workstations, and stress,
     334–335
Conceptual age, 136
Conflict
  about work policies and practices,
     305
  adversarial management and, 305
  competing for resources, 305
  ineffective communication and, 304
  marital, 324–325
  misunderstandings vs. disagree-
     ments, 304, 314–315
  negative attitudes and, 135
  organizational change and, 304–306
  personality clashes, 305–306
  positive view of, 303
  root causes of, 303–309
  values conflicts, 116–117

Conflict resolution
  Alternative Dispute Resolution pro-
     grams, 316–317
  assertive behavior for, 306–309
  avoiding defensive behaviors in,
     311–312
  dealing with difficult people, 306,
     307
  firing the client, 305
  importance of, 19, 20
  lose/lose approach, 309–310
  parable of the orange, 311
  role of labor unions in, 317–320
  in team building, 285, 309
  types of negotiating styles, 312–313
  win/lose approach, 309
  win/win approach, 310–311
Conflict resolution process, 314–317
  clarifying misunderstanding or dis-
     agreement, 314–315
  clarifying perceptions, 315
  defining problem, 315
  generating options for mutual gain,
     315–316
  implementing options with integrity,
     316
Conscious choice, in right livelihood,
     414–415
Conscious Life, A (Cox, Cox), 93
Consideration dimension, of leader-
     ship, 286, 287–288
Constructive criticism, 190–191
Control, external vs. internal, 91
Conversational etiquette, 267
Conversations with God (Walsch), 116
Core values, 111–112. *See also* Values
"Corporate counselor" leaders, 292
Corporate crime, 120–125
  corporate scandals, 8, 11, 32, 33,
     117, 121, 152
  employee sabotage, 216
  employee theft, 109, 129
  preventing, 122–125
  whistleblowing, 123–125, 130
Corporate culture. *See* Organizational
     culture
Corporate values, 119–125
  ethics initiatives and codes, 121–122,
     123
  ethics training, 122–123
  in global marketplace, 125–126
  good corporate citizens, 119–120
  hiring process and, 122
  See also Values
Corrosion of Character, The (Sennett),
     110
Country club management, 283
Courtesy, 237–238
Creating True Prosperity (Gawain), 416
Critical listening, 41

Critical thinking, in value clarification, 111
Criticism
  constructive, 190–191
  giving negative feedback, 201–202
Cross-functional teams, 281
Cultural differences
  language differences, 32–33
  in nonverbal communication, 36, 37
  in professional presence, 256–257
  value conflicts and, 304–305
Cultural influences, 256
Culture
  attitude formation and, 138–139
  emotional makeup and, 211–212
Curiosity, 158
Cyberlingo, 32
Cynicism, 144

Data smog, 334
Day-care centers, 392
"Dealing with People You Can't
  Stand," 306, 307
Decision-making
  self-esteem and, 93
  in team building, 285
Defensive behaviors, avoiding, 311–312
Depression, 346, 351–352, 417
Desires, sixteen basic, 157–158, 417
Developmental psychology, 87
Dialogue groups, 238
Diet
  emotional eating, 213
  guidelines for healthy, 424–427
  See also Health and wellness
Differences, developing sensitivity to,
  370
Dining etiquette, 265
Director style, 66–68, 73
  flexing to, 76
Disabled workers, 7
  companies enabling, 365
  discrimination against, 364–365, 373
  making good impressions on, 367
Disagreements, 304, 314–315
Discrimination, 360–368
  affirmative action plans, 373–375
  age, 361–362
  bigotry, 379–380
  defined, 360
  disabled workers, 364–365
  gender, 360, 383, 404
  pregnancy, 396
  race, 362–363
  religion, 363–364
  responding to, 368
  sexual orientation, 366–367
  subtle forms of, 367–368
  ways of overcoming, 369–372
  See also Work force diversity

Diversity
  developing tolerance, 358, 368, 374
  dimensions of, 356–357
  in higher education, 378–379
  prejudiced attitudes toward, 357–360
  valuing, 356
  See also Discrimination; Work force
    diversity
Diversity awareness program, 370
"Diversity Dialogue: Building an Inclu-
  sive Workplace," 372
Domestic abuse, 211–212
Dominance, 60
Dominance continuum, 60–62, 66
Don't You Dare Get Married Until You
  Read This! (Donaldson), 324
Dot.com companies, 8, 24
Dot.com–The Search for Sanity in a
  Wired World, 332
Do What You Love . . . The Money Will
  Follow (Sinetar), 414
Downshifting (Saltzman), 89
Dress for Success (Molloy), 260
Dress standards. See Career apparel
Drug abuse, 346, 347
Drug companies, on campus, 351–352

Eating, as basic desire, 158. See also
  Diet
Economics. See Money; Wealth inequality
Education
  intellectual growth, 419–420
  value formation and, 114
  See also Training and development
    programs
Effective Teaching and Mentoring
  (Aloz), 105
8th Habit, The (Covey), 277
E-mail, 46–49
  company policies for, 47
  impact on formal communication
    structure, 43
  language usage for, 48
  subject line in, 47–48
  tips for, 46
  using appropriate addresses, 47
Emotional balance
  barriers to, 207–208
  as daily challenge, 206–207
  interdependence of, 9
  self-disclosure and, 188
  strategies for achieving, 220–223
Emotional competence, 207
Emotional eating, 213
Emotional expression, 207–208
Emotional intelligence, 207
  for leadership, 291–292
  self-awareness and, 18
Emotional Intelligence (Goleman), 18

Emotional labor, 209
Emotional landscape, charting, 221
Emotional styles, 217–220
  accommodation, 219
  capitulation, 217–218
  fine-tuning, 221–223
  gender differences in, 219–220
  overexpression, 218–219
  strategies for identifying, 220–221
  suppression, 217
Emotions
  as communication filter, 34
  coping with anger, 212–215
  coping with grief, 227–228
  cultural conditioning and, 211–212
  defined, 206
  expressing, 222–223
  facial expressions and, 36
  impact of stress on, 338
  motivation and, 156
  moving beyond negative, 222
  negative attitudes and, 135
  romance at work, 226
  self-disclosing, 192
  self-esteem and, 89, 91–92
  taking responsibility for, 222
  temperament and, 210
  unconscious influences on,
    210–211
  in value clarification, 111
  in workplace, 208–209
  See also Anger; Workplace violence
Emotive style, 65–66, 67, 73
  flexing to, 76
Empathic listening, 42
Empathizer, 136
Empathy
  importance of, 136, 138
  in leadership, 287
Employee assistance programs (EAPs),
  347
Employee attitudes
  appreciation of coworker diversity,
    141–142
  corporate culture and, 138–139
  health consciousness, 141
  honesty, 142
  interpersonal skills, 140
  openness to change, 141
  organizational efforts for improving,
    147–148
  self-motivation, 140
  strategy for improving, 236
  team spirit, 141
  workplace costs of negative, 235
  See also Attitudes
Employee behavior, 10–14
  family influence on, 13–14
  job influence on, 13
  management's influence on, 12

Employee behavior (*continued*)
  organizational culture and, 11–12,
    138–139
  personal characteristics and, 13
  team influence on, 12–13
*Employee Burnout: America's Newest
  Epidemic*, 346
Employee development programs. *See*
  Training and development programs
Employees
  burnout, 346–347
  as leaders, 292
  managing relationship with boss,
    293–294
  See also Work force
Employee theft, 109, 129
Empowerment
  motivation through, 166–167
  self-esteem and, 101
Energy, 231, 232. *See also* Positive en-
  ergy/experiences
Entrance and carriage, 262–263
Environment, importance of, 246
Ergonomics, 335
Ethical choices
  corporate values and, 119–125
  guidelines for making, 118–119
  personal values and, 118–119
  scenarios for practicing, 121
Ethics
  codes of, 122
  defined, 118
  in international business, 125–126
  pledges, 123
  training, 122–123
  See also Values
Ethnicity, 359, 373. *See also* Race
Ethnocentrism, 359
Etiquette, 264–268
  cell phone, 266–267
  conversational, 267
  defined, 265
  dining, 265
  gender-related, 400–401
  Handyman, 265
  meeting, 266
  networking, 267
Excess zone, 72, 77
Exercise. *See* Physical fitness
Expectancy theory, 163
Expectations
  changing employee, 304
  changing job, 409
  leadership communication of, 288–289
  of others, as motivator, 167
External locus of control, 91
External motivation, 157
Extroversion, 65
Eye contact, 36, 264

Facial expressions, 36, 262
Families
  balancing work and, 389–390,
    391–392, 405–406
  as basic desire, 158
  child care challenge, 392–393
  influence on worker behavior, 13–14
  transitions, and stress, 337
  value formation and, 113–114
  workplace stress related to, 329
Family and Medical Leave Act (FMLA),
  393
Fear
  distrust cycle, 195–196
  negative attitudes and, 135
Feedback
  in active listening, 40
  for breaking habits, 429
  in communication process, 30–31
  generational differences in, 113, 169
  giving negative, 190–191, 201–202
  in Johari Window, 185, 187–188
  from leadership, 289–290
  self-disclosure and, 184
  360-degree feedback, 188, 201,
    202–203
  See also Positive reinforcement
Feelings. *See* Emotions
Feminine Mystique, The (Friedan), 383
Fierce Conversations (Scott), 40
Fifth Discipline, The (Senge), 420
Fight or flight syndrome, 331
*Final Accounting–Ambition, Greed and
  the Fall of Arthur Anderson* (Tof-
  fler), 117
Financial planning, 417–418. *See also*
  Money
Fire in the Belly (Keen), 223
First impressions, 254–256, 257. *See
  also* Professional presence
*First Impressions–What You Don't
  Know About How Others See You*
  (Demarais, White), 256
Fish! philosophy, 133, 151–152
Flexibility, 145
Flextime, 394
Foreign Corrupt Practices Act (1977),
  125
Forgiveness, 190
Formal communication channels, 43
Four Agreements, The (Ruiz), 90, 92
Free Agent Nation, 6
Fun, for managing stress, 342–343
Future
  impact of past on, 90
  visualization for creating, 112

Gain sharing, 244
Gay and lesbians, discrimination
  against, 366–367

Gender bias, 360, 373, 383
  glass ceiling, 388–389
  hidden discrimination barriers, 389
  pregnancy discrimination, 396
  sexual harassment, 395–398, 404
  wage gap, 387–388
  for working fathers, 391–392
Gender differences
  in career problems and challenges,
    387–392
  and changing traditional roles,
    383–387
  in communication style, 35, 398–400
  in emotional style, 219–220
  new organizational etiquette,
    400–401
  understanding and respecting,
    398–401
  words of caution about, 399–400
  See also Men; Women
Generation X
  motivators for, 168–169
  values of, 113, 116–117
Generation Y (Millennials)
  importance of job design to, 165
  motivators for, 168–169
  values of, 113
Gestures, 36, 37
Getting to Yes (Fisher, Ury), 313, 316
Glass ceiling, 388–389
Global union movement, 323
Goal-setting
  for breaking habits, 429
  major principles of, 97
  motivation and, 140, 163–164
  self-esteem and, 96–98
Grapevine, 43–44
Gratitude, 240
Gratz v. Bollinger, 379
Great Depression, 15
Grieving process, in workplace,
  227–228
Grit, 170–171, 174
Group membership, 12–13. *See also*
  Teams/team building
"Group think," 144
Grutter v. Bollinger, 375, 379
Guaranteed Fair Treatment process
  (GFT), 217, 317
Guided imagery, 98

Habits, power of, 428–429
Handshake, 263–264
Happiness
  choosing, 142–143
  role of learning in, 421
  sources of, 416
  value-based, 157
Hawthorne studies, 15
Healing and the Mind (Moyers), 423

Health and wellness
  alcohol in moderation, 426
  avoiding fatty foods, 426
  avoiding sodium, 426
  balanced and varied diet, 424–425
  benefits of exercise, 339–340, 419, 427
  fiber and starch for, 426
  interdependence of, 9
  as nonfinancial asset, 419
  organizations promoting, 141, 249, 419
  reducing calorie intake, 425–426
Health insurance, 162, 304
Helpers' high, 341
Hidden area, of Johari Window, 185, 186
Hierarchy of needs, 16, 160–162, 234
High self-esteem, 91–92
Hiring procedures
  for achieving diversity, 372
  affirmative action plans, 373–375
  integrity screening, 122
  screening unstable persons, 216
Homophobia, 366
Honesty, 142
Honor, 158
Horizontal channels, 43
Hostile work environment, 397, 404
Hours. See Work schedules
How Full Is Your Bucket? (Rath, Clifton), 236
Human relations, 4–10
  behavioral sciences and, 9, 284–285
  benefits of, 20
  defined, 4, 9
  importance of, 5–8
  information age and, 4–5
  major themes in, 17–19
  relationship management challenges, 8–9
  total person and, 9, 10, 429
Human Relations Abilities Assessment Form, 22, 428
Human relations movement, 14–16
Human Side of Enterprise, The (McGregor), 16, 163, 282–283
Hungry Spirit, The (Handy), 423

Idealism, 158
Image, 257. See also Professional presence
Immediate gratification, 119
I'm OK–You're OK (Harris), 211
Impersonal communication, 29–30
Impoverished management, 283
Incentive programs, 243–245
  criticisms of, 244–245
  effectiveness of, 249
  for health promotion, 141, 249, 419

list of common, 244
  noncash vs. cash, 244
Incentives, 157, 166
Incivility, in workplace, 6–7, 140, 268
Income inequality. See Wealth inequality
Independence, 158
Individuality, team building and, 293
Industrial psychology, 15
Industrial Revolution, 14
Inflexibility, 141
Informal channel (grapevine), 43–44
Informal organization, 15
Information overload, 333–334
Information technology
  adjusting to rapid changes, 141
  balancing with empathy, 136
  blogs, 47
  computer workstations, 334–335
  effective communication and, 29
  e-mail, 46–49
  for employee training, 166
  impact on human relations, 4–5
  information overload and, 333–334
  Internet addiction, 333
  technostress and, 332–335
  virtual offices, 45
  voice mail, 45–46
Inner critic, 98–99
Inner Edge, The (Pearson), 336
In Search of Excellence (Peters, Waterman), 16
Integrity, 110
Integrity tests, 122
Intellectual growth, 419–421
Intelligence standards, 207
Intensity zones, 71–72
Internal locus of control, 91
Internal motivation, 157
Internal values conflict, 116–117. See also Values
International business, values and ethics in, 125–126
Internet addiction, 333, 350
Interpersonal communication
  vs. impersonal communication, 29–30
  importance of, 5–8, 140
  See also Communication
Interpersonal relationships
  positive energy for improving, 231–233
  vs. role relationships, 196–197
  See also Relationships
Interruptions, 42, 270
Intimate distance, 36
Intrapreneurship, 24, 166
Iron John (Bly), 385
It's Not About the Bike (Armstrong), 170

It's Not Business, It's Personal (Lichtenberg), 105

Jargon, 32, 33, 38
Job design, motivation and, 164–165
Job enlargement, 165
Job enrichment, 165
Job interviews, professional presence at, 268
Job rotation, 165
Job sharing, 395
Johari Window, 185–188
Journal writing
  for anger management, 213
  for identifying emotional patterns, 220–221
Just Ask a Woman (Quinlan), 433

Labor market. See Work force; Workplace
Labor unions
  anti-union employers, 318–319
  "card-check neutrality" process, 319
  contemporary issues for, 318–320
  global union movement, 323
  role in conflict resolution, 317–320
Language
  as communication filter, 32–33
  in e-mail messages, 48
  gender differences in, 398–400
  jargon, 32, 33
  using clear and concise, 38
Laughter, for managing stress, 342–343
Layoffs
  handling of, 216–217
  increase of, 6
Leadership
  challenges in New Economy, 278–282
  character and emotional intelligence of, 291–292
  consideration dimension of, 286, 287–288
  defined, 277
  empathy and, 136
  employees as leaders, 292
  five practices for exemplary, 278
  four basic styles of, 285–286
  incompetent, and stress, 336–337
  Leadership Grid model, 283–284
  vs. management, 277–278
  respected leaders' advice on, 299–300
  situational, 290–291
  structure dimension of, 286, 288–290
  studies on effective, 282–285
  team-building skills for, 285–290
  See also Leadership skills; Management; Teams/team building
Leadership (Giuliani), 282, 299

Leadership Challenge, The (Kouzes, Posner), 278
Leadership Grid model, 283–284, 286
Leadership skills
  climate of open communication, 287
  coaching, 290, 298–299
  communicating expectations, 288–289
  dealing with performance problems, 290
  discovering employee values, 287–288
  providing feedback, 289–290
  providing for success, 287
  recognizing accomplishments, 287
  taking personal interest in employees, 287
Learned Optimism (Seligman), 143
Learning opportunities
  in breaking habits, 428
  importance of, 419–421
  motivation and, 166
  See also Training and development programs
Leisure time
  loss of, 412–413
  as nonfinancial asset, 421–422
Life plan
  changing habits, 428–429
  choosing right livelihood, 414–416
  defining nonfinancial resources, 418–423
  developing healthy lifestyle, 424–427
  importance of developing, 409, 413–414
  making your own choices, 429
  planning for changes, 427–429
  redefining success, 410–414
  relationship with money, 416–418
  See also Health and wellness; Nonfinancial resources; Work/life balance
Life purpose
  defining, 112
  statements, 171
Limitations, accepting, 93
Linguistic style, 398–399
Listening skills, 39–42
  active listening, 40
  critical listening, 41
  empathic listening, 42
Little Book of Forgiveness, A (Miller), 190
Lose/lose approach, 309–310
Loving Each Other (Buscaglia), 222–223
Low self-esteem
  characteristics of, 91
  identifying sources of, 93
  negative attitudes and, 135
  See also Self-esteem

Magnetism, 272
Maintenance factors, 162–163
Make Yourself Memorable (Sherman), 272
Management
  abusive behavior of, 216
  adversarial, and conflict, 305
  assertiveness training for, 61, 306–308
  authority-compliance, 283
  country club, 283
  defined, 278
  glass ceiling issue, 388–389
  impact on employee attitudes, 138
  impoverished, 283
  vs. leadership, 277–278
  managing relationships with, 293–294
  middle-of-the-road, 283
  participative approach to, 284
  "position power" of, 34–35
  role expectations for, 196
  team, 284
  Theory X vs. Theory Y, 163
  tips for young managers, 294
  training, for workplace violence, 217
  women in, 359, 385, 388–389
  worker behavior and, 12
  See also Leadership; Leadership skills
"Management Women and the New Facts of Life" (Schwartz), 389–390
Managerial Grid, The (Blake, Mouton), 283–284
Managers as Mentors: Building Partnerships for Learning (Bell), 95
Managing Your Mouth (Genua), 201
Manners. *See* Etiquette
Man's Search for Meaning (Frankl), 148
Marriage
  conflict in, 324–325
  discrimination based on, 373
  financial compatibility in, 418
Maslow on Management (Maslow), 162
Material possessions
  self-esteem and, 89
  as value, 119, 415
Matures
  motivators for, 168
  values of, 113
Media, value formation and, 114–115
Mediation, 318
Meditation, 341–342, 423
Meeting etiquette, 266
Men
  balancing career and family, 391–392
  burden of stress on, 386
  changing roles of, 385–387

  communication style of, 35, 398–400
  conflicting role messages for, 386–387
  health issues for, 392
  organizational problems for, 391–392
  See also Gender differences
Men Are from Mars, Women Are from Venus (Gray), 398
Mental health, 419. *See also* Health and wellness
Mental illness, 344–347
Mentors
  corporate programs, 96, 97
  power of, 105
  seeking support of, 95–96
  using multiple, 96
Messages
  in communication process, 30–31
  sending clear, 38–39
Middle-of-the-road management, 283
Military experience, discrimination and, 373
Minding the Body, Mending the Mind (Borysenko), 171
Mirroring, 57
Misunderstandings, 304, 314–315
Modeling, 115
"Mommy track," 389–390
Money
  defining relationship with, 416–418
  incentives, 244, 245
  pride vs., 250
  in right livelihood, 415
  See also Wealth inequality
Money management, 344, 416, 417–418
Monitoring anxiety, 333
Moral development, 110. *See also* Values
Motivation
  basic desires and, 157–158
  for breaking habits, 428
  characteristics of, 159
  complex nature of, 156–159
  defined, 156–157
  generational differences in, 168–169
  importance of, 18
  internal vs. external, 157
  See also Self-motivation
Motivational factors, 162–163
Motivational theories, 159–164
  expectancy theory, 163
  goal-setting theory, 163–164
  hierarchy of needs, 160–162
  motivation-maintenance theory, 162–163
  TheoryX/Theory Y, 163
Motivation-maintenance (two factor) theory, 162–163
Motivation strategies, 164–167
  empowerment policies, 166–167

expectations of others, 167
incentives, 166
job design, 164–165
learning opportunities, 166
for self-motivation, 169–171
Multicultural communication, 32–33
Multicultural Manners–New Rules of Etiquette for a Changing Society (Dresser), 257
Multitasking, 348
My American Journey (Powell), 282
MyPyramid, 424–425

Name of Your Game, The (Atkins), 78
Narcissism, 240
Narcissistic Process and Corporate Decay (Schwartz), 303
National Depression Screening Day, 352
Nature, time with, 423
Needs
hierarchy of, 160–162
positive experiences, 233–235
Negative attitudes
root causes of, 134–135
strategy for reducing, 236
workplace costs of, 235
See also Attitudes
Negotiating styles, 312–313
Negotiation. *See* Conflict resolution
Networking etiquette, 267
New Economy
challenges for, 24–25
education and training for, 419–420
leadership challenges in, 278
work schedules in, 14, 336
New Professional Image, The (Bixler, Nix-Rice), 255
No Contest: The Case Against Competition (Kohn), 244
Noise pollution, 335
Nonassertive behavior, 306, 308
Nonfinancial resources, 418–423
health and wellness, 419
intellectual growth, 419–421
leisure time, 421–422
spirituality, 422–423
Nonverbal messages
body language, 35–37
facial expressions, 262
for identifying communication style, 72–73
law enforcement analysis of, 53–54
Now, Discover Your Strengths (Buckingham, Clifton), 94, 95

Office Romance, The (Powers), 226
100 Absolutely Unbreakable Laws of Business Success, The (Tracy), 145
One Minute Manager, The (Blanchard, Johnson), 16, 233–234, 237, 238

1001 Ways to Reward Employees (Nelson), 235, 242
Open area, of Johari Window, 185, 186
Open-mindedness, 144–145
Optimism, 143–144
Order, 158
Organizational change
conflict and, 304–306
stress and, 330, 331, 332
See also Change
Organizational communication, 42–45
barriers to self-disclosure, 193–197
formal channels, 43
informal channel (grapevine), 43–44
methods for improving, 44–45
upward communication, 44–45
using technology, 45–49
See also Communication
Organizational culture
employee attitudes and, 138–139
employee behavior and, 11–12
for managing diversity, 369–372
positive energy and, 230–231, 246
Overexpression, of emotions, 218–219
Overtime pay, 245

Participative management, 284
Passages (Sheehy), 156
Passion for Excellence, A (Austin), 268
Past experiences, self-concept and, 90
Pathfinders (Sheehy), 156
Pay for knowledge, 244
Peer group, 137
Peer reviews, 203
Pension fund obligations, 152
People and events, influence on values, 113
People Styles at Work (Bolton, Bolton), 73
Perception, in expectancy theory, 163
Perfect Madness–Motherhood in the Age of Anxiety (Warner), 390
Performance
coaching for peak, 290
dealing with problems in, 290
technological monitoring of, 333
See also Motivation
Personal communication. *See* Communication
Personal competence, 207
Personal distance, 37
Personal growth, in right livelihood, 415–416
Personality, 57
Personality clashes, 305–306
Personal needs. *See* Life plan; Work/life balance
Personal space, as nonverbal message, 36–37

Personal Styles and Effective Performance (Merrill, Reid), 59
Personal values. *See* Values
Pessimism, 143–144
Phobias, 345
Physical activity, as basic desire, 158
Physical appearance, 35. *See also* Professional presence
Physical fitness, 339–340, 419, 427. *See also* Health and wellness
Physical strokes, 234
Physical symptoms, of stress, 338
Physiological needs, 160, 161
Playfulness, 133, 151
"Position power," 34–35
Positive Energy (Orloff), 232
Positive energy/experiences
actions and events that create, 232–233
human need for, 233–235
importance of environment, 246
for improving relationships, 231–233
Positive reinforcement, 235–240
active listening, 238
barriers to, 240–243
for breaking habits, 429
courtesy, 237–238
defined, 236–237
identifying commendable actions, 241–242
incentive programs, 243–245
making time for, 241
misconceptions about, 241
phrases and actions for, 242–243
power of praise, 237, 238
power of pride, 238–240
shared responsibility for, 243
for teamwork, 243
Theory of the Dipper and the Bucket, 236
See also Rewards
Positive self-talk, 98–100
Power, as basic desire, 158
Power of Apology, The (Engel), 190
Practice, in changing behavior, 428–429
Practice of Management, The (Drucker), 116
Praise, 237, 238
Prayer, 423
Pregnancy discrimination, 396
Prejudice, 357–360
bigotry, 379–380
childhood experiences and, 359
defined, 357
economic factors in, 360
ethnocentrism and, 359
stereotypes and, 357–359
worker diversity and, 141–142
See also Discrimination

Pride
 vs. money, 250
 positive energy and, 238–240
 tools for building, 250
Primacy effect, 254–255
Primary dimensions, of diversity, 356–357
Problem-solving style, 312, 313
Production incentives, 244
Productivity, reexamining ideas about, 245–246
Professional identity, self-esteem and, 89
Professional presence, 253–268
 avoiding incivility, 268
 business casual look, 261–262
 career apparel, 258–260
 cultural influences on, 256–257
 defined, 254
 entrance and carriage, 262–263
 etiquette guidelines, 264–268
 facial expressions, 262
 handshake, 263–264
 image-shaping components, 257, 258
 importance of class, 272
 importance of first impressions, 254–256
 at job interview, 268
 personal branding, 253, 273, 420
 surface language, 257–258
 voice quality and speech habits, 263
 See also Career apparel; Etiquette
Professional Presence (Bixler), 254
Profit sharing, 244
Prosperity, 416–417
Psychological disorders
 on campus, 351–352
 stress related, 344–347
 therapy options, 347
Psychological Types (Jung), 58
Psychology, 9, 87
Public distance, 37
Punished by Rewards: The Trouble with Gold Stars, Incentive Plans, A's, Praise, and Other Bribes (Kohn), 244–245
Pygmalion in the Classroom (Rosenthal, Livingston), 167

Quid pro quo, 395–396

Race
 discrimination, 362–363, 373
 myth of, 362–363
 as social identity, 363
 traditional nonwhite categories, 363
 wealth inequality and, 360, 388
Rage, 213
Random Acts of Kindness, 240–241, 248

Reaching Out–Interpersonal Effectiveness and Self-Actualization (Johnson), 60
Really Fit Really Fast (Ulene), 212
Receiver
 in communication process, 30–31, 37–38
 considering preferences of, 39
Reengineering the Corporation (Hammer, Champy), 16
Reference group, 137
Reflective style, 68, 69, 73
 flexing to, 76–77
Reid Report, 122
Reinforcement. *See* Positive reinforcement
Reinforcer, 234
Relational symptoms, of stress, 338
Relationship behavior, 291
Relationships
 interpersonal vs. role, 196-197
 personal vs. professional, 144
 positive energy for improving, 231–233
 repairing with self-disclosure, 189–190
 strengthening with self-disclosure, 184, 188
 three types of, 8–9
Relationship strategies, for customers, 209
Religion
 discrimination based on, 363–364, 373
 healthy spirituality, 423
 value formation and, 114
Repetition, for clear messages, 38
Resilience, for managing stress, 343–344
Resources
 competing for, 305
 nonfinancial, 418–423
Respect, generational differences in, 113
Responsibility
 apologizing, 181–182, 190
 in effective communication, 37–38
 for emotions, 222
 self-motivation and, 171
 taking, 23
Rewards
 attitude formation and, 137
 incentives, 157, 166, 243–245
 intrapreneurship programs, 166
 motivation and, 157
 programs, criticisms of, 244–245
 reexamining ideas about, 245–246
 See also Positive reinforcement
Right livelihood, 414–423, 432–433
 conscious choice in, 414–415

 as more than money, 415
 personal growth in, 415–416
 See also Life plan
Rights and Wrongs of Ethics Training (Rice, Dreilinger), 119
Road Less Traveled, The (Peck), 170
Role expectations
 as communication filter, 34–35
 for men and women, 383–387
 for supervisors, 196
Role models
 attitude formation and, 138
 values and, 115
Role relationships, vs. interpersonal relationships, 196–197
Romance
 as basic desire, 158
 in workplace, 226
"Rule follower" leaders, 292

Sacred Bull: The Inner Obstacles that Hold You Back at Work and How to Overcome Them (Bernstein, Rozen), 183
Safety needs, 160, 161
Saving, as basic desire, 158
Schedule creep, 421
Schedules. *See* Work schedules
Scientific management, 14–15
Seasons of a Man's Life (Levinson), 156
Secondary dimension, of diversity, 356–357
Security needs, 101, 160, 161, 234
Sedona Method, The (Dwoskin), 217, 218
Self-acceptance
 importance of, 18
 self-esteem and, 93
Self-actualization needs, 161
Self-assessment, 22, 61, 199
Self-awareness
 of communication style, 57, 58, 60, 81
 importance of, 18
 interdependence of, 9
 self-disclosure and, 184
Self-concept, development of, 87–90
Self-description, 182
Self-destructive behaviors, 91
Self-discipline, 170–171
Self-disclosure
 for accuracy in communication, 183
 apologizing, 181–182, 190
 benefits gained from, 183–184
 to boss, 294
 constructive criticism, 190–191
 defined, 182
 developing appropriate, 188–193

discussing disturbing situations, 191–192
effective expression of anger, 213–215
feedback styles and, 187–188
of feelings and emotions, 192
impact of role relationships on, 196–197
importance of, 19
Johari Window on, 185–188
organizational barriers to, 193–197
overwhelming others with, 193
practicing, 197–198
for reducing stress, 183
repairing relationships with, 189–190
self-awareness and, 184
vs. self-description, 182
sharing personal secrets, 193
for strengthening relationships, 184
time and place for, 192
trust and, 19, 193–196
Self-disclosure indicator, 197
Self-efficacy, 86, 163
Self-esteem
adulthood measures of, 89–90
authentic vs. false, 87
as basic need, 161
building, 92–100
characteristics of low and high, 91–92
decision-making and, 93
developmental process, 87–90
goal-setting and, 96–98
guided imagery for, 98
identifying sources of low, 93
impact on behavior, 90–92
importance of, 8, 18
interdependence of, 9
mentors for developing, 95–96
NASE definition of, 86–87
negative attitudes and, 135
organizational support for, 100–102
positive self-talk for, 98–100
power of, 85–90
self-acceptance and, 93
self-efficacy and self-respect in, 85–86
strength building and, 94–95
Self-Esteem at Work (Brandon), 85
Self-fulfilling prophecy, 163, 288
Self-managed teams, 279–280
Self-motivation
comfort zone and, 171
developing grit, 170–171
employers' valuing of, 140
strategies for, 169–171
taking action, 171
work/life balance and, 171
See also Motivation
Self-preoccupation, 240–241
Self-promotion, 248–249

Self-respect, 86
Self-talk, 98–100
Semantics, 32
Sender, in communication process, 30–31, 37–38
Serenity Prayer, 145
Service economy, 6
Seven Habits of Highly Effective People, The (Covey), 18, 156, 254, 428
Seven Laws of Money, The (Phillips), 414
Seven Spiritual Laws of Success, The (Chopra), 240
17 Essential Qualities of a Team Player, The (Maxwell), 293
Sexism. See Gender bias
Sexual harassment, 395–398
forms of, 395–397
how to deal with, 397–398
lawsuits, 404
Sexual orientation discrimination, 366–367, 373
Silence, in conversation, 42
Situational Leader, The (Hersey), 291
Situational leadership, 290–291
Six Pillars of Self-Esteem, The (Branden), 85
Slang, 32, 38
Sleep, for managing stress, 339
Sociability, 63
Sociability continuum, 62–65, 66
Social competence, 207, 286
Social contact, 158
Social contract, 4
rewriting, 304
Social distance, 37
Social endorsement, 74, 76
Socialization, 137
Social Life of Information, The (Brown, Duguid), 5
Social needs, 160–161
Sociology, 9
Solitude, 343, 421
Soul of a Business, The (Chappell), 122, 423
Speech habits, 263
Spirituality
healthy, 422–423, 431
value formation and, 114
Spirituality 2005, 422
Status, 158
Staying OK (Harris, Harris), 211
Stereotypes, 357–359
Stock options, 249
Strengths
assessing, 294
building, 94–95
Stress
from computer workstations, 334–335

defined, 330
fight or flight syndrome, 331
incompetent leaders, 336–337
long hours/irregular schedules, 336
major causes of, 331–337
mental, 330
noise pollution, 335
organizational change and, 332
psychological disorders related to, 344–347
responding to, 330–331
self-disclosure for reducing, 183
symptoms of, 337, 338
technostress, 332–335
of traditional male roles, 386
work and family transitions, 337
workers', costs of, 329–330
Stress for Success (Loehr), 330
Stress management strategies, 337–344
deep breathing, 340–341
exercise, 339–340
5-minute stress busters, 342
helpers' high, 341
laughter and fun, 342–343
meditation, 341–342
resilience, 343–344
sleep, 339
solitude, 343
vacations, 350–351
Stress of Organizational Change, The (Pritchett, Pound), 330, 331, 332
Strikes, 304, 318
Stroking, 234
Structure dimension, of leadership, 286, 288–290
Stubbornness, 141
Style flexing, 59, 75–78, 294
Success
developing life plan for, 413–414
leadership providing for, 287
loss of leisure time and, 412–413
need for new models of, 411
redefining, 410–414
Success Principles, The (Canfield), 22–23, 235, 414
Suggestion programs, 244
Supervisors. See Leadership; Management
Supportive style, 68–70, 73
flexing to, 77
Suppression, of emotions, 217
Surface language, 257–258
Swimming to Antarctica (Cox), 176
Synergy, 279

Table manners, 265
Talents, identifying, 94, 95
Tales from the Boom-Boom Room, Women vs. Wall Street (Antilla), 404

Task behavior, 291
Tattoos, 261–262
Team management, 284
Team recognition plans, 243
Team spirit, 141
Teams/team building
  behavioral science principles on, 284–285
  benefits and challenges for, 7, 279
  communication channels in, 42–43
  conflict resolution in, 285, 309
  cross-functional teams, 281
  employees as leaders, 292
  employee's role in, 292–294
  factors in team effectiveness, 281–282
  Hall's contribution to, 284
  influence on worker behavior, 12–13
  Leadership Grid model on, 283–284
  leadership skills for, 285–292
  as learning unit, 420
  managing relationships in, 9
  in Marine Corps, 281
  McGregor's influence on, 282–283
  qualities of valued members, 293
  self-managed teams, 279–280
  virtual teams, 297
  See also Leadership
Technology. *See* Information technology
Technostress, 332–335
Telecommuting, 45, 173, 395
Temperament, 210
10 Natural Laws of Successful Time and Life Management, The (Smith), 110
Tether anxiety, 332
"Thank you," saying, 238, 240, 241, 267, 428
Theory of the Dipper and the Bucket, 236
Theory X/Theory Y managers, 163
Theory Z style of management, 16
Therapy options, 347
They All Laughed: From Lightbulbs to Lasers (Flatow), 91
360-degree feedback, 188, 201, 202–203
Time and the Soul (Needleman), 344
Time/timing
  for clear messages, 38–39
  in expressing anger, 214
  managing, for stress reduction, 344
  of self-disclosure, 192
Tolerance
  community tools for, 374
  declaration of, 358
  personal tools for, 358
  workplace tools for, 368
"Too busy" syndrome, 241
Total person, 9, 10, 78, 429. *See also* Life plan; Work/life balance
Traditional roles, changing of, 383–387

Training and development programs
  for enhancing diversity, 372
  for enhancing self-esteem, 100–102
  ethics training, 122–123
  for intellectual growth, 419–420
  motivating through, 166
  for total person, 9, 10
Tranquility, 158
Transactional Analysis (TA), 16, 211, 234
Transitions, and stress, 337
True Wealth (Hwoschinsky), 418
Trust
  attitude of, 135
  fear/distrust cycle, 195–196
  impact of lack of, 194–196
  importance of, 18–19, 116
  self-disclosure and, 19, 193
  in team building, 285
Trust: A New View of Personal and Organizational Development (Gibb), 195
Twelve-step programs, 347, 423
20 Communication Tips@Work (Maisel), 30

Ultimate Secret of Getting Absolutely Everything You Want, The (Hernacki), 431
Ultimate Weight Solution, The (McGraw), 213
Uncertainty, negative attitudes and, 135
Unconscious
  factors in self-concept, 87
  influences on emotions, 210–211
  motives as, 159
Unconscious mind, 210
Union Network International (UNI), 323
Unknown area, of Johari Window, 185, 186–187
Upward communication, 44–45

Vacations, 350–351, 421
Values
  attitudes and, 134
  avoiding values drift, 115–116
  character and integrity, 110
  corporate, 119–125
  defined, 111
  defining life's purpose, 112
  education and, 114
  ethical choices and, 118–119
  family influence on, 113–114
  formation of, 110–116
  generational differences in, 113
  in global marketplace, 125–126
  happiness based on, 157
  harmony of personal and organizational, 119

  identifying core, 111–112
  interdependence of, 9
  leadership interest in employee, 287–288
  media and, 114–115
  modeling and, 115
  religion and, 114
  right livelihood and, 415
  self-esteem and, 89
  values clarification process, 111
  See also Corporate values
Values conflicts, 116–117
  in diverse work force, 304–305
  internal, 116–117
  leadership concern for, 288
  with others, 117
Valuing diversity, 356. *See also* Diversity; Work force diversity
Valuing Diversity (Griggs, Louw), 359, 369
Vengeance, 158
Verbal strokes, 234
Versatility, in communication style, 74–78
Vertical channels, 43
Violence
  cultural conditioning and, 211–212
  media and, 115
  in workplace, 215–217
Virtual offices, 45
Virtual strike, 318
Virtual teams, 297
Visualization, 98, 112, 144
Voice mail, 45–46
Voice quality, 263, 270
Voluntary arbitration, 318
Volunteering, for managing stress, 341
Volunteering Thanks (Boyd), 240

Wage gap, 7, 387–388
Wardrobe engineering, 260
Wealth inequality
  growth of, 7
  race and, 360
  women and, 387–388
Web-based counseling, 347
Wellness. *See* Health and wellness
What Color Is Your Parachute? (Bolles), 22
What Every Successful Woman Knows, 420
What Should I Do with My Life? (Bronson), 410
When Talking Makes Things Worse! (Stiebel), 314
Whistleblowing, 123–125
  checklist for, 125
  examples of, 124, 130
  legal protection for, 130
Whole New Mind, A (Pink), 136, 245

Who Moved My Cheese? (Johnson), 143, 152–153
Why Am I Afraid to Tell You Who I Am? (Powell), 184
Why Pride Matters More Than Money (Katzenbach), 238, 250
Win/lose approach, 309
Win/lose style, 312, 313
Win/win approach, 310–311
Women
  balancing career and family, 389–390
  as business owners, 382
  changing roles of, 383–385
  child care challenge, 392–393
  communication style of, 35, 398–400
  conflicting role messages for, 387
  discrimination against, 359, 360, 373
  domestic abuse of, 211–212
  hidden discrimination barriers, 389
  in management positions, 359, 385, 388–389
  "mommy track" for, 389–390
  organizational problems for, 387–390
  pregnancy discrimination, 396
  wage gap for, 387–388
  in workforce, 7, 383
  See also Gender bias; Gender differences
Women & Self-Esteem (Sanford, Donovan), 85
Women's movement, 356, 383
"Worker bee" leaders, 292
Worker behavior. *See* Employee behavior
Work force
  aging, 361
  changing expectations of, 409
  disabled workers in, 364, 365
  employee burnout, 346–347
  parents in, 329

  recent changes in, 6
  women in, 7, 383
Workforce America! (Loden, Rosener), 356
Work force diversity
  appreciation of, 141–142
  dimensions of diversity, 356–357
  economics of valuing, 368–369
  forms of discrimination, 360–368
  growth of, 7, 355–356
  individual efforts to enhance, 369–370
  leadership challenges with, 278
  managing, 369–372
  organizational diversity programs, 370–372
  prejudiced attitudes, 141–142, 357–360
  tools for tolerance, 368
  value conflicts and, 304–305
  See also Discrimination; Gender bias
Working Life, The (Ciulla), 112
Working with Emotional Intelligence (Goleman), 10, 184, 291
"Working Wounded" (Rosner), 150–151
Work/life balance, 14
  companies supporting, 9, 25, 405–406
  financial vs. nonfinancial resources, 418–419
  for men, 391–392
  self-motivation and, 171
  for women, 389–390
  See also Life plan
Workplace
  anger in, 212, 213
  competition for resources in, 305
  coping with grief in, 227–228
  core values and, 112
  cost of negativity in, 235
  costs of worker stress, 329–330

  emotional factor in, 208–209
  50 best companies for minorities, 371–372
  New Economy challenges, 24–25
  100 best companies, 4, 23, 139, 147–148
  100 best corporate citizens, 120
  personalizing, 250
  romance in, 226
  satisfying individual needs in, 161
  in service economy, 6
  team environment, 7
  threat of incivility, 6–7, 140, 268
  upheaval and restructuring, 6, 20, 22, 409, 411
Workplace violence, 215–217
  causes of, 216
  employee sabotage, 216
  preventing, 216–217
Work policies and practice, conflict and, 305
Work schedules
  as cause of stress, 336
  compressed workweek, 394
  flexibility in, 166, 393–395
  flextime, 394
  impact of downsizing on, 411, 412
  job sharing, 395
  loss of leisure time and, 412–413, 421–422
  in New Economy, 14, 336
  overtime, 245
  schedule creep, 421
  telecommuting, 395
  vacations, 350–351, 421

You and Me (Egan), 222
You Don't Have to Go Home from Work Exhausted (McGee-Cooper), 343
You Just Don't Understand: Women and Men in Conversation (Tannen), 398